# THE PATHOLOGY OF MAN

## A STUDY OF HUMAN EVIL

# ALSO BY STEVEN JAMES BARTLETT

*Reflexivity: A Source Book in Self-Reference*

*When You Don't Know Where to Turn*
*A Self-Diagnosing Guide to Counseling and Therapy*

*Self-Reference: Reflections on Reflexivity* (co-edited with Peter Suber)

*Conceptual Therapy: An Introduction to Framework-Relative Epistemology*

*Metalogic of Reference: A Study in the Foundations of Possibility*

*Validity: A Learning Game Approach to Mathematical Logic*

# THE PATHOLOGY OF MAN

## A Study of Human Evil

*By*

### STEVEN JAMES BARTLETT

*With a Foreword by*

Eric A. Zillmer
*and*
Irving Greenberg

**CHARLES C THOMAS • PUBLISHER, LTD.**
*Springfield • Illinois • U.S.A.*

*Published and Distributed Throughout the World by*

CHARLES C THOMAS • PUBLISHER, LTD.
2600 South First Street
Springfield, Illinois 62704

©2005 by CHARLES C THOMAS • PUBLISHER, LTD.

ISBN 0-398-07557-3 (hard)
ISBN 0-398-07558-1 (paper)

Library of Congress Catalog Card Number: 2004063718

*Printed in the United States of America*
*R-3-CAMRDY*

**Library of Congress Cataloging-in-Publication Data**

Bartlett, Steven J.
    The pathology of man : a study of human evil / by Steven James Bartlett ;
with a foreword by Eric A. Zillmer and Irving Greenberg.
        p. cm.
    Includes bibliographical references (p. ) and index.
    ISBN 0-398-07557-3 -- ISBN 0-398-07558-1 (pbk.)
    1. Good and evil--Psychological aspects. 2. Pathology. I. Title.

BF789.E94B37 2005
170--dc22

                                                                    2004063718

*Dedicated to the few*
*whose qualities of person and of mind,*
*whose strength of conviction, courage, and aversion to cruelty,*
*keep them from aggression, blind conformity, obedience, and complicity.*

# FOREWORD

by ERIC A. ZILLMER

Carl R. Pacifico Professor of Neuropsychology, Drexel University, and author of
*The Quest for the Nazi Personality: A Psychological Investigation of Nazi War Criminals*

Steven James Bartlett's *The Pathology of Man* marks the most comprehensive examination of human evil to date. Drawing from different fields of study, including psychology and epistemology, Bartlett sets out on a *Tour de Force* of delineating the parameters on human evil.

Bartlett asks the question how exactly is it possible for humans to engage in acts of destruction, genocide, mass murder, and torture? This is an ambitious goal but one that Bartlett masters by writing with great clarity and by carefully reexamining published accounts together with providing a fresh perspective on the topic.

The resulting text is a most welcomed addition to the field and provides for fascinating reading. *The Pathology of Man* is a timely, scholarly, and important piece of work that should appeal to anyone who is interested in understanding human evil.

✧

by IRVING GREENBERG

President, Jewish Life Network/Steinhardt Foundation
Chairman, United States Holocaust Memorial Council 2000-2002

This book is stunning, upsetting, gripping. A generation after the Holocaust and a century after the greatest mass murders and destructive wars of all time, Bartlett sets out a theory of human evil as a ubiquitous disease and humankind as the pathogen/parasite which is rapidly spreading and, in the process, killing its hosts (be they other humans, other species of life, and nature itself).

While Bartlett's review of theories of human evil behavior and of the literature is illuminating and often fascinating, the conclusions are unrelenting and devastating.

The universal character of human evil and the likelihood of its further spread in the form of destructive and genocidal acting out is affirmed. The book offers no anodyne, no easy choices, and warns against the pathology of hope, that is, escape into wish fulfillment rather than facing up to the issue.

Nevertheless, the book is a moral act of the highest order. In essence, Bartlett insists that the first step to check a highly dangerous fatal disease is to diagnose its presence, to confront all evasions and refute all denials of its virulence. This paves the way for the development of possible cures. If the book leaves us with no respite and no paths of redemption from evil, it leaves us troubled enough and aroused enough to want to do something. That is no small contribution.

These prefatory comments would be incomplete without mentioning the erudition, the intellectual insight and playfulness, the gallows humor and the self-restraint which deepen and lighten this book.

# ACKNOWLEDGMENTS

Research for this book spans many years, as do relationships with people whose encouragement and guidance I would like to acknowledge here. The acknowledgments I would like to make relate to the three main disciplines which are the focus of this book and which I have had the opportunity to study: pathology, psychology, and epistemology. Special thanks are due to

MELVIN CALVIN, Nobel Laureate in Chemistry of the University of California at Berkeley, for his memorable and warm encouragement in connection with my search for new antibiotics.

THOMAS N. FAST for his generous guidance and free run of the microbiology lab at the University of Santa Clara.

WILLIAM ALTUS, of the University of California, Santa Barbara, for his insightful direction as my interests in pathology grew to include psychiatric pathology.

ROBERT M. HUTCHINS, Founder and Director of the Center for the Study of Democratic Institutions, for his encouragement that I would contribute to what, in the introductory volume of the *Great Books of the Western World*, he called "The Great Conversation." His breadth of mind, intellectual sharpness, generous humanity and spirit, and statesmanship in the nearly forgotten meaning of that word are greatly missed.

GABRIEL MARCEL for backing research reported in this book, and for making it possible for me to study with Paul Ricoeur at the Université de Paris.

PAUL RICOEUR, whose wide range of interests and scholarly knowledge, coupled with an intellectual fearlessness and creative capacity, made it possible to turn the usually dry and intellectually humdrum dissertation experience into the development of a method and approach which, now some 40 years later, I am still tilling.

C. F. VON WEIZSÄCKER, Director of the Max-Planck-Institut in Starnberg, Germany, for his support of research reported in Part III of this book. Like Hutchins and Ricoeur, von Weizsäcker was sufficiently at home in a non-compartmentalized openness to inquiry not to be threatened by it. I therefore wish to express my indebtedness to him for offering a supportive environment in which research of this kind could be undertaken.

THOMAS MALONEY, clinical psychology in Clayton, Missouri, who became an important colleague and close friend. I owe much to him, and now to his memory, for his willingness to provide me with a practicum as his co-therapist.

RAPHAEL J. BECVAR for his stimulating teaching, intellectual exchange, and friendship, and whose systems approach to individual psychotherapy and family therapy left an enduring appreciation.

KAREN M. BARTLETT, my wife, love, and friend, for her steadfast support and encouragement over the years, and for the time and intelligence which she devoted to help me to improve the writing of this work.

Above all, PAUL ALEXANDER BARTLETT, novelist-artist and my father, and ELIZABETH BARTLETT, poet and my mother, for a culturally rich upbringing in which the values of intellectual courage and honesty, independence of mind, and compassion were foremost.

Finally, I am indebted to the country of my birth, Mexico, for making clear to me that fine education relies less on modern classrooms and expensive facilities, and more upon respect for learning and culture, values that cannot be purchased. I wish to acknowledge my indebtedness to small rural schools in Mexico which communicated these values to me. Mexico has comparatively few published psychologists and philosophers to its credit, especially who publish in English. Although I have dual citizenship, I affiliate with Mexico whatever intellectual contributions I have been able to make.

✧

## CREDITS

Thanks are due to these authors and publishers for permission to use the following:

The graph of world population growth, in Chapter 17, from *Beyond the Limits: Confronting Global Collapse*, Envisioning a Sustainable Future by Donella H. Meadows, Dennis L. Meadows, and Jørgen Randers. Copyright 1992 by Donella H. Meadows, Dennis L. Meadows, and Jørgen Randers. Used by permission of Chelsea Green Publishing Company.

# CONTENTS

## PART II: THE PSYCHOLOGY OF HUMAN EVIL

## PART III: THE CONCEPTUAL PATHOLOGY OF MAN

# THE PATHOLOGY OF MAN
## A STUDY OF HUMAN EVIL

# INTRODUCTION

*Destructiveness and cruelty...constitute a paradox: they express life turning against itself.... They are the only true perversion. Understanding them does not mean condoning them. But unless we understand them, we have no way to recognize how they may be reduced, and what factors tend to increase them.* – Erich Fromm (1973:9)

Human violence, brutality, hatred, and cruelty—expressed in wars, murders, bigotry, and persecution—ought not to surprise us. As this study makes clear, these emotions and behaviors are to be expected, indeed we should be able to foresee them, to predict them, and, perhaps someday, to control them.

We cannot yet control them. As we shall see in the course of this work, most men and women do not welcome such control. Not yet, and perhaps not for a very long time. But at least we can understand the unattractive side of human existence, and in understanding, not passively forgive, but rather stand firm in a willingness to judge, condemn, and act when men and women feel and behave in ways that bring about the intentional suffering of others, and often their own in the process. When a reader puts this book down, he or she should no longer be able to say, "I don't understand what makes people do such terrible things." That people do such things is not only not surprising, it is, as we shall see, to be expected.

The topic of evil and rarely the more specialized topic relating to *human* evil have customarily been considered within the frameworks of religion, mythology, literature, symbolism, anthropology, moral philosophy, and ethics. The word 'evil' still summons up connotations for many that involve the dark powers of witches and demons, or else theodicy, with its efforts to accommodate or adjust theistic religion to the reality of evil in the world, or perennial philosophical discussions of good and evil, or the disputations of theologians, or the socially concrete descriptions of anthropologists. Mythologies have tried to account for evil, religions have sought to give men and women ways to cope with it, moralities have attempted to lessen it, and literature has narrated accounts of it. Certainly the word 'evil' most frequently has these associations, which are irrelevant to this book's focus, and which I cannot neutralize even if I intend to ignore them. This book is about none of these things: There are no other-worldly spirits to be found within these pages, no moral philosophy, no theological apologetics, no anthropology of symbols and myths. Having subtracted away these connotations, the word 'evil' may seem to many to become so deflated and shrunken in upon itself that it stands in need of a clarified, alternative meaning.

In the fields of pathology, psychiatry, and psychology there exist precedents, however, for its descriptive use that avoid these connotations. There, 'evil' is used to point to a connection between our species and a group of emotional responses, attitudes, and patterns of thought and behavior that together cause great suffering and destruction, often involve cruelty and aggression, and have resulted and continue to result in countless deaths and untold individual misery. No author to date, however, has undertaken a comprehensive study of human evil from the standpoint of these disciplines.

There is perhaps no equally neglected subject of such fundamental importance to humanity and to other forms of life that share this world than the subject of human evil. Leading psychologists, including Freud, Jung, Menninger, and Fromm, have long urged the need for its study. But psychological research that has directly confronted human evil has been exceedingly meager. A computerized search, for example, through the holdings of more than ten million volumes in the Library of Congress reveals only a light handful of books relating to the psychology of human evil. One cannot help but feel dumbfounded that this topic of such enormity and consequence has been so little investigated.

Why is there evil in the world? Why is man a creature whose history and personal life are so filled with suffering—suffering for which man himself is so often clearly the cause? The question, Why is there evil?, seems evidently to be on a par with the question, Why is there pain? But the question specifically concerning *human evil* is, as we shall see, inherently different from both of these. There, man is both victimizer and victim, both agent and subject, both he who destroys and inflicts suffering, and he who is destroyed and suffers at his own hand.

It is incontestable that human evil is one of man's most serious and pressing concerns if mankind is to endure. His social history is a bloody continuum of war, mass murder, individual and communal hate crimes, and the grief these have brought to countless millions who remain behind, bereft, to suffer and struggle on. Instead of a reduction in atrocities against life, civilization's march to the beat of progress has witnessed an ugly compounding of these forms of pain during the twentieth century. Two world wars, a multitude of local wars, and genocides in Europe, the Middle East, Central and South America, Asia, and Africa have killed and disabled an incredible number of people. The toll of humanity acting on itself during the twentieth century alone is so large it is impossible for the mind to fathom. More than 100 million lives were lost in wars, and more than one billion people were killed in genocides. (See Chapters 9, 11, 12, and 14.) To this must be added unrecorded numbers of individual and gang murders, judicial executions, infanticide, as well as the other many ways that human beings brutalize one another and deal out suffering. It is easy to lose sight of the fact that what appear on paper as unimaginably large numbers represent individual men, women, and their children whose lives were savagely cut short, or who were permanently maimed, physically or emotionally, for a variety of expressed justifications and because of inarticulate mass hysteria and insanity. The total number of people who, in one century, have suffered at the hands of others or who have been killed is horrifying and overwhelming.

The magnitude of this carnage and cruelty has no precedent in world history. Unfortunately, mass violence is only the larger manifestation of a pattern of human violence, malice, and viciousness that has developed and taken up unquestioned residence in the minds and actions of individual men and women. We have also witnessed the distressing growth of individual violence, brutalities of hate, "thrill murders," vicious hazings, school mass killings, and gang assassinations, which have gained intense momentum during the past decades, many of these crimes concentrated in the juvenile population.

Erich Fromm called such destructiveness and cruelty human evils. But in an age intoxicated by moral relativism, any such judgment, Fromm's included, has been opened to debate. Partially as a result of paralysis brought about by relativism, the destructive manifestations of human hatred, pride, envy, and greed remain unchecked, and are, as this book will make clear, actively encouraged in ways that are far from subtle, but which nonetheless are for the most part ignored both by our religious and political institutions and by reflective psychology and philosophy.

On the one hand, there exists a huge body of literature about the subject of evil, about goodness and evil, and about their treatment within the world's many mythologies and religious doctrinal viewpoints. This tremendous body of literature has encouraged man to believe that he has explained, that he can cope with, and that he is able ultimately to rationalize the existence of evil in himself and in others of his species.

On the other hand, no studies exist which provide a comprehensive analysis of the psychology of human evil, and none exist that relate an analysis of human thought processes to the psychology of human evil. An understanding of the reasons for man's destructive behavior calls for an examination of both the psychological and epistemological origins of human evil. A psychological study is called for in order to understand what it is about the average human being's world of feelings and behavior that predisposes him or her to evil. An epistemological study is called for to determine what it is about both the average person's patterns of thinking and the specific contents of the individual's mental life that support and encourage human evil. Nowhere in the literature do we find a work devoted to an inclusive, integrative, scholarly study of the psychology and epistemology of human evil. The present book responds to this need. Its principal purposes are these:

(1) The study is solidly grounded within the framework of pathology and the theory of disease. Here the book breaks new ground by offering a clear, empirically based, and theoretically sound understanding of human evil as a widespread, real, non-metaphorical pathology. The book critically evaluates the principal established theories of disease, and formulates a unified, framework-relative theory of disease from the standpoint of which it is appropriate to classify human evil as a pathology which is *not* a deviation from an accepted norm, but rather is a *normal state*. This is a radical departure from the conventional view that pathology must be understood as deviation from normality, and provides the necessary psychological foundation which the banality of human evil has in the past not had.

(2) For the first time, diagnostic judgments concerning human evil that have been expressed by numerous psychiatrists, psychologists, ethologists, and quantitative historians are brought together, discussed, and critiqued. Leading contributors in these areas of research have sought to understand human evil, but they have for the most part considered the topic only in passing, or in the context of general studies of human aggression and destructiveness. In no other work can one find a comprehensive discussion of the subject of human evil as it has been examined by such psychiatrists and psychologists as Freud, Jung, Menninger, Fromm, and Peck, by such psychologically-focused quantitative historians as Wright, Sorokin, Rashevsky, and Richardson, by such ethologists as Lorenz and Eibl-Eibesfeldt, by obedience psychologists Milgram, Miller, and Mixon, by psychologists of genocide and terrorism, and by psychologists who have studied the nature of what I will call "moral intelligence."

(3) For the first time, the author directs attention to mankind's role as a true pathogen, a pathogen no previous pathologist has studied. Here, the concept of human evil is broadened within the framework of disease theory to show that the human species is *auto-pathological* in many ways, destructive to itself and a danger to the continued existence of the species. We shall see that man's psychological constitution and conceptual structure frequently bring about and foster cruelty, suffering, and death, and accomplish these things in a wide variety of sometimes subtle and often very manifest ways. We shall find that mankind is inherently self-injuring and self-destructive; its destructiveness is at times limited to conflicts among individual members of the species, and at others comes to infect entire societies. Within individuals, self-destructive pathology may take the form of suicide; within societies, it may take the form of revolutions or genocide. When explicitly self-destructive forces are not

engaged, human destructiveness is expressed in conflicts between individuals in the many forms of emotional and physical abuse and murder, and between societies in the form of wars. At the same time, the human species is a *global pathogen* in terms of its worldwide destructive effects on other species. A connection is therefore made between the psychiatric-psychological understanding of human evil and ecology. From this standpoint, human evil becomes recognizable as a real, non-metaphorical pathology that results in destruction not only to members of the human species, but to other species as well.

(4) While there has been surprisingly little research specifically devoted to the psychology of human evil, there has been a total absence of research linking an epistemological study of man's characteristic patterns of thought with the results of empirical and humanistic psychology. Here, new ground is also broken by showing how human aggression, destructiveness, and cruelty to members of the species are fostered and maintained by human patterns of thought and by a conceptual vocabulary that encourages a certain interpretation of the world, which itself is pathological. Man is, after all, not only a creature whose behavior expresses what he feels, but what he thinks. The book therefore concludes by considering epistemological pathologies of human thought that underlie much of the pathology of human behavior.

The present study seeks, then, to examine the relationship between a psychological understanding of human evil and an epistemology of characteristically human ways of thinking. The psychology of human evil deals with the affective component in man responsible for human evil; the study's epistemological focus deals with the conceptual vocabulary used by man in his representation and interpretation of reality, which, in turn, affects his attitudes and actions. In the reflexive interplay between thought and feeling—between, that is, the subjects of epistemology and psychology—we find a group of processes that create, promote, and sustain the phenomenon of human evil. The evil which mankind is capable of realizing is a direct outgrowth of his affective and cognitive constitution.

The book is divided into three parts: Part I lays a foundation using central concepts of pathology, theories of disease, and epidemiology. From the standpoint of the resulting framework, human evil is identified as a non-metaphorical and widespread pathology. Part II discusses and analyzes contributions by leading psychiatrists and psychologically-focused researchers that are relevant to the study of human evil. Part III considers the work of several epistemologists—those who have shared a concern to analyze concepts by means that resemble those used in psychotherapy. Here, the goal is to make evident major and deeply rooted patterns of human thought that are associated with the psychological phenomena studied in Part II.

The book's intention in these three parts is to propose a combined psychological-epistemological approach to phenomena which, throughout mankind's history, have shown us to be creatures capable of behavior that is highly destructive—to ourselves and to other forms of life. The book attempts to identify what it is about human psychology and about familiar ways of conceptualizing the world that leads to pathological behavior.

The theory that is developed has a hypothetico-deductive character: From the standpoint of this general theory, we should be surprised if the human species had *not* behaved throughout history as it has; in this way, a form of retrodictive confirmation of the theory is possible. And from the standpoint of the theory proposed, we should expect the continuation of certain specifically human patterns of destructive behavior in the future; here the theory is open to falsification.

✧

There is a strong avoidance-wish among many people that prevents them from recognizing the ugly side of the human species. It is a very nearly automatic resistance, sometimes a repugnance, to consider, even as an abstract possibility, the hypothesis that mankind may in reality not be a source and model of goodness, but rather, and to a significant extent, possesses many of the characteristics that we tend to associate with pathology. This automatic resistance or repugnance usually appears to be both emotional and intellectual in nature. It is deeply rooted—so much so that many people whom one believes to be open-minded and committed to truth in inquiry, as soon as the topic of human evil is brought to their attention, feel called upon to proclaim man's native goodness and the praiseworthy qualities of the species, in a kind of reflex arc that blinds our species to its own failings. This very human *resistance* to view man dispassionately—to judge the extent and degree of his psychological and conceptual attraction to hatred, violence, destructiveness, and cruelty—is itself one of the dominant factors in a dynamic that perpetuates human evil. Man's unwillingness to judge his species impartially and to place the basis for his evil in the clear light of day is one of the key features, and perhaps the cornerstone, of the psychology and epistemology of human evil. There is, as we will see, a profoundly rooted, and paralyzingly entrenching, psychological and epistemological basis for this resistance.

As is normally the case in matters that inflame emotions and cloud the mind, there are multiple causes for this recalcitrance against seeing mankind in a diminished light. There usually is, of course, pride in one's species. There may be psychological denial, a wish to insulate oneself from observations and conclusions unpleasant in nature. There may be self-kindling idealism, the wish and even the need to candy-coat one's interpretation of life. There may be intransigent religious commitments at stake. To allay these forms of resistance, there appears to be a need for the researcher who studies human evil to reassure his readership that, in spite of the restricted focus any study must have, there *do* exist phenomena which fall outside the class of those considered. We do therefore take for granted from the outset the existence of such things as human goodness, human dignity, integrity, and compassion. There exists beauty in the natural world, and in many human creations of poetry, music, and art. There is much that human beings have created that is wonderful, inspiring, and good. Although the focus of this volume is delimited, there is nothing here that denies or depreciates these things. But just as concrete, detailed descriptions of examples of good health are largely irrelevant in a medical compendium of diseases, so are instances of human goodness largely irrelevant to our present focus. The world is many-colored and many-shaded; it is not black or white. Mankind is both good and evil, and individuals exist who exemplify all the shades that nature and society at any time can produce.

If this study successfully gives evidence for the claims it makes, then a strong case against the human species will have been made. But the case against man—and this presumably needs to be emphasized and emphasized again—does not entail that a case *for* man cannot be made. However, *that* case does not need to be made nearly as much as the negative, diagnostic case—for man's capacity to pat himself on the back is endemic and cannot be significantly discouraged. He is, in fact, so much in love with himself and his species that he is blind to many of its shortcomings, prefers to remain so, and will energetically oppose efforts to focus serious attention on them. He therefore considers that anything that paints his portrait in a particularly bad light must express misguided misanthropy.

Readers who do not like the conclusions that this book reaches will doubtless dismiss them by labeling this study and its author misanthropic. This would be a mistake of understanding and judgment. Of course no one can devote years of a life seeking to understand human evil without being affected by the cumulative comprehension of many centuries of bloodshed, the hollow anguish of so many victims, the ease with which ordinary people agree to become willing participants in group murder, and their recalcitrance to know what they do. I do not believe that anyone should wish to remain unaffected by these things, least of all the investigator himself. The way I have been affected is in my recognition that humanity more frequently scores high in the category of the exceptional, kind, creative individual, and exceedingly low in the categories of group prejudice and hatred, and its resulting herd behavior. The majority is, by definition, not made up of the few who have sought to bring to the world a taste of beauty or the savor of truth. The majority is made up of generally quite ordinary people, each an individual, but most still, as we shall see, comparatively primitive in terms of what will later be called *moral intelligence*. Educational attainment, social status, race, color, and creed do not exempt individual human beings and their groups from moral incapacity and stupidity. The book's conclusions therefore imply a judgment both of the individual, to the extent that he or she exhibits behavior and patterns of thought and emotion that are pathological, and of the human collective, where variations among individuals are averaged out.

There are two divergent purposes in understanding. The highest has always been regarded as a type of understanding that is an end in itself, where the simple act of knowing improves the self and makes more meaningful one's sense of place in the universe. The search for truth for truth's sake comes from this motivation. Then, there is the contrasting purpose of the engineer, who wishes to implement results in order to advance social ends, to progress, to produce utility, and thereby to improve the world.

This study is unapologetically the work of a scholar who wishes to know, for that reason alone. Beyond this, no one can reasonably hope to improve the human condition and the condition of the world without the ability to control, at the very least, humanity's predilection for violence and destruction, the species' runaway reproduction, and its environmental rapacity. This study of human evil is intended as a first step in reaching a level of understanding of ourselves that can perhaps, if sufficient time remains for our species, lead to effective control over our greatest shortcomings.

# PART I

# PATHOLOGY AND MAN

# PART I

# PATHOLOGY AND MAN

Pathology and the related concepts of disease, infectiousness, and contagion have traditionally been applied to phenomena that deviate in some way from a set of norms, most frequently norms that are endorsed by society. There are, however, real pathologies that are not deviations from a norm, but rather afflict an entire group. In the case of the human species, the field of pathology has been slow to recognize the existence of universal disease—that is, pathology that afflicts the majority so that a state of disease is a normal condition, not a deviation from health that affects only a minority.

In this section, a framework of understanding is developed in terms of which human evil can be studied using the theoretical resources of pathology. A framework-relative theory of disease is presented which sees individual mental illness and social and conceptual pathology in a new light. From this standpoint, the phenomenon of human evil can be effectively and accurately understood for what it is.

Readers whose main area of interest is the psychology of human aggression and destructiveness may be tempted to skip to Part II. Those who do this are likely to reach an understanding of human evil that is at best fragmentary and incomplete for lack of a unifying theoretical framework. They will see malignant human traits in their particularity, but not the larger picture within which it is compelling to call them pathologies in the true meaning of this word. Part I makes clear how, from the standpoint of the science of pathology, it is legitimate, justified, and of explanatory value to recognize the human species as a pathogen and as pathogenic to itself. This first part of our study is essential to any reader who would see that human evil is a real, non-metaphorical pathology, a pathology that affects billions usually without their knowledge but with their full complicity.

11

# CHAPTER 1

# PATHOLOGY AND THEORIES OF DISEASE

## DISEASE THAT IS NOT METAPHOR

In many languages there is a common metaphorical way of speaking: It is to label *as a disease* any phenomenon or condition that the speaker wishes to portray in a disparaging light and so emphasize its undesirability. This facile vocabulary of depreciation is not limited to use of the word 'disease', but draws upon a variety of kindred expressions that come from the clinical language of medicine: And so it has become commonplace to speak of rampant commercialism and materialism as "diseases," of city sprawl as a "blight," of "contagious "enthusiasm, and of "infectious" laughter. Or we may label a comedian's humor as "sick," and "sick" also may be a declining stock market and television commercials that are in bad taste. Such metaphorical extensions of language that has a clinical flavor are widespread and often applied unthinkingly.

Metaphorical "diagnosis" is a mental habit to which we have become accustomed, and, like most mental processes that have become automatic, has slipped away from reflective control, becoming a fashion that deadens sensitivity to genuine pathologies. For outside the tangible context of organic/physical disease, when a phenomenon is called a "disease," the prevailing tendency is either to assume a figurative meaning, or to assume that a private fiction has been elevated to the status of a public referent.

There exist, however and unfortunately, very real diseases that are not solely a result of disruptions of organic functions, though many may have a physical basis. Our metaphor-ridden, loose employment of what sounds like clinical language derived from physiology, medicine, and psychological diagnosis has rendered suspect any clinical judgment that refers beyond the most familiar forms of pathology. When every disagreeable condition is called a disease, the meaning of 'disease' is quickly lost on what Clifton Fadiman called "the scrap heap of popular misuse."

This book is about phenomena that constitute real, non-metaphorical, non-fictitious diseases. We need to recognize clearly what our conceptual vocabulary means when true and legitimate pathology is in view. The present chapter and those that follow it in this Part I seek to establish a common basis of understanding between the author and the reader, so that the clinical vocabulary used in this study has a clear and well-grounded meaning. To this end it will be important to be able to presuppose on the part of the reader a general under-standing of the nature of pathology; something of its history and the development of the concepts of infectiousness, contagion, and antibiosis; the types of organic disease; and an understanding of the main theories of disease that have been proposed.

## THE NATURE OF PATHOLOGY

The word 'pathology' is derived from the Greek 'πάθος' or 'pathos', meaning suffering or disease, and more broadly it refers to feelings such as sadness, misery, and loneliness. Pathos gradually has come to be associated with "anything bad that befalls anyone" (Link 1932:134), a meaning upon which a number of current theories of disease tend to focus, as we shall see. The term 'pathology' traces its lineage in English back to 1597, when the word was first used in Jacques Guillemeau's *French chirurgerye, or, All the manualle operations of chirurgerye*. There, "pathologia" is said to "treatethe of the cause and occasione of the sicknesses." Today, the term 'pathology' is still used in much the same way to refer to the science or study of disease.

Diseases can be classified as acute, chronic, or latent. Furthermore, they may be infectious, metabolic, genetic, environmental, nutritional, etc. They may affect only a few individuals, or a large proportion of members of a society. The term 'pathology' as it is used in this book refers to a broad spectrum of diseases or disorders, extending from the familiar biologically-based conception of disease to less familiar forms of psychological pathology, social pathology, and conceptual pathology. In all of these applications, the term 'pathology' is used with a non-metaphorical understanding of its roots in the general theory of disease, which includes among its purposes the therapeutic concern to eliminate the πάθος that conditions of disease produce.

Pathology, so understood, is the scientific study of disease. Its focus may be microorganic, biochemical, genetic, physiological, anatomical, nutritional, environmental, psychiatric, or cognitive—taking into consideration any of a wide range of causes and conditions that variously contribute to the incidence of disease. Pathology seeks to formulate general principles involved in the occurrence of disease; it proceeds by means of empirical analyses of pathologic processes and reactions. To accomplish these ends, pathology focuses attention upon the physiological state of an organism as well as upon conditions in the organism's environment that must be satisfied in order for the organism to live and function effectively. As a result, the study of pathology does not begin, or end, with a study of specific disease entities such as the tubercle bacillus or the malaria virus, but its scope is more inclusive, involving relationships between organisms and their respective, frequently specialized, environments. For often, changes in an organism's accustomed environment are associated with the development of pathologies that affect the organism's ability to function. In short, pathology is at once medical and ecological. And, as we shall see later on, the limited, common-sense association of pathology with biological disease proves to be excessively narrow when we confront the reality of psychological, social, and conceptual pathologies, all of which possess the defining characteristics of disease. It is therefore important that we have a clear understanding of those characteristics before proceeding. The characterization of disease has, as we shall see, evolved through history.

## A SHORT HISTORY OF PATHOLOGY

The most basic and intuitive way to understand disease is in terms of a breakdown in the normal state of an organism. That normal state involves a delicately maintained dynamic of inner and outer balance that relies upon a multiplicity of genetic, biochemical, physiological, and environmental processes controlled by mechanisms whose complexity is often not fully understood. From this point of view, disease is the result of a disruption of an organism's normal inner homeostasis, a concept developed by Walter Cannon in 1928 to describe an organism's stability as a biological system. From this point of view, disease comes about as a result of the disturbance and breakdown of conditions that play a vital role in the organism's interactive relationship with its environment. Pathogenesis describes how such a breakdown occurs.

The theory of disease as homeostatic breakdown appears historically to have been the most ancient. It is rooted in the view of disease developed by Hippocrates, who was born about 460 B.C. on the small Aegean island of Cos. Hippocrates and his followers thought of disease as a natural event that comes about as a result of an imbalance among the four humors of the body: blood, phlegm, yellow bile, and black bile.

The next step in the evolution of pathology had to wait for more than five hundred years, when Galen (129 A.D. – c. 216), born in the town of Pergamum (today known as Bergama, in Turkey), extended and refined the doctrine of the four humors. His humoral approach to disease then remained the dominant theory for more than a thousand years. Even after a millennium, emphasis was still being placed on the role of "the four temperaments," on phlegmatic, choleric, sanguine, or melancholy influences.

It took until approximately 1500 for the theory of disease to evolve to its next phase in the hands of Andreas Vesalius, who was born in Brussels in 1514 or 1515 and died in 1564. Vesalius based his work on extensive experience in human dissection, so that for the first time a medical theory of disease was formulated on a solid empirical foundation. In 1543, he published *De humani corporis fabrica libri septum* [On the Fabric of the Human Body in Seven Books], often now referred to as the *Fabrica*. Interestingly, this was the same year in which Copernicus published his major work, *De revolutionibus orbium coelestium* [On the Revolution of the Celestial Orbs]. So, within the span of a single year a revolution began that was to affect how mankind would view both the microcosm of his body and the macrocosm of the universe. But like any revolutionary contribution to human knowledge, the reaction to Vesalius's work, as it was to Copernicus's discovery, was one of outrage as old beliefs were proved fundamentally wrong.

The modern era of pathology began with Giovanni Batista Morgagni (1682-1771), who served as professor of theoretical medicine in Padua. Over a period of some fifty years, he summarized seven hundred autopsies, the majority of which he performed himself, while others were done by his teacher, Valsalva. It was the first time that systematic, logical connections between the symptoms of disease and autopsy findings were formulated within the framework of a general classification of diseases. Morgagni's life's work, *De sedibus et causis morborum* [On the Seats and Causes of Disease], was published in 1761.

In the year of Morgagni's death, a French physician, Marie-Francois-Xavier Bichat was born. He was to live a brief life, dying soon after his thirtieth birthday. In spite of a life cut so short, he influenced the development of pathology by asking how diseases arise in affected tissues, rather than in entire organs. This trend toward the increasingly small-scale localization of disease was carried a step further by Rudolf Ludwig Carl Virchow (1821-1902), who was responsible for moving the focus of pathology from tissues to the cellular level. The cell was identified as the basic biological unit of plants and animals by Theodor Schwann (1810-1882), and building on this basis, Virchow, along with Robert Remak (1815-1865), concentrated research in pathology on this basic unit of biological structure.

From Hippocrates' theory of humoral imbalance to the late nineteenth century, a period of nearly two thousand years, pathology progressed, then, from a metaphorical conception of physiological homeostasis to an understanding of organs as the seat of disease, to tissue and then to cell pathology.

This process of progressive refinement that has pushed the boundaries of human awareness in the direction of the increasingly small has not stopped. Research in molecular pathology was begun in the mid-twentieth century, when sickle-cell anemia was traced to abnormal hemoglobin. Soon, atomic diseases were identified with the advent of nuclear medicine. Today, more than a century after Virchow's work, the question has been raised whether some pathogens—mycoplasms and viruses—may in fact originate *de novo*. And more recently, Stanley Prusiner, recipient of the Nobel Prize for Physiology or Medicine in 1997, formulated the prion (pronounced "pree-on") theory of disease, in which the responsible pathogen appears to be an infectious protein. Prions differ from all other known infectious pathogens in several respects. Foremost among these, and worthy of note in this overview of types of pathogens, prions do not appear to contain a nucleic acid genome that codes for their progeny, as do traditionally recognized organic pathogens, which include viruses, viroids, bacteria, fungi, and parasites. The discovery and classification of pathogens comprise, in other words, an open-ended and evolving project.

Advances in pathology have experienced the acceleration characteristic of many branches of science. Remarkably, it was only a century ago that medicine "did not know the cause of a single important human disease" and was able to do very little to prevent or to cure disease. (Hudson 1983:141) "In a single century the understanding of disease increased more than in the previous forty centuries combined." (121)

## INFECTIOUSNESS, CONTAGION, AND ANTIBIOSIS

Since these three concepts will have direct application in this study of human pathology, let us look briefly at their historical development. In the evolution of medicine, the idea that some diseases are infectious and could therefore be transmitted from one person to another was first studied systematically in an Arabic text published in approximately 900 A.D., the *Book of Treasure*. In the West, the Jewish Old Testament gave early expression to the idea of contagion in its descriptions of leprosy. But it was the destructive power of recurrent waves of bubonic plague that gradually forced the public to accept the reality of contagion, an acceptance that grew over a period of centuries. In his treatise *On Plague*, the fourteenth-century Arabic physician Ibn al-Khatib wrote: "The existence of contagion is established by experience, study, and the evidence of the senses, by trustworthy reports on transmission by garments, vessels, ear-rings; by the spread of it by persons from one house, by infection of a healthy sea-port by an arrival from an infected land." (Hudson 1983:143)

Two centuries later, al-Khatib's view of contagious disease was developed further by the Renaissance physician Girolamo Fracastoro (1478-1553). Fracastoro wrote two works that have been important to historians of disease: his poem "Syphilis sive morbus Gallicus," from 1530, and his prose work in three books, *De contagione et contagiosis morbis et eorum curatione*, published in 1546 (Fracastoro 1930/1546). The interest of historians of medicine has been drawn to these works due to Fracastoro's emphasis on "seeds of disease" as an explanation for the plague and typhus, perhaps anticipating the microbial theory of disease by several centuries.

In Fracastoro's time, it was commonly recognized that even during the most devastating epidemic, some individuals did not get sick. Two explanations were given, but neither could yet be proved or disproved. "Either the lucky individual did not come into contact with the noxious agent of plague, or what was more likely, his or her resistance had been so strengthened that the body was able to maintain its equilibrium and not succumb to the external changes." (Nutton 1990:231; Fracastoro 1930/1546:60)

The infectious nature of disease and the phenomenon of contagion had to wait until the nineteenth century before significant advances in knowledge came. But, fortuitously, it turned out that therapeutic advances were possible in spite of deficient knowledge: For example, Ignaz Phillip Semmelweis (1818-1865), born in the area that is now Budapest, urged the use of chlorine wash as a disinfectant, and by its means during the mid-1800s was successful in reducing the incidence of puerperal fever that killed many women following childbirth. Semmelweis's analytical ability saved the lives of many women by means of a simple technique of antisepsis—long before the streptococcus cause of the disease was identified.

By approximately 1859, Louis Pasteur had become concerned with the nature of contagious disease, but his research was slowed by demands placed on him by the French silk industry, for which Pasteur was able to confirm that a protozoan was responsible for silkworm disease. By 1876, Pasteur had become convinced that microorganisms responsible for fermentation in wine and beer had their counterparts in organisms that cause disease in humans. In particular, he was able to develop a rabies vaccine without ever observing or identifying the virus that caused it.

It was not long until Robert Koch (1843-1910) discovered the life-cycle of anthrax bacteria, cultured them, and was able to verify that they cause anthrax in animals. In 1882, Koch discovered the bacteria that cause tuberculosis, basing his work on the research of a French army surgeon, Jean Antoine Villemin (1827-1892), who had been able to infect animals with tuberculosis from human beings, proving that it was contagious.

Progress then came rapidly. Before 1900, microbiological agents responsible for a range of diseases were correctly identified, among them botulism, cholera, diphtheria, dysentery, gonorrhea, meningococcal meningitis, plague, pneumococcal pneumonia, typhoid, tetanus, as well as numerous bacterial infections due to streptococci and staphylococci. The so-called germ theory of disease was solidly established by the beginning of the twentieth century.

This brief account of discoveries relating to the infectious nature of diseases would not be complete without mentioning the role of antibiosis in combating disease. In general terms, antibiosis is the name of any of a multitude of ways in which one organism can inhibit the growth of another, or kill it. In 1889, Villemin named the phenomenon of antibiosis, while Pasteur appears to have been the first to demonstrate its existence on the microorganic level. But the real importance and usefulness of antibiosis was first discovered in 1928 by Alexander Fleming (1881-1955), when he noticed that one of his staph cultures was contaminated by mold, and his attention was drawn to the area of antibiosis that formed around the mold colonies: Immediately outside the borders of the mold colonies a zone formed in which the staph bacteria did not grow. This no-growth zone, called a ring of inhibition, is where compounds produced by the mold form an inhospitable, toxic environment for the bacteria. In one of the famous accidents of scientific discovery, the mold that happened to contaminate Fleming's staph culture was the bread mold, *Penicillium*, whose secretion, penicillin, became a life-saving medicine for the treatment of a range of bacterial infections. It is of interest to note that Fleming's work finally gave modern sanction and proof to a practice in use more than 3,400 years ago. According to the Ebers medical papyrus written in 1552 B.C., Egyptians prescribed "bread in rotten condition," a natural source of penicillin, for the very ill.

Antibiosis is not limited to the microorganic world. Some plants secrete chemicals that inhibit the growth or kill neighboring plants that otherwise would compete with them. For example, the black walnut tree (*Juglans nigra*) produces juglone, which kills many herbaceous plants within the area of the walnut's root system. Similarly, in the deserts of the western United States, antibiotic inhibition among different plant species prevents them from growing too close together, a state of affairs essential to their survival in an environment of scarce water.

The phenomenon of antibiosis in which one organism produces toxins that inhibit the growth or kill other organisms will later become important in studying a number of ways in which colonies of human organisms exert an antibiotic effect upon numerous other species, and sometimes upon one another.

## TYPES OF ORGANIC DISEASE

So far we have emphasized diseases that can be traced to a specific agent, a bacterium, virus, perhaps a prion. However, there are evidently numerous diseases that are not the consequence of an infectious microscopic agent. One major class of diseases of this kind is environmental disease. For example, in the early 1950s when a Japanese industrial plant dumped mercury into Minamata Bay, the inorganic and comparatively less toxic mercury was converted into highly deadly methyl mercury, was absorbed by sea life, and was in turn eaten by human beings, fatally poisoning many. Numerous environmental diseases have so far been identified, among them: berylliosis, contracted from exposure to beryllium, which is used, e.g., in the making of fluorescent lights; bagassosis, which results from inhaling a residual product in the manufacture of sugar from sugar cane; byssinosis, from inhaling cotton dust; coal miner's pneumoconiosis or Black Lung Disease; liver cancer among workers handling vinyl chloride; green-tobacco sickness among harvesters of tobacco; respiratory illness among meat packers. (Hudson 1983:6) It is clear that environmental diseases come about as a result of activities that people engage in, which bring them into contact with toxic materials they handle or manufacture. Diseases of this kind cease to exist when people cease those activities, or when they take effective safety measures to protect their health.

Where environmental disease is treated by curtailing exposure to and ingestion of toxins, *nutritional disease* is treated in the opposite way, by supplementing what the organism ingests. Although nutritional diseases have certainly existed for millennia, it was not until the first half of the twentieth century that vitamin deficiency diseases, their causes, and treatments were discovered. Once a nutritionally adequate diet is supplied, the diseases no longer afflict people.

Another class of non-communicable diseases is *metabolic*. It has been hypothesized that the majority of metabolic disorders arise as a result of genetically determined abnormalities present from birth. For instance, deficiency in the production of an enzyme essential for the metabolism of the amino acid phenylalanine leads to a disease called phenylketonuria. It usually appears within a few weeks of birth and, if not treated, interferes with normal mental development. In contrast, some metabolic diseases begin later in life, e.g., gout and adult-onset diabetes.

Early in the second half of the twentieth century, medicine began to understand immune mechanisms used by the body to defend against infectious agents. A new classification of *autoimmune disease* was established for disorders that result when the immune system becomes self-destructive. For example, lupus erythematosus is thought to result when the immune system malfunctions and attacks its own connective tissue. Similarly, multiple sclerosis appears to be the result of an autoimmune attack on the insulating material, myelin, that sheaths nerves; Grave's disease appears to be the result of an autoimmune attack on the thyroid; rheumatic fever, the apparent result of an autoimmune attack on joint cartilage. Autoimmune disease is an example of a reflexive, or self-referential, systemic disorder. Close parallels to autoimmune disease are found in certain reflexive psychiatric and conceptual pathologies, as we shall see later on.

More recently, during the past two decades, the medical understanding of disease has evolved rapidly due to developments in molecular genetics. The new approach to disease is characterized by the view that mutated DNA alters the production of certain polypeptides involved in the formation of proteins required for normal cellular functioning. The resulting abnormal functioning produces *disease on the genetic level*. Medical understanding in this area is accelerating as genomic research advances, permitting medical researchers to identify how a propensity to develop a given disease is genetically encoded.

So far, this short summary of the principal classes of disease has tended to focus on the identification of specific causes or agents, whether microorganic or inorganic, genetic, autoimmune, nutritional, or environmental. However, it is becoming increasingly evident that certain major, widespread diseases may not be of this kind. Some may be the result of a combination of factors which, in relation to the genetic and physiological make-up of a given individual, produce effects that are *self-compounding*. Some types of cancer may be of this sort.

> Despite frantic efforts, the causes of cancer, of arteriosclerosis, of mental disorders, and of the other great medical problems of our times remain undiscovered. It is generally assumed that these failures are due to technical difficulties and that the cause of all diseases can and will be found in due time by bringing the big guns of science to bear on the problems. In reality, however, search for *the* cause may be a hopeless pursuit because most disease states are the indirect outcome of a constellation of circumstances rather than the direct result of single determinant factors. (Dubos 1987/1959:102)

This observation was made by pioneering biologist and ecologist René Dubos in 1959. It is worth quoting further from him:

> Thus, any factor that upsets the equilibrium of either one of these two ecological systems— the internal and external environments—can become a determinant of disease. As all components of both systems are interrelated, any disturbance in either of them—even though minor and not damaging in itself—can set in motion secondary effects which become destructive to the organism. Because the process of living necessarily involves all these complex interrelationships, any given pathological process is the resultant of a multiplicity of diverse influences, and all its phases are affected by the adaptive responses to anything that impinges upon the organism. (110-1)[1]

## THEORIES OF DISEASE

A variety of theories of disease has been proposed over the years. Since this book's focus is pathology applied to phenomena that are not commonly thought of as falling within the framework of disease, it is important that we understand how disease has been described from the point of view of general theory in order to establish a solid basis from which to proceed.

Perhaps the most intuitive conception of disease is the view which is based on the concepts of biological function and statistical normality. From this point of view, disease is simply malfunctioning that is not normal. This is an ancient, naturalistic way to understand disease. To be diseased from this point of view is for an organism to be in a state that is less

---

[1] Writing several decades before Dubos, geneticist George K. K. Link proposed a similar multifactorial account of disease. He cites hereditary conditions that may predispose an organism to disease, influence its susceptibility to infection, and affect the infection's virulence. From Link's point of view, disease "is not the effect of a single cause, but the resultant of causes infinitely numerous...the consequence of the state of the universe a moment before." Link (1932:164).

than statistically normal for its species; disease brings such a state about. Recently, this theory of disease has come more descriptively to be called the *biostatistical theory*. Its proponents claim that it is a value-free theory of disease, one that does not make recourse to normative concepts. (Cf. Humber & Almeder 1997)

Like many intuitive and simple accounts, the biostatistical theory is too simple: From its point of view, an organism is healthy if it satisfies the standards of statistical normality for its species; but this, as we shall see later, is clearly mistaken given the existence of certain chronic disease conditions that are statistically widespread and indeed normal for a given species. Secondly, the biostatistical theory is insufficiently restrictive, since certain conditions, e.g., intellectual genius or artistic creativity, would, because they are statistically abnormal and may involve social malfunctioning, thereby be classifiable as pathologies. Though they may at times be maladaptive in relation to socially desired functions, a theory of disease that is forced to regard genius and creativity as diseases is not particularly promising.[2]

A similarly naturalistic conception of disease has been proposed by the theory of *disease as loss of adaptive responsiveness*. From this perspective, disease is understood to come about when there is a change in the ecological equilibrium that has evolved between a species and its environment. Dubos, as we have seen, urged this view. When members of a species are exposed to a new pathogen, a severe epidemic of disease can occur. With the passage of time, however, adaptive responses tend to occur both in the afflicted population and in the pathogen, which gradually restore a state of equilibrium between them. Once this occurs, although the pathogen may still be present throughout much of the population, its degree of infectivity may be reduced or even cease. Following this line of thinking, the World Health Organization has proposed: "[Health] is not merely the absence of disease or infirmity...[but] the ability of a system (for example, a cell, family, society) to respond adaptively to a wide range of environmental challenges (for example, physical, chemical, psychological, and so on)." Disease, in the view advocated by the World Health Organization, is a failure of adaptive response "...resulting in disruption of the equilibrium of the system." (Caplin 1981:36) The theory of disease as loss of adaptive response leads to an approach to treatment that one is tempted to call more "holistic," since the overriding concern is less to focus efforts on alleviating the immediate symptoms of disease and more to restore the conditions necessary for optimal health.

If such a theory is useful, it is by virtue of its generality; but as a result of its very generality it tends to be excessively inclusive. For example, a pathological condition that may affect a large portion of a population may, in fact, be highly adaptive; yet it may be a condition we would regard as detrimental in ways not specifically relevant to an organism's adaptive response to its environment. Sickle-cell trait, for example, is the result of abnormal hemoglobin. When parents, both of whom have sickle-cell trait, have a child there is a 25 percent chance that the child will develop sickle-cell anemia, a potentially debilitating disease. Before the advent of modern treatments for this condition, the average life-expectancy of people with sickle-cell anemia was only about 45. Yet, sickle-cell trait can be beneficial to populations living in the tropics where malaria is rampant. Individuals with sickle-cell trait turn out to be resistant to malaria: When their red blood cells are invaded by the malarial parasite, the cells stick to the walls of blood vessels, become deoxygenated, and are de-

---

[2] There are further problems with the biostatistical theory, another of which can be mentioned here, and that is the confusing double role that the concept of normality is forced to play in such claims as abnormality is "a deviation from the *normal* range" and "disease is a *normal* process." [My emphasis.] (Hurst 1992:14)

stroyed, taking the malarial parasite with them. The discovery that this hemoglobin abnormality was the cause of sickle-cell anemia was made in 1948, when the science of molecular pathology, as we noted earlier, was born. There are other medical disorders that affect large proportions of populations, appear to be environmentally adaptive, yet are classified as diseases. The question whether they are "true" diseases is a question relating to nosology, the classification of disorders, to which we shall turn later.

A third theory of disease, still intuitive in nature but applicable to widespread, chronic disease, is the theory which equates disease with *malady*. Unlike the concept of biostatistical normality, the concept of malady is intrinsically normative since it entails the unavoidable judgment of what constitutes *harm* for a particular organism. As shall gradually be made clear, the identification of disease by man and the choices he makes to treat disease are both inescapably normative.

The equation of disease with malady has been made familiar by today's main mental health nosology handbook published by the American Psychiatric Association, in the *Diagnostic and Statistical Manual*'s definition of 'disorder'. There, emphasis is placed on the life-negating conditions of pain, disability, important losses of freedom, and death. (American Psychiatric Association 1987:xxii, 401) As recent proponents of this theory have expressed this, pain, disability, significant loss of freedom, and death are "harms" or "evils" that any rational person would wish to avoid. (Gert, Culver & Clouser 1997; Culver & Gert 1982; Clouser, Culver & Gert 1997) Their use of the word 'evil'—freed, however, from its associations with traditional moral, ethical, or religious doctrines—is intentional, to underscore the normative nature of judgments that a condition is harmful: "Since harm is necessary for disease, and harm is an evaluative notion, the concept of disease is evaluative. Whether a bodily condition is part of normal functioning is beside the point; the main question is whether or not the bodily condition causes harm." (Kaufman 1997:276)

Disease considered as malady therefore introduces morality explicitly into the theory of disease—something that many scientists resist in their wish for the moral neutrality of value-free analyses. Unfortunately, it is not possible to satisfy that wish when disease is in view, as a moment's reflection will make evident: What we identify as a disease is a function of purposes that we ourselves define. Peter Sedgwick has made this clear: Farmers consider the blight that attacks corn or potatoes to be a disease, yet

> ...if man wished to cultivate parasites (rather than potatoes or corn) there would be no "blight," but simply the necessary foddering of the parasite-crop.... Outside of the significances that man voluntarily attaches to certain conditions, *there are no illnesses in nature....* The fracture of a septuagenarian's femur has, within the world of nature, no more significance than the snapping of an autumn leaf from its twig: and the invasion of a human organism by cholera-germs carries with it no more the stamp of "illness" than does the souring of milk by other forms of bacteria.... [I]f some plant-species in which man had no interest (a desert grass, let us say) were to be attacked by a fungus or parasite, we should speak not of a disease, but merely of the competition between two species. The medical enterprise is from its inception value-loaded; it is not simply an applied biology, but a biology applied in accordance with the dictates of social interest. (Sedgwick 1973:30, 31)

In an effort to free the theory of disease from the framework of social interests, some researchers have proposed an alternative theory of disease, which defines disease in terms of the *disruption of an organism's functioning*. From the standpoint of the individual leaf, it might whimsically be hypothesized that its falling at the end of the year is due to a disease, especially if one believed that the browning of deciduous leaves in the Fall was a pathology. But once it is realized that deciduous leaves die at the end of each season of growth, and that this phenomenon is a natural process, it becomes hard to interpret the fate of the individual leaf as a sign of disease, in spite of evidence at first glance that its functioning as a leaf has been disrupted.

This reflection may make one wonder, in much the same way, whether many of the "diseases" that we recognize today may merely be signs of larger natural processes not yet identified. But, in the meantime, whether or not each of us may be a leaf attached to a larger tree, whose browning, dying, and falling is part of a "natural process," we may yet insist that the individual's suffering, the harm to which he or she is victim, is a good enough reason to intervene medically in an effort to reduce that harm and suffering. It is at this juncture, when a choice to engage in treatment occurs, that medicine cannot escape the moral foundation on which the identification of disease rests, as we shall see more fully later on.

A fourth and last theory of disease should be mentioned, and that is the *pragmatical theory of disease*.[3] It seeks to identify and describe diseases as a function of an organism's needs. The motivation for this approach to disease identification has come from Georges Canguilhem, who pointed out that "the impetus behind every ontological theory of disease undoubtedly derives from therapeutic need." (Canguilhem 1978/1948:11) The pragmatical theory of disease offers an intuitive conception of disease, whose spirit is captured by the following passage:

> The kind of health that men desire most is not necessarily a state in which they experience physical vigor and a sense of well-being, not even one giving them a long life. It is, instead, the condition best suited to reach goals that each individual formulates for himself. Usually these goals bear no relation to biological necessity; at a time, indeed, they are antithetic to biological usefulness. (Dubos 1987/1959:278-9)

Among competing theories of disease, the pragmatical theory is particularly sensitive to human or other goals that a pathology can undermine and often defeat. The theory is important because of its self-conscious weighting of an organism's objectives in relation to conditions that can block their attainment. The pragmatical conception of disease recognizes that disease identifications are a function of goals that we endorse, and in this sense links our understanding of pathology with how we construe an organism's purposes.

## A FEW REFLECTIONS ON THEORIES OF DISEASE

As one considers this assortment of alternative theories of disease, one cannot help but be struck by the obvious fact that we have not yet reached a stage of advanced and integrated understanding of disease. Certainly, the competing theories of disease variously overlap. But terms are still applied loosely, and there is no universal agreement in terminology. The pragmatical theory of disease, for example, is sometimes also referred to as the functionalist theory of disease, since it attempts to define disease descriptively in terms of the range of an organism's needs—which may extend from normal biological functioning to individual goals to socially desired performance. At the latter end of the spectrum of needs, a pragmatical or functionalist theory of disease often introduces what are transparently social and political considerations, which we shall turn to consider in the next chapter.

---

[3] See, for example, Agich (1997). Agich uses the term 'pragmatic', with its connotations of usefulness and practicality. In the text, I instead use the word 'pragmatical', drawn from semeiotics, to emphasize the essential relativity of disease to the interests of the afflicted organism.

As we can see, the various theories of disease we have discussed tend in different ways to approach the issue of values. The biostatistical theory tries as a matter of principle to avoid introducing values in its analysis of disease; the theory of disease as loss of adaptive responsiveness loses any pretension of value-neutrality when individual adaptive needs are taken into consideration; the theory of disease as malady is explicitly and unapologetically normative; and the last theory of disease we have considered, the pragmatical theory, reflects at least whatever norms are implied by an organism's needs, interests, and individual and group goals. Since the issue of values tends in this way to thread in and out of the various theories of disease, let us consider for a moment the general role of values in deciding what is and what is not disease.

The origin of the word *'value'* is the Latin *'valere'*, which means *health*. This is no etymological accident. How we understand health is linked essentially with what we value. Health is associated with our abilities to undertake what we care most about. It is when these abilities are impeded that we speak of disease.

René Dubos expressed the view that disease is, in the final analysis, a human, value-laden construct imposed on indifferent nature. (Dubos 1987/1959:30-128) Some researchers have drawn a parallel between breaches of law, which society calls "crimes," and malfunctions of the body, which involve a parallel kind of breakdown or violation with respect to the regulatory principles of physiology.[4] It has been argued that this analogy between a citizen's conformity to social law that implies honesty and an individual organism's internal functioning in accordance with regulatory principles of biological functioning that imply health is no more than a matter of "merely conventional classification." (Cf., e.g., Margolis 1976:239) From this point of view, on the one hand, we call certain acts and conditions crimes and diseases only because of our prior acceptance of standards of honesty and health that are no more than conventions.

On the other hand, there have been those who wish for more than a conventionalist position. Philosopher Lawrie Reznek put the matter this way:

> The concept of disease is a normative or evaluative concept. Judging that some condition is a disease is to judge that the person with that condition is less able to lead a good or worthwhile life. And since this latter judgment is a normative one, to judge that some condition is a disease is to make a normative judgment.... It is because the concept of disease is normative that we judge that conditions causing mental retardation and not genius are diseases. This normative view of the concept of disease explains why cultures holding different values disagree over what are diseases.... Judging that some condition is a disease commits one to stamping it out. And judging that a condition is not a disease commits one to preventing its medical treatment. (Reznek 1987:211, 171)

This way of construing disease immediately opens the door to the charge of relativism, the cousin of conventionalism. Reznek admits that "cultures holding different values disagree over what are diseases." But like most disease theorists, Reznek is not happy with relativizing the conception of disease, which can take the motivating wind from the sails of those who would treat it. He argues:

---

[4] As a literary aside: Raskolnikov, in Section 6 of Part I of *Crime and Punishment*, reflected on his conviction that an "eclipse of reason and loss of will-power attacked a man like some disease, developed gradually, and reached its climax a short time before the crime was actually committed; it continued the same way at the moment of the crime and for a short time afterwards, according to each individual; then it passed off like any other disease."

> Normativism does not commit us to Relativism. When I judge that Hitler is an evil man, I am making a value-judgment. However, I do not commit myself to the view that Hitler is an evil-man-for-me, but not an evil-man-for-the-Nazis. This would be to judge that I am both against Hitler and for him in the same breath, and this is incoherent. Once I have judged that Hitler is an evil man, I judge that those who disagree are wrong, and set myself against them. So if I accept that disease judgments are normative, this does not mean that I have to accept that any condition is only a disease-for-me. (211)

Though this may be an admirable position to take, it lacks justification. The position Reznek defends is formulated by means of a series of dogmatic assertions, each subject to question. We are forced to ask: Is it possible to defend a normativist theory of disease without incurring relativism?

One response was proposed by the disease-is-harm theorists:

> [A] malady can be said to be a condition that involves the incurring of harms. All the harms are instances of the basic harms (or evils): death, pain, disability, loss of freedom, and loss of pleasure. These are harms that every person acting rationally wants to avoid. This explains why and in what way malady (or disease) is a normative term. The concept involves values, certainly, but they are objective and universal values. Like colors, these values are universal and objective because there is general agreement about them. Most people make a distinction between different colors, e.g., between red and green, in the same way; those who cannot are regarded as color blind. There is a similar universal agreement among people about the nature of the basic harms and about the undesirability, absent an adequate reason, of experiencing them. (Gert *et al.* 1997:184)

Another author commented in a similar vein: "The existence of common or even universal illness testifies, not to the absence of a normative framework for judging pathology, but to the presence of very wide-spread norms." (Sedgwick 1973:33)

This suggestion, of course, reduces universal values to social consensus, which may, or may not, exist. Perhaps this is the best that we can do: urge, and then hope for, the eventual realization of a complete consensus of judgment among people. But, at best, this is a theoretically weak position with little persuasive force behind it. If by calling a condition a disease we are implying, or stating outright, that there exist preferred alternative states (of "health"), are these preferences anything more than arbitrary claims that rest on sociocentric and ultimately anthropocentric self-interest?

One way in which we may find an answer to this question is to consider the connections between pathology, politics, and clinical judgment, to which we turn in the next chapter.

# CHAPTER 2

# PATHOLOGY, POLITICS, AND CLINICAL JUDGMENT

## THE POLITICS OF DISEASE

During the twentieth century, a number of critics of standard classifications of diseases became vocal, pointing to the social and political interests that are vested in recognizing certain conditions as illnesses or diseases. These critics of nosology, of the taxonomy of disease, have argued that medicine is motivated to label many biological and mental conditions as "disorders," "illnesses," "diseases," or "pathologies" because medicine subscribes to prevailing human social goals, cultural biases, and political interests. According to this view, medical practitioners, knowingly or unconsciously, have their own agendas. By pointing their diagnostic fingers at the "dysfunctions" identified in their disease nosologies, they defend sets of values which the specified "disease entities" threaten or oppose.

Ivan Illich has argued that medicine is guilty of inventing diseases. As Illich has expressed this:

> All disease is a socially created reality.... In every society the classification of disease—the nosology—mirrors social organization.... "Learning disability," "hyperkinesis," or "minimal brain dysfunction" explains to parents why the children do not learn, serving as an alibi for school's intolerance or incompetence; high blood pressure serves as an alibi for mounting stress, degenerative disease for degenerating social organization. (Illich 1976:172-4)

When it comes to nosologies proposed for mental illness, even more patently obvious are the social and political agendas that lie behind the claims that certain conditions constitute pathology. In the previous chapter, we noted Peter Sedgwick's contention that illness and disease are human constructs. For Sedgwick, mental illness must either have an underlying physical-organic cause, or else it is purely an expression of social value-judgments about the patient. (Sedgwick 1973:36; see also Sedgwick 1982)

This is the position defended with bravado by psychiatrist Thomas Szasz, the twentieth century's scourge of establishment-psychiatry's wish to remain unchallenged in its preferred nosologies. Szasz has argued:

> Disease means bodily disease. Gould's Medical Dictionary defines disease as a disturbance of an organ or a part of the *body*. The mind (whatever it is) is not an organ or part of the body. Hence, it cannot be diseased in the same sense as the body can. When we speak of mental illness, then, we speak metaphorically. When metaphor is mistaken for reality and is used for

social purposes, then we have the making of myth. The concepts of mental health and mental illness are mythological concepts, used strategically to advance some social interests and to retard others. (Szasz 1973:97)

We live in a time when truth is frequently at the mercy of "political correctness," a time when many people see nothing wrong with equating socially and politically popular positions with what is true. Not only is such advocacy not disturbing to them, but by many it is considered obligatory.[1] There is no clearer way to put in historical perspective the currently popular equation of truth with political and social interest than to consider some of the most troubling examples in which human beings have used disease nosology in underhanded and invidious ways.

People are naturally inclined to *label* and so to stigmatize conditions and behaviors which they consider undesirable or wish to discourage. At the more "benign" end of the spectrum, for example, is the suggestion that *grief* is a disease: it is, after all, suffering, and it can be prolonged to such an extent as to interfere with normal living. (Engle 1961) This mid-twentieth century gesture to pathologize a potentially devastating emotion that is part of normal living is reminiscent of physician Leopold Auenbrugger, who in the eighteenth century identified the disease "nostalgia," from which, he believed, military draftees suffered. He drew attention to their painful emotional symptoms, but he later discovered that, in fact, many of them suffered not from "nostalgia," but from an underlying physical disease of the lungs, tuberculosis. (Hudson 1983:3-4)

Many of yesterday's diseases have undergone a process of gradual extinction so that most physicians today are ignorant even of their names. Lardaceous liver, gleet, chlorosis, febricula, status thymicus—diagnoses that had clear meanings to the doctors whose diagnostic vocabulary included them, have fallen into disuse and, now, obsolescence. Similarly, suicide, which was considered to be a sin in the eighteenth century, was transformed into a crime in the following century, and was, in 1967, officially pronounced to be a disease by the head of the National Institute of Mental Health. (Hudson 1983:4)

These are a few examples at the less damaging end of the spectrum. At its other end, we come to what are now recognized to be the most notorious attempts to embed racism in medical diagnosis. Whether they were originally "well-intentioned" or not, and whether they were legitimate, meaningful diagnoses that at the time identified genuine diseases, is left for the reader to judge:

A decade before Confederate guns opened fire on Fort Sumter igniting the American Civil War, a southern physician by the name of Samuel Cartwright was appointed by the Medical Association of Louisiana to chair a committee consisting of three physicians and himself. The task of the committee was to "investigate the diseases and physical peculiarities" of the black population. The committee's findings were summarized in a paper written by Dr. Cartwright, "Report on the Diseases and Physical Peculiarities of the Negro Race," and published in 1851 in a reputable medical journal, the *New Orleans Medical and Surgical Journal.* Today, any reader of Dr. Cartwright's essay will be struck by several aspects of his long and clearly written paper. First, the tone of the paper gives the strong impression that its author was a physician genuinely concerned with the medical well-being of his patients, many of whom were black slaves. Second, he was evidently also concerned for the well-

---

[1] An excellent and inadequately well-known work is that of Cheney (1992). "Having to mold ideas to fit prescribed ideologies is demeaning to individuals and damaging to societies. Being able to pursue the truth where it may lead is one of the blessings of liberty—and one of democracy's greatest strengths." (51) In the same connection, Bloom (1987) is highly articulate and insightful. A quasi-sequel may be found in Bartlett (1993).

being of slave owners, in the sense that proper medical treatment of slaves was of obvious benefit to their owners. In other words, there is an implied acknowledgement in Dr. Cartwright's paper of "vested interest" in maintaining the health of black slaves, who are property that ought conscientiously to be cared for. His paper has become a classic and scandalous example of how vested interest of this kind—how a social or political agenda—can influence the diagnosis of disease. But bear in mind the prevailing tone of the paper: one of medical caring and attentiveness that wished to benefit both black slaves and their owners. He remarked:

> [A]mong the whole multitude of medical schools in the United States, there is not one that has made any special provision for instruction in regard to three millions of people in the Southern States, and representing half the value of Southern property, differently organized in mind and body from any other people, and having diseases requiring peculiar treatment.... Some provision in our schools especially devoted to the anatomy and physiology of our negroes,—to the treatment of their diseases,—to the best means to prevent sickness among them,—to improve their condition, and at the same time to make them more valuable to their owners, and governed with more ease and safety,—would be sending Science into a new and wide field of usefulness, to reap immense benefits for the millions of both races inhabiting the South. (Cartwright 1851:703-4; alternatively, see Gregg 1970/1851, which restates though distorts Cartwright's views)

Dr. Cartwright believed that special diseases affected black slaves, harming their health, and which, as a result, interfered with their socially and politically desired performance. In his paper, he identified a number of "diseases of Negroes," including several respiratory disorders (for which he advised good housing with adequate heating, warm blankets, and hot teas); various specialized fevers (giving a recipe for a medicinal potion and other suggested remedies); Frambæsia, a contagious disease due to lack of hygiene (for which there is no other effective remedy than deuto-chloride of mercury combined with guaiacum and dulcamara); and three other diseases, which it may be of interest to describe in more detail.

"Negro consumption" is, according to Dr. Cartwright,

> ...a disease almost unknown to medical men of the Northern States and Europe. A few Southern physicians have acquired some valuable information concerning it, from personal experience and observation; but this knowledge is scattered in fragments about, and has never been condensed in a form to make it of much practical utility. (Cartwright 1851:704)

Dr. Cartwright reviews the ways in which this malady has been misdiagnosed, summarizes its symptoms (whitened mucous membranes, called by slave overseers "paper gum disease," rapid pulse under exertion, blood with "very few red globules"), and then asserts that the disorder is not physical, but lies "in the mind, and its cause is generally mismanagement or bad government on the part of the master, and superstition on the part of the negro." Dr. Cartwright observed that black slaves are "very jealous and suspicious," and "...if they are slighted or imposed on in any way, or over-tasked, or do not get what they call their rights, they are apt to fall into a morbid state of mind, with sulkiness and dissatisfaction, very plainly depicted in their countenances." (705)

"Negro consumption," Dr. Cartwright wrote, is caused by an "erythism [sic] of mind," a little "like the erythism of the gravid uterus in delicate females." The cure for "Negro consumption" is simple: to remove "the original cause of the dissatisfaction or trouble of mind, and by using every means to make the patient comfortable, satisfied and happy." (Cartwright 1851:706-7) He expressed the conviction supported by experience that a slave who is governed with a firm but caring hand will wish to remain with his master.

The doctor goes on to identify two other diseases: *drapetomania* (from δξαπέτης, a *runaway slave*, and μαυια, *mad* or *crazy*), which is "the disease of mind causing him to abscond," (Cart-wright 1851:707) and *dysæsthesia æthiopsis*, a disease that causes slaves to "break, waste and destroy everything they handle,—abuse horses and cattle,—tear, burn and rend their cloth-ing, and paying no attention to the rights of property...." (710) From the point of view of their white owners, such behavior on the part of black slaves, protesting against conditions of enslavement, unquestionably constituted *disorders* in the literal sense that these forms of behavior *produced disorder* within the social system; hence Dr. Cartwright felt justified in identifying them as "diseases." Was he wrong? He saw that the conditions of "Negro con-sumption," *drapetomania*, and *dysæsthesia æthiopsis*—all, it is interesting to note, diagnosed as *mental* disorders—led to dysfunctional behavior relative to the prevailing set of social norms.

Dr. Cartwright's analysis at the time was influential and enjoyed the company of similar beliefs such as the idea that freedom for blacks brings about mental illness. For example, John C. Calhoun, Secretary of State, writing about 1844, asserted: "Here is proof of the necessity of slavery. The African is incapable of self-care and sinks into lunacy under the burden of freedom. It is a mercy to give him the guardianship and protection from mental death." (Thomas & Sillen 1972:17) In this view, if emancipation led to mental illness, no less would it lead to physical illness: Medical journals after the Civil War reported that fundamental biological changes were taking place in black people, which would lead with "unerring certainty" to the gradual extinction of the race. (21)

After the Civil War, it was only a small step to take—although it took an entire century to make this questionable advance—for a similar claim to come into circulation, namely that desegregation unsettles structured ways of life in which habitual Black roles were defined. Desegregation, it was argued, is manifestly an "anxiety-producing" disturbance of established patterns of living. As a result, "[t]he black man, assailed by the ambiguities of cultural change, succumbs to severe emotional disorders." (Thomas & Sillen 1972:124) The Chair-man of the Psychiatry Department of the University of Virginia, Dr. D. C. Wilson, advanced this theory in a paper read before the American Psychiatric Association meeting as recently as 1956. In his paper, he "emphasized the harmful impact of the loss of 'definite status' once enjoyed by the blacks." (125)

But to turn back to the America of two centuries ago: Equally distinguished, allegedly legitimate medical research was reported by Dr. Benjamin Rush, who in 1792 claimed to have discovered the underlying cause for the "disease of being black": Dr. Rush discovered the "disease" when he came across a case of what he interpreted to be a spontaneous recov-ery from the disease of *Negritude*. A black slave named Henry Moss was suffering from a disease now recognized as vitiligo, which results in localized skin depigmentation. The de-pigmented areas were white, indicating to Dr. Rush that being black is a congenital disease for which there must be a cure. The state of being a black person, that is, *Negritude*, he there-fore claimed, was in truth a variety of leprosy, the only symptom of which is a darkening of the skin. (See Reznek 1987:17-8)

✧

Surely, one cannot have better illustrations of the subtle, sometimes insidious, ways in which social and political agendas can infiltrate medical diagnosis. Where is one to draw the line—between fictions that serve an agenda and "real" disease?

Let us turn from the pre-Revolutionary Era, when the vested interest of the slave-owner was rooted in his slaves' productivity and labor, to the economy of modern times which places high value on low unemployment. In a country inspired by the work ethic, it should come as no surprise that the American Psychiatric Association has identified a "mental disorder" that is expressly a sign of a *work malfunction*. In America's bible of psychiatric disorders, the A.P.A.'s *Diagnostic and Statistical Manual of Mental Disorders*, the *DSM* identifies a disorder that hinders an individual from gainful work. It is called an "adjustment disorder, with work inhibition" (or, *DSM* code 309.23, for insurance purposes). The *DSM* diagnostic description is short and to the point:

> The essential feature of this disorder is a maladaptive reaction to an identifiable psychological stressor.... The maladaptive nature of the reaction is indicated...by impairment in occupational (including school) functioning.... [T]he predominant manifestation is an inhibition in work...occurring in a person whose previous...work performance has been adequate. Frequently there is also a mixture of anxiety and depression. (American Psychiatric Assoc. 1987: 329, 331; in American Psychiatric Assoc. 1994 and 2000, absorbed under code 309.9)

American psychiatry appears here to have responded to social and political interests by equating mental health with the way our society, and in particular its economy, wishes Americans to work in order to live. One cannot help but wonder whether this is really so far from the way psychiatry was used in the former Soviet Union to label its political dissidents "mentally ill." When the limitations placed on individual liberty permeate deeply enough in a society, it is to be expected that practitioners of its medicine will strive to maintain them.

Homosexuality is another example. This "condition" or "sexual preference" has a long and tattered history, extending from acceptance among the Greeks, to punishment for many centuries as a religious or moral sin, to persistent persecution by members of ordinary society, continued today against the backdrop of a long-standing dispute within the American Psychiatric Association whether to include the diagnosis of *homosexuality* in the A.P.A.'s *DSM*.

> [S]cience is often not central to the decision to include or exclude a diagnosis from *DSM*. The dispute over the inclusion of homosexuality in *DSM* was not about research findings. It was a 20-year debate about beliefs and values.... Spitzer's reasoning was tortuous. [He was the psychiatrist in charge of the A. P. A. Committee appointed to study the issue.] In order to answer the question of whether homosexuality is an illness, Spitzer felt it was necessary first to define mental disorder. This, he decided, is a behavior that is accompanied by subjective distress or a generalized impairment in social effectiveness or functioning. Since Spitzer had met at the A. P. A. meeting gays who did not suffer from subjective distress because of their sexual orientation and who were obviously high functioning, he felt that homosexuality could not be considered a mental illness. (Kutchins & Kirk 1997:56, 69-70)

One of the A. P. A. committee heads commented at the time that "You don't devise a nomenclature through a vote."—But, after much deliberation, no hard experimental research, and much political and expedient soul-searching, this is precisely what the A. P. A. did. (71) A tally of votes pronounced that homosexuality is not a disease.

Certainly, there is a basis for wondering to what extent disease classifications are contrived in order to suppress behavior that is judged to be socially undesirable. From this perspective, one wonders to what extent a favored nosology, like the one endorsed by the *DSM*, serves as a *behavior management tool*. A good example is provided by the eighteenth century's diagnosis of clitoral organism as "perverse." Treatment was sometimes provided in the form of surgical removal of the offending organ. (See Actor 1871/1857 and Barker-Benfield 1983) Today, one and a half centuries later, the pendulum has swung and clinicians endorse clitoral organism as a vital female sexual response.

If the foregoing assertions by experts are questionable—that grief, nostalgia, suicide, "Negro consumption," *drapetomania, dysæsthesia æthiopsis*, Negritude, homosexuality, and clitoral orgasm are genuine pathologies—others have similarly argued, perhaps with more clinical persuasiveness, that anti-Semitism and racism are diseases.

## ANTI-SEMITISM AND RACISM AS DISEASES

Lev Semenovich [Leon] Pinsker (1821-1891) was a Russian Jewish physician who fought the 1848 epidemic of cholera in Moscow and the 1854 epidemic of typhus among Russian soldiers in the Crimea. He was a witness to the 1881 pogrom in Odessa, where Pinsker practiced medicine. This experience motivated him to write *Auto-Emancipation*, published in German in 1882. (Pinsker 1944/1882) The mass-generated rage against Jewish people in Odessa convinced him that this phenomenon was not a passing occurrence, but a chronic pathology. Pinsker looked at these events through the eyes of a physician. He came to the conclusion that the forced migratory existence of the Jewish people, condemned always to be asylum-seekers, evicted from country after country for more than two thousand years, gave the Jews a "wraith-like" image: The Jews, never fitting in, never accepted because of their differences, produced "...a strange, peculiar impression upon the imagination of the nations. And if the fear of ghosts is something inborn, and has a certain justification in the psychic life of humanity, what wonder that it asserted itself powerfully at the sight of this dead and yet living nation?" (Pinsker 1944/1882:78)

The psychological response among non-Jewish people to this forever-alien group living among them was fear: fear of difference and the antagonism and hatred that such fear produces. Pinsker called this phenomenon *Judeophobia*:

> Judeophobia is a form of demonopathy, with the distinction that the Jewish ghost has be-come known to the whole race of mankind, not merely to certain races, and that it is not dis-embodied, like other ghosts, but is a being of flesh and blood, and suffers the most excruciating pain from the wounds inflicted upon it by the fearful mob who imagine it threatens them.
>
> Judeophobia is a psychic aberration. As a psychic aberration it is hereditary, and as a disease transmitted for two thousand years it is incurable.
>
> It is the fear of ghosts which, as the mother of Judeophobia, has evoked that abstract, I might say Platonic hatred, thanks to which the whole Jewish nation is wont to be held re-sponsible for the real or supposed misdeeds of its individual members, and to be libeled in so many ways.... (Pinsker 1944/1882:78)

Pinsker recognized that Judeophobia was a highly *infectious* state of mind, easily transmit-ted from one person to another. He called it a an aberration of the human mind, a psychosis, a cancer. (Pinsker 1944/1882:80, 109) He believed that Judeophobia has become so deeply engrained in non-Jews that it has become "innate and ineradicable." (54, 90) Since the diseased state cannot be eliminated, he concluded that it was futile to combat it. His message to Jewish people was therefore: "We must reconcile ourselves once and for all to the idea that the other nations, by reason of their inherent natural antagonism, will forever reject us. We must not shut our eyes to this natural force which works like every other elemental force; we must take it into account." (54)

On the basis of this analysis, which today may seem more like a social psychiatric diagnosis, Pinsker urged Jewish people to form their own independent country. From his point of view, social, political, and religious independence are the only possible means to deal with "the war of destruction" that for millennia has been declared against Jews.[2]

---

[2] Pinsker, in a letter dated December 2, 1883, to Dr. Isaac Ruelf (1834-1902), who was rabbi of Memel

Pinsker sought, then, to understand the phenomenon of anti-Semitism in terms of pathology, using the clinical vocabulary of ideas familiar to him in medicine. Second, he could conceive of no treatment that could be effective against this pathology; the phenomenon of anti-Semitism must then be accepted with practical finality; and he therefore counseled Jews to form their own state. *Auto-Emancipation* became an influential work, culminating a half-century later in the establishment of modern Israel.

From a critical point of view, it is evident that the justification Pinsker offered for labeling anti-Semitism a disease rests on observations and analysis that he made as a result of his own experience and on the basis of his knowledge of history. His justification rests, in other words, on a perception of facts, integrated by means of clinical, diagnostic judgment. —Clearly, it is here, in connection with "clinical judgment," that so much of the validity of disease-identification rests. We will discuss the central role of diagnostic judgment in later chapters.

Less than half a century after Pinsker's death in 1891, psychoanalyst Otto Fenichel gave a lecture in Prague, in April, 1937. The lecture had the title "Psychoanalysis of Antisemitism." (Later published, Fenichel 1940; revised and reprinted, Fenichel 1946) Fenichel was apparently unaware of Pinsker's earlier work, yet the conclusions he reached were very similar. Fenichel described the phenomenon of anti-Semitism in these terms: "...whole masses of people are filled with senseless and contradictory feelings of hatred against a certain race. Logical thinking has lost all power against these emotions, the irrational, the original blind destructive instinct suddenly breaks out against an innocent object." (Fenichel 1940:25) These observations led Fenichel to judge:

> The antisemite arrives at his hate of the Jews by a process of displacement, stimulated from without. He sees in the Jew everything which brings him misery, and not only his social oppressor but also his own unconscious instincts, which have gained a bloody-dirty-dreadful character from their socially caused repression. He can project them on to the Jew because the actual peculiarities of the Jewish life, the strangeness of their mental culture, the bodily...and religious...peculiarities and their old customs make them suitable for such a projection. (Fenichel 37-8)

During the next decade, in 1946, a collection of papers was published under the title *Anti-Semitism: A Social Disease.* (Simmel 1946) It contained papers by a group of psychologists and psychiatrists, all of whom shared in the clinical judgment that anti-Semitism is a social pathology. Gordon Allport described it as a "contagious and complex evil." (In Simmel 1946:viii) Ernst Simmel classified it as a "mass psychosis" (39) that spreads like "an infectious disease." (40) According to him, the individual anti-Semite is not psychotic, but is *normal.* But "when he becomes a member of a mass, ...he loses certain qualities which determine normality and thereby becomes instrumental in helping to produce a mass delusion, belief in which is shared by all the other group members." (44)

A few years later, with WWII still in recent memory, a further study was published, Nathan W. Ackermann's and Marie Johoda's *Anti-Semitism and Emotional Disorder: A Psychoanalytic Interpretation* (1950). Again, in the clinical judgment of the authors, anti-Semitism is recognized as "a symptom of social pathology," built on prejudice that sometimes, in some

---

and author of a book, *Aruchat Bat Ami,* which offered a national solution to the Jewish problem faced by Russian Jews and Jews around the world.

Pinsker wrote with almost prescience of the Holocaust that was to follow. He urged Jews not to mark time, but to use the calm before the gathering storm to establish their own country: "Let 'Now or never!' be our watchword. Woe to our descendants, woe to the memory of our Jewish contemporaries, if we let this moment pass by!" (Pinsker 1944/1882:105).

societies, becomes the social norm. (2, 6) Although anti-Semitic prejudice can at times become normal for a society, Ackermann and Johoda judge that "it can never be normal in the psychiatric sense" (6), but is always a sign of underlying pathology. On a personal, psychological level, according to the authors, anti-Semitism is a deeply seated, irrational, and futile defensive attempt to compensate for the weakly defined sense of identity that so many people have. Their weak personal identity leads them to embrace conformity, surrender their tenuous individuality, and affiliate themselves with groups whose rallying cry is prejudice, which provides them with a delusional feeling of strength.

The importance of these two books, written close to one another in time, during and shortly after WWII, is, first of all, their classification of anti-Semitism as a psychiatric pathology, and, secondly, the emphasis both studies place on the unfortunate, periodic, social *normality* of anti-Semitism. This is a comparatively rare insight in the history of psychiatry: to identify a pathology as being the consequence of a psychological malfunction that is *normal*. In their clinical judgment, the authors and contributors to these books situate the phenomenon of anti-Semitism within a larger framework of understanding that has much in common with the perspective of the present book, in which, repeatedly and in conjunction with many manifestations of human evil, we see normal people succumb to, or willingly embrace, pathological attitudes and behavior.

We turn now to look at an associated, instructive, and ugly manifestation of human hatred and aggression, the phenomenon of racism. Edward Franklin Frazier (1894-1962) was an American sociologist who taught at Morehouse College in Atlanta, Georgia, where he organized the Atlanta University School of Social Work. He was forced to leave his teaching position shortly after the 1927 publication of his paper, "The Pathology of Race Prejudice." (Frazier 1927; reprinted in Cunard 1969, to which subsequent citations are made) In his controversial paper, Frazier argued that race prejudice exhibits the same characteristics as insanity: (1) dissociation, involving "the splitting off of whole systems of ideas" which then become "exempt from the control of the personality"; (2) any "pertinent stimulus may arouse the whole complex...to be projected into consciousness," so that "all thinking is determined by the complex"; (3) the resulting delusional system is supported by "the same mechanisms of rationalization that normal people employ to support beliefs having a non-rational origin"; (4) the delusional system is impervious to objective fact, so that incompatible evidence is met with distortion by rationalization, designed to preserve the inner consistency of the delusional system; (5) violent behavior frequently objectifies repressed unacceptable wishes through the mechanism of projection; (6) the delusional system is used as a universal framework of interpretation, so that a person under the influence of race prejudice will "interpret everything that happens in his environment in terms of his particular delusion"; (7) the pathology produces "social incapacity": people become incapable of rendering just decisions, and resort to violence, maiming and murdering members of the hated group (Frasier's understated comment: "such behavior is distinctly anti-social"); and, finally, (8) the pathology affects an entire group of people. (Cunard 1969:116-8) In connection with the last characteristic, Frazier quoted Nietzsche: "Insanity in individuals is something rare—but in groups, parties, nations, and epochs it is the rule."

After he was dismissed by Morehouse College, Frazier received a fellowship from the University of Chicago, where he completed his Ph.D. in 1931. He then taught at Fisk University, and then went on to teach, beginning in 1934, at Harvard.

It should come as no surprise that Frazier's contention—that racism comprises a genuine pathology, a true mental disorder—has made little headway in gaining public or professional recognition in the intervening years. In 1975, the Committee of Black Psychiatrists recommended the inclusion of racism as a mental disorder in *DSM*. The Committee was unsuccessful. (Kutchins & Kirk 1997:231) During preparatory work for a recent edition of *DSM*, Dr. W. T. Hamlin proposed that "Racist Personality Disorder" be included. His proposal was simply ignored, apparently without discussion. (232) Other authors who have examined racism as a legitimate mental disorder include Skillings & Dobbins (1991), Poussaint (1999), and Dobbins & Skilling (2000).

✧

Anti-Semitism and racism make up a pair of similar and related conditions, each of which engenders hatred and violence among large groups of people. Even when these conditions are carefully analyzed and diagnosed, as in the work of Pinsker and Frazier, professional and public agendas are often obstructive. Researchers who ask for an impartial forum in which to discuss diagnoses that run counter to social and political preferences will not be rewarded. They run the risks of persecution, at worst, to indifference and disregard, at best. It is all-too-clear that the willingness of professional groups or of the public to identify a phenomenon as a pathology must meet the prior test of satisfying already existing and favored social and political values—some would say "prejudices."

> Clinicians operate in particular institutional settings and wider social contexts and these influence...the actions open to them as well as their ways of deciding which of these actions to undertake (their mode of practice). These influences are, in the extreme, of such dominating force that they are appropriately referred to as ideologies." (Dowie & Elstein 1988:27)

This fact about human propensities is itself supported by the close connection that exists between the ways we tend to recognize diseases, and the sets of values upon which our disease classifications rest, as we noted in the last chapter when discussing theories of disease. This connection works, or cuts, both ways: On the one hand, it functions to define human conditions that we are motivated to identify as diseases, and, on the other, it serves as a basis for dismissing, often without due hearing, diagnostic judgments that conflict with prevailing social and political preferences.

## SOCIAL CONSEQUENCES OF DISEASE LABELING

How human beings classify their own attitudes, physical and mental conditions, and behavior is not a purely academic affair, for classifications can carry important consequences. On a concrete and practical level, how we classify these phenomena can determine how we respond to them when we encounter them in others. Classifying a particular condition as a disease, a pathology, or a disorder can raise sensitive issues: whether it is appropriate to make the condition a subject of medical study; whether its study will qualify for research funding; whether those with the identified disorder will receive medical care under insurance provisions; whether victims of the disorder are considered by the public to be contagious, or are otherwise stigmatized and shunned; whether individuals with the disorder will be held by the courts to be legally responsible for their actions; etc. How conditions are conceptualized, by professionals and by the public, determines in large measure how people with a given condition will be treated. In short, there are very concrete physical, mental, social, and financial consequences that follow in the wake of the decision to call a condition a disease.

For example, some insurance consultants argue that a condition is not an illness if it is correctable by education and training. So stuttering, since it is often correctable by these

means, would not be an illness. One consultant wrote: "Stuttering is the behavioural manifestation of a group of speech disorders—some of which are clearly neurological, some
apparently psychological, and some not yet defined. In the strictest sense, it is the sign of a
disorder, not an illness in and of itself." (Preston 1983) Others have argued that insurance
companies ought to pay for therapy to treat conditions like stuttering. Their arguments often
take the form of claiming that such conditions clearly disrupt normal functioning. "This
being the case, stuttering would be a deviation from the normal healthy state. The stutterer is
not free from disease or dysfunction, and he does not enjoy all his parts functioning normally. Therefore, stuttering is an illness." (135)

Theories of disease and the relativity of values that they entail therefore bring with them
very definite and important consequences—to individuals who have the identified conditions, to their families, to medical researchers, funding organizations, insurance companies,
and to the larger society, where the attitudes and behavior of the public are accordingly
shaped. It is important to emphasize the central role that is played in this system of interre-
lations by the human decision to place the label of *disease* on a phenomenon. We turn now to
discuss the basis for this decision in clinical judgment.

## THE ROLE OF CLINICAL JUDGMENT

It should be clear that numerous factors tend to enter into the willingness or the
unwillingness of professionals or of the public to call a condition a disease. In particular, as
we have seen, social and political agendas may affect a decision to label a condition as a
pathology, disease, disorder, or illness. Here, I wish for a few moments artificially to exclude
these factors from consideration in order to take a closer look at the phenomenon of clinical
judgment itself.

Clinical judgment involves a capacity that presupposes an individual understanding or
depth of perception gained from an intimate, sustained, analytical, and reflective study. It
requires an intimate understanding that is detailed and drawn from firsthand experience of
the phenomena in view. It ideally requires a sustained study that has occurred over an
extended period of time—sufficient time to make possible multiple observations under
varying conditions of a clinical subject, who may be an individual patient or a social group.
Clinical judgment is analytical in that it seeks to identify distinguishable major factors, which
may include environmental influences as well as personal concerns and values that are
important to the subject, who, again, may be an individual patient or a social group. Further,
clinical judgment is reflective in its ability to establish connections among similar and contrasting observations, calling for a capacity to generalize and to apply the resulting comprehension to new situations.

To be capable in this sense of clinical judgment, an individual must possess mental
characteristics that include a sensitivity to values and to nuances of physiology and behavior:
He or she must be able to recognize what values are compromised by a given pathology, and
take note of often subtle variations in physical symptoms and behavior that provide clues to
the nature of the disorder. While the diagnostic clinician must be highly analytical in orientation, he or she must also sometimes be intuitive, that is, able to "fill in" gaps in knowledge
and make "leaps" when there is a gap in a chain of inferences. Each of these ways of processing information is evidently subject to error; a single error in a chain of inferences and
intuitions can lead to incorrect diagnosis. And so it is necessary to add that clinical judgment
ideally requires accuracy both in the clinician's observations and in the conclusions he/she
draws from them.

All of these characteristics of approach and mental functioning are unapologetically "loaded terms" in that they do not lend themselves easily to algorithmic representation. Indeed, to understand fully what these loaded descriptive terms mean tends to presuppose the complex of abilities that together makes up "clinical judgment." —This is a circular statement, to be sure, but not viciously circular. It is the circularity involved, e.g., in the claim that to know fully what life means, one must be alive; to know fully in what clinical judgment consists, one must have certain specialized and specific abilities. It is the undeniable presence of this circularity that renders clinical judgment difficult if not impossible to teach.[3] Some medical practitioners come to possess true clinical judgment; many do not. The same appears to be the case with other varieties of judgment that are cultivated in the highly variable soil of individual consciousness, as in moral, artistic, and musical judgment.

Clinical judgment requires, in this perspective, a person who is endowed, then, with a certain relatively high degree of intelligence, who is perceptive, able to recognize connections where others may not, and who can of course articulate his or her findings. To this must be added a further ingredient, which I will call "minimum assumption."[4] Judgment that is exercised in keeping with the principle of minimum assumption is judgment that literally is based on the smallest possible number of assumptions. Ideally, one makes none at all: as Newton avowed, "*hypotheses non fingo*" ["I do not make assumptions"]. Adherence to minimum assumption is what keeps the clinician's feet on the ground, so to speak: maintaining contact with strict observational data and minimizing the introduction of speculative constructs.

This sketch of the qualities of mind and outlook required of one who possesses clinical judgment is inherently *fuzzy*. As in recently developed fuzzy logic, some of the descriptive terms that have been predicated here of clinical judgment have incompletely defined meanings; a number of the characteristics do not have clear boundaries and so overlap. If we possessed total clarity in this area, we could hope for a democratization of clinical-diagnostic abilities among all equally well-informed practitioners. Unfortunately for those who wish for equalization in all areas of society and individual life, clinical judgment still remains an elitist possession in a world in which inequality of mental and physical abilities is still the rule. For those inclined to look to an algorithmic representation of abilities through computer modeling, such a depiction of clinical judgment will have little appeal. For those with an interest in artificial intelligence and expert systems, where there is an interest in reproducing or simulating the cognitive skills of experts, it may have slightly more attraction, but still not satisfy.

In spite of the fuzzy nature of the abilities involved, and our lack of complete understanding of them, we are in an age that is attempting, with some success, to automate these skills. Computer-assisted medical decision-making is in its infancy. (See, e.g., Reggia & Tuhrim 1985.) Elaborate, test-data-specific algorithms have been formulated that can identify many diseases with a high degree of reliability.

What, however, of detecting as yet unidentified diseases? Algorithms are useful in reducing a universe of known alternative pathologies to a restricted set of most promising alternative therapies that are effective and compatible with known symptoms and test-results. The identification of as yet undetected pathologies is not the intended purpose of computer-assisted decision methods. —Here, one must still rely upon human clinical

---

[3] An important focus of research into the nature of clinical judgment relates to protocol analysis, in which competent experts describe their own cognitive diagnostic process. See, e.g., Kassirer, Kuipers, & Gorry (1988), in particular the section "Protocol Analysis" (214-17) An early proposal to use protocol analysis in this way is described in Bartlett (1978a).

[4] After Reginald O. Kapp's modern term for Occam's Razor in his important but little-known work, Kapp (1962/1960).

judgment which involves human abilities that are admittedly comparatively rare.

But rarer still than conventional clinical judgment among medical practitioners is the ability to frame new diagnostic ideas, to identify and conceptualize pathologies that have not been recognized before. This is especially true of disorders that have become so prevalent as to be accepted as normal, to which we have become habituated and in that sense blind. To recognize such dysfunctions for what they are requires that we step outside the familiar conceptual framework that we ordinarily use without question and turn a critical and dispassionate eye on patterns of human behavior, emotion, and thought that we use as unthinkingly and comfortably as we do a well-worn shoe. A challenge is therefore presented to us: to make use of the existing conceptual vocabulary of disease identification as a bridge that permits us to recognize important disorders that were previously unknown.

To this end, the next three chapters develop a new and comprehensive theory of disease in terms of which we can situate and study human disorders that have their sources in mental illness, social pathology, and pathologies of everyday thought. The inclusive frame of reference that is proposed will allow us to apply central concepts of epidemiology to reach an understanding of the human species that makes clear how man is a true pathogen, destructive to himself and to other forms of life, and how human pathology involves disorders which are universal and indeed normal. The final chapter in Part I will then consider historical precedents in psychiatry for linking human pathology with "evil," and will explain how the term 'evil' is used in this study to refer to specific and real human pathologies which we have too long ignored and denied.

# CHAPTER 3

# FRAMEWORK-RELATIVE PATHOLOGY

## THE FRAMEWORK-RELATIVE THEORY OF DISEASE

We have seen how the principal theories of disease have attempted to deal with the role of values in the identification of disease, and have looked at a number of ascriptions of pathology to a range of human conditions—to such everyday problems in living as grief and nostalgia, to homosexual preference, to race-specific conditions such as "Negro consumption," *drapetomania*, and *dysæsthesia æthiopsis*, to hate-engendering conditions such as anti-Semitism and racism. We have noted that some of these conditions were thought to originate in underlying physical dysfunctions and some in mental disorders. But regardless of their sources, diagnostic judgment has claimed that each is in some way harmful or destructive, that it is not desirable, and, usually, that the condition is in some way treatable; and further, when it is not treatable (as in Pinsker's theory of anti-Semitism), this fact may point to potentially constructive ways to respond to it.

In this section, I introduce a more comprehensive, theoretically more sophisticated approach to understanding pathology. To this end, we need to step up one rung of the ladder of increasing theoretic generality to observe that whenever a condition is judged to be a disease, pathology, or disorder of some kind, it is because there has been a breach or a violation of rules that we or others with special interests of their own do not want to see broken.[1] In the case of *drapetomania* and *dysæsthesia æthiopsis*, for example, southern slaveholders obviously did not wish slaves to run away or to destroy property. In the case of homosexuality, heterosexual conventions serve as the rules that "straight" society wishes to preserve. In the case of physical diseases—whether they are due to specific microorganic or inorganic agents, or whether they are genetic, autoimmune, nutritional, or environmental in nature—rules that describe desirable physiological functioning are broken. Finally, in the case of psychiatric pathologies, mental illnesses or disorders identify conditions that are judged to interfere with socially approved, normal functioning. Such pathologies violate rules that describe how, from the point of view of the surrounding society and perhaps also from the individual's point of view, it is appropriate or desirable to function.

The same is true for the treatment of any alleged pathology: The therapeutic intention is

---

[1] Georges Canguilhem was one of the first theorists of disease to take note of the relationship between the concept of norm, as it is used to characterize health, and requirements imposed by rules. See Canguilhem (1978/1943:239).

to alleviate the harm that the pathology is believed to cause by restoring an organism's functioning so as to conform to the particular rules that have been breached. In short, in both the identification of a condition as a disease and the establishment of methods of treatment of the alleged disease, there is an implied and inescapable relativity to a set of values, to the fundamental values held by the treating physician and often, but not always, by the patient.

From the standpoint of the framework-relative theory of disease that I propose in this work, a pathology exists as soon as it has been identified as such by means of what is accepted to be competent clinical judgment. —At first glance, this claim may seem counterintuitive, if not outrageous, for it appears virtually to legitimate *any* clinical ascription of pathology, however biased it may be. However, as we will see in greater detail in Part III, whenever a condition is identified as a pathology, this happens because a particular frame of reference is employed in terms of which (i) clinical judgments concerning that pathology derive their meaning and may compel, or fail to compel, assent, and (ii) a range of potential therapies is in principle suggested.

One of the few disease theorists to recognize these facts was Robert P. Hudson, a physician who was Chairman of the Department of the History and Philosophy of Medicine at the University of Kansas. Dr. Hudson wrote:

> It must not be thought that simply because we now agree a given disease never existed that in fact it did not exist, because of course it did. It existed in its place and time. [For example:] Patients developed the symptoms of catarrhal jaundice; physicians made the diagnosis, in which other physicians concurred; and the illness was treated the way physicians treated catarrhal jaundice. And these are the elements needed to prove the existence of a given illness, then or now. (Hudson 1983:8-9)

In short, when a condition is identified as a pathology, this does not occur in a vacuum, but in a context colored by values which define objectives that are frustrated by the condition. Furthermore, this context of reference is situated within an overall frame of reference to which prevailing medical experts give their credence, derive a sense of their own professional identities and purpose, and offer possible treatments. Disease identification occurs in this heavily laden atmosphere: For those who breathe that atmosphere, the recognition that a given condition constitutes a disorder is inherently persuasive. It is a quite different matter to ask whether a certain condition—*drapetomania*, for example—ought today, in terms we now accept, to be considered a pathology. A reasonable answer to this question can be given, for which the reader is asked to be patient.

It follows from a framework-relative understanding of disease that a given pathology will often suggest a group of potential approaches to its treatment. Hudson (1983:193) seems to have had precisely this in view when he claimed, "...disease concepts tend to dictate approaches to treatment." If, for example, a doctor believes a disease is caused by a bacterium, it is plausible for him to seek to develop a suitable anti-bacterial agent. Specific approaches to treatment in turn help to define concepts of disease that best conform to and throw light upon the therapies employed; and in this sense, "therapy has helped shape concepts of disease." (Hudson 1983:193) For example, when cinchona bark, the source of quinine, was found to be useful in treating malaria, this fact led to the suspicion that, underlying the fever, there might exist a distinct, identifiable disease. The relationship between a disease and therapies that are recommended for its treatment is therefore an interactive one, in which the conception of a disease often points to a range of possible forms of treatment, and in which established therapies affect how the pathology is understood.

I have referred to "rules" that variously may be "violated" or "breached," thereby producing the kinds of physiological or mental breakdown that medical experts characterize as pathological. In addition, there are two theoretically complementary and informative alternative ways to conceptualize pathology from a framework-relative standpoint. The first of these claims that disorders, diseases, or pathologies arise as a result of different types of "error." The second claims that the identification of a condition as a pathology is an instance of problem-solving judgment. Let us look more closely at each of these claims about the nature of disease.

Georges Canguilhem in his work, *The Normal and the Pathological*, characterized pathology in terms of the concept of error.

> At the heart of these problems is that of error. For at life's most basic level, the play of code and decoding leaves room for chance, which, before being disease, deficit or monstrosity, is something like perturbation in the information system, something like a "mistake." ...And if we admit that the concept is the answer that life itself gives to this chance, it must be that error is at the root of what makes human thought and its history. (Canguilhem 1978/1943:21-2)

In his book's last chapter, "A New Concept in Pathology: Error," Canguilhem focused on the identification of diseases that involve "biochemical errors" or "innate chemical malformations" such as those that appear to be involved in hereditary metabolic diseases. Canguilhem did not skirt the larger dimensions of pathology, moving, with characteristic French intellectual boldness, and within the compass of a single sentence, from the biochemical domain of the very small to the nature of human thought: "There is... no difference between the error of life and the error of thought, between the errors of informing and informed information." (Canguilhem 1978/1943:277) It is, as we shall see, one of the purposes of Part III of the present study to establish the basis for the connection between these two as yet unbridged areas of pathology, between disease as it has traditionally been understood and "errors of thought" which comprise a newly recognized variety of pathology.

An alternative way of characterizing pathology from a framework-relative standpoint is in terms of the general theory of problem-solving. There, a problem is defined in terms of a perceived gap between an initial condition or situation and a desired goal-state. (For more detailed discussion, see Bartlett 1978b.) A problem, understood in this way, is explicitly identified as a function of endorsed values and in terms of objectives to which those values lead. From this point of view, the state of an individual, for example, who is afflicted with a physically debilitating condition, occupies a position on one side of a "gap," the other side of which is occupied by an ideal, desired goal-state, the physical well-being of the patient. The gap constitutes the problem that defines the disease, and as a gap specifies what we believe to be lacking. Treatment of the disease, which is therapy, consists of a solution to the problem, bridging the gap. If therapeutic intervention is effective, the desired goal-state is brought about.

All three of the above theoretical characterizations of pathology from a framework-relative point of view will be used subsequently in this book: the conception of pathology as involving, alternatively, a breach of rules, an error, or the manifestation of a problem to be solved. All three approaches acknowledge the inescapable role of values in defining what is desirable and what is not.

Each approach can be transformed into the others: Violated rules can be construed in terms of the occurrence of error, which the rules in question proscribe. And the incidence of error, in turn, can be represented in terms of the perception of a gap between what is and what is desired, i.e., in terms of discrepancies disclosed in comparing an existing situation with a goal-state. Similarly, error-detection can be represented in terms of detection of breached rules; and rules that are violated can be interpreted in the language of problem-solving as "gaps" that identify deviations from consistently followed rules. Finally, to complete the circle, problems can be construed in terms of the perception of misfit—when errors or rule-violations are detected.

It should be clear from the foregoing that any judgment of disease is relative to a frame of reference in terms of which certain functional or conventional rules are broken, a physiological or mental error in functioning occurs, or a problem is posed whose solution we are motivated to find. From the framework-relative standpoint we shall employ, it can always be asked whether an identified pathology remains pathological within a wider context of reference. As with the individual leaf that browns and falls, the life of an individual, or of a society, may, within a wider picture, lose its identity as a pathological condition, and come to be viewed as a natural phenomenon, or a phenomenon that, though undesirable for the organism or the society, may in some way benefit or conform to the stability of a more encompassing environment. As optimistically observed by the good Bishop Berkeley:

> [O]ur prospects are too narrow: we take, for instance, the idea of some one particular pain into our thoughts, and account it *evil*; whereas, if we enlarge our view, so as to comprehend the various ends, connexions, and dependencies of things, on what occasions and in what proportions we are affected with pain and pleasure, the nature of human freedom, and the design with which we are put into the world; we shall be forced to acknowledge that those particular things, which considered in themselves, appear to be *evil*, have the nature of *good*, when considered as linked with the whole system of beings. (Berkeley 1999/1710:94, §153)

As will be made clear later on, this possibility of progressive enlargement of one's frame of reference does not, however, undermine the correctness and persuasive force of clinical judgment that is formulated within a more restrictive context of reference. Our approach is, in other words, *relativistic* but not *relativist*: There exists a relativity of judgments of pathology to appropriate frameworks of reference, but, as we shall see later, it is not true by virtue of this relativity that judgments of pathology become tentative or uncertain.

## GENERAL VARIETIES OF PATHOLOGY

There are four main degrees of pathology that determine the spectrum of disease: lanthanic, chronic, active, and acute. The name of the first, lanthanic, is derived from the Greek '*lanthano*,' which means 'to escape attention.'[2] Lanthanic disease is involved when one has a disease, but is not aware that one does. Lanthanic disease is the state of being ill while in a state of ignorance that one is sick. Those who are afflicted by this degree of pathology may be relatively asymptomatic, or asymptomatic for the pathology in question yet exhibit misleading symptoms characteristic of another pathology. This mixture of ignorance and pathology will come to dominate much of the later discussions in this book. And as we shall see, ignorance of the afflicting pathology may itself constitute one of the determinative characteristics of the disease.

---

[2] This term was suggested by Dr. Katerina Haka, who applied the same Greek root as chemists in naming the lanthanide (rare earth) elements. Cf. Feinstein (1967:145), where the term is used in the following sense: "If the patient came to the doctor complaining of blindness (due to ocular cataracts), and if the symptom of angina pectoris is noted during the routine 'review of the systems,' the patient is lanthanic. Another example of a lanthanic patient with coronary artery disease is an asymptomatic man who, during a 'routine check-up,' is noted to have pathognomonic abnormalities in his electrocardiogram."

The second, third, and fourth degrees of pathology—chronic, active, and acute—require no elaboration.

These four degrees of pathology apply to each of the four principal varieties of pathology which will be distinguished here: physical, mental, social, and conceptual. Physical pathology is of course the most familiar variety. As noted earlier, it is often possible to trace diseases that are physical in nature to specific agents that may be microorganic or inorganic, genetic, autoimmune, nutritional, or environmental. And some physical diseases, e.g., cancer, may prove to come about as a result of the interaction of multiple factors.

## THE CONCEPT OF MENTAL ILLNESS

The study of pathologies that affect the mind is essentially frustrating. Mental pathologies have proved to be less easily defined than physical disease, and their origins are a good deal less clear. As yet, there exists no single, universally agreed upon definition of mental illness, and there exists as yet no unitary theory of mental disorders. Instead, theoretically distinct approaches to psychotherapy and counseling now number in the hundreds, while studies of their therapeutic effectiveness are legion and the conclusions drawn from them often contradictory.[3] The field of mental illness is not for those who have a taste for theoretical clarity and distinctness.

At one end of this fog-covered battlefield stand the opponents to mental disease classification: They have argued in different ways that mental illness does not involve genuine disease, that proponents of mental illness seek merely to pathologize personal problems encountered in the course of ordinary living, and that enthusiasm for constructing psychiatric deviancies has grown in direct response to social and political pressures to permit individuals to escape from personal responsibility for their own behavior. Erwing Goffman, R. D. Laing, Michael Foucault, and Thomas Szasz number among those who have argued this.

On the other side stand the mental disorder nosologists, the diagnostic labelers, who have been responsible for a veritable proliferation of systems of classification for pathologies believed to afflict individual minds.[4] The American Psychiatric Association's series of *Diagnostic and Statistical Manuals of Mental Disorders* perhaps best represents proponents of psychiatric classification. Editions of *DSM* have been published since 1952, with intervals between newly revised editions becoming shorter and shorter in recent decades. As additions and revisions become more frequent, so do the number of contributors become more numerous: Where a handful of authors were responsible for *DSM-I*, more than a thousand members distributed among more than a dozen work groups were involved in the most recent edition. It would be wise to question the proliferation of disorders that one thousand contributors recommend. A steadying and salubrious effect would be exercised by *DSM*'s principal diagnostic rival—were only American mental health practitioners better aware of it. It is the World Health Organization's manual, known as the *ICD* (*The International List of Causes of Death*). Publication of the *ICD* began over one hundred years ago. *ICD-10*, for example, was published in 1992, in which the section devoted to mental disorders is a concise 77 pages long. *DSM-IV-TR*, by way of contrast, is 943 pages long. Within the relatively short period of 32 years, from 1968 to 2000, between the *DSM-II* and *DSM-IV-TR*

---

[3] For a comparison of principal approaches to psychotherapy in terms of their effectiveness in treating specific disorders, see Bartlett (1987). For a discussion of studies of therapeutic effectiveness, see Bartlett (1990).

[4] An informative and extensive historical comparison of psychiatric nosologies may be found in Menninger, Mayman, & Pruyser (1967/1963:419-89).

editions, the *DSM* was expanded by 824 pages.

It is instructive to consider how the A. P. A. goes about establishing the existence of a new mental disorder. The process involves these steps: A group of psychiatrists must agree to a listing of manifestations of an atypical behavior that they link to an underlying condition. They formulate a theoretical description of the condition based on their shared clinical judgment. A set of diagnostic criteria is specified, by the use of which the condition can be uniquely identified. The diagnostic criteria are reviewed by the propounders of the new disorder. A decision is reached to determine how many of the proposed criteria must be met in order for a diagnosis of the new disorder to apply. Discussions then take place, opposition to the new disorder is answered, and a vote is taken. (For further discussion, see Kutchins & Kirk 1997:127, 252.) When a majority is satisfied, a new psychiatric disorder is recognized. It is assigned a *DSM* diagnostic code, and from then on the disorder "exists" and patients satisfying the diagnostic criteria are perceived to be afflicted by it.

Between the two extremes we have mentioned—between denial of the existence of psychiatric illness, on the one hand, and assertion of its existence in endlessly proliferating varieties, on the other—it is incumbent upon us to sink a surveyor's marker if we are to proceed with any sense of direction across constantly shifting sands. The position I will take in this study is straightforward and in keeping with the framework-relative theory of disease already described: We recognize that disease identifications are relative to values that we endorse, so that conditions that conflict with social or political goals may then sometimes be labeled pathological. But in the same breath it is necessary to add that many social and political goals do not accord with competent clinical judgment, which seeks to ascertain and weigh the degree of harm to the individual or harm to a population which a putative pathology causes. In the account proposed here, clinical judgment remains the final arbiter. What this means is that we refuse to accept any psychiatric nosology wholesale,[5] but will require an explicit framework-relative analysis of any putative pathology, to identify its harms and weigh them in terms of individual and social interest, before it is considered valid. What such an analysis involves in specific detail will gradually be made clear in subsequent chapters.

With this general standard of judgment before us, perhaps the most informative definition of individual psychiatric pathology we can give is the following stipulative definition: A psychiatric pathology or mental disorder occurs when significant harm results to an individual by virtue of a failure of mental functions which either he or she values, or which others in that individual's social environment value. A psychiatric pathology in this sense is no different from an organic pathology: Both define a problem, a gap between what is and what we desire, a gap that makes evident to reflective judgment both that there exists a definite chasm between what is and what ought to be, and that this state of affairs results in harm to the subject. It is important to point out that this definition, unlike most definitions of disease, does not rely upon a standard of normality. Deviation from statistical normality has, as we shall see, no place in the general theory of pathology developed here.

Before moving on to consider the category of social pathology, some mention should be made of a middle-zone between individual psychological and social pathology, where the phenomenon of *psychological epidemics* is appropriately placed. It is well-known that groups are susceptible to collective emotional arousal that may assume epidemic proportions. The emotions that infect a group tend to consist of hatred, fear, and aggression, usually in

---

[5] The wholesale acceptance position has been argued, e.g., by MacFarquhar (1997): "*DSM*...is periodically revised in response to arguments about usage and usefulness, but new disorders do not represent claims to fresh biological knowledge. Which is to say that yes, a particular mental disorder is whatever *DSM* says it is."

combination. Disease theorist Robert P. Hudson wrote about such psychological epidemics that affected the behavior of people during the plague years in the later Middle Ages. (Hudson 1983:47) Anatol Rapoport devoted a chapter in one of his books to "psychological epidemics" (Rapoport 1960:47-59) commenting that "wars, both internal and external appear...as instances of vast pandemics with high mortality." (49) He went on to observe:

> ...the psychological epidemic can be taken as formally analogous to the organic kind. In an organic epidemic, the infected and infectious individual transmits the disease to a number of others, who, in turn, transmit it. The transmission is "nonconservative," that is, the giver of the disease is not thereby deprived of it. Ordinarily, if there were no limiting factors, every such epidemic would ultimately involve every individual alive, because in all likelihood a chain of links exists (through which contact is possible) from any individual to any other. (49)

The limiting factors in organic epidemics include: natural immunity (not everyone who is exposed to the disease will develop it); time-limited infectiousness (an infected individual is contagious for only a finite period of time); immunity conferred by the disease (growing numbers of individuals who have a natural immunity to the disease reduce the number of potential carriers); decreasing virulence of the pathogen as the epidemic progresses; and measures that may be taken by the exposed population against the pathogen (e.g., quarantine, closing public places, etc.). Rapoport observed: "If what is spread is not an organic disease but an attitude, a behavior pattern, or a piece of news, quite similar limiting factors can be listed." (51-2)

The concept of psychological epidemic is not metaphorical, but refers to a real phenomenon whose dynamic is fundamentally the same as is found in an epidemic of organic disease. The dynamic has been studied by mathematical epidemic theory, which reveals "the underlying similarity of the *mathematical structure* of the events." (Rapoport 1960:53 citing Hailey 1957) We will have occasion to discuss psychological epidemics in greater detail in later chapters.

## SOCIAL PATHOLOGY

If individual men and women can become mentally ill, it is plausible to expect that the groups they form may come to exhibit similar characteristics of mental disorder. As Dubos (1939:207) commented: "The sickness of the individual is not readily differentiated from the sickness of society." Mental illness, but of a kind and on a scale that affects entire segments of the human population, is what I mean by social pathology.

As we look back today, it seems like an ironic and prescient coincidence that four authors, during the years before the outbreak of World War II, should have attempted to bring public attention to bear on the phenomenon of social pathology, which frequently precedes and, they believed, brings about mass warfare. During the years 1920-1939, Vernon Lee (the pseudonym of Violet Paget), Caroline E. Playne, Leo C. Rosten, and Robert Waelder published a number of works, all of which, in different ways, urged that attention should be given to this phenomenon.

Vernon Lee's work (Lee 1920) is a play, sandwiched between two very long prose commentaries. It is not a work of a scholar or a professional psychologist, but it nonetheless contains a group of psychologically astute observations. Lee (or Paget) was outspoken in her condemnation of human evil, which she believed is in great measure a result of collective psychology.

Caroline Playne's book (Playne 1925) is a detailed historical study of psychological conditions and factors that led, in Germany and in France, to the spread of a "collective neurosis," a "group-dementia," which, in turn, resulted in the devastation of World War I.

Sociologist Leo Rosten's paper (Rosten 1935) shares the same framework. He spoke explicitly of "social pathology," and attempted, like Playne, to identify psychological "poisons which infect the public mind" and thereby lead to mass destruction.

Sociologist Robert Waelder's publications (Waelder 1934 and 1939) are the most psychologically detailed and specific. In them, he describes the conditions that lead to "collective psychosis," directs attention to the forms of emotional gratification that individuals receive as a result of their group allegiances and violent behavior, and shows how such collective psychosis brings about war.

Any reader of these works will recognize that the authors were not speaking metaphorically when they referred to the phenomenon of social pathology. They described in concrete and careful detail how a social pathology spreads within a population, and how this phenomenon satisfies widely accepted criteria of disease and disease transmission. Other authors since then have studied the same phenomenon. In later sections in this book, we will have occasion to discuss in more detail the contributions that Lee, Playne, Rosten, Waelder, and others have made to an understanding of social pathology.

## CONCEPTUAL PATHOLOGY

The view that human emotions and behavior are influenced by how we think is an ancient one. Much of the history of western philosophy has consisted of self-conscious appraisals of how we think about the world and ourselves, often with a view to affecting how we are to feel and behave. Although heightened intellectual clarity has been sought by western philosophers for more than two thousand years, and many competing schemes for the interpretation of reality have been proposed, philosophy and the theory of disease have had virtually nothing in common. Until relatively recently, in the present author's research and publications, no philosophical attempt to clarify human thinking has explicitly sought to show that human beings suffer from unrecognized diseases or *pathologies of thought* that are destructive to human life and to other forms of life on this planet.

The development of psychotherapy during the last century has led to the recognition that human beings at times need therapy in connection with affective, behavioral, and cognitive disorders—that is, in connection with problems that individuals experience and suffer from which concern their emotional lives, how they behave, and how they are able to perform mentally. As we have seen, an increasingly wide range of mental disorders has been identified, admittedly in the face of open skepticism and criticism by some.

The parallel notion that many heavily relied upon human ideas or concepts are themselves in need of real, non-metaphorical therapy is a comparatively new idea. Plato's allegory of the cave depicted the human condition in openly metaphorical terms, suggesting that mankind is imprisoned by views that the majority holds without question. During the first half of the twentieth century, Ludwig Wittgenstein spoke, again metaphorically, of helping the imprisoned escape from the bewitchments of language that trap us within the "fly-bottle" of our confusions (he was referring mostly to philosophers). Then Gilbert Ryle spoke of "category mistakes," while John Wisdom placed philosophy and psychoanalysis side-by-side and spoke of "mental cramps" and "philosophical stress," using what he called "words with a clinical flavor" to underscore the kind of riddle-encumbered thought in which philosophers are prone to entangle themselves. Stephen Toulmin coined the word 'cerebroses' to refer to intellectual neuroses. There have been others who have similarly sketched figurative, quasi-therapeutic relationships believed to exist between their favored approaches to philosophical analysis and erroneous philosophical thought. But none of these approaches has reached out to ordinary humanity, and to those in other disciplines, to suggest that commonly accepted ways of thinking may be dysfunctional or pathological.

Beginning in the early 1960s, I took this step in my own work, which has led to the development of an analytical method to detect and treat what I have called "*conceptual pathology.*" In a series of publications, I have elaborated the theory that many ideas or concepts which are central to everyday human thinking, and many of those, or their cousins, which are central to scientific thought, are inherently dysfunctional in the sense that they involve widespread conceptual pathology that renders their use self-defeating. These efforts have sought to close a separation that has existed for many centuries between philosophy and the theory of disease, and in the process to avoid the impressionistic, metaphorical suggestions that philosophers have made in the tradition that leads from Plato to more contemporary proponents of intellectual self-examination. Part III of this study describes the new field of study of human conceptual pathology and shows how pathologies of thought are inextricably involved in the phenomenon of human evil.

✧

In this chapter, I have distinguished, as yet only in broad, introductory outline, four varieties of pathology: physical, mental, social, and conceptual. Of these, all but the first variety will concern us in this work. We shall see that a continuum links together the mental pathologies studied and treated by psychiatrists and psychologists with social and then with conceptual pathologies, many of which are still largely unrecognized.

# CHAPTER 4

# EPIDEMIOLOGY, UNIVERSAL PATHOLOGY, AND THERAPY

## BASIC CONCEPTS OF EPIDEMIOLOGY

Since certain of the central concepts of epidemiology will be applied in later discussions of human pathology, a short overview of epidemiology is given in this section.

Epidemiology is the general theory of the determinants, frequency of occurrence, and distribution of disease. The *distribution* of a disease typically has to do with the extent of its geographical diffusion; *frequency* is measured in terms of the relative incidence of the disease within a given population; and the *determinant* of a disease is identified when an epidemiological theory is formulated that explains the distribution and the frequency of the disease, usually through the detection of a specific pathogen or toxin. During its history, epidemiology has focused primarily on the dynamics of infectious disease transmission, and especially on disease epidemics attributable to specific, individual pathogens. Secondarily, epidemiology has been concerned with outbreaks of disease caused by toxic agents occurring in the environment. In the past century, epidemiology has broadened to include the study of chronic disease, as chronic disorders have come to play an increasingly significant role as major causes of death in industrialized countries. Epidemiologists now consider some chronic diseases to comprise epidemics. The broadening of the meaning of both terms, 'epidemiology' and 'epidemic', so as to encompass chronic disease reflects a change in perception during the twentieth century. One now routinely speaks of an epidemic of any disease, whether it is infectious or chronic, whenever it occurs with a greater than normal frequency. In this sense, heart disease in the United States, for example, has become epidemic.

Epidemiology distinguishes between the prevalence and the incidence of a disease. '*Prevalence*' refers to the proportion of a population that has contracted a disease, whereas '*incidence*' refers to the rate at which new occurrences of a disease develop during a specified period of time. Clearly, the prevalence and incidence of a disease are strongly interrelated: The prevalence of a disease is a function both of its incidence and of the average duration from the onset of the disease to its conclusion in the individual, by acquired resistance or death. (For a more detailed discussion of these concepts, see Hennekens & Buring 1987.)

It is important to note that when the prevalence of a disease becomes epidemic, this tends to occur in waves, as the incidence of the disease rises to a peak and then subsides. The pathology spreads when each new case results in two or more additional cases. Whenever this happens as a consequence of a specific pathogenic agent, the pathogen must

46

evidently reproduce at a rate greater than the affected host population. Similarly, the pathology diminishes when this dynamic is reversed, when each new case results in fewer than one subsequent case, for then the effects of the pathogen wane within a population of increasingly disease-resistant individuals. The dynamics that control an epidemic are essentially stochastic, that is, the positive or negative rate of spread of the pathogen is a matter of probability, namely, the probability of spread of the pathogen from one diseased individual to another individual who is susceptible to the infection. By the time an epidemic has run its course, most of the members of the host population have become resistant to the pathogen. At this point, epidemiology considers that the population has developed immunity to the pathogen, or has developed "herd immunity." However, with the passage of time, herd immunity is lost as individuals in the population lose the immunity they have acquired, as those who have become resistant to the disease die, and as a new generation is born which is vulnerable to the pathogen. By studying and explaining these interrelationships, epidemiology shows how the waxing and waning of herd immunity coincides with the appearance of epidemics in waves.

It is more common for pathologies to affect a population sporadically or endemically, rather than in epidemic proportions. A disease occurs *sporadically* when the incidence of the disease within a given population is only occasional. Alternatively, a disease may occur *endemically* when the relationship between the determinant pathogen and the host population is one of approximate homeostasis. When the balance between them is lost, an epidemic may result.

Epidemiology typically identifies distinct stages in contracting a disease. Together these stages are called *pathogenesis*. They consist of *inoculation*, the pathogen's invasion of a host organism; *incubation*, the period elapsing between inoculation and onset of symptoms; and *infection*, when the pathogen has become established in the host and further spread of the disease occurs.

Pathogens vary considerably in their degree of *virulence*, that is, in their capacity to infect potential host organisms. The degree of virulence of a pathogen is relative to the degree of susceptibility of the host population; in fact, virulence and susceptibility are two measurements that can be used to specify the same result.

Epidemiologists differentiate diseases in terms of their determinants: When the cause is believed to come from within the individual diseased organism, disease is characterized as *idiopathic*; when caused by an infectious pathogen extrinsic to the organism, disease is said to be *communicable*; when brought about by a non-infectious pathogen, disease is said, as one would then expect, to be *noncommunicable*; and when a disease is brought about by medical treatment itself, because the treatment reflected poor clinical judgment or because of unexpected or unavoidable side-effects, it is called *iatrogenic*.

Epidemiology accepts the existence of what in an earlier chapter I have called lanthanic diseases—those that escape detection for long periods because they remain relatively symptomless or are otherwise camouflaged by more evident disorders. Among epidemiologists, the term 'latent' rather than 'lanthanic' has gained wider acceptance. *Latent* pathologies are diseases that are incipient in the sense that, over time, it is expected that they will manifest symptoms, or will undermine an organism's health in ways that decrease its resistance to other diseases.

With the extension of the term 'epidemic' to chronic disease, noted earlier, epidemiology has taken a step toward recognizing potentially *universal* disease, for it is not hard to conceive of a population, all of whose members are to varying degrees afflicted by a chronic disorder. This shift in the way pathology is understood is a significant one, and is seldom discussed. Usually, epidemiology has reserved the application of the term 'epidemic' to outbreaks of either infectious disease or disease caused by toxic agents, both of which may afflict a limited population. Epidemics were, in other words, conceptualized within a theoretical framework that presumed that their effects were contained. When the containment assumptions are lifted, however, a so-called "pandemic" or run-away epidemic can result with consequences that may approach universality, something which as yet has not been recognized to occur outside of theoretical models.

## THE CONCEPT OF UNIVERSAL DISEASE

Disease theorists have traditionally tended to limit their pronouncements of pathology to abnormal conditions and dysfunctions, that is, to deviations from a norm. Most theorists appeal to the standard of biological normality, in terms of which deviance and thereby pathology are identified. Though disease theorists admit the existence of chronic disease, the majority do this only in the limited sense in which a chronic disorder may affect a part of a population, resulting in dysfunctions that are evident departures from that population's norm. Pathology historically has not been open to the concept of disease that may affect an entire population, producing conditions and symptoms that are normal for that population. And it is precisely this that is meant by *universal pathology*.

Such a conception has, however, been proposed by a few researchers. They have been receptive to the view that disease may become so widespread as to be normal, that is to say, universal. To introduce the concept of universal pathology, I would like to review the work of a handful of twentieth century authors, none of whom, however, has developed the concept of universal disease in any systematic or precise sense, as early efforts to break out of habitual blinders tend almost always to be impressionistic and unscientific. We should be able, however, to look beyond these shortcomings and give our attention to the phenomenon of universal disease that concerned them.

During the second decade of the twentieth century, English biologist and sociologist Morley Roberts (1857-1942) proposed the hypothesis that cancer is erroneously understood: It was conventionally thought to be a disease like many others, caused by one or more microbiological agents or toxic conditions, although the actual, specific causes were not known. Roberts believed that this way of approaching cancer was fundamentally mistaken. In its place, he argued that cancer functions as a potentially adaptive response of the organism to changing environmental conditions: Since we live at a time when environmental conditions are changing rapidly, he reasoned, it is natural for the incidence of cancer to increase, as in fact it has.

According to Roberts, "malignant metastatic growths" occur on the cellular level as instances of potentially adaptive variation: "[T]umours are just as much products of the machinery of evolution as any normal growth." (Roberts 1926:291) In his view, only a tiny percentage of malignant variations are survived and function as successful, adaptive responses of the organism to changing environmental conditions. But, from an evolutionary point of view, Roberts argued, cancer is a normal phenomenon. (299)

On this basis, Roberts advanced the daring, controversial thesis that the evolutionary development of man's comparatively larger brain may constitute a maladaptive and pathological growth. He was, as far as I can tell, the first person ever to have raised the question, "Can we by looking on the brain from any special point of view consider it as an overgrowth or even as a tumour?" (Roberts 1926:253) Roberts advanced the hypothesis that it was. He went on to say:

[T]he fore-brain endeavours to dominate the man. Its activities may indeed destroy him just as motor ideas and impulses can in history be shown to have destroyed peoples and nations, or, at the very least, endangered them. Cerebral control can thus take on a quasi-malignant character. (256)

...I infer that the fore-brain is a forced, quasi-morbid reaction-growth that tends to be stabilized and physiologized if the environment remains stable..., which continually enlarges and withdraws energy, after the manner of a tumour, from the body. (257)

There can be no doubt that what we, perhaps in our blindness, call the upward progression of the human race has always been accompanied, especially when advance seemed most rapid, by an increase in disease, and it would in no way be surprising if we learnt at last that the remarkable increase in the fore-brain was not only one of the causes of malignancy but was to be in the end one great cause of the extinction of man. If that proved to be a fact, such a result would but class man as one of the many races of animals which perished of special over-growths.... (261)

It is not my intent here to argue on behalf of Morley Roberts' provocative thesis, which he unapologetically recognized would be offensive to human species pride, and for which there as yet exists questionable evidence. His thesis does, however, illustrate an early use of the concept of universal pathology, though this phrase was not used by him. By his hypothesis, the human species developed as a result of an ongoing pathological malformation, one that is shared universally by all of its members. If true, human "evolution" would be the consequence of a pathology that has become universal.[1]

A little more than a decade later, Roberts published another book-length study (Roberts 1938) that extended his previous work. In it, he argued on behalf of a secondary thesis that was introduced only in passing in his 1926 book, that there exist "malignant metastatic growths" on the social plane (Roberts 1926:204) in the form of social patterns of behavior that are themselves pathological and which have developed in parallel with the tumour-like human fore-brain. Again, Roberts was a twentieth century innovator: His work appears to be one of the earliest in the century to have applied the concept of biological pathology to

---

[1] If Morley Roberts' hypothesis has been ignored by most evolutionary theorists, it has not been ignored completely. Thirty years later, C. Judson Herrick made the following observations:

The history of civilization is a record of slow but dramatic enrichment of human life interspersed with episodes of wanton destruction of all the accumulated riches of property and spiritual values. These episodic reversions to bestiality seem to be increasing in virulence and in the magnitude of the resulting disasters until now we are threatened with the loss of everything that has been won in our struggle for the better life.

In view of this record it has been suggested that the enlargement of the human brain has gone so fast and so far that the result is actually pathological.... So, it is claimed, the human cortex is a sort of tumorous overgrowth that has got [sic] so big that its functions are out of normal control and "race" erratically like a steam engine that has lost its governor.

This ingenious theory was published by Morley Roberts and quoted with apparent approval by Wheeler (1928: 46). Their arguments seem to be plausible in view of the past history of wars, revolutions, and crumbled empires, and the present world-wide turmoil that threatens total destruction of civilization. But the theory is neurological nonsense. The evolution of brains...has gone on for a long time normally and on the whole progressively, if by progress we mean an increment of biological values. (Herrick 1956:398-9)

Herrick's conclusion—that Roberts' theory is "neurological nonsense"—does of course beg the question by assuming that normality and pathology are incompatible.

social disorders in a non-metaphorical way.[2] He brought a knowledge of biological processes to bear in an analysis of social and political dynamics. He proposed that societies could be studied as "organisms" in terms that parallel the physiological organization of biological subjects. "[S]ocial pathology implied its correlative physiology and therefore a social organism which was a reality and no metaphor." (Roberts 1938:xii) Roberts therefore drew various parallels between the functioning of cells within an organism and the functioning of members of a country within that larger "organism."

Unfortunately in his published work Roberts nowhere gives a clear definition of the word 'pathology'; he gives no explanation how this term is to be applied to "social organisms"; nor does his book contain any specific, detailed analysis of social pathologies. So it is understandable if some readers might complain that it is difficult to understand precisely what Roberts had in mind. The one concrete example he gives of a socially cancerous disorder is that of a country's police turning against the state. For Roberts, nonetheless, the conclusions that result from his perspective were clear. Since his books are now so little known, I would like to quote for the reader a few additional sample passages:

> Every successive inquiry into the nature and functions of a great social or national group will confirm the conclusion that where protoplasmic units, however simple or complex, work together in symbiosis or communal life, they can best be considered as organisms and as such liable to the diseases and disorders which change or destroy them. (Roberts 1938:18)

> It is...by introducing into sociological thinking the conception of social pathology and thus linking it to the general theory of disease and disorder that the greatest advance can be made in the study of social phenomena. (22)

> The conception that disorder in a nation is disease...was, and still is for the most part, wholly alien from common thought. (36-7)

> If I venture to run the usual risk of rage, indignation, and ridicule by what may be looked on as a cold-blooded attempt to prove that war is as inevitable as disease and death, I believe it will be all to the good, provided that ignorance of the way organisms are built and live and die is dissipated. (7)

> [T]here may be in societies processes which can be called malignant without unduly straining scientific language. (98)

I have touched on three views that Morley Roberts argued in imaginative but serious and thoughtful terms: his theory of cancer, his hypothesis concerning the evolutionary development of the human brain as a malformation, and his belief that biological pathologies

---

[2] There are always roots below roots. Roberts credits the original idea to Henry Gawen Sutton's *Lectures on Pathology Delivered at the London Hospital* (1891), which was published after Sutton's death. The work contains most of Sutton's *Lectures on Medical Pathology* (1886), supplemented by lecture notes taken at Sutton's lectures in 1886, 1888, and 1891. According to Roberts, it was Sutton who first proposed the general idea of applying physiological ideas to social pathology. (Roberts 1938:xii.) "It was [Sutton's] conception of a society sick and suffering as a whole, which not only suggested a city, a state, a world, as organisms of different grades, but gave at once the powerful conception of a true social physiology and pathology." (36)

The interested reader, however, will find upon reading Sutton that Roberts was inclined to see in Sutton's writing much of what Roberts himself wished to say. About the closest that Sutton comes to Roberts' views is his statement: "[W]e come to recognise that disease, the distracted feeling in our wearied patients, is the outcome of society, and its individual disorder." (Sutton 1891:xv)

are often paralleled by pathologies on the social level. Before leaving Roberts' views, it may be of interest to mention another suggestion that he made. He proposed, unfortunately only in passing, that a "social organism" such as a nation is vulnerable to "infection" through the agency of "infectious ideas." (Roberts 1938:151) He did not define what such ideas are, but from other passages one can assume that he meant political, social, religious, or other ideas and ideologies that regularly serve to divide people and engender hatreds. Later chapters in this study continue and develop this line of thought.

To bring these ideas to bear on our discussion of universal disease: It is only a small inferential step to move from Morley Roberts' perspective to the hypothesis that human beings are universally afflicted by pathology in several ways: by virtue of an evolutionary development that has gone awry in producing a brain in great measure dedicated to designing weapons of global destruction; by virtue of pathological disorders that afflict forms of human social organization, which provide a pathogenic growth medium for mass fear and hatred; and by virtue of ideas and ideologies which themselves, in human minds and in human hands, inspire intolerance, hatred, and violence. Roberts did not systematically develop his conception of these malignancies, or demonstrate them in a way that can satisfy reasonable standards of proof. Nevertheless, the framework he proposed was, early in the twentieth century, intellectually bracing and challenging.

During the same decade political scientist Frederick L. Schuman published his *International Politics* (1933), a massive study much akin to Roberts' publications in its intent to place responsibility for mankind's worst offenses squarely upon human shoulders. Much of the force of Schuman's position can be effectively summarized by his quotation from Nietzsche: "the earth hath a skin; on this skin are diseases—for example: man." (66) Schuman elaborated as follows:

> Without necessarily accepting the unsavory implications of this figure of speech, one may nevertheless legitimately compare the spread of man and of man's culture over the terrestrial globe with the spread of a thin film of parasitic organic matter over the skin of, let us say, an orange. Microscopic living beings appear where conditions are most favorable in the crevices of the surface; they reproduce, expand, and create societies or colonies; the societies spread in the direction of the most favorable opportunities and the least resistance; they come into contact with one another, intermingling and at the same time changing their own character; new societies emerge out of the fusion; old ones die and wither away. First one area and then another nourishes a rich growth and the process goes endlessly on until the orange is no more, or until the condition of its skin no longer supports life among the organisms which have made it their home. (66)

Schuman used a distinctly clinical vocabulary to describe the worldwide human tendency to organize itself into national political units. He claimed that a "malady" which is "extraordinarily contagious" is responsible for nationalism. (Schuman 1933:300) Later, we will discuss some of Schuman's psychological observations concerning the gratifications that the human species obtains from its emotional investments in patriotic identification, paid for at an ongoing and ever-increasing cost measured in millions of lives. Here, I mention Schuman's study as a further example of the relatively infrequent extension of pathology so as to apply to normal, average people. From Schuman's point of view, the human species is afflicted by a universal pathology, one which "infects" the vast majority of men and women with the "nationalist germ" (300) that continues to cause so much suffering.

Another twentieth century researcher who has attributed universal pathology to man has been sociologist Alexander Rüstow, who, in a monumental 700-page work (Rüstow 1980), argued that the history of human civilization has been dominated by a pervasive "pathology," "sickness," or "disease" that Rüstow calls "domination." Rüstow contended that human forms of social organization, from nomadic times to the present, have involved a process of "superstratification," which has given objective reality to the sadistic portion of man's psychological makeup: "Let us not forget that this is the enemy we are facing. Diabolic is too mild an expression for such a degree of inhumanity." (666) (For a full exposition of the complex concept of superstratification, I refer the interested reader to Rüstow's study.)

A more intuitive judgment of universal pathology was made by psychiatrist Karl Menninger:

> Gone forever is the notion that the mentally ill person is an exception. It is now accepted that most people have some degree of mental illness at some time, and many of them have a degree of mental illness most of the time. This really should not surprise anyone, for do not most of us have some physical illness some of the time, and some of us much of the time? (Menninger, Mayman, & Pruyser 1967/1963:33)

Menninger may have extended the concept of disease more gently than Rüstow, but he still proposed that pathology can become so widespread and so chronic that it is genuinely universal. We shall consider Menninger's observations in greater detail in Chapter 8.

Writing soon after Menninger, Peter Sedgwick, whose work I commented on in an earlier chapter, and whom the reader will remember as a proponent of the belief that disease is a human construct ("there are no illnesses or diseases in nature"), did not rule out the possible universality of some pathologies: "The existence of common or even universal illness testifies, not to the absence of a normative framework for judging pathology, but to the presence of very wide-spread norms." (Sedgwick 1973:33) Sedgwick noted that entire communities can share a physical condition that they themselves consider normal, but which outsiders would judge to be pathological. He pointed out that the Rockefeller Sanitary Commission on Hookworm found that in some areas of North Africa this disease was considered to be a normal aspect of health. (32, citing Knutson 1965:49) Further, in a South American Indian tribe, dyschromic spirochetosis, a disease that causes colored spotting on the skin, was considered to be so completely "normal" that individuals not afflicted by it were judged to be pathological and were excluded from marriages. (Sedgwick 1973:32, citing Mechanic 1968:16) "Social and cultural norms...plainly govern the varying perception, either as essentially 'normal,' or as essentially 'pathological,' of such characteristics as baldness, obesity, infestation by lice, venereal infection, and presence of tonsils and foreskins among children." (Sedgwick 1973:33)

During the 1990s, the concept of universal disease gained further ground. Disease theorist Jerome C. Wakefield called such pathologies "statistically nondeviant lesions." As was observed by Sedgwick, Wakefield noted that their recognition is a function of prevailing social norms, and can include such conditions as arteriosclerosis, gum recession, malaria, etc. (Wakefield 1992:375) Wakefield went on to say: "In fact, there is nothing incoherent about a virtually universal disorder, as might occur as a result of an uncontrolled epidemic or radiation poisoning after a nuclear war." (378)

Not surprisingly, Wakefield criticized the narrow view of traditional pathology, which uses statistical deviance and normality to identify disease, for then, "the majority are debarred from being regarded as ill." (Wakefield 1992:378, quoting Kendell 1975:309) Not only would it not be possible to consider the majority to be afflicted with a pathology, but "excellence in strength, intelligence, energy, talent, or any other area is just as statistically deviant as its opposite." (Wakefield 1992:377) In short, the concept of universal pathology opens the door to the possibility that the majority of members of a species may be diseased. This, certainly, is the strong meaning of universal pathology.

Today, an increasing number of disease theorists accept the idea of universal pathology. Recently, for example, a disease theorist has stated: "Lack of optimum health, over the long term, contributes to physical disease, and to the extent that most of us are not nearly as emotionally healthy as we could be, we are in this arena 'subclinically diseased.' ...[M]ost of us are unhealthy, and therefore, diseased, most of the time." (Woodhouse 1997:341) And still another has argued: "Since it is conceptually possible for some diseases to be part of the species design, those diseases are not abnormal in the idealized sense; the diseased organism would be functioning as evolution 'intended.'" (Kaufman 1997:277)

✧

During the twentieth century, then, there has been a succession of views relating to the concept of universal pathology: Morley Roberts' impressionistic but suggestive studies early in the century; Frederick L. Schuman's theory of ideological contagion; Alexander Rüstow's thesis of universal social pathology; Karl Menninger's observation of the universality of mental illness; Peter Sedgwick's view that pathologies may sometimes afflict entire societies; Wakefield's willingness to admit virtually universal disorders; and, finally, the recent hypothesis that a disease may be part of the evolutionary design of a species—which comes full circle back to Morley Roberts' theory of evolutionary pathology.

I have devoted space here to these views in order to provide a foundation that we will build upon later when we study a variety of universal human pathologies in greater detail. Some adversely affect humanity from within, while others harm non-human forms of life as a result both of humanity's destructive behavior and the erosion of conditions of life that the proliferation of the human species brings about.

## MAN AS PATHOGEN

A pathogen is an organism that is destructive to other life; a self-pathogen is destructive to its own life. An organism becomes pathological when a number of conditions together are satisfied: First, the organism must reproduce at a rate sufficient to dominate competing forms of life, so that the speed of its reproduction assumes the character of a disease or an epidemic within a given context of reference. The context in view may be the life of a single host organism, it may include one or even multiple communities of hosts, or the context may be widened still further to include the biosphere of an entire planet. (Whether there exist pathogens able to function on an interplanetary scale is not yet known to our species, but there is nothing inherently unimaginable about such a possibility.)

In the case of an individual host organism, we call a pathogen *disease-producing* when it is capable of reproducing at a rate which, in a period of time that varies with the pathogen and the individual host, will overwhelm and potentially destroy the host. We call a pathogen *epidemic-producing* when an entire community of host organisms is involved in this way, so that the proliferation of the pathogen is destructive to a great portion, and potentially the totality, of the community. When we consider a planetary environment consisting of many millions of individual species, a pathogen that results in acceleratingly widespread species extinctions can, in default of an expression in our existing vocabulary, be called a *global pathogen*. The reproductive proliferation of such an organism, when it leads to snowballing extinctions of other species, and to the destruction of planetary conditions essential even for its own survival, is a phenomenon that can justifiably be called a *planetary disease* of pandemic proportions.

The second defining characteristic of a pathogenic organism is that members of its kind pass on from one to another information that specifies how they are to interact with their host environment in ways that are inherently destructive to that environment itself. The transmission of this information among members of the pathogenic group, and from generation to generation, may be by genetic means, through the learning or training of its young, or by a combination of these. When a pathogen's activity is essentially limited to its immediate environment within individual host organisms, its successful reproductive proliferation insures that its future generations will continue to be destructive to their respective hosts. A pathogen is "successful" to the degree that its reproductive spread continues to be destructive to its environment, yet not so destructive as to undermine the conditions for the pathogen's own survival. There should be no need to elaborate further for the reader to perceive the applicability of the concept of pathogenicity to successively wider environments: A pathogen may afflict communities of like host organisms, or communities of diverse organisms, until an entire planetary environment may come to be adversely affected.

There is a third defining characteristic of a pathogen, one that is especially significant in the context of this study: A pathogen must typically be capable of resilient change, so that it is capable of adapting itself to changes in the host environment that threaten its survival. Many bacteria and viruses have excellent resiliency in this regard: They are capable, through a process of selection over a period of successive generations, of adapting progressively to toxic threats to their continued existence that may be introduced into their environments. Many can comparatively quickly, over the course of relatively few generations, acquire immunity to a wide range of new toxins. The increasing appearance of antibiotic-resistant bacterial strains is an example of this type of pathogen-preserving resiliency.

In the chapters that follow we shall consider the hypothesis that the human species has come to be such a pathogen; in Chapter 17, we examine this hypothesis in detail. If it is true, then we should expect that the above three pathogenic traits will apply to the human species: First, we should expect to find that mankind's rate of reproduction is accelerating at a rate characteristic of the unrestrained growth of a pathogen, evidenced by a progressively advancing encroachment of population in relation to finite land and resources, and, in the process, displacing or directly destroying other species. These are topics that fall within the purview of population studies and ecology, which will concern us later.

Secondly, we should anticipate that from one generation to the next the human species passes on attributes in the form of knowledge, skills, and a characteristic psychology and epistemology that support and encourage the continued destruction of the conditions necessary for the survival of a significant number of other forms of life. To the extent that human beings are auto-pathological as well, we should expect to find that we pass on attitudes and behaviors that encourage self-destructive activity, including the progressive destruction of conditions essential to our own survival.

Since man is a reflective creature, capable at least to some extent of self-regulating behavior, the third characteristic of pathogenicity becomes especially important: When a species is both reflective and self-regulating, its resiliency as a pathogen in the face of environmental change is likely to take on a quite different aspect than it does in "lesser" disease organisms: For such a reflective species—that is, for man—it can be essential to its continued role as pathogen that its individual members, and more importantly that communities of men and women, *remain ignorant, both psychologically and cognitively*, of the destructive effects of their reproductive and other behavior. Psychologically and conceptually complex organisms that we are, human beings have at their disposal a wide array of subtle and ingenious mechanisms to prevent them from becoming conscious of the consequences of their actions, by means of which they might thereby check themselves. Some of these mechanisms will be our focus in later chapters.

## RELATIONSHIPS BETWEEN THERAPY AND PATHOLOGY

In Chapter 3, I introduced the notion that a framework-relative understanding of the relationship between a disease and potentially effective therapies for its treatment is a dynamically interactive one, so that how a given pathology is understood may suggest possible ways that are believed to be appropriate to treat it. Reciprocally, therapies that are successful will affect how the disease is conceptualized. The following relationships between pathology and therapy are worth recalling: First, when a disease is judged to involve a breakdown of *rules* that define an organism's desired state or level of functioning, it is natural to seek methods capable of restoring the organism's functioning in conformity with the rules that have been breached. Second, when researchers believe that a pathology arises due to a fundamental *error* in functioning, it is likely that they will seek out therapies that aim specifically at error-correction. In the case of conceptual pathologies, we will look for methods to identify and then eliminate the specific forms of error that are involved. Third, when a disease is identified because we perceive a harmful state that is separated by a noticeable gap from the state of health we desire, then a *problem* of pathology is formulated, a problem that prospective therapies will attempt to solve.

Each of the three main alternative, interrelated approaches used in identifying pathologies may lead to similar or identical therapeutic approaches. For example, a geneticist may consider a genetic malformation to arise because a rule that prescribes "correct" or "optimal" encoding for a trait or function has been broken. By framing the disorder this way, the geneticist may seek a treatment to optimize and preserve correct functioning according to rule. Alternatively, the geneticist could choose to study the malformation in terms that stress the occurrence of an error of genetic sequencing, and then seek to discover appropriate error-correcting interventions. Both approaches may be combined when the researcher uses the conceptual vocabulary both of violated rules and of errors of encoding to define a problem of pathology. No one approach to disease identification is exclusionary; each approach to conceptualizing a disease can shape, or it can dictate, methods of treatment.

Often, unfortunately, a disease cannot be effectively treated, at least not by known means. When effective treatment does not yet exist, a knowledge of the prognosis of the illness becomes an essential tool and can be more important than therapeutic concern. The history of medicine bears this out. During the period of early Greek medicine, for example, being able to describe a patient's prognosis was a more realistic goal than therapy: "Predicting the outcome of a given episode of illness, and filling in symptoms forgotten by the patient, was more readily possible than effecting a cure, which was slow if successful and uncertain in any event." (Hudson 1983:80)

As we shall see, certain of the mental, social, and conceptual pathologies dealt with in this book have, unfortunately, no known effective treatment. The best that we can then hope to accomplish is to understand their nature and prognosis.

In a world in which ignorance and uncertainty prevail, it is helpful to recognize that some diseases can be effectively treated even when we know very little about them. As mentioned in an earlier chapter, Pasteur, for example, was able to develop a rabies vaccine without ever identifying or observing the virus that causes it. Another well-known example of effective treatment in a situation of deficient knowledge is that of Londoner John Snow, who during the mid-1800s showed that tainted water was the source of cholera epidemics. It was not until many years later that *Vibrio cholerae* was identified by microbiologists. Still another example is the successful reduction of scurvy among its sailors when the British Navy began to provide them with a diet containing fresh vegetables and fruit. It was not until several hundred years later that vitamin C was discovered, whose deficiency leads to scurvy. Other examples include the suspicions of pathogenic relationships between oral contraceptives and circulatory disease, and between smoking and coronary heart disease—again, years before these suspicions could be documented and the pathological determinants identified. (After Hennekens & Buring 1987) Some of the human pathologies this book identifies may be of this kind: treatable even though we are still ignorant of their sources.

A general theoretical meta-view of relationships between pathology and relevant therapies must include an understanding of the role of prevention, which is often the most effective method to eliminate a disease. Here, too, effectiveness is possible even within a context of ignorance: For example, between 1779 and 1817, Johann Peter Frank (1745-1821) published six volumes of carefully detailed studies of matters of concern to public health. Interestingly, the title of his substantial work was *System einer vollständigen medizinischen Polizei* [A System of complete medical policing]. Many of the measures he recommended, ranging from prenatal and perinatal care to water purification and garbage disposal, offered highly effective preventive treatments for a multitude of diseases, the causes of which would remain unknown for long periods of time. Johann Peter Frank was, as the honest title of his work made clear, a policeman in the uniform of a public health official: He urged the *need to control the activities of ordinary people for their own well-being*. He accepted the ignorance of the public, and was convinced that widespread pathologies could be dealt with by effective public health policing. To control widespread pathologies—and especially in terms of the present study's focus on man as a pathogen—there is, as we shall see, sometimes no other way, offensive though this may be to those with opposing political attitudes.

⬦

The relationships between pathology and treatment are, in short, complex and sometimes vague and indeterminate. Paracelsus's dictum, "the physician must be exactly acquainted with the illness before he can know with what medicine to conquer it" (Hudson 1983:195), is a generality that simply does not hold. As we have seen in the history of medicine, pathology can fortunately sometimes be effectively treated even when a disease is poorly understood and its determinants are not known. And when effective therapies are not available, pathology can sometimes be prevented, even in the absence of knowledge and the presence of uncertainty. Sometimes the external environment can be altered—as when standing water and marshes are drained to deter the reproduction of the mosquito that spreads yellow fever; sometimes inner conditions can be changed—as when a vaccine is injected to strengthen the body's immune reaction to the yellow fever virus, should an infected mosquito evade preventive measures. (After Hudson 1983)

In connection with the varieties of psychological and conceptual pathology we shall subsequently discuss, the essential interrelatedness of effective therapies and corresponding pathologies will be taken seriously, for the relations between the two are not metaphorical. It is ideal when we can know the source of a pathology, and a lesser ideal when we know a cure but do not know the source. "[A]lthough the discovery of cures may seem of greater significance than the discovery of the sources of disease, the latter type of knowledge carries the greatest payoff in the long run." (Rapoport 1957:269). In some cases, we shall be able to find therapeutic counter-measures, whether of the rule-correcting, error-correcting, or problem-solving varieties. In other more refractory cases, we shall be able to offer no therapeutic measures at all, but will, when possible, outline corresponding preventive measures. It will be our concern to enlarge our awareness of pathologies that bring about human evil, to diagnose them, to treat them when possible, and to suggest ways in which they can be prevented when they are untreatable at the time. After running this gamut, we shall in the end still find that certain major, widespread, human-engendered pathologies appear to resist all of these efforts, and for those, prognosis will have to be our best guide to what we may rationally expect.

# CHAPTER 5

# PATHOLOGY AND THE CONCEPT OF EVIL

## HISTORICAL PRECEDENTS

From the standpoint of the framework-relative theory of disease, we have observed that the identification of any pathology occurs within a context of reference that is unavoidably saturated with values: There is a set of goals the realization of which is frustrated by the condition; these goals express what a patient and/or attending physicians care about; and their cares, in turn, are situated within a larger frame of reference that defines both the belief-systems of medical experts and the range of potentially effective therapies which their understanding of the condition suggests. The context in which any judgment of pathology occurs is inherently value-relative in these ways. They define the human motivations to treat pathology by rule-correcting, error-correcting, or problem-solving strategies.

Within this general framework in terms of which disease is understood, we have seen that the relationship between a given pathology and therapeutic approaches that may be used to treat it is a mutually influential one, so that the way in which a pathology is conceptualized affects approaches to its treatment, while the set of prospective therapies associated with a clinician's judgment of pathology very often suggests how the pathology is conceptualized.

If we accept that judgments of disease and correlative approaches to therapy involve a relativity to values, it becomes immediately evident that pathology may be defined as a function of negative values. This is, in fact, what common usage expresses, as in the words 'dis-ease', 'dis-order', 'dis-comfort', etc. Pathology is fundamentally the negation of the positive values that define what we desire. In subsequent chapters, certain very widespread human psychological and conceptual propensities will be called pathological in this sense, and these pathologies will be grouped together under the general classification of "*human evil.*" It is time to discuss this classification and to provide a justification for linking such forms of pathology with the concept of evil.

✧

The word 'evil' has been associated with numerous meanings, most of which are irrelevant to this study. Historically, most of the associations have been mythological or theological; others have related to moral philosophy and ethics. The majority of these associated conceptions do not relate to our focus, which will steadfastly be maintained on a certain group of specifically psychological and conceptual phenomena that affect human beings.

There is, however, some historical precedent for the application of the term 'evil' to the general varieties of human pathology that we will study, as well as precedent for using the word 'evil' in the context of psychiatry. I would like to draw attention here to a few of the more important historical roots.

Readers familiar with the history of psychiatry will be aware that the development of this particular branch of medicine was heavily overshadowed for many centuries by the spirit of supernaturalism. "The church in her thirst for domain has ever had an envious eye on the alluring field of medicine. Long after internal medicine and surgery had been wrested from her grasp, she clung tenaciously to the practice of treating infirmities of the mind. Were not her ministers indeed divinely commissioned as physicians of the soul?" (Farrar 1909:288)

Psychiatry's development during the late 1800s was considerably retarded thanks to the resolute efforts of philosophers like Kant, Schelling, and their contemporaries, who instructed that the study and treatment of mental pathology were the proper province of theology and philosophy (which, so they claimed, have the best interests of the soul at heart), and not the domain of psychology. As a result of their campaigning, the study of mental illness was set back a good two generations while the mentally ill continued to be treated by moralists disguised in physician's attire.

During psychiatry's long and difficult birth, theology and the treatment of psychopathology eventually came to be understood as inappropriate bedfellows, and they fortunately parted company. But if we look back at a few of the earliest applications in psychiatry of the word 'evil', we will not be surprised to find signs of a still determined domination by religious dogma.

Let us draw our first historical examples not as yet from psychiatry itself but from ancient Hebrew, where some of the oldest roots lie (see Taylor 1985): Of approximately thirty words that refer to ways in which men and women may sever their relationship with God, there are three words in particular that relate to the phenomena we will have in view. The three Hebrew words are *psh´*, `*awon*, and *ht*. Interestingly and perhaps coincidentally, these three words, expressing forms of disapprobation or negative valuation, parallel the three senses of pathology that I have distinguished: pathology conceived of in terms of rule-violation, error-occurrence, and problem-perception:

The ancient Hebrew word *psh´* referred to a breach in the Covenant relationship, and more generally to the breaking of a social or international relationship. By extension, it meant rebellious behavior, usually translated into English as 'transgression'. The meaning of the word *psh´*, then, parallels the conception of pathology as a rule-violating disorder. The second Hebrew word, `*awon*, meant 'twisted' or 'wrong', and has frequently been translated into English as 'trespass' to suggest a wrongful or mistaken straying off a path onto prohibited ground. In this, the term resembles the conception of pathology that focuses on the occurrence of error in the sense of a violation of constraints, of what is permitted. The third Hebrew root word, *ht*, originally meant 'missing a mark' in the sense of falling short of a target; and this meaning closely resembles our definition of a problem in terms of falling short of a desired goal.

The three words *psh´*, `*awon*, and *ht* together refer to ways in which dis-order is brought about, a disruption that results in the rending of the order of things, which is judged negatively, disapprovingly, and in a condemnatory manner. Such a disruption, disturbance, or destruction of order was thought to be "evil." It is in this sense that dis-ease has traditionally been thought to involve a breach of the natural order. Further, it is interesting to note that in the ancient Hebrew usage, evil was considered to be a "contagious" defect or disfigurement of the person. (Taylor 1985:30) And as we have seen earlier, infectivity and contagion are characteristics typically associated with many pathologies.

The choice to refer to certain diseases as "evil," however, requires stronger justification than these loosely drawn analogies to words in ancient Hebrew. There are other, more substantial historical roots, and beyond these there are, as we shall see later on, additional solid grounds for this choice of terminology.

Historically, few psychologists and psychiatrists have made an explicit connection between human evil and pathology. Among those who have suggested a connection of this kind, three psychiatrists are worthy of note here. They significantly influenced the later development of psychiatry, and, in different ways, judged certain forms of mental illness to arise from human evil or, as we shall see, from closely related moral deficiency.

Johann Christian August Heinroth (1773-1843) was a German psychiatrist who has now largely been forgotten. His name is known today mostly to historians of medicine, who associate Heinroth with his claim that the origin of mental illness is sin. (Heinroth 1818 and Heinroth 1823) In advocating this doctrine, Heinroth followed Schelling, who felicitously dispatched the topic of mental illness in his 1810 *Stuttgarter Privatvorlesungen* by equating insanity with sin. Heinroth's treatment of the topic was more clinically deliberate, more detailed, but still heavily religious.

It is easy to dismiss Heinroth's approach today as the work of a well-meaning religious crackpot, taking pride for having freed the study of mental illness from theological and moral entanglements. Yet Heinroth, in spite of his religious narrowness and dogmatism, was a significant contributor to the development of psychiatry. He was, for example, one of the first physicians to urge humane treatment of the mentally ill. He was one of the first to describe the psychiatrist's role with respect to his patient in terms that come close to those now accepted.

> What impresses us today are [Heinroth's] views anticipating some contemporary notions, such as the disassociation of the schizophrenic, the importance of defenses for the economy of the personality, the therapeutic role of the psychiatrist in terms of transference and counter-transference, and the beneficial effect of the removal of the patient from his environment and placement in an institutional setting. (George Mora in his Introduction to Heinroth 1975/1818: lxvi-lxvii)

Medical historians Gregory Zilboorg and George Henry (1941:301) observed:

> Heinroth was probably the first clinical psychiatrist to sense the need of a unitary concept in psychology, like that of the total personality of today. He was probably the first to whom the ideational content of the mentally sick presented not merely a set of aberrations but a psychological process full of meaning.

Furthermore, the first use of the words 'psychiatry' and 'psychosomatic' has been attributed to Heinroth. (Farrar 1951)[1] He was also apparently the first professor to teach psychiatry in Germany, beginning in 1811. (Mechler 1963) He was extremely prolific, writing a steady succession of books about psychiatry, about anthropology, and even a four-volume collection of poetry and philosophy. He was a friend of Goethe and a contemporary of

---

[1] According to Farrar (1951), Heinroth's *Lehrbuch* (1818) appears to have been the first to use the word 'psychiatry'. However, Mechler (1963) claimed that Heinroth was the first to have "made use" of the two words 'psychosomatic' and 'psychiatry'; the latter, according to Mechler, was coined by Reil, in Reil & Hoffbauer (1808-12). However, we should note that Reil actually advocated the German term *'Psychiaterie'*, which did not become fashionable. Heinroth instead used the German word *'Psychiatrie'*, which has remained in use ever since.

Kant. By all accounts, he appears to have been a thoroughly humane and caring person and physician.

And yet he was a moralist to the extreme. Not only did he link mental health with the moral precepts of religion, but physical health as well. For him, many physical diseases had their basis in moral evils. And, as a psychiatrist, he considered mental illness to be a consequence of "moral disease." One of his most comprehensive definitions of mental illness was this: "The complete concept of mental disturbances includes permanent loss of freedom or loss of reason, independent and for itself, even when bodily health is apparently unimpaired, which manifests itself as a disease or a diseased condition, and which comprises the domains of diseases of temperament, spirit and will." (Heinroth 1975/1818:xxiv and §55) His definition is indeed not that distant from the more fully developed characterizations of mental disorder recommended today. And yet Heinroth firmly embedded his concept of mental illness in religion. He identified human evil as the origin of mental pathology; Heinroth also judged its consequences, mental illness itself, to be evil:

> The forms of soul disturbances...show us a deviation, a regression, or a total standstill in the growth of soul life. Thus, both the inclination and the stimulus, and their product, must be definitely recognized as *evil*. This consideration is completely ignored by conventional views on the morbid conditions of the psyche.... [F]rom our point of view...disturbances of the soul are precisely the ripest fruit of moral disease. This is the true substance of all soul disturbances: it is *evil* in general. (218)

In spite of his compassionate outlook and temperament, Heinroth placed the shortcomings of human nature in a central position in his account of mental illness. He wrote: "We thirst for evil from early youth and it is granted to us until we are more than satiated with it. No one loves good, everybody loves evil; and the excess of evil is a disturbed mental life." (Heinroth 1975/1818:219) Heinroth judged human nature to be evil and sought support for his psychological theory in the Gospels, which was for him a natural step to take.

Our earlier discussion of words in ancient Hebrew that refer to evil concerned ways of speaking of man's breach of his Covenant relationship to God. In much the same way, Heinroth argued that "there is no mental disease, except where there is complete defection from God." (Heinroth, quoted in Farrar 1909:290) He proposed that mental health is only possible within a life of piety. He believed that madness is a natural consequence of sin, and therefore restoration of faith is the only effective therapy for mental illness. From his point of view, when mental illness occurs, "[a]n evil spirit abides...in the mentally deranged...." (290)

Heinroth was quick on his rhetorical feet. Recognizing that some would consider his opinion that the insane are children of the devil to be nonsense, he argued that his view is no less questionable than the belief that the righteous are children of God. He went on to reason: "In short, we find the essence of mental disease in the partnership of the human soul with the evil principle—and not merely in partnership, but rather in its entire subjection to the latter. This is the complete explanation of the lack of freedom or unreason in which all the mentally disturbed are involved." (Heinroth, quoted in Menninger et al. 1967/1963:290n)

Heinroth's psychology of mental illness, which included a systematic classification of mental disorders, repeatedly emphasized that psychic disorders arise from the voluntary pursuit of evil. In his nosology, Heinroth identified a single inclusive category of mental disease, which he called *vesania*. It was divided into distinct subordinate orders, genera, and species. His psychiatric nosology sought to bring to light how different varieties of sin are correlated with different psychological consequences. (Menninger et al. 1967/1963:51; for a detailed description of Heinroth's psychiatric classification system, see 446-7.) The only suitable therapeutic response to human evil, according to Heinroth, is "moral treatment," in which the personality of the psychiatrist assumes a role of central importance.[2] And for Heinroth, as we have noted, moral treatment consists primarily in persuading the patient to cultivate religious piety.

In spite of Heinroth's numerous positive contributions to the development of psychiatry, his religious fervor did not stand him in good stead, even with contemporaries. The English psychiatrists D. H. Tuke and J. C. Bucknill quoted the following several passages from Heinroth, and concluded with their own emphatic and disparaging comment:

> "Insanity is the loss of moral liberty. *It never depends upon a physical cause,* it is not a disease of the body but of the mind—a sin. It is not and cannot be hereditary, because the thinking *ego,* the soul, is not hereditary.... The man who has during his whole life before his eyes and in his heart the image of God, has no reason to fear that he will ever lose his reason.... Man possesses a certain moral power which cannot be conquered by any physical power, and which only falls under the weight of his own faults." It would seem impossible to compress within a single paragraph a larger amount of false and mischievous psychological teaching. It should only be retailed after being duly labeled "POISON." (Bucknill & Tuke 1879/1858:36n; see also Tuke 1892:I:231, 545)

Writing a half century later about Heinroth, medical historian Clarence B. Farrar remarked:

> Page after page of his text-book, published in 1818 while he was associate professor at Leipsic, we pore over, fancying that we are in the depths of some mediæval treatise on theology. His psychology he draws from the gospels, much as others have attempted to reconstruct geology from Genesis. The life of mental health is the life of piety. The etiology of madness is sin. Repentance and a return to faith are the means of cure. (Farrar 1909:289-90)

Farrar concluded, with some irony: "Views such as those we have just been reviewing are happily seldom heard to-day, and then usually from two sources, namely, from certain quarters of the church, and from patients who are suffering from depressive psychoses." (290)

Interestingly, Heinroth did not subsume mental illness entirely under the category of human evil. He was perhaps the first psychiatrist to suggest that *human stupidity* is a valid diagnostic category. As we shall see in Part II, a number of twentieth century psychiatrists have come to rather similar conclusions. Heinroth classified "*stupidity*" as a "precursor form and symptom of disease," and more specifically as

> ...the precursor and symptom of *foolishness.* It is a sign of a depressed but at the same time irritable nervous system, of general slackness induced by an effeminate way of life, miseducation, and general lack of cultivation of the intellect or will. If any help is still possible, and an outbreak of foolishness can still be prevented, severe and harsh somatic and psychic discipline, as well as reeducation, can be the only treatment. (Heinroth 1975/1818:373)

About half a century after Heinroth classified mental illnesses, a somewhat similar psychiatric classification was proposed in England by psychiatrists D. H. Tuke (1827-1895) and J. C. Bucknill (1817-1897). They proposed a classification of mental disorders that involved three categories: what the authors called metaphysical, symptomatic, and aetiologi-

---

[2] This was the so-called method of therapeutic milieu centered on the personality of the psychiatrist, introduced by Phillipe Pinel in France, by William Tuke in a modified form in England, and by others. Cf. Heinroth (1975/1818:xxxviii).

cal. (Bucknill & Tuke 1879/1858:46-54; see also Menninger *et al.* 1967/1963:447-8) The first category was especially interesting as an extension of Heinroth's approach to mental pathology: By "metaphysical," Bucknill and Tuke meant classifying forms of insanity according to the mental functions involved. The metaphysical category included such conditions as "diseases of the intellect" (idiocy and imbecility, dementia, mania, and delusional insanity); "diseases of the emotions or moral sentiments" (moral imbecility, melancholia and exaltation); and "diseases of the instincts" (uncontrollable propensities, loss of will). Heinroth's central role of sin in the genesis of mental disease was discarded, leaving a psychiatric classification that in great part remained explicitly and unashamedly moral.

Bucknill and Tuke identified what they called *"lesions of the intellect,"*[3] which involve cognitive impairments and can be associated with similar deficiencies on a moral level. These involve "a condition of the moral sense analogous to intellectual deficiency." (Bucknill & Tuke 1879/1858:243) Moral disease, according to them, may exist in various degrees. There is *"moral insensitivity,"* characterized by feeble moral powers and volition. (246) A more severe form is *"moral idiocy"*; here, the authors quote their contemporary, Dr. Maudsley, who observed: "there are certain beings who are truly moral imbeciles.... It is remarkable, indeed, what an acute intellect may sometimes coexist with an entire absence of the moral sense." (246) Finally, there is true *"moral insanity"*: "the patient is drawn away from his accustomed course, to the commission of acts which neither reason nor sentiment determines, which conscience rebukes, and which the will has no longer power to restrain."(242) They restrict the term 'moral insanity' to "that morbid condition which results in immoral acts without apparent intellectual disorder." (49) In their judgment, the prognosis for moral insanity is "unfavorable."

A few observations should be made at this point: First, readers familiar with contemporary psychiatric theory will recognize that the Bucknill-Tuke designation of moral insanity as a mental disease is no longer made. One plausible reason for this is that, for Bucknill and Tuke, "moral insanity" called for "moral treatment," and moral treatment, as will soon be clear, does not lend itself easily to scientific formulation.

Moral treatment was also in vogue among other practitioners of the time. (See Bucknill & Tuke 1879/1858:660-74) The phrase was used to convey a kinder, more sympathetic treatment of the mentally ill, and to highlight compassionate qualities of the physician's person that were to be expressed in therapy toward the patient. As Bucknill and Tuke expressed this:

> The subject of moral treatment is as wide as that of moral education; nay, wider; for it is education applied to a field of mental phenomena extended beyond the normal size by the breaking down of all the usual limits.... The moral treatment is not a science, it is an art—like eloquence, painting, music, poetry. However great a master of the art you may be, if you give rules, he alone will submit himself to them who is your inferior. (Bucknill & Tuke 1879/1858:674)

Moral treatment, in short, is not science.

Second, moral treatment and the associated category of mental illness that Bucknill and Tuke called "moral insanity" do not reflect today's preference in psychiatry for mental

---

[3] French psychiatrist Pinel also used language like this. In the chapter "Can Mania Exist without Lesion of the Understanding" in Pinel (1801:155), he wrote: "...when I resumed at the Bicêtre my researches..., I was not a little surprised to see many madmen, who at no time had manifested any *lesion of the understanding*, and who were under the dominion of a sort of instinctive fury, as if the affective faculties alone had been diseased." (Quoted in Bucknill and Tuke 1879/1858:241; my emphasis).

pathology labels that are constructed to appear, at least on the surface, to be value-neutral. And yet, as we shall see in later discussions of pathologies that comprise forms of human evil, something of fundamental psychiatric importance has been lost in the recent desire to avoid explicit and perhaps more honest moral terms.

It is worth noting that Bucknill and Tuke were careful to explain (I will use contemporary language here) that the cognitive skills of intelligence and of moral decision-making can develop independently of one another. Pathological deficiencies in one area do not necessarily affect the other. This recognition will become important later on when we consider the topic of human moral intelligence.

Bucknill's and Tuke's category of "moral insanity" was established so as to group together under one heading forms of human behavior that are essentially destructive in nature. Since their opus is today seldom found in libraries and is seldom cited, I again would like to quote from them:

> A class of cases demanding much consideration and discrimination must now occupy our attention. They are mainly of a destructive character...and may be distinguished...by the term "Emotional Insanity *proper*," or what is ordinarily understood as Moral Insanity.... That intellectual power and the perception of moral truth do not necessarily exist in the same degree with the same person, that they do not always develop themselves *pari passu* are propositions which, as the result of common observation, obtain general acceptance. But that there should be anything like congenital defect of the moral sense (*anomia* of Dr Rush[4]), in conjunction with intellectual powers not strikingly deficient, is a proposition not generally recognized, or so easily established. It is obviously one which must be carefully considered in the description of mental diseases. (Bucknill & Tuke 1979/1858:239)

Readers who have not cultivated a taste for moral matters in psychiatry and who may feel such reflections are too "metaphysical" in the modern, disparaging sense of the word may be persuaded to feel increased forbearance if they are reminded that Bucknill and Tuke, who urged acceptance of moral insanity as a diagnostic category, were among the first psychiatrists to assert unambiguously that all mental disease is organic in origin. This was a considerable, progressive step beyond Heinroth. Bucknill and Tuke significantly influenced the subsequent development of psychiatry in urging research into the organic basis of mental illness. They were not metaphysicians, but physicians with their feet on the ground.

> All disease, therefore, in our opinion, is organic. Not only is this so with diseases which often come under the common observation of the physician...but mental and nervous diseases also, of every kind and form. Not a thrill of sensation can occur, not a flashing thought or a passing feeling can take place without changes in the living organism; much less can diseased sensation, thought or feeling occur, without such changes; changes which very frequently we are not able to detect, and which we may never be able to demonstrate, but of which we are, nevertheless, certain. (Bucknill & Tuke 1979/1858:495)

✧

Bucknill's and Tuke's empirically-focused work marked the beginning of the permanent separation of psychiatry from religion. The psychiatric association of human destructiveness and moral insanity with human mental pathology would subsequently be transformed. As we shall see in later chapters, this shift away from religious associations has strengthened as a

---

[4] The Dr. Benjamin Rush we encountered in Chapter 2, who believed he had discovered the underlying cause for the "disease of being black."

number of contemporary psychiatrists have given new meaning to the use of the term 'evil' to refer to specific mental pathologies.

## ABOUT THE USE OF THE WORD 'EVIL' IN THIS WORK

There is a little bit more to be said concerning the psychiatric connection between human pathology and the concept of evil. I would like to turn the reader's attention once again back to linguistic use itself: In English, the word 'evil' can be used in both its adjectival and substantive senses. According to the *OED*, the adjectival sense appears now to be little used in contemporary colloquial English, and has given way to the word 'bad'. The substantive meaning of 'evil' is more frequently expressed in current usage, but here, too, ordinary use has come to favor terms such as 'harm', 'misfortune', 'hurt', and 'diseased'. The direct ascription of evil to a person, when an individual is portrayed as evil—in the sense of being profoundly bad, morally wicked, the perpetrator of heinous acts, etc.—has, according to the *OED*, become rare to the point of obsolescence in ordinary discourse. (For further discussion, see Pocock 1985.) One author commented about this loss of the word's meaning: "The disappearance of evil as a concept is one of the most extraordinary features of modern society." (Macfarlane 1985:57)

Much of this book involves an attempt to regain the forcefulness and specificity that has been lost as a consequence of this increasing obsolescence of usage. Human evil, in the restricted and specific sense in which I will use it, refers to apparently voluntary destructive behavior and attitudes that result in the general negation of health, happiness, and ultimately of life. The term is therefore associated with suffering and harm that man can, if he wishes, avoid. When this study is not directly involved in developing a general theory of human evil, the human evils we will have in view will be concrete and specific. The ancient, often vague, superstitious notion of evil—as an independent, objectified, malevolent power that takes the form of a mysterious shadow, frequently covert, invidious, little understood and so associated with darkness, the demonic, or witchcraft, and producing unfocused fear—will have no place in this study. It will no doubt remain a favored subject-matter for theologians, mythologists, anthropologists, literary critics, poets, and writers of ghost stories. However, a traditional and central connotation of the term 'evil' will be retained, and that is the connotation that brings to mind with a particular expressive and compelling force certain phenomena that are essentially destructive of life, happiness, and welfare—for this is a significant part of the meaning of 'evil', which the word continues to communicate successfully.

There is another reason why I have chosen to use the word 'evil' within a framework that eschews mythology, the supernatural, metaphor, and symbolism, and seeks to adhere to strict standards of empirical science and rigorous analysis. To call a person or a group evil still carries a moral sting; it expresses a *condemnatory judgment* that is, as we shall see, *maximally strong*. From this point of view, there is no judgment of condemnation that is stronger, that is as uncompromising, that involves a greater degree of unflinching radical moral rejection in the clear censure that it expresses.

Human evil in the sense in which it will be studied here is also *descriptive* of a general category of pathology, which includes the subordinate pathologies that we have already characterized as mental, social, or conceptual. —I exclude physical disease from the category of human evil since it is a variety of pathology that is generally *inflicted* upon human subjects, rather than representing conditions that men and women often *prefer* to have. In excluding physical disease, I seek to differentiate human evil from those non-human causes of suffering that include, in addition to physical disease, natural catastrophes and poverty, for example. A distinction is therefore made here between human evil and *misfortune*, which falls outside the scope of this study.

In spite of the mental cobwebs and irrelevant, undisciplined associations that continue to cling to the word, 'evil' is still the best and really the only word the English language offers that is at once maximally condemnatory and descriptive of the phenomena that we will subsequently study.

## DIAGNOSIS AND PATHOLOGY

The diagnosis of any situation is not, of course, its remedy; nevertheless, any diagnosis makes any situation more tolerable, or less intolerable. – Pocock (1985:43)

Clinical diagnosis has several purposes: First of all and most importantly, it seeks to detect when harm is occurring. Diagnosis becomes reflective and technical when it analyzes harm in terms of a violation of rules of normal, optimal, or ideal functioning, or in terms of errors in biological or mental processing that have taken place. Abstractly expressed, the first phase of clinical diagnosis is to detect within a framework dedicated to the alleviation of harm when there is a gap between what is and what is desired; in short, as I have expressed this before, to formulate a problem to be solved. Second, diagnosis seeks to group together symptoms that may initially have been judged to be unrelated into a "constellation," and then to connect this set of symptoms with an existing condition. Third, diagnosis situates the detected harm, related symptoms, and existing condition within a classification of pathologies, in an effort to throw light on the nature of the condition that is now judged to constitute a pathology, and thereby to identify potentially effective ways in which it can be treated.

There are two fundamentally distinct types of clinical diagnosis that are seldom differentiated, largely because one variety is so rarely exercised. On the one hand, there is routine clinical diagnosis, whose goal is to make connections between a patient's symptoms and suffering, a uniquely specified disease, and one or more therapeutic solutions. This is the usual meaning of clinical diagnosis. On the other hand, there is a second variety of diagnosis that is involved in the detection of new pathologies. Much of the process of routine clinical thought also takes place here: There is an awareness of a fundamental harm, of suffering, of a loss of function, capacity, freedom, or happiness; a set of symptoms is identified; and last, an attempt is made to place the condition and constellation of symptoms within an existing classification of diseases. At this final juncture, however, there is a departure from traditional diagnosis: The clinician sees that the existing classification system is inadequate. The familiar, established nosology does not recognize the identified condition as a pathology. Perhaps the clinician perceives that connections need to be made among symptoms habitually assumed to be unrelated. And sometimes the condition itself, though attended by suffering and productive of harm, has long been assumed to be normal.

The form of diagnosis that is involved in the detection of hitherto unrecognized disease involves a kind of awareness and reflective thought that is significantly different from routine diagnosis. In some ways, the detection of new pathologies is a form of creative thought. It brings with it a new way of perceiving the habitual world.

The two varieties of diagnosis may be most clearly differentiated when we consider the very different kinds of sets of criteria that may be relied upon in order to show that each variety of diagnosis is *incorrect*. A routine diagnosis can be shown to be incorrect in several possible ways: It may be that the clinician has neglected to take into account symptoms or other diagnostic data pertaining to the underlying pathology, which he or she has simply failed to notice. Or, some of the test results may be wrong, because they were performed incorrectly, or because error was introduced in their interpretation. It may be that the clinician has correlated or mapped existing symptoms and other diagnostic data incorrectly within the prevailing nosology. Etc. No matter what the specific reason may be, what makes it possible to determine that a routine diagnosis is incorrect is the existence of consensus among practitioners—as to how tests are to be performed, how results are to be interpreted, and how symptoms and test data are to be correlated with an accepted classification of diseases.

Diagnostic judgment that is involved in the detection of new diseases is obviously not of this kind; it cannot benefit by an established consensus of clinical judgment, but it is not limited by such a consensus, either. While it is theoretically simple, though sometimes concretely complex and time-consuming, to demonstrate that a routine diagnosis is incorrect, it is not simple to prove the incorrectness of a clinical judgment that purports to identify a new disease. Stanley Prusiner's contention that there exists a new class of pathogens is an example: After years of research effort by Prusiner, research associates, and collaborators, proof—in the form of gradually accreting evidence—appears gradually to be taking shape to demonstrate that specific prions are indeed the epidemiological determinants of some forms of spongiform encephalopathy. (See the earlier reference to prion research in Chapter 1.) Establishing the existence of a new physical pathology may take years of effort and a concerted struggle against the prevailing mindset.

The diagnosis of new pathologies, like any original enterprise that is not built upon the shared convictions of previous generations, is a risky undertaking. It is usually also a thankless occupation, since it often questions the prevailing conceptual system, the habitual diagnostic vocabulary, and familiar ways of thinking about disorders.

Subsequent chapters in this book are devoted to efforts to diagnose what have until now remained largely unacknowledged or undetected pathologies. Because this is an area that is especially susceptible to individual variations in perspective, it is important whenever possible for us to consider the clinical judgment expressed by others. Although the consensus of a few researchers is a small consensus, it is sometimes more illuminating and persuasive than a consensus of only one, hence the particular need in this book to consider the work of others.

Chapters in Part II bring together for the first time a wide spectrum of diagnostic judgment expressed primarily by psychiatrists and psychologists, all of whom have been concerned in their respective ways with the phenomenon of human evil. In Part III, as we ascend the slopes toward greater theoretical generality, we will encounter relatively fewer contributions by previous thinkers, so that a certain amount of ground-breaking effort will be required.

✧

## THE PATHOLOGY OF MAN: SYNOPSIS OF PART I

In this and the preceding four chapters a theoretical framework has been established for the chapters that follow. Since a good deal of ground has been covered, it may be useful before proceeding to highlight and comment upon our working hypotheses and the main conclusions we have reached.

Having considered certain of the main theories of disease and noted a number of their shortcomings, I proposed a framework-relative theory of disease, which emphasizes that the recognition of a disease is always relative to the frame of reference in terms of which it is identified. As we have seen, this framework-relative understanding of pathology is explicitly normative, since both the identification and the treatment of any disease are recognized to be functions of accepted values. From this point of view, what may be identified as a pathology in one frame of reference may cease to be in another, perhaps more inclusive, context. This framework-relative conception of disease, however, does not imply, as we shall see later, that the recognition of a condition as a pathology must be provisional or tentative.

I have suggested that normal functioning, on a biological, psychological, social, or conceptual level, may often result in harm. In this sense, it is evident that individuals are routinely harmed when such harm is to the advantage of their social group or species. Leaves die and fall in order that trees may thrive; men and women lose their lives in order that their nations may be secure and prosper. And human societies routinely suffer harm and inflict harm upon one another. Normal functioning is therefore not used in this work as a determining standard of health, and therefore it is not used as a determining criterion of pathology when health is disrupted. Instead, optimal and sometimes ideal functioning will at times offer more useful and meaningful criteria. From this perspective it makes sense to say, for example, that the majority of the members of a social group may suffer from a pathology that brings about the less than optimal functioning of its individual members and causes harm to them or to others.

I have associated two meanings with the phrase 'human pathology': At this point both express only what I intend to be taken as working hypotheses: (1) the hypothesis that mankind is afflicted by universal, lanthanic, or previously undetected, mental, social, and conceptual pathologies; and (2) the hypothesis that human beings comprise a species that itself has come to act as a pathogen both to itself and to other forms of life. In subsequent chapters we shall review evidence presented by a wide range of researchers that strongly supports both hypotheses. We shall ask whether patterns of human conduct that have been documented over many centuries can be adequately and minimally explained by these two hypotheses, and whether they permit us successfully to *predict* future human behavior. In relation to the theory of human pathology developed here, we shall find that it is also possible *retrodictively* to confirm the conclusions reached, in the sense that, if our conclusions are accepted, we should be *surprised* if human beings had behaved differently than they in fact have. The conclusions we shall reach are therefore appropriately judged in terms of criteria of past explanatory as well as future predictive value. The general results of this study are non-discursive, non-speculative, in part empirically based, and in part deductively demonstrable.

The notion that there may exist universal human pathologies implies the use of inclusive norms or universally accepted values. Subsequent chapters show that most human beings are afflicted by varieties of pathology that result in harm. Such harm may be of numerous kinds, but all can and do result in suffering, loss, or tragedy. There is, as we shall see, sufficient agreement among researchers, about both the nature of these harms and the desirability of avoiding them, for us to conclude that they constitute widespread pathologies.

This approach clearly involves a radical shift of perspective as we extend the concepts of disease and pathology to the "normal" population. In particular we will make a radical shift beyond the traditional definition of disease in terms of deviation from normality. By applying norms of optimal or ideal functioning universally, it will be possible to identify varieties of individual and group human pathology that share the properties of self-destructiveness and destructiveness to other forms of life.

In this fundamental shift of perspective there exists an interesting parallel with recent research concerning the prion theory of disease, to which I have made earlier reference. Prusiner and his colleagues believe that prion disease-transmission requires the presence of the normal form of a certain cellular protein that becomes converted into pathogenic form. In a parallel way, as we shall see, so do the psychological, social, and conceptual pathologies we shall study require the "normal form" of certain essentially human characteristics of emotion, social grouping, and conceptual functioning. Found in most members of our species and in their social collectives, these normal, average, and ordinary characteristics provide the basis for the pathologies of feeling, attitude, and behavior that typify forms of human evil.

In the course of this first section of the present study we noted ecologist René Dubos' observation that many pathologies which afflict the individual similarly afflict the social collective. In much the same vein, we saw how socio-biologist Morley Roberts proposed that human societies are to be understood as organisms that develop their own corresponding forms of pathology. I have situated one of the major forms of social pathology, psychological epidemics, in the middle-zone between individual psychological and group/social pathology. In the phenomenon of psychological epidemics we shall see the occurrence in the individual of forms of pathology that are transmissible and contagious. We shall find that there exist widespread "harmful beliefs," pathological states of mind, that warrant classification as diseases. The notion that there exist "infectious ideas" (Roberts) or "errors of thought" (Canguilhem) will bring us to the framework proper to conceptual pathology, the subject of Part III.

During the remainder of this book, much of our interest will be diagnostic, to demonstrate that human evil constitutes a major and unrecognized category of pathology. As we have already commented, diagnosis is itself therapeutic, even in the case of pathologies for which no cure is available. Diagnosis identifies characteristics of a condition that might otherwise escape detection, and places the condition within a context of concern; in short, diagnosis poses a problem to be solved. The clear formulation of a problem is itself a step toward possible solutions. As Menninger remarked: "One does not complete a diagnosis and then begin treatment; the diagnostic process is also the start of treatment. Diagnostic assessment *is* treatment...." (Menninger *et al.* 1967/1963:333)

The general variety of diagnostic judgment that will most concern us is judgment that is at once clinical and evaluative. Our specific focus will be the diagnosis of widespread pathology within a context of self-conscious evaluative judgment. We shall find that in recognizing *pathology that is largely normal* clinical judgment will become linked to judgment that is condemnatory, and in a manner that does not incur the weak tentativeness of relativism. From this point of view, our use of the term 'evil' will have a descriptive role as well as express the strongest possible moral rejection. When diagnostic and evaluative judgment are combined in an assessment of the human condition, our earlier observation—that there are far-reaching consequences which follow from the recognition that a condition is a disease—will be seen in a new and different light.

When all has been said, our acceptance of the phenomenon of human evil will have a certain finality about it: We must then seek ways to deal with it as it is.

# PART II

# THE PSYCHOLOGY OF HUMAN EVIL

# PART II

# THE PSYCHOLOGY OF HUMAN EVIL

Nowhere in the literature of psychology do we find a comprehensive study of the psychology of human evil. Nevertheless, the subject has not escaped the serious attention of psychiatrists and psychologists. Historians and ethologists with an interest in human psychology have also studied the phenomenon. In this section, I discuss the work of leading twentieth century psychiatrists and psychologists, quantitative historians, and ethologists who have shared the concern to study human evil—ideally, in order to lessen its control over humanity, and to improve our capacity to control ourselves.

In the earlier chapters of Part II, I describe and comment on the work of leading individual thinkers who have contributed to the psychological understanding of human evil. In later chapters of Part II, I shift to a topically-oriented study of psychological dimensions of human evil, which include: the psychology of genocide and terrorism, the human pathology of war, the psychology of human obedience, the phenomenology of hatred, the nature of moral intelligence, the pathology of collective stupidity, and the ecological pathology of the human species.

Part II offers the reader a unitary and comprehensive psychological framework in terms of which we can understand human aggression, cruelty, and destruction. Human evil is seen to be a widespread human pathology, one that afflicts individuals as well as social groups. The concepts of pathology, universal disease, infectiousness, and contagion, which were developed in Part I, are applied to the class of phenomena that form the subject-matter of Part II.

Throughout the chapters that follow, I seek to stress that human evil is by no means a mysterious element in the constitutional makeup of human beings, but that it can be clearly understood to be multi-factorial: That is, human evil is not the result of one particular human characteristic, but is rather the product of a well-defined group of human psychological attitudes and dispositions that are inherently pathological.

# CHAPTER 6

# FREUD AND THE PATHOLOGY OF AGGRESSION

S igmund Freud (1856–1939) was the first major twentieth century psychiatrist to formulate a clinical judgment concerning human evil. In a succession of works written over a period of decades, Freud gave a description in terms that are clear and direct of emotional, mental, and behavioral traits that he associated with human evil. Freud's perception and interpretation of mankind's aggressive and destructive side remained consistent throughout his professional life. The diagnostic judgment that he expressed can be isolated from Freud's general theory of psychoanalysis, so that it will not be necessary for us here to become deeply involved in the complexities and ambiguities of psychoanalytic theory.

Freud's understanding of human evil and of human destructiveness in particular involves three components: his general theory of human aggression, his concept of psychological projection, and to a lesser extent his notion of narcissism. In this chapter, I examine each of these subjects, discuss the relationships between them, and show how they combine in Freud's clinical understanding of the phenomenon of human evil.

## THE DYNAMICS OF HUMAN DESTRUCTIVENESS

Over the course of many years, Freud developed his instinct theory, in which he sought to focus attention on a group of dominant human psychological impulses which he believed to be largely unalterable, to be innate, and which represent tendencies of human beings to respond, without the involvement of reason, in complex and yet specify ways to events in the external world. One of these instincts, the human instinct of aggression, became for Freud a problematic subject. His analysis of human aggression went through a number of phases, first subordinating human aggression to sexuality (Freud 1953-74/1905:158), and then gradually recognizing aggression as an independent force in human psychology. (To trace the development of his position, see Freud 1953-74/1905:193n; Freud 1953-74/1909:140; Freud 1953-74/1920:52-55; and Freud 1952/1930:790-1.)

Although Freud came only gradually to this recognition, his understanding of human aggression remained constant over a period of years. The mirror he held up does not reflect a pretty picture of the psychological constitution of human beings, but it is a tribute to Freud's intellectual integrity that he did not shirk from representing human aggression as truthfully and forcefully as he could. This is how he described what he observed:

The bit of truth behind all this—one so eagerly denied—is that men are not gentle, friendly creatures wishing for love, who simply defend themselves if they are attacked, but that a powerful measure of desire for aggression has to be reckoned as part of their instinctual endowment.... *Homo homini lupus* [man is to man a wolf], who has the courage to dispute it in the face of all the evidence in his own life and in history? This aggressive cruelty usually lies in wait for some provocation, or else it steps into the service of some other purpose, the aim of which might as well have been achieved by milder measures. In circumstances that favour it, when those forces in the mind which ordinarily inhibit it cease to operate, it also manifests itself spontaneously and reveals men as savage beasts to whom the thought of sparing their own kind is alien. (Freud 1952/1930:787)

Freud referred to the "human love of aggression" as an "ineffaceable feature of human nature."(788) The "lust for killing," according to him, is a fundamental, instinctual wish. (Freud 1961/1927:13) As a result, he claimed, the majority of human beings—and here so-called "civilized people" are not exempt—are under the control of aggressive drives:

There are countless civilized people who would shrink from murder or incest but who do not deny themselves the satisfaction of their avarice, their aggressive urges or their sexual lusts, and who do not hesitate to injure other people by lies, fraud and calumny, so long as they can remain unpunished for it; and this, no doubt, has always been so through many ages of civilization. (Freud 1961/1927:14)

Subordinate to human aggression is one of its specific manifestations, sadism. Sadism, according to Freud, is a pathology in which the instincts of aggression and destructiveness become exaggerated. It is therefore a disorder which exhibits, in an especially clear way, the inner dynamics that underlie the human compulsion to engage in aggressive behavior: "In sadism, ...even in the blindest frenzy of destructiveness, one cannot ignore the fact that satisfaction of it is accompanied by an extraordinarily intense narcissistic enjoyment, due to the fulfillment it brings to the ego of its oldest omnipotence-wishes." (Freud 1952/1930:791) What is true of the sadist also holds true, usually in an attenuated or camouflaged state, of human beings, generally: "...there are present in all men destructive, and therefore anti-social and anti-cultural, trends and...in a great number of people these are strong enough to determine their behaviour in human society." (Freud 1961/1927:8) Feelings of satisfaction, of deeply seated emotional gratification, are often to be found underlying acts of human aggression. Indeed, there is a close connection between aggressive behavior and its emotional gratification. In Freud's judgment, human intelligence and cultural development do not and cannot stand in the way of the inner forces that are involved here, for they are simply too powerful. And so he wrote, "...man is a creature of weak intelligence who is ruled by his instinctual wishes." (61-2)

Central to much aggressive behavior is the phenomenon of hatred. Freud's clinical observations concerning human hatred led him to judge that hate is a more primitive and more fundamental emotion than love. "The relation of hate to objects is older than that of love. It is derived from the primal repudiation by the narcissistic ego of the external world whence flows the stream of stimuli." (Freud 1952/1915a:421) This is a disturbing picture of man in which aggressive and destructive emotions and the forms of behavior to which they lead are motivated by psychological satisfactions that men and women and even children receive from them. As Freud observed, "...most of our sentimentalists, friends of humanity, champions of animals, have been evolved from little sadists and animal-tormentors." (Freud 1952/1915b:758)

The satisfactions gained through instinctual aggression are not, according to Freud, amenable to reason. Let us see why this is so.

## PSYCHOLOGICAL PROJECTION

The term 'projection' was introduced by Freud relatively early, in 1894-6 (Freud 1953-74/1894:43-69 and Freud 1953-74/1896:159-188), when he characterized projection as a more or less covert psychological strategy that attributes to another person unpleasant or unacceptable emotions. By 1912, Freud (1962/1912-13:61) had modified this description and made it more specific so that projection became an emotionally defensive process of attributing an individual's own feelings to others or to the world, generally, in a manner so as to avoid consciousness of those feelings. In this second sense, a projection results when one attributes to others one's own rejected propensities.

According to Freud, psychiatric pathology can develop as a result of ego boundary problems, that is, due to an individual's difficulties in maintaining a clear definition of self. When boundaries of the self are excessively vague, the separation between the ego and the external world also becomes vague. In infancy, according to Freud, this separation is as yet unclear. The infant's experience is of undifferentiated unity, an "oceanic feeling," which is felt as emotional bliss. The memory of that experience, he claimed, leaves an indelible print on us all in the form of a wish to return to the infantile state. Pathologic disorders involve a range of attempts to regain this lost experience. As a consequence, the boundary line between self and world can blur, so that internal, psychical events are inappropriately attributed to others or to the world. (Freud 1952/1930:768) This is projection as Freud came to conceive of it.

Unfortunately, projection is not limited to manifest cases of psychiatric pathology; it affects much of human experience. It is normal for primitive people, for example, to project "their own evil impulses into demons." (Freud 1962/1912-13:64) Later in the same work, Freud added: "Spirits and demons...are only projections of man's own emotional impulses. He turns his emotional cathexes into persons, he peoples the world with them and meets his internal mental processes again outside himself." (92)

The same kind of emotional projection that is habitual among primitive people has played a primary role in the evolution of mankind's view of the universe, which Freud described in terms of the three distinct stages of animism, religion, and science. Each stage involves the tendency of human beings to give "omnipotence" to the objects of their thought:

> At the animistic stage men ascribe omnipotence to *themselves*. At the religious stage they transfer it to the gods but do not seriously abandon it themselves, for they reserve the power of influencing the gods in a variety of ways according to their wishes. The scientific view of the universe no longer affords any room for human omnipotence; men have acknowledged their smallness and submitted resignedly to death and to the other necessities of nature. None the less some of the primitive belief in omnipotence still survives in men's faith in the power of the human mind, taking account, as it does, of the laws of reality. (Freud 1962/1912-13:88)

Freud suggested that primitive man's animistic projections onto his outer world may be similar to the overvaluation of private psychical phenomena characteristic of neurotics, who exhibit a strong preference for their own internal world over an external, shared world. (See Freud 1962/1912-13:159) Freud did not, however, take the obvious next step, compatible with his outlook, to ask explicitly whether both religion and science involve similar types of "overvaluation"—in the one case, overvaluing internal wishes by projecting them into religious dogma, and in the other case, overvaluing human interests by projecting them into the goals of human science. For in all three cases—in animism, in religion, and in science—we encounter an all-too-human tendency to propound conceptions of an external world that conforms to human wishes. In this sense, overvaluation, projection, and homocentrism go hand-in-hand.

So far, I have described Freud's concept of projection as a human propensity that involves an inappropriate and surreptitious "transplanting" (Freud 1962/1912-13:160) of emotions from the private world of the individual to the common world of other people and external events. This is the most familiar conception of projection, and it is one that has exerted a formative influence on the development of projective psychology, particularly in Rorschach research. There are, however, two less familiar but theoretically distinct forms of projection that Freud mentions, though he does not elaborate upon either in detail. In fact, it is not clear that Freud himself realized that he had more than a single kind of projection in view. In future chapters, we shall have occasion to apply the concept of projection to a variety of phenomena relating to human pathology. It will therefore be important to have a clear understanding of the various types of projection.

If we call the more familiar variety of projection *emotional* projection, we might call the second variety *reifying* projection. Here is how Freud described it:

> Under conditions whose nature has not yet been sufficiently established, internal perceptions of emotional and intellective processes can be projected outwards in the same way as sense perceptions; they are thus employed *for building up the external world*, though they should by rights remain part of the *internal* world. (Freud 1962/1912-13:64; my emphasis)

A *reifying projection* may be thought of as a kind of inappropriate ascription of external existence to phenomena that are inherently internal. By means of this variety of projection, man populates his external world with objects drawn from inner experience. It is an illegitimate but convincing reification of subjective life.

Later in the same work, Freud pointed to a different variety of projection when he wrote: "[P]rimitive man transposed the structural conditions of his own mind into the external world.... The technique of animism, magic, reveals in the clearest and most unmistakable way an intention to impose *the laws governing mental life* upon real things...." (Freud 1962/1912-13:91; my emphasis) Here, Freud introduced a third kind of projection, which I will call *rule-prescriptive*. A rule-prescriptive projection expresses a belief that events in the external world will conform to the rules that regulate inner experience. Like the other two forms of projective belief, emotional and reifying, rule-prescriptive projection involves an inappropriate, unjustified extension that goes beyond the world of inner, psychic phenomena.

The two passages I have quoted are significant, for they involve an important departure from an essentially affective understanding of projection. In these passages, Freud speaks more as a cognitive philosopher and less as a psychiatrist, for he is talking about issues that involve less the constitution of inner, psychic life, and more about those that relate to abstract and general relationships between consciousness and a world considered to be external to it. The two varieties of "projection" that Freud had in view in the passages just quoted are not of the kind that involves an unconscious ascription to another of an individual's rejected innermost feelings. If this reading of Freud is correct, they are, instead, varieties of projection that *give* the world its character: Reifying projection gives the world its "externalized" constitution, while rule-prescriptive projection underlies the belief in the external world's regulation according to the rules to which mental life itself happens to conform. The projection outwards of internal perceptions is, in Freud's words, "a primitive mechanism, to which, for instance, our sense perceptions are subject, and which therefore normally plays a very large part in *determining the form taken by our external world.*" (Freud 1962/1912-13:64; my emphasis)

In this way, Freud touched on the epistemological problematic that concerned Kant, though there is nothing in his text to indicate that he was aware of this. It is a problematic which later, though in different ways, concerned philosophers such as Russell and Carnap, who were also interested in this "construction of the external world." Here, perhaps it is fair to say that Freud slipped—rather uncharacteristically for him, given his bias against philosophical analysis—into non-psychological extensions of the meaning of 'projection'—into speaking, that is, about subjects not basically psychological. It is clear that Freud wished to refer to the "transplanting" not of *feelings* that one rejects, which is the result of emotional projection, but rather to very different kinds of matters: first, to *realities* that come to assume the status of externally existing objects as a result of the reifying projection involved, and, second, to conformity with *rules* that we projectively believe to hold in the "external world" that is formed as a result.

In later chapters, we will return to discuss further these three varieties of projection that Freud did not differentiate. I will subsequently refer to the familiar psychological variety specifically as *emotional projection*, and to the two that I have distinguished here as *reifying projection* and *rule-prescriptive projection*. The three varieties of projection will be grouped together under the general heading of *psychological projection*, as a reminder of their Freudian origin, and despite the essentially non-psychological content of reifying and rule-prescriptive projections. As we shall discover, all three varieties of projection play major roles in an understanding of human aggression and the broader subject of human evil.

To make this claim plausible to the reader at this early stage, it may be helpful to anticipate our later discussions a little bit: It should come as no surprise that the three varieties of psychological projection interact and combine to produce, inflame, and maintain psychological conditions that nourish human aggression. In suggesting this, I would like for a moment to step outside the context of Freud's thoughts about aggression: One has only to consider different social, political, or religious groups of human beings, and then build into our understanding of their psychological functioning the fact that each individual group member will typically project undesired emotions upon other people who are, or are believed to be, different in some respect. Each person will further reify his preferred perceptions, judging them to comprise undeniable objective realities. And while engaged in this thoroughly predicative-attributive process, he will insist that external events, and other people, in particular, conform to the rules that govern his own cognitive and emotional world. When many differently disposed individuals or groups confront one another, these projections fly fast and loose, as each person and his social collective first insist upon the primacy of his and its own projectively constituted reality, and then seek to eradicate any points of view which might invalidate that reality. —And, of course, to this end, the most concrete and effective method to prevent the invalidation of one's own preferential reality is by physically eliminating the other whose perspective disagrees. In this way, human projection leads easily and directly to violence.

Psychological projection, made up, then, of emotional projection, reifying projection, and rule-prescriptive projection, will prove to be fundamental to our understanding of how a wide range of phenomena involving human evil comes about: These concepts make it possible to clarify the origin, for instance, of crimes of hate, racial and religious prejudice, genocide, and the roots of ideological conflict. And yet, though psychological projection is central to such understanding, it is, as we shall see, only one aspect of the many-sided, complex phenomenon of human evil.

Before bringing this discussion of psychological projection to a close, it is important to mention its connection with *narcissism*. Earlier in this chapter, I pointed out how, according to Freud, psychiatric pathology can result from ego boundary problems. From our brief discussion of psychological projection, it should be clear that as the dividing line between self and world becomes amorphous and unstable, projective predications are encouraged and indeed facilitated. For, when an individual's sense of self in relation to the world is blurred, as it is in narcissism, it becomes all the easier to project inner states and mistake them for outward realities.

The concept of narcissism, as Freud understood it, is more restricted in scope than it later became in the history of psychiatry. Freud's view of narcissism was based in part on earlier ideas proposed by Havelock Ellis and Paul Näcke. For Freud, narcissism is expressed, for example, in the "attitude of a person who treats his own body in the same way as otherwise the body of a sexual object is treated." (Freud 1952/1914:399) Narcissism also is exhibited, he claimed, when "...a person suffering organic pain and discomfort relinquishes his interest in the things of the outside world, in so far as they do not concern his suffering. Closer observation teaches us that at the same time he withdraws libidinal interest from his love-objects: so long as he suffers, he ceases to love." (402) Similarly, for Freud, the hypochondriac becomes narcissistic when he withdraws his attention from the world of others and instead invests his interest in his own self-absorption. (403) In addition to narcissism found in organic illness and hypochondria, Freud mentioned a third expression of narcissism, found in the behavior of those who are in love (404), for love characteristically promotes an exclusionary absorption of the self in the encompassing, gratifying feelings of love. Furthermore, individuals who show a "disturbance in libidinal development" (for example, homosexuals, according to Freud) are prone to narcissism: "They are plainly seeking themselves as a love-object and their type of object-choice may be termed *narcissistic*." (405)

Underlying these specific manifestations of narcissism is a "primary narcissism" that exists in every person, and which is involved in his or her choice of sexuality. Although Freud did not intend this to be a universal generalization, many men when in love retain a form of emotional dependence that is characteristic of the relationship of the child to his mother or her substitute, and which Freud called *anaclitic*, in contrast to *narcissistic*. On the other hand, many women, he came to believe, do not develop this kind of emotional investment in the other partner, but rather become self-absorbed in a type of emotional "self-sufficiency": "such women love only themselves with an intensity comparable to that of the man's love for them." (Freud 1952/1914:405) Freud remarked that such narcissistic women are, as a rule, "the most beautiful" and "have the greatest fascination for men." (405) In addition to these more familiar forms of narcissism, Freud commented in passing that great criminals, and also humorists, frequently possess a "power of retaining a blissful state of mind" that enables them "to keep at arm's length everything which would diminish the importance of their ego." (405)

All of these expressions of narcissism reveal the human tendency to *overvalue*, mentioned earlier. In fact, overvaluation of an individual's preferred choice of "love-objects" perhaps, more than anything else, characterizes Freud's understanding of the manner in which the narcissist invests his or her emotional energy in ways that become hermetically sealed, so that all emotional paths in the end curve back upon the self as center of a universe of one.

When the mechanisms of psychological projection are incorporated into the narcissist's world, the groundwork for a significant portion of human aggression is laid. As we shall see later, the concepts of psychological projection and narcissism are used by many of the researchers we shall consider who have sought to understand human evil.

## THE GRATIFICATIONS OF WAR AND ITS INEVITABILITY

As any student of human history knows, there is no class of events that so fills mankind's recorded past as warfare. Were one to delete reference to wars from the history books, their covers would collapse upon very nearly empty bindings. Why do men engage in war? is a question many have asked but relatively few have tried to answer in terms that are psychologically concrete and specific. Freud's response to this question was simple and candid: Men engage in war because they enjoy it and because warfare satisfies a deeply felt need and urge.

Freud observed that primitive people like to kill, and that killing is part of their way of life. Where the majority of other animals have an instinctual aversion that impedes them from killing members of their own species, mankind, Freud claimed, does not. (Freud 1952/1915b:763) Unfortunately, the civilizing effects of advanced societies exert little influence over the human predilection for killing other people. Freud expressed a sense of disillusionment over "the brutality in behaviour shown by individuals, whom, as partakers in the highest form of human civilization, one would not have credited with such a thing." (757)

If civilization does not prevent or suppress aggression, unfortunately neither does intellectual endowment. World War I shocked Freud when he saw

> ...the narrow-mindedness shown by the best intellects, their obduracy, their inaccessibility to the most forcible arguments, their uncritical credulity for the most disputable assertions.... Students of human nature and philosophers have long taught us that we are mistaken in regarding our intelligence as an independent force and in overlooking its dependence upon the emotional life. Our intelligence, they teach us, can function reliably only when it is removed from the influences of strong emotional impulses; otherwise it behaves merely as an instrument of the will.... Thus, in their view, logical arguments are impotent against affective interests.... Psycho-analytic experience has, if possible, further confirmed this statement.... The logical infatuations into which this war has deluded our fellow-citizens, many of them the best of their kind, are therefore a secondary phenomenon, a consequence of emotional excitement.... (Freud 1952/1915b:760-1)

The radically destructive form of "emotional excitement" that leads to war has its roots, according to Freud, in illusions that function so as to "spare us emotional distress, and enable us instead to indulge in gratification." (757) These are emotionally turbulent and muddied waters, for, on the one hand, wars obviously bring great suffering and devastation, and yet, on the other, in Freud's judgment, they comprise an intensely gratifying experience for many. Without war: "Life is impoverished, it loses in interest, when the highest stake in the game of living, life itself, may not be risked." But with war: "Life has, in truth, become interesting again; it has regained its full significance." (762)

Human illusions are the grinding stones of the mills of war in which individual lives become the grist. Mankind seeks to justify its illusions by means of what Freud called "judgments of value," which are determined by human "desires for happiness." In other words, what men judge to be of value conforms to what they believe will bring them happiness, and in this perverse process that proceeds from wished-for gratification to destructive aggression on behalf of those interests, people make judgments of value that play the role of "attempts to prop up their illusions with arguments." (Freud 1952/1915b:801) Like individuals, nations are dominated by their immediate emotions far more than they are led by their intellectual faculties. Their stated interests "serve them, at most, as rationalizations for their passions; they parade their interests as their justification for satisfying their passions." (761)

A few years before his death, Freud was contacted by Albert Einstein, who initiated a now famous exchange between the physicist and the psychoanalyst. In his long letter to Freud dated July 30, 1932, Einstein asked Freud:

> Is there any way of delivering mankind from the menace of war? It is common knowledge that, with the advance of modern science, this issue has come to mean a matter of life and death for civilisation as we know it; nevertheless, for all the zeal displayed, every attempt at its solution has ended in a lamentable breakdown. (Einstein & Freud 1991/1933:3)

Characteristically, Einstein had already come to his own original answer to the question he posed for Freud. Einstein wrote:

> How is it possible for [the small group of those in government power] to bend the will of the majority, who stand to lose and suffer by a state of war, to the service of their ambitions? ...An obvious answer to this question would seem to be that the minority, the ruling class at present, has the schools and press, usually the Church as well, under its thumb. This enables it to organise and sway the emotions of the masses, and make its tool of them.
>
> Yet even this answer does not provide a complete solution. Another question arises from it: How is it these devices succeed so well in rousing men to such wild enthusiasm, even to sacrifice their lives? *Only one answer is possible. Because man has within him a lust for hatred and destruction.* In normal times this passion exists in a latent state, it emerges only in unusual circumstances; but it is a comparatively easy task to call it into play and raise it to the power of a *collective psychosis.* (5; emphasis added)

Freud responded to Einstein's letter in September of the same year. His thoughtful response to Einstein's questions supported many of the physicist's own observations. Freud agreed with Einstein that to avoid war, human beings will have to relinquish their cherished preference for national sovereignty: "There is but one sure way of ending war and that is the establishment, by common consent, of a central control which shall have the last word in every conflict of interests. For this, two things are needed; first, the creation of such a supreme court of judicature; secondly, its investment with adequate executive force." (Einstein & Freud 1991/1933:13) But this utopia is unlikely: Human beings, Freud observed, receive an instinctual gratification from killing their enemies. "You are amazed that it is so easy to infect men with the war-fever, and you surmise that man has in him an active instinct for hatred and destruction, amenable to such stimulations. I entirely agree with you. I believe in the existence of this instinct and have been recently at pains to study its manifestations." (15)

In principle, though evidently not in practice, people could avoid the destructiveness that results from their instinctual aggressiveness if they were capable of independent thinking. But, according to Freud, the majority are not.

> That men are divided into leaders and the led is but another manifestation of their inborn and irremediable inequality.... In this context we would point out that men should be at greater pains than heretofore to form a superior class of independent thinkers, unamenable to intimidation and fervent in the quest of truth, whose function it would be to guide the masses dependent on their lead. (Einstein & Freud 1991/1933:18).

As a consequence: "The upshot of these observations...is that there is no likelihood of our being able to suppress humanity's aggressive tendencies." (17)

Stepping back from the specific answer that he gave to Einstein's question, we should note that Freud made two interesting observations in passing: First, perhaps intending some humor in the context of dark thoughts about mankind, he referred to his personal opposition to war, which he shared with Einstein, as a "constitutional intolerance, an idiosyncrasy in its most drastic form," and "not merely an intellectual and affective repulsion." (Einstein & Freud 1991/1933:20-1) He did not elaborate. If he was serious, perhaps he meant to suggest that resistance to war is not only abnormal for the human animal, but unnatural and atypical to the point that its presence in an individual can be regarded as a dispositional disorder. Indeed, from this point of view, we should not be surprised when the majority finds fault with those who oppose war, at times going so far as to pronounce them psychiatrically abnormal misfits. I suspect that this would be to press Freud's incidental remarks too far—but when a psychiatrist speaks seriously of an "idiosyncrasy in its most drastic form," a potential association with mental disorder comes naturally to mind.

Second, Freud hypothesized that human warfare, which is "practically unavoidable," may in the end be "biologically sound." In suggesting this, he wrote: "Why do we, you and I and many an other, protest so vehemently against war, instead of just accepting it as another of life's odious importunities? For it seems a natural thing enough, biologically sound and practically unavoidable. I trust you will not be shocked by my raising such a question." (Einstein & Freud 1991/1933:19) Perhaps Freud was thinking of human warfare as an ecologically sound governor that limits population overgrowth. We shall never know; for again, he did not elaborate.

Einstein and Freud shared a "hatred of war" (Freud's expression); they agreed that there exists in man a pervasive collective instinct (Freud), or infectious psychosis (Einstein), that gives him a lust for hatred and destructiveness. Freud's conclusion, and it was clearly offered as a clinical judgment on his part, is that war is unavoidable precisely because it provides the great majority of human beings with instinctual psychological gratification. If his outlook is bleak, he offered the vague hope, that "whatever makes for cultural development is working also against war." (Einstein & Freud 1991/1933:21)

## THE PATHOLOGY OF CIVILIZATION

Of Freud's principal contributions, the ideas of individual neurosis and psychosis are likely to be among the most familiar to the general reader. But Freud did not restrict his analysis of mental illness to individuals. Sometimes, he argued, we are justified in claiming that an entire human social group has become neurotic. The basis for this extension of psychiatric diagnosis beyond individual psychology was established early in Freud's work, in his notion of a collective mind:

> I have taken as the basis of my whole position the existence of a collective mind, in which mental processes occur just as they do in the mind of an individual.... Without the assumption of a collective mind, which makes it possible to neglect the interruptions of mental acts caused by the extinction of the individual, social psychology in general cannot exist. (Freud 1962/1912-13:157-8)

Here lies an historically important transition from individual to social psychology. Once made, it was a natural consequence for Freud to apply diagnostic concepts drawn from the first area to the second. In doing this, he argued that civilization itself, due to its psychologically inhibitory and regulative effects, frequently leads to psychiatric disorders. He extended his account of this process by asking: "would not the diagnosis be justified that many systems of civilization—or epochs of it—possibly even the whole of humanity—have become *neurotic* under the pressure of the civilizing trends?" (Freud 1952/1930:801)

Freud recognized that there is an important difference between the diagnosis that an individual is ill and the clinical judgment that an entire society has become psychologically pathological: In Freud's view, when a psychiatrist judges that an individual is neurotic, it is on the basis of observing a deviation of the patient's feelings, attitudes, and behavior from what the psychiatrist takes to be "normal." However, Freud observed: "No such background as this would be available for any society similarly affected; it would have to be supplied in some other way." (Freud 1952/1930:801) Freud again leaves the matter without further clarification and does not explain what kinds of diagnostic standards exist or might be developed for this purpose. Here, the reader will be reminded of our earlier discussion of universal pathology, since a neurosis that afflicts an entire society is such a disease. Second, the reader will recognize the issue of cultural relativism that Freud's remark poses implicitly—for by what supra-cultural standards is one to judge the deviance of a whole society? We shall have occasion to return to both of these issues in the chapters ahead.

There is a second important difference that we should note when individual and society-wide neuroses are contrasted: In the individual case, it is sometimes possible for members of his or her family or social group to exert pressure upon the person judged to be neurotic, and so encourage, or coerce, the individual to receive appropriate therapy. But in the case of neurosis affecting an entire social group—as when the majority of people in a nation are infected by a shared psychological pathology—there is no parallel, persuasive way to bring "the patient" to therapy: Freud therefore raised the question: "what would be the use of the most acute analysis of social neuroses, since no one possesses power to compel the community to adopt the therapy?" (Freud 1952/1930:801) Freud was one of the first to pose the following two questions, which are essential to the diagnosis and treatment of social pathologies: By what criteria are society-wide mental disorders to be recognized? And, by what means (including means of enforcement) are they to be treated, if at all?

I have tried to make explicit a few of Freud's pioneering reflections in this area that are generally not well known. As with many great thinkers, occasional original but ungerminated seeds of thought lie scattered among the footnotes and passages of text that their author did not elaborate upon. Freud acknowledged the challenges that arise if we take society-wide pathology seriously. He wrote: "In spite of all these difficulties, we may expect that one day someone will venture upon this research into the pathology of civilized communities." (Freud 1952/1930:801) To a large extent, our focus in future chapters will be to this end.

## CLOSED SYSTEMS OF BELIEF

Earlier in this chapter, we saw how Freud sought to account for human enmity, destructiveness, and cruelty in terms of psychological projection and narcissism, which form major constituents of the emotional constitution of a species dominated, he claimed, by instinctual aggression. We also looked at the way in which Freud sought to understand animism, religion, and science in terms of what he called the "omnipotence" with which human beings endow their wishes. The preceding section focused on Freud's judgment that much of the human urge to go to war is derived from illusions which simultaneously function to spare us distress, to provide us with self-gratification, and which are justified by means of judgments of value we use to "prop up" our desires by means of argument.

In Freud's account of human aggression there are two main dimensions of aggression that need to be distinguished—an emotional dimension and an ideational dimension. The emotional side of human aggression is certainly the more familiar. But human emotions link up quickly with ideas: Prejudice, hatred, and gratification in an enemy's suffering and extermination are the emotional ingredients in the human need to rally in support of preferred systems of belief. Human passions are often closely tied to preferred *ideas*, so that emotional fervor becomes a function of infatuation with a favored set of ideas.

Freud considered two varieties of belief-systems that predominate among human beings: religion and philosophy. He wrote at some length about religion, while his analysis of philosophical belief-systems is sparse. The judgments of value to which human beings make recourse when seeking to justify their illusions are usually either religious or philosophical in nature. As we shall see later in connection with ideologies, both religion and philosophy lead to systems of belief that are essentially *closed*; they are *exclusionary*, each boasting that its beliefs are true and others false; and each purports to *take into account all relevant evidence* by rejecting, in an automatic reflex of self-validation, putative evidence offered from the standpoint of any competing belief-system. Freud did not formulate the matter in these terms, but as we have seen he spoke in terms closely related to these of the omnipotence that men attribute to their preferential thoughts and the "realities" they project.

Religion, according to Freud, circumscribes the possible choices that are open to human beings

> ...by urging upon everyone alike its single way of achieving happiness and guarding against pain. Its method consists in decrying the value of life and promulgating a view of the real world that is distorted like a delusion, and both of these imply a preliminary intimidating influence upon intelligence. At such a cost—the forcible imposition of mental infantilism and inducing a mass-delusion—religion succeeds in saving many people from individual neuroses. But little more. (Freud 1952/1930:776)

Religion for Freud is "mental infantilism" because the ideas that religion propounds as creed and doctrine are devised so as to make human helplessness tolerable. The ideas themselves, according to Freud, are "built up from the material of memories of the helplessness of his own childhood and the childhood of the human race." (Freud 1961/1927:23).

In short, the belief-systems of the various religions are nothing more, in Freud's view, than delusions created to make a harsh world psychologically more comfortable. That the teachings of religion are delusional was evident to Freud from three things:

> When we ask on what their claim to be believed is founded, we are met with three answers, which harmonize remarkably badly with one another. Firstly, these teachings deserve to be believed because they were already believed by our primal ancestors; secondly, we possess proofs which have been handed down to us from those same primaeval times; and thirdly, it is forbidden to raise the question of their authentication at all. (Freud 1961/1927:33).

Freud went on to say:

> We can now repeat that all of them are illusions and insusceptible of proof. No one can be compelled to think them true, to believe in them. Some of them are so improbable, so incompatible with everything we have laboriously discovered about the reality of the world, that we may compare them—if we pay proper regard to the psychological differences—to delusions. (40)

And so he concluded: "Where questions of religion are concerned, people are guilty of every possible sort of dishonesty and intellectual misdemeanour." (41) From this point of view, Freud believed it was clinically justifiable to call religion "the universal obsessional neurosis of humanity." (55) A neurosis is a perspective toward reality that functions to minimize pain—and in this, religion is a *successful* neurosis, even helping to prevent the development of individual neuroses in religious believers: "devout believers are safe-guarded in a high degree against the risk of certain neurotic illnesses; their acceptance of the universal neurosis spares them the task of constructing a personal one." (56)

Freud's criticism of philosophical belief-systems is similar to his criticism of religion, for both involve, as we shall see, the inappropriate ascription of internal states to reality. He "caricatured" religion as an "obsessional neurosis," and commitment to a philosophical system as "paranoic delusion." (Freud 1962/1912-13:73, 95) We need to understand these terms clearly. An obsessional neurosis occurs in an individual when certain thoughts, ideas, words, or images repeatedly and insistently intrude into consciousness. These invasive and recurring contents of awareness have their origin within the individual, but are often interpreted by the person as originating from an outside, alien source, and often are presented with a high degree of vividness. The obsessed individual is led impulsively to perform repetitive acts that have a ritualistic character. —For Freud, much in this diagnostic description accurately fits religious belief: It fits the tendency in believers to interpret all events in terms of their favored set of doctrines, their propensity to situate the source for their enlightenment outside themselves, and the ritualistic nature of religious behavior and ceremony.

In a parallel way, Freud judged that commitment to a philosophical system resembles paranoiac delusion. Paranoid thinking occurs when an individual routinely interprets events in a manner that is self-referential, considering himself to be the locus of whatever is happening around him—as when he comes to believe that a conversation taking place at a distance between strangers must be about him. Paranoid thinking often is associated with a sense of grandiosity, which confers upon the person an unjustified and magnified belief in his own importance. Delusional systems of belief in paranoia may be elaborate, and constructed in a manner that makes the paranoiac's belief-system impervious to outside influence—in a word, unshakable.

Freud observed that commitment to a philosophical system involves some of these same characteristics: There is a tendency for the proponent of a philosophical approach to interpret all events in its special and preferred terms, i.e., all claims and interpretations made from its point of view invoke, self-referentially, its own favored tenets. There is an unmistakable grandiosity about philosophical systems: each claims to have discovered the truth. Many are elaborately constructed, and in a manner that makes them relatively immune to revision even when confronted by evidence that conflicts with their first principles. (See Bartlett 1986.)

Freud's purpose in characterizing religion and philosophy as obsessional and paranoid, respectively, was, I believe, not to make facile and disparaging psychiatric diagnoses, but to point to the fact, in his judgment, that faith in religion and adherence to a philosophical doctrine involve neuroses and delusions that are, as he put it, "social structures: they endeavour to achieve by private means what is effected in society by collective effort." (Freud 1962/1912-13:73) In other words, the belief-systems that religious or philosophical proponents advocate are pathological, Freud suggested, on the level that is the focus of social psychiatry.

Stepping back from these claims, we see in Freud the beginnings in psychiatry of a fundamental and general concern with ways in which ideologies lead to pathology. Freud's explicit focus on religion and to a lesser extent on philosophy was a reflection of a broader analysis of ideology and its connection with human aggression that he did not undertake, a subject to which we shall return in future chapters.

## THE THERAPEUTIC TREATMENT OF HUMAN AGGRESSION

In reconstructing Freud's view of how instinctual human aggression might be treated effectively, his outspoken criticisms of universal love and altruism force themselves into our discussion. For universal brotherly love is what the major religions commonly teach as the most promising remedy for human aggression and destructiveness, and this remedy is, in Freud's judgment, a solution that will not and cannot work.

Preaching and practicing universal love, given mankind's emotional constitution and the unequal endowments and attainments of individuals, is simply absurd:

> The command to love our neighbours as ourselves is...a superlative example of the unpsychological attitude of the cultural super-ego. The command is impossible to fulfill; such an enormous inflation of love can only lower its value and not remedy the evil. Civilization pays no heed to all this; it merely prates that the harder it is to obey the more laudable the obedience.... [The] ideal command to love one's neighbour as oneself...is really justified by the fact that nothing is so completely at variance with original human nature as this.... I will not withhold the two principal objections we have to raise against this view. A love that does not discriminate seems to us to lose some of its own value, since it does an injustice to its object. And secondly, not all men are worthy of love. (Freud 1952/1930:801, 787, 783)

It is not only psychologically unrealistic, indiscriminate, and unjustified to be called upon to love one's neighbor as oneself, it is also an imperative that runs counter to what individual men and women, according to Freud, actually feel when others rouse their hostility. Freud here quoted Heine:

> Mine is the most peaceable disposition. My wishes are a humble dwelling with a thatched roof, but a good bed, good food, milk and butter of the freshest, flowers at my windows, some fine tall trees before my door; and if the good God wants to make me completely happy, he will grant me the joy of seeing some six or seven of my enemies hanging from these trees. With my heart full of deep emotion I shall forgive them before they die all the wrong they did me in their lifetime—true, one must forgive one's enemies, but not until they are brought to execution. (From Heine's *Gedanken und Einfälle*, quoted in Freud 1952/1930: 786)

If men and women naturally harbor such feelings of antagonism toward their adversaries, and feel gratified when they suffer or die, it is absurd to expect or to hope for them to love those who also feel enmity towards them. "I imagine now I hear a voice gravely adjuring me: 'Just because thy neighbour is not worthy of thy love, is probably full of enmity towards thee, thou shouldst love him as thyself.' I then perceive the case to be like that of *Credo, quia absurdum*" [I believe, because it is absurd]." (786) Attempts to persuade individual men and women, and their societies, to love their neighbors are misguided and absurd. How, then, can mankind seek to remedy its worst defects? Freud gives three answers. All presuppose the need to assess mankind's psychological makeup accurately: In treating people, in trying to lessen their aggressive and destructive constitution, it is essential to recognize that appeals to reason are irrelevant: "arguments are of no avail against their passions." (Freud 1961/1927:9) Any effective remedy against human aggression will, Freud believed, have to make recourse to and appeal to the forces of human emotionality.

Freud's first answer is that, for the greater part of humanity, coercive social control is necessary:

> It is just as impossible to do without control of the mass by a minority as it is to dispense with coercion in the work of civilization. For masses are lazy and unintelligent; they have no love for instinctual renunciation, and they are not to be convinced by argument of its inevitability; and the individuals composing them support one another in giving free rein to their indiscipline. (Freud 1961/1927:8-9)

Social control can, at least ideally, be achieved in two ways, according to Freud. Primarily through threat of punishment and promise of reward, human beings are encouraged to internalize the moral precepts that civilization advocates. Much of this process occurs during childhood; a sense of conscience is formed; and aggression is, in Freud's view, turned inwardly so that the individual becomes an agent capable of a certain degree of self-control.

In this civilizing process, guilt plays a central and significant role. Guilt is the second means used by society to control aggression, and became a central focus of Freud's research: "[M]y intention [is] to represent the sense of guilt as the most important problem in the evolution of culture, and to convey that the price of progress in civilization is paid in forfeiting happiness through the heightening of the sense of guilt." (Freud 1961/1927:796) For Freud, guilt arises out of the fear of losing love—love of one's parents or love of one's social group. Guilt also arises as a result of a person's fear of external authority, or fear of the internal authority of an internalized conscience. As a consequence, good, ethical behavior is often reducible to the conformity of people to social norms out of fear. (793) But the result of such conformity to moral precepts out of fear is moral hypocrisy.

> Civilized society, which exacts good conduct and does not trouble itself about the impulses underlying it, has thus won over to obedience a great many people who are not thereby following the dictates of their own natures.... Anyone thus compelled to act continually in the sense of precepts which are not the expression of instinctual inclinations, is living, psychologically speaking, beyond his means, and might objectively be designated a hypocrite, whether this difference be clearly known to him or not. It is undeniable that our contemporary civilization is extraordinarily favourable to the production of this form of hypocrisy. (Freud 1952/1915b:759)

This is not empty name-calling, but Freud's attempt to identify clearly what is involved in persuading and coercing the majority of people to follow the dictates of civilized conscience. If Freud is correct in his assessment here, it should come as no surprise that it requires very little suspension of measures of control for individual men and women to revert to extreme aggressive behavior and brutality. We shall particularly encounter this phenomenon in later chapters on the mass-killing that is characteristic of genocide and war.

In addition to internalizing morality by punishment and reward, and controlling it through the power of guilt, Freud suggested a third answer to the question, How can human aggression be reduced? He devoted little in his writing to formulating this approach, and so left its elaboration to the future. Freud claimed that civilizing constraints on the majority can only accomplish so much: In fact, under the veneer of civilization, rather little is accomplished when it comes to genuinely felt, non-hypocritical morality. Freud therefore mentioned, in remarks that are very brief, the notion that ethics can be employed in a therapeutic capacity: "Ethics must be regarded...as a therapeutic effort: as an endeavour to achieve something through the standards imposed by the super-ego which had not been attained by the work of civilization in other ways." (Freud 1952/1930:800) Were ethics to develop an explicitly therapeutic orientation, or, alternatively, if psychiatry and psychotherapy were once again to develop an interest in "moral treatment" (reminiscent of the psychiatry of Bucknill and Tuke, described in Chapter 5), a "therapeutic ethics" would face two challenges: moral therapy for the individual, and its equivalent therapy for entire social groups.

When the level of moral development of a nation or social group is barbaric and inhumane, its "treatment" faces two obvious and intractable difficulties: How are we to establish justifiable criteria by means of which the entire social group can be diagnosed as pathological, if by the term 'pathology' one has the customary meaning in view of dysfunctional deviation from "normality"? And, secondly, how is such "treatment" to be enforced when a whole society is involved? Therapeutic ethics is, as yet, an idea in search both of a cogent theoretical basis and of methods of implementation. The solutions that Freud proposed for the treatment of human aggression—punishment and reward, inculcation of guilt, and a therapeutic ethics—are sober, attempt to be practical, yet questionably offer much hope for combating human evil.

## FREUD AND HUMAN EVIL

As we have seen, Freud did not think highly of the largest portion of humanity, nor did he respect the level of moral or intellectual development of the majority of men and women. One seldom encounters the word 'evil' in his writing, though he occasionally used it. He spoke of "evil human tendencies" that he believed cannot be eradicated. (Freud 1952/1915b:758) For human aggressive instincts are, he claimed, "elemental": They are part of the human psychic constitution, and common to all men.

In another work, Freud (1962/1912-13:99) referred to "unconscious evil impulses" that men and women have. He had in view the same kinds of behavior that we commonly associate with human evil: malice, killing or injuring others, causing undue suffering, etc. In yet another work, Freud again referred to evil, in this way: "Those who love fairy-tales do not like it when people speak of the innate tendencies in mankind towards aggression, destruction, and, in addition, cruelty..... [N]o one wants to be reminded how hard it is to reconcile the undeniable existence...of evil with [God's] omnipotence and supreme goodness...." (Freud 1952/1930:790)

Freud's psychiatric judgment of mankind, as we have seen, is far from favorable. If there is a phenomenon that we may justly call "human evil," it is for Freud widespread, indeed a normal part of the human constitution. In speaking of everyman's attitude toward his neighbor, Freud wrote:

> Not merely is this stranger on the whole not worthy of love, but, to be honest, I must confess he has more claim to my hostility, even to my hatred. He does not seem to have the least trace of love for me, does not show me the slightest consideration. If it will do him any good, he has no hesitation in injuring me, never even asking himself whether the amount of advantage he gains by it bears any proportion to the amount of wrong done to me. What is more, he does not even need to get an advantage from it; if he can merely get a little pleasure out of it, he thinks nothing of jeering at me, insulting me, slandering me, showing his power over me; and the more secure he feels himself, or the more helpless I am, with so much more certainty can I expect this behaviour from him towards me. (Freud 1952/1930:786)

If we are to be adults with mature judgment, we cannot, Freud believed, escape the following conclusion: "The time comes when every one of us has to abandon the illusory anticipations with which in our youth we regarded our fellow-men, and when we realize how much hardship and suffering we have been caused in life through their ill-will." (787)

This for Freud is human evil. The normality and universality of feelings of the kind that he described affected him deeply. If human evil cannot be eradicated, and if we at present have no effective therapeutic measures against it, then the prognosis for humanity's future is open to doubt: "The fateful question of the human species seems to me to be whether and to what extent the cultural process developed in it will succeed in mastering the derangements of communal life caused by the human instinct of aggression and self-destruction." (Freud 1952/1930:802)

## NO CONSOLATIONS

Freud's experience of his fellow man and the clinical judgment he reached after years of psychiatric practice did not lead him to make a positive appraisal of the human species. He recognized that it is expedient for any man, and especially for an author of books, to make "humble obeisance on suitable occasions in honour of the high-minded nature of men; it will assist him to become universally beloved and much shall be forgiven unto him on account of it." (Freud 1952/1930:791) But he chose not to do this. Freud recognized the strength of human species pride, and although he was known for his commitment to the advancement of his work and his reputation, he nonetheless was willing to express an unpopular negative judgment of mankind. The clinical judgment that he formulated required intellectual honesty and personal courage.

As a psychiatrist, he recognized that human beings need to be comforted; and certainly there is much in life that is made easier by consolation. "My courage fails me...at the thought of rising up as a prophet before my fellow-men, and I bow to their reproach that I have no consolation to offer them; for at bottom this is what they all demand...." (Freud 1952/1930:802) It is a difficult position for an author: to express a point of view known by him to be unpopular, while at the same time recognizing that his theory offers no genuine remedies for the problems it identifies. —Why write a book that is guaranteed to be ineffective? "No doubt I might be asked here what is the point of writing these things if I am certain that they will be ineffective." (Freud 1961/1927:45)

And so, why did he do this? His response, given toward the end of his life and toward the end of his work, *The Future of an Illusion*, is direct and candid: His purpose was to help man to overcome his infantilism, the infantilism to which his ideologies cater, and the emotional infantilism that is at the basis of his aggressiveness and destructiveness. The purpose in writing about such things is to call upon men and women *to grow up* emotionally and intellectually. "[I]nfantilism is destined to be surmounted. Men cannot remain children for ever; they must in the end go out into 'hostile life'. We may call this *'education to reality'*. Need I confess to you that the sole purpose of my book is to point out the necessity for this forward step?" (Freud 1961/1927:63)

And yet, we should remember what Freud believed about any constructive steps forward that might be proposed: "I am certain that they will be ineffective." (Freud 1961/1927: 45) His call to maturity is one to which most men and women are deaf, though through no fault of their own. He offered no consolation for human evil. It is a fact about man that is final, that must be accepted, and it cannot be changed.

# CHAPTER 7

# JUNG'S UNDERSTANDING OF HUMAN EVIL

Evil has become a determinant reality. It can no longer be dismissed from the world by a circumlocution. We must learn how to handle it, since it is here to stay. How we can live with it without terrible consequences cannot for the present be conceived.... We stand face to face with the terrible question of evil and do not even know what is before us, let alone what to pit against it.... The old question posed by the Gnostics, "Whence comes evil?" has been given no answer by the Christian world.... Today we are compelled to meet that question; but we stand empty-handed, bewildered, and perplexed, and cannot even get it into our heads that no myth will come to our aid although we have such urgent need of one. – Jung (1991/1961-3:170-3)

[I]t is plain to any unprejudiced mind that the forces of evil are dangerously near to a victory over the powers of good. – Letter from Jung in Philp (1958:19)

Among leading twentieth century psychiatrists and psychologists who have studied human evil, after Freud we come to Jung. Carl Gustav Jung (1875-1961) was born into a Swiss religious family that had members of the clergy on both his mother's and his father's side. His father, too, was a pastor. Jung seems to have been a lonely boy, frequently distressed by his father's growing religious doubts. He was subject to vivid dreams and fantasies, which biographers believe probably laid the basis for his later interests in the irrational, mythic, and symbolic. As a teenager, he was attracted by philosophy; his readings in philosophy, combined with his fertile imagination and introspective preoccupations, led him to pursue a path away from the family's religious orientation. He chose medicine, and then specialized in psychiatry. Jung, however, never shook his family's religious heritage: Much of his later work was devoted to the psychology of religion. He read extensively in literature and mythology, applied myths and symbols drawn from his readings to his dream and fantasy life, and came to view certain dimensions of his personal experience as universals of human experience.

Jung is today remembered for suggesting the extrovert-introvert distinction, and also for his controversial claim that commonalities of human experience are somehow passed on to successive generations in the form of "archetypes" (from the Greek '*archetypos*' meaning 'original pattern'). Jung combined the claim that these primordial, inherited patterns of awareness induce similar feelings in different people with the related claim that there exists a collective human unconscious composed of inherited instincts and forms of perception that usually remain unconscious in the individual.

Jung's interest in the psychology of religion led him to the belief that psychological archetypes are not fully represented in Christianity, but are expressed more richly in Gnosticism, alchemy, mythology, and symbolism. As a result, Jung's theoretical perspective—as a psychiatrist—took a form that was to become arcane and considerably less systematic than other researchers we shall consider in this volume who have studied the phenomenon of human evil. For this reason, it is a good deal harder to glean from Jung's writings a clear description of the clinical understanding he came to have of human aggression, destructiveness, and cruelty.

My decision to include a chapter about Jung was made very much *in spite of* Jung's unsystematic, abundantly symbolic, and unscientific bent, for which he has already been appropriately criticized by others. (See, e.g., Kaufmann 1980:III:298, 300, 304, 375, 408, 424 & *passim*.) A wide range of indictments has been placed at Jung's doorstep, from muddle-headed and impressionistic, to confused, contradictory, and naively intuitive. Freud, for example, in writing about Jung's work, complained:

> ...it is...as its critics (Abraham, Ferenczi, Jones) have stressed, so unclear, opaque, and confused that it is not easy to take a position about it. Wherever one touches it, one must be prepared to hear that one has misunderstood it, and one does not know how one is to arrive at a correct understanding. It presents itself in a peculiarly vacillating way.... (320, quoting Freud 1963/1914)

Although Jung was a sloppy thinker who often indulged in a natural preference for fairy tales, he has been perceived by many, including a significant number of psychiatrists and psychotherapists, to have been an important ally in the fight against the kind of disenchantment with the world that some feel can stem from scientific rationalism.

It is my belief after devoting many long and sometimes painful hours to Jung's writings that the clinical judgment concerning human evil that he advanced on the basis of a lifetime's experience as a practicing psychiatrist merits a hearing. Let us then, in a spirit of sympathetic reading, reconstruct Jung's psychological understanding of the phenomenon of human evil in a way that frees it as much as possible both from vagueness and obscurity, and from his periodic discussions of evil within a religious context.

## JUNG'S STARTING POINT

Like many western psychiatrists, Jung considered the individual to play a central role in the psychological health, or the pathology, of society. Jung was sensitive to the psychological dimensions of human society and history, and deeply aware of the shortcomings of human groups, yet he believed that constructive change, if it is to occur, must take place within the individual person. "[P]sychopathology of the masses is rooted in the psychology of the individual.... The psychologist believes in the individual as the sole carrier of mind and life." (Jung 1967-83/1946a:218, 225) Meaningful, positive development within the individual is, however, decidedly difficult, perhaps even improbable, since it faces a substantial psychological obstruction: the fact, according to Jung, that man is a herd animal. Human instinctual drives, and fundamental preferences and values, originate in the human social consciousness of the herd. Its group mentality and the affiliative conformity it encourages in people are not conducive to individual growth and the realization of individual potential.

Human beings, though on the surface many appear to be civilized, are, according to Jung, "inwardly...still primitives." (Jung 1967-83/1954:269) "[M]ankind is, in essentials, psychologically still in the state of childhood—a stage that cannot be skipped. The vast majority needs authority, guidance, law. This fact cannot be overlooked." (Jung 1967-83/1916-17:237) Jung observed that in any civilized community, people living at its lowest levels exist "...in a state of consciousness little different from that of primitives. Those of the...[middle] strata live on a level of consciousness which corresponds to the beginnings of human culture, while those of the highest stratum [modern men] have a consciousness that reflects the life of the last few centuries." (Jung 1967-83/1928:75) Positive change within the individual psyche is, in other words, blocked or compromised, according to Jung, first, by humanity's herd mentality, second, by the fact that, from a developmental and evolutionary point of view, the vast majority of people are psychologically primitive, and, third, by the fact that distinct levels of consciousness generally characterize people depending upon their social level. Improvements in man face all of these obstacles. And so, from the outset, Jung's understanding of man takes into account a complex of forces that makes positive transformation within the individual implausible to achieve.

Mankind's herd consciousness, its primitive level of psychological, intellectual, and moral development, and the stratification of levels of consciousness generally correlated with social level, together contribute to humanity's vulnerability to what Jung called "psychic epidemics." The "mass man" is a ready subject and victim to the herd's political movements, which for Jung are the most common and virulent causes of human psychic epidemics. In one of his works, Jung suggests that it would be easy for him to "construct a political theory of neurosis, in so far as the man of today is chiefly excited by political passions." (Jung 1967-83/1916-17:19) (He did not go on to do this.)

The "political passions" that arouse men and women of course are linked to their preferred group ideologies. The human impulse to embrace a favored ideology is, Jung believed, little different from an addiction. It is like an addiction in that an ideology drives people to embrace a set of beliefs on behalf of which they will struggle and often go to their deaths. Like the ultimate results of any addiction, its consequences—to the individual and to his social group—are undesirable. "Every form of addiction is bad, no matter whether the narcotic be alcohol or morphine or idealism." (Jung 1965:329)

## JUNG'S ACCOUNT OF HUMAN EVIL

We need more understanding of human nature, because the only real danger that exists is man himself. He is the great danger, and we are pitifully unaware of it. We know nothing of man, far too little. His psyche should be studied, because we are the origin of all coming evil. – Jung (1977:436)

[T]he principal and indeed the only thing that is wrong with the world is man. – Jung (1967-83/1945:216)

Jung flatly rejected the so-called *privatio boni* argument endorsed by much Scholastic moral philosophy, which claimed that evil is the absence or privation of good. For Jung, evil is no more the absence of good than darkness is simply and no more than an absence of light. Evil has a substantial reality of its own; it is not to be accounted for simply by subtracting or suspending those values that determine what is good.

With a preference for metaphor, Jung developed his theory of human evil in terms of a pictorial allusion which he called "the shadow," borrowed from Nietzsche but given new meaning. In Nietzsche's (1924/1880:186) "The Wanderer and His Shadow," the shadow is portrayed as a co-inhabitant of the self, with whom internal dialogue is possible, who is bound to the world of ordinary things and ordinary living, who pursues the "smallest and most ordinary details" of daily existence. Jung changed this image and instead described man's shadow as the largely suppressed, undesirable portion of the personality: "the sum of all those unpleasant qualities we like to hide, together with the insufficiently developed functions and contents of the personal unconscious." (Jung 1967-83/1916-17:65, n. 5) "By *shadow* I mean the 'negative' part of the personality, namely the sum of the hidden, disadvantageous qualities, inadequately developed functions, and contents of the personal unconscious."(103n)

Jung came to believe that there exists not only a personal unconscious, but also a collective unconscious, comprising the unrecognized, deficient, unattractive, and repellant side of a group, nation, or race. The collective unconscious is made up of instincts and forms of perception that Jung claimed are inherited. The individual usually does not become conscious of them. They are collectively shared by members of a given group, or, Jung suggests, they may be possessed universally, by all men and women. (Jung 1967-83/1916-17:144-5; Jung 1967-83/1919:137-8; Jung 1967-83/1920:310) He therefore proposed both a personal and a collective shadow to represent these suppressed realities.

The personal and collective shadows complement the individual's or the group's self-concepts, and embody the characteristics that the person and the group wish not to acknowledge. For the majority of people, whose identity is linked with that of the herd to which they belong, individual moral commitments conform to those of their encompassing social group. For most people, the personal and collective shadows tend to coincide with what the group judges to be "evil." (Frey-Rohn 1967:170) According to Jung, the collective shadow either is represented in the leader of a society or a nation, who reflects the herd's perception of evil, or is expressed as a mass phenomenon, as it can be in the form of psychological epidemics that infect the herd's members.

Jung's concept of the shadow, metaphorical and impressionistic as it is, becomes a little more specific when he ties it to the concept of projection, which he used in a way similar to Freud. Jung observed in people a tendency to transfer to others their own unappealing characteristics: "The shadow, therefore, is invariably projected onto 'others,' and in politics, the 'others' are one's political enemies.... We simply accuse our enemy of our own unadmitted faults." (Jung 1967-83/1957:280-1)

The human propensity to engage in this unacknowledged process of transferring disagreeable traits to others is compounded by the tendency of others, in turn, to behave toward us in the same way—i.e., *"projections provoke counter-projections."* (Jung 1967-83/1916:270) As a result, the psychology of the individual and the psychology of his group together insure that enemies will be created: The herd's projections are answered in kind by the opposing herd, and so the creation of enemies is assured. Once the enemy expresses antagonism, the hostility and aggressive drive of one's own social group are aroused. A cycle of mutual antagonism and conflict perpetuates itself and gains strength.

This self-reinforcing pattern can only be broken, according to Jung, if human beings can become conscious of their personal and collective shadows. As long as the processes of suppression and projection continue, men and women will forever need, and they will *want*, to make enemies, and their success in accomplishing this will be guaranteed.

Working in tandem with individual and group projection is a process that Jung called *psychic inflation*. It is similar to Freud's concept of overvaluation, discussed in the preceding chapter. Psychic inflation refers to a psychological tendency common to many people: They magnify and extend beyond themselves attributes they do not possess—such as great strength, courage, heroism, moral and religious superiority, etc. In the process, they experience a feeling of self-aggrandizement, of inflated self-importance, of being "superhuman." Psychic inflation may be personal, or it may be collective, so that a social group, a nation, or a race may indulge in it. The resulting magnification of self-worth has a compelling attraction to people, for, as Jung observed, "it offers easy compensation for personal deficiencies." (Jung 1967-83/1916-17:142) Often, psychic inflation becomes evident when an individual, or a people, feels powerless and inferior; then, according to Jung, an unconscious and pathological urge to compensate can arise, which finds its satisfaction in the identification of the mass with a powerful, maniacal leader. In obedience to him, the people lose their sense of impotence and gain the compelling reassurance that psychic inflation provides. In a complementary but opposite way, society offers people psychically deflationary roles, in which they can lose their sense of personal identity and deficiencies, and in an experience of psychological gratification submerge themselves in the collective. Religion and patriotism offer this experience for many.

For Jung, both phenomena of psychic inflation and deflation provide compensations for the awareness that most people have of their personal deficiencies, easing the burdens of individual responsibility and individual insignificance. In short, in both inflationary and deflationary roles, people find solace and meaning in herd conformity and in struggling on behalf of their group's goals.

As mentioned earlier, much of Jung's research interest came to focus on what he believed are universal patterns of thought and belief that arise from humanity's collective unconscious. These archetypes form the content of fairy tales, mythologies, art, and religions, and are frequently, Jung claimed, expressed within the individual's consciousness in the form of dreams. Jung's conceptions of archetypes and a collective unconscious have been much contested, and it is not relevant to my purposes here to discuss these issues; my interest is to suspend the question of the validity of Jung's vocabulary of ideas, and instead focus attention on the clinical judgment he reached concerning the phenomenon of human evil.

Whether or not human beings are genetically predetermined to experience reality and to defend their preferred fictions in universal, instinctual ways, Jung observed that people in fact behave in strikingly similar ways, as individuals and in social groups. Their patterns of emotional response and conduct suggested to him that there is a dimension or component of the human psyche that is the source of man's aggression, violence, and cruelty. If we look beyond its metaphorical nature, "the shadow" is a construct intended by Jung to represent these human propensities, which in his judgment are universal. He therefore claimed that the shadow is an archetype: It is "the most accessible" of the archetypes and "the easiest to experience...for its nature can in large measure be inferred from the contents of the personal unconscious." (Jung 1967-83/1949-58:13ff) Commentator Walter Kaufmann reflected: "One can see what Jung is driving at, but not only could it be said better and more clearly than he says it; what is more important here is that it could be said better without introducing any archetype." (Kaufmann 1980:III:367) Whether one agrees with Kaufmann or not, Jung's clinical judgment concerning human evil can be disentangled from the intricacies and obscurities of his mythology- and archetype-heavy perspective. Here is the way this can be done:

Human beings, according to Jung, when they respond to one another with hostility, aggression, and malignity, do this because, first of all, they are herd animals; second, because they refuse to acknowledge their own deficiencies, engaging in fast and furious projections and counter-projections that insure the creation and strengthening of enemies; third, because they achieve emotional satisfaction in conformity; and fourth, because they find emotional compensations in group self-aggrandizement and the merging of the individual into the collective. There is no mythology in this account, and no need to introduce archetypes: It expresses a psychiatrist's observations and diagnostic judgment.

Jung asked, "How am I to live with this shadow? What attitude is required if I am to be able to live in spite of evil?" (Jung 1967-83/1945:217) His answer consists of two parts: On the one hand, some change in mankind is possible and feasible, and for this there are some hopeful steps that can help men and women to develop personally and morally. On the other hand, much about mankind cannot, at least at present, be changed or improved, but it is still necessary to judge human failings, and to indict the species when this is justified.

Jung's theory of human neurosis is complex and often not clear. It appears to be this: Much neurosis, according to him, comes about due to a lack of human spiritual self-fulfillment. Psychological health requires that one come to terms with oneself: Jung's prescription for psychological well-being is a combination of the Socratic injunction to know thyself with the insistence that we face our deepest shortcomings. Specifically, this means that individual human beings and their social groups recognize human evil: "[K]nowledge of one's own personal shadow is the necessary requirement for any responsible action, and consequently for any lessening of moral darkness in the world. This holds good to an even greater extent in relation to the collective shadow...." (Frey-Rohn 1967:199) Men and women, however, do strongly resist coming to terms with their own evil. Jung's prescription is a moral challenge that requires fortitude and personal strength, a challenge it would be absurd to hope will be taken up with any enthusiasm by the masses. "Coming to terms with evil is...a moral task which calls for the highest exertions on the part of the ego. It means consciousness, sacrifice, and a constant relationship to the center of the self." (199)

Jung faced mankind's self-chosen blindness soberly. Without widespread human consciousness of human evil, and engaged as humanity is in universal denial, "[s]uch blindness to the evil present within man is both foolish and harmful: foolish because only the fool can disregard the conditions of his own nature; and harmful because 'it deprives us of the capacity to deal with evil.'" (Jung 1967-83/1957:297)

At one point in his writings, Jung sought to describe the collective hysteria that Hitler helped kindle. In that discussion, Jung referred to a form of hysteria, *pseudologia phantastica*, "that form of hysteria which is characterized by a peculiar talent for believing one's own lies." (Jung 1967-83/1945:203-4) He attributed the condition to Hitler, but its application within Jung's framework is certainly more general. People who have such a "talent for believing their own lies" are commonplace in this world, if Jung's observations and conclusions about man are right. Psychological projection, psychic inflation, and deflation are obviously ways in which human beings lie to themselves.

How does one motivate an inveterate and largely unconscious liar to recognize that he lies? Earlier, I noted that for Jung the key to the improvement of society lies in psychology, a premise shared by most psychiatrists who treat individuals. Jung believed that it was possible —within the context of individual treatment—for a person "to recognize his own shadow" and so "come to terms with himself." But he never was so optimistic as to suggest that in the real, foreseeable future such a transformation of consciousness would grip an entire society, nation, or race. The most and the best that Jungian psychiatrists can do is to make the first small steps within the confines of individual treatment. In speaking about the nature of human "complexes" and the treatment of human neuroses, Jung commented: "We psychologists have learnt, through long and painful experience, that you...can only help [man] to become sufficiently aware of [his complexes] and to start a conscious conflict with himself." (Jung 1967-83/1946a:225)

## JUNG'S INDICTMENT OF HUMANITY

Since much about mankind cannot be changed or improved in the foreseeable future, Jung urged the need for moral consciousness and judgment: From his point of view, the psychotherapeutic task of coming to terms with oneself is simultaneously the challenge of coming to terms with others and with their dominant forms of emotional and behavioral response. Just as it is necessary to maintain an unflinching honesty toward oneself, so is it necessary to be truthful in one's assessment of others. Both involve "moral judgment," an evaluative decision that "carries psychological consequences." (Jung 1991/1963:171) Here, I want to summarize the moral judgment, and indeed the indictment of others, that Jung came to after a lifetime in psychiatric practice.

During his adult life, Jung witnessed both world wars. He was deeply influenced by the devastation and the suffering that the two wars caused. "It has filled us with horror to realize all that man is capable of, and of which, therefore, we too are capable. Since then a terrible doubt about humanity, and about ourselves, gnaws at our hearts." (Jung 1967-83/1945:200) He saw that only a few minds were able to learn from the crushing human sacrifice that had been offered up in the first world war. The experience of war teaches most people little of enduring value.

> [T]he consciousness of the masses has not advanced since the first World War. Only certain reflective minds have been enriched, and their moral and intellectual horizon has been considerably enlarged by the realization of the immense and overwhelming power of evil.... (Jung 1967-83/1946a:221)

> Probably no one today would still be rash enough to assert that the European is a lamblike creature and not possessed by a devil. The frightful records of our age are plain for all to see, and they surpass in hideousness everything that any previous age, with its feeble instruments, could have hoped to accomplish. (Jung 1967-83/1946c:192)

After witnessing the widespread slaughter of two world wars, Jung judged that men and women, though on the surface their behavior is based on "respectable motives," in reality are creatures whose very "respectable motivation" allows them to release built-up hatred when they become part of the mass. In this observation, he anticipated Hannah Arendt's view of the banality of human evil.[1] It is worth quoting Jung at length:

> ...if people crowd together and form a mob, then the dynamisms of the collective man are let loose—beasts or demons that lie dormant in every person until he is part of a mob. Man in the mass sinks unconsciously to an inferior moral and intellectual level, to that level which is always there, below the threshold of consciousness, ready to break forth as soon as it is activated by the formation of a mass.... It is certainly a good thing to preach reason and common sense, but what if you have a lunatic asylum for an audience or a crowd in a collective frenzy? There is not much difference between them because the madman and the mob are both moved by impersonal, overwhelming forces.... Look at the incredible savagery going on in our so-called civilized world: it all comes from human beings and their mental condition! Look at the devilish engines of destruction! They are invented by completely innocuous gentlemen, reasonable, respectable citizens who are everything we could wish. And when the whole thing blows up and an indescribable hell of devastation is let loose, nobody seems to be responsible.... All one's neighbours are in the grip of some uncontrollable fear, just like oneself. In lunatic asylums it is a well-known fact that patients are far more dangerous when suffering from fear than when moved by rage or hatred. (Jung 1967-83/1938a:15; Jung 1967-83/1938b:48. Also appears in Jung 1967-83/1946b:231-2)

---

[1] Jung was unflinchingly open to recognizing human evil: For example, he wrote: "I am open to conviction if anyone can prove to me that the phenomenology of National Socialism belongs to the normal inventory of the psyche." (Jung 1967-83/1946b:238).

This passage combines a number of Jung's observations. He notes that when the individual becomes absorbed in the mass, he or she is swept up in the social collective's release of dormant, pent-up, primal aggression. Jung observed that so-called "normal" people are the perpetrators of evil, and that their behavior is often prompted by fear. And the passage foreshadows Jung's view that mental illness can afflict an entire society. Let us look more closely at these claims.

Human evil, according to Jung, is inherently contagious. "The sight of evil kindles evil in the soul—there is no getting away from this fact...." (Jung 1967-83/1945:199) The phenomenon of psychic inflation discussed earlier combines with the human tendency to project undesirable traits and emotions on others. The combination results in a mass infection, a mass mental pathology to which normal rationality succumbs. (See Odajnyk 1976:x) From this point of view, Jung concluded "war is really an epidemic of madness." (Jung 1967-83/1946b:233)

In another work, Jung wrote: "But can we say that a whole nation is hysterical? We can say it as much or as little of a nation as of an individual." (Jung 1967-83/1945:210) In a passage in which he discussed Germany's role in the war, he spoke of the "mental contagion that threatened every European." (212) —This is not a metaphorical variety of infectiousness, but a genuine "all-engulfing force of attraction," in which "each man clings to the next and each drags the other with him." (Jung 1967-83/1946b:230)

Normal people, according to Jung, act out their inner conflicts by participating socially and politically in the mass psychoses of wars and revolutions. (Jung 1967-83/1946b:235) "Psychic epidemics" involve a sequence of phases of increasing pathology beginning in individual neurosis, which spreads to infect a social group to the point of mass neurosis. Once expressed in mass political movements, patriotic fanaticism, or religious fervor, the contagion reaches a level of true mass psychosis, and a mass psychic epidemic is unleashed. (See, e.g., Odajnyk 1976:44)

During this process, capacities for individual thought and independent response are blotted out. As they are lost, the individual's moral sense is dissolved, so that the larger the herd in which the individual is absorbed, the lower its moral standards. "Any large company composed of wholly admirable persons has the morality and intelligence of an unwieldy, stupid, and violent animal. The bigger the organization, the more unavoidable is its immorality and blind stupidity...." (Jung 1967-83/1916-17:153) "Hence every man is, in a certain sense, unconsciously a worse man when he is in society than when acting alone; for he is carried by society and to that extent relieved of his individual responsibility." (Jung 1967-83/1946b:228) Actions that would abhor an individual acting on his own initiative and conscience become commonplace: "the greatest infamy on the part of his group will not disturb him, so long as the majority of his fellows steadfastly believe in the exalted morality of their social organization." (229)

It is important again to stress that in Jung's judgment the pathology is not metaphorical but real: The infection takes place in the minds of people, it sweeps away their capacities for individual, independent thought and action, and it attributes ultimate importance to the social herd. When the collective comes to assume ultimate significance, then the contagion "puts a premium on mediocrity," elevating the ordinary, the mundane, the common, so that "everything...settles down to vegetate in an easy, irresponsible way. Individuality will inevitably be driven to the wall." (Jung 1967-83/1916-17:153)

Central to Jung's moral indictment of man is the low regard that Jung came to have for human intelligence: "Much...that proves to be abysmally evil in its ultimate effects does not come from man's wickedness but from his stupidity and unconsciousness." (Jung 1967-83/1942:197) And low human intelligence is further diminished and shackled by individual conformity to the outlook of the social herd. Very much like Freud, Jung was condemnatory in his judgment that human stupidity and lack of awareness lead to much human destructiveness and cruelty. As we will see in later chapters, a number of other twentieth century psychiatrists have flirted repeatedly with the observation—one that suggests, but never quite establishes, a new diagnostic classification—that human stupidity and humanity's lack of awareness are twin forces that contribute to the phenomenon of human evil.

Many of Jung's observations and claims about human evil focus on the human call to war. Did he believe there is any reason to hope that mankind will end war and bring an end to the creation of weapons of mass destruction? A Jung commentator answered this question incisively: To try to put an end to human warfare "would be comparable to outlawing sexual intercourse." (Odajnyk 1976:110) As Jung expressed this, "man's war-like instincts are ineradicable and therefore a state of complete peace is unthinkable." (Jung 1967-83/1946a: 225) Elsewhere, he noted, as Freud did, that "*homo homini lupus* [man is to man a wolf] is a sad yet eternal truism." (Jung 1967-83/1946b:231)

## SIDESTEPPING RELATIVISM

Jung was not a philosopher. In fact, he expressed a positive disdain for philosophical reflection. Yet readers of Jung may justifiably feel that his thought and writing would have benefited by a systematic philosophical approach. Jung, however, had little good to say of philosophy. In his late sixties, he wrote a letter in which, when complaining about the thought of Heidegger, Kierkegaard, Hegel, and Nietzsche, he made a cavalier and probably exaggerated general assertion about philosophy:

> For all its critical analysis philosophy has not yet managed to root out its psychopaths.... In the critical philosophy of the future there will be a chapter on "the Psychopathology of Philosophy." ...There is no thinking *qua* thinking; at times it is a pisspot of all unconscious devils.... Often *what* is thought is less important that *who* thinks it. But this is assiduously overlooked. *Neurosis* contradicts every philosopher, for he is at odds with himself. In such cases philosophy is nothing but the systematized fight against one's own insecurity. (1943 letter from Jung to Arnold Künzli quoted in Kaufmann 1980:II:225-6)

Given Jung's tendency, similar to Freud's, to view philosophy as inherently psychopathological, it should be expected that he would make little attempt to provide us with a carefully reasoned philosophical justification for his outspoken indictment of mankind, reviewed in the preceding section. And, indeed, a justification of this sort is not to be found in Jung's writings. Is the moral judgment that he propounded, then, arbitrary and idiosyncratic, a matter of his private moral tastes? Or is it an expression, pure and simple, of his own personal and professional experience, and in this sense, does it rest on a phenomenological basis? Or is his judgment based upon criteria that, although not explicitly formulated by him, serve as universal standards, applicable to all men and women? —In short, does Jung's indictment of mankind avoid relativism? Or is "the shadow" recognizable only from the standpoint of a particular and special moral framework of reference, the adoption of which has no compelling force, and so is merely arbitrary?

Jung, as is often the case, is hard to pin down. On the one hand, he expressed moral ambivalence: "Being a doctor I am never too certain about my moral judgments. I too often find that something that is a virtue in one individual, is a vice in another one, and something that is good for the one, is poison for another." (Jung in a letter quoted in Philp 1958:20) Elsewhere, he echoed the same ambivalence:

People talk to me about evil, or about good, and presume that I know what it is. But I don't. When someone speaks of good or evil, it is of what *he* calls good or evil, or what *he* feels as good or evil. Then he speaks about it with great assurance, not knowing whether it really is so or whether what he calls good or evil really corresponds to the facts. Perhaps the speaker's view of the world is not in keeping with the real facts at all, so that an inner, subjective picture is substituted for objectivity. (From an extemporaneous address by Jung, reprinted in Stein 1995:84 from Bitter 1966/1959.)

In passages of this sort, Jung seems to reject the idea that there exist universal moral standards in terms of which behavior can be evaluated. For him, as one Jungian commentator wrote, "[t]here is no Archimedean vertex from which a final, absolute judgment on good and evil can be made." (Stein 1995:9) Another of his commentators, writing about Jung's understanding of human evil, claims that Jung repudiated

...any criterion by which a decision can be judged good or evil—considered psychologically. Any moral judgment based on absolute principles always does violence to the uniqueness of the particular case. From the standpoint of psychology, submission to collective morality, or to a dominant faith, is no less "good" than submission to the symbol of wholeness. Each situation is unique and always requires its own unique answer. (Frey-Rohn 1967:198)

Is moral judgment reducible, then, to the view that

...what's one man's poyson Signior,
Is anothers meat or drinke. (Beaumont & Fletcher 1976/1647: Act III, Sc. 2:45)

—echoing the voice of Lucretius, who centuries earlier claimed, "What is one man's meat is another man's rank poison." (Lucretius 1924/1473:IV:293: lines 637-8) Is Jung's strongly expressed negative moral judgment of man no more than this? If so, it would be thin gruel, with little content and no persuasive force.

Jung sometimes seems not to know what position to take. In one and the same paper, we find passages that appear to contradict one another. On the one hand, he wrote:

Where do we get this belief, this apparent certainty, that we know what is good and what is bad? ...Something that appears evil to one nation may be regarded as good by another nation. This *relativity of values* applies also in the realm of aesthetics: a modern work of art is for one person of supreme value, for which he is ready to lay out a large sum of money, whereas another person can make neither head nor tail of it. (Jung, quoted in Stein 1995:85; emphasis added)

On the other hand, a little later in the same work we find this claim:

...in the matter of good and evil, one can, as a therapist, only hope that one is getting the facts straight, though one can never be sure. As a therapist I cannot, in any given case, deal with the problem of good and evil philosophically but can only approach it empirically. But because I take an empirical attitude *it does not mean that I relativize good and evil as such.* I see very clear: *this* is evil, but the paradox is just that for this particular person in this particular situation at this particular stage of development it may be good. Contrariwise, good at the wrong moment in the wrong place may be the worst thing possible. If it were not like this everything would be so simple—too simple. If I make no *a priori* judgments and listen to the facts as they are, then I do not always know beforehand what is good for the patient and what is bad. (86; emphasis added)

In the first passage, he endorses a "relativity of values" and in the second, he claims not to "relativize." It is hard to know just what he had in mind; perhaps he was himself unclear.

Jung was not an original thinker when it comes to his philosophically unexamined general frame of reference. He accepted the traditional notion that good and evil are polar opposites, the view that each concept requires the other. "Just as the conscious mind can put the question, 'Why is there this frightful conflict between good an evil?,' so the unconscious can reply, 'Look closer! Each needs the other. The best, just because it is the best, holds the seed of evil, and there is nothing so bad but good can come of it.'" (Jung 1967-83/1916-17:181)

Some of the passages I have quoted point to a naive, unquestioned relativism, to an intrinsically unstable and uncertain basis for moral judgment, where each situation is unique and each case is different, and in relation to which "[i]deas of morality are often as widely divergent as are views on what constitutes a delicacy for the Eskimo and for ourselves." (Jung quoted in Stein 1995:89) But it would be incorrect to infer relativism from these characteristic passages, for Jung was firm and uncompromising in his claim that the phenomenon of human evil exists, and in his concrete claim that the records of the recent past "surpass in hideousness" those of any previous age. A recognition of the hideousness of human atrocities cannot be reconciled with "one man's meat is another's poison." —There comes a point when definite and decisive moral judgment is not only possible, but demanded.

To answer how judgment of this kind is possible within Jung's account will require that we step outside of Jung's framework for a moment, since he lacked or resisted the philosophical motivation to provide clarity about it. The belief I have come to in reading Jung is that he affirmed, with certainty, that we can have knowledge of evil—but only in situationally relative ways. To some readers, this statement may appear paradoxical, but it is not hard to show that it is paradoxical only on the surface. I believe what Jung intended is to combine two points of view: to reject relativism, while at the same time presupposing that one is, in my own words, "situationally sensitive." Put differently, in relation to a specific situation that is invested with moral issues, and from the perspective of an individual who has a certain degree of what I will later call "moral intelligence," it is possible to formulate solid judgments that are not provisional, tentative, or relativist.[2] It is true that, for Jung, unambiguous judgments of this kind cannot be made in all situations; indeed, only some situations are sufficiently clear to permit a morally intelligent individual to make reliable moral evaluations that avoid the ambivalence of relativism.

As we have seen, Jung formulated definite judgments concerning human aggression, among them: the human need for and enjoyment of violence, the human urge to identify with and become absorbed in the group body and mind of the social herd, and the tendency of social groups and of individuals to engage in psychic inflation and projection. When men and women combine these needs and tendencies, their hostility and aggression toward members of their own species are guaranteed, and their attitudes and behavior become malignant. Jung gave every indication that he considered these judgments to constitute clinical judgments, advanced by a psychiatrist on the basis of long experience with human subjects. In a similar way, Jung's explicitly moral judgments, when they go beyond the "one

---

[2] The need for a comparatively high level of moral development is, e.g., also stressed by Murray Stein in his discussion of Jung's prescription that the self come to terms with its own evil: "This self-examination is itself an exercise in moral awareness. To see one's own shadow clearly and to admit its reality requires considerable moral strength in the individual. It also requires the prior attainment of moral consciousness...." Stein (1995:18).

man's poison" simplification, are, I believe, no less intended by him to express clinical assessments.

Placed within the context of a psychiatrist's professional judgment of humanity, Jung's indictments of man are rooted in the phenomenology of his own experience as a clinician, but they express, I believe, standards of a sort that he intends to be applicable to all men and women. These "standards," however, are of a particular, fuzzy, and theoretically slippery variety, since they are intended by him to be situationally relative: relative, that is, to specific, individual contexts of reference in which a person who is endowed with sufficient moral intelligence is able to formulate a judgment with respect to a particular set of events.

Although such claims are expressed with vagueness and imprecision in Jung's writings, they are, when one thinks about them, exactly the kind of claims one should expect within a medical frame of reference. For what is medically in view is always an individual patient, an individualized disorder, and an individual physician whose clinical judgment expresses a diagnosis and points to a potentially effective treatment. But this is not relativism.

It is rather the perspective of a diagnostician, whose intellectual and moral capacities to recognize patterns and meaning need to be understood clearly. Jung's vagueness and imprecision can serve to point us in a constructive direction. They underscore the need to examine the as yet unclarified nature of a clinical frame of reference that makes it possible—in a non-relativist way—to assess and to judge characteristically human patterns of thought, emotion, and behavior that are self-destructive to the species, and in the process destructive to other species. Subsequent chapters in this book attempt to throw light on the nature of that frame of reference.

# CHAPTER 8

# RECENT PSYCHIATRY AND HUMAN EVIL:
## MENNINGER, FROMM, AND PECK

R emarkably few psychiatrists have studied the phenomenon of human evil. If one has in view exclusively psychological studies of the phenomenon of human evil itself—unadulterated, that is, by explanations drawn from theology, moral philosophy, or mythology—rare indeed are psychiatrists, or psychologists, who have given thought to this subject in their publications.

In this chapter, I review the studies with this focus that have been left to us by Karl A. Menninger, Erich Fromm,[1] and M. Scott Peck. There is a span of nearly fifty years between Menninger's earlier study and Peck's more recent one. In spite of the passage of half a century, we shall find, as we pass from one study to the next, that there is surprisingly little change in the psychiatric understanding of human evil which they present. The analyses given by these three eminent thinkers add to the foundation laid by Freud and Jung. The contributions of Menninger, Fromm, and Peck overlap in various ways and the conclusions they reached have much in common. Their shared perception of the need for a serious psychological study of human evil, perhaps more than the specific claims they propounded, is instructive and provides a stepping stone for subsequent research.

## KARL A. MENNINGER (1893-1990)

In 1938, Menninger published a substantial work, *Man against Himself*, in which he sought to understand human self-destructiveness. Unlike Fromm and Peck, Menninger did not speak explicitly of "human evil." In fact, in a work concerned with human destructiveness, human folly, and the horrors of man's inhumanity to man, Menninger did not take the step to apply the term 'evil' to these phenomena. Perhaps he believed that 'evil' is an excessively normative term that has no place in professional psychological research;

---

[1] Readers not familiar with Fromm's credentials may question his inclusion in this chapter since, unlike Menninger and Peck, Fromm did not hold a medical degree. He received a Ph.D. from the University of Heidelberg in 1922, then received training in psychoanalysis at the University of Munich and the Psychoanalytic Institute of Berlin. During this period, psychiatry was not the sole province of M.D.s, as was still evident in 1962 when Fromm held the position Professor of Psychiatry at New York University. But whether Fromm should be grouped with psychiatrists will not be important to the substance of this chapter.

perhaps he felt that use of such categories as good and evil reflect unscientific human judgment, and so should be avoided. His writings do not answer these questions, and the reader can only surmise what he thought about these matters.

And yet, his study is filled with moral valuations. Early in *Man against Himself*, Menninger declared himself unambiguously to be on the side of humanistic, moral judgment. Nowhere did he express a wish to adopt an impartial stance of value-free neutrality. In fact, Menninger explicitly underscored the need for individuals to cultivate moral awareness. The following passage is representative of Menninger's viewpoint:

> Whoever studies the behavior of human beings cannot escape the conclusion that we must reckon with an enemy within the lines. It becomes increasingly evident that some of the destruction which curses the earth is *self*-destruction; the extraordinary propensity of the human being to join hands with external forces in an attack upon his own existence is one of the most remarkable of biological phenomena.
>
> Men fly above ancient and beautiful cities dropping explosive bombs upon museums and churches, upon great buildings and little children. They are encouraged by the official representatives of two hundred million other people, all of whom contribute daily in taxes to the frantic manufacture of instruments designed for the tearing and ripping and mangling of human beings similar to themselves, possessed of the same instincts, the same sensations, the same little pleasures, and the same realization that death comes to end these things all too soon. (Menninger 1966/1938:4)

In this long work of nearly five hundred pages, Menninger sometimes speaks of individual malignancy and of the destructiveness of entire societies, but never of "human evil" as such. As we shall see, his views concerning human malignancy, this "enemy within the lines," are similar to Fromm's, which are somewhat better developed. Menninger discusses *individual malignancy* expressed in suicide, and in what he calls "chronic suicide," the self-defeating nature of martyrdom, asceticism, addiction, neurosis, and psychosis. Paralleling these disorders to which individuals succumb, but on the level of social groups, is the *self-destructiveness of entire societies*. It is expressed, Menninger contends, in the phenomenon of war, a form of self-defeating social suicide.

In this large work devoted to a study of human destructiveness, Menninger expressed hope that through the application of the psychoanalytic method mankind may be brought to a future in which his violent nature is reduced. In particular, Menninger had a deep faith in human intelligence:

> I believe that our best defense against self-destructiveness lies in the courageous application of intelligence to human phenomenology. If such is our nature, it were better that we knew it and knew it in all its protean manifestations. To see all forms of self-destruction from the standpoint of their dominant principles would seem to be logical progress toward self-preservation and toward a unified view of medical science. (Menninger 1966/1938:vii)

And like any scientist, Menninger recognized the potential usefulness of theoretically unified understanding: "I submit that to have a theory, even a false one, is better than to attribute events to pure chance. 'Chance' explanations leave us in the dark; a theory will lead to confirmation or rejection." (viii)

In Menninger's view, the main ingredient in the human propensity for self-destruction is individual and group narcissism. He considered narcissism to be a "toxemia" that takes a variety of forms, "[i]n the smugness of provincialism, in the stupidity of race prejudice and discrimination, in the vanity which exalts such gods as nationalism, social prestige, and financial aristocracy and surrenders everything to them...." (Menninger 1966/1938:437-8)

Menninger did not give a detailed and systematic exposition of his concept of narcissism, but anyone who reads *Man against Himself* understands what Menninger points to: Narcissism expresses an endemic human blindness, one that magnifies the reality and the importance of the cares of the self or of the social group, and denies and denigrates the reality and value of alternative cares. It is a form of self-enclosure, of self-containment, a blinding of consciousness to what is other than the self who considers itself to be privileged or special.

For Menninger, there is no more pronounced manifestation of narcissism than in war. He was deeply concerned with the underlying psychological cause of the innumerable wars that men have inflicted on themselves throughout human history.

> ...for all its social and economic phases, the phenomenon of war impresses one as the most dramatic exemplification of my main thesis.
>
> It surely is no longer doubted by any thinking person that there is no such thing as victory in war, that the conqueror like the conquered suffers irreparable loss. In this sense war, contrary to appearances, is virtually self-destruction. This suicidal bent of nations is coldly exploited by elements within each country whose international organization constitutes a grimly anomalous cancer thriving under the official patronage of the people whom it exists to destroy. (Menninger 1966/1938:464)

In search of an adequate psychological understanding of war, Menninger referred to the exchange between Albert Einstein and Sigmund Freud. Menninger accepted the following formulation of the problem given by Einstein, already familiar to us (see Chapter 6):

> How is it possible for the ruling minority to force the masses to observe a purpose which rewards them only with suffering and loss? Why do the masses permit themselves to be inflamed to the point of madness and self-sacrifice by these means? Do hatred and destruction satisfy an innate human drive which ordinarily remains latent but which can easily be aroused and intensified to the point of mass psychosis? And is it possible to modify human psychic development in such a way as to produce an increasing resistance to these psychoses of hatred and destruction? (Menninger 1966/1938:468 quoting Einstein & Freud 1991/1933; apparently Menninger's English translation)

In response to Einstein's questions, Freud, as we saw in Chapter 6, was not hopeful that mankind's appetite for war can be curbed. Menninger, however, was more optimistic. He applied the diagnostic framework of medicine to assess self-destructiveness as it is found in individuals and groups. The conclusion he reached is that self-destructiveness involves a "sickness," a "malignancy," a "cancer" in relation to which narcissism is a major contributing "toxemia." Therapy for this sickness, he argued, is possible: What is necessary is for the self-destructive individual to become aware that he is sick and a potential menace to himself. (Menninger 1966/1938:444-5) The same holds true, he claimed, for the self-destructive society or nation. In order for such a self-realization to lead to a lessening of human destructiveness, it must, he believed, take place within a psychoanalytic setting. And it is here that the practical constraints of reality set in, for how is an entire society to be treated within a psychoanalytic setting?

Sober as Menninger's study is, and deeply conscious that it is of the pervasiveness and devastating nature of human destructiveness, his recipe to resolve this most serious problem of mankind is, at best, that of a kindly dreamer:

> For if it be possible to change one individual, no matter how laboriously—if one person can be helped, by any of the methods which I have described, to be less destructive—there is hope for the human race. The special encouragement of the psychoanalytic method is that the individual's own intelligence can be utilized to direct his better adaptation, a diminution

in his self-destructiveness. Granted that it may be a slow process, such a transformation of self-destructive energy into constructive channels can gradually spread over the entire human world. "A little leaven leaveneth the whole lump." (Menninger 1966/1938:470)

Menninger therefore invested his hopes in the power of human self-knowledge, of the Socratic "know thyself": By its means men and women must first become conscious of the malignancy of their predispositions, and then become capable of curtailing them, and perhaps in the end become able to overcome the compelling force that these predispositions exert over them. In this process, Menninger emphasized how man's ignorance and negligent disregard of his own malignancy sustain and increase it. We shall later see how this phenomenon is part of a reflexively self-fueling dynamic of human destructiveness; as Menninger expressed this: "blindness or indifference to the existence of self-destructiveness are [sic] the devices it constructs for its continuance." (Menninger 1966/1938:470)

Menninger was aware of the fact that he was unable to justify his optimism. He believed that a hopeful outlook, like a purely pessimistic one, is a "fallacy." His admission is intellectually responsible and explicit: "It boots nothing that both optimism and pessimism are philosophically fallacious attitudes; it would seem inevitable that human beings fall into one or the other fallacy, and certainly the fallacy of optimism has more to its credit in the way of accomplishment than has the fallacy of pessimism." (Menninger 1966/1938:443) Menninger saw that human blindness and indifference to the sickness he wished to diagnose and treat contribute to its perpetuation, but he seemed reluctant to accept that optimism itself can serve as a form of blindness, one which holds out false encouragement that human beings will eagerly embrace as a panacea.

Later in this volume I will take issue with Menninger's prejudice in favor of optimism, and show that human hopefulness is indeed often a major obstacle to treating human evil. If hope can be false—leading mankind to deny the reality of human malignity—then Menninger probably wore blinders. He preferred to believe that mankind, through the exercise of intelligence and insight, can balance and at least sometimes overcome the effects of humanity's illness as a species, in the face of eventual and inevitable death.

> This magnificent tragedy of life sets our highest ideal—spiritual nobility in the face of certain defeat. But there is a lesser victory in the mere prolonging of the game with a zest not born of illusion and in this game within a game some win, some lose; the relentlessness of self-destruction never ceases. And it is here that Science has replaced magic as the serpent held high in the wilderness for the saving of what there is of life for us. Toward the temporary staying of the malignancy of the self-destructive impulse, toward the averting of a premature capitulation to Death, we may sometimes, by prodigious labors, lend an effective hand. (Menninger 1966/1938:470-1)

## ERICH FROMM (1900-1980)

Nearly three decades after Menninger's study, Fromm published the first of three books relevant to our focus, *Beyond the Chains of Illusion* (1962), soon to be followed by *The Heart of Man: Its Genius for Good and Evil* (1964), and then by *The Anatomy of Human Destructiveness* (1973). Although Fromm's views changed to some extent from one work to the next, he expressed a continuity of concern in these studies.

### *Beyond the Chains of Illusion*

In *Beyond the Chains of Illusion*, Fromm raised the question, as did Menninger before him, Why is it that men, throughout their history, have been dominated by the compulsion to

wage war? Much of his book is an attempt to answer this question. Fromm's main observation is that man needs illusions in order to make his life bearable. Mankind's illusions take
the form of ideologies that assert the supreme importance of sets of preferred values. Society
erects its idols—they may be money, materialism, religious dogma, etc.—and then proceeds
to worship them. Members of the society transfer their emotional energy to their idols,
quickly forgetting in the process that it is they who empower their gods, and in so doing they
willfully lie to themselves. The population of a society comes to invest a huge amount of
psychological energy in sustaining and defending its preferred lies.

The majority of men and women, Fromm claimed, are inherently stupid and unable to
see through the lies in which they are so heavily invested. (Fromm 1966/1962:166-7) Wars
are fought largely to defend these illusions. Anyone who attempts to see through society's
lies is subject to ostracism and alienation, and so the fear of rejection and isolation discour-
ages individual incentive to penetrate the lies and to discover what is true.

Part of a long tradition running from Plato to Spinoza to Marx, Fromm argued that
intellectual and moral development in man is possible only when man becomes free, when
he summons the initiative and the capacity to become aware of his self-deceptions. "All that
the human race has achieved, spiritually and materially, it owes to the destroyers of illusions
and the seekers of reality." (Fromm 1966/1962:173) The capacity to destroy illusions,
according to Fromm, fundamentally requires *disobedience*:

> Man has continued to evolve by acts of disobedience [from the beginning of] his *spiritual*
> development...only because there have been men who dared to say "no" to the powers that
> be in the name of their conscience or of their faith. His *intellectual* development was also
> dependent on the capacity for being disobedient, disobedient to the authorities who tried to
> muzzle new thoughts, and to the authority of long-established opinions which declared
> change to be nonsense. (181)

But the reverse, mankind's urge to *obey*, is potentially lethal. Fromm argued that *obedience* may
plausibly lead to the end of human history. He observed that the majority of human beings
have an emotional constitution unchanged from the Stone Age, yet they now live with the
technical means at hand to bring about worldwide nuclear destruction. "If mankind commits
suicide, it will be because people will obey those who command them to push the deadly
buttons, because they will obey the archaic passions of fear, hate, and greed; because they
will obey obsolete clichés of state sovereignty and national honor." (181) "If we should all
perish in the nuclear holocaust, it will not be because man was not capable of becoming
human, or that he was inherently evil; it would be because the consensus of stupidity has
prevented him from seeing reality and acting upon the truth." (198)

As a result, Fromm, somewhat like Menninger, came to believe that hope for man must
be invested in his capacity to develop his intelligence. For Fromm, human intelligence is not
reducible purely to a set of intellectual skills, but demands the personal independence of the
genuine individual, supplemented by vitality and courage, all of which are necessary if he is
to dispel the veil of lies behind which he lives. However, Fromm's optimism on behalf of
this considerably enriched conception of intelligence was tempered by his recognition that
the vast majority of people wish nothing more than symbiosis, conformity, and safety. He
realized that the self-interests of the majority are deeply rooted in the desire to maintain the
very illusions that threaten man's survival.

Nowhere in this early work does Fromm mention "human evil." His focus, like Menninger's, is exclusively on the human propensity for violence and self-destruction. He
classified this propensity as an *illness*, specifically a *neurosis*, and hence as a *pathology*. Since he
was a trained clinician, one may expect that he used these terms judiciously and in their non-

metaphorical senses. In his use of the words 'neurosis' and 'pathology', Fromm deferred to Freud, who, we will recall, referred to collective neurosis and the "pathology of civilized communities." (Freud 1952d/1930:801) The reader will also remember that Freud himself recognized the difficulty presented by these two concepts: Both require some standard of judgment that goes beyond clinical *normality*. For a standard of normality is useless and cannot be applied when it comes to an entire society that has become pathological.

*Beyond the Chains of Illusion* leaves human self-destructiveness and violence still wrapped in considerable vagueness so that the following questions remain unanswered: If these human traits are signs of illness and pathology, what is the nature of the sickness? Is it an ongoing social contagion, or does it express a human constitutional disorder? And, as an illness, can it be treated successfully?

### The Heart of Man: Its Genius for Good and Evil

Following soon after the publication of *Beyond the Chains of Illusion*, Fromm published *The Heart of Man: Its Genius for Good and Evil*.[2] Although a somewhat shorter work, *The Heart of Man* presents Fromm's account of human evil more systematically and fully. In this work, Fromm described what he calls "the syndrome of decay" in which three elements participate in producing the phenomenon of evil. They are: the death instinct, narcissism, and incestuous fixation. Freud had claimed that the death instinct is an impulse to self-destruction fundamental to all living processes, and hence a part of normal biology. Fromm, however, argued that self-destructiveness is a *malignant* phenomenon that represents a form of *psychopathology*. Self-destructiveness is not normal, in Fromm's view, but arises when children are raised under essentially unloving conditions, in environments that do not provide stimulation, where fear is prevalent and life is uninteresting and routine.

Narcissism is a psychological incapacity to recognize the reality of what is other than the self. For Fromm, it is a pathological distortion that leads one to overestimate one's own position and undervalue and ultimately hate everything outside the self. Narcissism can similarly afflict social groups and entire nations: "'We' are admirable; 'they' are despicable. 'We' are good; 'they' are evil. Any criticism of one's own doctrine is a vicious and unbearable attack; criticism of the others' position is a well-meant attempt to help them to return to the truth." (Fromm 1964:82)

Incestuous fixation for Fromm is more general and inclusive than it was in Freud's account, for whom it meant blind attachment to the mother. For Fromm, it constitutes an impairment of judgment that can have as its object not only one's mother, but one's family, one's country, race, or religion. Blind incestuous fixation combines with narcissism to produce distorted judgments that are unquestioningly assumed to be absolute and true. These judgments become unshakable in large measure because the conviction that they are

---

[2] It is interesting to note that between the publication of *Beyond the Chains of Illusion* and *The Heart of Man*, Fromm published a small book (consisting of only some thirty pages of text by Fromm, supplemented by a number of brief commentaries by others), which had a quite limited circulation. This was *War within Man: A Psychological Enquiry into the Roots of Destructiveness* (Fromm 1963). The book is worth noting largely because it reflects Fromm's persistent concern to answer the question why human beings are destructive. The thesis he put forth in *War within Man* ties together four claims: People are destructive because the majority is "suggestible"; the violence of war requires the complicity of many; there exists a "necrophilous personality" that, while neither rare nor the rule, loves destruction; and it constitutes a pathology that is not a part of normal biology. War occurs, according to the view Fromm presented in this book, as a result of the suggestibility and by common agreement of the majority, and due to the central role in war of people who are themselves pathologically destructive.

unshakable is shared by all others who are affected by the same fixation. Fromm's conception of incestuous fixation is akin to the idea of an exclusionary belief-system—that is, an ideology—that distorts reason, results in the incapacity to experience another as fully human, and imprisons individuals and whole societies in sets of beliefs in relation to which the individual is not free to be himself, and cannot cultivate values and convictions of his own.

These three elements—the impulse to self-destructiveness, narcissism, and the impairment of judgment due to incestuous fixation, each of which is a psychopathology in its own right—together produce human evil, which Fromm called "the syndrome of decay."

> The person suffering from this syndrome is indeed evil, since he betrays life and growth and is a devotee of death and crippledness. The best-documented example of a man suffering from the "syndrome of decay" is Hitler. He was...deeply attracted to death and destruction; he was an extremely narcissistic person for whom the only reality was *his own* wishes and thoughts. Finally, he was an extremely incestuous person.... [H]is incestuousness was mainly expressed in his fanatical devotion to the race, the people who shared the same blood. (Fromm 1964:108-9)

The resulting total pathology, Fromm tells us, would at one time—some thousands of years ago—have been considered normal behavior: normal, that is to say, for individuals who acted like wild animals, whose animosities, violence, and cruelty could be freely unleashed.

> The same man would be a psychotic today. All archaic forms of mental experience—necrophilia, extreme narcissism, incestuous symbiosis—which in one form or the other have constituted the "normal" or even the "ideal" in regressive-archaic cultures because men were united by their common archaic strivings are today designated as severe forms of mental pathology. (120)

Fromm apparently had difficulty deciding to what extent human beings are "evil," and apparently felt more comfortable calling the phenomenon "the syndrome of decay." At one point in *The Heart of Man*, he wrote that the minority of people are afflicted with this "syndrome." ("Most likely it is only a minority of the population who are motivated by this syndrome." (Fromm 1964:111)). Ten pages later, while reviewing German history, Russia under Stalin, the Japanese rape of Nanking, and the violence of American lynch mobs in the South, he claimed instead that the majority of people have the pathology in latent form. ("For the majority the archaic form of experience is always a real possibility; it *can* emerge." (121)) Fromm's ambivalence over this question is made more evident by his suggestion that an empirical program of research should be initiated: He suggested that a "projective questionnaire" could be designed to discover "the incidence of people suffering from necrophilia, extreme narcissism, and incestuous symbiosis." (111n)[3] But no such questionnaire has ever been constructed and administered.

Although he remained undecided how widespread the psychopathology of evil is, he recognized that for many people it is only within an atmosphere of violence and destruction that they become fully themselves:

> ...the very fact that neither they nor those who are not so motivated are aware of the real motivation makes them dangerous carriers of an infectious disease, a hate infection, in times

---

[3] Fromm made the same proposal earlier in Fromm (1963), where he expressed the wish for an empirical study to determine what proportion of the American population is necrophilic, and then attempt to correlate these findings with such factors as economic position, education, occupation, etc., and finally study what conditions could change this orientation. (Fromm 1963:29n.)

of strife, conflict, cold and hot war. Hence it is important that they be recognized for what they are: men who love death, who are afraid of independence, for whom only the needs of their own group have reality. (Fromm 1964:111)

In spite of his willingness to recognize the worst side of man, Fromm remained hopeful that the psychopathology of evil could be treated. He spoke about the possibility that normal people may acquire a "certain degree of immunity" from the sickness. For this to happen, "...it is, of course, necessary to learn one thing: not to take words for reality, and to see through the deceptive rationalizations of those who suffer from a sickness that only man is capable of suffering from: the negation of life before life has vanished." (Fromm 1964:111)

Why do men and women succumb to this "infectious disease," to a contagion of hatred, violence, and destruction? As we have seen, in his earlier work, *Beyond the Chains of Illusion*, Fromm claimed that due to their basic stupidity people cannot free themselves from the shackles that bind them to lies that lead to violence. In his later work, *The Heart of Man*, he was inclined to express himself more tolerantly:

> ...most people fail in the art of living not because they are inherently bad or so without will that they cannot live a better life; they fail because they do not wake up and see when they stand at a fork in the road and have to decide.... If mankind destroys itself it will not be because of the intrinsic wickedness of man's heart; it will be because of his inability to wake up to the realistic alternatives and their consequences. (Fromm 1964:138, 142)

Where *Beyond the Chains of Illusion* squarely laid the blame for man's inability to wake up upon human stupidity, *The Heart of Man* does not point an accusing finger. Man needs simply to wake up. The judgment that human violence and atrocities are perpetrated while sleep-walking does not convey quite the moral sting that the indictment of the gross stupidity of the species does. And certainly each of the two alternatives would demand different practical solutions.

The view that one reaches after reading Fromm's *The Heart of Man* is that human evil is a form of psychopathology whose treatment lies in the possibility that individuals might be "awakened" from the conditions that imprison their minds and dictate their emotions. Whether the majority of people are sick in this fundamental way, Fromm could not answer. He expressed a hope that children will in time be raised in more loving and creatively stimulating environments. But it was to remain unclear in Fromm's writing what would have to change in order for men and women to wake up and repudiate their extreme narcissism, lust for destruction, and impaired and distorted judgment.

### The Anatomy of Human Destructiveness

This third work which we shall examine here is Fromm's longest attempt to formulate a general account of human evil. As is universally true, length of a work alone does not bring about an advance in thought. In the case of Fromm's long *Anatomy of Human Destructiveness*, the book adds relatively little to the foregoing discussion. One gets the impression from Fromm's *Anatomy* that he made a decision to "tone down" his theory further, to assume an even more diplomatic and less potentially abrasive stance, and, one is tempted to say, to mince words. For, in a book consisting of more than five hundred pages, only two pages now bear explicit reference to "evil." The position that Fromm propounded in *The Heart of Man*, which focused on the human pathology, sickness, and infectious nature of human evil, is not further developed in Fromm's *Anatomy*; in fact, it is largely ignored.

At the beginning of *The Anatomy of Human Destructiveness*, Fromm repeats his claim that human destructiveness and cruelty represent "malignant" aggression unique and endemic to the human species. As in *The Heart of Man*, he claims that malignant aggression is not "phylogenetically programmed" and is not biologically adaptive: "...it has no purpose, and its satisfaction is lustful." (Fromm 1973:4) Yet, later in the body of the book, he appears to reverse his claim that this malignancy has no purpose: "...life-thwarting passions are as much an answer to man's existential needs as life-furthering possessions: they are both profoundly human. The former necessarily develop when the realistic conditions for the realization of the latter are absent." (264) In other words, Fromm now suggests that the malignancy of the species answers basic human needs, and in this sense serves an evident purpose.

He goes on to stress the importance of developing a full understanding of man's malignancy: "Destructiveness and cruelty...are indeed destructive of life, of body and spirit, destructive not only of the victim but of the destroyer himself.... They are the only true perversion. Understanding them does not mean condoning them. *But unless we understand them, we have no way to recognize how they may be reduced, and what factors tend to increase them.*" (Fromm 1973:9; italics added) To this end, Fromm re-emphasized the leading idea introduced in *Beyond the Chains of Illusion*: that society provides individuals with ready-made illusions that pretend to provide meaning to life. "In our society, for instance, they are told that to be successful, to be a 'bread winner', to raise a family, to be a good citizen, to consume goods and pleasures gives meaning to life." (267) While the lies appear to succeed on the conscious level, they are breaking down, as evidenced, Fromm claims, by increased drug addiction, individual apathy, a widespread decline of intellectual and artistic creativity, and growing violence.

Perhaps the only significant brush stroke that Fromm adds to the picture he already painted in his earlier works is his observation that human evil is most frequently camouflaged by what appear to be positive human traits, a conclusion similarly reached by Hannah Arendt in her view of the banality of human evil. Human beings are victims of a fallacy of belief that convinces them that evil men and women can be recognized by their physical appearance and behavior.

> This fallacy lies in the belief that a thoroughly destructive and evil man must be a devil—and look his part; that he must be devoid of any positive quality; that he must bear the sign of Cain so visibly that everyone can recognize his destructiveness from afar. Such devils exist, but they are rare.... [M]uch more often the intensely destructive person will show a front of kindliness; courtesy; love of family, of children, of animals; he will speak of his ideals and good intentions. But not only this. There is hardly a man who is utterly devoid of any kindness, of any good intention. If he were, he would be on the verge of insanity, except congenital "moral idiots." *Hence, as long as some believe that the evil man wears horns, one will not discover an evil man.* (Fromm 1973:432)

Fromm's long treatise ultimately rests on an appeal to the same faith he expressed in his earlier books. It is essentially the faith of the humanist. But it is a faith that cannot help but seem both naive and short-sighted, given Fromm's own observations regarding the magnitude, pervasiveness, and malignancy of human destructiveness. Here is the way Fromm expressed this faith:

> The position taken in this book is one of rational faith in man's capacity to extricate himself from what seems the fatal web of circumstances that he has created. It is the position of those who are neither "optimists" nor "pessimists," but radicals who have rational faith in man's capacity to avoid the ultimate catastrophe. This humanist radicalism goes to the roots, and thus to the causes; it seeks to liberate man from the chains of illusions; it postulates that

fundamental changes are necessary, not only in our economic and political structure but also in our values, in our concept of man's aims, and in our personal conduct. (Fromm 1973:438)

## Fromm: In Summary

I have discussed Fromm's three studies of human evil in some detail. His publications have been widely read; he has come to be regarded as one of the century's leading humanistic psychiatrists whose thought has consistently been dominated by ethical concern; and his writing is clearly expressed, and though at times it leaves important questions unanswered, it is to the point, and it is not adulterated to any significant degree by non-psychological intrusions from theology, moral philosophy, or mythology. For these reasons, Fromm's psychologically-focused account of human destructiveness and cruelty deserves renewed attention.

A comparison of the three of works shows Fromm to have been undecided about certain questions and ambivalent about others. He attributed human malignancy first to human stupidity, then to the combined forces of self-destructiveness, narcissism, and exclusionary thinking, and finally to the inevitable failure of society's illusions to provide for a sense of genuine meaningfulness. He began by asserting that the majority of men are stupid and cannot see through the lies they permit to govern their lives. He later came to claim that human evil, which he identified with "the syndrome of decay," afflicts either the majority of people, or perhaps only the minority, but he was not able to determine which. He believed that man's malignancy serves no purpose, has no evolutionary function and no biologically adaptive purpose, yet he acknowledged that violence, destructiveness, and cruelty satisfy basic existential needs when life-furthering conditions are absent.

Given the historical paucity of research on the phenomenon of human evil, independently of moral, theological, and mythological interpretations, it is perhaps no wonder that Fromm could not free himself from uncertainty and ambivalence. Yet, like Menninger, he was one of very few researchers to devote time and thought to a study of the psychology of human evil, and for the first time in human intellectual history to begin to give serious thought to the possibility that the species is afflicted by a genuine sickness that causes immeasurable suffering, a sickness which, more than any other factor, stands in the way as the most conspicuous and serious obstacle to humanity's future.

## MORGAN SCOTT PECK (1936–   )

As we have seen, Menninger and Fromm often appear to skirt about the edges of the issue of human evil. They sometimes seem to have lacked the public stamina to engage the leading questions head on, and one cannot help but wonder whether they resorted to circumlocutions and verbal hedging in an effort not to inflame the emotions of readers and so make their works unpopular. M. Scott Peck has perhaps been more candid in this respect.

Peck was the first psychiatrist to confront the phenomenon of human evil directly, to eschew moral, religious, and mythological explanations for it, to make no apologies to his readers for the affront to human pride that may be implied by an honest study of human evil, and most significantly to propose that evil should be considered a specific psychiatric disorder. Unfortunately, his work in this area has to a great extent been ignored by many contemporary psychiatrists and psychologists because of Peck's tendency to associate aspects of his work with religion. His psychiatric account of human evil is, however, as we shall see, independent of religious considerations.

Peck based his study of evil on Fromm's characterization of malignant narcissism. Seen through Peck's eyes, malignant narcissism involves primarily a basic unwillingness of individuals to submit their wills to ideals that go beyond their private desires, needs, and interests. Mentally healthy, non-narcissistic individuals submit their wills to the demands of conscience. Narcissistic people, in contrast, possess imperious wills, focus their energy in order to gratify their own desires, and frequently exhibit a startling ability to influence others to comply with their wishes.

M. Scott Peck proposed a new psychiatric classification of mental disorders in which human evil falls within the already established diagnostic category of "narcissistic personality disorder." He characterized human evil as a disorder that involves denial of personal responsibility, extreme intolerance to personal criticism, and rejection of personal imperfection. The disorder is further distinguished by:

- scapegoating behavior, which is consistently destructive and frequently subtle and difficult to perceive;

- a heightened concern with the individual's public image, usually accompanied by personal pretentiousness and public denials that he or she harbors any hateful feelings or vengeful motives;

- intellectual deviousness that enables the individual to deflect criticism and to appear always to be right;

- and, finally, a strongly entrenched need both for self-deception and for the deception of others: There is a need to maintain lies, and an inability or unwillingness to tolerate truth about oneself. The main title of Peck's book, *People of the Lie*, is derived from this central characteristic of human evil.

The malignant narcissism that forms the backbone of the pathology of human evil comes about, according to Peck, when a child is brought up by parents who are unloving or cruel, or when childhood is otherwise traumatic. The normal narcissism of the infant then comes to be preserved "as a kind of psychological fortress to protect the child against the vicissitudes of its intolerable life." (Peck 1983:81) An adult whose life unfolds wholly within the walls of such a fortress will tend to forfeit his or her independent ethical judgment to whatever social, political, or religious dogma that provides the greatest sense of refuge and comfort.

> They perhaps direct at least as much energy into their devious rationalizations and destructive compensations as the healthiest do into loving behavior. Why? What possesses them, drives them? Basically, it is fear. They are terrified that the pretense will break down and they will be exposed to the world and to themselves. They are continually frightened that they will come face-to-face with their own evil. (124)

And so, according to Peck, malignant narcissism is both caused by and maintained by fear: fear of the outside world, and fear of being forced to confront the unstable and unpleasant image of a self whose development has been stunted due to the demands of fear. The narcissistic individual therefore pours large amounts of emotional energy into maintaining the armor of the lies he has constructed. —He seeks, as Sartre would say in this context, to *not be* the person he is, and to *be* a person he is not.

While narcissism in early childhood is normal, it is an emotional state and an attitude of mind that adults are expected to outgrow. However, as is overwhelmingly evident, many don't. "We may think of evil...as a kind of immaturity. Immature humans are more prone to evil than mature ones." (Peck 1983:222) One is therefore able to understand, for this reason alone, why it is that young adults in their late teens and early twenties make the best soldiers, and also the most frequent criminals. They are most easily persuaded to accept the distorting lies upon which wars are fought, and to be afflicted by narcissism turned malignant, which places the immediate gratification of personal wants above social conscience and above the interests and suffering of others.

Human groups of all kinds, no less than individuals, are susceptible to the psychopathology of evil. Peck refers to "group lies," which include political and religious ideologies, nationalism, racism, etc. Each variety of group identification is associated with the wish by its proponents to cover up their own misconduct, violence, and cruelty. The willful cover-up of war crimes stands as a prime illustration of this aspect of group evil.

The malignant narcissism that afflicts groups often takes root in the pride felt by human beings when they act as a collective entity: "As the members feel proud of their group, so the group feels proud of itself.... [T]he military deliberately does more than most organizations to foster pride within its group. It does so through a variety of means, such as developing group insignia—unit standard flags, shoulder patches, etc...." (Peck 1983:225) Pride coupled with the belief that the malignant narcissist is always and uniquely right lead to a shared feeling among members of a narcissistic group that they are superior to other groups, and that the values they propound are "better" than those held by others. For each narcissistic group, there is a set of lies upon which its members feed, and from which they derive a feeling of communal identity and cohesiveness. Patriotism is nothing more than national narcissism; spiritual righteousness is religious narcissism; racial supremacy is racial narcissism.

All of the ways in which people group themselves in exclusionary collectives have the potential to become malignantly narcissistic. All provide individual members with the emotional benefits that come from diffusing personal responsibility throughout the group, so that no one person is considered personally liable for atrocities committed in the name of the group. This diffusion of responsibility automatically promotes individual laziness: Since no one is willing to be considered apart from the collective mass, there is a seductive dynamic that lulls members of the group into an emotionally gratifying stupor of intellectual lassitude. This combination of group pride and individual laziness leads directly, according to Peck, to human evil.

M. Scott Peck interviewed soldiers who were going to Vietnam. Their attitude and outlook is typical of what happens when collective pride, intellectual laziness, and credulity mix:

> The enlisted men knew nothing...about the war and its relationship to Vietnamese history. Ninety percent of the junior officers knew nothing. What little the senior officers and a few junior officers did know was generally solely what they had been taught in the highly biased programs of their military schools. It was astounding. At least 95 percent of the men going off to risk their very lives did not even have the slightest knowledge what the war was about. I also talked to Department of Defense civilians who directed the war and discovered a similar atrocious ignorance of Vietnamese history. The fact of the matter is that as a nation we did not even know why we were waging the war.
>
> How could this have been? How could a whole people have gone to war not knowing why? The answer is simple. As a people we were too lazy to learn and too arrogant to think we needed to learn. We felt that whatever way we happened to perceive things was the right way without any further study. And that whatever we did was the right thing to do without

reflection. We were so wrong because we never seriously considered that we might not be right. With our laziness and narcissism feeding each other, we marched off to impose our will on the Vietnamese people by bloodshed.... (Peck 1983:249-50)

Like Menninger and Fromm before him, Peck nurtured a hope that mankind can be treated for the sickness of human evil. For Peck, "the hope for healing human evil," the subtitle of his book, lies in psychotherapy and in education. On an individual level, psycho-therapy, when it is at its best, seeks to "combat lies." Although difficult in practice, it is in principle possible to break through the rigid defenses of the narcissistic personality by directly confronting the lies that perpetuate it. The main portal to the soul who hides behind a defensive maze of lies is through the door provided by fear: A person who is evil—that is, sick in the sense of having the new psychiatric disorder identified by Peck—is a person who is dominated by fear: fear which is unpleasant and which requires emotional energy to keep at bay. The evil individual's fear offers the main opening for therapeutic intervention. The therapist, Peck claims, needs to be authoritarian and compassionate, but confrontational. But Peck admits that individual therapy to treat the disorder of human evil is difficult and challenging, and often ineffective.

To treat human evil in large populations, Peck could propose no other remedy than the hope of mass education:

> Children will, in my dream, be taught that laziness and narcissism are at the very root of all human evil, and why this is so. They will learn that each individual is of sacred importance. They will come to know that the natural tendency of the individual in a group is to forfeit his or her ethical judgment to the leader, and that this tendency should be resisted. And they will finally see it as each individual's responsibility continually to examine himself or herself for laziness and narcissism and then to purify themselves accordingly. They will do this in the knowledge that such personal purification is required not only for the salvation of their individual souls but also for the salvation of their world. (Peck 1983:253)

Most readers will likely agree that this is a heroic and also naively romantic statement of hope. Peck admits that he is dreaming. At best, an educational system capable of teaching average, middle-class children, not to mention neglected ghetto or delinquent children, to "purify themselves" of laziness and narcissism is so distant and unrealistic a goal as to demoralize all but dreamers. One would wish for more effective, more practical, and realistic methods to combat human evil than this.

## RECENT PSYCHIATRY AND HUMAN EVIL

In this chapter I have tried to bring together a group of studies made by researchers of the last century who were trained in psychopathology, all of whom shared the belief that human evil is a phenomenon that must be understood and explained if man is to lessen and perhaps end his vicious behavior toward others of his species. Here, I would like to say a few words in retrospect about the works we have discussed.

Menninger, Fromm, and Peck agree in their clinical judgments that high priority must be given to understanding human evil, both for the sake of human self-preservation, and, we might add, for the development of a unified psychiatric theory. They furthermore are in agreement in applying, in various ways, the diagnostic vocabulary of medicine to the phe-nomena of human destructiveness, cruelty, and violence. They describe these phenomena in terms of malignancy, sickness, cancer, toxemia, and psychopathology.

Their individual analyses vary, yet have much in common: Menninger focused largely on the role of narcissism. Fromm stressed, in succession, the roles of human stupidity and self-deception; the syndrome of decay, a psychopathology made up of three component psycho-pathologies, each a malignant phenomenon in its own right: the impulse to self-destructive-ness, narcissism, and the impairment of judgment resulting from adherence to exclusionary belief-systems; and, finally, he returned full-circle to emphasize the role of the illusions that society persuades its members to accept. Peck specifically proposed a new psychiatric classification for the mental disorder underlying human evil; in agreement with Fromm and Menninger, he claimed that malignant narcissism is its backbone.

The term 'evil' is used extensively in only one of Fromm's books (in *The Heart of Man*, where evil is considered to be an infectious disease) and in Peck's *People of the Lie* (where evil is characterized as a psychopathology that justifies its own diagnostic category). Beyond these applications of the term, Menninger and Fromm used it almost not at all.

All three men shared the view that the etiology of human evil can be traced to narcis-sism. Fromm and Peck asserted that narcissism is promoted by an unloving childhood envi-ronment, or one that is uncreative, routine, and fear-ridden. Menninger, Fromm, and Peck were completely silent concerning a potential genetic origin of human evil and its sequelae. They were not, after all, biologists.

There is, in fact, comparatively little detailed discussion in any of the works we have considered about the actual genesis of human evil, of the specific human needs it may satisfy or, indeed, gratify. So far, among psychiatrists, it has been mainly Freud who referred, in passing, to the pleasures men and women derive from aggression and destruction.

Menninger, Fromm, and Peck were unanimous in their hopefulness that man can overcome the malignancies of violence, hatred, self-destruction, and cruelty. Certainly all three were highly idealistic.

- Menninger proposed that individual intelligence can act, so to speak, as the "little leavening" for the whole; that the Socratic method can help man to un-derstand himself and to become aware of the "magnificent tragedy of life" and of his "spiritual nobility."

- Fromm argued that mankind can come to see through the network of lies that help individual men and women live in emotional comfort by means of the exercise of human intelligence, supported by individual freedom and courage. He believed that, through the power of love, human beings will in time be able to insure that childhood environments are creative and mentally healthy. His hopeful view is balanced to some extent by his admission that most human beings do not *want* to develop individual freedom, courage, and intelligence, but want only conformity with their preferred group, and the emotional and physical security this offers.

- Peck concluded that individual psychotherapy is needed to help people over-come the malignancy that afflicts them, while education is needed to combat the social lies that lead to mass violence and destruction. Peck expressed the hope that in both individual psychotherapy and in general education it may be possible on a large scale to persuade individuals to engage in "self-purifica-tion," that is, to rid themselves of the laziness and narcissism that underlie evil.

In terms of a psychiatric understanding of the phenomenon of human evil, we see only a slight empirical or theoretical advance in going from Menninger to Fromm to Peck.

Specifically empirical evidence for their views is almost entirely absent. And, insofar as the development of a unified theory of human evil is concerned, we have instead a mixture of comments, anecdotes, and psychological observations from which it is difficult to identify a general, unitary theory. Certainly, their observations are embedded within perceptive, sensitive, articulate, and intelligent clinical judgments formulated by three thinkers who have devoted a great deal of personal energy and reflection to understanding human evil.

Individual clinical judgment, which we have discussed earlier in some detail (Chapters 2 and 5), is, unfortunately, less respected today than it should be. We are caught in an era that requires double-blind studies, which can be replicated by individuals of greater or lesser intelligence, and which are supported by means of dispassionately computer-processed, statistically weighted data, in order that we may feel confident of results reached. Certainly, within such a framework, whose limits the present study challenges, the independent judgments of Menninger, Fromm, and Peck cannot fail to appear to be both impressionistic and unjustifiably hopeful in outlook. Their studies leave many questions unanswered. Is human evil a genuine disorder and in this sense a disease? Is it instinctual and genetically based? Is it communicable? Can it be treated in any realistic, practical, and effective way? Menninger, Fromm, and Peck do not, in the end, bring us closer to satisfactory answers to such questions.

In making these criticisms, I do not intend to denigrate past efforts, but rather to point to an unfulfilled need for better understanding of a group of phenomena that has received shamefully little serious attention across the centuries.

# CHAPTER 9

# THE QUANTITATIVE HISTORY
# OF HUMAN SELF-DESTRUCTIVENESS

In this chapter I examine the extent to which human beings have killed one another throughout history. This is one very evident dimension that must play a role in any evaluation of the pathogenicity of a species to itself. Quantitative history provides a framework to assess the weight we should give to mankind's propensity for self-destruction. This specialized approach to human history measures quantitatively the aggregated facts of our species' self-destructive history in order to provide an empirically based understanding of how much we have been a danger to ourselves, and how much of a danger to ourselves we are likely to be in the future. As we shall see, quantitative history provides an additional means of understanding the psychology of human aggression and destructiveness.

A principal topic in a study of human evil concerns the overwhelming historical evidence of man's propensity to engage in both collective and individual murder of members of his own species. The existence of separate nations has inextricably been linked to war, both civil and international. In much the same way, the conditions of individual existence have frequently been associated with the perpetration of individual murders. In this chapter we consider a historically based, psychologically focused study of these phenomena that place starkly in relief the impulse of human groups and individuals to kill one another.

During the decades before and after World War I a small number of researchers was deeply struck by the prevalence of war in human history. The political and social instability preceding the first world war gave scholars the incentive to engage in soul-searching, and then the devastation of the Great War on a previously unknown scale provided researchers with further impetus to understand the pervasiveness of human conflict throughout history. What is particularly interesting about much of this research is the extent to which it was undertaken in a spirit of scientific analysis. For the first time in studies of world history, quantitative methods that had proved their value within hard science began to be applied within a discipline that had until this time been rooted in the humanistic tradition of narration, interpretation, and rhetoric.

The field of quantitative history is dominated by the contributions of Lewis Fry Richardson, familiarity with whose research is still largely confined to specialists. The studies of three other major figures added to Richardson's, forming the basis for the discipline of conflict resolution as we know it today. Before turning to Richardson's work, I would like briefly to comment on the work of Quincy Wright, Pitirim Sorokin, and Nicolas Rashevsky. Some of their work precedes Richardson's, some was contemporary with it, and some was published after Richardson's death, so a linear chronology will not be in view. It is rather my intent to review some of the most important conclusions reached by these quantitative historians, in relation to which Richardson's contributions play the principal role.

## QUINCY WRIGHT (1890-1970),
## PITIRIM ALEKSANDROVICH SOROKIN (1889-1968),
## AND NICOLAS RASHEVSKY (1899-1972)

In different ways, Wright, Sorokin, and Rashevsky sought to measure the extent to which the history of human behavior has been dominated by deadly conflicts, and to identify the main psychological forces responsible for our species' history of strife and bloodshed. Wright published many works; of these, three studies should be mentioned here: *The Causes of War and the Conditions of Peace* (1935), *A Study of War* (1942), and close to the end of his life a collection of papers which he edited with Evan and Deutsch, *Preventing World War III: Some Proposals* (1962).

In *The Causes of War*, Wright observed that, from the beginning of the seventeenth century through the first quarter of the twentieth century, there have been some 2,300 battles in Europe alone, or an average of approximately seven a year. In his later, more detailed two-volume work, *A Study of War*, Wright assembled a much larger group of data. There, he analyzed 278 wars from 1480 until 1941. He found that the main European powers were engaged in 2,659 battles—an average of approximately six battles a year. During a wider span of time, the 800 years from 1100 to 1900, Wright's data show that the principal European countries were at war 49 percent of the time. For the United States alone, Wright (1942:I:237) observed: "The United States, which has, perhaps somewhat unjustifiably, prided itself on its peacefulness, has had only twenty years during its entire history when its army or navy has not been in active operation during some days, some-where." In other words, during only about 12 percent of the years of this country's hstiory was the U.S. military *not* occupied in warfare.

How does a quantitative historian answer the question, What is man's psychological motivation for his overwhelming degree of investment in and dedication to deadly conflict? Here is part of Wright's answer:

> ...the *cause of war lies in the fact that human beings do not generally and persistently consider peace more important than numerous other conflicting objectives.* Justice, reform, progress, prestige, prosperity are frequently if not generally more effective stimuli of group action than peace and any of them, if adequately propagandized, will lead people to the state of mind characterized as war. ...[C]onflict is far more interesting to human beings than harmony, and opinion is more precious than life.... [M]en have always preferred to fight for their opinions than to live in peace." (Wright 1935:15-16)

Wright was one of the first historians of war to characterize the human urge to engage in warfare as a *collective psychosis*. His early psychologically-focused analysis of war reached results similar to those of later psychiatrists and psychologists of war, which we shall discuss in Chapter 14.

> War may, for a time, offer...dual satisfaction to many. The soldier senses to the full and with moral satisfaction his participation in the group's great task, but at the same time he is free without inhibitions of conscience to satisfy his individual aggressions against the persons and the property of the enemy. Thus the elation marking the early stage of war flows from the complete reconciliation it offers to the individual's conflicts, but the unreality of this adjust-

ment gives it the character of a *collective psychosis* and renders its participants impervious to rational appeal until the illusion is dissipated. (Wright 1935:122, my emphasis; Wright notes the related research of Waelder 1934.)

Wright's lifelong study of the history of war made evident what subjects most arouse the interests of the majority of people. According to him they are, in order: war, sex, the lives of celebrities, sports, and crime. Of these, three out of the five have to do with *conflict* (war, sports, and crime). It is but a small step to ask "Why is it that so many men like war or can be brought to like it?," a question that had been posed earlier by John Carter (1926) and Leo C. Rosten (1935), whose publications were familiar to Wright, and are discussed in Chapters 3 and 14. Wright did not give a definite answer to this question. On the one hand, he formulated the hypothesis that man's violent predisposition may be genetically based: "On hearing of a conflict situation, people instinctively prick up their ears. Perhaps this is a biological inheritance." (Wright 1942:II:1097) At the time Wright wrote this, little empirical data was available to support or reject the hypothesis. Today, more than a half century later, the question concerning the possible genetic basis of violence is still far from having been settled, as we shall see in Chapter 10. On the other hand, Wright likened the species' violent inclination and obsession with conflict to a "general fever" (1942:II:1199), expressing—metaphorically or realistically, it is not clear which—the view that the human predisposition to violence and warfare is a kind of collective *disease*: "the virus once developed in one section of the human population, like a cancer in the human body, will under present conditions spread to other sections and involve the whole in war." (1942:II:1224)

Whether war results from biological inheritance or social pathology, Wright recognized the central role of emotional gratification, which the majority of men and women derive from conflict. The emotional satisfaction they receive may be stimulated by news of a distant war, or come directly through active participation in it. Wright made clear that the causes of war are not only psychological. Human conflict is multi-causal, he claimed, encompassing "material, economic, historical conditions, on the one hand, and symbolic, psychological, and ideological opinions, on the other." (Wright 1942:II:1115-6) His multi-causal perspective has much in common with the later development of a general systems theory of conflict, which he anticipated: "not only are the pertinent factors difficult to measure, but they are all to some degree dependent upon each other and continually changing in response to changes at any part of the total situation.... [W]ars occur because the family of nations is such a complex and dynamic mechanism that disturbances of its equilibrium are inevitable." (Wright 1935:10,11)

Wright was one of the first historians to raise the question whether states go to war because of hostility against the enemy, or whether they instead find an enemy because they want to go to war. (Wright 1935:112) He recognized the interest in conflict on the part of the majority of people, especially when it is played out on an international scale. From a psychologist's perspective, this mass interest in warfare and preparation for it is an irreducible fact: "Even if the charm, utility and social function of war could be eliminated, war would still recur so long as people devote major attention to preparing for it." (124) The conclusion Wright (1935) came to is that the growing dynamic complexity of an increasingly crowded world combined with the mass psychological appeal of conflict together cannot help but bring about war. He noted that

> ...[t]he technology...of peace [is] virtually nonexistent. Whereas the military is an old and respected profession, there is no comparable profession concerned with the maintenance of peace.... [The] yearly outlay of funds to prevent war and to increase our knowledge of how to resolve international conflicts without war is infinitesimal." (Wright 1935:9)

Wright faced the future realistically: "If peaceful coexistence of states is assured there will be no third world war; but peaceful coexistence cannot be maintained unless people desire it more than they desire the immediate destruction of ideologies which they deem immoral." (434)

Like Wright, Pitirim Sorokin is known for his commitment to quantitative historical analysis. His most substantial study is his four-volume work, *Social and Cultural Dynamics* (1937-41). It presents a panoramic view of the history and dynamics of human societies. He sought to apply the model of mathematical physics that moves from observations of nature to an interconnected group of formalized principles. Sorokin appears to have been the first historian to undertake a comprehensive study of the history of war as a function of numbers of human casualties. He analyzed 967 wars: in Greek history (24 wars); in Roman history (81); in Austrian (131); in German (240); in English (176); in French (185); in Dutch (23); in Spanish (75); in Italian (32); in Russian (151); and in Polish and Lithuanian history (65). He showed that during a total period of 876 years, 411 years, or 47 percent, involved wars. (Wright's corresponding result was 49 percent). Out of a total of 35 quarter-century periods, only three periods did not contain serious wars. (Sorokin 1957:542)

Sorokin showed that from 1101 to 1925, the principal powers of Austria, England, France, Russia, Germany, Poland, Spain, Italy, and the Netherlands were engaged in wars that resulted in growing numbers of casualties (civilian deaths are not included):

| Century | Size of Army | Number of Casualties |
|---------|-------------|---------------------|
| 1101-1200 | 1,161,000 | 29,940[1] |
| 1201-1300 | 2,372,000 | 68,440[2] |
| 1301-1400 | 2,947,000 | 169,929[3] |
| 1401-1500 | 6,910,000 | 364,220[4] |
| 1501-1600 | 16,707,300 | 896,185[5] |
| 1601-1700 | 25,796,000 | 3,711,090[6] |
| 1701-1800 | 31,055,500 | 4,505,990[7] |
| 1801-1900 | 24,233,800 | 3,625,627[8] |
| 1901-1925 | 60,425,000 | 22,035,150[9] |

[1] Only Austria, England, France, Russia.
[2] Only Austria, England, France, Russia.
[3] Plus Poland for one quarter
[4] Plus Spain
[5] Plus Italy and the Netherlands

[6] Plus Germany (all nine)
[7] All nine countries
[8] All nine countries
[9] All nine countries

Adapted from Sorokin (1957:548-9)

We see that although army size during these centuries increased by a factor of 52, casualties increased by a factor of 748. "This means that regardless of the size of the army, recent and modern wars have tended to become more devastating in their killing and wounding power." (Sorokin 1957:550) Casualties among soldiers increased from 2.5 percent during the twelfth century to nearly 39 percent during the first quarter of the twentieth century. Sorokin noted: "losses in the First World War amounted to 30 to 40 percent of the armies, and in the Second World War up to 100 percent, instead of the 1, 2, and 5 percent as in the wars before them." (551) He observed: "The above percentages reflect in absolute figures the progressive perfection of the means of exterminating human life in the wars of the last four centuries, especially the twentieth." (550)

Sorokin's dynamic analysis of the causation of war, which is multi-causal like Wright's, sought to avoid losing sight of what is psychologically fundamental: In looking at the genesis of wars, Sorokin noted that the majority of people and the majority of their leaders have consistently exhibited a pattern of stupidity and self-destructiveness:

> The majority, led by ignorant politicians and the selfish "power-elite"...carry on their hopelessly stupid policies, instead of decreasing the catastrophes they have increased them.... [T]hese blind leaders of blind human sheep have not given the human race either lasting peace or real security or true freedom. Neither have they established a just, harmonious, and noble order in the human universe. Instead they have released the deadly forces of hate, mass murder, insanity, and tyranny, and have brought mankind to the verge of apocalyptic self-destruction. (Sorokin 1963:266)

Also like Wright, Sorokin characterized war as an "epidemic of insanity among the masses and particularly among the power-elites." (1963:267) In this connection, we have already noted that an immense change in magnitude occurred during the twentieth century in the lethal power available to human beings to kill one another. The conclusion Sorokin was led to after a lifetime of research was not hopeful: Even if all American adults should become Ph.D.s, even if a thoroughgoing moral and religious rebirth should overtake the entire population, even if all constructive political and economic remedies were to be implemented, still "there is no chance for a lasting peace and for interhuman harmony, internal or external." (Sorokin 1963:272)

Before turning to Richardson, the quantitative approach of Nicolas Rashevsky deserves brief mention. Rashevsky sought to develop a general mathematical approach that would serve as a deductive science of human society, that is, an abstract theory of human relations. His goal was to formulate a mathematical sociology, modeled after progress in physics and biology. Of Rashevsky's publications, the work most relevant to our discussion here is his *Mathematical Theory of Human Relations: An Approach to a Mathematical Biology of Social Phenomena* (1947), in which he applied methods of mathematical biology to certain social phenomena. This book contains his "Outline of a Mathematical Theory of War" (1947:Chapter XXIII: 187-95), in which he showed how variables representing sociological changes lead to instabilities—a goal similar, as we shall see, to Richardson's. Foremost among these instabilities are the phenomena of civil and international war. Rashevsky's mathematical sociology of conflicts presaged the development of game theory as it applies to conflict situations. He attempted to formalize what he called a "satisfaction function," which represents generalized cases in which an individual tries to maximize his own satisfaction regardless of other individuals. (1947:156ff) His quantitative account of war, never fully developed, describes in mathematical terms how war ends: either through the physical destruction of one of the warring groups, or else through a breakdown in a group's morale. Richardson, as we shall see, described the latter phenomenon in some detail and called it "war fatigue." It plays the role of one among a number of variables that together make explicit the conditions and causes of war.

I turn now to examine the generally neglected work of Lewis Fry Richardson, who, more than anyone else, can be credited with the establishment of the field of quantitative history and specifically the area of study that has come to be known as conflict research.

## METEOROLOGY AND DEADLY HUMAN CONFLICTS:
## LEWIS FRY RICHARDSON (1881-1953)

Richardson was a respected British physicist specializing in meteorology when he decided to shift to psychology later in his life. He retired early, at the age of 59, to devote himself to psychologically-focused, quantitative studies of deadly human conflicts. His interest in the psychology of war began as a result of his voluntary service in the ambulance corps in WWII, during which he wrote a monograph, *Mathematical Psychology of War* (Richardson 1993:II:64-100), a work he was forced to publish privately. His two important later works, *Statistics of Deadly Quarrels* (1960) and *Arms and Insecurity: A Mathematical Study of the Causes and Origins of War* (1960a), also failed to attract a commercial publisher's interest and were preserved by Richardson on microfilm. During his life, his work was neglected, little understand, and sometimes ridiculed, but since his death the learned world has slowly come to appreciate his research. It was not until 1993 that his collected works were published (Richardson 1993). Richardson is now credited with wide influence: Systems theorists have embraced Richardson as an early pioneer in the field (von Bertalanffy & Rapoport 1963:v refer to Richardson as "the first to pursue the systems approach on a large scale"); fractal geometer Benoit Mandelbrot has acknowledged Richardson's research as a revelation and a profound influence upon his own work (Ashford 1982:260; Mandelbrot 1982); while Richardson's war data have been made part of conflict research databases around the world (Richardson 1993:21).

During his life, Richardson's professional reputation was made in the field of meteorology. His basic approach to numerical weather forecasting has become the foundation for nearly all present-day weather prediction. Richardson's biographers have been inclined to characterize Richardson's shift from meteorology to a study of human conflicts as a radical shift in which little from Richardson's meteorological approach carried over into his studies in psychology and history, but in fact this is not the case. Richardson's approach to weather forecasting and his approach to quantitative history and psychology have much in common from a theoretical point of view.

> Foreign affairs as they appear day by day in the newspaper: the text of the despatch, the facial expression of the ambassador as he comes away from an important interview, the movement of warships, these may be likened to the eddying view of a wind. Whereas the theory here presented may be likened to an account of the general circulation of the earth's atmosphere. (Richardson 1939:3)

Shared by both approaches is the presupposition that statistical regularities can be detected in phenomena when considered on a large-scale. The numerical data used in weather prediction are complex, the variables in numerical forecasting equations that take these data as values are interlinked with one another, and the quantified patterns that meteorologists look for in their data and represent in mathematical form express patterns of relative stability or instability from which forecasts can be derived. The final step of derivation is one that remains partly intuitive, instructed by the memory of the history of similar weather conditions. All of these statements are true, *mutatis mutandis*, of the phenomena studied in human conflict research. When Richardson decided to move to the field of psychology, he brought with him, then, a repertory of mathematical methods useful in formalizing statistical data relating to large-scale events. Wars, because they involve numerous participants and because there are many individual wars that can serve as data, are much like meteorological storms in that they are multi-causal events involving linked variables whose values lead to patterns of instability. Richardson sought to provide an objective mathematical representation of the most important causes and conditions that lead to the types of social and political instability that result in war, sustain war, and eventually bring war to an end.

Richardson's work is important in an assessment of human pathology because of its firmly rooted footing in the empirical data of history, and because of its methodological strictness in an area that is generally clouded by emotional distraction. For the first time in the history of social theory, notwithstanding the contributions of Wright, Sorokin, and Rashevsky, Richardson established a quantitative framework for a "social physics," a phrase with its own history that dates back to Comte (1856), and subsequently used by various authors (e.g., Haret 1910; Stewart 1948; Fürth 1952; cf. also Rapoport 1960) who sought to discover analogues of physical laws in principles governing social behavior. Richardson's approach was intellectually pioneering. He compiled large collections of data in relation to which he formulated plausible assumptions and then deduced consequences from them, which then could be tested by actual observations.

### Richardson's Analysis of Deadly Quarrels

Richardson's interests in the fields of meteorology, psychology, and finally conflict research were linked by a single, unifying concern: In each field of study, Richardson wished to represent by means of mathematical methods the behavior of irregular phenomena that characteristically form systems whose internal dynamics often lead to instability as a result of the collaboration of numerous causes. He recognized that many physical, psychological, and social processes cannot be modeled in terms of simple, predictable physical or mathematical systems, but require mathematical methods capable of representing essentially irregular behavior. The mathematical theory of irregular behavior was just beginning to be developed at the time, with the introduction in 1926 by van der Pol of nonlinear differential equations, whose solutions specify oscillations at a particular frequency that may then, slowly or suddenly, shift to another frequency. The mathematics of irregular behavior is particularly well-suited to an analysis of unstable systems.

With these mathematical tools, Richardson sought to study the instability-producing factors that precipitate deadly human conflicts. Such a study requires a solid empirical foundation consisting of a sufficiently inclusive set of data to make it possible to reach a level of theoretic generality that can be expressed mathematically. A great deal of Richardson's time and energy therefore was devoted to collecting and organizing data relating to the history of deadly human conflicts. Here, I would like to summarize some of that data, since this evidence provides perhaps the clearest and most detailed picture of man's propensity, as revealed by his history, to kill members of his own species.

In his *Statistics of Deadly Quarrels*, Richardson classified deadly conflicts according to the number of people who died as a result of them. He defined the *magnitude* of a deadly conflict as the logarithm to the base ten of the number of people who died because of that conflict. A quarrel of magnitude 0 would then indicate that one person was killed ($10^0$); a quarrel of magnitude 7 would indicate that 10 million people were killed ($10^7$). Richardson studied more than 300 wars that occurred between 1820 and 1945, and brought together data from many historical, military, and police records. What he produced was an inventory for that period of man's self-destructive aggression. Individual murders are represented at one end of the range, in the rightmost column of the following table, and WWI and WWII in the second column from the left (Richardson 1960:143):

| Magnitude | 7 ± ½ | 6 ± ½ | 5 ± ½ | 4 ± ½ | 3 ± ½ | Murders[*] |
|---|---|---|---|---|---|---|
| Number of conflicts | 2 | 5 | 24 | 63 | 188 | 6,000,000 |

In wars of magnitude $4 \pm \frac{1}{2}$ through $7 \pm \frac{1}{2}$ (wars in which up to $10^{4.5}$ and up to $10^{7.5}$ people were killed, i.e., in which there were from 31,623 to 31,622,777 lives lost), Richardson concluded that approximately 46.8 million people were killed during the 126-year period in question. In wars of magnitude $1 \pm \frac{1}{2}$ through $3 \pm \frac{1}{2}$, 2.9 million were killed. In connection with individual murders, he estimated that 9.7 million people were killed (apparently allowing for judicial executions). The cumulative total number of deaths that resulted from these wars and individual murders, according to Richardson's calculations, was approximately 59 million persons, which comes to an average of approximately half a million people killed each year over the 126-year period. What is especially noticeable about Richardson's sad tally is that the heaviest losses of life occurred at the two ends of the range: that is, in connection with two world wars and as a result of individual murders. Smaller wars, of which there were many from 1820-1945, resulted in comparatively fewer deaths.

How deeply is one to be affected by these numbers? On the one hand, the fact that human beings through wars and murders during a 126-year period killed 59 million persons is appalling and an indictment of our species. But is the degree of mass and individual killing that Richardson documented so carefully, in the end, significant? —Certainly, to make such a question meaningful, the term 'significant' has to be weighed in its "larger" sense—for the individual deaths were unquestionably "significant" and deeply tragic on a personal level to the individuals and their immediate families. Richardson was clearly concerned with this question. He calculated the number of deaths from *all* causes, not only from wars and murders, during the 126-year time period. From this total, it was only a step to calculate the percentage of deaths attributable to wars and murders. In fact, as it turns out, the percentage is quite small: only 1.6 percent. As Richardson commented: "Those who enjoy wars can excuse their taste by saying that wars after all are much less deadly than disease." (Richardson 1960:153)

To place Richardson's characteristically dry remark in perspective, the Editors of Richardson's *Statistics of Deadly Quarrels* added their own comment in a 1960 footnote (Richardson 1960:161), pointing out that Richardson's figures concerned only past, non-nuclear wars. To bring estimates more up-to-date, they summarized the testimony presented before the U.S. Joint Congressional Atomic Energy Sub-Committee in 1959, which, at that time, showed that in a "moderate-sized" nuclear war, one person in four in the United States would be killed within a matter of hours. To be sure, there has been considerable "improvement" in the killing power of nuclear weapons since 1959, from which fact the reader's imagination can no doubt extrapolate beyond the immediate 25 percent fatality-rate made public four decades ago. Employing an updated imagination, the reader will see that those who enjoy war can today derive considerably less comfort than they used to, given the considerably larger percentage of dead predicted to result from a general nuclear war.

---

[*] The figure of 6,000,000 murders has been corrected in this table. Richardson's figure in his original table ($6 \times 10^4$) is a typographical error, evident from his text on pages 125 and 145. However, Richardson's estimate of six million murders must be increased to ten million to include so-called "judicial executions." See Sutherland (1962:474).

To determine the degree of aggression of individual countries during the period 1820-1945, Richardson (1960:173) provided the following summary of the number of conflicts in which various countries have been involved:

| Range of magnitude | 7.5 - 6.5 | 6.5 - 5.5 | 5.5 - 4.5 | 4.5 - 3.5 | 7.5 - 3.5 (totals) |
|---|---|---|---|---|---|
| Britain | 2 | 0 | 1 | 25 | 28 |
| France | 2 | 0 | 4 | 15 | 21 |
| Russia | 2 | 0 | 6 | 10 | 18 |
| Turkey | 1 | 0 | 8 | 6 | 15 |
| China | 2 | 2 | 4 | 7 | 15 |
| Spain | 0 | 1 | 2 | 8 | 11 |
| Germany (or Prussia) | 2 | 0 | 5 | 3 | 10 |
| Italy or Piedmont | 2 | 0 | 3 | 5 | 10 |
| Austria | 2 | 0 | 2 | 5 | 9 |
| Japan | 2 | 0 | 2 | 5 | 9 |
| U.S.A. | 2 | 1 | 2 | 4 | 9 |
| Egypt | 0 | 0 | 0 | 7 | 7 |
| Greece | 2 | 0 | 1 | 3 | 6 |

It is interesting to note that there have occasionally been peaceful nations. By way of contrast with the countries named in the above table, Sweden's total in the last column would be zero.

Richardson's study of the more than 300 wars that took place between 1820 and 1949 includes a careful description of the causes and conditions of each war, and, as we have noted, the number of war dead. The amount of labor that Richardson devoted to his exhaustive historical research was considerable. His is the most complete and detailed analysis of wars that exists for the period, and it provided a "tragically sufficient" (Richardson 1993:xiv) basis from which statistical regularities can be observed.

From his many years of research Richardson concluded, as Wright and Sorokin also did, that wars do not occur with any periodicity, but rather their distribution in time appears to be random, though large wars are becoming more frequent. One researcher expressed the observation of the randomness of war in this way: "The numbers of outbreaks of war each year, and the outbreaks of peace, each agree closely with a Poisson distribution, with the disturbing implication that these events may be occurring purely by chance." (Sutherland 1962:474) More clearly and persuasively than any researcher before him, Richardson observed that deadly human conflicts, whether they are wars between nations, civil wars, incidents of gangsterism, or individual murders and socially approved executions, are phenomena whose behavior is irregular, and therefore subject to analysis by means of statistical methods applicable to large numbers of events. He noted that the lack of organization found in phenomena exhibiting irregular behavior is characteristic of chaos. "Mathematically the characteristic of chaos is that the probability of a complicated event contains among its factors the probabilities of the simpler events." (Richardson 1993:572)

Richardson called his quantitative history of human conflict "chaos restricted by geography and modified by infectiousness." (Richardson 1950:254; see also Richardson 1960:297) Today, a half-century after Richardson placed his manuscript of *Statistics of Deadly Quarrels* on microfilm, the mathematical theory of chaos has become an established area of study.

Interrelated discoveries, often mutually confirming, have occurred in a wide range of disciplines, from fluid mechanics and the physics of turbulence to mathematics, meteorology, chemistry, cardiology and immunology, cell growth and the biological architecture of organisms, human neuroscience, and artificial intelligence. An increasing amount of scientific attention is being devoted by a variety of disciplines to systems exhibiting irregular and unstable behavior. It is clear as one reads Richardson within the context of contemporary work, that here, in connection with chaos theory, his mind had advanced beyond the circular ruts of the mental habits of his time. He was at home in analyzing phenomena whose behavior is essentially irregular, in terms of a statistically-based understanding of the dynamics of unstable systems of events that involve chaos. The history of human self-destruction, through wars, civil conflicts, and individual murders, exhibits, he claimed, just such behavior.

## Richardson's *Mathematical Psychology of War*

In his early work, *Mathematical Psychology of War*, Richardson made a number of general psychological observations concerning the causation of war. He began his monograph with a quotation from William James's *Principles of Psychology*, which describes some of the factors that are involved in human aggression:

> The cooling advice which we get from others when the fever-fit is on us is the most jarring and exasperating thing in life.... Such is the inevitable effect of reasonable ideas over others—*if they can once get a quiet hearing*, and passion's cue accordingly is always and everywhere to prevent their still small voice from being heard at all. "Let me not think of that! Don't speak to me of that!" ..."Haec tibi erit janua leti" [this will be for you the doorway to death], we feel....
>
> The strong-willed man, however, is the man who hears the still small voice unflinchingly, and who, when the death-bringing consideration comes, looks at its face, consents to its presence, clings to it, affirms it, and holds it fast, in spite of the host of exciting mental images which rise in revolt against it and would expel it from the mind. Sustained in this way by a resolute effort of attention, the difficult object ere long begins to call up its own congeners and associates and ends by changing the disposition of the man's consciousness altogether. (Richardson 1993:64)

Several topics expressed in this passage were to exert an influence on Richardson, as we will see: James's characterization of human hatred as a "fever-fit," the general resistance among the majority of people to reason, the will of the majority to hate, and hope in the capacity of the occasional rational man to rise above the majority's passions of hatred and aggression.

In his *Mathematical Psychology of War*, Richardson sought to give an account of the main psychological factors involved both in the causation of war and in the establishment of peace, among them: the desire for conquest, retaliation for casualties, destruction of wealth, "war as a joyful adventure", "the defence of that which is held dear," vengeance, rivalry, business advantages, war as a source of income, the security of rulers, fear, pain, fatigue, the desire for change, the prospect of military success, duty to the dead, habituation to casualties, pity for the adversary, racial antipathy and cohesion, reason and intuition, justice, the destruction of militarism, religion, and the sense of guilt. In short, Richardson gave a detailed inventory of many of the emotions and motivations that contribute to human conflict. His approach to psychology was influenced by the theory of instincts developed by psychologist William McDougall (1871-1938), and he often cited McDougall's (1908) study. Within this context, Richardson considered war to be an expression in man of "instinct."

> The view here put forward is that the warlike striving of either side is largely, though not entirely, an instinctive reaction to the stimulus of the warlike striving of the opposing side. By an instinct is here meant an inborn tendency to perceive a certain state of affairs, and thereupon to feel in a particular way, and to act towards a corresponding end. A tendency, that is to say, which one might easily follow without considering it; and to resist which, if one judged it desirable to resist, would require an effort of will. (Richardson 1993:66)

Richardson's concept of instinct is probably best understood in terms of an analogy that he used to explain it. Habitual mental dispositions, Richardson observed, are similar to water flowing down a bank of soft mud: Channels are soon formed in the mud, and these establish pathways along which the water then tends to flow. Once the flow is stopped, the channels formed in soft mud tend to close up, while pathways that have been eroded in hard mud or rock remain, and do not close up through disuse. (70) These more permanent channels are what Richardson called "instincts." Although the language of human instincts is no longer in vogue among many psychologists today, instincts for Richardson are simply patterns of behavior that are comparatively immune to change, and so are relatively permanent features of human psychology. The question whether mankind's instinctual aggression and warlike nature are genetically determined or culturally based was not taken up by Richardson; from his point of view, they are specific and undeniable facts about human psychology, and in that sense are givens which the investigator of human conflict must accept.

Richardson's psychology of war is a psychology of the herd, best understood, he argued, in terms of statistical generalizations, rather than in terms of the psychology of the few individuals (philosophers or the heads of businesses) "who are accustomed to take long views. This type of man has his instincts well under control and is quick to realize logical necessities." (70) Richardson observed that human beings appear, in contemporary words, to be "hard-wired" to engage in war, and they do clearly derive emotional gratification from deadly conflicts. To be sure, the gratification experienced by the majority of the people whose country is at war is a function of the intensiveness and seriousness of the conflict and of the number of casualties their nation suffers: "it may be noticed that a very little warlike activity...is not tiring but is rather pleasing to a nation as whole...." (73) The degree of human gratification derived from war is situationally relative and evidently a matter of degree.

Psychologically counterbalancing the pleasure that men and women derive from war is the fatigue that sustained deadly conflict eventually causes. "[T]here are limits to all things human, and so we must...take account of fatigue." (66) Richardson's mathematical formulation seeks to express the interconnectedness of a group of important psychological variables. They include: human pleasure in violent conflict and "vigour-to-war," and the tendency for a limit to be set on these emotions by fatigue as suffering increases and casualties mount up. And then, overlaid upon fatigue is what more recent psychologists have termed "psychic numbing," or, as Richardson expressed this, "the deadening effect of habituation to continual casualties." (90)

Richardson invested a great deal of time and effort to provide a mathematical formulation of relationships among these psychological variables. According to him, on the one hand, there are a number of advantages in being able to represent phenomena in mathematical terms, and especially is this true for phenomena the understanding of which is clouded by emotion: Richardson claimed that the work of translating into formalism requires a careful scrutiny of the ideas expressed; formalism makes it easier to deduce implications; and it encourages brevity, and thereby reduces the mental labor of keeping complex systems of ideas simultaneously present in the mind. On the other hand, there are, to be sure, disadvantages of mathematical formulation, which Richardson also readily noted: The definiteness that formalism suggests may be spurious, "existing in the equations but not in the phenomena to be described"; and formal brevity "may be due to the omission of important things, simply because they cannot be mathematized." (67) He was the first major contributor to quantitative history to recognize the clear need to step beyond human emotionalism in order to come to grips with the central psychological forces that impel human beings to kill one another. Richardson sought to respond to this need through mathematical formalization.

### Richardson's Epidemic Theory of War, War-moods, and War-weariness

Richardson observed that human conflicts tend to spread in much the same way as does disease during an epidemic. He called the emotional hunger that gradually overtakes a populace and leads to war "war fever." He observed that war is genuinely, and not metaphorically, *infectious*, since it is possible to witness a growing *contagion* within a nation, as the emotions of the majority are stirred by leaders and by the media, kindling resentment into hatred, and hatred into the violent compulsion to kill the enemy. Richardson was interested in studying this phenomenon in order to bring the actual epidemic process to light.

Richardson's attention was drawn to the mathematical theory of epidemics, which seeks to characterize in terms that are clear and precise the dynamics of infection, transmission, and spread of disease. (See Chapter 4 in the present book.) He became acquainted with the work of W. O. Kermack and A. G. McKendrick (1927). Kermack and McKendrick proposed that for a given disease and for specific recovery and death rates, there will correspond a certain critical or threshold density of population. When this threshold density of population is exceeded, then the greater the population density is at the onset of an epidemic, the less it will become by the end of the epidemic. In other words, an epidemic reaches a degree of virulence when the population density is relatively great, and the epidemic increases or spreads as long as the unaffected population of people remains greater than the threshold density. (Kermack & McKendrick 1927:701) Kermack and McKendrick were of course speaking of the role of routinely recognized disease organisms in the etiology of epidemics; Richardson introduced the idea that the human propensity to engage in large-scale deadly conflicts obeys many of the same patterns of infection and transmission.

One of the results of Kermack's and McKendrick's mathematical theory of epidemics is that as long as a population is increased by "unaffected individuals" (those who as yet have not been infected by the disease while the critical population threshold continues to be exceeded), there will exist a corresponding increase in the probability of a catastrophic epidemic. In other words, epidemics that develop slowly, allowing for a prolonged delay in the outbreak of a truly virulent epidemic, pose the greatest risk of leading to "an almost complete extinction of the population." (720) Using this framework, Richardson based his application of epidemic disease theory on the observation that the human "eagerness for war" bears all of the characteristics of a "mental disease infected into those in a susceptible mood by those who already have the disease in the opposing country." (Richardson 1950:235 and 1993:558) Richardson asked whether the Kermack-McKendrick model of the rate of spread of an epidemic, such as an epidemic of bubonic plague, would be applicable to war fever. Although there are clear parallels between the two processes, Richardson noted that there are also differences. For example, the Kermack-McKendrick theory does not account for the long persistent phase of a war, followed by its comparatively sudden end.

the same six stages as a medically recognized disease epidemic: an incubation state, a state of infection and then transmission to others, a state of immunity (possessed by those individuals who are not caught up by the war fever), a state of recovery (those willing to accept terms of peace), and the state to which much deadly conflict leads, death. Late in his life, Richardson published two long papers in which he developed these ideas. (Richardson 1948, 1948a) In a section entitled "Analogies with Disease," Richardson wrote that the phrase "war fever" suggests:

(i)    infection, of course mental, by sights and sounds;
(ii)   a rise of excitement, analogous to rise of temperature in fever;
(iii)  that some people may be immune to these warlike excitements;
(iv)   that others may acquire immunity, alias war-weariness, as the result of a long bout of fighting;
(v)    that war-weariness may fade away after the end of the war. (Richardson 1948:160)

Richardson gave the contagiousness of war fever a central role in the mathematical theory that he formulated to describe the dynamics of psychological epidemics that lead to war. Richardson's mathematical model, which represented the six possible states of infection by means of six simultaneous differential equations of the second degree, is of sufficient complexity that he does not offer a solution to the equations. Instead, he shows how the waxing and waning of the war moods that are identified within his model correspond reasonably well to patterns of real behavior that are confirmed by historical data. In this original effort, he was surprisingly successful, causing one of his commentators, T. H. Pear, to state flatly of Richardson's theory: "it is the only one which has survived the test of quantitative comparison with historical fact." (Pear 1950:254)

Central among the psychological factors responsible for the infectiousness of war fever is, according to Richardson, man's emotional enjoyment of war, which Richardson called "the love of fighting for its own sake." (Richardson 1960:26) And intimately associated with the emotional satisfaction that the majority of people derive from conflict is of course the psychology of hatred. Richardson's observations concerning the phenomenon of human hate are sparse. In a short paper read at the Twelfth International Congress of Psychology and published near the end of his life, he commented: "...when we are given reasons for hating a foreign nation we should consider *also*: (*a*) that we, or our compatriots, may harbour a subconscious hatred which is seeking an object; (*b*) that every piece of news is a selection; and that its selector has usually a wide choice among different emotional tones." (Richardson 1949:167)

These remarks are cryptic. If one reads this passage within the overall framework of Richardson's research, it is plausible that he intended the following view: First, the majority of men and women are emotionally so constituted that hatred is a natural and fundamental response to many situations involving others. The human propensity to respond by means of felt hatred is, however, not entirely explained by the objects toward which hate is directed, but, as Richardson suggests, the emotion is "there" awaiting and seeking an outlet. Second, when an outlet is offered, the emotional realization of hatred, and its expression in behavior, provide a variety of pleasure that reinforces and so encourages the further expression of hatred.

Hatred, as we shall see in Chapter 16, has remained a little-studied phenomenon, one that is both self-fueling and self-reinforcing. It is a phenomenon that plays a fundamental role in human pathology, in human evil. In Richardson's incomplete analysis of this emotion he was led to ask whether there is "an irreducible minimum of hatred" that human beings may be brought to feel. (Richardson 1949:167) He answered rhetorically: "If the whole world were politically united, so that there were no human enemies, would abstractions like dirt, disease, ignorance, poverty, falsehood, ugliness, and cruelty seem sufficiently *exciting* to direct our latent pugnacities all in beneficent directions?" (167) Richardson was not optimistic that mass hate can meaningfully be reduced.

We now turn in concluding this chapter to the question, Under what conditions, in Richardson's analysis, do wars come to an end? We have mentioned the emotion of war-weariness, an emotion that Richardson observed in societies once a certain threshold of prolonged suffering with sufficient numbers of casualties has been exceeded. Before this threshold has been exceeded, Richardson found that it is futile to try to halt a war in progress. "[I]nfluential public men have tried to stop wars before intense war-weariness had developed, and they have signally failed." (See Richardson 1948:158, where he gives examples of unsuccessful attempts.) War-weariness comes about not only as a result of the suffering of prolonged war and mounting casualties, but because of the free, and sometimes the involuntary, expression of defeatism by members of the population. Richardson observed that in a symmetrical war (in which both sides are of equal strength), if there were no defeatists, an end to the struggle "could not come until every person in both nations had been killed." (Richardson 1948a:210) Public demoralization, combined with sufficiently pronounced suffering and a sufficient number of war dead, are the main ingredients that predispose a nation to accept a cessation of hostilities.

How much is too much suffering? How long must a war be, how painful must it be, to induce war-weariness? Richardson does not answer the first part of this question, although we may note that Quincy Wright hazarded an estimate: "Perhaps four or five years of the strain of war is as much as people organized in the modern state can stand without resting." Wright 1935:32) In his *Statistics of Deadly Quarrels*, Richardson (1960) found that, statistically, war-weariness sets in when the less populous of two warring countries has lost somewhere between .05 and 5 percent of its population—although there have certainly been wars in which it took many more war dead to convince the participants to end the conflict: At the extreme end of the range was Paraguay's war of 1870, in which 83 percent of its population had to be killed before sufficiently intense war-weariness set in. In 1918, Serbia lost 22 percent of its people before weariness set in. At the other end of the range, "only" 4 percent of the German population had to succumb to bring about war-weariness in 1945. In order to agree to end their involvement in WWII, "only" 1.2 percent of the Japanese population had to die to produce the same effect. (Richardson 1960:299)

## Richardson's Research and the Outlook for the Future

Richardson's quantitative inventory of humanity's bloody history is still unsurpassed for its comprehensiveness, detail, and the accuracy of its mathematical modeling of mankind's commitment to kill members of its own kind, whether by individual murder and judicial execution, or by "murder writ large," as Carl Sagan (1980:326) called war in his discussion of Lewis Fry Richardson's work. The outlook that Richardson came to have on the basis of the many years that he devoted to a study of deadly human conflicts was not, as we have already noted, optimistic. Some twenty years after Richardson's death, another careful quantitative study of wars was published by Singer and Small (1972), covering the period from 1816 to 1965. Their results were also not hopeful. They found that during this period 93 international wars occurred. Out of 150 years, there were only 24 years without war. They did not find that there was any discernible battle-death threshold at which nations became sufficiently war-weary to withdraw from war.

About a decade later, Carl Sagan became interested in Richardson's ground-breaking work. Sagan graphed Richardson's results relating to the steadily increasing destructiveness of wars, and then extrapolated his findings to offer a reasonable estimate of how long it will probably be until the trend noted by Richardson toward larger wars would reach a point where a war occurs that is so devastating that it kills all human life (see Sagan 1980:327). For this purpose, Sagan accepted Richardson's plausible quantitative-historical result that the greater the number of people killed in a war, the longer it takes for such a war to occur.

In the two charts below, I make a similar assumption in charting the anticipated number of people who will, on average, be killed in relation to increasingly long intervals of time between deadly conflicts.

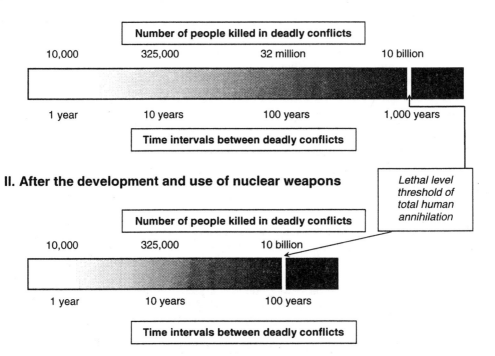

## I. Before the advent of nuclear weapons

## II. After the development and use of nuclear weapons

**The projected risk of total annihilation of the human population before and after the advent of nuclear weapons.** The horizontal scale above each shaded bar represents the number of people whose deaths from deadly human conflicts can be expected over time. The horizontal scale below each shaded bar represents the anticipated time intervals between deadly human conflicts, i.e., how long it is necessary on average for a deadly human conflict to occur that kills the indicated number of people. The vertical white bars mark the point where the human population reaches its lethal level, based on its size at present and in the immediate future.

As can be seen in the foreshortening of the second chart above, the development of and decision to use nuclear weapons has very likely reduced substantially the time interval until nuclear holocaust. (The two charts are based on Richardson's data and Sagan's (1980:327) extrapolation of Richardson's results.)

The light-to-dark gradient in each of the shaded bars gives a graphical representation based on Richardson's data of the increase in the number of deaths that are to be expected in relation to increasingly long intervals of time. The present total world population is in the order of six billion people. Allowing for a two-thirds increase in the total population in the foreseeable future, and under the assumption that mankind had not developed nuclear weapons, Chart I represents the expectation that a war large enough to kill up to 10 billion people would probably not occur for as long as a thousand years. The vertical white line toward the right end of the shaded bar represents the lethal level threshold for our species, based on its present and short-term projected population. (On the lethal level concept, see Chapter 17.) When that lethal level is reached, a deadly human conflict would occur that is sufficiently catastrophic as to terminate human life.

Chart II, however, takes into account the development of nuclear weapons and the decision to use them for the first time, in WWII. It is reasonable to argue that, once human beings begin to use nuclear weapons against one another, the time interval necessary in order to bring about Armageddon will almost certainly be reduced, and reduced very considerably. Since nuclear weapons technology has proliferated and become greatly more deadly since WWII, Sagan reasoned that "we may have only another few decades until Doomsday." (Sagan 1980:328) The vertical white line toward the right end of the foreshortened shaded bar in Chart II shows how the lethal level for our species has been brought significantly closer to the present as a result of human improvements in ways to kill one another on a large scale.

Like Richardson, Sagan felt a deep reverence for human and other life on this world. He did not make his extrapolation from Richardson's data in a spirit of frivolity. He concluded from his interpretation of Richardson's data: "This is merely another way of saying what we have known for decades: the development of nuclear weapons and their delivery systems will, sooner or later, lead to global disaster." (Sagan 1980:328) He summed up the international situation leading to probable imminent human extinction in words that Richardson would surely have endorsed:

> Every nation seems to have its set of forbidden possibilities, which its citizenry and adherents must not at any cost be permitted to think seriously about. In the Soviet Union these include capitalism, God, and the surrender of national sovereignty; in the United States, socialism, atheism, and the surrender of national sovereignty. It is the same all over the world. (329)

## IN CONCLUSION

Richardson's central intellectual interest throughout his life focused on the properties of complex dynamic systems that bring about instability. As we have seen, in meteorology his interest took the form of weather prediction, where extreme instability of atmospheric conditions leads to storms. In human affairs, Richardson's interest led him to investigate the infectious nature of the mass emotional storms that lead to conflict. Both forms of turbulence are intrinsically multi-causal and of a sufficient degree of complexity that mathematical formalization is not only useful, but, Richardson believed, essential to human understanding and, potentially, to control. A mathematical representation of meteorological conditions is today accepted unquestioningly as essential; in studies of human conflicts, the forms of psychiatric turbulence that are involved have so far been successfully analyzed and formalized to a much lesser extent.

Richardson's main contributions to conflict research were these: First, he was a pioneer in collecting and organizing a huge amount of quantitative data about mankind's long historical record of wars. Second, he was one of the first researchers to apply mathematical epidemic disease theory to the infectiousness of war enthusiasm within a framework of serious psychological analysis. Third, he developed a hypothetical set of equations that attempts to make explicit the connections between the principal variables that are associated with mass psychological instability antecedent to war. In this work, Richardson's hope, which he recognized to be highly idealistic, was that through the use of self-conscious and rigorous methods it would eventually be possible to develop a medically preventive approach that can reduce or eliminate the spread of psychological epidemics that lead to war. He believed that the only truly basic solutions capable of leading to conflict-reduction are to be found within psychology, where the human motivations that lead to conflict and permit its resolution can be studied. Although Richardson did not explicitly study the phenomenon of human hatred, he recognized the self-fueling nature of the human "vigour-to-war" that underlies the various manifestations of social and political instability, which, in turn, incline mass groups to kill one another.

In this chapter, I have had two main topics in view: the extent to which human history has been devoted to warfare, and the psychologically-based conclusions that quantitative historians of war have reached. As we have seen, Wright and Sorokin collected a huge amount of data in quantitative studies of many hundreds of wars. Their data establish the astonishing degree to which the history of the human species has been devoted to civil and international war. Neither Wright nor Sorokin detected any discernible periodicity of war, nor any basis for the belief that humanity is progressing in a direction of reduced warfare. Instead, they were in agreement that the measurable trend in history is in the direction of increasingly catastrophic wars. We saw that Quincy Wright's extensive study of war led him to conclude that the increasing dynamic complexity of an increasingly crowded world, combined with the mass psychological appeal of conflict, together cannot help but bring about war. A lasting peace would require the majority of people to prefer peace to their pet ideologies, something he accepted as extremely improbable. Sorokin similarly concluded that there is no chance for a lasting peace even if ideal remedial conditions are satisfied.

In subsequent chapters, we shall discuss the work of researchers who, like quantitative historians Rashevsky, Sorokin, Wright, and Richardson, were concerned to understand human evil, but from different perspectives. We shall consider a variety of psychological analyses that relate not only to war, but to such subjects as genocide and terrorism, the pathology of human obedience, and the human incapacity for empathy. In the next chapter, we consider research that has focused on studies of the behavior of the human species. We look at the contribution that has been made by ethology to a gradually developing picture of human evil.

# CHAPTER 10

# THE PATHOLOGY OF A SPECIES: ETHOLOGY AND HUMAN EVIL

Ethology, the comparative science of animal behavior, is a new discipline that was established during the last quarter of the twentieth century. But, like most approaches, ethology has roots—in the work, for example, of Charles Darwin (1872), who studied expressive behavior in animals and people, and appears to have been the first to apply an evolutionary approach to the comparative analysis of behavior. Other pioneering researchers in ethology have included biologists Charles Otis Whitman (1899, 1919), Jakob Johann von Uexküll (1909, 1920, 1957), Oskar Heinroth (1910), and Wallace Craig (1918). However, it was not until the Nobel Prize was awarded in 1973 to three ethologists that the discipline came into its own. Konrad Lorenz, Nikolaas Tinbergen, and Karl von Frisch shared the prize. It was the first time that the Nobel Prize was awarded to behavioral scientists.

Although the human species evidently falls within the scope of study of ethology, there has been an appreciable amount of human resistance to human ethology. Tinbergen (1907-1988) made man's self-chosen ignorance of his own behavior the subject of a paper. In it, Tinbergen called the willful blindness of our species to its own patterns of behavior "the enemy within." (Tinbergen 1968:1418) He made several observations about mankind's "mental block against self-scrutiny" (1411):

> The majority of people bridle as soon as it is even suggested that studies of animal behavior could be useful for an understanding, let alone for the control, of our own behavior. They do not want to have their own behavior subjected to scientific scrutiny; they certainly resent being compared with animals; and these rejecting attitudes are both deep-rooted and of complex origin. (1411)

In the same vein, Lorenz commented on mankind's tendency to reject whatever offends human species pride. According to Lorenz, there are three obstacles that stand in the way of human self-knowledge: mankind's irrational recalcitrance in accepting his evolutionary origin; his passionate adherence to a belief in free will, which takes the form of defiance in accepting that his behavior is subject to natural laws of causality; and the heritage of idealistic philosophy, which construes empirical explanation applied to the human species as devaluation. These three obstacles prevent man from gaining the insight necessary to control his behavior. (Lorenz 1966:223)

Perhaps largely as a result of such sources of human resistance to human ethology, few ethologists have devoted serious effort to a study of man's behavior; instead, they have generally confined their research to nonhuman animals. Konrad Lorenz has been an exception to this trend, along with his former student and now well-known ethologist, Irenäus Eibl-Eibesfeldt. Most of this chapter will focus on Lorenz's extensive human-centered and psychologically-focused research, though I will also summarize some of the work of Eibl-Eibesfeldt. It will not be my intent to review the recent literature of human-centered studies in ethology, but to focus in some detail on the pioneering approach and psychologically-centered conclusions reached by Lorenz and Eibl-Eibesfeldt.

## KONRAD LORENZ AND ETHOLOGY

Konrad Lorenz (1903-1989) was born in Altenburg, Austria. He was the son of an orthopedic surgeon who wanted his son to study medicine. Lorenz complied; he received an M.D. degree in Vienna in 1928. He went on to receive a Ph.D. in zoology in 1933. A decade later, when he was nearly forty, Lorenz was appointed Professor of Psychology at the Albertus University of Königsberg. His broad background in medicine, zoology, and psychology was to influence Lorenz to extend ethological research to include psychological dimensions of human behavior. Specifically, Lorenz wanted to expand the scope of research of evolutionary biologists to include a concern for patterns of both physical and mental behavior that have evolved as a result of selection pressures. Applying this approach to the human species, he sought to identify patterns of human behavior as well as thought that owe their existence to evolution. It is here that his approach diverges from the behavioral studies of many other ethologists. In one of his early works, Lorenz wrote: "...comparative behavioral research is concerned more directly than any other natural science with the human species as such and is therefore called upon more directly than any other to occupy itself with the science of the human mind." (Lorenz 1996: xxxi) As a result of Lorenz's focus, one of his biographers has appropriately called his approach "psychological ethology." (Evans 1975:80)

Once the tools of evolutionary biology were applied to human psychology, it was natural for Lorenz to portray certain patterns of human psychological behavior as innate, inborn, or genetically programmed. If significant patterns of human psychological behavior have resulted from evolutionary development, then it must be the case, he claimed, that these patterns of response have become part of man's inborn psychological constitution. Such an approach by ethology to the human subject would predictably arouse the ire of anti-instinct humanists, and so it has. The question is an empirical one, and plausibly will, given time and further research, be answered on the basis of empirical evidence. From another point of view, the interplay between genetic programming and environmental conditions may in fact be so intimately intertwined as to make a clear-cut division between inborn and acquired behavior a pseudoproblem, and perhaps even theoretically impossible.[1] In terms of the functional-descriptive approach taken here, the descriptive accounts of human behavioral patterns provided by Lorenz are penetrating and insightful. On this basis, he arrived at a clinical judgment regarding pathologies that are evident in those patterns of behavior.

---

[1] Writing in the 1930s, one of the first biologists to urge the abandonment of the conceptual separation of the innate and the acquired was J. Y. Kuo. All behavior, according to him, consists of reactions to stimuli, and these in turn essentially involve interactions between an organism and its environment. The notion that there is a relationship, one that pre-exists its theoretical representation, between the organism and the conditions of its environment, is no less questionable, Kuo argued, than the assumption of innate ideas. See Lorenz (1981:7) and Kuo (1932).

To gain a clear picture of the main conclusions that ethology has reached in understanding human behavior, it is important to characterize the method used by much ethology and in particular by Lorenz for it stands fundamentally in opposition to the experimental-quantified paradigm that dominates contemporary science. The method proposed by Lorenz, as much and perhaps even more than the conclusions to which he arrived, will prove relevant in later chapters.

## Epistemology and Gestalt Perception

Lorenz's science...is resolutely descriptive; and worse still, in this numerically encompassed world, he is often describing qualities. – Nisbett (1976:184)

From an epistemological point of view Lorenz was unusually reflective about the method he advocated as an ethologist thanks to his life-long interest in clarifying the preconditions of human knowledge. To his background in the three fields of medicine, zoology, and psychology he added a determination to pay attention to epistemological issues raised by ethology, for it is "even more necessary in ethology than other branches of biology to know the limitations of one's own perceiving apparatus." (Lorenz 1977:18) Since Lorenz wished to include human psychological processes within the scope of behavior studied by ethology, inner processes became for him as important to study as outer expressions in overt behavior. In this, he followed in the footsteps of his teacher, Jakob Johann von Uexküll.

Von Uexküll is known for having developed a theoretical vocabulary that avoids subjective terms when describing the inner states and processes that take place within an animal's nervous system. His representation of the animal's inner world is based on objective observations of its behavioral responses. In order to depict the experience that an animal has of its environment (its *Umgebung*), von Uexküll sought to reconstruct, in terms of empirical observations made by human scientists, how the animal's world of experience (its *Umwelt*) is functionally determined by the sensitivity and range of its sensory apparatus. From this epistemologically sophisticated biological point of view, von Uexküll recognized the reality of the innumerable individual worlds of animal and human subjects. Belief in the existence of any kind of single "extrasubjective" universe, in which all organisms live, he repudiated as unnecessary and inappropriate.[2] (See Lorenz 1970:276)

Although Lorenz did not accept all of von Uexküll's conclusions, Lorenz wrote that "ethology...owes more to his teaching than to any other school of behaviour study." (277; see also 274-5) As a result of von Uexküll's influence, Lorenz argued that experience comprises a genuine reality that can be studied. It includes both the perception of objects in the physical world as well as emotions, which have their source within the organism. "What is real, thus, is not at all only the physically definable and quantitatively verifiable, but also everything sensed and felt." (Lorenz 1987:236-7) The important, and for some, the controversial, step that Lorenz made in advocating this approach was to claim that "our subjective experiential processes possess the same degree of reality as everything that can be expressed

---

[2] Von Uexküll occasionally strayed from this strict point of view, as when he referred in a Kantian fashion to the concept of "nature" that lies beyond the appearances that are given in individual *Umwelten*: "The role which nature plays as the object of different scientists' worlds is highly contradictory. Should one attempt to combine her objective qualities, chaos would ensue.... Behind all the world..., there lies concealed, eternally beyond the reach of knowledge, the subject—Nature." (von Uexküll 1957:80)

in the terminologies of the exact natural sciences."[3] (5-6)

When it comes to an ethological study of human behavior, Lorenz added a second epistemological proposition: that inner states and their outward expression are essentially interconnected. "I wouldn't know where to draw the line between internal thought, which is not directly observable, and behavior, which is observable and is the result of [thinking]." (Evans 1975:5) In this way, by admitting all experiential data to have a degree of reality that is on a par with the "extrasubjective" reality reputedly studied by most science, and by emphasizing the essential interconnectedness of human inner and outer behavior, Lorenz established the theoretical foundation for what was to become his contribution to human psychological ethology. It would become possible to study, using the tools of empirical science, the inner, complex psychological behavior of human subjects as well as outward manifestations of those inner phenomena.

In order to study biological systems of this degree of complexity, especially keen powers of human observation are needed. Lorenz spoke of "persons gifted in Gestalt perception" (Evans 1975:12), a manner of speaking that has offended some of his critics through its claim to an elitism of human ability which they believe has no place in an egalitarian meter-reading paradigm of empirical science. Since "Gestalt perception" plays a central role in Lorenz's approach, we need to understand more fully what Lorenz meant by this phrase.

The concepts of Gestalt and Gestalt perception are fundamentally qualitative in nature. Lorenz described Gestalt perception in a number of complementary ways: It is most basically an ability that requires both intelligence and intuition to see a pattern in observations, "to winnow a few grains of knowledge out of a heap of information." (Lorenz 1970:I:xvi) Gestalt perception is what many call *induction*, a process that Lorenz characterized as "abstraction of a general law out of the observation of many special cases in which it prevails." (II:xix) Alternatively, Gestalt perception is what some have called "a clinical eye." (II:8) Lorenz argued that Gestalt perception is not mysterious, for it is used, though to different degrees, by everyone: It is the cognitive ability "...to disentangle the essential configuration common to all dogs from the background of inessential differences and which permits [one] to perceive, in the aunt's peke, the neighbour's dachshund, and the butcher's mastiff, *one* common Gestalt, that of *the* dog!" (II:253)

Gestalt perception, in short, is pattern recognition, the perception of lawfulness, the ability to detect principles that explain and encompass variation. Lorenz recognized three things about it: it develops in people with unreliable variability, it does not lend itself to quantified understanding, and it cannot be taught. (Lorenz 1970:II:313) So understood, one could anticipate that Gestalt perception would not be accepted as a popular analytical tool in the contemporary democratized model of empirical science. During his entire professional life, Lorenz was confronted—and indeed was often blocked—by the unquestioned conviction among scientists that has become dominant: that only through experimental means—in which every human scientist is placed on an equal basis with every other, in which the role of the human observer is minimized and emphasis is placed on duplication of experimental results under reproducible conditions—can valid empirical results be obtained.

---

[3] In making this assertion, Lorenz, although he does not refer to Husserl's work, placed himself firmly within the framework of Husserl's conception of phenomenology as a rigorous science. There is much in Lorenz's thought that resembles scientific phenomenology as advocated by Husserl early in his life —for example, the provision that descriptions need to be presuppositionless: "A simply prodigious amount of time, spent in presuppositionless observation, is necessary in order to collect and store the factual material which the great computing apparatus [the human brain] needs in order to be able to lift the gestalt from its background." (Lorenz 1981:47) What Lorenz was referring to here when he spoke of lifting "the gestalt from its background" will be made clear in the discussion that follows in the text.

Lorenz's opposition to the prevailing view acknowledged that Gestalt perception is essentially elitist. And yet this fact does not, he pointed out, invalidate Gestalt perception. But it may, first of all, underscore why it is that Lorenz's approach to human ethology has faced opposition, and secondly and perhaps more importantly, as we shall see, help to identify the way in which many of Lorenz's ethological conclusions are ultimately justified.

## The Hierarchy of Human Capacities

Before we turn to consider Lorenz's ethological observations concerning human aggressiveness, it is important to make explicit the frame of reference he applied to questions of value. For, as we shall see, his ethology of human aggressive behavior is linked with value judgments that place such behavior in a largely negative light and condemn it. Just as Lorenz refused to allow himself to make claims to knowledge without making his epistemological presuppositions explicit, in the same way he wished to make explicit the presuppositions involved in evaluative judgments about human behavior.

Value theory, or axiology, comes into the picture whenever evaluative rankings are made, as when it is said that one scientist has better observational skills than another, that the neurological complexity of one species is higher than another and hence is worthy of greater compassion, or that human aggressiveness has assumed a degree that is pathological and is in this sense undesirable. Lorenz's approach to ethology involves several evaluative rankings of this kind. He spoke, for example, of the way in which human beings value complex organisms more highly than those that are simple:

> We cannot help feeling that organic systems are the more valuable the more highly integrated they are, in fact, our accustomed way of calling some animals higher and some lower is the immediate outcome of this inescapable value judgment. Its axiomatic nature is easily demonstrated by the following thought-experiment. Visualize yourself confronted with the task of killing, one after the other, a cabbage, a fly, a fish, a lizard, a guinea pig, a cat, a dog, a monkey and a baby chimpanzee. In the unlikely case that you should experience no greater inhibitions in killing the chimpanzee than in destroying the cabbage or the fly, my advice to you is to commit suicide at your earliest possible convenience, because you are a...monstrosity and a public danger. (Evans 1975:227; cf. also Lorenz 1966:226 and Lorenz 1970:II:325)

What is at stake in this context is the existence, or its absence, of human compassion, a capacity unequally distributed among human beings. It is a capacity, like the observational ability of Gestalt perception, that can be ranked by the degree to which individuals possess it. Using compassion as a standard, we make evaluative judgments of our own behavior and that of others. When human beings lack compassion, this is, according to Lorenz, a psychological deficit; it is an "inability." (Evans 1975:233-4) And so, individuals can suffer from "value-blindness" in the sense that they are deficient in the capacity to recognize value—again in much the same way as a person may be deficient in a capacity to perceive Gestalts. Not having a trace of "sympathetic feeling" is an indication of an individual's deficient capacity for empathy. (Lorenz 1970:II:325) As we shall see, Lorenz associated such a deficiency with human pathology.

In addition to ranking individual human beings in terms of their capacities for Gestalt perception and compassion, Lorenz also applied the standard of intelligence, which is also self-evidently variable among people. Lorenz's assessment of the level of general human intelligence is low:

> If I had to believe that an all-powerful God had created humans as they are represented by an average of our species today *intentionally*, as they are, I would in truth be in despair about God. If these beings who are often not only so evil in their collective actions but also so dumb are supposed to be the likenesses of God, I then must say: "What a pitiful God!" (Lorenz 1987:242)

Lorenz occasionally referred in his writing to "the man of high value," "the fully superior person," or "the fully valuable person." What he seems to have meant by these characterizations is a person who combines the attributes of high intelligence and high moral worth. High intelligence is a human attribute that one understands comparatively clearly, but high moral worth calls for clarification. Lorenz does not provide much to go on. In an early paper written in 1940, which later became bitterly controversial for retrospective political, and not ethological, reasons, Lorenz wrote:

> The fully superior person [*Vollwertige*] reacts against contemporaries manifesting inferior traits by keeping away from them. But this reaction from a superior person is felt by the person with inferior traits [*Ausfallstypus*] as extremely galling, and he responds to it with boundless hatred. Where there is a sizeable group of persons with inferior traits, the fully valuable person who rejects them becomes highly unpopular. (Nisbett 1976:84, quoting Lorenz 1940:71)

Unfortunately, in writing about this topic Lorenz made recourse to some of the jargon associated with the National Socialist political environment of his time. He was to be hounded for many years due to the language he employed.[4] In response, he insisted that his choice of scientific language was altogether politically innocent. If one detaches Lorenz's observations from this potential taint, one is left with an ethologist's attempt to provide a picture of human variability that focuses on the unequally distributed capacities of intelligence, compassion, and high moral worth—the last trait being particularly in need of a more satisfying elaboration than is to be found in Lorenz's writings. Even ethologists—ironically including those who may choose to study the preceding three human traits—are similarly themselves unequal, and unequal as well when it comes to their individual observational skills and diagnostic insight. Lorenz accepted these variations. The persuasiveness of his ethological conclusions about the human species depends, as we shall see, on our willingness to accept the variability in individual human beings of these unequally distributed abilities.

## Pathology as a Source of Knowledge

> I do not think that a healthy philosophy of values can develop without a sense not only of what is good but also of what is evil. –Lorenz in Evans (1975:127)

The heading for this section is taken from a lecture that Lorenz gave in 1971 (Lorenz 1975). In it, he argued that when a biological system becomes pathological, its structure can

---

[4] In later years, Lorenz was unswerving in rebutting his critics: On the one hand, he condemned his own "naive error" (Lorenz quoted in Cox 1974:20) of using expressions popular at the time, but devoid for him of concrete political application, and, on the other hand, he maintained the scientific legitimacy of his observations. It is not my intention to discuss this issue here; it has been treated elsewhere in detail. See, e.g., Eisenberg (1972), Cox (1974), Nisbett (1976), Kalikow (1978 and 1983), Chorover (1979), Lewontin, Rose, & Kamin (1984), Richards (1987), Proctor (1988), Lerner (1992). My reason for mentioning Lorenz's politically controversial paper is to make explicit the way in which his comments about "superior" individual human beings became tainted, for some critics, by association with the language in use during an ugly period of German history.

more easily be understood when its pathology is understood. In other words, he saw in the identification of pathologies an opportunity to understand the organism better: "the pathological disturbance of a system, far from being an obstacle to its analysis, is indeed very often the key to it." (Evans 1975:174; see also Lorenz 1977:5) Throughout much of his research relating to human ethology, Lorenz stressed, in particular, the need for a study of the pathological behavior of the human species.

Combining his training as an ethologist and a physician, Lorenz identified a variety of malfunctions in human society that he claimed are clearly pathological in nature. (See, e.g., Lorenz 1977:5) He observed forms of society-wide, highly destructive pathology in human civilization that have the character of disease and specifically of mental illness. (See, e.g., Lorenz 1987:204) He urged the need for a study that would make use of the "diagnostic methods of medical science in order to study human civilization and the human mind." (Lorenz 1977:18) According to Lorenz, most of the pathology that afflicts our species has to do with psychological disorders associated with social and moral behavior. If there is any hope for mankind, it is imperative, he believed, that we reach a scientific understanding of these dysfunctional and destructive kinds of behavior. What is needed, although Lorenz did not use this phrase, is a pathology of man: It would comprise a reflective, scientific "self-examination" of human society, something that has never existed in human history, in much the same way as objective science had to wait for Galileo to be inaugurated. (245) Such a pathology of man "requires us to break down the barrier between the humanities and the sciences at a point where it is stoutly defended on both sides." (19) The reason for the need to bridge humanistic and scientific understanding is due to the inherently psychological and moral nature of the pathologies in question. Psychology and axiology have traditionally developed from roots deeply embedded in the humanities, but here the pathologies in question demand scientific, not purely humanistic, study.

Given Lorenz's training as a physician, it is to be expected that his understanding of disease would be based on the medical model. Lorenz was aware of the difficulties, even for a physician, in defining disease. Comfortable with qualitative and sometimes "fuzzy" understanding, Lorenz did not insist on a precise definition of disease. Instead, he emphasized the diagnostic skills of human experts, for it is their judgment that determines what is to qualify as pathological. "The diagnostic faculties of the physician...are to be found in their looking at a living system and, purely perceptually and, initially, without deliberation or reflection, being able to see that in the system something is awry. This accomplishment is the very same one known as the 'clinical eye' of the experienced physician." (Lorenz 1987:217)

Before turning in the next section to examine Lorenz's observations concerning the human species and its pathologies, it may be helpful to sum up what we have come to understand about his approach: First, the abilities of individual human beings are unequal, so that one must expect that individual capacities—of intelligence, compassion, and moral development—will be unequally distributed. In particular, the human capacity to recognize value, especially moral value, is undemocratically distributed, since compassion exists to widely varying degrees in individual human beings. Perhaps only "the fully superior person" is constitutionally—in terms of intelligence as well as moral development—able to distinguish what is morally right from wrong in a dependable manner in situations that incite many people to hostility and violence. Second, the ethologist's own specialized skills of observation and integrative pattern recognition are also unequally distributed, even among ethologists. Third, the ability to recognize pathology is similarly itself unequally shared.

These various inequalities of human capacity are, for Lorenz, an inescapable fact about reality. It is not a popular viewpoint today, which is not to say that it is mistaken. The observations Lorenz made about the human species are, whether one likes this or not, made from this hierarchical, non-egalitarian frame of reference. One might suspect that Lorenz, who wished for theoretical consistency, might even believe that the conclusions that he reached could only be recognized as valid to the degree that the reader has a certain level of requisite abilities, intellectually and morally. And we do occasionally find hints of this acknowledgment in Lorenz's writing, as when he commented that it has required a reader of a certain intelligence "to have read thus far" in one of his books. (Lorenz 1966:96) Accustomed as we are to maintaining at least the polite pretension of egalitarianism of mental capacity, this honesty may rankle some. But books do require of their readers different levels of intelligence, a fact that is undeniable and unavoidable.

Once these prerequisites of individual mental and moral capacity are satisfied, Lorenz believed that his conclusions about the human species followed. It is important to underscore that the validity of his conclusions is framework-relative in this way. Let us now see what those conclusions are.

## Human Aggression

[T]he imagination of man's heart is evil from his youth.... – *Genesis* 8:21

Even in connection with patterns of behavior that Lorenz judged to be pathological, he maintained the point of view of a scientist interested in the possible evolutionary function of that behavior. In the case of man, Lorenz observed that aggression between human beings, i.e., intraspecific aggression, has in the past evidently had an important survival value for the species by helping to limit its population growth. (Lorenz 1966:31) Intraspecific aggression also has the effect of dividing up the environment and its resources in a manner so that a larger population can exist than might otherwise be possible. (47) Under most circumstances and in most species, "we find that aggression, far from being the diabolical, destructive principle that classical psychoanalysis makes it out to be, is really an essential part of the life-preserving organization of instincts." (48)

Though aggression has species-preserving benefits for many animals, in the case of the human species, mankind has come to be violently aggressive toward its own members to a degree and with a destructive power that no longer have survival value. Instead, human aggression has, according to Lorenz, gone awry, becoming truly pathological. Human aggression has become, in Lorenz's words, the "greatest of all dangers" (Lorenz 1966:29), not only to man but to other species. Once our species developed weapons, began to use clothing, and accepted social organization, "an evil intra-specific selection must have set in." (157) Lorenz called this a "hereditary evil," and set out to "show how the misfunctioning of this social form of intra-specific aggression constitutes 'evil' in the real sense of the word, and how...[mankind's] social order...represents a model in which we can see some of the dangers threatening ourselves." (157) Lorenz's purpose in identifying pathological patterns of human behavior was to find ways of counteracting those pathologies, and to resist accepting such behavior as "something metaphysical and inevitable." (30)

Human aggression has become pathological, according to Lorenz, because people have no in-built inhibitions against killing their own kind. Most carnivorous species that are biologically well-equipped to kill one another do have such inhibitions, so that their aggressive behavior toward one another for the most part is dissipated harmlessly. In man, however, no such inhibitions are in force; he is, after all, when considered purely in terms of his natural biological endowment, a comparatively vulnerable, omnivorous creature deficient in the natural weapons that would allow him to kill large animals. But during his short evolutionary history he has developed weapons of ever-increasing destructiveness, and designed them so that they could be used at increasing distances, both physically and emotionally, from his opponents. At this point, with no significant inhibitions to deter him, mankind, according to Lorenz, became a pathologically self-destructive species.

In comparison with other species, mankind's aggressive behavior closely resembles the behavior of rats—for rats, like people, are incited to hatred by their awareness of others who belong to their own species but who are perceived to differ from them. The murderous intraspecific aggression of rats resembles its human counterpart:

> What rats do when a member of a strange rat clan enters their territory...is one of the most horrible and repulsive things which can be observed in animals. The strange rat may run around for minutes on end without having any idea of the terrible fate awaiting it; and the resident rats may continue for an equally long time with their ordinary affairs till finally the stranger comes close enough to one of them for it to get wind of the intruder. The informa-tion is transmitted like an electric shock through the resident rat, and at once the whole col-ony is alarmed by a process of mood transmission which is communicated in the Brown Rat by expression movements but in the House Rat by a sharp, shrill, satanic cry which is taken up by all members of the tribe within earshot.
>
> With their eyes bulging from their sockets, their hair standing on end, the rats set out on the rat hunt. (Lorenz 1966:161-2)

The result to the intruder is a violent death. What is the purpose of such murders, of such group hatred between clans of rats? Lorenz came to believe, with the group hate of people as well as of rats in view, that such behavior "is really a diabolical invention which serves no purpose." (163) It is evident that group hatred of this kind fails to serve a species-preserving value. Killings between rat clans "serve neither spatial distribution nor the selection of strong family defenders—for among rats these are seldom the fathers of the descendants." (163-4) Lorenz noted that the same predisposition to violent behavior against those who are differ-ent is expressed in the human phenomenon of bullying. When an individual diverges from conventionally accepted social norms, it is characteristic of men, women, and children to gang up on that person in a display of the group's readiness to defend its habitual behavior. (259)

If human aggression has become life-threatening to a degree that makes it legitimate to consider it a pathology, we may ask whether any other species are similarly pathological. According to Lorenz, the human species has a monopoly on truly large-scale murder. Ants, like rats, may also make war on their own kind. Hyenas sometimes do this, too, as does a certain species of lizard, and to a limited extent the Indian elephant may attack and kill other elephants. Certain monkeys and lions also may kill members of their own species, as when a male takes over a leadership position and kills the offspring of his predecessor. The diver, a northern loon, sometimes kills to defend territory. But, in the final analysis, the list of species that will engage in intraspecific killing is short and none compare with man in destructive-ness.

Lorenz observed that human aggression, whether or not it is genetically based, is cultivated and fostered through violence-gratifying entertainment and through the glorifica-tion of violence in both human entertainment and real life. When the National Commission on the Causes and Prevention of Violence (1969) concluded that violence on television and film is highly destructive and should be eliminated, Lorenz noted that the media's emphasis on violence may lessen or remove already unstable human inhibitions against violence, "creating a social climate which increasingly tolerates them." (Evans 1975:40-1)

According to Lorenz, militant enthusiasm in human groups is aroused when members of the group believe they are threatened, when they believe that the threat originates from a group that opposes their preferred values, when the members of the group stimulate and reinforce one another's level of militant arousal, and when their agitation is focused against a common enemy by a charismatic leader. Lorenz observed that mankind's combativeness is due to the propensity of human beings of their own volition to divide themselves into opposing camps "because this is the adequate stimulus situation to arouse militant enthusiasm in a satisfying manner." (Lorenz 1966:271) The emotional gratification of herd togetherness "is greatly enhanced by the presence of a definite, threatening enemy whom it is possible to hate." (285) In this connection, Lorenz quoted Erich von Holst's remark:

> If ever a doctrine of universal salvation should gain ascendancy over the whole earth to the exclusion of all others, it would at once divide into two strongly opposing factions (one's own true one and the other heretical one) and hostility and war would thrive as before, mankind being—unfortunately—what it is! (271)

Lorenz explained this pattern of human behavior in terms of what he calls a "hydraulic model" of aggression: By this, he meant that people build up aggressive pressure, whether or not there are environmental reasons for this. Once a certain explosive pressure is bottled up, people will break free from social constraints and let aggression loose. If Lorenz were alive today, one can imagine that he would regard such phenomena as "road rage," "air rage," "shopper's rage," etc., to be human behavioral expressions of pressure that has built up and that breaches the easiest channel. As a consequence of his hydraulic account, Lorenz proposed that mankind should provide more opportunities for the redirection of aggression into harmless channels, such as sport. But other ethologists, Tinbergen and later Eibl-Eibesfeldt among them, saw the herd excitement of sports enthusiasts in a different light, since for spectators as well as athletes, the unrestrained freedom to express aggression in sport can be self-reinforcing rather than cathartic, and influence human behavior outside of the arena. (Nisbett 1976:161; Eibl-Eibesfeldt 1972:77n) It seems odd that Lorenz himself did not examine the possibility that aggressive sports may exacerbate human aggression, given his misgivings over the emphasis on violence by the media.

An important psychological factor that promotes aggression is ideology, according to Lorenz, for ideology blurs the boundary between internal thought and the behavior which is its result. (Evans 1975:5) Lorenz spoke of "dangerous thought habits" (167), which encourage people to fight for ideals they hold in common, often with a force that renders irrelevant both what it is that the ideals themselves stand for, as well as their intrinsic value. (Lorenz 1966:267) Human groups invest zealous devotion in the symbols they create, which they come to believe possess an autonomy of their own. In this process of idolatry, the emotional security of the group is heightened. The group's symbols, once they have acquired an imaginary autonomy, become independent sources of motivation for human aggression. (See Lorenz 1966:75)

And so the autonomy that man gives to his ideologies and the transcendence over himself that he accords to his moral ideals foster human aggression. Ideological convictions are often so strongly ingrained that "[m]en may enjoy the feeling of absolute righteousness even while they commit atrocities." (Lorenz 1966:269) Furthermore, the emotional investment that people make in their preferred ideologies is utterly impenetrable to reason. Mankind's "dangerous thought habits" repel reasoning like a raincoat; people listen with their emotions, and not with their minds:

> In reality, even the fullest rational insight into the consequences of an action and into the logical consistency of its premise would not result in an imperative or in a prohibition, were it not for some emotional, in other words instinctive, source of energy supplying motiva-

tion.... It is hard to believe that a man will refrain from a certain action which natural inclination urges him to perform only because he has realized that it involves a logical
contradiction. (247)

When human aggression takes over, reason ceases to control thinking or behavior. Lorenz
recalled the Ukrainian proverb: "When the banner is unfurled, all reason is in the trumpet."
(269) The inflamed emotional state of the aggressive herd resembles a group panic attack of
"...men fundamentally disciplined and self-controlled, rushing blindly along, closely huddled,
all in the same direction, with eyes protruding, chests heaving, and trampling underfoot
everything that comes in their way, exactly like stampeding ungulates, and no more
accessible to reason than they." (149)

In effect, human aggression subverts intelligence. Lorenz expressed this in terms of the
close connection between human aggression and human stupidity.

> Man...has become so clever that he sufficiently comprehends the natural preconditions of his
> life in order to destroy them, but he is not smart enough to maintain these natural precondi-
> tions.... I consider the collective stupidity of mankind—which is somehow incapable of
> learning from truly negative experiences and turning them into good—very great indeed.
> (Lorenz 1990:163, 131)

This was not an attempt to administer a misanthropic slap to the face of the human species,
but an ethologist's candid observation of the limitation of certain human capacities. Human
stupidity, a deficit of intelligence that Lorenz observed to be refractory to improvement, is
seldom identified by psychologists of aggression as a principal factor in promoting and sustaining mankind's aggressiveness and destructiveness. Lorenz felt strongly justified in this
diagnosis of human stupidity, as did Tinbergen, who wrote that as a species we may ultimately succumb due "to our own stupidity." (Tinbergen 1968:1418) A later chapter in the
present volume specifically examines the pathology of human stupidity (Chapter 18).

In Lorenz's implied estimation, one of the signs of human stupidity is the species'
resistance to efforts that would improve its condition by guiding human reproduction
through the selection of individuals of high intelligence and moral development. Eugenics
applied to the human species has yet to outlive its ugly Nazi connotations, and probably for
this reason Lorenz in his writing often seemed intentionally to avoid an outright recommen-
dation of human eugenics. But he makes a point of underscoring mankind's success in
manipulating the genetic constitution of other species. As a result of human selection, dogs,
for example, have come to possess many of "those attributes regarded as human virtues: the
capacities for love and for fidelity, courage and fortitude, bravery and obedience." Within a
relatively short evolutionary span of time, selective reproduction controlled by man has led
to "creatures...that excel us in all these qualities." (Lorenz 1987:43) Yet, selective family
planning remains socially and politically objectionable, in spite of successes with nonhuman
animals.

## Lorenz's Critics

Lorenz's theory of human aggression has been criticized for three principal reasons: that
it does not acknowledge the extent to which some nonhuman species engage in aggression
toward their own members, that it places excessive emphasis on the claim that human
aggression is a genetically inborn trait, and, as we have already noted, that the observations
upon which the theory is based are most often qualitative in nature. In connection with the
first criticism, later in Lorenz's life evidence of intraspecies aggression among an increasing

number of nonhuman species began to accumulate. He had no difficulty accommodating the latest discoveries, which he felt did not diminish the validity of the observations he made about human aggression. (See Evans 1975:36, Nisbett 1976:155ff) As for the second criticism, relating to the claim that human aggression is inborn, one needs to recognize that Lorenz did not claim in his principal study of human aggression (Lorenz 1966) that human aggression is genetically based. (Cf. also Lorenz 1987:158-9) We should do well to ignore the issue, since we are interested here only in observable facts that shed light on the dynamics of human aggressive behavior. Whether human aggression will prove to be genetically encoded is a question whose answer evidently does not lie within the covers of a book written today, but in the laboratories of the future. It is with the third criticism that we are primarily concerned.

Most directly related to the present study is Lorenz's conclusion that human aggression is a pathology. A close reading of Lorenz suggests that this conclusion rests on three subordinate claims: first, that the nature and extent of human aggressiveness form a dangerous obstacle to the survival of the species; second, that human aggression is an aberrant behavior, many magnitudes more serious in its destructiveness than the behavior of other species; and, third, that it is morally to be condemned. The first two factual claims are clearly on different levels of discourse or conceptualization compared with the third, which involves a value judgment. Lorenz believed that the two factual claims legitimized his application of the term 'pathology' to human intraspecific aggression, while the third claim legitimized his choice of the word 'evil'.

We recall that Lorenz was trained as a physician, and that he cultivated a life-long, serious interest in epistemology and theory of value. For Lorenz, evil and pathology are not loose metaphors, but concepts applied with self-awareness to phenomena observed carefully and patiently. We also recall that Lorenz, in reaching his conclusions about mankind, presupposed on the part of fellow researchers a certain level of intelligence, pattern recognition, compassion, and moral development; and certainly these must also be present to a sufficient degree in his readers if they are to understand and accept his research conclusions. If one is to evaluate behavior, and not merely count, measure, and graph it, one is forced to make use of a qualitative reference frame—for values are not to be found in numbers. Those who insist upon quantification as the sole criterion of scientific meaningfulness will generally not find Lorenz's observations or his conclusions to their liking. A rigid insistence upon quantification reflects an "ideological limitation," as Lorenz put it. (Nisbett 1976:149) As we shall see in Part III of this book, epistemological self-understanding of the kind that Lorenz wished brings with it the tools that make legitimate and theoretically compelling many of the qualitative conclusions that he reached.

## Mankind's Future

An unprejudiced observer from another planet, looking upon man as he is today, in his hand the atom bomb, the product of his intelligence, in his heart the aggression drive inherited from his anthropoid ancestors, which this same intelligence cannot control, would not prophesy long life for the species. – Lorenz (1966:49)

Although Lorenz tried to express optimism about the human species from time to time, the picture one assembles after a careful study of Lorenz's writing is not one of hope. As a scientist, he had a low opinion of speculative predictions, and yet, as an ethologist, he described what he saw: pathological patterns of human behavior that have come to possess a life of their own. The pathologies he observed include human overpopulation, environmental destruction, a species-wide selfish desire for immediate gratification, susceptibility to ideological indoctrination (cf. Nisbett 1976:176), coupled, as we have seen, with a generally low level of moral development and pronounced stupidity. Among the consequences of such patterns of psychological and physical behavior are aggression and destructiveness, directed toward ourselves and other species.

Perhaps the most direct prediction Lorenz made is this: "If I am compelled to prognosticate—something that I do not like to do and that I do only with certain provisos—then I would have to say that things will have to get much worse before they get better. There must be a turning point, because otherwise mankind has had it." (Lorenz 1990:103) The turning point for the species, according to Lorenz, will likely involve escalating crises due to overpopulation. Here, Lorenz again compared human society with that of the rat, bringing in the dispassionate perspective of a fictitious alien observer:

> If...our Martian naturalist knew of the explosive rise in human population, the ever-increasing destructiveness of weapons, and the division of mankind into political camps, he would not expect the future of humanity to be more rosy than that of several hostile clans of rats on a ship almost devoid of food. And this prognosis would even be optimistic, for in the case of rats, reproduction stops automatically when a certain state of over-crowding is reached while man as yet has no workable system for preventing the so-called population explosion. (Lorenz 1966:238)

If Lorenz were called upon to identify one factor that incarnates human stupidity, it would be mankind's unrestrained reproduction, an observation with which Tinbergen agreed. (See Nisbett 1976:161) Lorenz repeatedly tried to drive this observation home in various of his books: "All the dangers that threaten mankind today result, in the final analysis, from overpopulation.... Of course, one tries to find countervailing measures, but these solutions not only seem ineffective but indeed are." (Lorenz 1990:149; cf. also Evans 1975:73)

Like Morley Roberts, Karl Menninger, Quincy Wright, and Alan Gregg, whose work is discussed in other chapters,[5] Lorenz saw an accurate parallel between the proliferation of the human population and the growth of a cancer:

> If you look at a cancer under the microscope, a cross section with cells of healthy tissue, it looks exactly like an aerial view of a city in which the old sections are surrounded by new, irregularly built regions or else by those that are monotonously geometric.... The parallels between the formation of malignant tumors and cities in a state of cultural decay are very wide-ranging. (Lorenz 1990:37-8)

Toward the end of a life devoted to the observation of animal and human behavior, Lorenz came to feel that, with respect to mankind's future, "the main problems that face us today are ethical and moral." (Evans 1975:46) We find in Lorenz's writings two possible paths that are open to mankind if we are to become a morally enlightened species. One is selective family planning, or eugenics, which as noted Lorenz apparently felt is unpromising in the present political climate. What little optimism remains is the hope that we can

> ...reduce the enthusiasm for war. You cannot teach a person *not* to be enthusiastic, but you can teach him what to be enthusiastic *about:* what heroes to imitate, what heroes to be enthusiastic about.... You can teach a person what cause to embrace, what causes are worthy of embracing.... We must get accustomed to the fact that war is not functional any more. With

---

[5] See, e.g., the discussion of Roberts (1926) in Chapter 4 of the present volume; of Menninger (1966) in Chapter 8; of Wright (1942) in Chapter 9; of Gregg (1955) in Chapter 17.

nuclear weapons, war means suicide. I think that the elimination of war should be the major
task of social education today. (45)

Yet, Lorenz himself was pessimistic that social education can really make a meaningful
difference in reducing the pathology of evil that he observed in human behavior and human
thinking. He referred to the widespread belief that, "given proper education, all men can be
turned into angelically ideal citizens," and commented: "If there is anything more dangerous
than founding public policy on a lie, it is living in a fool's paradise." (Lorenz 1970:I:xiv)[6]
Later chapters in this work will make evident why it is that human evil is so resistant to our
best-intentioned efforts.

## IRENÄUS EIBL-EIBESFELDT

[M]en with the emotional baggage of stone age hunter-gatherers today engage in private car
races on the highways, and, as leaders of the superpowers, control weapons and armies capable of igniting the world. – Eibl-Eibesfeldt (1989:719)

In this section, I will summarize, but not discuss in detail, certain of the observations
and conclusions of Irenäus Eibl-Eibesfeldt, whose research, perhaps more than that of other
ethologists since Lorenz, has been concerned with the ethology of human evil. I do not
discuss the work of other post-Lorenz ethologists due to reasons of space, and not rele-
vance. In comparing the work of Lorenz and Eibl-Eibesfeldt, we shall find that the conclusions they reached are complementary and often identical.

Eibl-Eibesfeldt (1928- ), whose training in ethology took place under Lorenz's supervi-
sion, shared Lorenz's belief that ethology can make significant contributions to the solution
of certain of the large-scale problems that face mankind. To a great extent, this belief, even
among ethologists, is still unfashionable. An excess of caution among researchers prevails,
which limits their willingness to address larger problems. In an effort to respond to his
professional peers, Eibl-Eibesfeldt has combined Lorenz's qualitative method with a disciplined empirical approach. He has sought to collect data that demonstrate the existence of
universal patterns of behavior among human beings in all societies, and is perhaps best
known for his carefully documented observations of certain human facial expressions, which
ethological evidence shows are universal. In his numerous publications, Eibl-Eibesfeldt has
described and discussed certain other ethological observations relating to the human species.
Among them are the following (which do not reflect the chronological order in which they
appear in Eibl-Eibesfeldt's publications):

In connection with the species as a whole, mankind will remain its own greatest
enemy—as long as we are unable to bring the propensity for human aggression under
control. (Eibl-Eibesfeldt 1972:1) Mankind today is responsible for behavior that jeopardizes
our survival, as well as that of other species. Such behavior "may be considered as pathological and thus as evil." (Eibl-Eibesfeldt 1982:58; cf. also Eibl-Eibesfeldt 1993c) Furthermore,
the behavior of the human species has resulted in an ecological crisis due to massive overpopulation, environmental depredation, and depletion of global resources. It is plausible that
this destructive behavior will lead to violent international conflict over the last existing
resources. (Eibl-Eibesfeldt 1989:421)

---

[6] Although Lorenz was an outspoken critic of education as a panacea for human aggression, he also
occasionally defended it, as when he wrote: "All of these high hopes [for human improvement]
depend, of course, on education...." (Evans 1975:267) But admittedly he had no concrete idea how
education could be expected to perform this magic, given mankind's present psychological structure.

Human aggression serves specific functions, among them: territorial acquisition, defense of property, of social relationships, of social rank, etc. (Eibl-Eibesfeldt 1989:391) Human aggression is universal: Hunters and gatherers, contrary to the romantic view of some anthropologists, are not peaceful. (Eibl-Eibesfeldt 1979:131-161) It is evident "[t]hat men killed each other in the Stone Age, and in all other ages as well...." (Eibl-Eibesfeldt 1979:127; cf. also Eibl-Eibesfeldt 1970:506ff) Although human aggression is universal and serves certain functions, there exist "pathological forms of aggression" in genocide, sadistic murder, torture, etc. But Eibl-Eibesfeldt has, by his own choice (Eibl-Eibesfeldt 1989:408), generally avoided the study of such extreme forms of aggression, admittedly a serious limitation for an account of human aggression.

Eibl-Eibesfeldt has argued on behalf of a "functional point of view" in ethology, stressing the need for a study of the adaptive value of behaviors. In the case of human aggression, the phenomenon is sufficiently complex, according to him, so that it cannot be reduced entirely to genetic factors, or entirely to environmental conditions. When we understand such complex phenomena functionally, we see how they serve as responses to an organism's adaptive needs and interests. (Eibl-Eibesfeldt 1979:95, 114, 168) For example, ethological evidence confirms the existence of a universal human propensity to obey authority. From the standpoint of functional understanding, it makes no difference whether obedience to authority is the result of an inborn or a learned disposition. (Eibl-Eibesfeldt 1979:94-5) In Eibl-Eibesfeldt's view, it is sufficient and informative to recognize how obedience to authority serves human adaptive needs.

Eibl-Eibesfeldt has observed that people glorify aggression throughout the world in the form of heroes, symbols representing aggressive animals (the eagle, lion, bear, etc.), flags, national holidays that celebrate aggressive acts in history, etc. (Eibl-Eibesfeldt 1972:74) The human spectator's enjoyment of violence, brutality, and sadism, as in aggressive films and sports, arouses aggressive feelings, which can spread beyond violent entertainment into real life. (77n) Specifically, human aggressive behavior has a definite tension-releasing effect, but this is short-lived; the long-term effect of habitually discharging aggression (e.g., by watching violent sports, television, and films) is to reinforce aggressiveness, since "every drive system becomes entrained by repeated action." (Eibl-Eibesfeldt 1989:384) Adding to this is the fact that people imitate or learn from socially approved models of behavior. Although not fully endorsing Lorenz's hydraulic theory of aggression, Eibl-Eibesfeldt has observed that men are "often motivated aggressively without apparent external causes." They feel an appetite for aggression, and some seek aggressive confrontations. (380)

Aggression by human groups leads to the formation of "group cement," which bonds people together into strong, emotionally unified collectives. (Eibl-Eibesfeldt 1972:165) Fear simultaneously strengthens the inner bonds of the group, and encourages fear of enemies and loyalty to a defending leader. (Eibl-Eibesfeldt 1970:503) Under conditions which promote group fear, human populations "become infantilized," responding easily to leaders who offer them security. (Eibl-Eibesfeldt 1982:64) Furthermore, according to Eibl-Eibesfeldt, it is a natural human tendency to cluster in small groups (Eibl-Eibesfeldt 1970:509), which in turn is associated with so-called "pseudospeciation" and the consequent dehumanization of other groups: That is to say, human groups willfully seek to identify, or create, group distinctions that enable them to differentiate and distance themselves from others. "A human being has the ability to convince himself that others are not fellow humans.... In my opinion one of man's most dangerous abilities is this of dehumanizing his fellows, for only through this mechanism can he become a merciless killer." (Eibl-Eibesfeldt 1970:511)

Eibl-Eibesfeldt has found that the related phenomenon of bullying among children appears to be universal: They "mock those who deviate in their behaviour or appearance from the norm and they do it in all cultures we have studied so far." (62) Related to the phenomenon of bullying among children is society's willingness to permit it, for the permissive upbringing of children tends to produce highly aggressive adults. (Eibl-Eibesfeldt 1972:82; Eibl-Eibesfeldt 1989:392, citing Rothchild & Wolf 1976)

In connection with war, Eibl-Eibesfeldt has observed that war is a universal human phenomenon, found in all societies. Like Lorenz, he has noted that intraspecific killing is extremely rare among other higher vertebrates, and is prevented by inborn inhibitions. (Eibl-Eibesfeldt 1979:6n, 92, 131-61; Eibl-Eibesfeldt 1993c:145) In his view, man's propensity to war is the result of cultural evolution. War historically has served a variety of functions (for instance, acquisition of territory and resources) and, in this context, according to Eibl-Eibesfeldt, should not be considered pathological. (Eibl-Eibesfeldt 1979:123, 180, 186; Eibl-Eibesfeldt 1993c:145) However, fear between opposing groups has become dangerously self-reinforcing, leading to increased aggression on a scale of destructiveness that today does justify the judgment that it is pathological. (Eibl-Eibesfeldt 1982)

In connection with human patterns of thinking, Eibl-Eibesfeldt observed that people are subject to certain "compulsions or delusions of thought," which, although they have an evolutionary basis, are "deceptions inherent in the inaccuracy of our thinking apparatus." (Eibl-Eibesfeldt 1979:167) However, he did not elaborate upon this idea in any detail, as Lorenz also failed to do in connection with "dangerous thought habits," mentioned earlier. Finally, according to Eibl-Eibesfeldt, human beings are not inherently rational. What people prefer often has no rational basis: "we feel values without being able to give reasons for them." (Eibl-Eibesfeldt 1979:232)

Eibl-Eibesfeldt's theory of human aggression can be expressed in condensed form as involving a characteristic sequence of steps: The aggressor—whether an individual or a group—begins the escalating process by propounding a view that the opposing individual or group is less than human. When this attitude does not rid the aggressor of the problem posed by the enemy, the aggressor tries to evade individual responsibility by camouflaging aggression toward the enemy under the veil of duty and obedience to orders. When these attitudes and corresponding behavior still do not suffice, the aggressor further inflames his or her group's emotions by defensive posturing, citing the need for retaliation, exalting its group's violence and heroism, and in the process dismissing moral scruples. (Eibl-Eibesfeldt 1979:189)

On the basis of a lifetime's ethological research focused in large measure on the human species, Eibl-Eibesfeldt has claimed that mankind's survival requires that we recognize the following:

- Whether or not aggression has a genetic basis, human groups can develop effective control over their aggressive behavior through knowledge of its causes. (Eibl-Eibesfeldt 1970:505-6)

- Specifically, a primary and essential condition of world peace is effective birth control. The "biological time bomb" is real. (Eibl-Eibesfeldt 1972:229)

- Peaceful coexistence among human groups is possible, but requires education for peace, tolerance, and willingness to understand. (Eibl-Eibesfeldt 1979:241)

Unfortunately, Eibl-Eibesfeldt, like most of the researchers whose work is discussed in the present volume, has favored what he believes to be constructive recommendations, but has failed to indicate how—in a manner consistent with his observations of the human species—they can be realized. How are we to change environmental conditions so as to lessen human violence and cruelty? How are we to institute world-wide effective birth control? How are we to educate for peace, tolerance, and mutual understanding? How are we to accomplish these things, given mankind's ethologically evident shortcomings? —These pressing and by no means unexpected questions remain unanswered. Eibl-Eibesfeldt's uninformative recommendations for the future therefore cannot help but seem idealistic and perhaps naive.

Moreover, his observations about human aggression are intellectually more difficult to come to grips with than Lorenz's, because Eibl-Eibesfeldt is not consistent in his use, or avoidance, of explicitly moral norms. Although, as we have seen, he sometimes uses morally evaluative words like 'evil', the general inclination expressed in his writing is to avoid the application of moral concepts to large-scale patterns of human behavior, and to evaluate such behavior, instead, in terms of adaptedness. In his substantial work, *Human Ethology*, he wrote, for example: "The ideal norm is measured with the yardstick of adaptedness. Statistical norms tell us nothing about the way conditions should be." (Eibl-Eibesfeldt 1989:708) And so, for Eibl-Eibesfeldt, human warfare in the past—when it did not yet have the potential to bring about Armageddon—served certain adaptive functions, and so was not, in his view, pathological.[7] But, he tells us, now that human warfare can bring about world-wide devastation, the fear between human groups, which leads to war, is genuinely pathological, it is "evil." For an author who employs morally condemnatory concepts, one is disappointed that there is no clear theoretical explanation of the connection between human pathology and theory of value, and, on a less abstract level, that there is no attempt to situate "pathological forms of aggression" (as in the Holocaust) within Eibl-Eibesfeldt's description of human aggression, which must therefore be judged more limited in scope than Lorenz's.

For a more comprehensive account of human aggression, its pathology, and the basis for judgments concerning human evil, we must look elsewhere, as we shall do in subsequent chapters.

---

[7] And yet, as we have seen in earlier chapters, many pathologies do certainly serve specific functions, and many of these are clearly adaptive, as in the case, for example, of individuals whose "mental illness" is the most adaptive behavior they have been able to find. Psychiatrist Ronald Hargreaves, for example, when attempting to understand a mental disorder would ask what its survival value to the patient may be. (Evans 1975:173) Virtually any pathology serves definite functions, when assessed from an appropriate point of view. To counter-balance this recognition, we recall that the identification of a condition as pathological is an expression of judgment that it is undesirable.

# CHAPTER 11

# TOWARD A UNIFIED PSYCHOLOGY OF GENOCIDE

If [history] had a voice, it would sound as one long moan of anguish.... [M]ake real to your-self the vision of every blood-stained page—stand in the presence of the ravening con-queror, the savage tyrant—tread the stones of the dungeon and of the torture-room—feel the fire of the stake—hear the cries of that multitude which no man can number, the victims of calamity, of oppression, of fierce injustice in its myriad forms, in every land, in every age—and what joy have you of your historic reading? One would need to be a devil to un-derstand it thus, and yet to delight in it.... And if anyone soothes himself with the reflection that such outrages can happen no more, that mankind has passed beyond such hideous pos-sibility, he is better acquainted with books than with human nature. – Gissing (1918:223-5)

[M]ay God preserve us from all that we can get accustomed to. – Singer (1982:134)

## INTRODUCTION

This and the next have been the most difficult chapters in this book for the author to research and write. No words can communicate what happens to one's soul after studying the many horrors everyday people have inflicted upon others for reasons that range from the absurd to the fanatical. Detailed descriptions of genocide and of the Holocaust in particular turn killing and human suffering into a pornography of murder and brutality. Such accounts tell us what many of us would prefer not to know—when man becomes a mon-strosity to himself, and the human evil he perpetrates is hideous, obscene, and contemptible. If pages can be said to have been written in anguish, these have.

In the previous chapter we touched on the controversy over the question whether human aggression is mainly acquired or primarily genetic. The study of genocide has fol-lowed a parallel pattern, asking instead whether the perpetration of genocide is mainly due to situational factors, or whether genocide is primarily a consequence of normal people engaged in gratifying deeply rooted psychological needs. On the one hand, situational arguments cite such forces as the psychopathology of leaders (e.g., Victor 1998), the "culture of cruelty" that comes to be established in a genocidal society (e.g., Katz 1993), or the frustration of basic human needs that leads people to desperate, monstrous behavior (e.g., Dollard *et al.* 1939; Staub 1989; Berkowitz 1989). On the other hand, arguments that have come from individual and group psychology point to the results of obedience studies (e.g., Milgram 1974), to the psychology of prejudice (e.g., Allport 1954) and the psychology of extreme hatred (e.g., Goldhagen 1996), and to the desire for vengeance and the fear of retaliation (e.g., Kressel 1996).

When attempts are made to focus upon one or a small number of causes of genocide there is a temptation to become reductionist in order to simplify a complex phenomenon, as well as to localize blame and to devise potential solutions. Human reality, however, is not theoretically "neat." There exist numerous predisposing or contributing conditions that lead to genocide, but they have not been brought together within the framework of a unified psychology of genocide. In this chapter, I want to place the numerous leading accounts of these predisposing conditions side-by-side so that we may gain an inclusive picture of the variable conditions that incite groups of people to engage in the mass killing of other groups of people who are perceived to be "different." It will then be possible to put the pieces together into a whole which is the emotional constitution of the normal person, and to offer a simplified, but not over-simplified, unitary account of the psychology of genocide. To this end, I want in this chapter to discuss psychological accounts of genocide that have been proposed, recognizing that the predisposing conditions they have identified are part of a continuum of emotions found in the majority of people. In the next chapter, I turn to a more specific consideration: the psychology of the Holocaust. There, I consider the pathology of anti-Semitism and its role in the Holocaust, and then examine the psychology of five different groups that played distinct roles in the Holocaust: the Nazi leaders, the German physicians who contributed to the atrocities, the individual submissive bystanders and nations who passively stood by, the individuals who refused to participate in mass murder, and those who actively resisted. We will then try to reach some clarity about what the psychology of genocide teaches us, and discuss some of the solutions to this human evil that have been proposed. Last, we will look at genocide in terms of its bearing on moral relativism. In the course of these discussions, I see no reason to burden the reader with graphic depictions of the innumerable atrocities which any reader can find elsewhere, and so the point of view here is predominantly theoretical in an effort to understand and explain.

Some preliminary perspective is useful before we begin. The word 'genocide' was coined in 1944 in a book by Raphael Lemkin, *Axis Rule in Occupied Europe*. The word combines the Greek '*genos*', meaning race or tribe, with the Latin '*cide*', to kill. 'Genocide' has come to be applied to the mass murder of any group of people, perpetrated for whatever reasons, and it is in this extended sense that I will use it here.

It is plausible to say that genocide has been practiced for the duration of human history—for as long as human beings separated themselves from one another into competitive groups and then chose to kill the members of opposing groups. Those who have studied individual genocides have urged the need for a specific psychology of genocide. On a basic level, one researcher has claimed: "The only hope lies in understanding the human impulse to hate and, more important, the forces that transform that impulse into action." He goes on to say: "Traditional explanations based on economics and politics provide part of the answer, but the deepest understanding emerges from psychology." (Kressel 1996:2, 8) Another genocide scholar has commented: "There is a substantial historical and descriptive literature on...genocide and mass killing...but surprisingly little analysis of the psychological, cultural, and social origins, except in the case of the Holocaust, but even here no in-depth psychological-cultural analysis exists." (Staub 1989:28)

The need for a specifically psychological focus has, to some extent, been impeded by the widespread feeling that genocide is such a powerful and irrational force in humanity's emotional constitution as to be intractable to intellectual understanding, and that even if such understanding were reached, it would remain helpless in lessening that force. As one author put it: "An intellectual understanding of genocide constitutes a very weak defense against the pressures, emotions, and beliefs that typically lead to mass murder." (Kressel 1996:273). Certainly many who have studied genocide have come away with a belief that this is so.

Further, as one might expect, research concerning the psychology of genocide has been impeded by human denial and self-deception. As psychiatrist G. M. Gilbert put this, after a close study of the Nazi leaders in Nuremberg: "It is possible to look at things without fully perceiving them, to divert one's attention from the unpleasant to the pleasant, to suspend the process of rational inference in mid-air, and to distort one's insights to avert anxiety." (Gilbert 1950:275) He goes on to say that such self-deception is not "merely a defense mechanism of the weak, the immature, the inadequate and ultrasuggestible. To a large extent, it is part of the normal adjustive process of the human quest for security in a world of conflicting values." (276 )

Perhaps more than anything else, these three things—a sense of the helplessness of intellectual understanding, the tendency to engage in denial, and a need for self-deception— have stood in the way of many who might otherwise have tried to bring genocide within the compass of psychological study. However, in spite of these deterrents, significant research, largely since World War II, has resulted in a number of general, psychologically-focused accounts of genocide. Among them is the thesis that every genocidal killer is "pathologically ill": "[T]he man within him is pathologically ill. Nature has struck him with the illness of sadism, and this disease has penetrated into the very fiber of his being." (Kaplan 1973:87) Alternatively, it has been proposed that "it takes only one person to lead a people to geno- cide"—a charismatic leader who seeks to solve the problems of a nation by recourse to scapegoating. (Victor 1998:217) A broader perspective has occasionally been advocated, as in the theory that it takes a suitably constituted people to be roused to genocide: "[T]he leader's power rests on the people's availability to violence." (Charny & Rapaport 1982:196) And, as we have noted already, there is a tendency to blame the situation. As one author has asked: "Is evil done by evil men, or by ordinary people who are responding, not to malevolent drives within themselves, but as creatures of social forces beyond their control; as ordinary men, trapped in an evil situation?" (Zillmer *et al.* 1995:176) In this vein, one author has proposed that people are "beguiled" into doing evil as a result of a society's "packaging of evil" in a belief-system that makes evil acceptable to ordinary people who might not other- wise commit it. (Katz 1993) —General theories of genocide offer a wide choice of where responsibility is to be localized: that it is the killers who are sick, that genocide is incited by a charismatic leader, that it takes a suitably aroused people, or an appropriately motivating situation. Plausibly there is truth in each account.

A more inclusive approach has been recommended by Staub (1989). In Staub's view the main factors responsible for genocidal killing include the compartmentalization of bureau- cratic roles, a tendency to use euphemistic language ("the Final Solution," etc.), obedience to authority and the desire to obey, existing psycho-social conditions in a society, prevailing ideologies and prejudices, the role of the family, the personality structure and psychopa- thology of individual leaders, the degree to which the actions of victims may cause a back- lash of violence against them, the role of difficult life conditions, the psychological needs fulfilled by scapegoating, and the devaluation of enemies which results in a suspension of normal moral inhibitions against hurting and killing others. Staub's analysis is detailed, insightful, and clearly motivated by an interest in comprehensiveness. The wide range of interrelated variables, such as those just enumerated, of course makes it challengingly diffi- cult to reach specific and concrete conclusions concerning the psychology of genocide and its possible treatment. What is required is a more systematically integrated theoretical frame- work that has yet to be provided.

## CONDITIONS THAT CONTRIBUTE TO GENOCIDE

Drunk with evil, he feels in himself the lightness of heart and peace of mind which a good conscience and the satisfaction of a duty well done bring. – Sartre (1948:50)

As we have begun to see, many predisposing conditions underlie genocide. To see some integrating order in their number, it is useful to place them along a continuum, for they form overlapping, interlinked, and mutually reinforcing emotional and cognitive constituents of human reality. The individual's internal emotional and conceptual makeup may be located at one end; the relationship of the individual to his or her immediate personal reality is placed in the middle range; and at the opposite end is placed the individual's more external relationship to his or her social group and the relationships among different social groups.

### The Individual's Emotional and Conceptual Makeup

In connection with the emotional constitution of the individual, genocide theorists have identified the following contributing conditions: The individual who agrees to participate in mass murder has been described in terms of a *personality of hatred*. Kressel (1996), for example, has sought to determine "whether there is such a thing as a hater's personality, a collection of traits that predisposes a person to initiate or join in acts of mass hatred." (10-11) Goldhagen (1996) similarly points to the "phenomenological reality" of the perpetrators (21, 22), urging the need for a "microphysics" that would describe the inner states of genocidal killers (24). As yet, a detailed phenomenological study of human hatred has not be undertaken. A separate chapter in the present work is devoted to that subject. (See Chapter 16.) Certainly, we should expect that much of the emotional urge to commit genocide is to be found in the inner world of the hater. To this end, Goldhagen (1996) has made the experienced inner hatred of the average person central to his "extreme hate" theory of the Holocaust. He has argued that the intense anti-Semitic hatred of the ordinary German people—"as profound a hatred as one people has likely ever harbored for another" (389)—must be recognized as central in any attempt to explain the Holocaust.

Closely associated with the hater's personality is the *joy of killing* experienced by perpetrators of genocide. The present volume returns repeatedly to the inference that people would not behave as they do, with such regularity and consistency, unless they receive some emotional benefit from their behavior. The joy men and women experience in killing one another stands out as an ugly aspect of human evil, one that is frequently swept under the carpet of denial. In Klee, Dressen, and Riess's (1991) book, *"The Good Old Days": The Holocaust As Seen by Its Perpetrators and Bystanders* (the title of which is taken from *Schöne Zeiten*, the memory album of Kurt Franz, the last commandant of the Treblinka concentration camp), the authors refer to the soldiers' joy in killing as a psychological addiction: "Some were positively addicted to it and 'could not have enough of it'.... Ordinary soldiers of the Wehrmacht who came to watch would sometimes ask to join in, borrowing guns to share the sport and shooting Jewish children as they ran, 'like hares.'" (Klee *et al.* 1991:xiii)

The public mass executions were in many ways a festival. In Kovno (Lithuania) locals—among them mothers and their children—applauded as each Jew was beaten to death in front of them. Cheers and laughter rang out. German soldiers stood by and took photographs. The military authorities were aware of this but did not intervene. German soldiers were sometimes prepared to travel long distances in order to obtain the best places at the bloody "shooting festivals." (xx)

By no means was this a unique event, but one that played out numerous times elsewhere, before equally enthusiastic crowds.

In Kaunas, Lithuania, where Einsatzkommando 3 operated, the Jews were clubbed to death with crowbars, before cheering crowds, mothers holding up their children to see the fun, and German soldiers clustered round like spectators at a football match. At the end, while the streets ran with blood, the chief murderer stood on the pile of corpses as a triumphant hero and played the Lithuanian national anthem on an accordion. (xii)

These chilling events make evident that, when conditions are right, even among children and their mothers, human beings find mass killing to be stimulating and emotionally satisfying. Witnesses made this clear: "Each time a victim was beaten to death they started to clap." "Cheers and laughter" broke out at the mass murder in Kovno. Soldiers sat "on rooftops and platforms watching the show," an execution held on August 7, 1941, in Zhitomir. (Klee *et al.* 1996:*passim*) Goldhagen (1996) refers to the testimony of a former German police official who served in Cracow, who admitted that the men serving with him "were, with a few exceptions, quite happy to take part in shootings of Jews. They had a ball!" (396)

The My Lai massacre in Vietnam evidenced the same thing: "The boys enjoyed it." (Hersch 1970:56) The "killing was done in a festive mood." (Katz 1993:107) Genocide historians Chalk and Jonasson have therefore observed: "The historical record, from ancient times to the present, amply testifies to the ease with which people can extinguish the lives of others, and even take joy in their deaths." (Chalk & Jonasson 1990:14) The pleasure that human beings experience in killing others is an undeniable and contemptible precondition for mass murder.

Furthermore, *psychological projection* plays an important part in the motivation of people to engage in mass killing. The reader will recall our earlier discussion of projection (see Chapter 6). Here, it is enough to recognize the way in which psychological projection functions, especially during periods of high stress, to embody and magnify in the targeted enemy group all that has become an individual's focus of hatred. Projection also functions to externalize and amplify the individual's prejudices, investing them in the identity he or she receives from group belonging. Projection goes hand-in-hand with psychological *splitting*, the name for the process of dividing a grandiose conception of the self from others, or of defining who belongs to one's favored group and who does not, who is a "true believer" of one's chosen ideology and who is not, which we shall discuss at greater length in connection with the psychology of terrorism (see Chapter 13). In genocide, splitting combines with projection so that what an individual most hates and devalues is attributed to the target group whose alien nature is magnified. At the same time, the individual's sense of self is expansively projected and merged with his own group:

The boundaries of the self are weakened. The 'I' becomes embedded, enveloped, and defined by the "we." This makes emotional contagion easier, a form of empathy...called "empathic joining." It exists even among animals; for example, it causes the spread of fear and the propensity for flight in heard animals. In human groups the speedy spread of feelings can lead to lynchings or mob violence. Emotional contagion is both a means of mutual influence and a source of satisfaction for group members. (Staub 1989:238)

As a result of this emotional merging of group members, similarly disposed members share in one another's projections and splitting. The psychological benefits of group belonging, of emotional kinship, comradeship, or mutuality, are evident: By belonging to the herd, the individual gains an inflated sense of power, emotional support, and connection. With the feeling of group-exaggerated power and puffed up personal importance comes a new awareness of one's own identity, which is projected into the individual's conception of his preferred group. It is by virtue of such a projection that it can make sense to the group member to risk his or her life on behalf of the group, which in the individual's mind has come to assume an autonomous existence that transcends his own. At this point, psychological projection involves a serious *thought disorder*, which we shall examine in Part III.

It is often claimed that the emotional attractions of belonging are strongest for those whose sense of identity is weak or "burdensome" (Staub 1989:77). A weak sense of personal identity can be associated with a weak will. One is reminded of Aristotle's distinction between "people of weak will, who do wrong against their real wishes and intentions, and vicious people, who do wrong contentedly and with conviction." (Prins 1994:299) *Belonging to a group* lowers an individual's inhibitions, and fosters in the group member stronger convictions than he or she might otherwise have when alone. Belonging to a group transforms people of weak will so that they will frequently behave in ways they might ordinarily reject on their own. The sense of group-belonging promotes the emotion of contentedness and pride in obeying the group's urgings, and in the process buttresses the individual's convictions that have received the group's endorsement. Through membership in the herd, Aristotle's two kinds of people can, in this essentially projective way, become one.

A comparatively *low level of moral development* may be associated with weak personal identity and weak will. The psychology of moral development is a topic of its own, directly related to a study of human evil, and calls for separate consideration. (See Chapter 18.) In the context of the psychology of genocide, it is important to recognize the strong role that a people's degree of "moral intelligence" plays in fostering, or in resisting, mass killing. We shall return to this topic later on.

Genocide researchers have identified another, still generally "internal," process that characterizes people who engage in mass killing. *Doubling* is the name for the ability that many perpetrators of genocide develop, which permits them to engage in acts of cruelty and atrocity and yet return home to a life of calm and caring domesticity. The "decent" man, husband, and father develops a separate sense of identity from the mass murderer that he becomes when he is "on the job, wearing his uniform." "He can do what he does because his doubling is part of a functional psychological equilibrium." (Lifton 1986:465) "The two selves seem encapsulated, walled off from each other to avoid internal conflict." (Staub 1989:143) The perpetrator of mass hate crimes can, in this way, maintain a separate part of himself that remains "untainted" and "acceptable"—to himself, his family, and his group.

So far, I have referred to conditions that contribute to genocide that are, for the most part, emotionally based and have their origin in the affective makeup of the individual. In addition to these, there are a number of conditions contributing to genocide that are more conceptual in nature—that is, which concern the thought processes of individuals, rather than their affective constitution. Let us look at several of these.

The perpetrators of genocide are often considered to be "fanatics" by members of an unsympathetic or opposing group. In the latter's view, the designation of "fanatical" is intended to underscore the judgment that mass killers are intensely uncritical in their excessively zealous devotion to a set of objectives or to an all-encompassing ideology. What this common view catches a corner of is the fact that perpetrators of genocide tend to be devoutly committed to the purposes they support in a particularly self-enclosed fashion that blinds them to alternative points of view, thereby making it impossible for them to recognize or respect points of view other than their own. Their frame of reference is, in other words, rigid and exclusionary. One researcher, referring to the Gestalt test results of Nazi leaders Dönitz and Streicher, commented: "[B]oth found it very difficult to alter their attitudes or opinions or to view issues from a perspective different than that which they held." (Zillmer *et al.* 1995:171) As we shall see later on, it is a characteristic of ideology—of the system of ideas itself—to make a "change of perspective" somewhere between difficult to impossible. When perpetrators of genocide are labeled "fanatical," what we seek to draw attention to is the *framework inflexibility* of the self-encapsulating belief-system which *defines their preferences* and to which they are committed.

A second and seldom appreciated characteristic of systems of belief is their persuasive *reality consistency*. This is a phrase coined by J. R. R. Tolkien, whose fairy tales have been the delight of millions. In a nonfiction essay, Tolkien (1965) wished to explain the power of some stories to create a belief in the reality of the fictitious worlds they depict. He came to feel that the most effective stories are those that create in their readers a sense of "the inner consistency of reality." (47) An effective story, from Tolkien's point of view, is one whose reality consistency is so persuasive that the reader is convinced of that reality. Tolkien cites *The New Testament* as one of the most effectively reality-consistent books. Reality consistency evidently applies beyond tales told to children. The hermetically sealed belief-system of the fanatic has, for him or her, exactly this feeling of reality consistency. The reality consistency of ideology is shared by effective fantasy. As Tolkien admitted: "It can be put to evil uses. It may even delude the minds out of which it came." (55) The world, as seen from the fanatic's perspective, is intrinsically persuasive and persuasively real—to the exclusion of all others.

The reality-consistent ideologies that motivate people to commit mass murder are, moreover, *ideologies of hate*. They are systems of belief that target a specific group of people as the object of hatred. The internal dynamic of human hatred (see Chapter 16) and that of ideology are inherently *blinding*. Kurt Möbius, former Police Battalion member who contributed to the genocide in Chelmo, made this point clearly in testimony that he gave on November 8, 1961:

> I would also like to say that it did not at all occur to me that these orders could be unjust. It is true that I know that it is also the duty of the police to protect the innocent, but I was then of the conviction that the Jews were not innocent but guilty. I believed the propaganda that all Jews were criminals and subhumans and that they were the cause of Germany's decline after the First World War. The thought that one should disobey or evade the order to participate in the extermination of the Jews did not therefore enter my mind at all. (Goldhagen 1996:179)

It follows from its exclusionary, blinding nature that once an ideology of hate is embraced by a society, mass killing on behalf of the ideology elicits the group's moral approval, while opposition to the mass murder is censured. The moral approval that a society gives to mass killing is a powerful force. As one Holocaust researcher observed: "The moral approbation that the work [of killing Jews] met explains why only a small minority of Police Battalion 101's men asked to be excused from killing, and why the officers could rely upon volunteers to fill out the killing squads." (Goldhagen 1996:261)

I have so far spoken of the extreme hate to which people are subject, the existence of exclusionary ideologies that promote hate, and the reality consistency of the awareness that such belief-systems promote. Closely related to these psychological and conceptual preconditions of genocide is the thesis that *"ideas can kill."* At first glance, this thesis seems patently ridiculous, given our unquestioned acceptance of the childhood refrain, "sticks and stones can break my bones, but words (and by association also ideas) can never hurt me!" Unfortunately, this pat reassurance is far from the truth. Among genocide scholars, Goldhagen

(1996) in particular has been mindful of what I shall later call the pathological power of ideas. In concluding his long study, he emphasized the central role in the Holocaust of a single hate-generating idea: "This study of the Holocaust and its perpetrators assigns to their beliefs paramount importance.... Germany during the Nazi period was inhabited by people animated by beliefs about Jews that made them willing to become consenting mass executioners." (455) Ideas and patterns of human thought can, as in the mass murders of genocide, assume a leading part in the human tragedy of self-destructiveness. Later in the present volume, in Part III, we shall have occasion to look in some detail at certain of the ways in which ideas and patterns of thinking become pathological and promote human aggression and destructiveness.

I have referred to the way in which the ideology of perpetrators of genocide defines many of their preferences. Such a characterization is an understatement. What is realistically at issue is a deeply rooted and powerful emotional bond that comes to be established between members of a genocidal group and its hate-engendering system of beliefs. The group affirms its beliefs through a complex of rituals and public emotional appeals that *exalt* the group's ideology. Flags are waved, national anthems are played, parades are held, bands play, patriotism is glorified, etc. Genocide historian Helen Fein has centered attention on this aspect of a group's investment in belief. She noted that for genocide to occur the convictions of the perpetrators must be exalted by them, often through a legitimating myth or political ideal. (Fein 1979:8) The processes used by a society to exalt its "preferred" beliefs are, as we shall also see in Part III, conceptually as well as emotionally pathological.

### The Individual's Personal Reality

At this point, we have reached the middle area of the continuum of interrelated psychological conditions that contribute to genocide. Here, the relationship of the individual to his or her immediate personal reality frequently involves awareness of harsh conditions of living with which he or she is forced to contend. These conditions may be extremely difficult, physically and emotionally draining, and acutely frustrating. They are strong sources of motivation for the individual to insist aggressively upon change. Ervin Staub has observed that

> ...people often respond with thoughts, feelings, and actions that do not change real conditions but at least help them cope with their psychological consequences.... Hard times make people feel threatened and frustrated. Threats to the physical self are important, but so are threats to the psychological self. All human beings strive for a coherent and positive self-concept, a self-definition that provides continuity and guides one's life. Difficult conditions threaten the self-concept as people cannot care for themselves and their families or control the circumstances of their lives. (Staub 1989:5, 15)

Observations like these have been the basis for the frustration-aggression theory, formulated by Dollard, Miller, Mowrer, and Sears (1939), and further developed by Staub (1989), Berkowitz (1989 & 1993), Baron and Richardson (1992), and others. Dollard and his collaborators sought to show that *frustration* is a precondition for human aggressive behavior, and that extreme frustration invariably produces some form of aggression as its consequence. When aggression, for whatever reasons, cannot be directed against the origins of frustration, it tends to be redirected against targets that are more accessible. Frustration, in this view, is the natural expression of "deprivation experiences":

Infants who have not yet learned to talk will attack people who take something away from them or refuse to do what they want. I have observed in very different cultures that infants strike their mothers when they fail to give them the breast quickly enough or do not give them a share of some tidbit. They also protest if they are interrupted at play. Every interruption of an enjoyable activity, every obstacle in the way of a goal-directed activity, every frustration of a wish, first of all rouses aggression. That applies universally to us human beings and is the basis of the frustration theory of aggression. (Eibl-Eibesfeldt 1979:105)

It is tempting, on the basis of the substantial body of evidence collected by frustration-aggression theorists, to believe that all human aggression originates from frustrated basic needs. But as Eibl-Eibesfeldt has observed: "The fact that frustration of every kind encourages aggression does not prove that frustration is its only cause." (Eibl-Eibesfeldt 1979:114) The conditions that contribute to human aggression, and specifically to genocide, are, as we have begun to see, complex and numerous.

### The Individual as Part of a Social Group

Located toward the end of the continuum of conditions that contribute to genocide are those which involve the individual's more external relationship to his or her social group, and the relationships between social groups. These predisposing conditions are numerous, while some are interlinked. *Pseudospeciation*, discussed in Chapter 10, and *ethnocentrism* form an interlinked pair. We recall that pseudospeciation refers to the willful propensity of human groups to identify, or manufacture, group distinctions that enable them to differentiate and distance themselves from others. Ethnocentrism is itself an expression of pseudospeciation, for ethnocentrism is a group's insistence that it is special and uniquely good. Ethnocentrism results in prejudicial perception of other groups: "[P]eople's perception...of outgroups is that 'they are all alike, different from us, and bad besides.'" (Fiske & Taylor 1991:133) Ethnocentrism, like many other psychological conditions that contribute to genocide, appears to be both normal and unlikely to change. Harvard social psychologist Roger Brown has observed:

> It is not just the seeming universality of ethnocentrism that makes us think it ineradicable but rather that it has been traced to its sources in individual psychology...and the source is the individual effort to achieve and maintain positive self-esteem. That is an urge so deeply human that we can hardly imagine its absence. (Brown 1986:534)

Pseudospeciation and ethnocentrism frequently involve four additional interlinked conditions which also contribute to genocide: *stereotyping, dehumanization, euphemistic language*, and *psychic numbing*. Each of these paves the way for the next. Kressel (1996) has pointed out that stereotyping is a normal human propensity, which serves a purpose that has clear emotional benefits. Stereotypes "are easy to use, and though they sometimes lead to erroneous judgments, they often do not." (233) Stereotyping is so widespread as to be a stubbornly enduring feature of human psychology. Though it is at times associated with heinous human behavior, stereotyping facilitates judgment, as Kressel observes, saving time and the need to think. The frequent consequences of stereotyping are dehumanization, often supported by the use of euphemistic language, and psychic numbing. It is easy to see how these bedfellows can arouse one another, for when a negative stereotype is used to caricature a group of people, it immediately becomes easier to add further negative characterizations that reduce the group to a subhuman level. For Hitler, the cultivation of such "indifference"—"like that of an animal to the suffering of its opponent—was critical in elevating the new German to be the 'beast of prey' that would rule the earth." (Victor 1998:110 ) The devaluation of others that is involved is clearly illustrated in a Nazi indoctrination pamphlet, *The Subhuman*, which urged the following view of the Jew:

> The subhuman man [the Jew]—the creation of nature appearing wholly identical in all biological respects, with hands, feet, and a species of brain, with eyes and a mouth, is in reality something quite different, a dreadful creation, a mere first draft of a human being with facial features resembling those of human beings—but mentally and spiritually inferior to any animal. The inner life of one of these people is a hideous chaos of wild and uninhibited passions: a nameless will to destroy, desire in its most primitive form, the most manifest vileness. (Victor 1998:111 quoting von der Gruen 1980:200-1)

Such dehumanization led, without encountering resistance, to the Nazis' decision (which was acted upon) to burn children alive, "in order to spare the two-fifths of a cent per child it would have cost to have gassed them first...." (Davies 1977:57)

The use of systematically misleading language contributes to dehumanization when euphemisms replace more compassionate expressions. Language can affect how we perceive and judge the world, a thesis argued long ago by linguists Benjamin Lee Whorf and Edward Sapir. As another author has noted:

> The power of language to color one's view of reality is profound. In many instances, the most significant factor determining how an object will be perceived is not the nature of the object itself, but the words employed to characterize it.... Words...act as a force for justice or a weapon of repression, an instrument of enlightenment or a source of darkness. (Brennan 1995:1)

Euphemistic language in the service of genocide appears universally to fall into eight categories, as analyzed by Brennan (1995:3). Such language tends to emphasize any of the following: human deficiency (applying words such as 'stupid', 'defective', 'inferior', etc.), a status lower than human (using 'subhuman' or 'nonhuman'), resemblance to animals ('bestial', 'brute', etc.), parasitism ('vermin', 'lice', etc.), infectivity ('pestilence', 'plague', 'contagion'), reduction to the inanimate ('thing', 'material'), equation with waste ('garbage', 'trash'), or denying a people's status as genuine persons (attributing psychological, social, or legal nonexistence to persons). Psychiatrist Douglas M. Kelley, who studied the Nazi leaders in Nuremberg, had this to say about the degrading and devaluing power of euphemistic language: "The power of the spoken word has been emphasized over and over. As a matter of fact, human beings in their present state of development are more moved by words than by reason. We allow ourselves to be overcome by emotional assault and battery...." (Kelley 1947:198)

The "emotional assault and battery of words" contributes to what has variously been called *psychic numbing*, constriction of affect, emotional deadening, or simply sedation of compassion. Euphemistic language can deaden empathy, but habituation to cruelty and killing appears to be most directly responsible for extreme emotional deadening. The capacity to feel compassion toward others can be completely blunted after regular exposure to brutality.

> When our emotions are overwhelmingly unpleasant or painful, we anesthetize ourselves; soldiers become able to tolerate mangled bodies, and the capacity for horror becomes blunted. While this diminishes suffering, it also makes us insensitive to the suffering of others, especially when the other is defined as different, the member of an outgroup, or an enemy bent on our destruction. (Staub 1989:45)

Some can experience emotional numbing very quickly, as did this Vietnam veteran:

> Flying over a group of civilians in a helicopter, he was ordered to fire at them, an order he did not obey. The helicopter circled over the area and again he was ordered to fire, which again he did not do. The officer in charge then threatened him with court-martial, which led him to fire the next time around. He vomited, felt profoundly distressed. The veteran reported that in a fairly short time firing at civilians became like an experience at a target-shooting gallery, and he began to enjoy it. (Staub 1989:134n)

Another cluster of interconnected factors that contribute to genocide includes the common human *need to be led* and its expression in *conformity* and *obedience to authority*, the *supersedure of a society's moral standards* by the commands of its leaders, and the relative *ease in creating an enemy*, which is often an outgrowth of the previous three factors. Psychologists have recognized that two main elements influence an individual's willingness to follow orders to inflict harm or death: the need to be led, already mentioned, as well as *the willingness to obey*. The first refers to the need to follow, to be told what to do, to be told what to believe and who is the enemy and who the friend. People who find it difficult to make decisions independently, especially when conditions of living become difficult, are more prone to wish to be led by those whom they accept as authorities. This kind of dependency is a form of emotional immaturity. It is a

> ... common and normal variety of immaturity reaction in adult social behavior.... We refer to the common tendency to avoid mature social responsibility in assuming the adult role, to submit to protective leadership and authority, to accept decisions "from above" in order to avoid the anxiety of having to make them, and to submit to paternalistic influences generally. In short, it represents a desire to reap the benefits of youthful irresponsibility in adult life. This regressive tendency can take place in the life of any individual in any culture, and it may take place by social facilitation in the life of an entire nation. (Gilbert 1950:267)

Freud (1921) pointed out that when emotional regression of this kind occurs, emotions intensify and intellectual functioning is curtailed as the individual merges his identity with that of his group. The emotionally regressed adult world comes to resemble that of the child, a world dominated by a need for immediate gratification, magical thinking, and primitive rationality. As we have noted, regression of this kind occurs when life becomes especially stressful. And so: "When the going gets rough, the sleeping infantile monster awakens to its a career of destruction and cruelty." (Rubenstein 1966:24)

Distinguishable from the human adult's propensity to regress emotionally when under duress is the willingness to follow orders out of respect for authority, the wish to "do one's duty," and the need to be thought well of by others. The desire to be led implies a weakness or deficiency of a certain kind, while the willingness to obey involves an individual's self-identity and self-esteem, which express what he or she regards as sources of pride and value. The need to be led and the willingness to obey are often fused in those who commit genocide: Dependency upon authority to provide the lead is often coupled with a need to conform, to accept and respect what others consider to be important, and to wish for their approval. The psychology of obedience has come to play an important role in understanding what brings men, women, and even children to commit callous and brutal acts. It has been thought by some psychologists to be at the root of human evil. We will therefore consider this topic in some detail in a later chapter. (See Chapter 15.)

These predisposing conditions—the need to be led and the willingness to obey—work in tandem with the ease with which everyday people will surrender their moral principles to the dictates of a leader. The commands of those whom the people believe to be authoritative are quickly allowed to supersede the individual's or the community's moral precepts. By permitting this, individuals and communities surrender their conscience to their leader's judgment and divest themselves of moral responsibility for their actions. Once this state of affairs has been realized, "... any person or group may be slaughtered if so ordained by the absolute sovereign. He accomplishes this by the simple device of designating them as enemies of the state." (Gilbert 1950:306). As Hermann Goering (Reichsmarschall, Luftwaffe-Chief, and President of the Reichstag) commented:

> ...it is the leaders of the country who determine the policy, and it is always a simple matter to drag the people along, whether it is a democracy or a fascist dictatorship or a Parliament or a Communist dictatorship.... That is easy. All you have to do is tell them they are being attacked and denounce the pacifists for lack of patriotism and exposing the country to danger. It works the same in any country. (307-8)

There are of course many calls to violence to which the public of any country will give credence. Three methods that are widely relied upon by leaders are the insistence upon vengeance against the target group for actual or imagined injuries, urging the public against the enemy out of fear of retaliation for atrocities one's group has already perpetrated, and the perception that mass murder is an effective means of reaching a set of objectives. The decisions by the United States to bomb Afghanistan and invade Iraq after the terrorist destruction of World Trade Center appear to involve these elements. The leader's perception of events, under the influence of the inconclusive Persian Gulf War, quickly becomes a matter of public acceptance. Appeals by leaders intended to inflame public fervor rely on the fact that, as emotions of hostility and aggression snowball, reason is increasingly excluded. As Kelley (1950:6) observed: "It is an established scientific fact that a person who is thinking with the emotional (thalamic) brain centres cannot think intellectually (cortically). Hitler had an entire people thinking with its thalamus."

The range of conditions that contribute to genocide is, unfortunately, as we will see in detail in the next chapter, part of the psychology of the normal citizen and the normal leader. Everyday people—people who are not extraordinary in any way, who live domestic lives of comparative peacefulness—share in an emotional and cognitive constitution that allows and at times encourages them to rally behind and to participate directly or indirectly in genocidal killing. Psychologically focused studies of genocide make evident that the joy of killing is not an uncommon human trait, and everyday experience offers ample confirmation of the fact that human beings, in so many ways, have an appetite for violence, aggression, and destruction.

## SUMMARY: THE CONTINUUM OF PREDISPOSING CONDITIONS

The conditions that predispose human beings to commit genocide form an interconnected continuum. We have noted that generally low levels of moral development can combine with mankind's habitually projective and hate-expressive ways of construing inner experience. Weak-willed individuals with weakly defined personal identities embrace conformity. They engage in splitting their idealized group from the rest of humanity and in doubling so they can engage in morally vicious behavior. And they are convinced of the righteousness of their behavior by the reality-consistency of their self-enclosed belief-systems. On such a solidly established basis in the psychology of the normal person, an ideology of hate can develop with relative ease. It easily becomes self-exalting, thanks to ways that human beings have found to glorify their own social groups to the exclusion of others. Hardships of living often add frustration. Differences among groups are emphasized or manufactured where none exist. Ethnocentrism adds its ingredient of social narcissism. Stereotyping and euphemistic language further contribute to dehumanization and emotional deadening. The desire to surrender to leadership and a willingness to obey authority combine to produce groups of people whose individual and group moral standards give way before, and are superseded by, the commands of their leaders. The "enemy" is easily created and, once created, snowballing public emotionality disables the capacity to reason.

The emotional and conceptual conditions that contribute to genocide are pervasive and deeply entrenched. It is no longer a perceptive question to ask why genocides occur, for it would be surprising if they did not.

# CHAPTER 12

# THE HOLOCAUST AND HUMAN EVIL

[T]he extermination of the Jews of Europe is perceived by many as the ultimate standard of evil, against which all degrees of evil may be measured. – Friedländer (1997:1)

Today we still gape in unbelief that such a holocaust was possible in our "civilized" world, refusing to see how true it was to man's nature.... – Becker (1975:117)

From the standpoint of the Holocaust's victims, the Holocaust is unique: It is such an extreme expression of human evil as to be dumbfounding and incomprehensible, and therefore unspeakable. Yet from the standpoint of the scientist, the Holocaust is not special or unique, and it is not unintelligible. For the scientist, to emphasize that the Holocaust is a unique and indecipherable event is to relegate the Holocaust to the category of a single gross and terrible human aberration—which the behavior of its perpetrators, as we shall see, is not. We unfortunately find the same forces of hatred, violence, cruelty, atrocity, and mass murder in other genocides. Among them, the Holocaust stands as the most horrifying obscene eruption of human evil in man's history. It is as different from other genocides as a devastating disease pandemic is to localized and more limited infections. But the same fundamental pathology is involved, the same human evil. It is possible for us to know why the Holocaust, and other genocides, happen and why others are likely in the future.

Genocides are more common than many people realize. There is a larger context in which the Holocaust took place. One might expect that the Holocaust would stand at the top of the list of genocides that occurred during the twentieth century, but in fact it is third. In the order of the magnitude of mass murders involving a million people or more, during the years 1917-1987, 61,911,000 people were killed in the U.S.S.R.; in Communist China, 35,236,000 people (1949-1987); in Germany, 20,946,000 (1934-1945); in Nationalist China, 10,075,000 (1928-1949); in Japan, 5,890,000 (1936-1945); in Cambodia, 2,035,000 (1975-1978); in Vietnam, 1,659,000 (1945-1987); in Poland, 1,583,000 (1945-1947); in Pakistan, 1,500,000 (1971); in Yugoslavia, 1,067,000 (1944-1987); and in Turkey, 1,000,000 (1915-1918). (Rummell 1994:11) Individual lives and aspirations were ended, cruelly and often painfully, at the average rate during the years in question of more than 5,000 people a day.

The psychology responsible for these mass killings is clear and evident for those who wish to study it. And, as I shall argue in a later chapter, these expressions of human evil should not be forgiven even though we understand them. The Holocaust represents a single expression of human evil that deserves our attention as scientists because much is now known about the psychology of its participants.

## THE PATHOLOGY OF JEW-HATRED: THE HUMAN NEED FOR PREJUDICE AND PERSECUTION

Anti-Semitism is not merely the joy of hating; it brings positive pleasures too.... It is fun to be an anti-Semite. – Sartre (1948:26-7, 47)

[If there were no Jew] we should have then to invent him. It is essential to have a tangible enemy.... – Hitler quoted in Rauschning (1940:237)

As the Holocaust is to genocide, so is anti-Semitism to prejudice. An understanding of anti-Semitism captures much about the nature of human prejudice. The reader will recall that a number of authors discussed in Chapter 2—Pinsker, Fenichel, Ackermann, Johoda, Allport, and Simmel—argued that anti-Semitism is a pathology. They held that anti-Semitism involves a pathological process of displacing or projecting hatred upon a group of people chosen for this purpose because they are perceived to be different. The persecution of the Jews that results from this process of distortion gives to anti-Semites a fortified sense of their own otherwise inadequate personal identity. The man who has difficulty believing in himself will have much less difficulty believing in his chosen group, his country, his race when these are magnified by his hatred toward other groups. His provincialism and bigotry become ready substitutes for his own deficiency, and they provide him with a group-sponsored source of strength not his own. This delusional and fortifying character of anti-Semitism caused Pinsker, Allport, and Simmel to judge that anti-Semitism is a true mass social psychosis, a psychosis of hatred that is infectious. Simmel recognized that Jew-haters are in general psychiatrically *normal*, and yet the hatred they express when part of an emotionally fused collective is psychotic. Ackermann and Johoda recognized that anti-Semitism is socially pathological, yet prejudice against Jews can become a *social norm*, as it did in Nazi Germany. The psychology of individual Jew-haters may be psychiatrically normal, and anti-Semitism may become an accepted norm in a society, and yet it is appropriate, they argued, to identify anti-Semitism as a pathology.

To say that anti-Semitism is a pathology yet can be normal is to say that hatred of Jews, or of any identifiably different group of people, can become what I have called in this book a *universal pathology*. It is comparatively rare, almost unheard of, in the history of psychiatry to identify a pathology as being the consequence of a psychological malfunction that is normal. But it is this—the rarely acknowledged yet ubiquitous pathology that afflicts the psychologically normal person—that much of this book is about.

If we ask why psychologically normal people develop and even cultivate hatred toward groups that differ from them, we must again come back to the emotional functions of such hatred. Nietzsche took note of this: "To behold suffering gives pleasure, but to cause another to suffer affords an even greater pleasure." (Nietzsche 1956:198) In Nietzsche's view, human beings experience an undeniable *joy in persecuting*. Allport (1954) sought to identify the psychological benefits that come from targeting persecution through scapegoating. He refers to "functional prejudice." It serves as the "crutch" that the insecure person needs. "It must give reassurance for past failures, safe guidance for present conduct, and ensure confidence in the future." (396) In these ways, prejudice against others can function so that it can "become part of one's life tissue, suffusing character because it is essential to the economy of life." (395) Prejudice is then "more than an incident in many lives; it is often lockstitched into the very fabric of personality.... To change it, the whole pattern of life would have to be altered." (408) Prejudice does, in the final analysis, often function as a unifying force in an individual's view of the world:

> The emotional ferocity of the crudest anti-Semitism makes it easy to forget that anti-Semitism can provide an extensive cognitive interpretation of the world. Above all, crude anti-Semitism is based upon a belief that Jews have immense powers of evil in the world. Modern anti-Semitic dogma asserts that Jews control both communism and capitalism and that they aim to dominate the world in a régime which will destroy Western civilization. All facts are explained in terms of this pervasive and perverse belief. (Billig 1978:132)

Prejudice and persecution do not usually bring sadness and remorse to the victimizers, but rather a sense of strengthened identity, pleasure, self-satisfaction, superiority, and power. Prejudice and persecution are Siamese twins: Together they generate a heightened and invigorated belief in the victimizers' supremacy. The fact that prejudice and persecution *benefit* bigots and persecutors is often overlooked or denied.

Prejudice and persecution usually involve scapegoating. Scapegoating is one of the specific ways in which human beings use exaggerated and distorted human differences as a pretext for aggression. For example: "They [the Jewish people] are worse than cholera, than lung pest, than syphilis...worse than a conflagration, famine, the break of a dam, extreme drought, the worst locust plague, poison gas—worse than all of these because these elements destroy only the German people, those [the Jews], however, Germany itself." (Malitz 1934:45, quoted in Goldhagen 1996:398) Or, in the ironically contrasting context of the Third Century, A.D., Tertullian remarked: "They take the Christians to be the cause of every disaster to the state, or every misfortune to the people. If the Tiber reaches the wall, if the Nile does not reach the fields, if the sky does not move or if the earth does, if there is a famine, or if there is a plague, the cry is at once, 'The Christians to the Lions.'" (Allport 1954:243) As soon as people perceive, or imagine that they perceive, that another group differs from them, the machinery to deride and scorn the other group is ready to put into motion. (See, e.g., Sherif *et al.* 1955; Sherif 1966; Tajfel *et al.* 1971; Tajfel 1978, 1981, 1982) People will opportunistically divide themselves into opposing groups, even when there is no "objective" need for this, since by so doing they manufacture an enemy toward whom they can direct their antagonisms. As Sumner (1906) noted long ago: "Each group nourishes its own pride and vanity, boasts itself superior, exalts its own divinities, and looks with contempt on outsiders.... [E]thnocentrism leads a people to exaggerate and intensify everything...which is peculiar and which differentiates them from others." (13) Once group differentiation—the real Tower of Babel Phenomenon—has set in, pride in belonging to one's own group becomes central. The fear and aversion that tend automatically to be aroused in the face of another group's differences make it easy to project upon others whatever abuses serve the interests of superiority. Scapegoating is in this way an effective means of inflating self-importance. As Sartre wrote:

> By treating the Jew as an inferior and pernicious being, I affirm at the same time that I belong to the elite. In contrast to most modern elites, which are based on merit or labor, this elite closely resembles that of an aristocracy determined by birth. There is nothing I have to do to merit my superiority, nor is there anything I can do to lose it. It is given once and for all.... [The anti-Semite] finds the existence of the Jew absolutely necessary. Otherwise to whom would he be superior? (Sartre 1948:27-8)

Prejudice and persecution are essentially projective. The negative feelings and images that people project into their conceptions of others are frequently not based in reality, but are expressions of bigotry. The persecution of others who are perceived in this way is built upon projection. This point of view has led to the observation: "It may very well be that unless and until we have tools for containing projection processes, most of the heroic efforts we make toward world justice and peace will be to little avail." (Charny & Rapaport 1982:191) These and other authors have pointed to the need to study the various forms of projection processes, but this work remains to be done. Much of the discussion in Section III of the present study serves this objective. Here, it is important to recognize that, while projection is central to human prejudice and persecution, it is, by definition, relatively impervious to a group's self-awareness. Sources of projective hatred will always be located in the hated group, and not in the prejudiced and persecuting group.

From the public's point of view, anti-Semitism was the motivation for the Holocaust; some Holocaust scholars also have made this claim, for example Goldhagen (1996):

> [The Germans] were internally motivated killers, moved by a boundless hatred of Jews.... Many factors were necessary for Hitler and others to have conceived the genocidal program, for them to have risen to the position from which they could implement it, for its undertaking to have become a realistic possibility, for it then to have been carried out.... With regard to the motivational cause of the Holocaust, for the vast majority of perpetrators, a mono-causal explanation [hatred of Jews] does suffice. (403, 416)

And yet, as we shall see, the emotional and cognitive reassurance and heightened self-importance that bigots and persecutors gain by these means are not, by themselves, a complete explanation for the Nazis' motivation. To make this clear, I turn now to look more specifically at the Holocaust, and at the psychology of three groups: the Nazi leaders, ordinary enlisted men, and doctors who served in the concentration camps.

## BROADENING THE CULPABILITY OF THE HOLOCAUST: SOME CALL IT MADNESS, BUT IT IS NORMAL

> [N]ormal and average human beings can be manipulated into inhumane behavior.... [T]he need is great to study the normal man from this aspect rather than continue to regard such behavior either as incomprehensible or as evidence that the person involved is somehow aberrant, abnormal and atypical.... – Milton Erickson (1968:279)

It is not well known that the suffering and mass killing during WWII primarily of Jews, but also of other ethnic groups and of the mentally and physically ill, took place in a huge number of death camps, and was perpetrated by hundreds of thousands of participants. Many readers may be under the impression that there existed only a handful of concentration camps, perhaps a dozen or so. In fact, there were more than 2,400 camps that participated in the extermination program. (Victor 1998:198) As many as two million Germans were involved in killing innocent people. (93) A quarter of a million people among the SS alone worked to search for, apprehend, and imprison Jews. (198) The contributors to the Holocaust included men and women in many professions: police, prosecutors, judges, attorneys, and law clerks who conspired to arrest and sentence innocent people; government functionaries who compiled lists of Jews, issued documents, and restricted personal freedom; civilian citizens who, often knowingly, acquired property, homes, and jobs taken from Jews; approximately a million transportation workers who were involved in the shipment of Jews to extermination sites; physicians, who oversaw much of the extermination process itself, as we shall see later; large corporations that used slave labor, often working underfed people to their deaths; and last, but not least, the many everyday Germans who stood by, "accessories and beneficiaries of crimes," passively and unwilling to resist the events that unfolded. (122; see also Greenberg 1977:17n)

Even German children were involved. They were educated for killing in various ways: through games, weapons training , and indoctrination. Young recruits to the SS

> ... were required to observe and participate as assistants while others beat, tortured, and killed prisoners. Those who did not faint were rewarded.... Some SS men were given dogs to rear as their own and then ordered to strangle them. Others were given infants for target practice. Still others were forced to kill Jewish babies in front of the babies' mothers. Voicing scruples and flinching when witnessing or performing such acts were called softness, unmanliness, weakness, and cowardice before the enemy. (Victor 1998:110-11)

This was not, however, an exclusively German phenomenon. Germans who directly and indirectly contributed to the mass killings "acted no differently from the equally numerous and 'ordinary' Austrians, Rumanians, Ukrainians, Balts, and other Europeans who became the most willing operatives of the murder machinery functioning in their midst." (Friedländer 1997:4) In addition to these groups, "there were far too many cases of willing, active, enthusiastic Polish assistance to the Nazi murderers." (Donat 1965:100) Yet the majority of atrocities were perpetrated by Germans. Though Hitler was a magnetic, spellbinding leader, it required, as we saw in the preceding chapter, a population that was "available" to respond to his will to induce hysteria. "[T]he evidence suggests that a great majority of the German population found ways to accommodate the Nazi regime, despite whatever inner reservations they might have had." (Johnson 1999:16) Not only did the general population comply with Nazi measures, but, as we shall see, "average German citizens formed the core of both the reserve police battalions and the German army." (18) As a result of these and other observations, Holocaust scholar Eric A. Johnson concluded that the Nazi regime's

> ...implementation and effectiveness depended on the voluntary choices and local actions of individual German citizens.... [The] horrendous acts [of the Holocaust] would not have been imaginable without the loyalty, complicity, and silence of the German population.... Hitler, the Nazi Party, the SS, and the Gestapo did not murder the Jews alone. They led the charge certainly, but it took nearly the entire German population to carry out the Holocaust. (Johnson 1999:27, 375, 379)

This point is often overlooked by those who engage in a witch hunt, intent upon placing blame on the extremism of leaders rather than upon everyday, average people. Human evil is not madness. It is normal, "sane" by conventional standards, yet pathological.

Hannah Arendt (1964) was responsible for stressing its "banality," but she stopped short of identifying human evil as a universal pathology. Instead, she placed blame for the horrors of the Holocaust primarily on "circumstances that make it well-nigh impossible for [the perpetrator] to know or to feel that he is doing wrong." (276) Situational factors, in Arendt's view, "impair" the normal person's "ability to distinguish between right and wrong." (277) Such people are not "perverted" or "sadistic," they are "terribly and terrifyingly normal." (276) This view has been echoed in Holocaust studies since then. Kressel (1996), for instance, observed:

> Contrary to popular opinion, few perpetrators evince signs of mental illness or severe psychological disturbance.... Few of Hitler's followers met formal criteria for any diagnosis of psychopathology. Most cannot be distinguished from others in a normal population on the basis of their mental health.... [T]he preponderance of crimes of mass hatred can be traced to those whom psychologists would regard as "normal." (259)

Similarly, Katz (1993), in a study of Paul Kremer (an SS doctor), Rudolf Hoess (head of Auschwitz), and Lieutenant William Calley (U.S. platoon commander in the massacre of the My Lai villagers), claimed: "evil, even evil on a horrendous scale, can be practiced by very ordinary sorts of persons" (7); "an ordinary person may not only do evil, but do evil innovatively and enthusiastically and on a grand scale" (18); "[o]rdinary caring people do take part in extraordinary evil." (36) Others who lived through the horrors made the same observation: "Monsters exist, but they are too few in number to be truly dangerous. More dangerous are the common man, the functionaries ready to believe and to act without asking questions...." (Levi 1985:394) Other Holocaust scholars have written:

> What kind of men were these who accepted murder as their daily work? They were perfectly ordinary people, with one difference: they could act as members of the "master race".... Those who commit crimes of initiative seek out opportunities to kill or otherwise participate. Some meet the criteria for psychopathology, but most do not. (Klee *et al.* 1988:xix, 262)

The result of these and other similar observations has been an increasing recognition that human evil is the result of normal people behaving in ways that, as these terms are understood, are neither psychotic nor mystifying. "I began to recognize that the difference between the Germans and other men was not very great. Given similar conditions of political and social stress, most of us could commit very terrible crimes." (Rubenstein 1966:216) Not only are the common man and woman willing to commit barbarities, but so are those who are well educated: "[C]ontrary to much supposition, the people directly involved in the murder enterprise were not gutter riff-raff. More frequently than not, they were men with university or professional training behind them. In some instances, former pastors were active leaders of the work of death." (47)

In a detailed study of the infamous Police Battalion 101, consisting of approximately 500 men sent to Poland in June of 1942, Browning (1992:1) noted that these "middle-aged family men of working- and lower-middle-class background..., too old to be of use to the Germany army..., raw recruits with no previous experience," quickly became mass killers. They were ordinary men who deferred to authority, sought career advancement, and worked within a bureaucracy that diffused personal responsibility. In concluding his study, Browning raised the question: "If the men of Reserve Police Battalion 101 could become killers under such circumstances, what group of men cannot?" (189)

A parallel and detailed study was made by Zillmer *et al.* (1995), who examined the psychological profiles of 200 rank-and-file Nazis, Danish collaborators, and German military occupation personnel who received prison sentences or were executed for war crimes and crimes against humanity. Again, the conclusion reached was straightforward:

> Although our image of the Nazis tends to be that of thugs and murderers, the current analysis suggests that many ordinary people became involved in atrocities who did not demonstrate any particular inclination toward violence.... [T]he German conduct as such is not enigmatic or related to a national character. In this sense, no contemporary historian of Nazi Germany would argue today for the existence of a psychopathic Nazi personality. Historical and psychologically informed inquiries have reached this conclusion on vast and solid evidential foundations. (117, 8)

Studies of the kind I have touched upon here all point to the same conclusion: normal people commit cruel and horrifying acts. This is not a complex statement, although it may be hard for optimistic and ingenuous readers to accept. One would not, however, expect that psychologically-focused Holocaust researchers themselves would suffer from a related naïveté, and yet they do. Zillmer *et al.* (1995), for example, summarized personality traits of many of the perpetrators of the Holocaust. They include "oversimplification" and use of inaccurate stereotypes, an ineffectual "problem-solving style," "altered self-esteem," "diminished regard" for others, weak abilities to think independently, susceptibility to influence, etc. The authors went on to say that these traits "are not pathological in and of themselves and are actually frequently found in the U.S. population." (181) They argue that "[t]hese personality characteristics are not universally pathological, in the clinical or psychiatric sense...." (179) —This of course is an innocent tautology, for in applying conventional standards of mental health based on a standard of normality, no normal personality characteristics are, by definition, universally pathological. The authors admit that "under certain social circumstances, just about anyone could have joined the Nazi movement, but that there were individuals who were more likely to join." (181) And yet who were these people? They were everyday, ordinary people who share the common traits listed above. Do these normal, often decent people suffer from any sort of pathology, then? The answer for anyone for whom "diagnosable" means "abnormal" must of course be "no." As long as "diagnosable" is confined to what is "abnormal," any pathology sufficiently widespread so as to be the norm for a population cannot be detected—the sieve of conventional standards of mental health simply has too wide a net. And so the authors' conclusion follows: "These personality traits are...not considered diagnosable." (181) Such a conclusion is of course valid—unless, that is, we come to feel that there are compelling reasons to broaden what we mean by pathology.

The "human evil is undiagnosable" conclusion has often led Holocaust researchers in search of an explanation to throw up their hands in dismay, since their hands are tied by the rigid equation, disease = abnormality. Here is a common result of this way of thinking: "At the present time we as psychologists have been unable to satisfactorily [sic] explain the motivations and personality organizations that prompted...war trial criminals to such grotesque and inhumane actions." (Borofsky & Brand 1980:399)

We come inevitably, then, to the core dilemma in a study of the psychology of genocidal behavior as it was expressed in the Holocaust: On the one hand, we may accept the conclusion that the behavior and mental outlook of Holocaust perpetrators is an expression of human evil that is normal, and which, for this reason, since it is not an abnormality or aberration, is not subject to psychopathological investigation. This result then makes it impossible to diagnose and treat conditions that are utterly normal. Or, on the other hand, we can identify human evil as a pathology, or group of pathologies, that psychology can recognize and perhaps treat. Psychiatrist Milton Erickson has been one of the few to urge the second approach:

> It is time that society—particularly its psychologists and psychiatrists—takes a realistic view of the nature of undesirable and destructive human behavior and the extent to which, under stress or without stress, the individual, the group or an entire society can be led to enact it.... [N]o effort is made to investigate scientifically the extremes to which the normal, the good, the average, or the intellectual person or group will go if given the opportunity.... (Erickson 1968:278)

—For it is here, in the psychology of the normal, good, average, and sometimes intellectual person and group, that the roots of human evil, hideously expressed as that evil was during the Holocaust, are to be found. *Without a theory of universal pathology, our hands are bound and we cannot comprehend the obvious. Psychology presently is in the position of applying a diagnostic yardstick that is blind to human evil.*

The millions of human perpetrators who were direct and indirect contributors to the Holocaust were, as numerous studies have shown, for the most part psychologically ordinary and normal. Yet we know that normal human beings are usually not motivated to commit atrocities unless circumstances are right. J. M. Steiner therefore proposed the idea of the "sleeper," "who lies dormant until circumstances or specific events will activate him or her and produce behavioral traits not apparent before." (Steiner 1980:431) Staub added: "Most persons are sleepers to some degree, inasmuch as they have a violent potential that can be triggered by specific conditions." (Staub 1989:134) The motivations that inspire people to "awaken" and commit acts of radical evil result from basic predispositions that have their roots in ordinary human emotions and thought. As Staub remarked, "Evil that arises out of ordinary thinking and is committed by ordinary people is the norm, not the exception.... Great evil arises out of ordinary psychological processes that evolve, usually with a progression along the continuum of destruction." (126) Let us look at these processes in more detail.

## THE PSYCHOLOGY OF THE NAZI LEADERS

I wonder how I could have done these things.... – Hans Frank, Nazi Governor-General of Poland, quoted by Gilbert (1950:147)

While "circumstances" and "situational factors" played a role in the mass murder of millions of people and the devastation of Europe, it is important to understand the personalities of Germany's leaders, for it was they who led ordinary men and women in a mass orgy of human destructiveness. Psychologically-focused attention has been given to the Nazi leaders, enough so that we know a good deal about their emotional and mental constitution.

Initially, when Nazi leaders were captured and examined it was thought that psychological testing would show them to be aberrant monsters, psychotic sociopaths. But, instead, they were found to be essentially normal people. Most were articulate. They were men who were motivated by sincerely held beliefs, committed to doing their jobs well and motivated by a desire for professional advancement, respectful of authority and obedient to it, disciplined and willing to accommodate to experiences that habituated them to brutality. And most of the leaders were intelligent—in fact, they were highly intelligent. The human traits of obedience and of dedication to ideology and duty are frequently associated with fanaticism, but high intelligence should give us pause.

Of the Nazi leaders tried in Nuremberg, 21 were tested using the Wechsler-Bellevue Intelligence Test, Adult Form-I. The results, for many readers, may be surprising. The following list gives their measured intelligence: Schacht (IQ 143), Seyss-Inquart (140), Göring (138), Dönitz (138), Papen (134), Raeder (134), Frank (130), Fritzsche (130), Schirach (130), Ribbentrop (129), Keitel (129), Speer (128), Jodl (127), Rosenberg (127), Neurath (125), Funk (124), Frick (124), Hess (120), Saukel (118), Kaltenbrunner (113), and Streicher (106). (Zillmer *et al.* 1995:48) Their mean IQ was 128, which falls at the superior to very superior end of the range of human IQs (an IQ above 140 is considered "genius"). Some of the Nazi leaders held doctoral degrees, one held a law degree, one an economics degree, one a chemistry degree.

Three comments about the high IQs of the Nazi leaders are in order: First, it is evident that these men who led Germany to commit the most barbarous acts in human history were highly intelligent, by conventional psychometric standards. Second, we should not be surprised by their level of intelligence, since comparatively high intelligence is not unusual for leaders in any field. Third, their high intelligence makes it clear that intellectual capacity has no bearing on an individual's moral development. The test results of the Nazi leaders should make anyone doubt the belief that high intelligence goes hand-in-hand with kindness and compassion. *There is perhaps no clearer evidence that intellectual intelligence and what I will later call moral intelligence are not linked.*

> It must be borne in mind that the IQ indicates nothing but the *mechanical efficiency* of the mind, and has nothing to do with character or morals, nor the various other considerations that go into an evaluation of personality. Above all, the individual's sense of values and the expressions of his basic motivation are the things that truly reveal his character. (Gilbert 1961:34)

Psychiatrist Douglas M. Kelley, known for his Rorschach testing of the Nuremberg prisoners, provided a candid clinical and personal account of each of the Nazi leaders. He described Hermann Göring, for example, as

> ...a brilliant, brave, ruthless, grasping, shrewd executive, ... a man of charming manner (when he chose to be charming) [with] a keen imagination and a good educational background..., great drive, and a sense of humour.... [He showed an] extreme fondness for and tenderness toward his family and friends.... His letters to his wife and child indicate not only his strong love, but his effervescent emotions.... [H]e loved animals and felt that they should be protected.... For these creatures; for his friends, for his family, nothing was too good. [Yet,] he had no sense whatsoever of the value of human life, of moral obligation, or of the other finer attributes of civilized man when they conflicted with his own egocentric aims. (Kelley 1947:43-4, 50-2, 54)

Dr. Paul Josef Goebbels, who was the Reich Minister of Propaganda, "was well educated, original in his ideas, possessed of an excellent memory." (68) Baldur Benedekt von Schirach, who headed the Nazi program to indoctrinate German youth, "was an executive of great imaginary powers, ...with great drive, ...enthusiastic, ...of good family, well educated, and handsome, a young man of keen imagination and considerable creative and literary ability." (74) Joachim von Ribbentrop, chosen by Hitler to be his chief foreign diplomat, was described by Margaret Blank, his secretary for many years, as a lover of classical music, a fine violinist, a lover of art with a special interest in contemporary painting, a person who

> ...takes warm human interest in his employees, even the smallest ones, be it a case of illness or damage suffered through bombing, and he sometimes extends his interest even to their whole families. He then sends the best doctors to the patient, expects a daily report, and will pay all the expenses. He makes big presents and grants a generous vacation. I myself had opportunity to experience to a great extent this warm, human sympathy. (89)

Where Göring was an art collector, Streicher was a collector of books. "He had a vast library, containing the rarest manuscripts and...finest volumes, collected—that is, stolen—from Jews." (119) Hans Frank, Gauleiter of Poland, who sent millions of people to execution, "was of medium height, active, intense and extraordinarily well-read.... He was interested in art and, in his days of power, sought out artists and scientists whom he persuaded to give lectures for him. He was particularly fond of music and...preferred Beethoven, Mozart, Chopin, and Strauss to Wagner." (147) Wilhelm Frick, Hitler's first Minister of the Interior, held a law degree and a doctorate from the University of Munich. He was "just an average friendly appearing fellow in a sports jacket, his grey hair cut extremely short—G. I. style. This deceptive mildness was one of his main sources of strength, since no one could easily realize that his smooth face hid a vicious, ruthless killer." (153) Like other Nuremberg Nazi leaders, Eichmann was certified as "normal" by half a dozen psychiatrists. (Kressel 1996:9) One of them, after examining Eichmann and finding him to be normal, admitted that he is "more normal, at any rate, than I am after having examined him." (Arendt 1964:25)

The psychiatric conclusion that Eichmann was "perfectly sane" led Thomas Merton to comment: "I do not doubt it at all, and that is precisely why I find it disturbing." (Quoted in Charny & Rapaport 1982:17-18)

The Nazi leaders were not psychotics, but men who were ambitious, patriotic, and who, in spite of their often intellectual brilliance, educational level, cultural interests, artistic sensibility, and positive personal qualities, possessed a level of moral intelligence that was abysmally low.

After getting to know the Nazi leaders on a personal basis and as subjects whom he carefully tested, Kelley had this to say about them in conclusion: They were "essentially sane" and they "knew precisely what they were doing during their years of ruthless domination." (Kelley 1946:47)

> From our findings we must conclude not only that such personalities are not unique or insane but also that they could be duplicated in any country of the world today. We must also realize that such personalities exist in this country and that there are undoubtedly certain individuals who would willingly climb over the corpses of one half of the people of the United States, if by so doing, they could thereby be given control of the other half. A realization of this fact and an understanding of the types of personality capable of such action is an important step along the path for prevention of such an occurrence. (47)

Psychiatrist G. M. Gilbert came to the same conclusion:

> The suggestion is often made by both clinicians and laymen, when inquiring about the examination of Nazi leaders, that "these men must have been a lot of psychopaths to have done what they did." That statement rests on the popular assumption that since atrocious crimes are abnormal manifestations of social behavior, the people who participate in them must be abnormal. We have...detected a flaw in that assumption. (Gilbert 1950:280-1)

Nazi Rorschach researcher Molly Harrower (1976:350) came to a similar conclusion: "[W]ell-integrated, productive and secure personalities are no protection against being sucked into a vortex of myth and deception, which may ultimately erupt into the commitment of horror on a grand scale." She found no "underlying common denominator" in the test results of the Nazi leaders. And yet indeed there was a common denominator where one did not expect to find it—in their underlying psychological normality. In a similar vein, a later Rorschach study of the Nazi leaders came to the conclusion that their pattern of responses bore more similarity to a standardized sample of six hundred "normal" U.S. citizens than to any psychiatric group including schizophrenics and depressives. (Porpora 1990:18 referring to Zillmer *et al.* 1989)

In recent years, the "logic" of evaluating the Nazi leaders has undergone a reversal. Not long ago, it was thought by many, the public as well as some researchers, that the perpetrators must have criminal minds and be mentally deranged—but this fact, most argued in the same breath, ought not to excuse them from their execrable actions. Now we see that, for the most part, Nazi leaders as well as the men they led were merely psychologically normal and in some cases intelligent people—"decent" in some ways, and yet willing to commit the worst of atrocities. But, as in the past, we now say that this fact does not excuse them from the evil they perpetrated. If the perpetrators were, by conventionally accepted standards, psychologically normal, and if the horrors they perpetrated are not to be excused on grounds that they were normal, we are left with the need to distinguish the normal and pervasive pathology of human evil from the psychology of individuals who are exceptions to that evil, who refuse to participate in it, or who actively oppose it. I will do this in later sections of this chapter.

## HEALERS IN THE SERVICE OF MASS MURDER:
## THE NAZI DOCTORS

Of all professional groups, that of physicians is reputed to be motivated by human compassion. Doctors take a professional vow to confine their medical practice to compassionate care that will not cause harm. In this context, the behavior of Nazi physicians provides a telling indication of the difficulty ordinary people experience—even in the medical profession—in resisting inner and outer forces that lead them to commit monstrosities against others.

Nazi doctors played a much more central role in the mass murders of the Holocaust than is generally realized. At Auschwitz, for example, physicians supervised the killing of approximately one million people. (Lifton 1986:18) The part they played extended considerably beyond the familiar patient-doctor relationship: Nazi physicians had the duty to make "selections" as prisoners walked down the "ramp" when they arrived at concentration camps. The "selection" of prisoners was usually made quickly and determined who would live and who would be murdered. The doctors also made "selections" later, during day-to-day camp life and when prisoners required medical attention. People with diseases believed to be contagious were "selected," as were the disabled and many of the old. But the physicians' duties did not end here. They also supervised the gas chamber executions, determined how much poison gas was needed, and decided when those who had been gassed were likely all to be dead. The doctors' interventions were sometimes even more direct: They were responsible for choosing which debilitated prisoners should be killed, and sometimes themselves carried out individual medical executions by injecting phenol intravenously or directly into the heart. The doctors signed falsified death certificates listing diseases that people did not have. They estimated how many inmates should be kept alive for the needs of slave labor. And the Nazi physicians decided how most efficiently to burn the vast numbers of human bodies so as not to exceed the capacity of the ovens. (18) Their "medical" duties were many. Medical doctors, ironically, were central in the mass killings.

Robert Jay Lifton interviewed a group of former Nazi doctors and was able to gain their confidence under a formal promise of anonymity. His purpose was specific: "My goal in this study is to uncover psychological conditions conducive to evil." (Lifton 1986:12) The doctors' testimonies tell us several things. First, it is clear that they found their work gratifying. "Every once in a while there would be a flash of nostalgia for the Nazi times, for an era when life had intensity and meaning, whatever the conflicts engendered." (11) Lifton interviewed a former *Wehrmacht* neuropsychiatrist involved in the treatment of psychological disorders of many *Einsatzgruppen* personnel.

> He estimated that 20 percent of those doing the actual killing experienced...symptoms of psychological decompensation. About half of that 20 percent associated their symptoms mainly with the "unpleasantness" of what they had to do, while the other half seemed to have moral questions about shooting people in that way. (15)

As we shall see in a later section of this chapter, relatively few of those who were directly involved in the mass killings asked to be relieved of this duty and be assigned elsewhere. Here it is enough to note that the doctors could request transfers from their extermination work with impunity. (109, citing Buchheim 1968:373)

Second, the Nazi physicians seem to have felt little remorse for the atrocities they committed. Lifton remarked, in looking back over the interviews he had with former Nazi doctors, that they showed virtually a "complete absence of moral confrontation, of acknowledgement of their own moments of evil or even of the degree to which they had been part of an evil project." (Lifton 1986:502) Third, the doctors' unspeakable work was facilitated by their use of euphemistic language, dignifying the hideous job on the ramps as *ärztliche Rampendienst* (medical ramp duty) and their choice of who would be allowed to live as *Selection*, which they associated with Darwinian "natural selection." (445) Fourth, they engaged in an inner process of psychological doubling, discussed in the previous chapter, which made a life of mass murder palatable by walling it off from their personal and home life. (465, referring to Kull 1985) Fifth, the Nazi physicians did not have especially strong inner moral barriers to surmount, for they were, for the most part, emotionally and cognitively normal. Lifton remarked on the "ordinariness of most Nazi doctors" whom he interviewed: "Neither brilliant nor stupid, neither inherently evil nor particularly ethically sensitive, they were by no means the demonic figures—sadistic, fanatic, lusting to kill—people have often thought them to be.... [O]rdinary people can commit demonic acts." (4-5)

An example of a Nazi doctor who in this fashion combined normality with the perpetration of evil was Eduard Wirths, M.D. Dr. Wirths seems to have been what his friends, acquaintances, and even Jewish prisoners under his control at Auschwitz perceived to be a good person, compassionate and gentle, "kind," a "gentleman," "conscientious," and "decent." He would treat Jews at night in his consulting room, "sometimes for injuries they had received at the hands of Nazis." (386) He showed

> ...concern about and friendliness toward prisoner patients.... Wirths used his medical authority to save lives. At Gestapo trials held in Auschwitz, he frequently testified to the medical capacity of an accused, usually a Polish civilian, to perform useful work, thereby arguing for the prisoner to be allowed to enter the camp as an ordinary inmate rather than be shot at the Black Wall.... He consistently took stands against brutality and random abuse of prisoners, was generally antagonistic to the ordinary criminals who took part in that abuse.... (386-8)

Yet he was the Nazi authority who was responsible for Auschwitz's "selection" system and for the camp's "medicalized killing" for a period of two years during which most of the mass executions were accomplished. (384) He was directly responsible for the murder of more than a million people. Dr. Wirths hanged himself after being captured by the British in September, 1945.

Finally, it is natural to ask whether doctors new to a concentration camp's routine of mass murder found it difficult to "adjust" to their new duties. Apparently they adjusted without difficulty: "The doctors...made a very speedy adjustment. The comments, questions, and doubts stopped soon after arrival. One doctor kept a diary in which there is no mention of difficulty in adjustment after the first few days." (Staub 1989:143)

We see then that the medical healers who placed their services at the disposal of the Holocaust's mass murders played a central role in the killings; those who lived to look back on their former days of military service have done so with bittersweet nostalgia; few of the doctors or others directly involved in the killings developed severe emotional reactions to their work; it was relatively easy for those who disliked their work to transfer to other duties, but few did; the physicians who supervised and engaged in the killing generally felt little remorse in retrospect; their work was facilitated by their recourse to euphemistic language and by doubling; doctors new to the tasks of medicalized killing found it comparatively easy to adjust to their new jobs; and in all these ways, the physicians who served the goals of the "Final Solution" appear to have been fairly normal, well-adjusted men.

## THOSE WHO STAND BY AND DO NOTHING:
## ALLOWING THE EVENTS TO HAPPEN

Don't let anybody tell you that they had no idea. Everybody sensed that there was something horribly wrong..., even if we didn't know all the details. They didn't want to know! It was too comfortable to live on the system, to support our families in royal style, and to believe that it was all right. – Hans Frank, Governor-general of occupied Poland, hanged at Nuremberg, quoted in Gilbert (1950:278)

He, standing behind the curtains, watched. The police beat women and children; he did not stir. It was no concern of his. He was neither victim nor executioner; a spectator, that's what he was. He wanted to live in peace and quiet. – Wiesel (1964:150)

Bystanders may be individuals, but they can also be entire societies and nations. When faced by events that are unpleasant, events that involve human atrocity and call upon moral courage to resist them, many bystanders prefer not to become involved. It can be a defensive choice motivated by self-preservation, or it can simply express an ostrich-like choice to evade responsibility, involvement, and the disturbance of one's own preferred status quo. Other motivating factors may enter in, as well. The psychology of bystanders has been studied in events that range from individuals who witness violence and murder but who are unwilling to intercede (as in the case of the 1964 murder of Kitty Genovese), to passivity on the part of entire nations when faced by human brutality, whether immediate and in their own lands, or abroad. In connection with the role of bystanders in genocides, much of the research has focused on the psychology of bystanders in the Holocaust, which will also be my focus here.

There exist two distinct and complementary ways in which most human beings react to mass killing once it starts: to join in the fray, or turn their heads the other way. Relatively few, indeed a very small minority, as we will see, resist mass killing. The majority will either willingly join in the violence, or they will comply, submit, and remain passive when faced by brutality. These are two sides of the same phenomenon and they have to do with the individual's and the group's psychological activity or passivity when confronted by mass murder.

It is often difficult to distinguish between simple passivity and silent complicity, since the behavioral manifestations of both attitudes are the same: inaction and absence of protest. During the Holocaust, both attitudes played a part. As has been documented in one study, "mass murder was carried out in full public view over a long period of time." (Klee *et al.* 1991:xx) For many people, as we noted in the previous chapter, the mass killings of the Holocaust provided "popular entertainment," a "public spectacle": German spectators, for example, visited the execution area in Leipaja, Latvia in what has been described as "execution tourism." (Klee *et al.* 1991:*passim*) When mass killing was not experienced as thrilling, it was often experienced dully—that is, with indifference.

Indifference characterized the attitude of the Allies during World War II when they systematically barred asylum to Jewish refugees from Germany, while, ironically, dictators Trujillo and Franco, of the Dominican Republic and Spain, opened their doors to Jews. (Charny & Rapaport 1982:200) Historians Arthur Morse (1968) and Judah Pilch (1968) have presented evidence that the United States was a well-informed accomplice to the Nazi Holocaust; they documented the indifference and inaction by American political leaders in spite of their growing awareness of the mass killings perpetrated in the course of Germany's "Final Solution." Staub remarked:

> In the United States there was strong resistance to immigration, even of refugee children. The number of immigrants actually allowed into the United States during the war years was well below the number that could be admitted without special legislation. The legal quota allowed sixty thousand immigrants a year, but only about six thousand actually got into the United States. (Staub 1989:157)

In a recent study of the role of America in genocides around the world, Power (2002:503) observed: "The United States has consistently refused to take risks in order to suppress genocide."

Pilch (1968) has shown how the English, French, and Swiss, along with the United States, established policies to prevent Jews from seeking sanctuary within their borders. The Evian Conference of 1938, the purpose of which was to discuss rescuing German Jews, was a failure due to the unwillingness of countries to accept Jewish immigrants. Not to excuse, but to explain, one Holocaust researcher noted: "[W]hen humanitarian issues are the only ones involved, most leaders opt for inaction." (Kressel 1996:268)

Taken together, the authors I have mentioned or quoted, among others, have shown us that numerous people—many ordinary Germans and citizens of other countries, as well as their leaders—knew about the terrible events of the Holocaust, but kept silent and did nothing. Some authors have claimed that silence of this kind *is* complicity, that knowing bystanders are guilty as accomplices to the Holocaust's mass murders, and that "[h]ad the silence been broken and the pretense...shattered, millions of Jews might not have died." (Johnson 1999:381) Staub (1989) has supported this claim:

> Even the behavior of governments can be strongly affected by bystanders—individuals, group, or other governments. Repeatedly when they faced substantial opposition, the Nazis backed away. They did not persist, for example, when Bulgaria (where the people protested in the streets) refused to hand over its Jewish population or when, within Germany, relatives and some institutions protested the killing of the mentally retarded, mentally ill, and others regarded as genetically inferior. (87)

There may be some truth in believing that had bystanders been more active the outcome would have been different, but of course this is speculative. My concern is not with what might have been had the facts been different, but to understand the psychology of those who stood by, unable or unwilling to trouble themselves with the plight of others.

There are several things that we know about bystander psychology. The now classic studies of Latané and Darley (1970) found that bystanders have a deeply rooted tendency to ignore crisis situations and to sidestep involvement, even when the crisis threatens to include them. The presence of other bystanders and their number tend to inhibit an active response by most individuals. Sheleff (1978) interpreted Latané's and Darley's findings as a sign that "diffusion of responsibility" occurs among bystanders, more so as the number of bystanders increases. But also contributing, one should note, are such factors as conformity, deficiency of empathy, and lack of moral sensibility, which bystander psychology must take into account. Seldom, in particular, is much attention given to the last two.

Bystanders, as do members of any crowd, lose themselves in the emotional state of the group and become—in their own minds—less personally accountable for their inaction. As the number of bystanders grows, they may furthermore become increasingly callous, less prompted to sympathy for victims, and more disposed to devalue life. (Sheleff 1978:18, discussing unpublished work by Ted L. Huston) The more bystanders who remain unswayed, the less chance there is that they will choose to intervene; and the more that bystanders believe there is no point in trying, the more they may "construe the victim as the kind of undesirable person who 'deserves' to suffer. The greater the injustice of the victim's fate the greater the efforts at condemnation and rejection." (Lerner 1970:207)

Apathy, inaction, the number of bystanders, their perception that they are impotent, conformity, lack of empathy and moral awareness, their tendency to turn against the victims, and their enjoyment of the victim's suffering—all of these are ingredients that foster and perpetuate inaction. There is, furthermore, the characteristic of bystanders to enjoy and dote upon the crisis itself. This is the human predisposition to enjoy catastrophe. William James found this in his own reaction to the San Francisco earthquake of 1906: "[E]verybody was excited, but the excitement, at first...seemed to be almost joyous. Here at last was a *real* earthquake, after so many years of harmless waggle!" (Sheleff 1978:45, quoting James) During widespread floods in England in 1953, the same phenomenon was observed: "[W]hile the flood waters filled the town, morale was extremely high in spite of the great threats to life..." A "euphoria" took possession of the public. (45, quoting witnesses) We see the same thing time and again as human beings are drawn irresistibly by their excited emotionalism to scenes of disaster and tragedy, to gawk, bathe gratifyingly in their tears, and share in the stimulation of the group experience.

These, then, are some of the common human emotions that contribute to the bystander's willingness to gaze excitedly upon victimization, or dully to avert his gaze, while doing nothing. As time passes, his fear of becoming involved, and the support and gratification he receives as a member of a community of bystanders, make any intervention he might initiate less and less likely. As he bears witness to brutality, so will he avert his eyes as brutality metastasizes into mass murder: In this way during the Holocaust, "bystanders to cruelty became bystanders to genocide." (Morse 1968:383)

Perhaps the worst part of this dynamic that perpetuates the bystander's emotional state that ranges from apathy to callousness to outright pleasure is that there is little evidence that bystanders learn from the past, or even from their own past mistakes. This phenomenon will become clearer as we later look more deeply into the subjects of moral intelligence and pathological human stupidity. From that perspective, we see that the silent, uncompassionate, and often callous and sadistic bystander is indeed afflicted with one of humanity's principal lanthanic pathologies (see Chapter 2), i.e., a destructive disorder that is unrecognized.

During the Holocaust, however, there occasionally occurred brighter sparks of constructive effort that originated from a minority of bystanders. We turn now to consider them.

## THE PSYCHOLOGY OF THOSE WHO REFUSE TO PARTICIPATE IN MASS MURDER

Helpful bystanders provide a different definition of reality. They break the uniformity of views and call attention to values disregarded by perpetrators and passive bystanders. They affirm the humanity of the victims. – Staub (1989:166), speaking of attempts to help the Jews of the French town of Le Chambon

In this section and the next it is important to emphasize that we are dealing with exceptions to human normality. Those who refuse to participate, directly or indirectly, in their group's sponsorship of killing comprise a very small minority. The history of genocides and wars makes this fact clear. The unwillingness to participate in these mass-approved acts of human destruction is, from a clinical point of view, an aberration, an exception to the rule. Exceptional individuals and exceptional groups do exist. Let us see what characterized their emotional outlook during the Holocaust.

The refusal to participate in mass murder can be of two kinds: There are those who refuse to contribute to the killing, and there are those who actively will oppose it. Here, I want to focus on the first group; in the next section, we shall consider the second.

Earlier in this chapter, I commented on the relative ease with which Nazi physicians could request transfers to less disturbing lines of work. Goldhagen (1996 and 1985) documented the relative ease with which ordinary soldiers could request and receive transfers when killing Jews and others became uncomfortable for them. There were very few who applied, and there were no punishments exacted for those who made such requests. (Goldhagen 1996:253ff) There even exists evidence that the men in at least nine police battalions "had been informed that they would not be punished for refusing to kill." (278)

> The Germans in nine police battalions, totaling 4,500 men or more, did indeed know that they did not have to take part in genocidal killing, yet they, with virtual unanimity, chose to kill and to continue to kill. Significantly, of these nine battalions, all but one were composed predominantly or substantially of reservists.... The men of these nine battalions form a sample sufficient to generalize with confidence about other police battalions. By choosing not to excuse themselves from the genocide of the Jews, the Germans in police battalions themselves indicated that they wanted to be genocidal executioners.... Germans could say "no" to mass murder. They chose to say "yes." (279, 381)

It is important that we take note of this freedom of choice that existed if we are to look at exceptional cases in which people refused to participate in the Holocaust's mass murder. Other options and alternatives did exist, as they so often do.

In 1942, a police battalion whose men were untrained for the tasks ahead was sent to Poland, to execute Jews. The commandant was distressed over his assignment; he tried to blunt his feelings with alcohol; he wept. He told his men that any who "did not feel up to it would be excused." (Victor 1998:94) Out of 500 men, a mere dozen asked to be excused, and they were. When the actual shooting of Jews began, a few more "balked"; they

> ...were spoken to harshly, but there was no insistence that individuals carry out the orders; coercion or fear of grave consequences were unnecessary in getting the majority to comply. Four hundred—80 percent—persevered in their assignment, shooting thirty-eight thousand Jews in a year and a half. (94)

What was the motivation of those who refused? "Years afterward, those who refused or evaded the assignment were questioned. They did not explain their noncompliance on moral grounds, but said they were too weak to do the killing—too weak to tolerate the disgust aroused." (95) As we shall see shortly, there were other motivations.

Two principal studies of Germans who refused to participate in mass murder deserve our attention. (Others that reached similar conclusions include Hinrichsen 1971; and Goldhagen 1985 and 1996.) Jäger (1982/1967) studied more than a hundred cases in which Nazi functionaries refused or managed to avoid carrying out execution orders. Kitterman (1988) extended and updated Jäger's study. The object of both studies was to investigate cases in which one or more people refused to participate in killing innocent people. It is enough here to concentrate on Kitterman's study, since it is the more inclusive and recent. In his study, those who refused included Generals in the Army and Police, officers in the Waffen SS, SD, and *Einsatzgruppen* execution units, enlisted men, and Nazi Party officials. Most refused to participate in mass murder on an individual basis, but there were about a dozen cases in which officers refused on behalf of their units.

Kitterman's study throws light on what appears to have motivated these people to refuse to participate in mass murder. (The qualification in using the word 'appears' is prudent because we are dealing with professed reasons that these individuals often gave in court for their refusal to participate in mass killing. However, since the reasons for their refusals after WWII were given in a social and political context that exonerated them, and indeed honored them for the positions they took, it is unlikely that these reasons were fabricated to avoid punishment, although they still may have been contrived.) The following were the personal reasons they gave for refusing to carry out executions: humanistic, religious or moral reasons (27.1%); claims that civilian executions are illegal (17.6%); assertions that perpetrating genocide would cause them personal emotional disturbance (8.2%); claims that such action would conflict with the individual's role or professional duties (8.2%); claims that executions of civilians would be "politically disadvantageous" (2.3%); and no reason given (48.2%). (Kitterman 1988:248-9) One man refused to execute women and children because he had a wife and children of his own. Three men refused simply on grounds that they would not shoot innocent people. (249) A few used a cleverly devised evasion tactic of legal argument, demanding that, before they would comply with execution orders, they be provided with legal documentation to show that those who were to be executed had been formally tried in courts of law and convicted, and then requiring that judges and prosecution attorneys be present at the executions. (249-50) Other ways to "opt out" of participation in mass killing included: allowing Jewish prisoners to escape; soldiers who threw their weapons away, "lost" them, or deliberately missed their targets; soldiers who simply resigned from military service or who were transferred to other duties because of their refusals. SS regulations themselves permitted soldiers "to be relieved from execution squads if they could demonstrate mental or psychological damage," which in principle opened this exit door for those who knew the regulations. (249-51)

There were, in short, a variety of potential strategies that Nazi functionaries used to evade the burden and crime of mass killing. Many situations provide loop-holes of one kind or another, often including the feigning of mental or physical illness. For would-be executioners to avail themselves of such ways out, a certain amount of individual initiative is of course essential. Not many have it.

And what were the consequences for those who refused? A number of studies have shown that they were generally insignificant. In Kitterman's study, those who refused experienced these consequences: no negative consequences at all (57.6%); placed under house arrest, charges then dropped (5.9%); threatened to be placed on report, sent to the front, or to be placed in prison (17.6%), the majority of which threats were not carried out; units broken up after their officers refused (2.4%); transferred to another unit or back to Germany (16.5%); demoted or simply not promoted (8.2%); ordered to drive officers to scenes of execution, dig execution pits, or participate in guard details (4.7%); resigned or were removed from their positions (3.5%); sent to combat units (3.5%); sent to concentration camps (1 individual, or 1.2%—who, incidentally, did not refuse to kill civilians, but was punished for brazenly informing his troops about military and police codes of criminal law, thereby undermining their "fighting ability"). (250-1) Goldhagen (1996) noted:

> ...it can be said with certitude that never in the history of the Holocaust was a German, SS man or otherwise, killed, sent to a concentration camp, jailed, or punished in any serious way for refusing to kill Jews.... [N]ot one SS judge has ever been found who adjudicated a case in which the accused was charged with refusing to kill Jews. (379; 578, n. 5).

What are we to conclude from this brief discussion of the psychology of those who refuse to participate in mass murder? Certainly, the psychology of the non-perpetrator must be understood as a function of the context in which he or she lives and works. In Nazi

Germany, as we have seen, the context was one of relative permissiveness, allowing Nazi functionaries who found it difficult to face the strain of mass killing to be transferred elsewhere, resign from service, or find less immoral alternatives. "[T]here was no need of compulsion, for volunteers were always available to replace the defectors, who were anyway very few: most men accepted their orders automatically and soon got used to the work." (Klee *et al.* 1991:xiii) I have summarized some of the evasion strategies that the men used to avoid killing innocent people, but the particular devices that they used are incidental. What is important is to recognize that it takes a certain kind of person sufficiently motivated to find the cracks in the system, to search for methods whereby he, and perhaps also the men under his command, can avoid participation in mass murder. What does it take to be such an individual? Clearly, someone who, compared to others, is capable of a certain degree of independent thought, who is emotionally self-reliant, is not imprisoned by a wish or need to conform, is not compliant or apathetic, who has a capacity for empathy with the suffering of others, and who possesses a certain level of moral sensibility.

In the next section, I look at the psychology of those who actively resist mass killing, for they embody these exceptional—and indeed humanly abnormal—characteristics more than most.

## THOSE WHO ACTIVELY RESIST

> [O]ne wonders how so many people could find the courage to dance to forbidden swing music, listen to outlawed BBC and other foreign-language broadcasts, spread jokes and epithets about Hitler and other Nazi leaders, and communicate their discontent with their government and society in myriad ways, but could not summon the courage and compassion to register abhorrence and thereby break the silence about the systematic murder of millions of defenseless and innocent men, women, and children. – Johnson (1999:459)

A very small, insignificant percentage of people is willing to resist the dictates of their leaders and the conventionally accepted views of their communities. During the Holocaust, only about 0.5 percent of Germans who lived through the period participated in any sort of active resistance against the Nazi regime. (Johnson 1999:261) Those willing to resist tend to make up a tiny minority in most populations, in the neighborhood of the percentage of those motivated to be conscientious objectors during wars, and often probably less. (Richardson's data, e.g., indicate that fewer than 0.3 percent of Britons called to military service during WWI resisted as conscientious objectors. Richardson 1948:151.) As noted in the opening quotation of this section, even in a political climate comparatively tolerant to dissidence, resistance seldom occurs. What makes these few people different?

Tec (1986), for example, studied the rescue of Jews by Christians in Nazi-occupied Poland. She found that many of the rescuers possessed personal qualities that made them comparatively independent of the conformist expectations of their society. They were, as a result, motivated to act without the need to rely on others for approval.

One might suppose that having a record in one's life of service to benefit others would predispose a person to resist mass murder. But as we saw earlier in this chapter, physicians are thought to be people of this kind, but "by 1942, 38,000 doctors—one-half of the total in Germany—were members of the Nazi Party and many of those chose to end, rather than preserve, millions of lives." (Zillmer *et al.* 1995:182)

Then there is the view that ordinary people share in a kind of "banality of heroism" (Zillmer *et al.* 1995) which surfaces during catastrophes and predisposes them to do good, to aid others in distress, and to pitch in to alleviate human suffering. But if this were true, one would expect acts of outstanding goodness to be fairly common. But they are not, certainly not during the Holocaust, as we have seen from the behavior of inactive bystanders, both individuals and their nations. What we might call the "mundanity thesis"—according to which, no matter what the act, "anyone could do it"—is misleading. It is expressed, for example, in the contention that "those who could have opposed [Hitler] were normal men, not heroes." (Zillmer *et al.*:183) But it was the normal men and women of Germany who followed Hitler, and the few, the very few, who resisted.

Some authors have pointed out that: "We are also beginning to sense that it is often primarily anger toward the offender rather than concern for the victim which induces intervention." (Geis *et al.* 1976:33) A study by Piliavin, Rodin, and Piliavin (1969) supported the view that the principal motivation of those willing to become actively involved "is not a positive 'altruistic' one, but rather a selfish desire to rid oneself of an unpleasant emotional state." (298) For example, a motorist was so intent upon catching a hit-and-run driver that he abandoned the badly injured victim at the site of the accident, who died within an hour at the hospital. (Geis *et al.* 1976:33) In such cases, people who are motivated to do something about an unjust situation may intervene "more out of hostility for the harm-doer and a desire to mete out immediate 'justice' than out of any feelings of empathy for a victim, or even any effort to help him." (Sheleff 1978:18)

Staub (1989) has thoughtfully sought to identify the characteristics of rescuers during the Holocaust. One of their main characteristics was "inclusiveness," by which Staub means the openness of people who are motivated to care and behave respectfully and morally toward people irrespective of their social status, ethnicity, or religion. (166) Another characteristic shared by some rescuers, according to Staub, is "marginality": "being a member of a minority religion..., being new to the community, having a parent from another country, or some other source of social separateness that allowed a different perspective and reduced fear of risking one's relationship with the majority group." (167) The willingness to resist a criminal regime like the Nazis' seems to generalize in the lives of people who resist: "People who agreed to hide some Jews briefly went on to care for them for years. A person who responded to the need of a friend continued by helping strangers." (167-8)

In connection with the characteristics of those who are motivated to resist the human evil of genocide we should re-emphasize the following: They are to an important degree able to step outside the prevailing context of awareness and values of their community or nation. They are exceptional people, for they are, literally, exceptions to the prevailing mentality. They are able to feel empathy and therefore tolerance and respect toward others. The suffering and deaths of others affect them deeply. Allport (1954) recognized that what is in question is a true "ability." In a section entitled "Empathic Ability," he commented:

> One important factor in tolerance is an ability we know little about. This ability is sometimes called empathy.... Just what the basis of empathic ability may be we cannot say. Perhaps it is a joint product of a secure home environment, aesthetic sensitivity, and high social values. For our purposes, it is sufficient to note that, whatever its origins, it seems to be a prominent feature in personalities possessing ethnic tolerance. (434, 436)

He referred to an early study of anti-Semitism (Evans 1952), which showed how tolerance is a function of a person's "value orientation toward life." The study measured college students' values and their prejudice against Jews. Those who were high in anti-Semitism ranked their values as follows, from highest to lowest: political, economic, religious, social, theoretical, aesthetic. Those who were lowest in anti-Semitism had values with virtually the opposite ranking: aesthetic, social, religious, theoretical, economic, political. This is, interestingly, one of the earliest studies that pointed to a correlation between aesthetic sensibility and freedom from prejudice.

People capable of resisting human evil, as in the mass killings of the Holocaust, are, to varying degrees, then, "marginal individuals": Their experience of the world allows for some measure of disengagement from prevailing ideas and values; they are more able than most to stand emotionally alone, without the crutch of group agreement; they may feel a certain amount of repugnance toward violence that harms innocent people and perhaps toward collectivism itself; they are more resistant to the emotional attractions of conformity, the gratifications of hatred, power over others, divisiveness, destructiveness and its adrenaline-producing capacity; and the list could be lengthened, as indeed it will be as we move to later topics in this book.

Generally put, although indeed counterexamples exist, those who resist human evil are exceptions to the normal man and woman, about whom most of this chapter has been devoted. We would be justified in considering them to be aberrations, deviations, or abnormalities, although in counter-intuitively good senses of these words. Their emotional and cognitive constitution, as we shall see, tends broadly to run counter to the pathology of human evil, which became pronounced and nearly universal in the Germany of the Holocaust.

Specifically in relation to the Holocaust, those who were motivated to resist human evil were, in a sense which we have yet to define, *morally more intelligent* than their fellow citizens and victimizers. Their stronger moral orientation toward human life made them less likely to comply with the demands of cruelty and dehumanization, and more likely to oppose these. I will have more to say about this in connection with the subject of moral intelligence. (See Chapter 18.)

## WHAT GENOCIDE HAS TAUGHT US

No study of mass hatred can conclude optimistically. Genocidal massacres and terrorist attacks will surely thrive in the future as they have in the past. – Kressel (1996:280-1)

This and the preceding chapter have sought to give an integrated account of certain of the principal observations and conclusions that have come from psychologically-oriented studies of genocide, considered generally, and of the Holocaust, in particular. If we learn anything at all from such an overview it is that "civilization" does not put a stop to human indifference to human evil. Normal people engage in genocide, killing other normal people for a variety of reasons. Certainly the human normality of genocide is a fact we would rather not acknowledge, even as psychologists. As Charny and Rapaport (1982:20) commented, "...even now, psychology books rarely contain an honest description of how the normal personality includes an explicit penchant for destructiveness."

I generally avoid reference to "human nature" in this book, and speak rather of the emotional and conceptual "constitution" of human beings as it is at present. And at the present time, that constitution, as is evident for all who would study it without the blinders of homocentric self-satisfaction, is recalcitrant to efforts to neutralize the numerous motivations that lead people to engage in mass killing. Psychology, in particular, which is the framework for most of the present study, has not been able to provide effective solutions that can be applied *en masse* to the rapidly proliferating human species. As one genocide scholar commented, "when one considers the energy that psychologists devote to fostering independence and new values in a single person, it seems doubtful that anyone could carry out such a complex restructuring of personality on a mass scale." (Kressel 1996:269)

Psychologically normal people give power to their rulers in order to gratify their own needs. Studies of genocide that focus on a leader's "twisted psychology" fail to recognize this. As long as people achieve emotional gratification from mass killing, this form of human evil will not end. In a later chapter, I summarize a number of the very substantial obstacles that mankind's present human emotional and conceptual constitution place in the way of any efforts to deter the pathologies that comprise human evil. Genocide is one of the expressions of human evil, and proposed solutions to it, even when it is recognized as a pathology, are, as we shall see, far from promising.

A historian once asked what needed to happen to the German people in order for them to accept a government intent upon mass murder. "Unfortunately, *nothing needed to happen*. In nations across the world, people accept government crime." (Victor 1998:221, my emphasis) *Nothing needs to happen* in order for psychologically normal, average, everyday people to accept and comply with a callous and cruel government intent upon a program of systematic dehumanization and murder of the members of another group or nation.

Psychiatrist Douglas M. Kelley, who studied the Nazi leaders in Nuremberg, was led to this recognition. Even the democratic conditions that prevail in the United States, he believed, are sufficient to permit a re-enactment of genocidal atrocities perpetrated against a dehumanized enemy. "I am convinced that there is little in America to-day which could prevent the establishment of a Nazi-like state.... It is a deeply disturbing experience to return from Nuremberg to America and find the same racial prejudices that the Nazis preached being roused here in the same words that rang through the corridors of Nuremberg Jail." (Kelley 1947:195-6, 197) He notes that the personal characteristics that made men like Hitler, Göring, Goebbels, Streicher, and Ley successful are to be found, for example, among American businessmen, and among politicians, salesmen, racketeers, and others. In saying this, Kelley was not singling out the U.S. from among other countries whose populations are intrinsically more moral. On the contrary, he was courageous and unbiased enough to see even within the democratic and "open" society of America the same psychological roots from which genocide flourishes.

Perhaps one of the most important lessons to be learned from a study of human genocide is that *we must not fall victim to faith in humanity*. As we shall see in the last chapter of this work, one of the greatest, and most unsuspected, sources of human evil and of the resulting lack of preparation to oppose it, comes from this faith. As one Holocaust author reflected: "We fell victim to our faith in mankind, our belief that humanity had set limits to the degradation and persecution of one's fellow man." (Donat 1965:103) "Especially disastrous was the victims' faith in universalism and modern humanitarian values. It disarmed them." (Greenberg 1977:19) If genocide and particularly Holocaust studies teach us anything, it is that we must not fall victim to this comforting delusion again.

To recognize that genocide is a normal human predisposition is not to accept that it is either excusable or forgivable. Not long ago, as noted earlier in this chapter, it was implicitly accepted among genocide researchers that perpetrators of genocide must have criminal minds and be mentally deranged, but that they should not, for this reason, be excused. The logic of judgment, with perverse irony, has now been reversed as further research has shown that perpetrators are, for the most part, in fact psychological normal people—but they should not, for this reason, be excused: "To be sure, to view the Nazis as merely ordinary and average persons should not be interpreted as an excuse for their immoral deeds and the terror, massacres, and genocide they have caused but rather as an attempt to understand them." (Steiner 1980:440)

We see that possession of comparatively normal psychology, i.e., a comparatively normal emotional and cognitive constitution, is far from rendering one immune to human pathology, but is in fact the basis for it. Normality does not exempt from moral condemnation the bigoted outlook of ordinary men, women, and children, and their hate-inspired behavior. —A statement of this kind finds its justification not within this pair of chapters that have focused on the psychology of genocide, but requires a specific explanation of the connection between the pathologies we have been considering and an explicitly moral-evaluative framework, which any approach to pathology must presuppose. We will take the steps needed to reach this understanding in the chapters that follow.

## PROPOSED SOLUTIONS

In separating this section from the previous one, I wish to draw attention to the difference between what we can learn from the psychology of genocide and how we might propose to treat this human evil. These are very different things, and they are often confused. Solutions that have been proposed to genocide presuppose what we learn from the subject—which is a matter of intellectual comprehension—and then suggest potential ways of healing this human pathology—which is a matter of practical problem-solving. Limitations of space do not permit me to discuss in any detail the main solutions that have been proposed. It will be enough here simply to recognize the immense gap between the following sample proposals I have chosen to mention, and reality. The obvious question, in the end, must then be raised, What, at least in principle, has to occur in human psychology for such suggestions to be realized?

In no particular order, here are some of the proposals that have been offered: To remedy man's genocidal predisposition, Holocaust survivor and author Elie Wiesel has urged the need to cultivate respect for the differences of others (not mere "toleration," which, in his view, implies derogation). (Televised interview with Charlie Rose, PBS, 12/22/1999) Psychiatrist Douglas M. Kelley, after his study of the Nazi leaders, urged that we "reform our system of education to teach students to think. We may even have to rebuild our language habits, eliminating those generalities which actually mean nothing, but which produce in unthinking persons strong emotional reactions." (Kelley 1947:201) Writing half a century later, George Victor (1998:217-18) also urged the need for "new methods of learning," which should embrace "moral training" and socialization, and the need to reduce the majority's "acceptance of charismatic would-be killers and...reliance on scapegoating to solve national problems." Similarly, Neil J. Kressel (1996) emphasized the need for higher education, which on the one hand he claimed fosters tolerance, and yet on the other tends to produce especially destructive leaders, for "it is the educated who are more likely to take the lead in devising schemes of destruction for others to follow." (240) He recognized the comparative ineffectiveness of attempts at moral education and concluded that "[t]he two best strategies for combating mass hatred are the relentless pursuit and punishment of the perpetrators of atrocities and the promotion of stable democracies wherever possible." (277)

Holocaust scholar and theologian Richard L. Rubenstein (1966), in speaking of the need to reconcile Jew and Christian, pointed to the need for people "to accept their own and each other's humanity." (58) This is to say a great deal relevant to the issue of genocide, in a few words. Israel Charny and Chanan Rapaport (1982) gave an articulate and more inclusive statement to the issue of what should be expected from us, given our understanding of the psychology of the person who "enjoys himself and life and cares for his family and friends" and yet "can destroy others without being aware of their humanity." They stressed the need to overcome scapegoating, by finding "new ways to control and reduce projection." (209) For, "[t]o the extent that a people rejects scapegoating another people in their everyday life and in their society's social and political institutions, it is doubtful that a leader can lead that people to genocide." (198)

During the course of this book I have pointed repeatedly to psychological projection as one source among others of many of mankind's most undesirable and harmful traits. If one wishes to reduce a complex subject to its oversimplification, one is tempted to sum up many of the emotional propensities that underlie humanity's genocidal tendencies in the following way: Many appear to arise through a combination of psychological projection and the emotional gratification which the process of projection provides. To bring these tendencies of prejudice and persecution which contributed so strongly to the Holocaust to life again, people need only to seek gratification for certain rather simple projective emotional and conceptual needs. From this point of view, any efforts that are effective in reducing the human projective propensity will help to weaken man's genocidal character. Projection is a subject to which we shall still have occasion to return a number of times.

In reflecting on proposed solutions to the problem of genocide, one cannot but be struck by their frequent vagueness, generality, ingenuousness, and often their impracticability. More to the point, as we shall see in the final chapter of this book, the proposals to reduce "humanity's inhumanity" have consistently been blind to the powerful barriers in man's emotional and conceptual constitution that swiftly render them ineffective.

## MORAL RELATIVISM AND THE HOLOCAUST: IS ONE MAN'S GENOCIDE ANOTHER'S ETHNIC CLEANSING?

In Chapter 20, we shall have the opportunity to deal with moral relativism as it concerns human evil. But in the immediate shadow of the preceding discussion of the Holocaust, a few words about moral relativism are in order. For perhaps nowhere among the individual topics with which this book deals is moral relativism such a burning problem as it is in connection with genocide and the Holocaust, in particular. As we have seen in the Holocaust, an entire population can become so consumed by its projected hatred that the majority of men and women will willingly contribute to mass murder, and do so in the interests of values which, for them, have an intrinsic and persuasive reality-consistency. Many Germans, even these many years after WWII, carry with them a conviction that, at the time, they were doing what was "right" and that they distinguished themselves in dutiful and disciplined service to their country and its "high ideals." We recall the defense founded on moral relativism offered by such Nazis leaders as Karl Dönitz and Rudolf Hoess, both of whom claimed that, relative to the established norms of their state, they were "good" citizens and "good" soldiers, which perhaps they were. (Zillmer *et al.* 1995:189-90)

We have seen in this chapter that normal people engage in mass killing. And we have seen that this fact raises the question whether mass murder is to be understood simply as a normal phenomenon, or as a universal pathology, a harmful, dysfunctional propensity shared by the majority of people. Whether man's genocidal propensity is "simply normal" or whether it bears the stamp of universal pathology, a second question has to be asked: whether genocide is ever "justified," as it was felt to be by many Germans. As Staub (1989) asked, "Are mass killing and genocide ever justifiable self-defense or understandable retaliation?" (11) He responded to this question as though it were self-answering by saying that of course they are not. And yet there is obviously a totally convincing rationale in the minds of perpetrators of evil. Simply to state flatly that they are wrong does not make them wrong, nor, more importantly, does it change the way they perceive the world. When we confront those who embrace belief-systems that endorse genocide, does our judgment rest only on opinion? We recall the words of Sartre (1948:7), who wrote: "This word *opinion* makes us stop and think.... It suggests that all points of view are equal; it reassures us, for it gives an inoffensive appearance to ideas by reducing them to the level of tastes. All tastes are natural;

all opinions are permitted."

The Holocaust not only raises the issue of moral relativism, it demands an answer, an answer that is definitive, rationally and morally compelling, in short, decisive. As yet no genocide researcher has offered such a solution, nor is such a solution to be found in moral philosophy where one might expect to find it. I give a solution in the chapters ahead. To recognize it as a rationally compelling solution and to be convinced by it will require of the reader his or her sustained interest, attention, and moral intelligence.

# CHAPTER 13

# THE PSYCHOLOGY OF TERRORISM AND HUMAN EVIL

## INTRODUCTION

Relatively little is known about the terrorist as an individual, and the psychology of terrorists remains poorly understood.... – Hudson (1999:25)

Terrorism, although real, is a vague, incomprehensible, unpredictable, and unexpected menace.... – Crenshaw quoted in Hutchinson (1978:25)

Contrary to these assertions, terrorism, as we shall see, is neither difficult to understand nor vague and unpredictable, while a good deal is known about it. However, the psychology of terrorism and studies of the individual psychology of the terrorist personality have made little headway in spite of attempts to explain these phenomena. The general ineffectiveness of psychological research relating to terrorism is widely recognized by the researchers themselves. There are three main reasons for the lack of meaningful progress in achieving a unified and useful psychological understanding of terrorism and of individual terrorists. First, as we shall see in this chapter, terrorism psychologists have been unable to agree upon a definition of terrorism, so the domain to be studied has been impossible to pin down. Second, a largely unquestioned belief has dominated much psychological research into the origins of terrorism. It is the belief that since only comparatively few people become terrorists, there must be something special about them, some set of psychological characteristics that sets them apart from others. In fact, numerous studies have shown that this is not the case, as we shall see. Third, there has been a widespread failure to recognize that terrorism and forms of socially approved violence differ insignificantly on the level of the psychology of the individual perpetrator. The result of this failure is a tendency to disconnect psychological studies of terrorism from other closely related human propensities that are neither mysterious nor incomprehensible. Let us examine these subjects one at a time.

Terrorism is an ancient form of political violence that dates back at least to 48 A.D. when the Jewish sect, the Zealots, began to infiltrate cities under Roman rule and assassinate Roman soldiers and Jewish collaborators. *Sicarii*, or dagger-men, killed or took highly placed officials hostage, and used poison to murder, intimidate, and arouse public alarm. During the past two millennia, terrorism has proliferated throughout the world. (For a brief history, see Laqueur 1987 and Reich 1998.) More than one thousand terrorist organizations are now active in more than 125 countries. (Taylor 1988:7) The spread of terrorism in the past half century has brought with it an increasing disregard and even contempt for the lives of innocent people. (Pearce 1977:174 and Merari & Friedland 1985:185) Even so, and despite the toll of life, for example, in the 2001 terrorist destruction of the World Trade Center, so far the number of civilian casualties due to terrorist groups has remained comparatively small, dwarfed, for example, by the number of deaths in the United States each year due to automobile accidents. (For instance, during the entire decade from 1973 to 1982, terrorism around the world resulted in the deaths of 3,509 people, compared to an *annual* U.S. highway death toll of 45,000 during the same period. Merari & Friedland 1985:188) The public's interest in terrorism and the fear that terrorist groups provoke are therefore greatly disproportionate, at least so far, in relation to the magnitude of the problem. Saying this is not to diminish the tragedy of individual lives lost to terrorism, but to comment on the past *relative* danger of terrorist groups. As one author remarked:

> Compared with the truly important problems of our time—the potential dangers of modern technologies, global debt, hunger in the Third World, overpopulation, certain new and incurable diseases—terrorism was, after all, a side-show.... [T]errorism directly affected the lives of only a handful of people. It did not cause major political, economic, social or cultural upheaval. (Laqueur 1987:298)

In a moment I will distinguish several forms of terrorism, one of which, to anticipate, is terrorism perpetrated in conflicts by states against other states. State-against-state terrorism has been the main exception to terrorism's general political ineffectiveness, for states have indeed used terrorist strategies to force the capitulation of their adversaries. Other forms of terrorism that have sometimes resulted in political change include terrorist strategies employed in wars of national liberation, civil, and revolutionary wars, and by resistance movements against foreign occupation.

The fact that in recent years terrorism has come to occupy center stage in public consciousness and government concern is not due, then, to either its political effectiveness or the comparative degree of its destructiveness, but rather to its psychological success in attracting attention. Given prospects for an increasingly devastating loss of lives and property as terrorists come to possess increasingly lethal weapons, and as terrorist incidents on a grand scale become increasingly capable of inciting widespread war, it is important that we understand as well as possible the terrorist's frame of mind in order to know what we should expect. As Reich (1998) has urged: "Demystification of terrorism is one of the most important public contributions the psychological approach could make." (260) Taylor (1988) has expressed the belief: "Although psychological analyses of terrorism are relatively limited, it might be argued that it is, in fact, in this area where most practical, as opposed to conceptual, knowledge might be gained." (11) As this chapter attempts to make clear, we do, in fact, know a good deal about the psychology of terrorism, what to expect of terrorism in the future, and something about how best to deal with it. Unfortunately, as we shall see, nearly all of these insights have been ignored by those most able to make use of them.

In this chapter, it will not be my intent to discuss current terrorist movements or appropriate responses to them, but rather to attempt to understand the terrorist mind, the rationale from the terrorist's point of view for his or her behavior, and in the process to identify certain pathologies of emotion and thought that are fundamental to terrorism. We shall find in the psychology of the terrorist many of the same emotional and conceptual characteristics that we found in those who commit genocide. In fact, many of the psychological observations relating to terrorism can be reduced to a problem we have already sought to solve. Unfortunately, many genocide researchers are unaware of the psychology of terrorism, while psychologists of terrorism frequently are unacquainted with the psychology of genocide. The gap that has existed between these two areas is bridged by human characteristics that are, as we shall see, constant and pervasive.

## THE PSYCHOLOGY OF TERRORISM

It is, as I have already mentioned, generally conceded by psychologists of terrorism that their efforts to understand the phenomenon have been ineffective, failing to provide either theoretical knowledge or practical terrorist identification methods. Psychological data and theorizing about terrorists have seemed to be on a different level of discourse than military intelligence, which can often suggest specific ways to fight an enemy. One reason for this situation was noted by Laqueur (1987:165): "No truly scientific (that is predictive and explanatory) theory with regard to terrorism has emerged, nor has there been any significant progress in this direction over the last decade." This is not surprising, given that the trend in psychology has favored experimental as opposed to observational methods. Terrorism and individual terrorists, after all, do not lend themselves to experimental study; control over variables is impossible; terrorists are not "cooperating subjects." Furthermore, empirical data is most frequently negligible and inadequate as a basis for generalizations. This is understandable since the psychology of terrorism is a fairly new area of study. Twenty years ago, only a handful of publications relating to terrorism was even listed in *Psychological Abstracts*.

In spite of the reluctance of many psychologists to yield to the necessity of observational methods in the study of terrorism, there is a growing realization across disciplines that terrorists are human beings, and if we are to understand their motivations, strengths, and weaknesses, we must know their psychology. Efforts to do this have proceeded along four main paths. One group of researchers has sought to detect forms of psychopathology in individual terrorists, usually under restrictive conditions: They have been captured and placed in prison, the authorities permit them to be interviewed, and the terrorists themselves agree to this. Second, there has been considerable interest in the psychological profiling of terrorists as an aid to identifying them before they carry out their objectives, and there has been some very limited success in doing this. Another group of researchers has looked for terrorist "group organizational pathology." And finally some psychologically-focused researchers have sought to discover origins of terrorism in a variety of family and social-environmental conditions. The most recent psychological leaning has favored the last two approaches, principally because of the limited value of profiling and out of a sense of discouragement because nothing special was found by the first group. However, discouragement would be a mistake, as I will show. The negative findings by those who have looked in vain for terrorist psychopathology are important and revelatory, although to see this we need to look at those findings in a new light. Before we discuss them, however, it is important to situate terrorism within a wider frame of reference than is customary in the literature.

## DEFINITIONS, THE PERVASIVENESS OF TERRORISM, AND ITS CHARACTERISTICS

Reality does not dictate definitions, it only sometimes shows us which are most useful in relation to a set of purposes. Among terrorism experts, there has been little agreement what terrorism is, but instead a swarm of definitions has clouded its study. Schmid (1983:119-58) assembled 109 competing definitions of terrorism, and since his book the proliferation of definitions has continued. There are good reasons for this exuberance. In history we see many varieties of terrorism, according to the nature of the conflict—sometimes between groups, sometimes between groups and states, often between states. As we shall note in passing, even on the individual level, in relationships between individuals, various forms of terrorism are as common as they are neglected by terrorism experts and by the majority of people when they think of terrorism. Due to this wide variety of levels and kinds of terrorism, most authors are obliged to discuss the issue of definition; even in the course of a single chapter, we need to do this.

Some of the main categories of terrorism include criminal, religious, ethnic, and political terrorism. Individual terrorists, terrorist groups, or entire governments may be involved. State-sponsored terrorism involves governmental support of terrorist organizations. Alternatively, governments sometimes terrorize their own citizens. And, most familiar to the public is political terrorism by terrorists groups against governments. In connection with the last two varieties, Frederick J. Hacker proposed the now familiar distinction between "terror from above" and "terrorism from below":

> ...terror, which is inflicted from above, is the manufacture and spread of fear by dictators, governments, and bosses. It is the attempt of the powerful to exert control through intimidation. Terrorism, which is imposed from below, is the manufacture and spread of fear by rebels, revolutionaries, and protesters. It is the attempt of the so-far powerless, the would-be powerful, to exert control through intimidation. Terror and terrorism are not the same, but they belong together, indissolubly linked by the shared belief that fear is the strongest, if not the only, effective human motivation and that violence is the best, if not the only, method to produce and maintain fear. (Hacker 1980:144; see also Hacker 1976)

Among the more integrative and nonspecific definitions that have been proposed for terrorism was one given in the context of a hearing by the U.S. Senate Subcommittee on Emerging Threats and Capabilities (U.S. Congress 2001:3): "Terrorism, most experts agree, is violence or the threat of violence in order to coerce others to alter their actions or refrain from actions." A similarly broad definition was proposed by the 1986 Vice-President's Task Force on Combating Terrorism: "The unlawful use or threat of violence against persons or property to further political or social objectives. It is usually intended to intimidate or coerce a government, individuals, or groups, or to modify their behavior or politics." (Quoted in Laqueur 1987:144) I could discuss a host of alternative definitions, but these two will suffice exactly because they stand out as being, some would say, excessively inclusive. For, although very likely not intended by their authors to include such things, both definitions cover a wide range of forms of terrorism—that is, intimidation through fear of violence—used not by political groups or organizations, but by individuals against other individuals. Some of these forms of violence include punishment, extortion, torture (on torture as a form of terrorism, see Hovens & Drozdek 2002), hate crimes, rape, child abuse, domestic violence, and even bullying in the schoolyard, for the wish to provoke fear in one's enemy and so to terrorize him or her is a propensity, after all, that makes itself known even among young children (on the child as terrorist, see Warneka 2002 and Stokes 2002).

In all its forms, terrorists attempt to intimidate using means that historically have been disproportionately small in terms of degree of physical destruction when compared with the strength of the emotions they hope their acts will arouse in their victims. Fundamentally the same strategy is used by terrorists no matter what their nationality, race, or system of belief. This is true throughout the gamut of terrorist acts, whether perpetrated by one individual against another, by a group against a state, or by a state against an enemy state. The psychological aggression they commit is of a special kind in that *the success of terrorists is in the hands of the victims,* for only if they are willing to respond to terrorist acts as the terrorists intend can terrorism obtain the emotional leverage it seeks. As one researcher has pointed out: "Terrorism wins only if you respond to it the way the terrorists want you to; which means that its fate is in your hands and not in theirs." (Fromkin 1975:697)

From a psychological point of view, and I will have occasion to emphasize this several times in this chapter, terrorism is a phenomenon that has the same origins as do forms of human response to conflict that are much more commonly encountered than is political terrorism by a group working to undermine an enemy state. It is important to recognize that terrorism can and does involve much more of human behavior than is customarily meant by the term. We need to acknowledge the pervasiveness of terrorism in all its forms, since otherwise we shall be looking for something special and unique in the psychology of terrorists and their groups, which, as we shall see, is not there.

Groups and states can participate in terrorism in four different ways: (1) group-against-group, (2) group-against-state, (3) state-against-group, and (4) state-against-state. We find the first combination, for example, in organized crime, as when one criminal group terrorizes a competing group. The second combination, group-against-state, is found, for example, when groups seek to overthrow a government, as in anti-colonial revolts, domestic terrorism, and international terrorism perpetrated by terrorist organizations, which at present is the most prominent form. The third combination, state-against-group, occurs, as we saw in the last two chapters, most especially in genocide, and it can occur in attempts by states to destroy terrorist groups that threaten their existence. The fourth combination, state-against-state, is seldom discussed in the literature as a form of terrorism, and yet terrorism of the worst kind is frequently takes place in wars between states. Overwhelmingly, the largest number of deaths due to terrorism occurs in connection with the last two varieties, in genocides and wars.

In all of these forms of violent conflict, terrorist acts appear to the perpetrators to be reasonable and necessary, part of a "rational strategy, with calculable costs and benefits." (Colvard 2002:359; cf. also Crenshaw 1998a:24 and Lande & Armitage 1997:419) The belief by terrorists that terrorism is a rational strategy is based on their recognition that a certain tactical threshold exists beyond which their enemies will, they hope, capitulate. This is the threshold that nations reach in war when their populations become "war weary" (see Chapter 9) to such a degree that a country's aggression turns into concession and capitulation. Terrorists seek to bring about this phase-change in their enemy's attitude. (Merari & Friendland (1985:194), for example, have graphed the relationship between the degree of stubbornness of the public to stand firm against terrorism, and the intensity of the terrorist threat. Their graph shows that once terrorist intimidation reaches a threshold, which varies with the situation, the public will capitulate.)

There are other characteristics universally shared by political terrorists and their groups. Foremost among these is that of "having a cause," of "seeing oneself as part of a grand design." Political terrorists share an interpretation of the world, an ideology, whose construction is immune to argument and resistant to contrary evidence. The ideology will compartmentalize, or split, people into those who are portrayed as good and worthwhile, and those who constitute the enemy, who are described in dehumanizing and abusive language. Furthermore, political terrorists share a belief in a desired future, which confers meaning upon the immediate violent struggle of the day; it is a belief that fundamentally involves projection, as we shall see later on. Another universal is the key belief among terrorists that killing innocent people will provide them with publicity, that publicity will cause panic, and that such panic will contribute to the destabilization of the enemy. (See Laqueur 1987:144.) Still another universal is found in the paired terrorist characteristics, the personal renunciation and the dedicated commitment of the terrorist, for political terrorism is difficult, intensely serious, life-threatening work. (See Livingstone 1982:34-5) Terrorists share a wish for attention, which media publicity offers; and of course for many there is the attraction of emotional stimulation and escape from the monotony of everyday life. A list of general characteristics of this sort could be lengthened; it contains no surprises and is what one would expect.

It is important to see that such characteristics do not tell us anything important about the "terrorist personality": They are descriptive of attitudes, of states of mind and general qualities of person, but not of individual psychology, that is, of individualizing traits that lend themselves to effective detection. They would not be especially helpful as a profile to identify would-be terrorists before they act. Such characteristics are, however, among the necessary conditions for terrorism to occur, and so they throw a certain amount of light on the phenomenon.

## THE FRAMEWORK- AND AUDIENCE-RELATIVITY OF TERRORISM

Terrorism in the sense of deliberate, planned violence against a person, group, a people, or a state in order to bring about political, social, religious, or other change is a *framework-relative* classification. It is framework-relative in much the same way that identification of disease is, as we saw in Part I of this book. And indeed terrorism has been likened to a disease: "Like a psychosocial smallpox, eruptions of terrorism are scattered all over the skin of today's world." (Akhtar 1999:350) Whether one identifies a condition as a disease or calls someone a terrorist, doing so is a function of accepted values. Terrorism is a negative label. Most terrorists therefore call themselves "freedom fighters," "revolutionaries," or give themselves other heroic appellations. Most do not regard themselves as terrorists at all, "but rather as soldiers, liberators, martyrs, and legitimate fighters for noble social causes." (Hudson 1999:38) "What is called terrorism thus seems to depend on one's point of view. Use of the term implies a moral judgment; and if one party can successfully attach the label 'terrorist' to its opponent, then it has indirectly persuaded others to adopt its moral viewpoint." (Jenkins 1981:3; see also Kellen 1982:10) To call someone a terrorist is automatically to adopt the position of adversary, of an opponent with conflicting values and beliefs. Terrorism is framework-relative in these senses.

The relativity of terrorism to one's context of reference can be a source of considerable hypocrisy, as Charles Yost, Ambassador to the United Nations, remarked:

> The fact is, of course, that there is a vast amount of hypocrisy on the subject of political terrorism. We all righteously condemn it—except where we ourselves or friends of ours are engaging in it. Then we ignore it, or gloss over it, or attach to it tags like "liberation" or "defence of the free world" or "national honour" to make it seem like something other than what it is. (Quoted in Taylor 1988:3)

It follows from its framework-relativity that terrorism is also an *audience-relative* phenomenon. Its audience-relativity needs to be built into whatever definition we give to terrorism. For terrorism is a kind of rhetoric of violence: Rhetoric seeks, traditionally by words alone, to persuade, to change the convictions of an audience, and as we have seen, this is what terrorism tries fundamentally to do, but by violent means. The audience-relativity of terrorism is what is responsible for the fact, alluded to earlier, that the success of terrorism lies in the response that an audience makes to it. It is the audience-relativity of terrorism that justifies calling terrorism a form of psychological warfare, and it is, as we shall see, the basis for one of the main counterterrorist strategies that has come from psychological studies of terrorism, but to which unfortunately little heed has so far been paid.

## PSYCHOLOGICAL HYPOTHESES TO EXPLAIN TERRORISM

In spite of limited data, some psychologists of terrorism have not been hesitant to offer hypotheses to explain it. In fact, a whole and varied spectrum of clinical diagnoses has been offered to explain terrorism. In an area of research in which a lack of empirical data is the rule rather than the exception, given the rarity of opportunities to interview and test individual terrorists, it is extraordinary to encounter so many competing diagnostic pronouncements in the literature. Here, in no particular order, is a sample of the range of diagnostic hypotheses that have been offered to explain terrorism: Paranoia, paranoid schizophrenia, borderline disorder, schizophrenia, passive-aggressive personality, and sociopathy (Berkowitz 1972); a physiological hypothesis of terrorism, according to which terrorist violence is in large measure the result of an "agitated tissue response" to stress (Hubbard 1983); the frustration-aggression hypothesis (Gurr 1970; Davies 1973; Margolin 1977; Berkowitz 1989); the negative identity hypothesis, which claims that negative identity comes about through the individual's rebellion against family and social values (Knutson 1981); the narcissistic rage hypothesis (Post 1990, Crayton 1983, and Pearlstein 1991); the "crippled narcissist" hypothesis, according to which terrorists have a "shared paranoid pathology," "inadequate personalities," and a "flawed sense of identity" resulting in "self-pathology" (Johnson 1992:293, 295-7, 301); psychoanalytic hypotheses that terrorism results from "regressive hope" originating in the mother complex, repressed hatred resulting from abusive parents, and blocked empathic development (cf. Taylor 1988:142 for discussion and sources); the hypothesis that terrorism can result from a collective delusional state (Crenshaw 1988:40); the view that terrorism relies on splitting and externalization (cf. Reich 1998:29); what one might call the "incentive hypothesis," that terrorism is the consequence of a group of general psychological incentives, including power, excitement, risk, stress, belonging, and social approval (Crenshaw 1998b:250), as well as hatred, revulsion, revenge, anger, and desire for political change (Reich 1998:272-3); older 1870s hypotheses of terrorist behavior: Cesare Lombroso's view that it is due to pellagra and other vitamin deficiencies, and views that terrorism is related to barometric pressure, moon phases, alcoholism, droughts, and cranial measurements (cf. Reich 1998:268); the more recent, less fanciful hypothesis that some terrorism is the result of "a predisposition toward violence and cruelty" (Laqueur 1999:236); the theory that terrorists are "mentally ill" (cf. Lande & Armitage 1997:426-31 and Coronado 1981); the hypothesis that terrorists are "deeply traumatized individuals" (Volkan 1997) who are generally "sexually inhibited young men, ...traumatized and struggling to achieve a sense of selfhood and a cohesive identity" (Akhtar 1999:352); and, finally, in case the reader is feeling a bit dizzy from this panorama of hypotheses based on so little evidence, we have the hypothesis put forward by psychiatrists David G. Hubbard and F. Gentry Harris, who examined 80 imprisoned terrorists in 11 countries, and found that approximately 90 percent had defective vestibular functions of the inner ear (see Coronado 1981:302).

This cursory listing of many of the hypotheses proposed to explain the psychology of terrorism and the individual psychology of terrorists should serve two functions: to make us aware how easy it is to slip into speculative excess when empirical evidence is scant, and to put before us an enumeration of human traits that may well characterize many individual terrorists, but which are, after all, shared by many people in the general population, people who do not become terrorists.

This brings us to the important topic of the terrorist personality, for it is in connection with studies made in this area that we should begin to gain an integrative perspective of what characterizes people who are willing to kill thousands not only without remorse, but with a sense of pride and with joy in their hearts.

## THE MIRAGE OF THE TERRORIST PERSONALITY: THE PSYCHOLOGICAL NORMALITY OF TERRORISTS

[T]errorists are recruited from a population that describes most of us. – Hudson (1999:30)

Some terrorism experts as well as the general public believe in the psychological abnormality of terrorists. (Cf. Reich 1998:269 for discussion and sources.) This belief has been urged, for example, by Parry (1976). He has claimed that "most political terrorists have not been normal.... Not all political terrorists are insane or mentally disturbed, but most are." (Parry 1976:23) This view, endorsed by Parry and a few others, has succumbed to the piecemeal, gradual accretion of evidence that it is not true, as we shall see shortly, and it has succumbed to plausible reasoning: For terrorists who are mentally ill are unlikely to possess the discipline and fortitude required of terrorists or of their leaders. (E.g., see Livingstone 1982:31)

The belief that terrorists are psychologically abnormal in the sense that they possess a shared set of aberrant traits is a belief that dissolves the closer to the subject we get. As Laqueur (1987:91) observed, "the differences between terrorists are more pronounced than the features they may have in common." It has become increasingly clear in recent years that terrorists for the most part are psychologically normal, and as normal people they share characteristics that we find in ordinary people who commit genocide (see Chapters 11 and 12). Among these characteristics are *dehumanization* of their victims—in terrorism studies referred to by some researchers as "moral disengagement" (Bandura 1998:161), "reduction of responsibility" (Groebel 1989:34), or regarding others as "instruments" (Lande & Armitage 1997:421); *prejudice* and *use of euphemistic and abusive language* (Taylor 1988:97, 100); *doubling* and *splitting* (Lande & Armitage 1997:428); *numbing* (Selg 1971:174 refers to sensibilities and compassion that are blunted); *belonging to the group* and *conformity* (Groebel 1989:31, 48; Hudson 1999:33); *enjoyment of violence*—called "exultant behavior" by Hubbard (1983:49); and, in particular, *projection*, about which more will be said later.

These emotional propensities that are found in ordinary people are found in terrorists, as they are found, as we shall see in the next chapter, in conventional soldiers and their leaders. Approaching the psychology of terrorism through the door of emotional normality will prove to be more informative than a presumption of terrorist abnormality. The emerging consensus among terrorism experts is that terrorists are simply psychologically normal people. Let us consider some of their findings.

In his review of the results reached by psychologists of terrorism, Hudson (1999:30) concluded: "There is considerable evidence...that international terrorists are generally quite sane." Hudson notes a number of studies that have reached this conclusion, among them Crenshaw (1981), who found "the outstanding common characteristic of terrorists is their normality." C. R. McCauley and M. E. Segal (1987) concluded "the best documented generalization is negative; terrorists do not show any striking psychopathology." Taylor and Quayle (1994:197) came to the conclusion that "the active terrorist is not discernibly different in psychological terms from the non-terrorist.... [I]n psychological terms, there are no special qualities that characterize the terrorist." Lande and Armitage (1997:428) concluded: "none of the studies to date have convincingly demonstrated a statistically higher frequency of mental illness in members of terrorist groups when compared with the rate of mental illness in the nonterrorist population from which they are drawn." Post (1985:103) noted that "behavioral scientists attempting to understand the psychology of individuals drawn to this violent political behavior [terrorism] have not succeeded in identifying a unique 'terrorist mindset'." Hudson (1999:51-2) concluded: "There do not appear to be any visibly detectable personality traits that would allow authorities to identify a terrorist.... [T]here is...substantial evidence that terrorists are quite sane." In testimony before the U.S. Senate Subcommittee on Emerging Threats and Capabilities (U.S. Congress 2001:8), Post observed: "The first thing to emphasize is that terrorists are not seriously psychologically disturbed. They are not crazed fanatics. In fact, terrorist groups expel from their midst emotionally disturbed individuals, just as the Green Beret squad would. They represent a security risk." Elsewhere, Post (1998:31) wrote: "In summary, most terrorists do not demonstrate serious psychopathology."

Numerous studies of terrorists in different countries have reached the same conclusion: In studies of German terrorists, "no conclusive evidence has been found for the assumption that a significant number of them are disturbed or abnormal." (Hudson 1999:30 quoting Rasch 1979) In Italy, a study of Red Brigade terrorists found no psychopathology or family backgrounds significantly different from others who are merely politically active. (Reich 1998:29; see also Taylor 1988:91-2) In Northern Ireland, the result was the same: "[T]here is no psychological evidence that terrorists are diagnosably psychopathic or otherwise clinically disturbed." (Hudson 1999:30 quoting Heskin 1984; see also Taylor 1988:92) Japanese Kamikaze pilots have been studied in detail; they appear to have been psychologically normal, serious, reserved, studious, and "above average in both culture and sensibility." (Taylor 1988:114 quoting Morris 1975) Later, young Japanese terrorists in the mid 1970s "were described variously as nice people, congenial, popular, terrific workers, and punctual. They baked cookies for neighborhood children and were meticulously neat." (Livingstone 1982:33) The results with Palestinian terrorists have been similar: Israeli psychologists tested Palestinians and other prisoners at the Al Ansur camp, "but found no consistent pattern of psychological imbalance among those interviewed." (Laqueur 1987:344) —In short, study after study, working within the acknowledged limits of comparatively scarce terrorist subjects, has reached the same conclusion concerning the psychological normality of terrorists. One might naturally then wonder whether terrorists differ psychologically in any appreciable way from conventional soldiers, for terrorists usually consider themselves to be soldiers on behalf of their causes.

As far as I have been able to discover, no psychologists of terrorism have studied the similarity in emotional constitution of terrorists and regular soldiers with the objective of determining specifically whether terrorists may be as psychologically normal as the soldiers of most armies. The next chapter in this study, on the psychology of war, attempts to respond in part to this issue. Here, some preliminary and general parallels sketched by others can be noted. In discussing the psychology of the Kamikaze pilots, Taylor (1988:115) wrote: "we should consider whether their actions differ that much, at least in psychological terms, from the willing sacrifices that have characterised the United Kingdom and United States servicemen in the First and Second World Wars, who from time to time have embarked on combat in the knowledge of a very low probability of survival." Livingstone (1982:41), for example, has raised the issue of religious ideology in a comparative context: "Many military and wartime political leaders have been men of deep and abiding religious faith, so why should it be any different with terrorists?" In a discussion of the possible emotional incentives to become a terrorist, Crenshaw (1998b:250) posed a similar question: "Do these incentives change from individual to individual or from group to group? Are they unique to terrorism? What is the difference, for example, between the terrorist and the soldier?"

The psychological observations and conclusions of terrorism experts point to a picture of the terrorist as an ordinary person, and to a recognition that there are no "special" causes of terrorism in the form of a unique set of explanations for it. Terrorism has unfortunately now become widely established as a "'normal' process of political activity" (Taylor 1988: 110), that is, an established political strategy. Observation and plausible reasoning together indicate that terrorism attracts individuals who are generally psychologically normal, and who are motivated by many of the same emotions and thought processes as any other group of people chosen at random. Which is to say that their behavior and attitudes are influenced by many of the same predisposing conditions as are ordinary people who make up the population at large. We noted earlier that psychological studies of terrorism have failed to discover individualizing characteristics that might help counterterrorism efforts to detect terrorists. Taylor's (1988:157) conclusion in this connection represents the general consensus: "Perhaps that is because all such characteristics are present in the general population."

After this abridged summary of research findings that point to the psychological normality of terrorists and to the nonexistence of a "terrorist personality," two reflections are in order. First, we should emphasize that the current "standard view" of the psychology of terrorism is to claim that it is perpetrated by the psychologically normal, and not by people who are afflicted by any form of pathology. The present study is in fundamental disagreement with this conclusion. Terrorism, I will argue, is not pathological because it is committed by individuals who are mentally ill; *terrorism is a pathology because it is committed by people who are, in respects that matter most, inherently normal.* Terrorists undergo the same habituation to brutality that butchers, public executioners, and ordinary soldiers undergo. Terrorism is not distinguished by its abnormal psychology, only by the particular kinds of ends to which terrorists put violence, atrocity, and murder.

Second, if the psychological sanity of terrorists continues to be borne out by future observations, as many suspect it will, this should serve as an important indication that *standards of sanity need to be revised upward.* The psychology of terrorism has yet to make this step. The need for elevated standards of sanity will be our focus in several future chapters.

Before leaving this picture of the psychological characteristics associated with terrorism, it is important to mention two fallacies in thinking which it is essential to avoid, and which even terrorism experts sometimes fall victim to. One is called the *fallacy of composition.* Simply due to the fact that members of a group share a set of characteristics does not entail that the development of the group involved that set of characteristics. For example, we have noted that terrorist psychology involves many of the same human emotional predispositions as the psychology of genocide. It does not follow from this, however, that a group's genocidal or terrorist propensity derives from splitting, doubling, projection, and the like, although these are observable properties that help us to understand genocide and terrorism. Similarly, it does not follow that terrorist psychology develops from such characteristics. The developmental source for these characteristics is, if we are to be honest, as yet unknown. Observation provides us with descriptive information, and not necessarily information about the genesis of a phenomenon.

The other fallacy that it is important to mention is the *fallacy of predictive reversibility.* It is fallacious to conclude simply because terrorists have certain psychologically normal characteristics in common that anyone with these characteristics is expected to become a terrorist. The most we can conclude from the fact that terrorists possess normal human psychological characteristics is that being normal in these respects does not prevent one from becoming a terrorist. The fact that our standards of sanity do not preclude being capable of killing thousands of others without remorse tells us something both about the psychology of terrorism and about the inadequacy of our standards of sanity.

A critical aspect of the psychology of terrorism that we have yet to discuss relates to the role of ideas in terrorist behavior. I turn now to look at that subject.

## IDEAS THAT JUSTIFY MASS MURDER

The English word 'fanatic' was first used in the seventeenth century to mean "excessive enthusiasm in religious belief" (Milgram 1977:58) Over time, fanaticism has come to refer to anyone who holds beliefs with maximum commitment, tenacity, and willful blindness to contradictory evidence. It is common to think of terrorists as fanatics, a term customarily intended to be pejorative. 'Fanaticism' is, however, a relative term much like 'terrorism'. What is deep conviction and zealous dedication in one society may be fanaticism for another. Whether a person is called a fanatic is decided by whether society withholds or gives the individual its approval. Terrorism expert Maxwell Taylor (1988:96) asked: "Is the Pope a fanatic for adhering to beliefs on contraception in the knowledge of...the spread of AIDS?... Was De Gaulle a fanatic for holding nationalistic (and sometimes romantic) views about France? As with terrorism, perhaps the concept lies in the eye of the beholder." Taylor went on to say that the intensity of the commitment of a football player, for example, is psychologically of a piece with the dedication of the terrorist—yet one inspires fear, the other applause.

The system of ideas that defines the fanatic's outlook circumscribes his world and gives it an exclusionary and positive meaning.

> How does a person take on the role of terrorist? The psychological transformation of a person who is acutely aware of his frailty, into a person who is an heroic and potentially destructive bearer of an ideological or religious message is a dramatic one. The terrorist group provides the structure for this transformation. It provides a new belief system; ...it holds out the promise of an extremely desirable outcome; it defines the terrorist act as morally acceptable; and, it presents a plausible way of achieving the outcome—all of which defines the terrorist act as serving the greater good. (Lande 1997:417)

The relationship between the fanatic believer and his system of beliefs deserves separate treatment (see Chapter 19). Here, I would like to reiterate several properties of ideologies that are responsible both for their attraction and for the extreme emotional, that is, fanatical, attachment they engender. As noted in Chapter 11, such belief systems are rigid, exclusionary, blinding, and self-exalting; they constitute inflexible frameworks of reference that are self-encapsulating, hermetically protected from external refutation; they offer a sense of reality consistency; they often target a specific group of people as the object of hatred; and they frequently provide a single-minded moral justification for mass murder. Once a group has invested its credence in such a system of belief, it is no exaggeration to say that ideas, which shape the fanatic's attitudes and behavior, can kill.

Although fanaticism is not found in classifications of mental illness, Taylor (1988:101) has compared it to obsessive-compulsive disorder. Both the fanatic and the obsessive-compulsive, he argued, share a pervading obsession which both of them

> ...energetically and compulsively pursue...in spite of social disapproval. The fanatic does not, however, perceive his obsessions as irrational or aversive. Such a perception is an important feature of obsessive-compulsive states, and in itself serves to distinguish the fanatic from them. On the other hand, there is a sense in which the fanatic might be said to be "driven" to do the things he does, which is a feature of compulsive states.

The objectives that the terrorist seeks compulsively to achieve and the violent means he or she chooses to attain them are, moreover, perceived to be inherently rational. This is a common perception in all violence, as Arendt (1969:79) observed: "Violence, being instrumental in nature, is rational to the extent that it is effective in reaching the end that must justify it." As Taylor (1988:112) remarked about the extreme acts of terrorists: "[W]e should note that they are far from irrational once we understand the assumptions on which they are based."

The terrorist's ideology not only confers rationality upon its ideas but exalts sacrifice made in its behalf by labeling such sacrifice heroism. By immersing themselves in service to ideals of heroism, terrorists acquire a sense of self-importance they may not have had as mere individuals. Their system of ideas equally confers moral acceptability, even moral superiority, upon them. Their organized beliefs provide the stability of a frame of reference that, furthermore, confers upon its adherents a sense of identity and social purpose. These things—a sense of dedication, rationality, heroism, moral superiority, stable identity, and social purpose—are all sources of human gratification. As one author expressed this:

> Just as there is a psychology of needs, so there is a psychology of rewards.... And the rewards of joining can be enormously satisfying. In some groups, terrorism can provide a route for advancement, an opportunity for glamour and excitement, a chance at world renown, a way of demonstrating one's courage, and even a way of accumulating wealth. (Reich 1998:271)

Comparatively little attention has been paid to the gratifications that terrorists receive through their adherence to their preferred systems of belief. Reich, quoted above, speaks of the "inadequate appreciation of the palpable and psychic rewards of belonging to terrorist groups." (271-2) He notes that these rewards are "almost totally unstudied by researchers seeking to understand why terrorists become terrorists, and why they continue to do what they do." (272) Adeniran and Alexander (1983) have written about the "exultant states" of terrorists, who, cast in a "heroic mode," become oblivious to stress and pain, and "are filled with an elation and pleasure comparable to that of a drug-crazed addict." (49, 51) In other words, the power of systems of belief over their human adherents is sizable. It is a power over themselves to which people are glad to submit.

Terrorists, like others who find encompassing and fulfilling meaning in their ideologies, can derive great pleasure from acting on behalf of their cherished ideas. Individual terrorists, immediately before blowing themselves up, for example, have been seen to give the "smile of joy," the *bassamat al-farah*, worn by martyrs as death comes. (Taheri 1987) And death does not have to be involved: Merely being a terrorist can simply provide one with "an exceptionally good time," words used by Michael Baumman, founder of the West German 2nd of June Movement. (Taylor 1988:153 quoting Kellen 1979)

Among forms of behavior and ways of thinking that are expressions of human pathology, terrorism brings emotional gratifications that involve several disorders of thought, to which I now turn.

## THE THREE PSYCHOLOGICAL PROJECTIONS OF TERRORISM: THE ENEMY, THE IDEAL FUTURE, AND THE AFTERLIFE

Three distinguishable psychological projections are usually involved in the outlook of terrorists. They represent forms of thought that, in Part III of the present study, are shown to be inherently dysfunctional and pathogenic because they lead to self-defeating behavior and contribute to a snowballing epistemological pathology. All three kinds of projection involve *disorders of thought* that must be recognized if we are to understand the psychology of terrorism. The psychology of terrorism has failed to recognize them and the essential role that they play in the terrorist's resolve to destroy. The three projections are these: projection of the enemy, projection of the ideal future, and projection of the afterlife. Each makes a different use of the idea of transcendence.

The first of these projections concerns the terrorist's conception of the enemy. The terrorist thinks of the enemy as a great malignity that stands before him, an obstacle to the fulfillment of his wishes. The enemy embodies what the terrorist hates; in the perpetuation of the enemy's existence he sees a threat to much of what he values. The dynamic of hatred is self-fueling, as we shall see in more detail in Chapter 16. That is, it concentrates attention in a narrowed field of vision in which intent and a willingness to engage in violence converge and strengthen one another. In the tunnel vision that results, the terrorist projects into his conception of the enemy many of the human ingredients that are emotionally most repugnant to him. It is a projection in the sense of the word that goes beyond the Freudian notion of projection of inner traits that one rejects; it is rather a collective projection of hatred built upon what he and fellow terrorists reproach and oppose. It would be a theoretically contrived proposition to claim that the terrorist's idea of the enemy is "actively constructed," for it is not. The idea of the enemy takes the shape it has in his immediate perception of it; nothing is voluntarily assembled; the enemy stands before the terrorist as an independent reality, a threat that has a malevolent autonomy. The only reasonable course of action, given this frame of reference, is to destroy the enemy. Nothing short of this can make sense. It is the very autonomy of the enemy that sparks the terrorist's hatred of it. In short, the terrorist's way of thinking about his adversary leads to his perception of the enemy as a detached, i.e., a transcendent, reality capable of bringing his efforts and his most cherished values to nothing. This is the terrorist's first projection. It is a reifying projection in the sense described in Chapter 6. The enemy assumes the proportions of a dehumanized object of hatred, an abstract object incarnated in its flag, its architectural monuments, its system of values, its music, and so forth. Innocent people who are members of the enemy group or state cease to be persons in their own right, and become mere counters or poker chips whose deaths weigh only, for example, in the war against a reified "Communism" or a jihad against the "Great Satan."

The second projection made by the terrorist is similar, but it has a temporal reference: It projects the terrorist's objectives into a hoped for future: into the cause, the grand design, of which he or she becomes a part. It establishes an endpoint on behalf of which the terrorist labors. As one psychologist of terrorism put it,

> All terrorists have one...trait in common: they live in the future, that distant—yet imperceptibly close—point in time when they will assuredly triumph over their enemies and attain the ultimate realization of their political destiny.... [A]ll terrorists exist and function in hope of reaching this ultimate, inevitable, and triumphant end. (Hoffman 1999:338, 340)

It is a supreme future which, like the transcendent enemy, stands separate and apart from the immediate world of the terrorist, with an independent and glorious reality of its own. The projected future is invested with a solidity not shared by mere dreams. For the terrorist, it expresses a vision and passion that has a reality that is almost palpable: It lies out there, ahead, and must be fought for in a struggle to reach what is *there*. It embodies a *promise*, which *will be fulfilled*. The future for which the terrorist is willing to work and even to die has such an existence. It is no tenuous and uncertain musing about what is possible, but a vision that compels him to take weapons in hand and if necessary kill thousands in order to reach it. This projection, too, is based on the idea of transcendence.

The third projection is substantially different in nature from the first two. It reaches beyond the present world, beyond the world in which the terrorist fights the malignity which is the enemy, and it reaches beyond this world's future. The world of the afterlife is another dimension of reality entirely. It is the ultimate promise, the carrot that is suspended from the end of a stick that is no longer part of this reality. This is transcendence in its most extreme form. The terrorist's conception of the afterlife is often vividly pictured in his imagination. The Islamic suicide-bomber, for example, may envision the promise of being loved by *hoors*, or celestial maidens. When he gives his life, it is not suicide to end personal suffering, or *intihar*, but *istishad*, the giving of one's life in an act of self-sacrifice in the name of Allah. For the individual terrorist, his act of self-renunciation is meaningful and rational, for the taking of one's own life is as framework-relative as other concepts we have described. As Taylor (1988:104-5) expressed this:

> [S]uicide can have a rational and logical basis.... We might well admire the individual who sacrifices his own life for another, or for a cause *we* hold dear. The biblical injunction [tells us that] "Greater love hath no man than this, that a man lay down his life for his friends." (John 16:13). Many men and women have soberly and deliberately given their lives for their fellows in acts of self-sacrifice, and sometimes these acts of self-sacrifice might well have political consequences.

A projective belief in an afterlife is indeed common to many religions. It is shared by some varieties of terrorism, but not all—Kamikaze pilots, for example, were not motivated by such a religious belief. (Taylor 1988:116) Yet, many people fervently believe in it. The majority of Americans hold fast to it:

> ...a 1994 poll showed that 77% of Americans believe in the existence of heaven and...look forward to a future existence there. 91% of these heaven-minded people believe that heaven is a leisurely place, stress-free, and peaceful. 70+% believe that when in heaven they will enjoy God's company, along with that of friends and family. (Pyszczynski *et al.* 2003:21, citing Panati 1996)

No matter how universal the projective belief in an afterlife is, the fabric of an imagined continuation of life after death is woven with fibers that ultimately, as we shall see in Part III, are devoid of the meaning intended by their believers. Belief in an afterlife is thoroughly projective and is based, like the previous two projections, on the idea of a transcendent actuality, of a separate mode of existence in an autonomous, presumed reality.

By virtue of the three projections I have described it can make perfect sense to a terrorist group member to risk his or her life on behalf of the group's projected realities: to battle the transcendent enemy, to struggle on behalf of a transcendent future, and perhaps to give up one's life in the present reality in the assurance of a life in the transcendent hereafter. All of these imagined, projected realities transcend the terrorist's own; they give his struggle a sense and direction; but they are all, as we shall see in Part III, expressions of nearly universal human thought disorders that are self-defeating and pathological.

## HUMAN EVIL AND TERRORISM

By this point, the reader will have before him or her several strands of evidence and argument that support the judgment that terrorism is a human pathology in much the same way that genocide is. A group of human psychological propensities has become familiar to us: projective thinking, dehumanization, doubling, splitting, use of abusive/euphemistic language, psychic numbing, and the gratifications that come from finding an emotional home in the struggle for a cause, from conformity with one's group, and from enjoyment of violence. We have seen how, in the estimation of the majority of psychologists of terrorism, terrorists are fundamentally normal people, and we recognize the other side of this coin, that normal people who are not terrorists have many of the same emotional predispositions. The trend in the recent psychology of terrorism has been to accept the psychological normality of terrorists, and then move on to look elsewhere for an explanation of their destructive and morally execrable behavior. Here, the present study parts ways with that conventional view, recognizing that terrorism is not a pathology because it is perpetrated by people who are mentally ill in the accepted meaning of this phrase, but precisely because it is committed by individuals who are inherently normal. Human evil, as this study attempts to show in many different contexts, is a many-sided pathology that is universal in that it afflicts normal people, and not just the occasional, deviant, psychopathological exception identified by current disease nosologies.

Laqueur (1999:93) noted that "[p]sychological, biological, and sociological attempts to explain violence and crime have almost extinguished the concept of evil and evil-doing that was familiar to earlier generations." He expressed the belief that this trend to embrace a set of categories of pathology to the exclusion of evil is fundamentally a mistake, for we need the concept of evil to understand terrorism:

> The imposition of psychiatric categories in order to understand the actions of political leaders...is dangerous and often misleading. There may be elements of mental illness in the behavior of these leaders, but within the dynamic of their group they may be considered perfectly normal. One needs the concept of evil to make sense of these individuals. (233)

Unfortunately, this observation has to date not been developed in the existing literature, and among other psychologists of terrorism it has yet even to be noticed.

Ironically, at the same time that the psychology of terrorism has drifted away from using the concept of evil, terrorists themselves have embraced it. For example, Donatella della Porta (1992:286) interviewed terrorists from groups in Italy and Germany. She noted that they "perceive themselves as members of a heroic community of generous people fighting a war against 'evil'." Menachem Begin, who was by many considered to be a terrorist during his fight for liberation against the British, wrote: "There are times when everything in you cries out: your very self respect as a human being lies in your resistance to evil." (Begin 1977:46) Terrorism psychologists Pyszczynski, Solomon, and Greenberg (2003:187) therefore have argued: "People need a worldview that provides a basis of self-worth and death transcendence, and they need to feel that they are contributing to some great cause—a heroic triumph over evil." —The concept of evil, in short, has an emotional appeal to terrorists as it does to non-terrorists. Neither group has a monopoly on the term. But where the terrorist's cause to overcome a perceived evil can bring about the injury and deaths of many thousands, the use of the concept of human evil to understand terrorism as a specific pathology is on a different level of discourse. It is the level on which we look from a theoretical perspective at human conduct, without the bias of special interest, and evaluate it in terms of the harm it brings about.

To make this completely clear, I need to widen the scope of terrorism to include individuals whose actions are approved by a government and by the majority its citizens. Alexander and Gleason (1981), for example, have discussed a definition of terrorism that was proposed by Brian M. Jenkins, a Rand terrorism expert. His definition specifically includes what I have called state-against-state terrorism (whereas most definitions of political terrorism fail to take this variety into account). Terrorism, from this point of view, involves violence carried out against civilians in order to achieve "maximum publicity" through acts that are "intended to produce effects beyond the immediate physical damage." (4-5)

Alexander and Gleason went on to comment: "This definition of terrorism would not limit the application of the term solely to nongovernmental groups. Governments, their armies, their secret police may also be terrorists." (5) In another comparatively rare study of state-against-state terrorism, Pilisuk and Wong (2002) sought to show how the most destructive terrorism has been perpetrated by governments. "The real mass murderers produce victims by the thousands and tens of thousands, many times dwarfing the tragic losses from the attack on the World Trade Center. These murderers are on the loose. They are called governments." (105) It is not hard to find examples of terrorist acts perpetrated by a government that elicit the approval of the majority of its citizens. Such acts are certainly among the most lethal terrorist triumphs, as noted earlier. Laqueur (1987:146) commented in this connection: "Acts of terror carried out by police states and tyrannical governments, in general, have been responsible for a thousand times more victims and more misery than all actions of individual terrorism taken together." The Holocaust stands as a monstrous example of state-against-group terrorism. Taylor (1988:41) therefore classified the Nazi extermination program as "the extreme of State Terrorism."

Rauch (2002) has sought to remind readers of a series of events which have been long ignored and which Rauch judges to be acts of terrorism of the kind in view here, perpetrated by a government and endorsed by the majority of its citizens. They concern the firebombing of Japan by the United States during the last war, followed by the atomic bombing of Hiroshima and Nagasaki. Beginning on March 9, 1945, the U.S. dropped napalm incendiaries from more than 300 B-29 Superfortress bombers on more than 60 Japanese cities, including Tokyo and Osaka. The action was directed by Major General Curtis LeMay, who later remarked that the victims were "scorched and boiled and baked to death." (22) The firebombing of Osaka alone killed between 80,000 and 100,000 people, more than were killed later in Nagasaki (70,000-80,000) and half as many as in Hiroshima (120,000-150,000). (22) Rauch argues that the firebombing of innocent civilians was a terrorist act, a "war crime, a terror bombing, if those terms are to have any meaning at all." (22) The subsequent use by the U.S. of the atomic bomb against the civilian population of Hiroshima has conventionally been justified as a life-saving tactic for Allied soldiers. Why the U.S. decided to drop another atomic bomb on the people of Nagasaki just three days later has not been answered, according to Rauch: "Neither President Harry Truman nor anyone since has provided a compelling answer." (22) America's firebombing campaign against Japan has been described as "one of the most ruthless and barbaric killings of non-combatants in all history" by a military aide to General Douglas MacArthur, as quoted by historian John W. Dover. (22) Under the definition of terrorism proposed by Jenkins, mentioned above, both the firebombing and the use of atomic bombs on Japanese civilians constitute acts of state terrorism. Similarly, Pilisuk and Wong (2002) argued: "Surely if targeting civilians is a defining characteristic [of terrorism], then the dropping of atomic bombs on Hiroshima and Nagasaki would qualify as state terrorism." (107) Pilisuk and Wong went on to point out the increasing tendency in recent wars to engage in the mass killing of civilians. They concluded: "It is entirely possible that modern technology has turned the conduct of war into a form of terrorism." (107)

The reason that I bring the tragic examples of Hiroshima and Nagasaki to the reader's attention is precisely because they were endorsed by a nation's government as well as by the majority of its citizens. Psychologically normal people approved of them, and normal people carried them out. The acts—the actual dropping of napalm and atomic bombs—were committed by "good and loyal citizens" who were obeying orders from a government in which they had invested their trust in a struggle for a cause against an undisputed enemy. Over Hiroshima, Major Thomas W. Ferebee was the bombardier of the B-29 Superfortress, the "Enola Gay." Colonel Paul W. Tibbets, Jr., was the pilot. The other B-29, the "Great Artiste," used over Nagasaki, was piloted by Major Charles W. Sweeney. These men were applauded by their society after the bombs took their toll. A half century later, Col. Tibbets continues to be honored in a book, *Duty: A Father, His Son and the Man Who Won the War* (Greene 2000). As we found in the last chapter, men and women with many "good" personal qualities, courageous people who will do their duty on behalf of their country, are often precisely the men and women who cause great harm and bring tragedy to thousands.

In conjunction with the two previous chapters on genocide and the Holocaust, the present chapter has tried to show how it is emotionally and cognitively possible for psychologically normal people who are motivated by a cause they sincerely believe in to kill countless others without compunction or shame. The pathology of terrorism lies here, in the cement that seems to join good and normal people with ideas that kill. The inclusion of the subject of terrorism in this book is a step toward situating terrorism within a broader perspective, as one among numerous phenomena that express forms of human pathology, or human evil.

## WHAT PSYCHOLOGY CAN CONTRIBUTE TO COUNTERTERRORISM

Largely because psychologists of terrorism have failed to find easily identifiable marks to help counterterrorism personnel single out would-be terrorists, psychological insights into the nature of terrorism that would be useful in counterterrorist measures have been largely ignored. It has been a kind of baby-and-the-bathwater phenomenon. Yet some very specific and practical recommendations have come from the psychological study of terrorism, and they are worthy of long overdue attention. The two recommendations that I will focus on here follow naturally from the recognition that terrorism is an audience-relative phenomenon whose success depends upon the response their audience gives to the acts of terrorists. For the warfare conducted by terrorists is a conflict in which the aggressor's success does lie, more than is generally realized, in the hands—or more correctly, in the minds—of the victims.

Psychologists of terrorism have reminded both those who read their publications and government leaders that the effectiveness of terrorism requires the participation, indeed the complicity, of the media in providing the attention that terrorists seek. Groebel and Goldstein (1989:94) referred to a "contagion of aggression" that results from terrorist publicity. The BBC came to recognized the contagion effect and placed a ban on live coverage of incidents of violence. In his testimony before the U.S. Senate Subcommittee on Emerging Threats and Capabilities (U.S. Congress 2001), Post urged a particular counterterrorism response. "One does not counter psychological warfare with smart bombs and missiles.... One counters psychological warfare with psychological warfare." (25) A key strategy is to adopt a policy like the BBC did. Government officials at the hearing heard the following specific suggestion that Post made, and passed over it without comment, perhaps assuming it was meant in jest: "I would like to see that $25 million reward for Osama bin Laden reduced to $1. I would like to see his name never mentioned. Osama who? I think this will not happen, but it really would be extremely helpful." (34) Colvard (2002:359), writing in the *British Medical Journal,* similarly urged that the best response to terrorism by small groups is "to do nothing more than what the same violation would provoke if it were a criminal act without political resonance." Psychologists Merari and Friedland (1985:189) came to the same conclusion: "[W]e hold that the response and counterstrategy ought to be largely indirect and to use psychological tactics. More specifically, we propose that the core of an effective containment strategy consists of denying terrorists the most essential condition for their success: namely, a responsive and excitable public." Terrorism is a struggle for attention; therefore the most obvious and effective counter-strategy is to withhold it. Merari and Friedland urged a policy of restraint in the media's reporting of terrorism (200), thereby denying to terrorists free publicity. Others who have studied the psychology of terrorism agree: Alexander and Gleason (1981:84) outlined what they believed would be the main contribution that a psychological understanding of terrorism would achieve:

> The specific psychiatric contribution could be the prevention of the terroristic contagion and the creation of conditions under which terror from above and terrorism from below may still not have lost their menacing characteristics but at least have been deprived of their present exciting entertainment value, imitation potential, and seductive attractiveness.

The counterterrorist strategy of systematically ignoring terrorist attempts to gain attention is a valuable, but disregarded, tactic once terrorists have perpetrated acts of destruction.

Psychologists of terrorism have also suggested counterterrorist measures that are preventative. Reich (1998:40) has put his finger on one of these measures: "In the long run, the most effective way of countering terrorism is to reduce external support, to facilitate pathways out of terrorism, and, most important, to reduce the attractiveness of the terrorist path for alienated youth." Hudson (1999:57) has summed up both of the preceding counterterrorism strategies in a general statement that contains the best advice forthcoming from the psychology of terrorism: "Rather than retaliate against terrorists with bombs or cruise missiles, legal, political, diplomatic, financial, and psychological warfare measures may be more effective."

Our psychological understanding of terrorism tells us that there is a way, in fact a combination of ways, in which a country can magnify the successes of terrorist acts and so unwittingly but actively contribute to the worsening of terrorism. By following this path, a country's response to terrorism will contribute maximally to the effectiveness and proliferation of terrorism. The psychological recipe is to do the following: to declare war on terrorism, to give it maximum publicity in the media, to place terrorism high on the priorities of fear of a people and their government, to portray terrorism as the unfathomable evil behavior of pathologically disturbed fanatics, and generally in these ways fuel panic that justifies both a hysterical, i.e., highly exaggerated, use of force and a perception of terrorists as members of a dehumanized and alien group.

A psychologically intelligent course of action to minimize terrorism, on the contrary, is to do none of these things, but instead to adopt psychological tactics that ignore and systematically downplay terrorist atrocities, intentionally relegate terrorist activities to the back pages of newspapers, minimize mention of them in the other media and by government officials, portray terrorists not as fighters on behalf of their causes, but as human beings who have become tragic pawns, duped by ideologies of fear and hatred, and generally to take a judo-like stance, stepping aside before the occasional onrush, and thereby sidestepping the kind of peak anxiety confrontation that terrorists aim to achieve. To be sure, spectacular and horrifying terrorist destruction is impossible to ignore and difficult to downplay. To lessen the attention we pay to such events would challenge our resolve, but with strong leadership, such resolve is possible. Ignoring terrorism will not make it go away, but denying it free rent for space in our minds will at least withdraw the support we otherwise unthinkingly give it.

Unfortunately, both the attention-denying and the preventative approaches to counterterrorism have fallen largely on the deaf ears of government policy makers and leaders. Merari and Friedland (1985:203) expressed the belief that this neglect has come about because government personnel are excessively involved in immediate considerations, with foresight often limited to the duration of their terms in office. In part because of this short-sightedness, government officials have been wary of "academic advice," which often is based on a wider and more long-range perspective.

In recent years, terrorism has grown in political and religious popularity, so much so that there is good reason to take Laqueur's recent warning, written in 1999, to heart: "Megaterrorism could well become what Florus, a Roman historian, wrote about a contemporary: *fax et turbo sequentis centuri*—the incendiary torch and the devastating storm of the coming century." (Laqueur 1999:282) Such a warning, made two years before the World Trade Towers came crashing down, is all the more reason why politicians and government officials need to pay long overdue attention to the straight-forward and practical recommendations that have come from studies in the psychology of terrorism.

Beyond these recommendations, however, we must recognize that counterterrorist strategies tend to be naive and blind to the fact that ordinary human beings share traits that fairly easily, under circumstances that occur frequently, render them not only capable of mass murder, but bring them enjoyment and satisfaction from their actions. We need to recognize that ultimately the only meaningful counterterrorist solution lies where no psychologist or psychiatrist has so far looked for it: After their repeated testimony as to the psychological normality of most terrorists, it can only strike one as incredible that *none* of their counterterrorist reflections has focused on what must be done so that psychological normal people are no longer "psychologically normal," but are instead the kind of people who cannot commits acts of intolerance, cruelty, and murder, and who are immune to ideological fervor and prejudice. As long as we remain without any answer to this fundamental challenge, counterterrorist measures themselves will remain limited and insignificant.

## THE INEVITABILITY OF TERRORISM

The highest ambition of the terrorist is to be the object of the government's and the public's anxious attentiveness. If the government and the public become a receptive and fearful audience to terrorist acts, terrorism has attained its most essential foothold. The attentiveness of the public and the government can become obsessional and perpetuate a state of administrative and public hysteria. The emotionality that is stirred up can result in a frenzy of efforts "to end terrorism" or "to win the war against terrorism." Efforts like this are misguided for they ignore the psychological inevitability of terrorist behavior. Hysterical governmental and public reactions to terrorism moreover ignore terrorism's roots that branch deeply, as I have tried to indicate, into normal human group and individual psychology. The psychology of terrorism is continuous with the psychology of genocide, as it is, as we shall see in the next chapter, with the psychology of war. Terrorism, genocide, and war involve substantially the same emotional conditions and the same dysfunctional thought processes. Like its companions, genocide and war, terrorism can be reduced, the efforts of terrorists can be undermined, but it cannot be eradicated.

The struggle against terrorism is not a military war that can be won. It makes no sense to declare war on psychologically normal predispositions, unless one engages in metaphor. As Kellen (1982:46) commented: "To thwart them, the whole world would have to transform itself into an armed camp." It is important to have a sober understanding of the conditions that bring about terrorism, including a recognition of the psychological characteristics that normal people and psychologically stable terrorists share. Such an understanding leads directly to the following conclusion: "Whether we like it or not, terrorism is a feature of modern political activity. It is unlikely that it will diminish and it is naive to imagine that it is something that can be defeated or eliminated." (Taylor 1988:188) Precisely because the psychology of terrorists is normal, and precisely because normal people who are not terrorists possess many of the same emotional and conceptual traits that contribute to terrorism, terrorism is part of the human equation and is here to stay. The wish to plunge one's adversary into a state of fear, through intimidation that injures or kills innocent people, is an enduring feature of human pathology.

# CHAPTER 14

# THE POPULARITY OF WAR AND ITS ROLE IN HUMAN EVIL

> We feel the popularity of war, and the ease with which the martial spirit of nations can be stirred—the enthusiasm stimulated by the appeal to force—is a basic fact that any complete theory of the cause of war must be able to explain. – Durbin & Bowlby (1940:36)

## BEAUTIFUL BELIEFS AND UGLY FACTS

Historian Will Durant remarked that during all of man's recorded history, there have only been 29 years in which a war was not taking place somewhere. (Hedges 2002:11) In the words of Walter Millis, war has been one of the most "enduring modes of relationships of men." (Millis 1961:53) As this chapter will make clear, war is *the* most persistent way in which groups of people have related to one another throughout history, the most harmful, and, to a great extent, in psychological terms the least well understood. Why are human beings so attracted to war? Why, when the surface is scratched, do we find so much human resistance to ending war?

War is not an accident. There are strongly compelling incentives for people to engage in war as much as they do. War brings multiple gratifications. It is, as we shall see, an activity that is as pathologically addictive as the most powerful narcotic, and it causes incomparably more harm. It is not an accident that people devote a substantial part of their nations' assets to prepare for war, to glorify war, to make courageous soldiering a heroic ideal, and to launch wars with determination, zeal, and unconditional commitment—all in a mental state which has been likened to delusional fervor, the involuntary pull of an irresistible drug that deadens consciousness of pain, suffering, and death—at least for a time, until, as Lewis Fry Richardson observed, war weariness overcomes at least one participating group. Then the warring sides lapse into an exhausted recovery period while collective amnesia sets in, until they are physically and emotionally braced to launch a new foray.

An extensive amount of thought and writing has been devoted to the psychology of war. Much of this research has centered on the question, "What is the psychology that drives men and women to go to war?" Two kinds of answers have been offered: One provides descriptions of the psychological causes of war, the key human motivations that encourage people to engage in collective killing. They enable people to participate in organized mass murder and to perpetrate atrocities in the name of patriotism or any of the endless supply of alternative political and religious ideologies. As we have already seen in previous chapters, these preconditions of collaborative killing include the manufacturing of differences (also called pseudospeciation), dehumanizing the enemy, doubling, splitting, emotional numbing, varieties of projection, fetishes of nationalism, revealed and absolute truths, cultivation of group identity and its glorification, the camaraderie of collective effort, etc. Psychologically-focused studies of genocide, terrorism, and war show that these general psychological and cognitive predispositions to commit violence are shared by human beings whether they engage in genocide, terrorism, or war.

The other set of answers to the question why people engage in war is of a different kind. Such answers relate not to specific psychological characteristics that allow people to participate in mass violence and to perpetrate atrocities, but instead point to fundamental emotional factors that lead people to *prefer* to remain in a unending cycle of collaborative mass murder. These emotional conditions lead people to *resist* efforts that might prevent them from killing one another by the millions without great hesitation, with fervor, often with enthusiasm. They are very effective blocks to the human willingness to end wars, and to end the war of the moment. It is important, then, to make the distinction between psychological conditions that *enable* people to commit mass atrocities, and those belonging to a different psychological category that *prevent* people from choosing to end war.

There is a need for a clear-headed psychology of war in order that we may understand war's popularity. A promising approach that has not been used in the past is to examine the psychological basis for the human resistance to give up war, which I propose to do in this chapter. As Dunn (1950:9) remarked, "Where else, one might ask, could wars begin save in the minds of men?" And as the Charter of UNESCO states, "Since wars begin in the minds of men it is in the minds of men that defences of peace must be constructed." (Cf. Pear 1950:17, 142) By examining the factors that motivate human beings to want war and to resist efforts to end war we shall make explicit a significant part of the psychology of war that has received relatively little attention.

The emotional and conceptual resistance of human beings to end war appears to be *primitive* not only in the developmental sense of the word but in a psychological sense that parallels the meaning of primitiveness in logic. There, a concept is judged to be logically primitive when it must be presupposed in order that the logical system in which it is used may serve certain purposes. A presupposition in logic, generally put, is a statement or condition that must hold in order for other statements that are based on it to be asserted as true or meaningful. In much the same way, a "psychological presupposition" refers to a mental or emotional state that must be in force in order for certain behavior and attitudes to be perceived as desirable, persuasive, and attractive. In this sense, the emotional and conceptual blocks to ending collaborative group violence serve as a primitive, presuppositional basis without which group killing would cease to have an appeal. This primitive basis complements and sustains the predisposing conditions, with which we are now familiar, that enable people to perpetrate horrors. Together, enabling predispositions and presupposed sources of gratification make up two sides of an equation that guarantees mass-initiated violence. People seek to protect their primary sources of gratification, and as we shall see, war offers them many. They are not readily relinquished. It is this resistance, reluctance, or disinterest that needs to be the focus of research—why it is that ending war has not been taken seriously, and why serious attempts have not been made to control it. From this point of view, the central reason that human beings continue to engage in war is because *they do not choose to do otherwise*. This is a tautology, but it is not empty of content. It is, in fact, instructive. This chapter seeks to identify and describe the emotional and cognitive presuppositions that make war attractive to human beings and which halt efforts to prevent or end war. These are the true obstacles to peace.

History provides abundant evidence of man's preference for war as a solution to group conflicts, evidence that he "prefers that form of settling disputes to peaceful means" (Mac-Curdy 1918:39), that "man tends to prefer the solution of various socio-political problems by means of war to their solution in any other way...." (Jones 1974:61) If men and women were desirous of peace, they would invest significant resources to further the causes of peace, but hardly a country in the world reserves a significant part of its national budget to study ways to foster peace. Instead, societies everywhere choose to ignore our species' indulgence in mass killing, and turn away in denial or disgust from glimpses in the mirror of their unattractive reflections. And so, in addition to the human resistance to ending war, we find a second-order resistance to facing this issue in the form of an aversion to recognizing the ugliness of our species' murderous behavior in war. It is a willful blindness which, if challenged, sparks shrieks of indignation and offence, and comprises a subject in its own right. Various authors have commented on this human recalcitrance, among them Glover (1933:73, 101), Chisholm (1946:30), and more recently Grossman (1995:xvi, 96).

It has been suggested by some psychologists of war that human warfare is a nonfunctional pathological condition of society. War, they say, causes great harm, while the emotional state of its participants resembles certain mental illnesses. War, from this perspective, is a pathology that serves no function: It is destructive and of no real benefit to mankind. Here, however, I take the opposite position. I argue that war is a *functional pathology*: It meets and it satisfies specific psychological needs in men and women and even children, needs that are so deeply seated and have so much attractive force that it becomes clear why war is so popular, why mass violence is fundamentally the most preferred way to settle human conflicts. Yet war now has sufficient destructive potential to qualify as one of our species' worst pathologies. In short, war is a pathology which the great majority of human beings do not *want* to cure.

## THE GRATIFICATIONS OF WAR: EXTREME SPORT AND SADISM

You will see the effect on people. They will acclaim it with enthusiasm; everybody is already looking forward to the first onslaught—so dull have their lives become. – Hesse (1969:149)

Human beings find intense satisfaction in war. In recognizing this fact, we do not ignore that war is a human horror that brings terrible suffering and extinguishes individual lives. But the satisfactions of war come in many compelling varieties. They may be divided into two main groups: those that intoxicate perpetrators of violence, and those that give them indirect satisfaction due to the suffering and destruction of their enemy. The first type of gratification closely resembles the emotional high of any so-called extreme sport, in which life is placed in an adrenalin-arousing balance. The second type of gratification is sadistic, for pleasure is derived from the suffering and deaths of others. As with any source of pleasure, the pleasures of warfare are emotionally attractive and are not voluntarily relinquished. They constitute one of the key psychological presuppositions that must be taken into account by those who seek peace. I would like to look more closely at these two kinds of satisfaction. Since there are no large-scale experimental studies of how much men and women *like* war, or how much soldiers who are engaged in mass killing *like* what they do, we must rely on observations that have been made over the years by psychologically-focused researchers. And there have been quite a few.

Robert Waelder (1934:105) remarked on the "true sense of liberation and joy" that the majority of people experience when they are free to express aggression without inhibition. This, he tells us, is the pleasure of the barbarian, the satisfaction that comes from the release of primitive emotion. According to Waelder, aggressive release brings emotional relief to the individual (122), it is an anodyne to the aggravations and disappointments of everyday, do-mesticated existence. War for many is an intoxicating experience, and it brings its own vari-ety of euphoria. The act of killing others, "fueled by fear, excitement, the pull of the crowd, and the god-like exhilaration of destroying, is often thrilling." (Hedges 2002:171) Anthony Loyd's book, *My War Gone By, I Miss It So* (1999/1942), describes the emotional highs that attract so many to war. In a similar, nostalgic vein we recall (see Chapter 12) the title given to his war photo album by Kurt Franz, Commandant at Treblinka, *Schöne Zeiten* ("The Good Old Times"). In the midst of WWII, a well-known television anchor man admitted: "War was almost fun." (Smith 1942:117) Aldous Huxley (1934:63, 58) observed: "For those who are not directly exposed to its suffering and death, war (at least when it is of short duration) is perfectly delectable.... Man loves emotions. War, among other things, is a source of intense emotions. This is the reason that men love war." For many, "war was the best experience of their lives." (Greene 2000:185) Charny and Rapaport (1982:118) speak of "the intoxication of group experiences" that comes when people give up their individuality and merge with their group.

In a perceptive essay, Leo C. Rosten (1935) wrote:

> If one talks to the soldiers of the last war one swiftly discovers that to the majority of them the war was heroic and thrilling.... (192) [T]he psychological remunerations of war are deep and manifold.... War is a nostrum for a vast assortment of psychic ills.... (193) [T]o the mass of men [war] means many precious things: romance to the miserable, action to the inhibited, power to the impotent, reward to all the unnoticed. The release of terrific tensions and grati-fication of terrible impulses—that is war.... Men denounce war—rationally. But psychologi-cally, in the deepest recesses of the personality—men like war. (195)

From this point of view, that of the participants, the causes of war are irrelevant to its immediate gratifications. In a recent study, Ferguson (1999) devotes a chapter to "the joy of war." He quotes the testimony of a wide range of people who found great pleasure in war, from an artist to a cavalryman. He quotes even Teilhard de Chardin, who was not immune to such feelings when he served as a stretcher-bearer: "You...see emerging from *within yourself* an underlying stream of clarity, energy and freedom that is to be found hardly anywhere else in ordinary life." (361) For the soldier himself, the adrenalin rush is addictive. "Once you've shot down two or three [planes] the effect is terrific and you'll go on till you're killed. It's love of the sport rather than sense of duty that makes you go on." (Grossman 1995:234 quoting Moran 1945)

The connection of war with sport is not an overextended metaphor. Berkowitz (1990:30; 1993:212), Goldstein and Arms (1971), and others have noted the growing evi-dence that the aggression encouraged in many sports can spill over into other areas of life. Soldiers themselves frequently express a kind of extreme sports attitude: "When Captain W. P. Nevill of the 8th East Surreys led his company over the top at the start of the Somme offensive, he just had time to kick a football towards the German lines before he was shot dead: sport and war had fused fatally in his mind." (Fussell 1975:27) Ferguson (1999:360) notes the attitude among many soldiers that war is simply "an extension of hunting," in much the same way that cavalry officers were traditionally encouraged to think. George W. Crile, a surgeon during WWI, remarked in his study of war on the close relationship between many sports and aggression:

> ...in all periods of life games consist of contest; of struggle, of attack and defense. In the playing of cards, chess, golf, billiards, tennis, baseball, football, the spirit of fight is ever pre-sent; fight not alone of the players, but of the spectators.... Football is perhaps the most

satisfying game to the full-blooded youth, as this gives him a savage grapple with naked hands with his fellows. (Crile 1916:55)

The cheering crowds with their passionate, determined, even vicious intensity to vanquish their opponents on the playing field and the cheering public that sends off its young men into battle have very much the same emotional constitution. What excites them in both cases is violent action whose stimulant is heady and addictive. In war, the sport becomes more intense and extreme.

It would be one-sided and a distortion to claim that popular enthusiasm and the extreme sport gratifications of war are the only reasons why men, and now increasingly women, enlist. There are, to be sure, many reasons they join up. Unemployment during difficult economic times can motivate many; personal reasons enter in; there is the desire for adventure, for change; there are many possible individual motivations. Yet, for those who have closely observed the people of war-hungry nations and their soldiers, the psychological fact stands out prominently that much of the capacity of war to elicit a resonant response in the human heart is due to the powerfully attractive and seductive pleasures that war brings. Steven Kull (1990:40-55) called it "the conscious attraction to destruction."

Among the emotional gratifications that war brings, then, are these: a state of heightened intensity and pleasurable arousal; the psychological rewards of a public bonded into a single unit of togetherness, whose troops find the same reassuring comfort in comradeship, the thrill of danger; the life-enhancing life-joy of being alive in the midst of death that can come suddenly at any moment; the heightened eroticism of sex in the midst of destruction. And there is the keen sense of pleasure that comes from playing a game where the stakes are especially high. As one Vietnam vet wrote:

War is a brutal, deadly game, but a game, the best there is. And men love games.... No sport I had ever played brought me to such deep awareness of my physical and emotional limits.... I had to admit that for all these years I also had loved it, and more than I knew. I hated war, too.... But I believe that most men who have been to war would have to admit, if they are honest, that somewhere inside themselves they loved it too, loved it as much as anything that has happened to them before or since.... That's why when we returned from Vietnam we moped around, listless, not interested in anything or anyone. Something had gone out of our lives forever, and our behavior on returning was inexplicable except as the behavior of men who had lost a great—perhaps the great—love of their lives.... [W]e were also mute, I suspect, out of shame. Nothing in the way we are raised admits the possibility of loving war.... I'm talking about why thoughtful, loving men can love war even while knowing and hating it.... (Broyles 1984:58, 55-56)

The short list I have given of the ways men and women find deep and intense enjoyment in war should not be over-generalized. These feelings are assuredly not felt by all the participants. Some are reluctant killers; some are resentful, nonconformist, and by shooting into the air avoid killing; a few as conscientious objectors are utterly averse to killing. But for the overwhelming majority, the public who can usually be rallied to support war, and recruits who can be counted on for their steadfast willingness to go into battle, what we have in view are the ingredients of heady drugs, of narcotizing experiences that deaden pain and drive human beings on in an orgy of killing and destruction. The causes of war, to repeat, are irrelevant from this standpoint. What matters—here, in the immediacy of felt experience—are the heightened emotions, the intensity, the satisfactions—all of which take place on a psychologically primitive level, immune to reason, independent of rational thought, emotions that are aroused with a spontaneity that can be suppressed, if at all, only with great difficulty.

Having summarized some of the varieties of direct emotional gratification that people gain from war, we turn to recognize the specific and unattractive second-hand pleasure that men and women can feel when they kill and injure others and destroy their property and their government—in other words, war as an expression of sadism. Edward Glover made this topic the subject of his now seldom read study, *War, Sadism and Pacifism* (1933), written when he was Director of Scientific Research at the London Institute of Psycho-Analysis. His thoughtful analysis of the psychology of war stresses two things: the degree to which human beings receive sadistic pleasure through warfare, and the degree to which we "succeed in remaining unaware of our sadistic urges." (43) His interest in the psychology of war led him to pay attention to the connections he perceived between aggressive behavior seen in children, aggressive sports, the cruelties of punishment and torture, ascetic practices of religious sects, and the sadistic attitudes and behavior characteristic of human beings at war. In all of these guises he found the connecting thread of sadism, which he associated in passing with *Schadenfreude*, the "tendency to gloat...over the misfortunes of others." (63) Glover concluded that the sadistic pleasures that men, women, and children feel contribute to their "readiness to tolerate or even welcome situations of war." (76) And so we are brought to the question, Is there incontrovertible evidence that people harbor and act upon such feelings?

The literature relating to the psychology of war abounds with observations by psychologists and testimonies by their human subjects that support Glover's cheerless conclusion. We have already noted ways in which people, whether they are onlookers or active perpetrators of war, find satisfaction in killing and destruction (see Chapters 11-13). Here, I would like to summarize some of the psychological observations and conclusions that support Glover's view. Once again there is a need to rely upon observation in an area where experimental studies have not been undertaken.

Baumeister (1997:224ff) has provided many descriptions of the enjoyment that killers claim they experience. Broyles (1984:61) described this in concrete terms:

> [O]ne of the most troubling reasons men love war is the love of destruction, the thrill of killing...all you do is move that finger so imperceptibly, just a wish flashing across your mind like a shadow, not even a full brain synapse, and *poof!* in a blast of sound and energy and light a truck or a house or even people disappear, everything flying and settling back into dust.

Glover (1933:13) referred to the same experience when he wrote of "the curious satisfaction" experienced by soldiers when they witness a direct hit. As Crile (1916:21-2) observed long ago, "man, whom we consider as civilized, as evolved to a higher plane than his savage progenitors, is thrilled by the death agony of his fellows." What is true of the adult stems from a basis in childhood: Glover's interest in tracing sadism in its various forms led him to claim that the adult's satisfaction from destruction is continuous with the child's hostile outbursts in the nursery. (14)

Much of the interest and pleasure that human beings take and receive from the suffering and deaths of others is no more than the public's drool when confronted by the sensational. Emotional stimulation excites no matter what its subject-matter. However, Glover's efforts to trace human sadism throughout its range lead one to recognize that hatred, which we have not singled out up to this point, is frequently, though by no means always, an ingredient in killing and the inflicting of suffering. It can and does play a role in war, though it is not the sole, or sometimes even the dominant emotion. Hatred itself, as we shall see later (see Chapter 16), serves as a stimulant of a particular kind. As Aldous Huxley noted: "Hatred is the equivalent of alcohol; general goodwill is a weak and watery beer. Give man a choice between the two stimulants; he will naturally take the stronger." (Huxley 1934:68).

No matter what its inner function and the source from which the sadistic pleasure is derived, there can be no doubt that men and women at war receive multiple gratifications from their efforts and their successes in killing and injuring one another. It would seem to make a mockery to use the words 'beautiful' and 'beatific' in this context, but the choice to use them is not mine. Broyles (1984:62) described a colonel's face after the corpses of the enemy were retrieved. It was "a look of beatific contentment...that I had not seen except in charismatic churches. It was the look of a person transported into ecstasy." Broyles described the "bliss" of combat, and spoke of "surrendering to an aesthetic that was divorced from that crucial quality of empathy that lets us feel the sufferings of others. And I saw a terrible beauty there...it is...an affair of great and seductive beauty.... War is beautiful." (62)

The phenomena of human sadism in war and of war's positively attractive appeal to human beings are old: Sometime during the fourteenth century, a troubadour "...sang that his heart was 'filled with gladness' when he saw 'both great and small / Fall in the ditches and on the grass / And...the dead transfixed by spear shafts.' ...'Lords,' he exclaimed, 'mortgage your domains, castles, cities / But never give up war!' " (Berkowitz 1993:377 from Tuchman 1978:16) Even now, seven centuries later, it is clear that the hearts of many people sing with pleasure at the sight of slaughter and suffering. But there are reasons for their attraction to war beyond immediate pleasure, as we shall see.

## WAR GIVES MEANING TO LIFE (AND DEATH)

War furnishes perhaps the most potent stimulus to human activity in all its aspects, good and bad, that has yet been discovered. It is a miniature of life in general at its sharpest pitch of intensity. It reveals all the latent potentialities of man, and carries humanity to the uttermost confines of the attainable, to the loftiest heights as well as to the lowest depths. It brings man a little closer to the realities of existence, destroying shams and re-moulding values. It forces him to discover what are the things that really matter in the end, what are the things for which he is willing to risk life itself. It can make life as a whole greater, richer, fuller, stronger, and sometimes nobler. It braces a nation, as an individual, to put forth its utmost effort, to the strange experience of bringing into action the whole energy of which it is capable. – Jones (1974:75)

What a species ours is that it should take organized, collective mass murder to bring out these life-affirming qualities! And so, in addition to providing a deep-seated emotional attraction for human beings, war is an unmistakable source of meaning for people. In this capacity, it serves important psychological functions that have less to do with enjoyment and more to do with purpose and determination in advancing personal and group interests. We have previously noted the need that human groups have for enemies (see Chapter 10). Wright (1935:24) pointed out that the enemy functions to secure and preserve the solidarity of a group. Volkan (1988:18-19) observed that people need enemies upon whom they can externalize and project what they most wish to reject in themselves, and in the process gain a group identity they can admire and immerse themselves in.

Under the extreme conditions of war, the reality that men and women experience is imbued with fresh meaning: They gain a sense of direction which their ordinary lives did not offer; their energies are focused, intense, and vital; they gain a meaningful identity from their involvement in their social group under potentially deadly conditions. During wars, the suicide rate declines, whereas during periods of peace it increases (Rosten 1935:193; Huxley 1934:58). In other words, simply because people are politically at peace it does not follow that they are at peace psychologically. War, paradoxically, is a psychologically stabilizing force. In the emotional extremity of war, ordinary lives are infused with meaning that comes from a heightened state of arousal that sharpens consciousness and magnifies the feeling that people are truly alive. This expanded consciousness of meaning needs to be distinguished from the varieties of emotional satisfaction described in the last section. War is a source of meaning in the sense that it liberates people from the ordinariness and monotony of every-day living. It raises them to what they believe is a higher level of awareness, opens out their perception, gives them a sense of nobility and purpose. And the price for these things to happen is mass murder and terrible suffering. The meaning that war gives to everyday existence, like war's pleasures, is, as we can see, multiple. It offers people the opportunity to focus their enmity and it provides a sense of direction and purpose. It offers an escape from the boredom of humdrum living, and fuses the individual's solitary identity with the en-hanced identity of his group, to give people a cause worth dying for. Jones (1974:61) raised the question "whether there is not in the human mind some deep need...which tends to bring about wars more or less regularly, and to find or create pretexts for wars whatever the external situation may be." We should be able to see that, indeed, this is the case.

In this section, I have tried to recognize some of the main varieties of meaning that men and women derive from war. But it is perhaps also important to balance the scales, recog-nizing that, from a reflective point of view, wars are meaningless if they are merely reducible to the psychological needs of individuals and groups to obtain momentary gratifications and illusory meaning, when these come at the expense of enormous losses of life. Samuel Du-mas, writing about the period before WWI, observed that in most wars, it is nearly impossi-ble to determine at the time, and even in retrospect, "who really was the aggressor" and to weigh "the rights and wrongs on both sides." (Dumas & Vedel-Petersen 1923:127) We recall M. Scott Peck's observation, noted in Chapter 8 of the present work, that some 95 percent of soldiers haven't a clue what the war they are fighting is about, and Quincy Wright's (1935:81) comment that it is virtually impossible for a soldier to know he is fighting on the "right" side. For almost never is it possible for the recruit to know whether the war of the moment is just or not. As a result, Dumas wrote: "We fear, accordingly, that the great majority of the soldiers who have sacrificed their lives in war did so for a very bad cause." (Dumas & Vedel-Petersen 1923:127)

Such a dispassionate reflection on human folly is, unfortunately, a small voice quickly drowned out by the chorus of excited shouts of governments and individual men and women urging each other on to the next war. For, as we shall see in the next section, people *want* war.

## PEOPLE *WANT* WAR

[I]f people didn't like to fight, there are no good reasons why they should do so much of it.
– Wells (1967:16)

In the previous two sections of this chapter, I have focused on gratifications and meaning that human beings derive from war. Here, I would like to focus on the degree to which men and women *want* these things. Much of the literature devoted to the human propensity to engage in war has focused on how wars might be prevented. But the assump-tion unquestioningly made in most of these studies is that people *want* to prevent war. In fact, as we shall see, many, perhaps most, people do not want this at all. Psychologist Rollo May (1985:212) described the experience of J. Glen Gray, a front-line captain in WWII and later an intelligence officer. Some years after the war, he returned to Europe under a Fulbright grant wishing to study the attitudes of the participants. He was surprised to discover that even families in war-torn countries missed the war—specifically, its heightened sense of adventure, the unity of a people against a common enemy, the dedication to a cause greater than themselves. A middle-class French woman, living comfortably with her husband and son, admitted: "My life is so utterly boring nowadays! ...Anything is better than to have nothing at all happen day after day. You know that I do not love war or want it to return. But at least it made me feel alive, as I have not felt alive before or since." Gray reminisced with one of his fellow soldiers, talking of the hardships during the war. Gray's comrade said of the war: "Sometimes I think that those were happier times for us than these." And Rollo May commented: "there was something like despair in his eyes.... Neither one of these people was longing for the old days in sentimental nostalgia; they were confessing their disillusionment with a sterile present. *Peace exposed a void in them that war's excitement had enabled them to keep covered up.*"

Robert Waelder, whose observations I have referred to earlier, found that:

War relieves them of the *responsibilities of daily life*, of fears brought about by the struggle for existence, fears which for many men are less bearable than fear of physical annihilation while sharing a common fate. In short, war relieves them of the fears experienced in solitude and offers the intoxication of merging completely into a community. And the constraint of culture which many people find burdensome slips away and leaves one again in the midst of a primitive existence which has certain charms. (Waelder 1939:49)

Here, we touch on human emotions of a different kind: They do not refer so much to specific pleasures derived from war, nor to a new meaning that life comes to have under the conditions of war, but rather to a *sense of relief* from the daily burden of burdensome life, something that many men and women unquestioningly *want*. War offers them a respite, a change of pace and of attention, a new set of interests and concerns. War is a *desirable* relief.

A source that tells us in no uncertain terms that human beings *want* war comes from the recognized roles of governments. As LeShan (1992:104) observed, no government in the world has an office whose responsibility is to insure and maintain peace. The U.S. Constitution designates which part of the government is empowered to declare war, but fails to indicate which branch of government is to seek and can declare peace. Countries have their Secretaries of War or Defense, but no Secretaries of Peace. Glover (1933:17n) pointed out:

[N]ot one country in the world spends a sou on investigating the psychological phenomena and motivation of war. On the other hand hundreds of thousands of pounds are available for research on cancer, leprosy, measles, foot and mouth disease, wheat rust, the boll weevil, the death-watch beetle, and sundry vegetable saprophytes.

As expressed by French pilot and author Antoine de Saint-Exupéry (1940:284-8), man's urge for war is an overwhelming attraction. Governments and individuals respond readily and eagerly "to heed the great call." (286) The history of human behavior, the organization of governments, and the psychological constitution of the normal person all make abundantly clear where human priorities are. They tell us in no uncertain terms that men and women not only *like* war and find in war the source of enhanced meaning in their lives, but war is an activity that human beings would not give up easily. Men and women *want* what war brings them.

## HUMAN MORAL DEVELOPMENT AND WAR

> Western civilization has recently [in WWI] lost ten millions of its best lives as a result of the
> exclusion of the intellect from the general direction of society. So terrific an object lesson
> has made it plain enough how easy it is for man, all undirected and unwarned as he is, to sink
> to the irresponsible destructiveness of the monkey. – Trotter (1920:256)

As we saw in Chapter 12, some people will refuse to engage in mass killing and some
will actively oppose it. The two groups tend to form comparatively small minorities in any
population. As Ferguson (1999:446) noted in looking back on past wars, "the evidence
clearly shows that those who had to be coerced into fighting were a tiny minority." Few
psychologists who have studied war have devoted attention to the psychology of this
minority. Those who have shared this interest have been inclined to focus on the subject of
moral development, moral maturity, or, as I will call it in a later chapter, moral intelligence.
Among those who have taken such an approach, Robert Waelder (1939:24) made several
observations that are relevant in this connection: He was concerned with the kind of human
psychological disposition required for peaceful co-existence. He came to believe that what is
essential is a comparatively rare degree of psychological "maturity," which for him involves a
highly developed conscience and capacity for individual judgment, and a strong individual
will to act upon one's dictates. He found that "[t]he great majority of men are, however, far
remote from this state." (41) Waelder claimed that conscience appears to reach the "degree
of stability" that people are capable of achieving only when they are in their thirties—in
other words, at an age older than most draftees. The human propensity to engage in war is
based, according to him, upon "the immaturity of most men." (46) Other psychologists
writing at the time of WWII made similar observations. G. B. Chisholm (1946:6) remarked
on the general lack, in sufficient numbers, of morally developed people. The majority remain
unaware and disinclined to pay attention to the basic psychological facts about themselves
that this chapter has identified, which lead, in Chisholm's view, to "neurotic" symptoms
despite the fact that they are normal:

> So far in the history of the world there have never been enough mature people in the right
> places. We have never had enough people anywhere who have been able to see and accept
> these facts and who are sufficiently well developed and responsible to tackle these prob-
> lems.... We have never had enough people anywhere who are sufficiently free of these neu-
> rotic symptoms which make wars inevitable.

In his long study of war, Wright (1942:1382-88) included an appendix, "The Analysis of War
by Social Psychologists," in which he refers to Waelder's view that wars are made possible by
the human tendency to revert to "the conditions of early infancy in which the suggestions of
the parent are blindly followed." (1383) The reader will recall Freud's similar observation
(see Chapter 6). Lee (1920:xlix-l) associated the human propensity to participate in war with
a general lack of intellectual development, that is, with human stupidity. In a similar vein, C.
Wright Mills, in his study of the causes of war (1958:77), referred to the "moral insensibility"
of people. Few psychologists have followed this line of investigation, perhaps because it
entails a negative diagnostic judgment of psychological normality. We shall, however, pursue
this issue in some detail when we examine the pathology of collective stupidity in a later
chapter (see Chapter 18). The widespread *prejudice in favor of normality* among psychologists has
so far served to shield from research any serious efforts to study man's propensity to war in

terms of the level of moral intelligence of its participants. We shall also consider this subject in detail later on (see Chapter 18).

## WAR: THE LESSONS NEVER LEARNED

Time could never obliterate these memories. The brain was permanently wounded. – Paul Bartlett (1998:31)

The incapacity to learn from past experience can be a sign of various disorders: Among them, such an incapacity may reflect a failure of memory, or a failure to perceive regularities or to register them in memory, or an inability to comprehend their significance, or an unwillingness or refractoriness to recognize that which, if remembered, is obvious. When it comes to a failure to learn the lessons taught by the huge number of wars over the centuries, of these four learning disorders, it is primarily the last two that to apply to human experience. Glover's (1933:12) observation rings true: "As the memory of the last great 'war to end war' dims, the incentive of common people to prevent the next outbreak loses energy, continuity and direction." A gradual process of forgetfulness does, certainly, set in. But it is not, I believe, the main force that disables human learning in connection with our species' long experience with war. The reader may recall a quotation from William James' *Principles of Psychology* which Lewis Fry Richardson placed at the beginning of his monograph, *Mathematical Psychology of War*, and which was quoted in Chapter 9. In that passage, James observes that the "fever-fit" of war is deaf to any criticism and obdurate in its desire to rush blindly into deadly combat. Only "the strong-willed man," who can hold fast to sobering reason, can resist the human attraction of destruction. Such a man is not the norm. The average person is deficient in these qualities, and so, if James is right, will be unable to learn the lessons of war.

As George Bernard Shaw (1919:xxix) pointed out, "...most people could not comprehend these sorrows. There was a frivolous exultation in death for its own sake, which was at bottom an inability to realize that the deaths were real deaths and not stage ones." Most people cannot comprehend what Shaw called "big catastrophes"—such as wars that kill many thousands or millions. What they are able to comprehend is on a much smaller scale, such as the sinking of the Lusitania or the destruction of the Twin Towers of the World Trade Center: "...the big catastrophe was too big for them to grasp, and the little one [is] just the right size for them." (xxxi)

It is not that human memory is in short supply, and it is not that the patterns of human war behavior are unclear, it is rather that, first of all, many men and women cannot "get their minds around" the magnitude of mass killing and destruction reaped by war, and, second, those that can seek by all means at their disposal to avoid doing so. Glover (1933:133) points to the factors of psychological inertia and emotional stupidity, which we shall see later play an important role. The average mind balks at the reality of killing others on a massive scale and shirks awareness of the enormity of large-scale suffering and devastation; what is not forgotten in the convenience of a collective amnesia that is willed is pushed beneath the carpet of consciousness. There are powerful psychological reasons for this behavior, some of which this chapter has sought to identify. Given that war confers the many emotional benefits that it does, pleasures as well as meaning, it is no surprise that mankind's learning curve when it comes to comprehending the lessons of obsessive war is shallow to flat.

# HOW EASY IT IS TO TURN THE ORDINARY PERSON
# INTO A KILLER

It takes little in wartime to turn ordinary men into killers. Most give themselves willingly to the seduction of unlimited power to destroy and all feel the heavy weight of peer pressure. Few, once in battle, can find the strength to resist. – Hedges (2002:87)

In this section I want only to comment on what should by now be obvious. The frequency of wars and the satisfactions and meaning that men and women obtain from war make evident that it must not be difficult to induce and train human beings so that they will commit mass murder. As in solving any crime, we have before us both the circumstances of known involvement of millions of people in wars throughout the centuries; we recognize how few have been the individuals who have said no to war; we realize what gratifications people have obtained from war; and, in a step of inference that is no step at all, accept the truism that people want what brings them gratification. The war evidence in the case against man could not be stronger. The human species willingly and willfully embraces war, gives to war first priority in global spending, socializes its young to accustom them to killing, glorifies war and its related symbols of patriotism, flags, anthems, military marches, pledges of allegiance, and the rest.

Grossman (1995) has studied the ways in which modern societies indoctrinate children into violence, and notes that these methods are identical to those used by the military to train recruits to kill. U.S. society in particular today *cultivates* violent behavior, according to Grossman. The methods used by the military to produce killers are also in wide use in the general society. Children are readily influenced in their attitudes and behavior to accept killing, to associate killing with pleasure, to dehumanize their enemies, and to respond violently when antagonized. From this point of view, school shootings, child hate crimes, and other child violence are predictable. Children as well as adults can with some ease be trained to be violent.

Given the foundation of psychological predispositions and emotional satisfactions that make human beings eager participants in armed conflict, it is only necessary, if Grossman is right, to accomplish a few things in order to nudge the mass into war: to persuade them to accept authority without question, to apply the methods of classical and operant conditioning and desensitization, and then to provide socially endorsed violent role models. In the next chapter, I discuss the psychology of obedience, which is a subject unto itself. Classical conditioning here refers to a process whereby soldiers are taught to laugh and shout immediate approval in response to their aggression and ferocity, so that they come to associate violence with pleasure. Operant conditioning in military training refers to a related process whereby soldiers are trained to respond in an unreflective reflex by firing, for example, at the sudden appearance of an enemy in the form of a pop-up silhouette. They are rewarded or reinforced for performing in the desired way. And desensitization in this context involves systematic efforts to dehumanize the enemy. As a result of such training, men and women can readily be taught to kill when prompted. The percentage of soldiers who can, by the use of these methods, be trained to kill when prompted (the "individual firing rate") has effectively been increased from 15 to 20 percent during WWII to 95 percent in Vietnam. (Grossman 2002:304) Grossman observed: "We know how to take the psychological safety catch off of human beings almost as easily as you would switch a weapon from 'safe' to 'fire.'" (332) The unavoidable conclusion in studying the human propensity to war is: "With the proper conditioning and the proper circumstances, it appears that almost anyone can and will kill." (Grossman 2002:4) This has been known by psychologists for a long time. Writing nearly a century earlier, Crile (1916:64) reached the same conclusion: "It is sufficient to say here that the behavior of an individual or a people, the dominant action patterns of whose brains have been formed by responses to the stimuli of killing, will be warlike, and cannot be otherwise."

The difficulties lie not in training people to kill, but in influencing them so that they will not. With a little training Grossman's "safety catch" is easily taken off human beings. The problem is to "understand where and what that psychological safety catch is, how it works, and how to put it back on." (Grossman 2002:332) Unfortunately, as long as human beings receive the psychological benefits that war confers, they will remain steadfastly recalcitrant candidates for peace.

## THE PATHOLOGY OF WAR

Madness is the exception in individuals, but the rule in groups. – Nietzsche quoted in Goleman (1985:161)

The idea that war is a pathology is ancient. Among the Greeks, Euripides, for example, called it "battle-madness" in his tragedy, "The Suppliant Women." Here, I would like to trace the history of the idea during the twentieth century. As we shall see, during this period many psychiatrists, psychologists, and other psychologically-focused researchers have classified war as a pathology.

As we saw in Part I of this book, many twentieth century psychologists and psychiatrists have resisted the idea that behavior that is normal and socially accepted may be pathological. But perhaps the least resistance has been felt by those who have studied the phenomenon of war. Waelder (1934), for instance, tackled this issue head-on. He argued that a kind of "perturbation of the reality sense" takes over the members of a warring group. It causes a shift in the way group members perceive the world. According to Waelder, the perception that results is "psychotic" in the same way that an individual may be psychotic; both involve distorted awareness that is immune to counter-evidence. He therefore spoke of "collective psychoses" which, however, afflict *psychologically normal* individuals. "[A]lthough each individual in the group is, for all intents and purposes, psychologically 'normal' (not 'sick'), yet the group in which he has membership can become psychotic." (89-90) In Waelder's view, "only 'normal' people are capable of being pulled into collective psychosis, since in order to function as a collective, they must be in communicative contract with others of their group (something which presupposes 'normality')." (91)

Toward the beginning of the twentieth century, in 1915, Bertrand Russell expressed the belief that nationalism is a form of madness: "Devotion to the nation is perhaps the deepest and most widespread religion of the present age. Like the ancient religions, it demands persecutions, its holocausts, its lurid heroic cruelties; like them, it is noble, primitive, brutal, and mad." (Russell 1971/1915:116) A few years later, MacCurdy's (1918) *The Psychology of War* sought to establish a clinical "analogy" between war and mental disease (6, 22). He argued that "[w]ar is a disease." (18) MacCurdy judged war to be a pathology because there is "no practice to which man in all his history has clung more tenaciously and irrationally than he has to the pursuit of war" (11), because war causes undeniable suffering, and because war involves a pathological shift in human perception. Very much like Waelder, he judged that war involves a profound shift from "normal mentality" to pathology. The transition

...is not occasioned by the addition of something from without, but by a change in combination or relative strengths of the forces that are already operative in "normal" mental life.... The fact that this alteration is sometimes a most profound one makes the analogy with...psychosis all the more exact. (14-15)

The task of the psychologist, according to MacCurdy, is to "discover, if possible, what tendencies of the normal mind upset the balance which exists apparently in times of peace, and thereby produce war." (15) The human "cruelty impulse," he recognized, "is not confined to warfare. It is an everyday observation that the behaviour of an American college student is more brutal in a football game than in his individual activities; he is not ashamed of it, in fact he positively enjoys it. More notorious is the violence of mobs." (26) The groundwork for war is laid by *normal psychology*, for violence and cruelty "have some attraction for every one of us." (28)

In the decade after MacCurdy's study, Playne (1925) examined "the neuroses of nations." She concluded that war is a form of "contagious group-lunacy" (455), a variety of "mass-madness" (61) that leads crowds to rejoice: "'At last! At last! We get what we want! We can *do* and *die!*' And they felt, in their hearts, intense relief that there was to be no more negotiating, no more thinking, no more heeding, only rushing on, on, gloriously, splendidly on, all traces kicked over, all bridles thrown away!" (463)

In the next decade, Glover (1933) presented evidence that war is a "mental pathology" (35): Like any form of insanity, he argued, war is "an attempt to solve some difficulty, some problem, a mass insanity if you like, provided you remember that insanity is simply a dramatic attempt to deal with individual conflict, *a curative process* initiated in the hope of preventing disruption, but *ending in hopeless disintegration.*" (45-6) Writing at about the same time, Rosten (1935) shared Glover's perception, arguing that war is a "disease" (189), an "insanity" (189), a "social pathology" (197).

In the following decade, Durbin and Bowlby (1940) characterized war in terms of the "infectiousness of fighting" (11) and judged war to be a "chronic disease of the social organism" (29, 31). Chisholm (1946:7) similarly judged the human need to fight war to be "a pathological psychiatric symptom." Such a judgment, according to Chisholm, has as much clinical justification as the claim that a phobia or the antisocial behavior of a criminal is pathological. "They are alike irrational behavior patterns resulting from unsuccessful development and failure to reach emotional maturity. It is evident that this failure is usual in the whole human race and has been so throughout historical time." (7) Chisholm urged the need for psychiatry to treat the pathology of war: "[A]fter all, this is a major illness." (33)

Another decade later, following WWII, Lentz (1955) introduced "the concept of the insanity or sickness of society" as a "pathological diagnosis." The following year, Saint-Exupéry (1965/56:78) characterized civil war as a "disease":

> A civil war is not a war, it is a disease. These men were not going up to the front in the exultation of certain victory; they were struggling blindly against infection.
>
> And the same thing was going on in the enemy camp. The purpose of this struggle was not to rid the country of an invading foreigner but to eradicate a plague. A new faith is like a plague. It attacks from within. It propagates in the invisible. Walking in the streets, whoever belongs to a party feels himself surrounded by secretly infected men.

Because such observations seemed to many to be metaphorical, Lewis Fry Richardson recognized the need to place them on firmer ground. (See Chapter 9). We recall that by 1950 he had applied epidemic disease theory to "war moods" and found that "[e]agerness for war can be regarded analogously as a mental disease infected into those in a susceptible mood by those who already have the disease in the opposing country." (Richardson 1993:II:558) Like Richardson, Rapoport (1960) realized that an effort was required to show that the diagnostic judgments of the past had a non-metaphorical basis. He sought to demonstrate that wars are —in reality and not in metaphor—"instances of vast pandemics with high mortality." (49) He characterized wars as "psychological epidemics," and stressed that "[t]hese analogies are not mere metaphors. They are based on an underlying similarity of the *mathematical structure* of the events, which affords the possibility of describing the various processes by similar types of mathematical equations." (53)

By 1980, Carl Sagan had become interested in the human predisposition to engage in war, became familiar with Richardson's research, and came to regard war as a "pathogen," an "illness of childhood." He stressed the need to study its causes and urged the need for society to "spend more on understanding and preventing, than on preparing for, the next war." (Sagan 1980:330) The judgment that war is a pathology was still being made at the end of the twentieth century, as when Paul Alexander Bartlett, my father, characterized war as a "collective insanity." (1998:151)

By the beginning of the twenty-first century, but still on the edge of human consciousness and not altogether explicit, the realization was beginning to dawn that we are proponents of a kind of "inverted standard" of mental health. According to it, we endorse the view that "psychologically normal" and "sane" people routinely go to war, but should they somehow develop compassion toward the enemy, they will go "insane." This point of view was ingenuously expressed by Major Thomas W. Ferebee, the bombardier who dropped the atomic bomb on Hiroshima. An interviewer recorded:

> I asked him his thoughts about the people beneath his bomb—the people who lived in the houses and the buildings that he saw being sucked up the bomb's stem toward the plane.
> "I would hate to think about someone in my family being down there," Ferebee said. "But it's just a part of war.... If you let yourselves think those kinds of thoughts, you might end up going nuts." (Greene 2000:263)

The judgment that war is a pathology has continued into the 21st century. Hedges (2002:48), too, refers to war as a "collective psychosis." —And so it has been asserted for the past hundred years, by researchers who have made the psychology of war their focus. There have been a few who have expressed dissenting views. The reader will recall, e.g., that Eibl-Eibesfeldt, whose research in human ethology was discussed in Chapter 10, argued that war (at least past wars of limited destructiveness) is not a pathology since it clearly "fulfills functions." (Eibl-Eibesfeldt 1989:418; cf. also Nettleship, Dalegivens, & Nettleship 1975) Such a view is, I submit, untenable. Pathologies of all kinds "fulfill functions"—it is just that the functions they fulfill are judged ultimately to be harmful and not desirable.

In this connection, Wright (1935:7) discussed biologist George K. K. Link's notion of "pathic events," which are "happenings or changes of living systems which do not fall within their range of easy tolerance or adaptiveness." (Link 1932:134, 136) Wright applied the notion of pathic events to war:

> What is a pathic event for one level of organization need not be for another. Thus the fall of a leaf in autumn is a pathic event for the leaf cells but healthy for the tree. Death, while pathic for individuals, may be healthy for society. Thus the applied sociologists may evaluate war differently according as he is interested in the integration of the world, of the state, or of the human personality. Under certain conditions, war may be pathic for the family of nations and for most of the participating individuals but healthy for the state. There may be conditions where it is healthy for all three. Under modern conditions it is probably pathic for all. (Wright 1935:7)

Jones (1974:74) was concerned with the question raised by Wright, whether the benefits of war may not be "greater than the total amount of harm done, terrific as this may be." Jones gave no answer.

The question can, in fact, be answered. Part of it is answered later in this chapter, and part in a later chapter, when we look more closely at the issue of moral relativism (see Chapter 20).

## THE INEVITABILITY OF WAR

> I must confess at once that I do not see any solution of the intricate evils of disharmonious relationship between nations, nor can I point out any path which may lead us immediately to the levels of sanity. – Rabindranath Tagore (1935:32)

Given man's stubborn continuation of his long history of wars succeeding wars, and now our recognition of the psychological benefits that war confers, benefits most people wish not to relinquish, it will not astonish the reader to be faced at this point with the assertion that war is inevitable. Many of the psychologists and psychiatrists whose studies I have discussed have reached this sad conclusion. Crile (1916:66) observed that the inevitability of war is a result of a set of human psychological conditions: "The war reaction of a people is the final expression of its action patterns; their conduct is natural, inevitable." The conclusion reached by another early study of war did not mince words: "The world will escape the blight of war when man has ceased to be human. The world will find peace when man is extinct. For man is war." (Carter 1926:351) Morley Roberts (1938:7), whose point of view was discussed in Chapter 4, as we will recall concluded: "If...I venture to run the usual risk of rage, indignation, and ridicule by what may be looked on as a cold-blooded attempt to prove that war is as inevitable as disease and death, I believe it will be all to the good, provided that ignorance of the way organisms are built and live and die is dissipated."

As Bertrand Russell pointed out in his study, *Why Men Fight* (1971/1915:6-7), human reason, which is under our control, cannot prevent war, not does it cause war. War can only be prevented, he argued, by "a positive life of impulses and passions antagonistic to those that lead to war. It is the life of impulse that needs to be changed, not only the life of conscious thought." As long as the emotional "life of impulse" of human beings remains fundamentally unchanged, war is inevitable.

Psychologists and social scientists who have studied war have, in near unanimity, reached Frederick L. Schuman's (1933:733) conclusion:

> The problem of peace at bottom is not the problem of security, of sanctions, of guarantees, of the renunciation of war, of pacts and covenants and procedures of pacific settlement.... This in turn is not a problem of mechanisms, but a problem of values, attitudes, ideologies, sentiments, emotions, loyalties, and allegiances. It is insoluble so long as the prevalent cult of the nation-state exalts national power to the skies as the alpha and omega of political action.

Many proposals have been made to deter human beings from their war propensity. Nearly all are utopian and implausible given the psychological forces which we have reviewed that attract people to war. The basic dilemma was stated many years ago by Durbin and Bowlby (1940:40, 48):

> If war is due to the fundamental aggressiveness of human beings, who tend to fight as individuals and in groups, then there are two solutions and two solutions only—either human beings must be changed or their aggressiveness must be restrained.... Thus, as we see it, there

are two ways and only two in which war can be reduced in its frequency and violence—one slow, curative, and peaceful, aimed at the removal of the ultimate causes of war in human character by a new type of emotional education—the other immediate, coercive, and aimed at symptoms, the restraint of the aggressor by force.

Unfortunately, we have not yet found ways to institute changes in basic human psychology, nor have we found acceptable ways to establish a world government capable of the kind of restraint by force that Durbin and Bowlby mentioned. As long as we are unable to make these changes, war is a psychological inevitability.

## WAR AND HUMAN EVIL

Nations would not go to war so often if the underlying makeup of homo sapiens made it psychologically impossible for them to kill each other in a grand scale. – Glad (1990:11)

By legitimating the moral atrocity of mass murder, war, clothed as it is in the psychologically attractive trappings of patriotism, heroism, and the ultimately good cause, is one of the main components of human evil. War, because it causes incalculable harm, because it gives men and women justification to kill and injure one another without remorse, because it suspends conscience and neutralizes compassion, because it takes the form of psychological epidemics in which dehumanization, cruelty, and hatred are given unrestrained freedom, and because it is a source of profound human gratification and meaning—because of these things, war is not only a pathology, but is one of the most evident expressions of human evil. To the extent that human beings receive the multiple gratifications described in this chapter, they will oppose efforts to withhold these satisfactions from them. Opponents to war must face this reality.

As C. Wright Mills commented: "We are at the very end of the military road. It leads nowhere but to death. With war, all nations will fall. Yet the preparation of World War III is the most strenuous and massive effort of the leading societies of the world today. War has become total. And war has become absurd." (Mills 1958:4) When war has reached a degree of infestation that it produces an international self-destructive contagion, the pathology which it comprises becomes antibiotic to the human species. The psychological dynamic that sustains war in the human heart and mind has the self-fueling, self-reinforcing, and self-destructive character of a pathology which few are willing to take note of because of its "unattractiveness." In the words of Erasmus (1794/1510), writing five centuries ago:

If there is in the affairs of mortal men any one thing which it is proper uniformly to explode, which it is incumbent on every man, by every lawful means, to avoid, to deprecate, to oppose, that one thing is doubtless war. There is nothing more unnaturally Wicked, more productive of misery, more extensively destructive.... Why need I dwell on the evil which morals sustain by war, when everyone knows, that from war proceeds at once every kind of evil which disturbs and destroys the happiness of human life? (1, 10)

The most fundamental psychological obstacles to peace are, then, the emotional gratifications that men and women receive from war, the supercharged meaning they derive from it, and, as we shall see in the following chapter on the psychology of human obedience, the utmost regard that human beings bestow on the dutiful, the disciplined, and the brave.

# CHAPTER 15

## "WE ARE SHEEP..." —OBEDIENCE AND HUMAN EVIL

The worst problem of all in any society is that the majority of human beings are sheeplike in their obedience and conformity to authority, even when they are instructed to commit heinous acts that go against their real values and beliefs. – Charny & Rapaport (1982:195)

T oward the end of the nineteenth century, psychologist George Romanes defended the thesis that there are certain meaningful and factual observations about the world that do not stand in need of experimental confirmation from empirical science. (See, e.g., Romanes 1883, 1888, 1895)[1] The observation that human beings possess a will to obey is certainly one of these. For human history as well as the testimony of our daily lives make clear that the majority of people receive emotional gratification from obeying the various sorts of authorities in whom they willingly and, for many, needfully invest their credulity. It is abundantly evident that average, normal, ordinary people will typically and voluntarily obey socially, politically, or religiously endorsed practices that harm others. This is one of the facts about mankind, Romanes would have argued, that does not call for scientific proof.

And yet the public as well as many academics do not welcome the view that their species is blindly compliant, obedient to social policies, national expectations, and ideological dogmas that urge the perpetration of harm upon designated enemies, and which condone

---

[1] Romanes did not devalue experimental evidence, but he argued that especially in psychology when experimental evidence is not possible direct observation must be supplemented by deductive reasoning:

> [N]o one can have a more lively appreciation than myself of the supreme importance of experimental or historical verification, in all cases where the possibility of such verification is attainable. But in cases where such verification is not attainable, what are we to do? We may either neglect to investigate the subject at all, or we may do our best to investigate it by employing the only means of investigation which are at our disposal.... [I]n the science of psychology, nearly all the considerable advances which have been made, have been made, not by experiment, but by observing mental phenomena and reasoning from these phenomena deductively. (Romanes 1895:12)

Once reasoning based on observation does provide a demonstration of a certain fact, we will sometimes find that "the proof itself is too complete to admit of any question." (Romanes 1889:400) There are, Romanes claimed, facts we can come to know about the world, and specifically about psychology, which do not rest on or require experimental verification.

atrocities to other people and other species. The observation that human beings are *sheep*, as praised regularly each December in Händel's *Messiah*, has encountered enough resistance so that a substantial number of psychological experiments have been undertaken to confirm what should, Romanes would say, be obvious. In this chapter, I discuss some of the most important and fundamental experimental findings and their interpretation. Since this is a chapter and not a book in its own right, I have chosen to limit most of my discussion to historically fundamental research, which has of course been followed by a profusion of individual studies that have not always given us a clearer or wider comprehension of the psychology of human obedience.

## MILGRAM'S EXPERIMENTS: OBEDIENTLY HARMING OTHERS

Foremost in the research relating to the psychology of human obedience are the well-known experiments designed by Stanley Milgram (1933–1984), which showed that the majority of people, even though they are not coerced under threat of any punishment, will obediently follow an authority figure's instructions that cause other people harm. Milgram's research focus grew out of his familiarity with the work of social psychologist Soloman Asch, for whom Milgram was a teaching assistant at Harvard in 1958 and 1960, and Milgram was further influenced by his awareness of the central role of obedience in the Holocaust. Asch had found that as a result of social pressure, most people are prejudiced by and will become a party to their group's perception and interpretation of events. They will, in other words, conform rather than engage in independent critical thinking and self-determination. In part as a result of Asch's influence, Milgram undertook a cross-cultural study of conformity in France and Norway in his doctoral dissertation. Later, his interest shifted to the subject of obedience, related to conformity, yet distinct from it. Where an individual complies with his group's preferences and decisions through *conformity*, he follows the instructions of those whom he recognizes to be in authority through *obedience*. Hence, in both conformity and obedience, the individual abdicates his capacity for critical judgment to an outside source.

Milgram was troubled by the degree to which the atrocities committed by Nazi Germany rested on the willingness and perhaps the need of people to obey. He wished to understand whether the phenomenon of obedience found in WWII Germany was an aberration. Before his experiments, he believed in the existence of "certain spontaneous resources in men that enable them to overcome pressure from authority." (Milgram 1974:194) It was therefore a considerable surprise, and a disappointment, when Milgram found that those spontaneous resources do not exist.

The design of Milgram's obedience experiments is now well-known. For readers unfamiliar with his work, suffice it to say here that, in general terms, a test subject was deceived into believing he was part of a "learning experiment" in which a mock "learner" in another room was given electrical shocks when he gave incorrect answers to questions posed to him. The test subject was asked to follow an authority figure's instructions to administer painful and potentially dangerous electrical shocks that were faked. In reality, the learner was a cooperating actor in another room who would cry out in pain, scream, and beg for mercy. Milgram found that a consistently high percentage of people—a majority of approximately two-thirds of all subjects—will in such situations obediently and under no coercion inflict pain on someone they do not know. They will do this even though they have been informed that the injury they are inflicting is potentially serious.

From an Emperor's New Clothes perspective, one ought to wonder whether this is really news about human psychology, for it is common knowledge that soldiers do this routinely. Obedience is not that hard to summon up in the breast of good, normal, and ordinary people, as we saw graphically illustrated by the perpetrators of the Holocaust, by any who engage in genocide, and, in the last chapter, by men and women who obediently and enthusiastically go to war. However, as we noted earlier, it seems that what is obvious to some requires experimental confirmation for many. Milgram, and a host of experimental psychologists since, have sought to provide it. Milgram devised a range of 18 situations to show how an average person will behave when given instructions and asked to obey them. What he found was that there exists in most people an easily tapped potential to shift their perception of events when they are in what he called an "agentic state." It occurs when a person surrenders his potential autonomy to outside authority.

> [T]here is a phenomenological expression of this shift to which we do have access. The critical shift in functioning is reflected in an alteration of attitude. Specifically, the person entering an authority system no longer views himself as acting out of his own purposes but rather comes to see himself as an agent for executing the wishes of another person. Once an individual conceives his action in this light, profound alterations occur in his behavior and his internal functioning. These are so pronounced that one may say that this altered attitude places the individual in a different *state* from the one he was in prior to integration into the hierarchy. I shall term this *the agentic state*, by which I mean the condition a person is in when he sees himself as an agent for carrying out another person's wishes. This term will be used in opposition to that of *autonomy*—that is, when a person sees himself as acting on his own. (Milgram 1974:133)

Socialization lays some of the groundwork for the psychology of obedience. We are taught compliance, to conform, to defer and submit to authority, to relinquish independent thinking in favor of the herd's inclinations, etc. And, as Milgram went on to say, we are given ideological justification for the conformity and obedience we are pressured to accept. "Ideological justification is vital in obtaining *willing* obedience, for it permits the person to see his behavior as serving a desirable end. Only when viewed in this light, is compliance easily exacted." (Milgram 1974:142) When compliance is obtained, people will, according to Milgram, obey in a state resembling sleep: Individual conscience is anaesthetized and behavior becomes automated.

> During sleep, a person's capacity for hearing and sight are [sic] sharply diminished, though sufficiently strong stimuli may rouse him from that state. Similarly, in the agentic state, a person's moral judgments are largely suspended.... The state produced in the laboratory may be likened to a light doze, compared to the profound slumber induced by the prepotent authority system of a national government. (155)

Milgram found that various psychological mechanisms serve to defend and preserve obedient behavior. They are basically identical to those we have already encountered in connection with the psychology of genocide, terrorism, and war: In Milgram's terminology, they include avoidance, denial, subterfuge, the desire for social reassurance, blaming the victim, noninstrumental dissent (meaning that the person obeys orders which he claims to oppose, but carries them out anyway, in deference to authority), etc. These mechanism have a purpose: They "*must be seen as subserving an overriding end: they allow the subject's relationship to authority to remain intact by reducing experienced conflict to a tolerable level.*" (Milgram 1974:162; original emphasis)

Once in the anaesthetized "agentic state" of obedience, the human individual is reduced to a dutiful automaton:

> The scene is brutal and depressing: [the subject's] hard, impassive face showing total indifference as he subdues the screaming learner and gives him shocks. He seems to derive no satisfaction from the act itself, only quiet satisfaction at doing his job properly.
>
> When he administers 450 volts, he turns to the experimenter and asks, "Where do we go from here, Professor?" His tone is deferential and expresses his willingness to be a cooperative subject, in contrast to the learner's obstinacy.... In his view, the learner brought punishment on himself. (Milgram 1974:46)

Other subjects did derive manifest satisfaction from their obedience in inflicting suffering on another. In fact, for them it was a "peak experience" in which they took pride for a job well done. A subject who inflicted the full 450 volt shock on the learner thought the experience was "terrific." "I was fascinated with it [and]...that night I went to a party; I have a couple of sisters-in-law that are nurses, you know, and they were fascinated with it, too.... I'm telling you it's something I'll never forget as long as I live." (87) All of which is of a piece with the heightened enthusiasm we have found in those who perpetrated atrocities during the Holocaust, and in terrorists and soldiers who have succeeded in a spectacular destructive act. It is similar to the heightened emotion of the successful bully and of the triumphant perpetrator of hate crimes.

Milgram observed that "...we find in common among soldier, party functionary, and obedient subject...the same limitless capacity to yield to authority and the use of identical mental mechanisms to reduce the strain of acting against a helpless victim." (176) These psychological buffers, in Milgram's words, "ease obedience to malevolent commands." After years of laboratory observations of obediently behaving human beings willing to inflict pain, the following scene became real and credible to him:

> As for the man who sits in front of a button that will release Armageddon, depressing it has about the same emotional force as calling for an elevator. While technology has augmented man's will by allowing him the means for the remote destruction of others, evolution has not had a chance to build inhibitors against these remote forms of aggression to parallel those powerful inhibitors that are so plentiful and abundant in face-to-face confrontation. (157)

From his experimental work, Milgram came to a number of conclusions, among them: (i) "with numbing regularity good people were seen to knuckle under to the demands of authority and perform actions that were callous and severe" (Milgram 1974:123); (ii) younger subjects tended to be more obedient; (iii) better educated people tended to be less inclined to obey uncritically, that is, they tended to exercise independent judgment and were more defiant of unjust orders; (iv) those in "the more moral professions of law, medicine, and teaching...showed greater defiance than those in the more technical professions, such as engineering and physical science" (205); (v) those who obediently follow orders to injure others are in the majority; and, most important, (vi) Milgram failed to find any psychologically distinguishing marks that would uniquely identify people capable of blind obedience to "malevolent authority." (157, 205) As we have seen in connection with perpetrators of genocide, terrorism, and atrocities in war, researchers find nothing in those who perpetrate human evil to distinguish them from ordinary, normal, and average folk. Searches for special, distinguishing marks of pathology to explain human pathology come up empty, leaving the conclusion that the mainstream of mankind is its source. Milgram concluded:

> The results, as seen and felt in the laboratory, are to this author disturbing. They raise the possibility that human nature, or—more specifically—the kind of character produced in American democratic society, cannot be counted on to insulate its citizens from brutality and

inhumane treatment at the direction of malevolent authority. A substantial proportion of people do what they are told to do, irrespective of the content of the act and without limitations of conscience, so long as they perceive that the command comes from a legitimate authority. (189)

There have been many variations and cross-cultural extensions of Milgram's work, of which I will mention only a very few here: In Germany, even after the trauma of WWII, a repetition of Milgram's experiment yielded an 85 percent obedience rate (compared to Milgram's 65 percent). (Mantell 1971) Experiments in Rome, South Africa, and Australia similarly found higher levels of obedience (Kelman & Hamilton 1989), as did studies in Jordan (Shanab 1977; Shanab & Yahya 1978) and in Holland (Meeus & Raaijmakers 1985). Space is not available here to discuss the further proliferation of obedience experiments; a concise, partial overview may be found in Miller (1986: Chap. 8).

Milgram was naturally concerned about the issue of obedience in his own country, the United States. He observed, for example, that

> ...the importation and enslavement of millions of black people, the destruction of the American Indian population, the internment of Japanese Americans, the use of napalm against civilians in Vietnam, all are harsh policies that originated in the authority of a democratic nation, and were responded to with the expected obedience. (Milgram 1974:179)

He referred to a study that showed that 51 percent of Americans would, like Lt. Calley, obediently follow orders to shoot all of the civilian inhabitants of a Vietnamese village. The authors of the study concluded that Americans feel they have no right to resist commands from legitimate authority, and perceive what Calley did at My Lai to be normal and acceptable because the mass killing was perpetrated in obedience to rightful authority. (Kelman & Lawrence 1972:210) Milgram expressed a personal observation:

> I am forever astonished that when lecturing on the obedience experiments in colleges across the country, I faced young men who were aghast at the behavior of experimental subjects and proclaimed they would never behave in such a way, but who, in a matter of months, were brought into the military and performed without compunction actions that made shocking the victim seem pallid. (Milgram 1974:180)

Again and again we run up against the same "obvious" conclusion. In experiments in which mock nuclear weapons were fired by a team against a distant enemy,

> ...the experiments suggest these conditions should elicit ready obedience, so it is not surprising that when the commander of a Polaris submarine was asked how it felt to be the man whose act could unleash the submarine's destructive power, he replied: "I've never given it any thought. But, if we ever had to hit, we'll hit. And there won't be a second's hesitation." (Frank 1982:84)

Obedience that can be called upon to cause the suffering and death of others is, as I will argue, a universal human pathology. Mixon (1989) sought to show that Milgram's laboratory results, demonstrating that two out of three people will obey orders that cause others to suffer, fall far short of what is true in reality, where close to 100 percent of people can generally be counted on to carry out the commands they are given by their authorities to injure and kill others:

> Milgram's prototypical situation showed 65 per cent of subjects obeying and 35 per cent defying. Those who take the percentages as a true estimate of what happens when

authorities issue commands to harm or kill suffer from a dangerous delusion. The proportion of subordinates who obey authorized criminal commands to harm or kill ordinarily is 100 per cent. (Mixon 1989:xiii)

Unfortunately, "[o]bedience to authority and compliance at the expense of personal ethics is unique to no one age or nation." (Rosenbaum 1983:45) The command to obey issued by Nazi youth leader of the German Reich and Gauleiter of Vienna, Baldur von Schirach, did not fall on deaf ears then, nor would it today when translated into different circumstances: "You must be faithful in heart to the mission with which our Führer has entrusted you—by blind obedience of the discipline imposed on you, and obedience to the orders given you, no matter what they may be." (von Schirach quoted in Neumann 1960:5) Milgram found that the majority of men and women are available and receptive to such orders; Mixon has argued that the majority includes nearly everyone.

## THE MEANING OF MILGRAM'S WORK

Far more of history's hideous crimes have been committed by obedient citizens than by criminals or rebels. – Mixon (1989:61)

The most common interpretation of Milgram's research has been to stress the relationship between obedience and authority itself—to emphasize that people, in following instructions or commands, are most fundamentally responding both to the respect, intimidation, or outright fear they experience when confronted by authority figures, and to the imagined loss of self-esteem, social approval, and even punishment that might result if they were to disobey. Such a synoptic statement encompasses a large body of literature on the subject of obedience, which there is not space here to discuss in detail. Suffice it to say that the general tendency in the literature has been to construe obedience as a situationally relative phenomenon, and in the process to a large extent to diminish or to ignore the importance of the *psychological normality* of the human propensity to obey even those directives that cause others harm. Here, I would like to summarize a group of interpretations, observations, and conclusions proposed by psychologically-focused researchers who have had an especially broad understanding of human obedience:

(1) Human obedience is much more widespread than we tend to recognize. It permeates many aspects of living; it enters into every choice we make when we comply with a wish that is not our own; it is so ubiquitous as to have become habitual and unconscious. (Mixon 1989:13) (2) People willingly allow their interpretation of the world to be influenced and often determined by those whom they see as legitimate authorities. In other words, people permit and perhaps prefer that authorities provide them with definitions of what constitutes desirable action. (Milgram 1974:145) (3) Human suffering that has resulted from people who have loyally and faithfully obeyed orders far surpasses any other evil. "Even a cursory glance at history should convince one that individual crimes committed for selfish motives play a quite insignificant part in the human tragedy, compared to the numbers massacred in unselfish loyalty to one's tribe, nation, dynasty, church, or political ideology, *ad majorem gloriam dei.*" (Koestler 1978:14) The most frequent excuse the obedient have given for atrocities they commit has been to emphasize their loyalty, patriotism, and stalwart response to the call of duty. (Mixon 1974:48) (4) Obedience offers the most facile justification for the perpetration of horrible acts, while those who choose to disobey in the same circumstances are compelled to justify their refusal and may be punished or lose their lives. (Mixon 1974:64)

(5) Democratic societies are internally inconsistent: On the one hand, they emphasize

equality and freedom; on the other, they deny both. For, like totalitarian nations, they have a hierarchical organization that discriminates between leaders and those who must follow, which is inconsistent with equality, and followers are compelled to obey the commands of their superiors, which is inconsistent with freedom. (Mixon 1974:64) (6) Obedience is usually "total," that is, even in Milgram's experiments subjects were almost always persuaded of the "acceptability" of the laboratory situation—"they stayed in their seats, 'in their assigned place', politely, psychologically demurred, and they waited to be dismissed by the authority." (Zimbardo 1974:567) This framework of acceptability permeates situations that call men, women, and children to obey. Few question it. Obedience is total in this sense.

(7) In terms of our psychological predictive ability, and our ability to explain history in the same terms retrodictively, it is generally irrelevant to take individual personality factors into account. Obedience, from a purely statistical point of view, can reliably be produced in the vast majority of people without knowing anything about them. This proposition means that, from a psychologically predictive and explanatory point of view, and for all practical purposes, we really do not need to know in great detail what exact psychological factors in the individual contribute to his or her willingness or need to obey. (Miller 1986:255) For, in the greatest majority of cases, obedience can be expected regardless of psychologically distinguishing characteristics. This conclusion is in opposition to a trend in current psychological and sociological research to search for psychologically and sociologically individuating factors that contribute to obedience. All that is necessary is that the human population in question be comparatively normal, a condition that must be granted in most varieties of human pathology which we have studied. This requirement leads to the next observation. (8) The obedience experiments taken as a whole have demonstrated what we should know without experimental proof, that

> ...without employing duress or force, ...an average, normal, intelligent individual would *of his own accord* inflict pain and misery upon a fellow human being, and, with sweating brow and inward fear and trembling, continue to inflict dire harm upon an innocent person, and continue grimly to the very limits possible of this behavior under no compulsion but a structured social situation. (Erickson 1968:278)

(9) There is therefore a need "to investigate scientifically the extremes to which the normal, the good, the average, or the intellectual person or group will go if given the opportunity...." (Erickson 1968:278) Several decades have now gone by, and still we have not defined the extremes to which normal people will go. Similarly, L. S. Wrightsman (1974:805) urged the need for research that would study obedience attitudes and behaviors on the part of large institutions and among such groups as students, patients, and soldiers. —And yet, as I began this chapter with reference to Romanes' willingness to endorse claims to knowledge for which a purely experimental basis is lacking, do we, in the light of so much history, really need further proof of the willingness of human beings to harm others when commanded to do this by their authorities?

There is, furthermore, (10) the dual hypothesis that people make some kind of choice when they obey, whether it is a self-conscious choice or an inchoate embracing of the orders they are given, and that they do this in order to gratify their own emotional needs. We will discuss this hypothesis in greater detail in the next section.

Finally, (11) it appears to be the case that the willingness to obey orders to harm others is closely associated with level of moral development. Here is a psychologically individuating characteristic that seems to be relevant to the capacity to commit the unthinkable, but, as we shall see in a later chapter, the level of moral development needed to resist the perpetration of horror is relatively high, so much so that the majority of men and women fall outside the range of consideration. Here, it is relevant to mention Lickona's early work (1976:5), in which he raised this point: "Kohlberg's Stage 5, for example would not rule out shocking the 'learner' in Milgram's experiments...or preclude dropping the atomic bomb on Hiroshima and Nagasaki...; Stage 6 would."

## THE PSYCHOLOGICAL BENEFITS OF OBEDIENCE

*USA Today*: "What were your thoughts when you dropped it [the atomic bomb on Hiroshima]?"

Tibbets [the pilot of the bomber]: "I had no thoughts, except what I'm supposed to do. I had an airplane full of people, and I had a couple airplanes with me. We had to get them out of the way of the bomb blast. The next thing we had to do was prepare ourselves for the shock wave that would be coming up. We did all of these things routinely. There was no problem. We had practiced and practiced." – Interview in *USA Today* quoted in Miller (1986:228)

[N]ever underestimate the power of the need to obey.... – Freud quoted in Grossman (1995:142)

It is in connection with the psychological payoffs that people receive from their capitulation to the orders of their authorities that the psychology of obedience might especially profit from more detailed experimental work. Psychologists who have studied human obedience are aware of the evidence provided by the psychology of genocide, terrorism, and war that psychologically normal people do receive clear and pronounced emotional gratification from their acts of obedience. I have identified many of the forms of such emotional and cognitive gratification in other chapters, so will not repeat those observations in detail here. Although we are always in a state of incomplete knowledge, it is clear enough to us already that many people—and we can reliably surmise at this point that the percentage is quite high—derive substantial psychological and ideological satisfactions from their choice to obey, and they comply with the orders they are given because in so doing they satisfy a variety of emotional needs. From this point of view, that of understanding the psychological and cognitive gratifications that come from obedience, it is no accident that Milgram and others have found that the great majority of people are available to be commanded, will proudly and dutifully undertake to carry our their orders, and will do this irrespective of the destruction they bring about in the lives of others. As social psychologist Don Mixon remarked, "the evil contingent upon obedience is indeed normal." (Mixon 1989:153)

In Chapter 11 which dealt with the psychology of genocide, I distinguished between the two main elements that influence an individual's willingness to follow orders to inflict harm on others or to kill them. They are the psychological need to be led, and the willingness to obey, which work together to facilitate the way in which average people will surrender their moral principles to the dictates of a leader. The need to be led, the reader will remember, refers to an emotionally immature dependency expressed in a need to follow, to be told what to do, to be told what to believe and who is the enemy and who the friend. The willingness to be led refers to the individual's wish for the approval of others in his group, gained through dutiful obedience to the group's authorities. The willingness to obey therefore involves a person's sense of self-esteem and identity in relation to his group; it is a source of pride and value; obedience in the name of the group is glorified. The need to be led and the willingness to obey are usually coupled with the need to conform, to imitate how others behave and to copy what others value.

The psychological benefit of subjugating oneself in obedience was noted by Arendt (1964:32) when she quoted Eichmann's reaction to the impending German defeat on May 8, 1945: "I sensed I would have to live a leaderless and difficult individual life, I would receive no directives from anybody, no orders and commands would any longer be issued to me, no pertinent ordinances would be there to consult—in brief, a life never known before lay before me." *To live a leaderless life* brings insecurity to many people, while life under a leader offers many rewards. To summarize some of the most important of these, there is (i) the satisfaction of acquiescing in an ideology, which offers a source of meaning and a pre-fabricated way interpreting events; (ii) the related satisfaction of surrendering to the herd or its authorities, to become a helpless cog-in-the-machine, which frees men and women from personal responsibility for their actions; (iii) the satisfaction itself that comes from conscientious obedience, from a job well done; (iv) the enjoyment of power, acquired through participation in group effort; (v) the sense of strengthened identity derived from obedient herd togetherness; and (vi) the emotional and cognitive security that come from having one's behavior and attitudes defined by authorities in whom one has invested faith.

## DISOBEDIENCE

> Disobedience, in the eyes of any one who has read history, is man's original virtue. It is through disobedience that progress has been made, through disobedience and through rebellion. – Oscar Wilde quoted in Mixon (1989:13)

In Chapter 12, dealing with the pathology of the Holocaust, I discussed the psychology of those who refused to participate in mass murder and of those who actively resisted the Nazi regime. Here, I would like to connect that discussion with Milgram's work. For one of the most interesting aspects of Migram's research has been the focus of little public or professional attention. This is the psychology of the rebel. Those who are psychologically and cognitively able to defy authority are in the small minority. Milgram gave the following description of a woman who refused in the context of one of the obedience experiments to comply with instructions to harm another person: "The woman's straightforward, courteous behavior in the experiment, lack of tension, and total control of her own action seems to make disobedience a simple and rational deed. Her behavior is the very embodiment of what I had initially envisioned would be true for almost all subjects." (Milgram 1974:85) Milgram found that she grew up in Nazi Germany; in her words, she had "seen too much pain" and therefore had the initiative to refuse to participate in cruelty. Milgram remarked that disobedience brings with it a sense of relief. "The remarkable thing is, once the 'ice is broken' through disobedience, virtually all the tension, anxiety, and fear evaporate." (152) Milgram traced the inner events that lead to disobedience:

> The sequence starts with *inner doubt*, tension that is at first a private experience but which invariably comes to assume an *external form*...; communication shades into *dissent*, as the subject attempts to persuade the authority to alter his course of action...; dissent is transformed into a *threat* that the subject will refuse to carry out the authority's orders. Finally, the subject, having exhausted all other means, finds that he must get at the very root of his relationship with the experimenter in order to stop shocking the victim: he disobeys. *Inner doubt, externalization of doubt, dissent, threat, disobedience*: it is a difficult path, which only a minority of subjects are able to pursue to its conclusion, but has the character of an affirmative act, a deliberate bucking of the tide. It is compliance that carries the passive connotation. The act of disobedience requires a mobilization of inner resources, and their transformation beyond inner

preoccupation, beyond merely polite verbal exchange, into a domain of action. But the psychic cost is considerable. (163)

That cost, according to Milgram, is a hollow feeling that one has been unfaithful to the society he belongs to, or to the society's cause, to which he is expected automatically to give allegiance. As a result, "[i]t is he, and not the obedient subject, who experiences the burden of his action." (Milgram 1974:164) The rebel is further burdened by his society's unequivocal and overt disapproval and even punishment. The history of conscientious objection is a story of the burden placed on those who possess independence of mind.

In spite of society's condemnation of those who think for themselves and defy authority, it is clear that disobedience plays a major role in the resolution of human conflicts. Richardson pointed out that while society routinely punishes dissenters (1948:171), wars in which both sides are evenly matched would, without the critical thinking of defeatists, not come to an end "until every person in both nations had been killed." (1948a:210) There is a need for iconoclasm, for the ability to see through the lies of blindly held belief-systems. Don Mixon concluded his study of the psychology of obedience with these words:

> I have written, in the literal meaning of the word, as an iconoclast.... I have written hoping to convince that only by breaking, and breaking with, the idol can we begin to create a society in which evil is not normal and liberty and equality are more than words used to describe degrees of bondage. (Mixon 1989:153-4)

Those who are capable of defying the inner and outer pressures to conform and obey make up an exceedingly small minority. As Mixon expressed this well, "...in relation to authorized criminal commands conscience is sovereign for only a tiny minority." (40) The public and its social psychologists both recognize that today there no longer exist common, agreed upon values. The consciences of the billions are tied by their umbilical cords to what they are instructed by their authorities to feel and think. The capacity to discriminate malevolent from benign authority is a capacity possessed only by very few. We shall attempt to understand in more detail what gives them this rare ability in later chapters.

## CONCLUSION: THE PATHOLOGY OF OBEDIENCE

Of course not all expressions of human obedience are malignant. But because the majority is generally available and enthusiastic to follow the commands given to it by its social, religious, and political authorities, and is often unable to discriminate malignant authority from benevolent, the potential for benign obedience to become pathological is realized in human affairs with overwhelming frequency. We recall from Chapter 8 that Erich Fromm singled out human obedience as a force that may plausibly lead to the end of human history. Like many of the elements of human pathology that I have sought in this work to identify, obedience is an expression of basic human inclinations, needs, and gratifications. And like other forms of human pathology, high levels of obedience are characteristic, as we have seen, of normal people. Milton Erickson, commenting on Milgram's obedience research, wrote:

> Now at last, here is a pioneer willing to say simply and emphatically, and to prove it by well-demonstrated scientific study in the laboratory, that normal and average human beings can be manipulated into inhumane behavior, and that the need is great to study normal man from this aspect rather than to continue to regard such behavior either as incomprehensible

or as evidence that the person involved is somehow aberrant, abnormal and atypical. (Erickson 1968:279)

We are on board a moving ship, ever in a state of imperfect knowledge. At present, we do not know whether the inclination and need to obey may have a genetic basis. We do know that the predisposition exists and is readily tapped by whatever authorities a people will recognize. It is further evident that there are clear psychological benefits that accrue to the obedient. And it is equally evident that the disobedient shoulder a heavy burden. Obedience is rewarded externally, and defying it exacts substantial inner and outer costs. When the many factors that contribute to, reinforce, and sustain obedience are considered, and the others that actively discourage disobedience are accounted for, the resulting dynamic is almost inconceivably hardy.

When a society is at peace, it is not that the psychologically normal majority "refrains" from aggression, it is only that they have not, yet, been called upon by their authorities to behave aggressively. Once called upon, obedience psychology informs us that it is very nearly a sure proposition that they will comply. The extreme acts they will perpetrate in the name of obedient duty are limitless. Conformity and obedience are the product of unexceptional men and women, while their opposite, found in rebellion and disobedience, often distinguish the exceptional individual; and yet they also characterize the defiant juvenile delinquent and the criminal. It is not a simple world in which one can conclude that all obedience is evil and all rebellion good. But it is all too evident from the evidence of the laboratory of reality, as well as from the laboratories of experimental psychology, that, precisely because obedience is so deeply rooted in the needs and gratifications of the normal person and group, its potential to become malignant is substantial.

The tendency of many obedience psychologists who have come after Milgram has been to emphasize situational pressures that elicit obedience, to confine the conclusions drawn from the psychology of obedience to "laboratory reality," and to refrain from extending those conclusions to the world as it exists beyond the lab. From a Romanes-like vantage point with which I began this chapter, this methodological naïveté does not, I believe, constitute a meaningful context in terms of which to understand the human propensity for evil. From a broader point of view, the obedience experiments will strike many reflective readers as intelligently designed, but incredibly naïve. For do we need controlled laboratory situations to mimic artificially the willingness we see everywhere, and indeed the eagerness, of individuals, groups, and nations, to inflict malicious violence and destruction upon innocent people? The laboratory of reality is unfortunately thoroughly sufficient to provide evidence in the extreme of the pathology of human obedience.

# CHAPTER 16

# THE PHENOMENOLOGY OF HATRED

*Not until we understand hatred and unearth its deeper roots can we make it harmless.*
– Stekel (1953/1929:II:462)

As we have already seen in this study, hatred plays a central role in many expressions of human pathology. Psychologically normal human beings experience hatred, which, like any emotion, comes in degrees, in many shades from dislike to contempt, to extreme and bitter hatred. And whether in the individual or the group, hatred can take many forms: in prejudice and persecution, in invective and abuse, in crimes of hate, in punishment and torture, in self-destructive behavior, domestic conflicts, rape, in the bullying of children by other children, children by adults, and adults by adults. The list could go on, for there are many ways in which people express their hatred through acts of malice and brutality. Hatred is, unfortunately, one of the emotional conditions that characterize being human; it is, as Gordon Allport (1950:154) put it, "a normal enough response." In order to comprehend and perhaps better cope with this source of human cruelty and destructiveness, we need to reach a clear understanding of the experience of hatred. What does it mean, in specific emotional and cognitive terms, for the individual and the group to hate?

Among human emotions, hatred has been studied by psychologists and psychiatrists surprisingly little. In particular, we would expect to find in the literature of phenomenological psychiatry and phenomenological psychology a systematic and detailed description of the experience of hatred, but few works in this area even mention the phenomenon in passing. In fact, to the author's knowledge, no serious, thorough study of human hatred has been made by phenomenological psychologists or psychiatrists. In one of the few works in psychology to mention this neglect, Pierre Janet (1932:213) noted that "[h]atred has been studied excessively little." Gordon Allport (1950: 150) commented that science has avoided the subject. Anatol Rapoport (1960:359) remarked, in connection with the study of human conflict, "...the psychology of hatred would seem to be the most directly relevant field," but acknowledged a lack of expertise to fill this need. Writing 70 years after Janet, McCauley (2002:7) observed: "The surprising fact is that, although a few psychoanalysts have discussed hatred, there is very little psychological research focused on hate or hatred.... [E]mpirical research on hatred, particularly research that distinguishes hatred from anger, is notably absent." Anger itself has been called "the forgotten emotion" because so little of the psychological literature has dealt with it (DiGiuseppe, Tafrate, & Eckhardt 1994); but compared with the attention given to anger, the psychology of hatred has fared even less well. In a recent psychological inventory of anger-related words (Kassinove 1995:6), 'hatred' does not even appear. Eissler (2000:29) commented on the "favorable emphasis" which psychology has given to studies of the emotion of love, and "the implied critical, if not contemptuous, neglect" of the psychology of hatred. In short, there is an almost total absence of psychological studies of human hatred, and no systematic attempt has been made to understand the psychological reality in which the hater lives.

A clear account of the human experience of hatred would tell us much about how reality is perceived by those who hate, how they experience others and are likely to behave toward them, and how hatred brings with it a well-defined group of emotions and cognitive states that have special value and meaning for individuals and groups who hate. With these ends in view, this chapter gives a brief introduction to the phenomenology of hatred, for which a separate book-length treatment is long overdue.

## BACKGROUND

During the first half of the twentieth century, a small, internationally represented group of psychiatrists and psychologists proposed to use a phenomenological approach to study human psychopathology and normal psychology. They were influenced by the work of philosophers who had sought to develop a method to describe human experience in a manner free from both the unexamined preconceptions of common sense and the metaphysical-epistemological presuppositions of contemporary science. The philosophers included Husserl, Heidegger, and Sartre, who, in turn, had been influenced by the phenomenological studies of nineteenth century psychologist Franz Brentano. If one wished, one could see the emergence of phenomenological psychiatry and psychology as a return to specifically psychological considerations after a long interlude during which phenomenology was the exclusive domain of philosophers. Ludwig Binswanger, Viktor von Weizsäcker, Eugene Minkowski, Menard Boss, Rollo May, J. H. van den Berg, and others took concepts and a general method that had been developed by the philosophers and gave them psychiatric application. They shared the wish to develop a descriptive science of experience that, if not entirely presuppositionless as ideally urged by Husserl, would at least be self-consciously aware and critical of the presuppositions it does make. Phenomenological psychology of normal experience and phenomenological psychiatry of psychopathological experience abstain from explanation and from the uncritical imposition of conventionally accepted categories of psychiatric diagnosis. Instead, they seek to understand how reality is experienced by the psychologically normal subject and by the psychiatric patient. From this point of view, no one is "mistaken" about the reality he or she experiences. It is therefore pointless for a therapist to seek to "adjust" an individual's world of experience to fit either that of the therapist or the norms of the surrounding society.

The phenomenological approach to psychology and psychiatry is usually caricatured, even by some of its adherents, as "introspective," and as such has been criticized and rejected by anti-subjectivist empiricists. This is a widespread and misleading error in understanding, for it presumes the validity of the inner/outer, subjective/objective preconception, a notion usually used naively and without reflection, which phenomenology, perhaps above all else, has sought to question. The distinction between subjective and objective experience is, after all, a conceptual one that has its historical roots in the philosophical frame of reference proposed by Descartes. The distinction between what is "inner" and what is "outer" has come to permeate our understanding of "ourselves in opposition to the world" to such an extent as to have become second nature; we forget that it is part of the vocabulary of a particular *theory* of experience; and so it tends to be uncritically accepted. The paired notions of "introspection" and "subjectivity" stand in need of careful analysis, without which they should be considered suspect. Uncritical acceptance of Descartes' dualism is, as Binswanger wrote, "the cancerous tumour of all psychology" (van den Berg 1980:32). Van den Berg went on to note: "It is this evil which phenomenology wishes to combat." (32)

There is unfortunately not space here to examine this issue. (See relevant sources cited in Chapter 19.) Suffice it to say that from a phenomenological perspective, whatever intelligibility can be found in the distinction between what is outer and what is inner must be based on what we can experience, and cannot be applied to experience itself as a kind of "container" "beyond which" lies what is "outer." This misplaced spatial metaphor was singled out by phenomenologist Erwin W. Straus when he wrote:

> Since the days of Galileo, subjectivity has been interpreted in spatial terms. Sensory qualities do not reside—to use Galileo's terminology—in things themselves; they reside in our minds. Today, we let them reside in our brains. From their supposedly original position, percepts are carried outward—through reality testing, projection, or some other voodoo procedure—and finally located in an external world to which none of us has any direct access. (Straus 1966:258)

Phenomenological psychology and psychiatry avoid the assumption of an inner/outer, subjective/objective dichotomy, and replace it with an understanding of reality as experienced differently by different individuals. Binswanger urged an approach that would enter into the individual's own unique world without importing preconceptions, as a precondition for understanding that world. Phenomenological psychology and psychiatry endorse what one might call the Principle of Ontological Equality of Life-Worlds: "Nothing gives us the right to regard our perception as being more true than that of the patient." (van den Berg 1955:36)

The reader will recall our earlier discussion in Chapter 10 of von Uexküll's approach to biology; here we may note that von Uexküll is to the scientific understanding of the unique worlds inhabited by living non-human organisms as Binswanger and other phenomenological psychiatrists are to the scientific understanding of the unique worlds inhabited by psychiatric patients. Binswanger himself deferred to von Uexküll on various occasions, as he did when he quoted these passages from him:

> It is nothing but mental inertness to assume the existence of a single objective world which one tailors as closely as possible to one's own environment, and which one has extended in all directions in space and time.... Only to the superficial observer it seems as if all sea-animals were living in a homogeneous world, common to all of them. Closer study teaches us that each of those thousands of forms of life possesses an environment peculiar to itself which is conditioned by and, in turn, conditions the "building plan" of the animal. (Binswanger 1958:196)

Rollo May expressed the human, phenomenologically equivalent thought in connection with mental illness: "[T]he mentally ill live in 'worlds' different from ours. Therefore, knowledge and scientific description of those 'worlds' become the main goal of psychopathology...." (May *et al.* 1958:213) From this perspective, the psychiatric patient does not make errors of understanding about the reality he experiences, and it is not the task of the psychiatrist to "correct his error." From a phenomenological point of view there is therefore a good deal more acceptance of individual differences than we find in the "socially correct," more rigidly constrained definition of mental health agreed upon by *DSM* contributors. The phenomenological therapist seeks to help the patient adjust to his own unique reality in the least painful way possible; the outcome may, or may not, consist of behavior and attitudes that conform to conventionally accepted reality. That is, good mental health may not mean "psychologically normal." (See Spinelli 1989:137)

> [T]o help is before everything to put oneself in the other's place, to make one's home in his existence, to learn to know the world in which he lives. Undoubtedly to help is not: to dictate a way to the person needing help without knowing or even wanting to know whether the way dictated can join up with his existence. (van den Berg 1955:102)

I need to turn now from these introductory comments about phenomenological psychiatry and psychology to what is my main interest in this chapter, to lay a groundwork for the phenomenology of hatred. (Readers who wish a fuller understanding of phenomenological psychiatry and psychology may wish to consult, e. g., van den Berg's "Historical Summary" (1972:125-139), Spiegelberg (1972), van den Berg (1980), de Konig & Jenner (1982), Kockelmans (1987), Spinelli (1989), Fewtrell & O'Connor (1995), and Sims (2003).) We therefore turn to consider reality as it is experienced by those who hate. We shall find in the phenomenological description of hatred much of the reason why it is such a pervasive emotional and cognitive state, and why it is resistant to efforts to reduce and eliminate it.

## THE PHENOMENOLOGY OF HATRED:
## THE HATER AND HIS WORLD

The reality of the person who hates can be described in a kind of "snapshot" that depicts the details of emotion and the experience of others as these are lived by the person during a short period of time. Alternatively, a description of hatred can be given in terms of the experience of hatred over longer durations that are more complex, contain more information, and yield a more comprehensive account to reflective understanding. It is the second approach that I will take here, summarizing descriptively what it is that characterizes the experience over time of those who hate intensely, whose hatred is strong and influences much of their lives. The decision to adopt this focus reflects the recognition that even when hatred is diluted in milder forms it still retains many of the characteristics that we observe in extreme hatred. When possible, I will refer to the few psychologically-focused sketches of hatred that have appeared in the literature. It is important to be reminded that we are not here seeking to develop an explanatory theory of hatred, but a finer description of the experience itself than is ordinarily given.

### A Definition of Hatred

To begin, we need a working definition of hatred. In its broadest sense, as we shall see, hatred combines three elements which, in no particular order, are these: (a) It is a decisively different way of construing reality—different, that is, from ordinary experience in which hatred is not prominent. When I speak of "construing reality," what I am referring to is an often inchoate collection of beliefs and feelings about reality, which is at once cognitive and affective, that is to say in which certain patterns of *thinking* as well as *feeling* predominate. (b) It is a specific *state of being*, that is, a unique way of being in the world that brings with it its own practical definition of reality, which disposes the individual who hates to *act* toward others in certain ways. And, (c), it is, as we shall soon see in more detail, a form of *human relationship*.

In its more familiar, concrete, and specific sense, extreme hatred is the desire to destroy another, to erase that person's presence from one's reality. This concrete focus of hatred has been reiterated since Aristotle sought to distinguish anger from hatred when he wrote: "The angry man wants the object of his anger to suffer in return; hatred wishes its object not to exist." (Aristotle, *Rhetoric*, Book II, as quoted by Horowitz 2001:543) Early in the twentieth century, psychologist Alexander F. Shand (in a section of a chapter devoted to the "Analysis of Hatred," Shand 1914:58-63) similarly expressed this by saying that hatred intends the destruction of the hated object. Shand's view was ahead of his time when he emphasized that hatred forms a "system" in the emotional life of the individual:

> That hatred is a system that, however much it may be held in check by other forces of char-
> acter, works for the destruction of the hated thing, as anger does only in its extreme forms,
> and in human beings works with a deliberate and self-controlled activity as one of its dis-
> tinctive marks, is generally recognized.... Destruction then becomes the prominent end of
> hatred. All means may be adopted for this end.... (Shand 1914:58)

Two decades later, in the early 1930s, psychologist Pierre Janet, in another of the few works partially devoted to the psychology of hatred (Part 2, Chapter 2, "La Haine et l'amour," Janet 1932:213-305), continued the Aristotelian tradition by identifying hatred with the wish for the other, or even for the self, not to be. The first can lead to murder, the second to suicide. (226-7) Janet did not provide a detailed description of the experience of hatred; he rather sought to explain it (arguing that anxiety and defensiveness are its source, as is the perception that one is persecuted or that one's interests are blocked).

Two more decades later, like Janet, Gordon Allport (1954:363) again deferred to Aristotle's observation that hatred "desires the extinction of the object of hate," and argued that hatred is more deep-rooted than anger. He was followed shortly thereafter by Sartre, whose brief treatment of hatred may be mentioned since his philosophical work, as noted earlier, exercised considerable influence on phenomenological psychology. In his opus, Sartre (1956) also accepted the Aristotelian view, though it was disguised in Sartre's less accessible, "hy-phenated" terminology: As Sartre expressed this, hate

> ...implies a fundamental resignation; the for-itself abandons its claim to realize any union
> with the Other; it gives up using the Other as an instrument to recover its own being-in-
> itself. It wishes simply to rediscover a freedom without factual limits; that is, to get rid of its
> own inapprehensible being-as-object-for-the-Other and to abolish its dimension of alien-
> ation. This is equivalent to projecting the realization of a world in which the Other does not
> exist.... [H]ate knows only the Other-as-object and attaches itself to this object. It wishes to
> destroy this object in order by the same stroke to overcome the transcendence which haunts
> it.... (Sartre 1956:411)

Although some other claims play an obscure role in this passage taken by itself, the gist of it is that, according to Sartre, the person who hates wishes to do away with the hated Other.

In keeping with the long Aristotelian tradition, we may accept the definition that hatred intends the destruction of what is hated, which may be another person, a group, a nation, or, reflexively, the hater himself, as can be the case in penance and self-mutilation, masochism, depression, and suicide. If this is the intention that defines hatred, what is the experience of hatred and how is reality perceived once the shift in perception that characterizes hatred takes place? As we shall see, hatred has its own special logic and its own ontology.

### The Partitioned Reality of Hatred

In earlier chapters, we have had occasion to note how the perception that others are different frequently inflames human hostility. The perception of difference tends to provoke people to mistrust, to dislike, and frequently to hate. To perceive difference, distance must be established between oneself or one's group and the hated object. Hatred, as we shall see, can provide that *distancing*. Perception undergoes an initial shift when the object perceived is identified as different and alien. Once it is, few conditions need to be satisfied in order for the object to be perceived as a real or imagined threat to the hater's interests and preferences. (Again, the contingent conditions that can precipitate hatred do not concern us here since we are interested in describing the experience of hatred, not explaining it.) When the object is perceived in this way, it is frequently disliked, devalued, and can receive the hater's contempt.

Central in this shift in perception are the directedness and concentration of hatred. Hatred is, above all else, a *focus of attention* that is a form of emotional and cognitive tunnel vision: The hater's concerns, his interests, his energy become focused. And what is this focus? It is rigidly constrained attention, to the exclusion of all else. In extreme hatred, as we shall see later, this focus can become obsessive and compulsive. In his hate, the hater sharply delimits the world in which he lives; he cordons off a special region in which his intensity is concentrated; his hate and the objects of his hate merge into a hard kernel, an exclusionary focus in which his hostility and odium are felt with a penetrating intensity.

Hatred is, in other words, *selective, separating,* and *differentiating.* The hater's attention is specific and concentrated in a manner that heightens the perception of difference. Hatred is essentially an emotion that differentiates the hater from the hated; it partitions the hater's reality. If love is understood as an emotion of fusion with the one who is loved, an experience which produces a collection of feelings that include warmth, being at ease, appreciating and being appreciated, caring and being cared for, then hatred is a parallel, contrary emotion. It is an emotion not of fusion but of fission, of separation, alienation, and radical detachment and differentiation from the hated. In hate, as we shall see, the hater develops a keen sense of his or her own separateness and sense of identity that is a function of the distance that hatred places between the hater and the depersonalized, hated object. One of the clearest depictions of the way in which hatred involves a perception of differentiation is this:

> Fundamentally, to love is to incorporate into the self the loved object insofar as it is satisfying and therefore a source of pleasure. To hate…is tied to the growth of internal tension, to dissatisfaction and displeasure; to hate is to reject, to expel, to put at a distance, but also *to constitute the object* by differentiating it from the self, that is to say to experience at first hand the inside-outside distinction. (Dorey 1986:81; my translation)

It is important to point out that the "inside-outside distinction" to which Dorey refers is a distinction the hater becomes aware of *within, and as part of, his experience;* a metaphysical "outside" of experience is not at issue here: In his hatred, the hater experiences himself, his interests, and his power more keenly because of the separation, the intensely felt division, that he feels between himself and the object of his hatred. Phenomenology often speaks of the "constitution" of objects: In this case, hatred provides a fundamental way in which the hated object derives its identity in the hater's experience as being separate and differentiated from his own sense of self. Within the hater's world there is constituted a clear, emotionally charged distinction and separation between what is familiar, valued, and part of the self, and what is alien, contemptible, and other. To say this is to recognize that hatred leads to an awareness of reality in which the person who hates, by virtue of his hatred, sees that he and others are broken apart—discrete and separate. In this way, hatred serves to divide reality into distinct pieces, and so has an ontological component. One of the first experiences by the infant of the differentiation of reality is when his needs are not met and his frustration gives way to primitive and intense hatred.

But while hatred is an emotion, it is also a state of mind that affects the hater's *thinking*. The hater's tunnel vision that perceives a fragmented reality is at the same time a *channeled*, *inflexible*, and *hard* way of thinking about his world. The channeled nature of his thought process, with its familiar shortcut routes and the economy of effort which they make possible, was noted by Allport (1950). Here, "the principle of least effort" regulates thinking:

> There is a marked short-run economy in holding a negative view of other people. If I can but reject foreigners as a category, I shan't have to bother with them—except to keep them out of my country. If I can then ticket all Negroes as comprising an inferior and objectionable race, I conveniently dispose of a tenth of my fellow citizens. If I can put the Catholics into another category and reject them kit and caboodle, my life is further simplified. To pare down again, I slice off the Jews, the Democrats, and labor unions. As for experts, professors, and reformers, they are easily exiled along with all the other "communists." Soon there isn't much left for me to worry about except my own group on Suburban Heights—and I can proceed at leisure to destroy them one by one through gossip. (159-160)

Hatred is not only channeled to offer the least mental and emotional effort on the part of the hater, but the attitude it promotes is *hard*: The hating person is resistant to seeing or thinking about things differently, and *he stubbornly does not want to*. In fact, he *wants not to*. Those who hate are in an affective and cognitive state that is recalcitrant to being changed, moderated, or reduced. Hatred is a rigid outlook that actively resists change. There are good reasons for this hardness and inflexibility, for the hater gains much, as we shall see, from the narrowly circumscribed, efficient reality in which he lives. It follows that, for the purposes of hatred, human beings will identify with their most immediate and smallest groups, since hatred encourages highly partitioned and concentrated affiliation. Whereas, through love, people will identify with the largest groups, membership in which gives them an expansive feeling and identity.

## Shand's Law: Neutralizing Moral Awareness

Furthermore, a thought process that is channeled, inflexible, and hard is essentially *blind*. The hater's circle of attention and hence of affiliation can be directed only to the realities to which his habitual paths lead. His circle of affiliation is defined and constrained by his exclusionary hatred, and so is his ability to see those he hates as beings like himself. His hatred blinds him to their feelings; his feelings toward them harden; and his attitude toward them becomes pitiless. In this connection, Shand (1914:119) formulated a psychological "law of hate," which has gone unrecognized and ought to bear his name. *Shand's Law* recognizes that hatred eliminates moral constraints and obligations, permitting those who hate to destroy the objects of their hatred using whatever means are available. The hated become mere objects that call out to be destroyed.

Here, we encounter the element of *contempt* for others and their suffering that is the cold core of human hatred. In keeping with Shand's Law, the hater's moral conscience becomes attenuated or neutralized. The hater's exclusionary, tightly focused, and hard perspective fosters his feeling of *personal superiority*, with which contempt is linked. As Izard (1977) observed:

> [T]he feeling of contempt is the feeling of being superior, of being better than someone, some group or some thing.... Contempt [is] the "cold" emotion.... It causes people to hurt others through acts of indifference.... The feeling of contempt toward a human being tends to depersonalize the target individual, to cause the person to be perceived as something less than human. It is because of these characteristics that contempt can motivate murder and mass destruction of people—"cold-blooded killing." (339, 95, 340)

Compassion requires a very considerable enlargement of an individual's usually narrow scope of attention in order to recognize the feelings experienced by another. This expansion of awareness is the very thing that hatred and the contempt it inspires do not allow.

The reality of the hater is therefore partitioned emotionally and cognitively. His feelings are blunted and his thought process is turned back on itself. The shift in perception that defines hatred has the effect of excluding compassion toward the hated other, while the hater's moral restraints are loosened or extinguished completely. When the earlier discussion in this study regarding the exclusionary nature of ideology is applied to this phenomenological understanding of hatred, we see that hatred in fact lays a psychological foundation that perfectly fits the immunity of ideology to contrary evidence. When dovetailed with an ideology, hatred promotes much of the cruelty and malignity that fill human history. The partitioned reality of human hatred provides an ideally suited "growth medium" for the cultivation of systems of belief that are resistant to opposing evidence.

## The Emotional Dynamics of Human Hatred

If hatred were an unpleasant emotion, men, women, and children would seek to avoid it. Instead, the reality of mankind's psychological constitution is clear: Hatred confers upon people many benefits, without which the world would be other than it is. My purpose in this section is to identify and place in relief some of hatred's main emotional benefits. We have already noted that hatred involves a narrowed form of attention that simplifies reality for those who hate, strengthens the hater's sense of self-identity, adds definition to his interests, and increases his feeling of power. And hatred, as we have seen, bars empathy by narrowly circumscribing the hater's experienced reality and by reducing or extinguishing his compassion for others. This limited, efficiently reduced world brings other benefits, which are deeply felt by the hater and are not relinquished easily.

Hatred gives the hater a sense of *emotional security*: By virtue of his hatred, his reality is more sharply etched; people, events, and ideas are more readily compartmentalized; he knows what his acceptable boundaries are, and so gains emotional security. Hatred similarly can give him *determination*, for from his hatred comes the motivation to cause suffering and to destroy what he hates. Further, his determination gives him *zest* for his task; his hatred becomes a source of energy for his actions. His narrowed focus gives him an *intensity*, typically expressed by his set jaw, his pulsing jaw muscles, his teeth on edge, his clenched fist, etc. —All of these emotions involve *tension*, and indeed hatred is a state of tension.

That tension is a form of *excitement*. Hatred gives the hater increased *alertness*, fuller wakefulness than he experiences in lackluster ordinary living. As Aldous Huxley (1934:68) observed: "Hatred is one of the most stimulating feelings.... Hatred is a feeling more intense and more invigorating than general goodwill." He went on to note that hatred is *intoxicating*. "Hatred is the equivalent of alcohol; general goodwill is a weak and watery beer. Give man a choice between the two stimulants; he will naturally take the stronger." (68) As we shall see later, the "intoxication" of hatred must be taken literally, for it is *addictive*. We may note that such observations about the stimulating nature of hatred are similar to the heightened and pleasurable awareness that we saw in connection with war: As Robert Nathan (1941:181) expressed this: "It was as if life itself, the feeling of living, were clearer and more intense— sights and sounds, the night, the moonlight, the distant guns, the deep shadows, clear, more brightly seen and felt, more sharply lived through."

While hatred brings the tension of excitement, it also *assuages anxiety*. As psychiatrist Edward Glover (1933:26) noted, hatred can function to protect those who hate from anxiety. But how can hatred produce both tension and yet assuage anxiety? Hatred is a pronounced state of tension, rigidity, and agitation, but one whose *relief* lies in causing the hated to suffer or be destroyed. And all the while hatred brings *immediate relief*, by distracting the individual who hates from his or her anxieties of ordinary living. This is why a novel whose story fills the reader's breast with hatred against the brutally unjust villain can help him to relax.

Hatred is furthermore an emotion that *magnifies itself*, is self-reinforcing or self-fueling: That is to say, every sign of the continued presence of the hated incites the hater to further hate. All the hater needs is to hear a certain tone of voice, an accent, a lisp, just a fragment that suggests the hater's presence: It may be in the shape of the nose or the fullness of the lips, in the color of the skin or the texture of the hair; it may be found in the clothing of the hated, its style—in fact, once hatred has transformed the perception of the hater, any sign, symbol, sound, sight, or smell of the hated can be sufficient to arouse and magnify it. As Kernberg (1990:184) noted: "Primitive hatred at a sustained, intense level...creates a vicious circle that not only perpetuates but pathologically increases hatred itself." Hatred magnifies the hated so that it assumes exaggerated, expanded proportions that can absorb all the attention the hater is able to give it. It is always able to absorb more. This makes the hated worthy of an enormous investment of attention and energy. The hated can assume the importance of a monolith, putting all else in the hater's world in the shadow of the detestation and contempt it inspires.

Finally, the emotional dynamic of hatred is powered by the *pleasure* which is experienced by those who hate. It is this pleasure that exercises a magnetic attraction upon those who are available, who stand ready, to hate. The pleasure it brings is central to the emotional dynamic of hatred, and because of its major role in attracting, perpetuating, and intensifying hatred this pleasure warrants separate consideration.

### People Love to Hate: The Pleasure in Hating

People feel fine when they are full of anger and hatred against someone else. – May Sarton, *At Seventy*, quoted in LeShan (1992:21)

It has been said that "[t]here is no point to sin if it were not the corridor to pleasure" (Gordon 1993:3). And so it is with the phenomenon of human hatred. Most of the few psychologists and psychiatrists who have given thought to the role of hatred in human psychology have searched for causes of human hatred, and have suggested explanations that claim to have identified various sources, as when Janet (1932) believed he had found the main source of hatred in human defense mechanisms, or when Allport (1950) traced hatred to blocked self-esteem and a frustrated desire to affiliate with others, or when Stekel (1953/1929) claimed to find the source for hatred in an obstructed will to pleasure and power, or when physiologist D. Stanley-Jones (1970) sought to reduce the "primary emotions" of love and hate to physiological reactions of lust and rage, or when Kernberg (1990) argued that hatred is the consequence of an inability to eliminate frustration through rage. Although without doubt there is some truth in all of these hypotheses, from a non-explanatory, phenomenological point of view, the most immediate basis for hatred can be found in the experience of pleasure which accompanies it. From this point of view, there may be no need to look for a cause of hatred beyond itself, for to hate is to experience pleasure of a certain kind. It has become commonplace to associate pleasure with hatred only in those who are labeled psychopathic and then to call it "sadism," but, unfortunately, as we shall see, hatred is an experience imbued with pleasure even for those who are psychologically normal.

There are other emotions often associated with hatred which also lead to pleasure. Walter Kaufmann (1980:III:165) observed: "[T]here is abundant evidence that human beings have experienced ecstasies...when making others suffer. Here a frightening economy comes into play. The torture of a few or even of a single human being can provide intense delight for a large audience." This was the emotion that Nietzsche called *Schadenfreude*. We noted in an earlier chapter that he wrote: "To behold suffering gives pleasure, but to cause another to suffer affords an even greater pleasure. This statement expresses an old, powerful, human, all too human sentiment...." (Nietzsche 1956: *Genealogy of Morals* II, §6). It is a feeling of "malicious joy." (§27) This is the gratification that people can derive from witnessing punishment, in causing others degradation and pain, in cheapening them, and in seeing their misfortune. (See, e.g., Portmann 2000; Ben-Ze'ev 1992, 1993.)

We need not hate those whose suffering brings us enjoyment, but the pleasure that results is no different from the clinical manifestations of pleasure in the experience of hatred, studied by Wilhelm Stekel and Otto F. Kernberg. Stekel (1953/1929) observed how people experience cruelty as joy in another's pain (I:28); how many of us take a "delight in the horrible" (I:38); how even children enjoy barbarous stories—"[t]he more gruesome the better" (I:32); how in human groups the "senseless urge to destroy" often appears without any need for a leader, but is a readiness for cruelty that lies dormant, there to be awakened (I:36); how brutality, far from being limited to a few psychopathological cases, is a normal predisposition: "The normal person...covers over or sublimates his infantile cruelty; he adapts himself to the demand of civilization; yet inwardly he remains cruel" (I:40). And, perhaps most importantly, Stekel recognized the human inability to accept these psychological facts of self-understanding: "We are unable to bear the truth, because we have not been educated to the truth." (II:462)

Like Stekel, Kernberg (1990) studied the way in which hatred leads to "highly pleasurable aggressive behaviors," to a "sadistic enjoyment in causing pain, humiliation, and suffering; and the glee derived from devaluing others." He went on to say: "Each of these behaviors might be rationalized as an expression of righteous indignation or even expressed in...explosive violence that obscures its very origin—sadistic pleasure—in the act of destroying the object of its hatred." (179-180)

The pleasure that Stekel and Kernberg examined is not a special emotion uniquely associated with human hatred, cruelty, and destructiveness. It comes with other emotions. As in the experience of hatred, there is a certain luxury that people feel in venting their spleen. Berkowitz (1973/1968:51) summarized research results which showed that angry people do often "(a) feel better, and (b) perhaps even experience a temporarily reduced inclination to attack their tormentors, upon learning that these persons have been hurt." In Chapter 14, we saw how soldiers frequently experience pleasure and satisfaction, even a form of ecstasy, in killing. (Cf., e. g., Gray 1967:45f, 50, 55; Moreno 1977:Chap. 4.) Similarly, prison guards can build up hostility toward their prisoners when prisoners mock them and heap invective upon them. Conover (2000:134) described the experience of guards when they discharge pent-up aggression toward their prisoners as a "thrilling release." In this connection, historian Peter Gay (1993) noted in his study of the Victorian period that people "...cultivate their hatreds because they get pleasure from the exercise of their aggressive powers.... Most people find that hitting out, whether calculated or spontaneous, yields greater satisfactions than holding in, at least in the short run; smiting the other's cheek is more delightful than turning one's own." (9, 526)

Film producer Claude Lanzmann when making the film *Shoa* could not help but be distressed by the behavior of the Polish townspeople whose homes remain near the former Treblinka concentration camp. During the Holocaust, they were known to have waved gleefully at the cattle cars loaded with Jews en route to their deaths. They waved at the Jews who stared from the cars, and graphically illustrated what was to happen to them by drawing their hands across their throats and laughing. When interviewed by Lanzmann decades later, their hatred was still there. Their love for their hatred, the pleasure they took in it, these were unmitigated: "It was a joyful gesture! And again today, when they repeat it, it is with the same joy. It is a gesture of absolute hatred." (Gantheret 1986:13; my translation) This is the "joy of hate" observed by Shand (1914:59) and Elmgren (1937:276). It can be a durable emotion, surviving the devastation and resisting the shame of the Holocaust and a world war.

The commission of horrors against others is intrinsically exciting to most people; it is evident in the stimulation they enjoy when watching films or reading about murders:

> The reading becomes exciting .... One murderous incident follows another.... My excitement mounts.... I flow into the next account of killing and become one with the murderer.... Part of me still says this could never be me.... But I am increasingly excited, and it is almost as if I am experiencing myself as one of the killers whom I swore I could never be.... If one can really bear listening inside, ...I believe all of us can also hear echoes and refrains of a muted excitement that resonates and vibrates to the very horrors being committed by others all around us. Within us too there beats a pulse of pleasure as we read about mass murders. (Charny & Rapaport 1982:28)

The pleasure experienced by those who hate can offer the same thrill, the same exhilaration.

### The Existential Rewards of Human Hatred

Human hatred confers a number of what I will call "existential rewards"—that is to say, psychological benefits that come with the experience of hatred, benefits which improve the ability of people to live with less anxiety, uncertainty, and insecurity. I have already commented on the way in which hatred serves to offset anxiety by stimulation that distracts the hater from the concerns and monotony of everyday living. There are other existential benefits that are closely linked with the experience of hatred. Readers will recall an earlier discussion in Chapter 12 in connection with prejudice and persecution, which bring a sense of strengthened personal identity to those who are intolerant. In a study of anti-Semitism, Frenkel-Brunswik and Sanford (1946:117) sought to show that intolerance against groups other than one's own can serve "an important function in keeping the personality integrated. Without these channels or outlets (if they should not be provided by society) it may be much more difficult, in some cases impossible, to keep the mental balance. Hence, the rigid and compulsive adherence to prejudices." Their observations concerning the psychology of prejudice are applicable to hatred in two ways: Like prejudice, hatred serves the purpose of psychic integration, and like prejudice, hatred can become compulsive and obsessive. I discuss the first here, and the second in a later section of this chapter.

As we have seen, hatred serves to differentiate the reality of the hater, separating and accentuating the division between the hated other and the hater's sense of self. This process of differentiation also provides the existential reward of *more pronounced self-awareness* on the part of the hater: He becomes more self-possessed, aware of his distinctive identity, aware of his strength, and he feels his strength grow. In this sense, hatred shares characteristics of mania: its elevated mood, its disproportionate enthusiasm, and its hyperactivity as the hater works toward his goal to bring suffering and destruction to the hated. In this connection, we recognize that the most direct way for individuals, as well as the groups they form, to deny or disregard their own sense of inferiority and baseness is to magnify or manufacture the inferiority, baseness, and culpability of others. The person who hates gains a strengthened sense of self, a self that is felt to be better, stronger, and more valuable in the contrast which hatred enables him to feel between himself and the hated other. In this way, the experience of hatred is an experience of self-affirmation that comes about through the rejection of what is contemptible in the other. Hatred can therefore serve as a fundamental experience of *self-integration*. Thus, the satisfaction some soldiers feel in hating "...appears to lie, not in losing themselves and their egos, but precisely in greater consciousness of themselves." (Gray 1967:56) The differentiating perception and the narrowly intense experience of human hatred concentrates a person's or a group's sense of identity. The same observations of course hold true of groups whose hate provides them with an intensified sense of identity, group integrity, and an exaggerated belief and manic exuberance in their own strength.

The encapsulated reality of the hater also brings *a sense of community* with those who share his hatred. Hatred is, after all, a basic form of human relationship. As LeShan (1992:136-7) remarked: "We know...that hostility, per se, *is* a relationship, and for many individuals it is far preferable to none. No man is truly alone when he has an enemy." (See also LeShan 1958.) One of the most effective and easy ways to overcome loneliness is to hate and to find others who hate the same things. The facility with which hatred can be shared—and, in fact, "communicated" in the sense of contagion, which is discussed later—enables individuals who hate to affiliate with others in a camaraderie of hatred.

Further, hatred can give people *a way to overcome some of life's disappointments*. The attractive and intoxicating power of hatred diverts the attention of those who hate from their problems and frustrations by giving them a cause around which they can center their lives. As Hanfstaengl (1957:283) commented: "The humbler people are, the greater the craving to identify themselves with a cause bigger than themselves...." Hatred provides them with a way to do this.

Finally, hatred can help people to *overcome their fear of death*. As Ernest Becker (1975) wrote:

> [B]y actively manipulating and hating we keep our organism absorbed in the outside world; this keeps self-reflection and the fear of death in a state of low tension. We feel we are master over life and death when we hold the fate of others in our hands.... [W]e have to conclude that men have been the midwives of horror on this planet because this horror alone gave them peace of mind, made them "right" with the world. (114, 116)

In this way, people can avoid awareness of death by absorbing their attention in their wish to bring about the suffering and deaths of others. It is not merely that their attention is distracted by their hatred, but their hatred defines a purpose that lies "beyond themselves" in a manner that can be so all-absorbing that hatred can be characterized as one of the ways people find to immunize themselves against the reality of death.

In summary, hatred, depending upon its degree, can bring certain specifically existential benefits to those who hate: It can give to those who hate a sense of personal integration and strength; it can provide them with the emotional security of membership in a community of similarly disposed haters; hatred can diminish consciousness of life's disappointments; and it can help people to cope with their fear of death. —Any state of emotion and of mind that can accomplish these important existential purposes for people will bind them intimately to their experience of it. They will, in varied and often camouflaged ways, but wholeheartedly, resist efforts to lessen or extinguish their hatred.

## The Human Need to Hate

Our need to hate is just as great as our need to love. –Stekel (1953/1929:I:29)

Wilhelm Stekel has been one of the few psychiatrists to recognize the human need to hate. In the late 1920s, in a rare work in which the psychology of hatred is central and from which the opening quote of this chapter comes, Stekel reached the following conclusion: "I have long ago answered the important question, which is primary in man, love or hate, in favor of hatred...." (Stekel 1953/1929:I:23) He came to recognize that "[t]he need to hate is quite universal.... The necessity for hate chooses the most varied disguises. Now it is ethics, now aesthetics, now religion or politics, nationality, which must furnish the pretext.... To be long deprived of hating makes one hate-hungry." (I:30-1) Stekel did not provide what here I have referred to as a phenomenology of hatred. His two-volume study is primarily a psycho-analytically-inspired interpretation of sadism and masochism; his observations relating to the psychology of hatred, disengaged from a sexually-based analysis, are confined to one chapter ("The Psychology of Hatred and Cruelty," I:22-44). He returned to the subject at the end of the second volume when he wrote: "The hater must...recognize the pathological character of his...position and knowing it, overcome it...." (II:462)

This is an ugly realization about mankind's psychological constitution, and many will seek to avoid it. It was present in the confession made by Joseph Goebbels: "I...want to be able to hate. Oh, I can hate, and I don't want to forget how. Oh, how wonderful it is to be able to hate." (Quoted in Boonz 1995:14) If the description of hatred given here is true to the hater's reality, the need to hate is, indeed, a near-universal human phenomenon. We have seen persuasive reasons why it would be, for rare is the person who does not experience the need for excitement and distraction, reduced anxiety, a strengthened sense of personal identity, and all the other emotional and cognitive gratifications of hatred that we have identified. Human beings experience a very real *need* for such things. Unfortunately, the satisfactions that come from human hatred generally have harmful consequences.

## The Incapacitating Nature of Hatred

Like many phenomena that, on one level, benefit psychic life, the emotional and cognitive benefits conferred by hatred exact certain costs. Hatred is a self-incapacitating, self-disabling experience as Shand's Law makes clear. As Shand (1914:119) put it, "[h]ate...tends to destroy all virtues, ideals, and duties that restrain it from its ends." To the extent that a person hates, his or her ability to value others is attenuated. This is a reflexively disabling experience, which the everyday expression "being consumed by hatred" points to. Hatred deactivates compassion; it is the antagonist of the human capacity to care for the other. For to the degree that a person feels compassion, his conviction that his preferred reality is supremely important is undermined.

Hatred not only disables compassion, it also can disable the hater's cognitive functions, specifically his ability to reason. His hatred is expressed in his narrow and intense focus of awareness, which ignores and renders unreal all that does not fall within its scope. As we have seen, his exclusionary consciousness is impervious to countervailing evidence. Hatred deafens him to reason, which he does not want to hear. For listening to reason has the potential of reducing the benefits he derives from hating.

In short, hatred involves a shift in emotional response and cognitive interpretation that disables both the emotional capacity to empathize and the cognitive ability to stand back from experience, to reflect and reason. The experience of hatred leads to a single-minded disregard of the feelings of those who are hated, and at the same time it disables the capacity to think clearly and to use the resources of reason. The individual who cultivates hatred does, in a certain sense, lobotomize himself.

## THE PATHOLOGY OF HUMAN HATRED

The truth is I cannot hate wholly enough to kill a man. I always know how he feels, too.
– Pearl Buck (1931-35:44)

Hatred is a response, as we have seen, that can satisfy a variety of human needs: It can answer the human need for stimulation, distraction, excitement, reduction of anxiety, and pleasure. Hatred can strengthen personal identity, fortify membership in groups, reduce life's disappointments, and assuage awareness of death. Hatred also functions in a basic way to define reality by differentiating the self from its opposition by giving people an intensity of focus that is efficiently exclusionary, narrowing to manageable proportions their range of perception and their affiliations, and, in the process, hardening their feelings and instilling in them pitiless contempt for others. Hatred, as emphasized earlier, comes in many forms and degrees. It is part of normal human experience, where it can take the form of momentary reactions of antipathy and antagonism, or enduring hatred. It can be outwardly focused, or it can be directed inwardly.

As we step back from the phenomenology of hatred, we need to raise the question, Should we pathologize hatred? Hatred is, after all, by definition destructive: harmful to others and at times to the hater himself. The term 'hatred' is, however, not even indexed in *DSM-IV-TR* (American Psychiatric Assoc. 2000), but then again neither are the terms 'anger' and 'aggression'. This neglect is consistent with the fact that, for the most part, the psychology of hatred has been ignored and absorbed into the general category of normal aggressive emotions. Yet the experience of hatred possesses certain of the key defining characteristics of pathology: It is, as we have already seen, frequently by its own intent *harmful*. And, like many pathologies, it can spread as a *contagion*. Hatred is infectious in three ways: As Sartre (1956:412) noted, the normal human response to being hated by another is to hate in return: "Hate demands to be hated." Hatred is also transmissible from one hater to a fellow hater: Hate groups depend upon this fact in order deliberately to provoke and raise the level of hatred. And hatred is also transmissible from the object of hatred to anyone who associates with it in a positive, friendly way: This is how "collusion with the enemy" inspires hatred.

While hatred can be destructive and contagious, it is nonetheless a normal emotion that comes naturally to people. It is rarely judged to be a pathology by psychiatrists. An exception is the claim by psychiatrist Willard Gaylin (2003) that human hatred is an aberration and as such constitutes a psychological disorder. As Gaylin expressed this: "Hatred is a severe psychological disorder. The pathological haters, whether Al Queda today or the Nazis under Hitler...are 'deluded,' and their self-serving and distorted perceptions allow them to justify their acts of hatred against an enemy they have created." (14-5) "Hatred is their disease...and we normal people must protect ourselves against it." (240) This view seeks to pigeon-hole human reality by placing those who hate in a special pathologized category of their own. Gaylin compartmentalizes hatred, linking it to paranoia: "Since paranoid mechanisms are at the heart of the phenomenon of hatred, to appreciate what goes on in the minds of those who devote their life to hatred, we must understand paranoia." (108) —The reader will recall that we saw the same tendency among some psychologists of genocide, the wish to localize and confine the responsibility for atrocity in a few psychopathologically aberrant leaders.

Considered from the opposite point of view, hatred is rarely judged by psychiatrists to be a symptom of good mental health. An exception is the claim by psychiatrist Kurt R. Eissler, who has defended the positive value of hatred. As Eissler put it, "I believe...the full capacity to hate with great intensity...belongs to health as much as freedom to love passionately." (Eissler 2000:29) He sought to defend what one might call "noble hatred," which in his words is a "rarely encountered ability" that can be placed "in the service of a worthy goal." (32) This variety of hatred, which has an explicitly moral component, is the hatred of "the person who is truly sensitive to injustice." (33) Eissler argued that such hatred is "a legitimate way of handling reality, a life driven by hatred and absorbed in the one purpose of realizing its goal." (36) Eissler was evidently sympathetic with the revolutionary, for whom "[t]he activation of compassion would only diminish the impetus of his attack against superior power." (41) He therefore spoke of "the ideal hater" who "is extremely efficient in managing reality, however one-sided that contact remains." (40)

And so we see before us two possibilities that define theoretical extremes: On the one hand, we may perceive hatred to be narrowly restricted to a small minority afflicted with a certain specialized "psychological disorder"; on the other, we may praise it as the legitimate response of those who are sensitive to injustice. However, there is a third possibility, which I believe expresses a broader truth, and that is the view that hatred is a normal emotional and cognitive state which is destructive and undesirable, and hence pathological. This view is not as radical as it seems. For one thing, the phenomenological reality of the hater shares many of the same characteristics as the world experienced by the obsessive-compulsive. In V. E. von Gebsattel's phenomenological description of "The World of the Compulsive," we find this passage:

> [O]ur thesis illustrates that the compulsive patient lives in a world different from ours.... What entered our awareness from this other kind of world is a sum of negations. What struck us above all was that the friendly, inviting powers of existence step back in favor of the hostile, repulsive ones. Everything that normally draws the individual into the world and invites him to fuse with it is condemned to a peculiar kind of ineffectiveness.... Indeed, it can also be plainly shown that the...characteristics [of the world of the obsessive-compulsive] are narrowness, ...monotony, and rigid, rule-ridden unchangeability....[T]he compulsive patient is forever in action. From early till late we see him in constant tension, ceaselessly at work to have it out with the enemy who...is "forever at his heels".... (von Gebsattel 1958:184-6)

We have seen that hatred is compulsive and obsessional in its reduction of reality to its exclusionary focus of concern; in its narrowly defined, intense directedness of its antagonism; and, in extreme hatred, in the extent to which hatred gains an obsessional life of its own, defining reality for the hater and defining important goals of his life in relation to that reality. To the extent that the obsessive-compulsive personality is judged to suffer from a psychiatric disorder, to the same extent, it is credible to argue, so does the personality dominated by hatred. "Disorders of hatred" share much in common with obsessive-compulsive disorders, and, one could argue, should be associated with that diagnostic classification.

From Kassinove's (1995) collection of papers, one could construct some plausible suggestions how a diagnostic classification of hatred might be undertaken in analogy with anger. Various "anger disorders" were proposed in a paper by Eckhardt and Deffenbacher (Kassinove 1995:27-47) using the diagnostic pattern of *DSM*. The rationale of their proposal can easily be extended to hatred, *mutatis mutandis*. Doing this would yield such diagnostic classifications as: "adjustment disorder with a mood of hatred," "situational hatred disorder without aggression," "situational hatred disorder with aggression," "general hatred disorder without aggression," and "general hatred disorder with aggression." Another of the papers included in Kassinove (1995), by Tsytsarev and Grodnitzky (91-108), proposed that criminal behavior undertaken in strong anger should be labeled as "pathological affect." (108) Similarly, a paper by Tafrate (109-129) discussed "anger disorders" and their treatment. On the basis of our foregoing description of hatred, it would not be difficult to develop a similar framework in which a constellation of "hatred disorders" could be defined. There already exists a familiar diagnostic "platform" that can accommodate disorders of hatred and hence hatred as a psychopathology. —But what would be the purpose in identifying hatred in this way? Would hatred disorders constitute just one more addition to the already bulging *DSM*?

Identifying human hatred as a legitimate pathology has the same value as judging any condition to be a disorder: It marks the condition as dysfunctional and undesirable, and articulates a commitment to work toward its reduction and possible elimination. The phenomenological psychology of hatred reveals to us an emotional and cognitive experience that exercises a magnetic attraction upon men, women, and children, is profoundly pleasurable to the point that it can become addictive, spreads infectiously in human groups, and is undeniably one of the most harmful of human psychological propensities. One need search no further to be justified in judging hatred to be *a psychopathology that afflicts the normal population*. Like many of the forms of human pathology studied in this book, hatred needs to be recognized and challenged for what it is: one of the main forms of human evil, responsible for much of the aggression and destructiveness of human behavior and thinking. By judging human hatred to be a pathology, we recognize that ordinary and psychologically normal individuals are the ground force that leads to the perpetration of acts of cruelty and violence against others. At mankind's present stage of development, hatred is an emotion and state of mind, as Richardson suggested (see Chapter 9), that exists in people as a disposition: It is "there" awaiting an outlet. As Allport (1954:364) put it, there is a "psychological readiness to hate," or, in Stekel's terms, "a readiness for cruelty" (Stekel 1953/1929:I:36).

From this perspective, we recognize that hatred is a natural human emotion associated with a restrictive, obsessional cognitive state. It does not serve the interests of scientific honesty and truth to claim otherwise. By judging hatred to be a form of pathology, we see it dispassionately as the source of much human suffering and take a stand in opposition to it. By taking such a stand, we voice the need for the long-neglected, serious study of this destructive state of mind and emotion, with a view to treatment. If hatred is pathological, it is not because it is an unusual, deviant emotion. It is commonplace. The pathology of hatred, like other pathologies studied in this book, is universal. Judging human hatred to be pathological is to see a normal state as a pathology, and to see human psychological normality in a new light.

# CHAPTER 17

# THE ECOLOGICAL PATHOLOGY OF MAN

One of the penalties of an ecological education is that one lives alone in a world of wounds.... An ecologist must either harden his shell and make believe that the consequences of science are none of his business, or he must be the doctor who sees the marks of death in a community that believes itself well and does not want to be told otherwise. – Leopold (1966:197)

In earlier chapters, we examined the phenomenon of human evil from a variety of perspectives, focusing on the psychology of human aggression and destructiveness as these are directed by people against others of their own kind. Unfortunately there is another side of the story: the destructiveness of mankind toward other species and toward the conditions required to support life. Like human aggression, obedience, genocide, propensity to war, and other subjects we have considered, human ecology can be considered from a psychological point of view. Man's environmental rapacity and destructiveness and his extermination of other forms of life are exercised sometimes with self-awareness, at times without it, but most commonly they are deeply entrenched in psychological resistance to acknowledge the malignant, pathogenic side of self-interested human activity. (See Bartlett 2002.)

Although this is a time of increased environmental awareness, there has been no serious study in the literature of ecology of the role of the human species in its capacity as a global pathogen. One might imagine that such a study would examine the environmental depredation and reproductive behavior of the human species, and draw attention to evidence of a non-metaphorical, malignant parasitism that has become planet-wide. This chapter seeks to make a beginning. To do this, it is important that we understand what parasitism is and describe certain key concepts of parasitology which apply to the role of the human species in relation to other forms of life.

## THE NATURE OF PARASITISM

Parasitologists have found it difficult to define parasitism due to the complexity of possible associations between different species. In its most general sense, parasitism is a relationship in which one organism, the parasite, derives benefit from its association with another organism, its host, while the host is harmed to a degree that varies from an insignificant degree of detriment to the loss of the host's life due to the damage done to it by the parasite. (See, e.g., Matthews 1998:12-13; Poulin 1998:66; and Marquardt, Demaree, & Grieve 2000:5.) Traditionally and in the public mind, parasites have been associated with invasive, usually microscopic, organisms that infect the host, live in its body, multiply, and cause temporary harm, permanent disablement, or death. The popular conception of a parasite leads people to think of tapeworms, hookworms, or perhaps a protozoan like *Plasmodium*, which causes malaria.

These are examples of so-called *endoparasites*, which may either inhabit spaces between cells in the host's body, or live within its cells, as in the case of bacteria and viruses. Intracellular parasites are frequently transmitted by a carrier, called a vector. In the propagation of malaria, for example, the anopheline mosquito is the vector for *Plasmodium*. In addition to endoparasites, there are *ectoparasites* that make their living from the surface of a host's body. They include leeches, lice, fleas, ticks, and some larger parasites, for example, vampire bats and the pencil-thin fish, the candiru, a species of catfish that inhabits rivers in Latin America. The candiru is a feared parasite that attacks human beings who happen to urinate while bathing in rivers. The candiru follows the stream of urine and swims forcibly up into an individual's urethra. Once its teeth have secured it within a person's vagina or penis, the fish can be removed only with great difficulty, if at all.

Beyond ecto and endoparasites, there are other forms of parasitism, in which one species exploits another: There is so-called *brood parasitism* in which, for example, the cuckoo usurps the nest of the reed warbler or the cowbird, throwing out its eggs or its already hatched nestlings, and laying its own eggs to replace them. *Social parasitism* is practiced, e.g., by some species of ants that enslave other ant species. And then, parasites themselves may become parasitized, a relationship called *hyperparasitism*: For example, a flea living on a cat may have a protozoan parasite living in the flea's intestinal tract.

Parasitism is distinguished from *parasitoidism*, also a relationship between two species, but one in which the parasite kills the host. Parasitoidism is, one might say, a terminal form of parasitism. It occurs, for example, in a wide range of insect species in which the female injects her eggs into the body of the host, or deposits them on its surface. The eggs hatch and the larvae proceed to devour the host. Parasitoidism is common in certain species of butterflies, moths, flies, ants, wasps, and bees.

It will be important in this chapter to understand several other terms from the vocabulary of parasitology, which identify some of the main ways in which organisms interact: *Symbiosis* is a broad category that includes associations that may be established between organisms of different species, called symbionts. Symbiosis is subdivided into mutualism, commensalism, and parasitism. Any association between two species that live together is considered to be symbiotic, whether they benefit, harm, or have no effect on one another. In *mutualism*, the associated organisms both benefit from the interrelationship. For example, certain bacteria and cattle live in a relationship of mutualism: The bacteria living in a cow's digestive tract both aid the cow's digestion and live in an environment that benefits them. *Commensalism* is a relationship between two species in which one profits from its association with the other, while the second is neither harmed nor benefited. Clown fish, for example, obtain shelter and security among the stringing tentacles of sea anemones, an apparently one-way benefit that does not cost the anemone. And in *parasitism*, as we have seen, one species is benefited and the other, to some degree, harmed.

There are other possible relationships between organisms. Among them, *amensalism* is a relation between two organisms of different species in which one remains unaffected while the other is noticeably harmed. The affected individual may be deprived of food or space in which to live, a result of *competition* between the two species, or it may be injured or killed, the result of *antibiosis*. (See the earlier discussion of antibiosis in Chapter 1.) Antibiotic amensalism and parasitoidism, then, are closely related. Strict antibiosis occurs when an organism secretes toxins that inhibit the growth or kill another organism; parasitoidism is generally less specific, killing its host in one of many possible ways as a result of its activity. And so, in the deserts of the western United States, chaparral prevents plant overcrowding in an environment of scarce water by means of antibiosis, inhibiting the growth of potential competitors in a defensive zone around each chaparral clump. Parasitoidism occurs when a wasp injects its eggs into a paralyzed caterpillar, and then hatch larvae that will consume from the inside and eventually kill their host.

In order for a parasite to maintain its natural life cycle, new hosts must be infected. The *infectivity* of a parasite is determined by its ability to find new hosts, and by the degree of susceptibility or resistance of the host to infection. Parasitism is often measured in terms of the *pathogenicity* of a parasite population. The pathogenicity of a parasite is a function of three things: its infectivity, the size of the parasite population in the host, and the amount of damage for which the parasite population is responsible.[1] The specialized vocabulary which makes it possible to differentiate distinct forms of parasitism will be useful to us later in this chapter as we consider mankind within the context of the millions of non-human species with which we share the world.

## PARASITOLOGY AS A BRANCH OF ECOLOGY

Valentin Aleksandrovich Dogiel (1882-1955) was a pioneer in approaching parasitology from an ecological viewpoint. Traditionally, parasitologists have studied the relationship of an individual organism to its local environmental niche, often a particular host's body. This focus upon a well-defined microcosm has been advantageous because it is sufficiently finite to facilitate controlled observations. In recent years, some ecologists have sought to extend Dogiel's work. They have attempted to broaden the scientific understanding of organism-environment relationships by including increasingly more encompassing layers of the earth's total system of ecology.

As a result of the more comprehensive perspective of ecological parasitology, the definition of 'parasitism' is being widened so that parasitism is understood to be a particular kind of ecological relationship between a parasite and the environmental conditions upon which it depends for its survival and reproduction, a relationship that causes some degree of harm to the parasite's environment. In the case where the necessary environmental conditions are provided by another organism's body, the relation is that of parasite to host organism. Calling such a relationship ecologically parasitic forces attention to be directed to two things: the dependency relation that exists between the individual organism and its requisite environmental conditions, and the cost to the environment that the parasite's continued existence, reproduction, and proliferation exact.

It is important to observe that the concepts of parasitism and predation are closely allied. As one parasitologist observed, "It has proved difficult to define parasitism and to draw the line between parasitism and predation." (Halvörsen 1976:100) What we identify as a host is, for the parasite, its prey, while, for the host, the parasite is predator. When predation becomes excessive, we see the extinction of one species by another. During the 1930s, in research now seldom remembered today, microbiologist G. F. Gause (1934a; 1934b;

---

[1] Parasitologist C. R. Kennedy has expressed these relationships in the following more precise form: *Infectivity* (I) = the parasite's host-finding ability + the susceptibility/resistance of the host. Then, *pathogenicity* = I × the number of parasites in the host × damage to the host/parasite. Cf. Kennedy (1976:4-5).

1934c) sought to throw light on the conditions that lead to the extermination of one species by another, or to their mutual destruction. In one series of experiments, Gause was interested in testing the theoretical assumption advanced by mathematicians that under stable conditions in a controlled microcosm populations of predators and victims would exhibit natural periodic fluctuations. Gause, however, found that these expectations are not always borne out. For example, when two populations of organisms, one of which is a predator and the other a prey, coexist in an environment that provides an abundance of food for the prey, the predators multiply greatly, devour all of the prey, and then die out themselves. This dynamic in which predator and prey populations both become extinct was not anticipated. (See Dogiel 1965:657-8) Gause's experimental work laid the foundation for the *lethal level concept*, proposed by H. D. Crofton (1971). Crofton saw that most parasite species are able to kill their hosts when they are present in large enough numbers. As one would expect, lethal levels vary from one parasite-host system to another. Crofton's concept will be useful in our later discussion of the dynamics of human population growth.

As advances in parasitology have brought the field into closer contact with ecology, they have made evident to us that parasitology and the study of infectious disease frequently share the same subject-matter. Many parasitologists now accept an enlarged definition of 'parasite' that includes the standard classes of pathogens, including viruses, as well as so-called "selfish DNA." Large portions of human DNA, as well as the DNA of other species, are apparently inessential for the purposes of normal biological processes. These segments of DNA have been termed "selfish DNA" or "genetic parasites." (Cf. Dawkins 1976; Combes 1995). It has been hypothesized that such DNA segments use companion genes in a "parasitic way" in order to replicate themselves. (Zimmer 2000:127)

The three fields, then, of parasitology, pathology, and the ecology of predator-prey systems share a common interest in investigating interactions between species whose activities and life cycles affect one another. The three fields are losing their traditional boundaries and beginning to fuse. At one end of the spectrum of use, the phrase 'microbial predators' (Zimmer 2000:128) is applied in the context of infectious disease theory; and, at the other, the phrase 'behavioral parasitism' is used to refer to larger forms of life that are not physiologically dependent upon their hosts, but nonetheless exploit them—e.g., birds that steal the food from members of another species (see, e.g., Barnard 1990). Within this widened frame of reference, the terms 'parasite', 'predator', and 'pathogen' have meanings that are essentially interrelated, differing principally according to the user's disciplinary identity, rather than according to subject-matter.

As parasitology comes to involve explicitly ecological considerations, the relation of parasite to host is translated into the relation of parasite-pathogen-predator to host-environment. The transformations in terminology and in conceptual outlook suggest that reality is understood in more integrative and yet more specific ways. For instance, it is now recognized that the environment of a parasite may possess a systems-related capacity to respond to the parasite in ways that actually *block* the parasite's survival. This proposal was first advanced nearly a century ago when ecologists coined the phrase 'environmental resistance' to refer to the responsive potential of a parasite's environment to block its growth and proliferation. (See Chapman 1928.) Environmental resistance is a concept whose meaning, within an ecological context, parallels to a certain extent that of antibiosis. (See Chapter 1.)

During the past two decades, environmental parasitology has enabled us to see more clearly how pervasive parasitic organisms are. Where the millions of species of animals and insects that live on plants used to be regarded as herbivores, it is increasingly common for them today to be classified as parasitic organisms. (See, e.g., Zimmer 2000:45) In recent years, parasitologists have discovered that the proportion of parasitic organisms in relation to free-living species is surprisingly large. One contemporary parasitologist observed: "As far as numbers of organisms is concerned the number of parasites greatly exceeds that of free-living animals." (Matthews 1998:16) Another author noted: "...parasites may outnumber free-living species four to one. In other words, the study of life is, for the most part, parasitology." (Zimmer 2000:xxi) To be concrete: while there are only some 4,000 species of mammals, there are between 8 and 100 *million* species of insects, making up more than half of all species of organisms. Of these, among the multitude of parasitic insects there are 200,000 species of parasitic wasps alone, while there are hundreds of thousands of species of insects that parasitize plants. There are more than 5,000 species just of parasitic tapeworms. When we also take into account parasitic species of bacteria, protozoa, fungi, plants, and larger animals, it becomes evident that by far the greatest majority of all forms of life engages in parasitism. If we include in the count parasitic viruses and parasitic DNA, parasitism pervades even the constituent genetic materials of life itself.

A study of the ecology of parasites has, in short, had a broadening effect upon our general biological understanding of life. A good example of this can be found in a newcomer to the life sciences, evolutionary parasitology, which has in recent decades emerged as a field of study. The discipline investigates parasitic relationships among organisms in order to improve our understanding of evolutionary patterns of descent. Evolutionary parasitology has brought a new awareness: "only now are...[we] realizing that parasites have been a dominant force, perhaps the dominant force, in the evolution of life." (Zimmer 2000:xxii) In addition to expanding the scope of parasitology to include evolutionary studies, environmental parasitology has deepened our awareness of the nature of the relationship between organisms and their required ecosystems. An organism's environment can promote its health, its illness, or its death. It has therefore become meaningful to speak of ecosystems that are healthy or diseased, depending upon whether or not they support the health of species that depend upon them. When an individual species pollutes the environment on a global scale, as the human species does, it acts as a pathogen that undermines the health of a vast range of ecosystems, bringing disease and death to hundreds of thousands of species.

Despite the increased scientific recognition of the ubiquity of parasitism, the human species to date has itself been studied by parasitology exclusively in terms of man's capacity to serve as *host* to endoparasites such as tapeworms and microbial pathogens, and to ectoparasites such as lice and ticks. The focus of parasitology has been homocentric in considering man only as a species preyed upon by other forms of life, by parasites that have traditionally been thought, in evolutionary terms, to be more primitive. As a result, the human species has not been studied specifically as an evolutionarily advanced parasitic species in relation to other organisms, or as a parasite species in relation to the global environment. But the concept of parasitism does not include in its meaning any *exemption* excluding its application to the human species. In what follows, we will begin to apply an understanding of parasitism to man.

## THE WORLD AS A GENERAL SYSTEMS HOST

As noted earlier, parasitologists have traditionally focused their attention on organism-environment relationships in a strictly localized manner, studying a given organism's ecological niche as a microcosm in comparative isolation from the complex network of relationships among other species that are not perceived to have explicit associations with it. The host of an individual parasite is usually, from this point of view, a specific, individual organism.

During the past several decades, largely as a result of the research and publications of James Lovelock, it has become popular among perhaps more whimsically inclined scientists and philosophers to regard the earth as a unitary "organism" in which the millions of individual microbial and larger plant and animal species live in their respective ecological niches as though as cells within a body of planetary dimensions. For many scientists, this theory of the earth as a super-organism—called "Gaia" after the Greek Earth Goddess, a name proposed to Lovelock by novelist William Golding—serves as an interesting and meaningful metaphor, but a metaphor only.[2]

Gaia theory is appealing, especially to those who are committed to preserving the natural environment. Gaia theorists have drawn attention to ways in which organisms and the natural cycles in which they function contribute collectively to global homeostasis. This is without doubt scientifically fundamental and important work—work whose value does not depend in any essential way on whether the global system does or does not comprise a genuine giant organism, a view about which many researchers have expressed reservations.[3] In addition to expanding our detailed knowledge of an interlinked biosphere, the Gaia conception of the planet as a dynamic system made up of interconnected and interdependent species has helped somewhat to diminish homocentrism. From this perspective, the human species is one among many, part of a complex, global system in which the existence of each affects others.

The interrelatedness of the general system that comprises the world is a fact we cannot escape. Within that general system, we see that the human species has evolved and has developed socially and politically as an unusually destructive and ubiquitous parasitic species. There are now few places on earth that remain unaffected by man's presence. *For the parasitic human species, the world has become its host.* And like the most damaging forms of parasitism, the human form is causing huge amounts of devastation, both to other species and to the biological and physical conditions required for their coexistence with man and for mankind's own survival.

## *HOMO PARASITICUS*

> After five million years of serving as a host to parasites, man has himself become one.

The claim that the human species is a true biological parasite has, as far as I have been able to determine, been proposed only metaphorically or in passing.[4] And yet, as I will try to

---

[2] Lovelock's theory was anticipated in general terms by the many poets and philosophers who have described the world in dynamic, organic terms. In language most closely resembling Lovelock's, humanist Dane Rudhyar (1971:21), for example, wrote: "... international scientific studies have shown irrefutably that the Earth as a whole is an organized system of most closely interrelated and indeed interdependent activities. It is, in the broadest sense of the term, an 'organism'." Lovelock's Gaia-related books include Lovelock (1979, 1988, 1991, 2000).

[3] One of the strongest objections to the scientific legitimacy of a Gaia "organism" was expressed by biologist W. Ford Doolittle: "The biosphere, Lovelock's Gaia, is not a replicating individual, and has no coherent heredity. If her parts contribute to global homeostasis, this cannot be for the same reasons that organs of an animal promote physiological homeostasis.... If individual species do collaborate as one whole, it can only be because some sort of interaction rule like Tit-for-Tat has been selected during their coevolution." (From a short contribution by Doolittle in Barlow (1991:235).)

[4] In terms of Gaia theory, in Barlow (1991:x), for example, we find in the Editor's Preface the following remark: "If Lovelock is on track with his Gaia hypothesis, there exists an organism far more

show, human parasitism is pervasive and can be recognized unmistakably using established criteria of parasitism.

The human species is a parasite species in a number of evident ways. In addition to satisfying the general definition of parasitism given earlier, a parasite species characteristically exhibits three properties. These are properties of special interest to parasitologists, and also properties that accurately describe human ecology. They are: *parasite opportunism, exponential growth,* and *parasite adaptability.* Together, these species traits more fully define parasitism.

Although parasite species do not always reproduce at rates that exceed those of non-parasitic species, the majority of parasite species are opportunistic. That is to say, if given the opportunity, their reproductive behavior is exploitative: If conditions necessary for their survival and reproduction are met, their populations will grow quickly and they will proliferate rapidly throughout environments that suit them. Parasite opportunism enables a parasite species to gain an ecological foothold, and once established, provided its survival needs are met, the species will reproduce exponentially. Parasite opportunism and the exponential growth that it fosters are functions of the third trait, a parasite species' adaptability.

The ability of a parasite species to adapt to changing environmental conditions is essential to its survival, as it is for non-parasite species. Many parasite species, however, seem to specialize in adaptability: Some are able rapidly to alter their own genetic makeup so as to evade detection by a host organism's immune system, a property that has made treatment of the AIDS virus, for example, so difficult. A moving target is much harder to hit. Other parasite species are able to exercise manipulative control over their ecosystems, and so transform their hosts' environments in ways that make living conditions more congenial. Manuals of parasitology are replete with fascinating examples of both strategies of adaptation.

The applicability to the human species of the three properties of parasite opportunism, exponential growth, and parasite adaptability is direct. Among larger animal species, mankind is without doubt the most successful opportunist. Environmental conditions and the natural availability of food and water do not need to exceed more than a bare minimum for people to gain a foothold, construct shelters, begin to modify their environment to make it conform to their needs, and start a chain of escalating reproduction. The ability of human beings to carve out niches even in the most inhospitable environments is truly astonishing, whether they are settlements in an arid desert, at high elevations, in the arctic, or in the hottest tropics. As one contemporary biologist put it, "if one feature sets humans apart from other animals, it is the breadth of the ecological niche that we presently occupy." (Flannery 1994:142)

An objective characterization of human adaptive skills applies, with few changes in wording, to the abilities of many non-human parasite species to accomplish precisely the same ends: Microbial parasites construct shelters for themselves, encapsulating themselves in the form of cysts, or growing thickened cell walls, or covering their surfaces with chemically resistant defenses. Many engage in biochemically modifying their food, as numerous species of protozoans have done for eons. Human ingenuity is matched on many levels of parasite life. When man cultivates land, when he domesticates and slaughters animals, even when he develops genetically modified foods, what he is engaging in are precisely processes that define parasitic life forms. When human beings cut down forests and put the land to human

---

complex and grander than we. Humans may simply be cells (benign or cancerous?) of a single planetary-scale organism." And in a recent semi-popular account of parasitism, Zimmer (2000:245) commented: "It is we who are the parasites, and Earth the host. The metaphor may not be perfect, but it chimes well."

use, there is no difference between the nature of this activity and that of any parasite that forces its immediate environment to meet its biological needs. Except in terms of scale. Man is the first known parasite species to manipulate the environment of an entire planet for its own purposes. The global environment has become the host organism for the human parasite.

Highly successful as an organism that transforms its environment to satisfy its own needs and interests, *Homo parasiticus* exhibits parasite opportunism and adaptability in their ecologically most penetrating, threatening, and destructive forms. The species opportunism and adaptability of mankind have led to the characteristically exponential growth curve of a flourishing parasite species, at least for a time.

## THE POPULATION BIOLOGY OF HUMAN PARASITISM

There has been more [human] population growth since 1950 than during the preceding 4 million years. – Lester Brown quoted by Associated Press (1999:2A)

What is exponential growth? In commonsense terms, as illustrated in the now well-known studies dealing with the exploding human population, *The Limits to Growth* (Meadows *et al.* 1972) and *Beyond the Limits* (Meadows *et al.* 1992), a population experiences exponential growth "when its increase is proportional to what is already there." (Meadows *et al.* 1972:29) The authors' example, taken from a French riddle, is worth recalling: Consider a pond on which water lilies double in population each day, and which will choke out all other life by the end of thirty days. For many days, the rate of reproduction of the lily population seems insignificant, "so you decide not to worry about it until it covers half the pond. On which day will that be? On the twenty-ninth day. You have just one day to act to save your pond." (Meadows *et al.* 1992:18) The population growth rate of the human species has decidedly been exponential—in fact, during the past few centuries, no other species in the world has had a population growth rate tantamount to man's.

Not all parasite species reproduce exponentially until they harm and perhaps destroy themselves and their environments. On the contrary, many parasite species that have attained evolutionary success seem to follow a biological principle of moderation. They appear to know enough not to exterminate their hosts. They are, in other words, capable of self-regulation. As one author put it, "they are expert at causing only the harm that's necessary, because evolution has taught them that pointless harm will ultimately harm themselves." (Zimmer 2000:245) In many of these parasite species, overcrowding itself functions as a feedback control upon their rate of reproduction. (Kennedy 1976:110) The human species, however, appears to have no built-in governor to rein in its instinctual reproduction, as the following graph of world population makes clear.

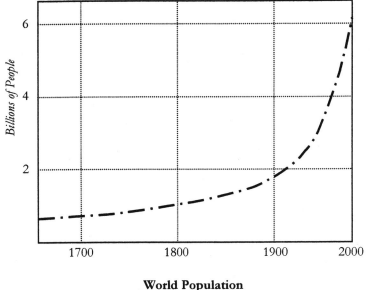

**World Population**
Meadows *et al.* (1992:4)

As we shall see, the exponential growth of the human species is the runaway growth of a pathogen in the process of killing its host.

If the human species suffers and will continue to suffer at its own hand it is due to lack of foresight, to what seems to be a constitutional human inability to make the future real in the species' consciousness. Reality, unfortunately, gives no special dispensation for the imagination deficit of a species. The accelerating rate at which human babies are now being produced may be difficult to imagine, as the human species brings more than 250,000 infants into the world *each day*, or some 150 births per minute. (Of the daily influx of a quarter of a million babies daily, we would need to ship 230,000 of them off the world *each day* in order to achieve a stable population, according to Hardin (1999:135).) The doubling time of the human species has now shrunk to 35 years. Mankind's enormous rate of reproduction mirrors the exponential, opportunistic growth of a parasite population during the early stages of infection of its host. In the case of man, the host is the planet itself and the diversity of species that have evolved on it.

Biologist Garrett Hardin has raised the question whether God gives a prize for the maximum number of human beings. "If we opt for life with nature we opt for fewer human beings and boldly assert that God gives no prize for the maximization of human protoplasm.... Can any trustee for posterity consent to a step-by-step sacrifice of the variety of nature, merely to make possible the maximum number of human lives?" (Hardin 1982:195) The answer, of course, is "yes," for progressive sacrifice of mankind's host is in keeping with the species' activity as a parasite. If the hypothesis formulated here is correct—that the human species is a true global parasite—*significant* reductions in human population growth will not come about as a consequence of humanity's voluntary efforts. This is not a matter of attitude, but of empiricism. Our species' population replacement rate is approximately 2.1. At this rate, a mother and father are replaced, while 0.1 percent allows for mortality of infants and young adults who have not yet procreated. In 1996, the average woman, however, bore 2.6 children. This amounts to a rate of reproduction nearly 24 percent *greater* than the replacement rate. Intelligent, reflective discussions of the optimal population carrying capacity of the world are highly unlikely, in the long run, to make a real difference in terms of humanity's rapidly accelerating growth rate.[5] Parasite psychology has deep roots.

There has been considerable debate concerning the earth's optimal human carrying capacity. Some judge, in terms of quality of life and the preservation of natural beauty, that the world's optimal carrying capacity has already been considerably exceeded. Paul Ehrlich, for example, has argued that the maximum sustainable world population is in the neighborhood of two billion—less than a third of today's population. (Ehrlich 1990) Biologist E. O. Wilson stands with him on this minimalist side of the population discussion. According to Wilson's calculations, "to raise the whole world to the U.S. level with existing technology would require two more planet Earths." (Wilson 1998:282)

It should not take graphs and calculations to prove that any organism's exponential reproductive rate cannot continue for long. Human ecology is no different from that of any organism: land and resources are finite. But the psychology of homocentrism is excessively strong, so much so that it is likely to require catastrophe to reduce human population significantly. To date, even warfare has not cut into population growth very much: From the beginning of World War I to the end of World War II, "only" some 250 million people were killed. (Piel 1994:124) This number of babies will be born in just the next two and a half years. Certainly global cataclysms can be envisioned that would have a more drastic effect in reducing the burgeoning human population, but it is tragic that so many individual people must suffer to curtail a species-driven heedless compulsion to reproduce. The grandson of Charles Darwin, C. G. Darwin, underscored this phenomenon when he called the human species *Homo philoprogenitus* (lover of many offspring). (Lovelock 1979:140)

My point in reviewing some of these perspectives on human population growth is simple: We are accustomed to thinking of the characteristic exponential growth rates of many parasites as applicable only to non-human organisms, and then usually to microorganic pathogens during the early stages of an infection—that is, when their population growth rates closely resemble man's during the twentieth century. We are not accustomed to taking a larger view of the world, situating the human species within that view, and then recognizing that the many psychological, social, and ideological forces that encourage human reproduction are no more than the particular expressions by the human species of the universal drive of any parasite species to reproduce itself. Membership in the human species makes such reflections more difficult: certainly they are frowned upon, dismissed, or denied—as one should *expect* as part of the behavior of a parasite species. For, after all, if mankind is globally parasitic, it is to be expected that his drives, attitudes, beliefs, and dogmas will express and reinforce his single-minded parasitic relationship toward other species and toward the world's resources.

---

[5] Although hope always sells best, and those who dispense less optimism are dismissed as so many profits of doom, there is substantial empirically-based evidence to support the claim that the human species is on a deadly course. Much of the psychological evidence is presented in this book. Physical evidence and the results of thousands of computer simulations based on it have been presented in studies like Meadows *et al.* (1972) and its successors, Mesarovic & Pester (1974) and Meadows *et al.* (1992). In the last of these studies, the authors comment: "In fact, in the thousands of model runs we have tried over the years, overshoot and collapse has been by far the most frequent outcome." (136)

## THE EXTERMINATOR SPECIES' BIODIVERSITY HOLOCAUST

If it moves, shoot it. If it grows, chop it down. – Rallying cry of Australia's settlers

Some humans have dreams...to make the deserts bloom and to make the depths of the sea and even Antarctica yield their bounty. As each year goes by, we come closer to developing the technologies that will allow us to realise these dreams. Each year we also feel an increasing need to utilise marginal lands in order to feed our growing populations. With our dreams fulfilled we will, I fear, see a wave of extinctions so vast as to dwarf anything that has gone before. For we will have become the exterminator species that broke all the rules. The one that could take not only all the resources of rich lands, but of poor ones as well. – Flannery (1994:101)

Paleontologists have found evidence in the fossil record of five major extinctions that have wiped out huge numbers of species. Each of these catastrophes to life has resulted in a loss of many thousands of species. Periods of mass extinction have sometimes lasted for thousands of years. After each mass extinction, it has then taken millions of years for new species to evolve. They have taken the place of the forms of life that were wiped out, but they did not replace them. The species that evolved were new, but those rendered extinct were lost forever.

The five documented mass extinctions were: (1) the most ancient, the *Ordovician* (approximately 440 million years ago; 25 percent of forms of life lost); (2) the *Devonian* (370 million years ago; nearly 20 percent of living organisms lost); (3) the *Permian* (250 million years ago; 54 percent of living species extinguished); (4) the *Triassic* (210 million years ago; 23 percent of living organisms rendered extinct); and, most recently, (5) the *Cretaceous* (65 million years ago; 17 percent of living organisms lost, including the dinosaurs). (See Morrell 1999a:42-56.)

Mass extinctions clearly are not new to the earth's history. What is new is a mass extinction caused by a single species. Such a mass extinction is in progress now. Unlike the mass extinctions of millions of years ago, the mass extinction that is underway is not being caused by catastrophic natural events, such as the impact of a meteor, a period of devastating volcanic activity, or a radical change in climate. It has been called the *Quaternary*, the sixth mass extinction, and it is being caused by the human species.

In the course of its history, mankind has found many complimentary attributes to underscore the uniqueness of the species and its separateness from other animals. Of the many self-ascriptions that philosophers, theologians, and scientists have tried to find with which to praise, elevate, or distinguish mankind, none has carried the force of the appellation that the species has earned during the past few centuries. During this period, the species has distinguished itself in a way that stands very much apart from its traditional characterizations as a featherless biped, a user of tools, the sole possessor of reason or of an immortal soul, as the player of games, or the user of language. The most recent designation that mankind has earned has placed the species in a direct adversarial opposition with the rest of the world: The new distinguishing mark of what Flannery (1994) has called "the exterminator species" makes the phenomenon of human parasitism explicit, by emphasizing the destructive relation of the species to both the physical and the biological world:

The exterminations that the human species is causing are global. All forms of life are being affected: microorganisms, plants, insects, fish, birds, and mammals. For example, biologist Stuart Pimm calculates that within the next century, fully 50 percent of the world's flora may be rendered extinct. Two thousand tropical and subtropical plant species are disappearing *each year.* One in eight species of plants is now at risk of extinction. Already, 11 percent of all species of the world's birds—1,100 species out of a total of 10,000—face extinction. Fifteen percent of bird species are expected to disappear from the Amazon basin within the decade, while 15 percent of the earth's forests will be leveled within the same period. (For a compilation of researchers' estimates of species extinctions per decade, see Groombridge 1992:203; also Morrell 1999a:46.)

What Pimm calls a "worldwide epidemic of extinctions" (Morrell 1999a:46) is occurring because of the collective behavior of our exponentially proliferating species. Natural land is "developed": houses, apartment complexes, industrial plants, and dams are built; the earth is paved over; forests are leveled; human toxic waste pollutes rivers, streams, the oceans, and the atmosphere; the world's ozone shield is increasingly destroyed; land is turned into desert. Already, the human species has degraded 40 percent of the total vegetated land surface on the planet, while it has co-opted or destroyed 40 percent of the food supply relied upon by all species of animals and microorganisms. (Ehrlich 1997:13) —All of these things are occurring as the human population explodes on an almost unimaginable scale, as human beings take up residence and displace other forms of life in virtually every possible habitat.

Mankind has become a world-devouring species, or, to use an appropriate term that has now become rare, it has become *pantophagous,* consuming all that it is capable of, ravaging the resources of its host with true parasite rapacity. The human species has developed a capacity and a will to devour an exhaustively wide array of resources. When one resource is depleted, human beings find ways to satisfy their needs by means of an alternative resource, which they then exploit.

Comparatively feeble, though heroic, gestures are being made to save a tiny fraction of the world's biodiversity. The Millennium Seed Bank at Kew Gardens, for example, hopes to be able to collect samples of 10 percent of the world's plants by 2010. Perhaps at some time in the future, a few that have been pulled into the lifeboat of refrigerated storage may, conditions permitting, be restored. The project is a band-aide, one might say, bravely applied to stanch a severed artery. An equally ineffectual wand to protect non-human species has been waved by legislation. In the United States, since the Endangered Species Act was passed in 1973, some 1,200 species have been listed as endangered or threatened. Of these, fewer than 2 percent have actually been protected over a period of three decades. (Data reported in *Discover,* January, 2000:66) It is not much of a success record. In reality, the gesture toward other forms of life is extremely weak. It is a matter of too little, too late. (For a picture of the relative insignificance of efforts to save species from human destruction, see Groombridge 1992:206-25, 233.)

As a matter of course, species come into existence, and they die out. We live at a time when it is beginning to soak into our consciousness that all things have their lifespans: on a larger scale, suns die and planets perish; on a smaller scale, forests become deserts, drastic changes occur in the global climate, species become extinct. More than 99 percent of all species that have ever lived have become extinct. However, by current estimates, the present rate of species extinctions is some *ten thousand times* the average evident from the fossil record. This year, while 92 million individual human infants are brought into the world, 30,000 non-human *species* will be brought to extinction as a result of human activity: more than 80 species are eliminated from the face of the earth *each day.* (McClintock 2000:65; Powell 2000:54) The death of an individual is a tragedy, but in the public consciousness the death of a species is only a statistic apprehended dimly if at all.

A standard of comparison is helpful if we are to grasp what is happening. During past extinctions, how many species have become extinct each year? Based on the fossilized re-mains of past extinctions, paleontologists estimate that as many as one species of mammal should normally be expected to become extinct perhaps every 400 years and one bird species every 200 years. These are thought to be maximum estimates: normal extinction rates in the past have probably occurred significantly less often. (Groombridge 1992:197) In comparison, and to use only a single country as an example, the United States threatens the extinction in the foreseeable future of the greatest number of reptiles (25 species), amphibians (22 species), and fish (164 species). For these groups of organisms, the U.S. is the top offending country in the world today. In exterminating birds, the U.S. ranks ninth (43 species). (Groombridge 1992:242)

The mass extinction we are witnessing may turn out to be the largest in the history of the planet. (Myers 1979:5) Already, based on the current rate of extinctions, which is accelerating (Ehrlich 1997:8; Flannery 1994:143; Groombridge 1992:204), ecologists estimate that some 50 percent of all living species will be destroyed. (See, e.g., Novacek 2001; McClintock 2000:65) We are witnessing a *biodiversity holocaust*[6] caused by a single species, our own.

The worldwide destruction of other forms of life by the human species appears to some biologists to be more a side-effect of its activity than an intended consequence. Ecologist R. V. O'Neill has described mankind's destruction of the world's biological diversity as "the metabolism of the dominant animal."[7] When a pathogen causes disease and death in an infected population, it makes little sense to call this intended. Mankind's species behavior as a pantophagous exterminator of life may be no different in this respect.

Some environmental parasitologists have used the expression 'anthropogenic impacts' to refer to environmental damage caused by man. One of the most destructive of these impacts concerns human toxic waste, and specifically human sewage, an inevitable biological by-product of human life. Sewage produced by the rapidly increasingly human population is routinely dumped into streams, rivers, and oceans. The waste is euphemistically called "outflows." Some of the sewage is treated, but most is not. The oceans of the world, in particular, have for centuries been regarded as vast dump sites that can accommodate unlimited human refuse. The scale of this pollution is huge and has still not been reliably measured. Just a single moderately sized modern city will, as a matter of course, dump billions of gallons of untreated waste. During a recent year, Portland, Oregon, for example, permitted three billion gallons of untreated sewage to "outflow" into local freshwater streams. During periods of heavy rain, the quantity of untreated sewage dumping increases, as the capacity of sewer and storm water drains is exceeded. Towns and cities without sewage treatment plants—which still include most communities in the world—are responsible for a major portion of human sewage pollution. Damage is done to non-human forms of life, and also very directly to people, who frequently depend on freshwater streams and rivers as a source of food or drinking water.

As of the year 2000, 58 *dead zones* were identified: These are areas of the sea bordering coastlines and which are now bereft of life. Dead zones come about when nitrogen-rich sewage, other human waste, fertilizer, herbicides, pesticides, industrial waste, and garbage are dumped into the oceans of the world. This waste can then feed a runaway growth cycle of algae, choking the water and depleting dissolved oxygen, a process called eutrophication. Sedentary forms of marine life, such as lobsters, clams, and mussels, are killed. Already, for

---

[6] A phrase coined by Stanford environmental biologist Stephen H. Schneider, from an interview published in *Discover*, January, 2001:60.

[7] O'Neill made this observation at a symposium, "Ecological Economics: Building a New Paradigm for Sustainability," at the 1994 annual meeting of the Ecological Society of America, August 7-11. For his concluding remarks at that symposium, see O'Neill (1996).

example, one-third of the Baltic Sea, an area of 38,000 square miles, is lifeless. Half of all estuaries in the United States are now oxygen-depleted. The number of dead zones in the world caused by "outflows" of human waste is expected to double within the next ten years.[8]

Parasites often damage their hosts as a result of by-products that they excrete. *Homo parasiticus* is no different in this regard. The waste that the species excretes—in the form of natural biological waste and industrial-chemical waste—is fouling the ecosystems of an accelerating number of microbial and large plant and animal species. As the human biomass increases and spreads, the waste products produced by the species increase proportionately. The world's rapidly multiplying dead zones are one direct consequence.

Mankind's present exponential rate of population growth cannot of course be continued indefinitely. A projection of the human population's waste products follows along similar lines. Even if the present rate of human reproduction can be reduced to a replacement value of 2.2 (so that real population growth is limited to only 0.1 percent), "the human biomass would eventually equal the weight of the world." (Wilson 1998:281) Human sewage, a topic as unpleasant as it is often neglected, would, however, long since have made man's habitat uninhabitable, and unlivable as well for a multitude of other species.

The oceans of the world, which make up most of the habitat volume within which the earth's organisms live, are rapidly being polluted, not only by human sewage and other human waste and run-off, but by the combined effects of oil spills, thermal pollution from the cooling systems of coastal power plants, and by heavy metal poisoning (e.g., lead, mercury, and arsenic). When these are added to the effects we have already mentioned due to the dumping of sewage, garbage, industrial waste, fertilizer, pesticides, and herbicides, the oceans, long thought to be impervious to human waste disposal, will reach a threshold beyond which it will be difficult—and, for innumerable forms of life, impossible—to return.

As the population growth of the human species persists, lethal levels for other species are reached. It is here that parasitologist H. D. Crofton's lethal level concept acquires its human application. The global population of *Homo parasiticus* has increased in density and distribution on a scale which, were we speaking of a non-human pathogen, we should unflinchingly call an infestation.[9] An ecological saturation point is reached at which the human species, in a monopoly of its own devising, engulfs many of the resources required to sustain life—displacing, poisoning, and actively killing other species in the process. It should be clear that the species, as a result, has become highly *infective* and *pathogenic* in the strict senses of these terms defined earlier in this chapter: For, as we have seen, the human species has developed the ability to spread into and dominate diverse ecosystems with relative ease, causing severe environmental harm and species destruction. This is *infectivity, on a global scale.* The already immense and yet still exponentially growing human population is directly related to the amount of damage for which the human species is responsible. Together, these factors determine the *pathogenicity* of the human species, which is also now global in scale.

In biology, the "niche exclusion principle" refers to the fact that, in relation to a given niche of resources, there is often one species that survives at the expense of others that depend on the same resources. The niche exclusion principle is the ecological equivalent of the principle of economic scarcity, which states that commitment to one alternative path of action rules out others that would have been possible. Ecology is the economic theory of life.[10] Biological resources are always finite, so that when an organism's population grows to

---

[8] Based on calculations by marine biologist Robert Diaz of the Virginia Institute of Marine Science.

[9] We recall that Frederick L. Schuman expressed a view similar to this more than seventy years ago (Schuman 1933). His view was described earlier in Chapter 4.

[10] One of the few ecologists to draw attention to some of the potential connections between economic

be sufficiently large, competing forms of life are excluded.

Earlier, I referred in passing to the research of G. F. Gause, who studied the phenomenon in which a parasitic or predatory species over-indulges itself to the point that both it and its prey die out. More than half a century later, University of Arizona biologist Paul Martin (1984) proposed what he called the "Blitzkrieg hypothesis." Both Gause and Martin have offered what are in essence specialized formulations of the niche exclusion principle, describing the destructive displacement of one species by another. Martin has argued that man exterminates other species wherever he goes in a veritable "Blitzkrieg." Martin found that significant numbers of species extinctions have occurred following soon after man's first arrival at any given location, that is, within a period of a few hundred years.

A similar result has been reached more recently by Ross MacPhee, curator of mammals at the American Museum of Natural History in New York City. MacPhee (1997) has studied species extinctions that occurred on the islands of the Caribbean since the arrival of Europeans 500 years ago. He noticed the same pattern: whenever human beings came on the scene, the extinction rate soared. He found that this "dreadful syncopation"—the arrival of human beings followed by numerous extinctions—has occurred not only during the past five centuries, but appears also to have taken place 11,000 years ago at the time of the extinction of the Siberian mammoths. And the same pattern of extinctions has followed in the wake of prehistoric man in many areas of the world, with the possible exception of Eurasia and Africa, where the human species evolved in parallel with other species.

When the Blitzkrieg hypothesis is applied to the worldwide human presence today, the extinction of huge numbers of non-human species is to be expected. In areas once rich in natural resources, the life cycle and activities of the human species reduce a world of biodiversity to a human *monoculture*—to an environment, that is, primarily fit only for man. (See Tilman 1982.) Once such a monoculture is reached, as it has been for increasingly large numbers of species in human cities, densely populated regions, and industrialized areas, general niche exclusion follows in the swath of Blitzkrieg devastation, and lethal levels for a great many organisms are reached. Then Gause's warnings to an over-eating, predatory-parasitic population remind us that our extensive biological and physical destruction can come to encompass ourselves.

✧

Humanity's host, as we have seen, is multiple. Our species has become dependent upon numerous plant and animal species and a wide range of environmental resources. I have argued that in an extended but non-metaphorical sense, the world itself—the physical environment, its natural resources, and the diversity of life they support—has become the host of *Homo parasiticus*. At the same time, our species causes organic and environmental harm of a magnitude that is believed to be on a par with the most devastating massive destruction to life this planet has ever witnessed.

We are adaptable, resilient, and innovative—characteristics of successful parasite opportunism—which means that our anthropogenic impact is spread across a wide variety of biological niches. Viewed in terms of the Blitzkrieg hypothesis and the niche exclusion principle, our species' parasitism makes clear that, as long as the exploding human parasite population continues to kill other organisms and to evict those that survive from the habitats

---

theory and ecology has been Paul Ehrlich. He devotes a chapter to this topic, "Ecology, Economics, and Equity," in Ehrlich (1997: 113-51). Another ecologist urging the establishment of bridges between the two disciplines has been R. V. O'Neill (1996).

they require in order to live, our exterminator species will continue to set—and to *be*—the lethal levels for those species.

## MAN, THE GLOBAL PATHOGEN

The reality is as simple as it is dramatic: modern societies are preparing for a scene for suicide. With increasing speed and determination they are destroying the basis of life on earth:
our own and that of many other species. – Otto Kinne in Ehrlich (1997:xiii)

In recent years, as we have seen, parasitology has awakened to ecology. Its enlarged focus is promising since it encourages a more inclusive comprehension of the destructive dynamic in which human beings are engaged. The ways in which our species interacts with the rest of the world involve human life on most levels: from the behavior of individuals in the privacy of their own bedrooms, to the behavior of businesses and nations seeking monetary profit and power. Homocentric values are the species' self-justification. Human parasitism is an individual and group psychological, social, political, and religious phenome-non. It finds its expression in the cult of motherhood, in the species' uncritical appetite for and infatuation with children, in beliefs that the earth and all other species exist for the pleasure and use of the human species. This last trait has been nurtured by species pride and its expression in religious dogma. Ecologist Paul Ehrlich (1997:37) has referred to it as "human exceptionalism," while biologist E. O. Wilson (1998) has similarly called man the "exemptionalist species": "In this conception, our species exists apart from the natural world and holds dominion over it. We are exempt from the iron laws of ecology that bind other species. Few limits on human expansion exist that our special status and ingenuity cannot overcome. We have been set free to modify Earth's surface...." (278)

Can mankind's parasitic relationship toward the world be changed? When by the end of this study we arrive at a more inclusive comprehension of the multiple forces that sustain the phenomenon of human parasitism, this question becomes harder, not easier, to answer. The changes that would be required are of such a magnitude, and penetrate to roots that run so deeply, as to make any kind of optimism unrealistic.

A difficult problem cannot be solved as long as the existence of the problem cannot be recognized. Naive hopefulness, rhetoric, sham, and species-induced denial block a clear perception of the ecological problem posed by the human species. We shall probably have to wait for the pressure of human overcrowding to build to a point that will force the issue upon human attention. But even then recognition is likely to dawn only gradually. For a time, the signs of overcrowding will not be recognized for what they are. In one imagined but realistic picture: "For a while the media will continue to ascribe riots and other violent upheavals abroad mainly to ethnic and religious conflicts. But as these conflicts multiply, it will become apparent that something else is afoot, making more and more places ungovern-able." (Kaplan 1994:54) The perspective expressed in Meadows *et al.* (1992:66) is more moderate in tone, but similar: "Long before the ultimate limits are reached, the human race becomes economically, scientifically, aesthetically, and morally impoverished."

There are a number of possible futures for the accelerating proliferation of a parasite species. (See, e.g., Leslie 1996) One mechanism that it is important to recall is environmental resistance. Earlier in this chapter, I referred to this concept, which identifies ways in which a natural ecosystem may come to resist the pathological reproduction of a parasite. In the case of the human species, many of our activities are obviously coming full circle to harm us, in the form of conditions of environmental resistance that have an increasing potential to suppress the human population. Among possible examples, one can cite global warming, ozone layer depletion, the spreading effects of human toxic waste, and the evolution of increasingly virulent micro-pathogens, many of which are developing antibiotic resistance as a result of man's injudicious overuse of antibiotics. Each of these represents a way in which environmental resistance is developing to block the proliferation of the human species.

It is useful to mention another parallel between ecology and economics, as disciplines often evolve in tandem without the knowledge of their practitioners. The concept of environmental resistance has its counterpart within economics:

> An exponentially growing economy taking resources from and emitting wastes into a finite environment begins to stress that environment long before reaching ultimate limits. The environment then begins to send signals and pressures to the growing economy—signals of resource scarcity, pressures from accumulating wastes. Those signals and pressures are negative feedback loops. They seek to bring the economy into alignment with constraints of the surrounding system. That is, they seek to stop its growth. (Meadows *et al.* 1992:115-6)

The corresponding environmental pressures will, over time, inevitably restrain human population growth.

If we were capable of seeing the planet from a distance, we should see that *Homo parasiticus* possesses all of the defining attributes of a global pathogen, one which is in a very short span of time undermining the health of the world as a livable ecosystem. To call the species a global pathogen is to judge it to be an *ecological malignancy*.[11] It is to regard many of the effects of the species as signs of disease. This is not to engage in name-calling. The concepts of disease, pathology, and parasitism are themselves applicable when the conditions of their applicability are satisfied. This is a benign tautology, for diagnosis is precisely a procedure of applying a set of criteria to an observed state with an intent to recognize a harmful process. *Homo parasiticus* satisfies the criteria of a disease-producing species, a species that has come to act as a global ecological pathogen.

Toward the beginning of this chapter, I briefly described the concepts of parasitoidism and amensalism. We noted that, in parasitoidism, a parasite kills its host, while in a relationship of amensalism, one organism remains comparatively unaffected at the same time that the other is noticeably harmed. Competition and antibiosis, we recall, are two forms of amensalism. Competition deprives an organism of its conditions of life. Antibiosis inhibits another organism's growth, and may bring about its death.

We are now in a position to recognize that the human species is pathogenic in certain specific ways: For the enormous number of species that mankind pushes into extinction, and the countless individual organisms we daily harvest, slaughter, and butcher for food, hunt as a sport, crush beneath the wheels of our vehicles, and kill in a multitude of ways and for other reasons, the human species is parasitoidal. For numerous species, man is amensal, either because our species directly competes for land or the conditions of life, or because human activities are themselves antibiotic for surrounding forms of life, as human waste and toxins are released into the environment, natural land is paved over, etc.

To say that mankind is a pathogenic species in these ways is not to engage in the use of metaphor. There is no more rampant and concrete expression of parasitoidism and amensalism on earth than man's—and, as we have noted, there never has been, for no other species has ever wrought the amount and degree of destruction to other species and to the general conditions of life as has the human species. The reader will recall behavioral parasitism in which exploitative organisms appropriate from members of another species their

---

[11] One is reminded of a similar claim advanced almost half a century ago: "The world has cancer and the cancer is man." (Gregg 1955:681)

requirements of life. This form of parasitism also characterizes the human species. The species is engaged in worldwide environmental exploitation in its own self-interest, exhibiting a degree and scope of behavioral parasitism unique among parasite species.

## IN SUMMARY

The viewpoint we have taken in this chapter toward the human species involves three attitudes not routinely accepted by the lay public, but which are increasingly endorsed by the scientific community: (1) We have refused to acquiesce in our species' unquestioned and self-proclaimed centrism. (2) We have approached the phenomenon of parasitism from an ecological perspective in which, (3) the concept of a parasite's host is understood in general systems terms, that is, as the interwoven network of interdependent associations the parasite species has with other species and with environmental conditions that sustain life.

Once these attitudes become part of our thinking about the natural world, it is not difficult to recognize that any ecosystem, even the encompassing ecosystem provided by the planet as a whole, can become diseased. In Part I of this book, we reached an understanding of disease in the specific sense of conditions and processes identified as harmful. Varieties of pathological harm were discussed, which result from individual or group organic, mental, social, or conceptual pathology. In the present chapter, my intention has been to identify and, in the space permitted, to some extent to clarify the nature of a widespread ecological pathology. It has resulted from a human psychology committed to the same goals shared by all parasite species: selfish, self-serving preservation, environmental exploitation, and reproduction at the expense of their respective hosts. The psychology of parasitism shares much with the psychology of narcissism, which previous chapters have discussed in a range of contexts, for in both parasitism and narcissism attention is confined to the immediacy of self-interest.

To see the human species in this way is to see mankind in a new light. We see the human species as one parasite species among many, recognizing that parasitism is the most pervasive way in which forms of life—from viruses to bacteria to protozoa to plants and animals—meet the exigencies of living. Among the defining characteristics of parasitism that apply to the human species, one in particular stands out as we consider the massive extinction of species for which mankind is currently responsible. It is genetic selfishness. In the human species, the genetic selfishness of the parasite has taken the form of our species' self-centeredness, our opportunistic exploitation of environmental resources, and our species' disregard of the degree to which human activity and reproduction displace and exterminate other forms of life.

The human species could, in a test of the imagination, approach the natural world differently. The opposite of parasitism is an approach to the world resembling altruism. If a species were altruistic in this sense, its behavior would involve acting in the interest of other species, even though doing so entails real cost to the altruist species. The cost that I am talking about would include self-restraint of our species' reproductive urges, a willingness to compromise its quality of living, etc.—all on behalf of species not its own.[12]

---

[12] On the human psychological and conceptual resistance to altruism toward other species, see Bartlett (2002). One of the few ecologists courageous or idealistic enough to espouse this degree of species unselfishness has been biologist Dan Janzen, who has worked to conserve the diversity of species in Costa Rica's Guanacaste Conservation Area. Janzen has been one of the few to resist linking the desirability of survival of a species with its benefits to man, in a way that is reminiscent of Christopher D. Stone's respect for the legal rights of natural objects in the environment, independent of human

Such an unselfish species, as far as we know, does not exist in the world. If one ever has, its self-sacrificing nature would not lend itself to competition and natural selection, and as a result it is plausible to believe that it would soon die out in the evolutionary process. It falls to individuals and occasionally to social groups to express altruism, usually toward members of their own species, at times toward members of other species. Ironically, human individuals who are altruistic toward their fellow man often are not toward other species. For human intraspecific altruism often rests on religious grounds that ennoble man while construing all other species as his chattel. Though altruism evidently exists among some individuals and groups, on the species level per se, altruism appears not to exist or to have evolutionary promise.

Perhaps someday it will, but if and when it does, the existence of species altruism will be a radical departure from the powerful self-centered and self-serving interests that have been vested with such intensity in parasite species, and which have acted as the motive force behind many millions of years of organic evolution.

---

interests, benefits, and profit. (Stone 1988/1972) Janzen has maintained: "Yes, you want to save this forest because you might find a new drug or new pest control or attract tourists, but none of these are [sic] the reason for wanting to keep this a wildland. For me, there's only one objective: that this biodiversity survive." (Morell 1999:83)

# CHAPTER 18

# MORAL INTELLIGENCE AND
# THE PATHOLOGY OF HUMAN STUPIDITY

At the end of this long middle part of a study which has focused on psychological dimensions of human evil, we need to pause and ask why it is that human beings have not learned, after some hundreds of centuries en route to a more civilized existence, to curtail their pathologies and to learn kindness and compassion toward one another and toward other forms of life. The lessons of human history are not difficult. But, for the great majority of people, there is a deeply seated recalcitrance to learn, to change, and to end the human-caused suffering and horrors. Here, in this very recalcitrance, we find one of the topics of this chapter, the pathology of *human stupidity*, which, as we shall see, is a main source and reason for our species' obstinate pursuit of continued aggressiveness and destructiveness. In this chapter, I will consider this nearly universal resistance to self-knowledge as belonging to the category of human stupidity, which comprises a specific although complex pathology of man. Stupidity of this kind makes it possible for people to continue to think and to behave aggressively, destructively, and often with great cruelty—without questioning, without misgivings, without remorse, but with pride and certainty that, by so doing, they do the best thing.

At the same time, we recognize that man's persistent commitment to aggression and destruction cannot entirely be attributed to human stupidity alone. In previous chapters, we have seen again and again in different contexts how men and women and even children can be morally deficient: insensitive to the consequences of their often self-serving and self-centered existences. In this chapter, I introduce the concept of *moral intelligence*, which when conjoined with a broad understanding of human stupidity, further answers the larger question, What is wrong with man? We shall see that deficits in general as well as in moral intelligence, along with dysfunctional conceptual functioning, with which we shall deal in Part III, are responsible for the widespread pathology of human stupidity.

## THE INCIDENCE OF HIGH MORAL DEVELOPMENT

One might suppose that research on the psychology of human moral development would throw light on the issues with which this book has dealt. But moral development research has been disappointing and frustratingly naïve. Psychological studies of moral development have generally avoided the crucial topic of human moral *behavior*. Specifically, there has been a lack of psychological research that would determine the moral levels of individuals by analyzing their actual behavior. Psychologists interested in moral development have instead focused on moral *reasoning* and *judgment* as these are expressed by subjects in artificial settings such as clinical interviews, tests or questionnaires, or in the classroom. For a realistic understanding of human moral action, there is an evident need to shift attention from these contrived settings to actual behavior. At present, what the psychology of human moral development offers are theories that identify *stages of moral reasoning* through which people progress, giving little attention to ways in which they actually behave when confronted by real moral choices. In the twentieth century, this emphasis on moral stages extends as far back as McDougall's 1908 study, which initiated a direction of research in psychology that has come to define the study of moral development. McDougall wrote:

> The fundamental problem of social psychology is the moralization of the individual into the society into which he is born as an amoral and egoistic infant. There are successive stages, each of which must be traversed by every individual before he can attain the next higher: (1) the stage in which the operation of the instinctive impulses is modified by the influence of rewards and punishments, (2) the stage in which conduct is controlled in the main by anticipation of social praise and blame, (3) the highest stage in which conduct is regulated by an ideal that enables a man to act in the way that seems to him right regardless of the praise or blame of his immediate social environment. (McDougall 1908:97)

A few decades later, Jean Piaget (1932) began efforts to identify discernible stages in the moral development of children. But where McDougall's theory referred to actual moral *conduct*, Piaget chose to study moral *reasoning*, a decision that was to place later psychological research on a footing that is one very large step removed from reality. Piaget observed that children develop a consciousness of moral rules in three stages, progressing from a habitual stage of automatic obedience, to a second stage at about the age of six when they accept as sacred and permanent moral rules that are stipulated by adults, and culminating in a final stage, beginning at about the age of 10, when children recognize that moral rules are laws based on mutual consent. As children develop morally, according to Piaget, they progress from *heteronomous* moral reasoning according to rules formulated and enforced by adults, to *autonomous* reasoning as they come to accept that justice is equalitarian and requires a person to make moral evaluations that are situationally specific. (Piaget 1932:57) We note that Piaget's theory of moral development claims that *every* child, unless handicapped or environmentally deprived, generally will advance to the highest stage.

Beginning in the late 1950s, Lawrence Kohlberg proposed a more elaborate structural theory of moral development with more finely distinguished stages. But unlike Piaget's theory, in Kohlberg's the majority of people do not reach the highest level of moral development. Like Piaget, Kohlberg focused on the *reasoning* and *judgment* expressed by his subjects, not their actual moral behavior in real life. Kohlberg's theory distinguishes six main stages in the development of moral reasoning or judgment: Stage 1 is characterized by obedience enforced by punishment; Stage 2 by conventional, instrumental hedonism; Stage 3 by conformity and approval-seeking from others; Stage 4 by dutiful obedience to authority in the interests of the social order; Stage 5 by legalistic adherence to the principles of a just social contract; and Stage 6 by justification of social values through reference to universal principles of conscience. (See, e.g., Kohlberg 1969:376; 1981:334.) Kohlberg sometimes added a seventh stage, characterized by adherence to principles of justice understood to reflect the larger cosmic order. (Kohlberg 1981:347, 401; 1984:213) He later dropped Stage 6 (as well as Stage 7) because of the difficulty in finding highly developed moral subjects.— "As far as we can ascertain all our Stage 6 persons must have been killed in the 1960s like

Martin Luther King. Stage 6 remains as a theoretical postulate but not an operational empirical entity." (Kohlberg 1984:425; see also 215, 271, 274.)

In the tradition established by McDougall, Piaget, and Kohlberg, the psychology of moral development has attempted to answer a group of questions, chief among them: Does moral development generally occur in human beings with their increasing age, experience, and education? Are there invariant natural stages through which they pass? Is such a progression from stage to stage universal across cultures? Can education contribute significantly to moral development? What is the relationship between *cognitive* moral development, as expressed in moral reasoning and judgments, and moral *action*? And, finally, what does moral development research tell us about the distribution of levels of actual moral behavior among people? The most intensive study has been made of issues raised by the earlier questions, while comparatively little has been devoted to the last two. Here, I want to consider the pair of neglected issues: the tenuous relationship that we find in most people between their degree of moral reasoning and their conviction that translates reasoning and judgment into action, and the disappointingly low incidence of people who show signs of high moral development. As I shall argue, human history provides more than adequate empirical evidence to reach reliable conclusions about both.

Although it was not Kohlberg's main purpose, research by him and his colleagues has thrown some light on the incidence of moral development stages in the general population. Here are some of the conclusions reached:

- There is a partial correlation between level of intellectual maturity and moral maturity. Children who have IQs that are below average tend also to be below average morally, but children with higher IQs are equally likely to be low or high in moral maturity. (Kohlberg 1984:64-5)

- Stage 5 moral reasoning tends not to occur until a person is 24 or older. Essentially no one reaches Stage 5 reasoning before the end of high school. (Kohlberg 1984:458) By the age of 35, there is still no sign of Stage 6 thinking. (Kohlberg 1984:1)

- Very few 30-year-olds show signs of Stage 5 moral thinking. Only ten percent of 40-year-olds in one study (Bakken 1983) showed moral reasoning between Stages 4 and 5, while the highest level attained among 50-year-olds (half of them) remained between those two stages. (Kohlberg 1984:459)

- The majority of American adults reason at Stages 3 and 4. Philosophers of law and Supreme Court Justice appear to reason at the higher Stages 5 or perhaps 6. (Kohlberg 1981:xxxiii) In connection with the morally important issue of the death penalty, for example, "only a minority of Americans have as yet attained a high enough developmental stage" to oppose capital punishment. (254)

- In a study of moral development by countries (Israel, Turkey, and the U. S.), the highest moral stage (intermediate between 4 and 5) was found among Israelis (20 percent of people ages 24-26, compared with 13 percent in the U. S.). In America, the age group having the largest percentage of Stage 4/5 individuals was found among 28-30 year-olds (13.5 percent). (Kohlberg 1984:612)

- The comparatively small number of people who reach Stage 5 in their moral thinking tend to have earned a graduate degree. (Kohlberg 1984:458) By profession, those in the humanities (e.g., German studies, political and social scientists) tend to have higher levels of moral reasoning than those in more quantitative disciplines (chemists or electrical engineers). (Portele 1985:201)

- Evidence of individuals who have reached Stage 6 of moral development appears to be limited to "a small elite sample, elite in the sense of its formal philosophical training and in the sense of its ability for and commitment to moral leadership." (Kohlberg 1984:270)

One researcher has characterized this tiny minority in the following terms:

> The people who develop in moral judgment are those who love to learn, who seek new challenges, who enjoy intellectually stimulating environments, who are reflective, who make plans and set goals, who take risks, who see themselves in the larger social contexts of history and institutions and broad cultural trends, who take responsibility for themselves and their environs. (Rest 1986:177)

These results, most of which are regarded as well-confirmed but still provisional, bear out that age, experience, and education are related to the level of moral reasoning reached by an individual. We see, for example, that younger people, under the age of about 24, are not inclined to reason about moral issues beyond the level of conventional, conformist obedience to authority. When they are recruited into military service, their level of moral thinking therefore makes them ready and easy subjects for indoctrination. We also see that high cognitive intelligence does not automatically insure high moral development, something we found in connection with the psychology of Nazi leaders. (See Chapter 12.) And we see that high moral development is confined to a very small minority.

Although the incidence of high moral development has not been a central issue in psychological research, in the commonsense spirit advocated by Romanes one cannot but resist the belief that more experimental results are needed to confirm what human history already shows us plainly: that the human majority has not reached a high level of moral development, and that those human beings who have constitute a small and elite minority. As moral development psychologist Thomas Lickona commented in another context, "...the reader may feel that—contrary to the honored axiom of scholarship—more research is not needed. His intuition is probably sound." (Lickona 1976:239) In earlier chapters, we have repeatedly observed, whether in connection with the psychology of war, genocide, or ecological destruction, that human beings for the most part are willing participants and perpetrators: Their level of moral development, as judged not by their expressed reasoning in an artificial laboratory situation *but by their actions in the real world*, is quite low. Furthermore, to the extent that moral development can be changed within the span of a person's lifetime, this can happen only to a limited degree (Kohlberg's efforts in moral education, when most effective, advanced a person only one stage). Morally directive schooling is offered only to the few, and its successful large-scale, international implementation remains dubiously utopian. Psychological research on human moral development has, from this wider point of view, been characterized by academic naïveté—an almost intentional disregard for historical evidence of the human *lack* of moral development. We recall, as Kohlberg himself acknowledged, that "[a]ll but one of the soldiers present at My Lai participated in the mass murders." (Kohlberg

1984:565) True moral development is unfortunately limited to the very few. The following section bears this out more fully.

## THE MORAL BRIDGE PROBLEM:
## THE GAP BETWEEN MORAL REASONING AND MORAL BEHAVIOR

[M]oral judgment alone does not produce moral action.... – Lapsley (1996:105)

Psychologists since Kohlberg have continued to find that only a minority reaches an advanced level of moral reasoning. Note again that reasoning, not behavior, has been the predominant focus. Kohlberg admitted that just because an individual reaches a high moral level of reasoning does not entail that he or she will act morally. Kristiansen and Hotte (1996:77) acknowledged this gap between moral reasoning and action: "Although intuitively it makes sense to assume that people use their general values in life to guide their more specific attitudes and behavior, ...this might not be as true as one might think." They refer to a study (Kristiansen & Zanna 1992) of some 300 students, which showed that exposure to a moral "self-confrontation procedure" "had absolutely no impact on participants' intentions or their actual behavior." (Kristiansen & Hotte 1996:78) Kohlberg candidly admitted that there was an evident gap between how people reason about moral issues and how they behave. "To act in a morally high way requires a high stage of moral reasoning. One cannot follow moral principles (Stages 5 and 6) if one does not understand or believe in them. One can, however, reason in terms of such principles and not live up to them...." (Kohlberg 1984:172) At one point, he commented on the lack of evidence showing that moral behavior is the result of holding high moral attitudes: "...the reason for this failure, we believe, lies in the fact that when confronted with a real moral situation individuals do not reason in terms of abstract moral values but rather define the situation in terms of concrete rights and duties." (575) Perhaps to say this actually goes too far, since it is plausible to believe that very little actual thinking goes on when many people act in ways that are morally decisive and irrevocable. Since few people reach Kohlberg's highest levels of moral reasoning, even fewer can be expected to translate their intentions into action.

Here we confront what I shall call *the moral bridge problem*, which refers to the gap between what may take place affectively and cognitively within a person who is confronted by a morally challenging situation, and how that person will behave. The moral bridge is quite rickety and offers slippery and unreliable footing for researchers who wish to cross it. Moral reasoning and moral judgment may seldom be related to deeds, and then only for a moral elite, or they may, paradoxically, be the basis for widespread behavior that is morally repugnant.

> History is replete with atrocities that were justified by involving the highest principles and that were perpetrated upon victims who were equally convinced of their own moral principles. In the name of justice, of the common welfare, of universal ethics, and of a God, millions of people have been killed and whole cultures destroyed. In recent history, concepts of universal right, equality, freedom, and social equity have been used to justify every variety of murder including genocide. (W. Mischel & H. Mischel in Lickona 1976:107)

The image of a moral bridge that might link moral judgment with moral behavior disappears in a fog that reminds us that reasons, judgments, and words can motivate atrocities, or they may have little or nothing to do with genuine moral deeds. There is often an emotionally compelling relation between dogmatist judgment and horrifying behavior, and often there may be no relation between sheer reasoning and compassionate behavior.

As one breathes in this misty atmosphere, we need to recognize that the psychological study of what has been called "moral judgment competence" resembles the drunk who searches for his lost keys beneath the lamp post because there is more light there. When people are called upon to describe their moral reasoning, what they express may have little if any bearing on how they will behave in extreme situations that exhibit human evil. In other words, it makes little sense to concentrate on moral reasoning if the majority of people do not engage in it, or will ignore it in morally challenging situations.

Until we are shown otherwise, it is reasonable to surmise that little, materially relevant, moral, reflective reasoning occurs before many people act. For half a century, psychology has been dominated by a naïve focus on moral reasoning and judgment. There is a clear need to shift attention back to McDougall's emphasis upon real conduct. When we return to reality we shall recognize that human history provides a more than adequate empirical basis to evaluate man's actual moral level of functioning. Elsewhere (Bartlett 1969), I have discussed the tenuous relationship between conviction and rationality, and have found in conviction that which welds reasoning to action, but only in individuals who have what in the present context I will call *moral intelligence*, to which I now turn.

## MORAL INTELLIGENCE

I think that one has to distinguish between two forms of intelligence, that of the brain, and that of the heart, and I have come to regard the second as by far the more important.... Experience offers proof on every hand that vigorous mental life may be but one side of personality, of which the other is moral barbarism. – Gissing (1918:41, 59)

[M]orality, by the very fact that we are intelligent, has its roots in intelligence. – Durkheim (1961:249)

As the reader will recall from Chapter 5, in his 1818 work Johann Christian Heinroth described what he called "moral disease" and identified this pathology with "evil in general." (§251) Heinroth's perspective became part of an intellectual current in psychiatry and psychology that has paid special attention to the moral dimension of human existence. In 1840, early psychiatrist Thomas C. Upham (1973/1840) discussed "moral sensibilities" and disorders of the "moral sentiments": He referred to "idiocy of conscience" and to "moral derangement," when the "moral sense" becomes "paralyzed, or, perhaps, extinct." (269, 357, 360, 362) In 1869, Francis Galton noted the extensiveness of individual human differences, and sought, as had Alexander Bain before him, for a connection between the intellectual and moral characteristics of individuals and their physical features. The inclusion of moral considerations within the scope of psychology was similarly reflected in a paper by Alfred Binet and Victor Henri (1895), in which they criticized existing intelligence tests for their over-simplification and urged the use of a variety of tests for distinct human mental capacities, including tests of memory, mental imagery, imagination, attentiveness, mechanical and verbal comprehension, suggestibility, aesthetic appreciation, the capacity to sustain muscular effort, visual judgment of distance, and moral sensibility. They suggested various ways of testing each of these ten functions, which they regarded as categories of human traits. A few years later, in an posthumous English translation of his work, Johann Christian Heinroth (1898) urged that efforts be made to study how adults and children could be educated "for moral and intellectual maturity."

Overlapping with some of these proposals, John Charles Bucknill and Daniel Hack Tuke (1879/1858) gave special attention to "moral sentiments," defining insanity as "a condition in which the intellectual faculties, or the moral sentiments, or the animal propensities—any one or all of them—have their free action destroyed by disease, whether congenital or acquired." (21) The nature of the mental disease which they had in view was, as the reader will recall from Chapter 5, organic brain disease, which is "marked by intellectual or emotional disorder." (21) They went on to describe specifically "moral or emotional insanity" (Section VI): "A class of cases...mainly of a destructive character." They identified a form of moral deficiency, which is expressed in the various degrees of "moral insensitivity," "moral idiocy," or "moral insanity." (Again, see Chapter 5 in the present study.) They recognized a fact now familiar to the reader, that a given person may possess excellent intellectual abilities and yet be deficient in moral sensitivity. They agreed with the observation that "there are certain beings who are truly moral imbeciles.... It is remarkable, indeed, what an acute intellect may sometimes coexist with an entire absence of the moral sense." (246)

With the passage of time it was only natural for psychologists to turn to the study of social intelligence, emotional intelligence, and moral intelligence. There is not space here to recount the evolution of these ideas in detail. Suffice it to mention that following Heinroth's emphasis on moral maturity, E. L. Thorndike (1920) proposed that there is a special kind of "social intelligence," distinct from traditional intellectual intelligence, which he understood as "the ability to understand and manage people." (275) Soon after, Charles E. Spearman (1927) observed that some people can generate for themselves the thoughts and feelings of others, by analogy with their own experience. He judged this ability to be an act that exhibits intelligence. A few decades later, social psychologists Bruner and Tagiuri (1954) recognized three abilities that are involved in the perception of others: the cognition of emotions based on observing the expressions of others; judgment of personality traits from their external behavior; and formation of impressions regarding others. Taft (1956) similarly sought to identify the abilities that are required to be a good judge of personalities.

In the following decade, J. P. Guilford (1967) offered a highly differentiated "multidimensional conception of intelligence" (467), in which he identified some 120 abilities that he believed to be distinguishable. He noted the existence of "social cognition," which "involves abilities quite differentiated from other intellectual factors of intelligence" (34), and described a factor of intelligence that he called "behavioral": "...to take care of the kind of information involved in cognition and in other operations pertaining to the behavior of other people. We know that we know to some extent what the other person is perceiving, attending to, feeling, thinking, and intending to do." (60) In this way, Thorndike's earlier recognition of social intelligence found its way into Guilford's theory.

Less exuberant intelligence researchers have since questioned the independence of Guilford's numerous intelligence factors, since many appear to be significantly correlated with one another. (See, e.g., Eysenck (1999:108, 110, and Figure 5.1, 62), who, though an outspoken critic of the multiplication of intelligence factors, even so sought to find a place for "social intelligence," and recognized a dozen factors that contribute to it.) Following in Guilford's footsteps, various psychologists have nonetheless sought to delimit specifically social and/or moral abilities, less strictly concerned with knowing whether the skills associated with intelligence are rigorously independent of one another. Salovey and Mayer (1990), Gardner (1993/1983; 1983), and Goleman (1995) have given special attention to "emotional intelligence," recognizing a set of distinct skills that are involved in discerning one's own emotions and those of others. Salovey and Mayer remarked on the existence of *deficits in emotional intelligence*, manifested when people are unable to regulate their emotions, becoming enslaved by them and unable to recognize emotions in others, often causing others to suffer. They proposed a conception of emotional intelligence that is essentially related to problem-solving skills. From this point of view, emotionally intelligent people will take emotional considerations into account when solving human problems, leading to behavior that is sensitive and respectful of their own feelings and the feelings of others. (Salovey & Mayer 1990:200-1)

> We have suggested that appraising and expressing emotions accurately is a part of emotional intelligence.... These skills are *emotionally* intelligent because they require the processing of emotional information from within the organism, and because it is clear that some level of minimal competence at these skills is necessary for adequate social functioning. (193)

Research relating to emotional intelligence has led other psychologists who have written primarily for a general audience to refer specifically to *moral intelligence*, but without throwing light on the nature of the skills involved. Gardner (1993:46) mentioned moral intelligence only in passing, deciding not to recognize it as a distinct form of intelligence in its own right due to his belief that moral reasoning and moral behavior are subordinate to the moral influences exerted by an individual's surrounding society. More recently, Coles (1997) used the phrase 'moral intelligence' in the title of a book on child-raising, crediting pediatrician Rustin McIntosh for the expression. Borba (2001) similarly used the phrase in the title of her book, also on raising children.

A review of the literature of the past century makes it clear that the psychology of human intelligence has included "moral skills" in our understanding of intelligence only by fits and starts. In the hundred years since Binet and Henri wrote, the vocabulary of traits and sensibilities fell into disuse for what were perceived as good theoretical and empirical reasons. The pendulum has now begun to swing the other way with the increasing recognition in moral psychology of the need once again to take into account both "markers of personality" such as self, identity, and character (Lapsley 1996:197, 198, 213), and sensibilities and sensitivities that are associated with an awareness of values (Rest 1986:24-5). Lapsley (1996:213) commented: "...there is now active speculation concerning just how the issues of character and virtue might be reintroduced into moral psychology in a more adequate way."

In the context of our study of human pathology, it will be of value if we formulate a working definition of human moral intelligence. In the light of earlier chapters, we see that moral intelligence has several interrelated components. An individual who is morally intelligent in the sense proposed here first and foremost *does not receive emotional gratification from the human evils described in this book*. Moral intelligence is thereby defined negatively, in terms of a psychological constitution from which has been subtracted those elements that make a negative contribution to human moral performance: In other words, the more an individual receives emotional and existential gratifications from such sources as narcissism, hatred, obedience, the excitement of violence, joy in witnessing the distress of others, ideological righteousness and empowerment, etc., the lower that individual's level of moral intelligence.

Second, a morally intelligent person must have a *fully functioning capacity for empathy*. Allport (1954:434) identified empathy as an "ability;" admitting that it "is an ability we know little about." Arendt (1969:64) went a step further, observing that the "inability to feel moved," to feel compassion toward others, is a "pathological phenomenon." Although she did not develop this notion, she made clear what she was pointing at when she commented on Eichmann's "inability to think from the standpoint of someone else":

> The longer one listed to him, the more obvious it became that his inability to speak was closely connected with an inability to *think*, namely, to think from the standpoint of somebody else. No communication was possible with him, not because he lied but because he was

surrounded by the most reliable of all safeguards against the words and the presence of others, and hence against reality as such. (Arendt 1964:49)

The ability to make another's existence and life-world real to oneself is the second component of moral intelligence. (For a detailed discussion of empathy, see, e.g., Hoffman 2000.)

Third is a matter of literal sensibility, which fundamentally involves *sensitivity* and also *taste*, in the meaning of that word which connotes discrimination, selectivity, discernment, and critical judgment. This component of human moral intelligence involves normative weighing tied to the sense of disgust that a morally intelligent person experiences when confronted by human evil.

Fourth is *moral conviction*. As we noted earlier in this chapter, there is a gap between moral reasoning and moral action which it has been difficult for moral psychologists to bridge. What is needed is an "affective cement" that welds moral perception and reasoning to behavior. Conviction, as commonly understood, serves this connective function; it acts as the bridge that unifies an individual's judgment, reasoning, and beliefs with behavior that conforms to them. Without conviction, reasoning falls on deaf ears; without conviction, there is no need for moral or reflective judgment to be expressed through behavior in real life. Seen in this way, conviction is a genuine ability, an ability to connect strongly felt emotions with behavior consonant with them. It is what enables someone who is persuaded by reflective thought or by moral principle to act consistently with that thought or principle. Unfortunately, conviction, without the other three components of moral intelligence, will by itself complete a circuit that leads to real behavior—which may or may not be moral. This is a phenomenon we see in the ideologically inspired fanatic and the gullible military recruit. Here, we recognize that conviction must take place in an affective and cognitive context that is essentially moral. The fact that moral intelligence has a complex, multiple-component structure like this is not so much an obstacle to its recognition by psychology, but rather an indication that we have not yet devised adequate measurement tests for all intelligent human abilities.

When a person possesses the group of abilities identified here he or she qualifies as a morally intelligent person, deeply averse to human evil; compassionate in understanding another's life, interests, and feelings; sensitive and critical in ways that lead the individual to feel disgust and contempt for cruelty, violence, and other forms of human evil; and convinced to a degree such that the individual's consciousness of moral principles is fused with a need to act consistently with those principles.

When a person lacks these abilities, he or she is morally *stupid*, and here I turn to examine a final topic in the psychology of human evil.

## THE PSYCHOLOGY OF HUMAN STUPIDITY

There is no escaping the impression of a factitious fatality that is pushing humanity in the direction of conflicts that can have no issue and no other possible results than the destructions of every kind that they guarantee. However cruel they may be, their cruelty will pale beside their stupidity, for the vanity of their effects, apart from the suffering they must entail, could have been foreseen.... – Paul Valéry (1933:127-8)

Why is it, I wonder, that people suffer, when there is so little need, when an effort of will and some hard work would bring them from their misery into peace and contentment.... Sheep, indeed. Man was made in the image of God. Is God a sheep? Because if He is, I understand why we are all so damned stupid.... The evil that is in Man comes of sluggish minds, ...for sluggards cannot think, and will not. – Richard Llewellyn (1940:101, 130, 232-3)

At what point in human history will members of the race stop their brutality, their destructiveness, and their many forms of behavior and thinking that at least sometimes they know perfectly well are harmful and wrong? Again and again people have had to experience war, genocide, prejudice and persecution, cruelty and violence in order to know that they bring great suffering, death, and destruction. The knowledge they gain each time is stored in the quickly fading memory of a society whose mentality resembles senility. Once the hostilities of the moment are over, forgetfulness promptly sets in. Soon we are again fully armed physically and mentally, and enthusiastic to begin the next fray.

It is not as though the psychological facts presented in this volume are new or difficult to comprehend. Most have been known to anyone with a willingness and an interest in understanding what motivates the ordinary person to look the other way or to perpetrate any of the many pathologies of man. In the remainder of this chapter, among the subjects we shall discuss is the phenomenon of our species' rejection of its awareness of its own pathology, a form of avoidance that we will understand in terms that define human stupidity, since it is stupidity, and stupidity alone, that most precisely applies to deliberate evasion of facts that, once recognized and acted upon, would spare man the seemingly endless grief and suffering that he causes himself.

Intelligence is a rating of a person's level of ability, and it therefore makes sense that intelligence is as varied as are distinguishable abilities. I have introduced the concept of moral intelligence as a way of rating a person's ability-level with respect to his relative immunity from human pathology, combined with his possession of empathy, sensitivity and taste, and moral conviction. Just as intelligence is a measurement and evaluation of an individual's abilities, so "stupidity" provides a vocabulary for referring to a person's deficiencies. Paralleling the concept of moral intelligence, then, is the related concept of *moral stupidity*, which we shall quickly see is basic to many of the phenomena of human evil we have so far studied. Anticipating later chapters, we shall discover a broad class of forms of conceptual or epistemological stupidity, and we shall find that the two human deficiencies of moral and conceptual stupidity explain much about the high incidence and persistence of human evil among psychologically ordinary men, women, and children.

## A Brief History of the Psychology of Human Stupidity

Nothing in the world is more dangerous than sincere ignorance and conscientious stupidity.
– Martin Luther King quoted in *Discover:* 9/2001:14

Despite an extensive literature devoted to the psychology of human intelligence, astonishingly little research has dealt with human stupidity. The few existing studies of human stupidity are furthermore generally unknown, and yet their contributions to our understanding of human pathology are of value and interest in their own right. Significantly, most were written by researchers in medicine, psychiatry, neurology, and physiology. There is not space here to offer more than a cursory review of the main works with this focus. Among the earliest is an impressive, scholarly study by English physician Sir Thomas Browne (1605-1682), which he called *Pseudodoxia Epidemica* [Epidemic False Beliefs], first published in 1646. Browne's interest was to provide a veritable encyclopedia of human "erroneous" thinking. He did not use the word 'stupidity', but it is clear that he had that phenomenon in view, for he observed of human beings:

Their understanding is so feeble in the discernement of falsities, and averting the errors of reason.... Thus the greater part of mankinde having but one eye of sence and reason..., therefore hopelessly continuing in mistakes, they live and dye in their absurdities; passing their dayes in perverted apprehensions, and conceptions of the world.... (Browne 1981/1646:15)

In the course of his book, Browne distinguished a number of causes of human error, among them general "human infirmity," credulity, laziness, misunderstanding, adherence to authority, and aversion to truths that are feared. All, we note, can be symptoms of human stupidity.

From Sir Thomas Browne we jump to the early twentieth century when German neurologist L. Loewenfeld published in 1909 what he believed was the first serious study of human stupidity, *Über die Dummheit: Eine Umschau im Gebiete menschlicher Unzulänglichkeit* [On Stupidity: A Survey in the Area of Human Inadequacy]. It has never been translated into English and deserves to be. Among the wide range of subjects he considered is the question of the normality of stupidity. Because such a large proportion of the general population is stupid [*beschränkt*], stupidity, he observed, is a normal condition [*innerhalb der Breite der Norm*]. (10) Characteristic of the reasoning of most disease theorists, Loewenfeld claimed that stupidity is not a pathological deviation [*krankhafte Abweichung*] precisely because it is a normal condition. He considered the relationship between stupidity and intense emotion, hatred, and fanaticism; mass stupidity; stupidity resulting from illness, brain injury, dementia, alcoholism, etc.; the organic basis of stupidity; stupidity and age, sex, race, social class, profession, environment, religion; stupidity as a factor in economic and social life; stupidity in art, science, politics; mass suggestibility; the epidemic spread of foolish ideas; stupidity and criminality; the diagnosis of stupidity; and other topics. Loewenfeld's outlook was generally optimistic; he made constructive suggestions for the ongoing "war against stupidity," relating, for example, to education, politics, and scientific progress.

In 1912, another German work was published, *Aus der Geschichte der menschlichen Dummheit* [The History of Human Stupidity], by Max Kemmerich. His book is a detailed inventory and critique of numerous human stupidities committed in the name of religion. Kemmerich considered religious stupidities to be one of the principal ways in which human masses are susceptible to the epidemic spread of stupefying ideas.

In 1919, French physiologist and Nobel Laureate Charles Richet published a study, *L'Homme Stupide*, apparently unaware of Loewenfeld's work. *L'Homme Stupide* is an early and important work in the history of the psychology of human stupidity. Richet offered this understanding of human stupidity:

Stupidity does not mean that we have not understood, but that we act as if we had not understood.

To know that which is good, and to do that which is bad; knowingly and deliberately to inflict pain upon ourselves; to recognise the cause of unhappiness and to fling ourselves upon that cause; that is stupidity....

It is not enough to create ingenious works. If they bring pain, illness, wounds and poverty, they show the stupidity of their creator. (Richet c. 1925/1919:17, 23)

Richet observed that people are uninterested in reducing their own stupidity, and have throughout history denied leadership to the highly intelligent—"The boundless stupidity of human communities has denied them any authority, while idolising the half witted." (42-3)—while they have persecuted its geniuses—"The more stupid and mediocre the masses, the more mercilessly do they persecute those who...strive to mitigate their mediocrity and their stupidity." (153) Richet remarked on "the incomparable stupidity of the human race" (53) in connection, for example, with its infatuation with war: "Their courage was magnificent but it was surpassed by their stupidity." (86) "It would be a thousand times easier to teach monkeys croquet than to convince men that peace is better than war." (85)

> That since the days of Homer, in spite of Plato, Aristotle, Cicero, Saint Augustine, St. Jerome, Leonardo da Vinci, in spite of Pascal, Voltaire, Montesquieu, Leibnitz and Kant, humanity should have found no better way of settling its quarrels than by the mutual slaughter of thirty millions [in WWI] of its best and bravest is the crushing, irrefutable demonstration of utter intellectual impotence. (83-4)

Richet also noted the ideological stupidity of the religions of the world in believing that each contains the whole and only Truth (106-7). He commented on the human predisposition to kill other species (138). He further observed how men are stupidly resistant to change for the better, and will voice all kinds of objections, which "can all be condensed into a single phrase, which sounds, like a funeral knell, at every step of progress: '*We are not interested.*'" (159) For physiologist Charles Richet, the only effective solution to stupidity of this magnitude and incidence is "a severe and lengthy process of selection" (162), and by this he meant eugenics, although he did not use this word.

In 1932, Columbia University Professor in psychology and philosophy Walter B. Pitkin, who had been tutored by Edmund Husserl and Georg Simmel at the University of Berlin, and who was influenced by William James, published a very lengthy work humorously called *A Short Introduction to the History of Human Stupidity*. Pitkin's study is abundantly illustrated with examples drawn from many facets of human life, and I can only mention here some of its main points. Pitkin commented on the lack of serious studies of human stupidity: "we must...come to understand the infinite variety of stupidities. Yet nobody has inquired into them." (8) Pitkin distinguished such general categories of stupidity as stupidities of action and of inaction, and discussed such forms of stupidity as obesity (the "stupidity of self-control" (76)), linguistic stupidity ("the common man thinks, reads, and talks in catch-phrases" (173), which help him to avoid thinking), socio-economic stupidity, political stupidity, the stupidity of war and its glorification, and, generally, "the stupidities of men which arise from attitudes toward and dealings with others of their species." (333) He distinguished several characteristics of stupidity, among them *lack of sensitivity* "which resembles death, sleep, blindness, deafness, and torpor"; *confusion* in situations that demand skills in observation and decision-making; *slowness* in "turning to account what one already possesses intellectually"; *inability to cut through to the heart of a situation or problem*; and "*the commonest and most disastrous of stupidities: ...those which result from the interplay of many functions.*" (26, 29, 37; original emphasis) Pitkin argued that evolution has selectively favored the stupid, who will work to suppress the more intelligent whenever possible. For Pitkin, human stupidity is best understood as a species-wide insensitivity: "stupidity is insensitivity, regardless of the psychic level on which it occurs." (49) From this point of view, he rejected human normality as a good: "To select as a standard the present normal member of a social group strikes me as itself evidence of imbecility. I should incline to reject normality in the social sense altogether; for the entire social life of our age seems to me...sickening in its innumerable deviations from good sense, the rules of health, and the broader principles of human happiness." (502-3) He concluded that stupidity is "the supreme Social Evil." (6)

In 1937, Austrian novelist Robert Musil published a short monograph, *Über die Dummheit* [On Stupidity]. It is not especially informative, but is worth noting in passing as an early work by an author with an academic background in psychology who recognized that to each form of human ability there corresponds a form of stupidity: "So hat jede Klugheit ihre Dummheit...." (26) [In this way, for each intelligence there is a corresponding stupidity.]

Moving on to 1947, Rupert Crawshay-Williams published a little-known work entitled

*The Comforts of Unreason: A Study of the Motives behind Irrational Thought.* As the title suggests, his principal interest was to identify the human psychological motivations for adhering to irrationality, that is, the "motivated distortions of reality" that tempt people to adopt irrational beliefs and theories about other people and about the world they live in. He did not connect his subject-matter explicitly with human stupidity, but stupidity is never far from the topics he analyzes. One of the principal values of his work is the emphasis he placed on the public's resistance to uncomfortable truths: the average person's opposition to clear thinking, his preference for irrationality (2), excitement (24), and his willful recourse to pleasant fictions. Together these processes allow the average person to "twist the evidence of unpleasant reality into a semblance of pleasant and satisfactory fantasy." (5-6)

In 1954, German physician Horst Geyer published a still untranslated work, *Über die Dummheit: Ursachen und Wirkungen der intellecktuellen Minderleistung des Menschen* [On Stupidity: Causes and Effects of Inferior Human Intellectual Performance]. Geyer divided his study into three sections, relating to stupid behavior that results from low, normal, and high intelligence. He considered human stupidity to be a type of error that is a general human phenomenon that needs to be understood as a function of normal psychology. Stupidity, he argued, leads to certain definite human advantages, while intelligence is often perceived as disadvantageous.

A last work on the psychology of human stupidity that I will mention here is a collection of papers edited by Robert J. Sternberg (2002). Some of the contributed papers imply that stupid behavior can be morally wrong and inexcusable because its perpetrators fail to utilize fully their existing knowledge and abilities. In particular, one of the contributors, Keith E. Stanovich (2002, 1993, 1994), drew attention to what he regards as a disability category, "dysrationalia," characterized by "the inability to think and behave rationally despite adequate intelligence." (2002:138)

From this short listing of the rare studies of human stupidity, three things stand out: First, their authors were uniformly aware of the remarkable lack of attention that has been given to this varied, dangerous, and destructive human deficiency. Second, the authors we have mentioned were unfortunately unaware of one another's publications. And, third, we should note that none of those who have studied human stupidity associated it with moral incapacities of the kind discussed in this chapter. As far as I can tell, *moral stupidity* has been entirely neglected. We shall return to this subject shortly.

Before proceeding, the reader may be reminded that many of the authors whose work we have discussed in previous chapters have shared a concern for the role of human stupidity in human pathology. Let us pick up a few of these threads:

- In Chapter 3, I argued in connection with lanthanic disease—pathology of which the diseased individual or group is ignorant—that "ignorance of the afflicting pathology may itself constitute one of the determinative characteristics of the disease." Human stupidity is of this kind, due to its reflexive inability to recognize itself. ("Are we perhaps so stupid that we cannot recognize stupidity when it thrusts its dull face against ours? Have we acquired a blindness toward our own blindness?" (Pitkin 1932:22))

- In Chapter 5, we noted that Heinroth appears to have been the first psychiatrist to suggest that *human stupidity* is a valid diagnostic category. Readers will recall that he considered stupidity to be a form and symptom of "disease" which involves "miseducation" and a "general lack of cultivation of the intellect or will." The only treatment that is available for stupidity, according to

Heinroth, is re-education and a rigorous psychological and physical discipline, about which he does not satisfy us with much detail. (Heinroth 1975/1818:373)

- Freud did not study the psychology of human stupidity explicitly, yet from Chapter 6 we recall his claims that people are incapable of independent thought, and that, if we seek to lessen our species' aggressive and destructive constitution, it is essential to realize that appeals to reason are irrelevant: "arguments are of no avail against their passions." (Freud 1961/1927:9)

- Jung was more explicit, mentioning both stupidity and morality in the same breath: In Chapter 7, we noted that the larger the human collective becomes, according to Jung, the lower its moral standards and the more "stupid" it becomes. As a result, "[t]he bigger the organization, the more unavoidable is its immorality and blind stupidity...." (Jung 1967-83/1916-17:153) We recall that Jung judged that most people are still psychologically primitive. Like Freud, Jung concluded that human stupidity and lack of self-awareness are responsible for much of human destructiveness and cruelty. "Much...that proves to be abysmally evil in its ultimate effects does not come from man's wickedness but from his stupidity and unconsciousness." (Jung 1967-83/1942:197)

- Similarly, Fromm judged that human stupidity comprises the greatest danger to man's future survival. We recall from Chapter 8 that he wrote: "If we should all perish in the nuclear holocaust, it will not be because man was not capable of becoming human, or that he was inherently evil; it would be because the consensus of stupidity has prevented him from seeing reality and acting upon the truth." (Fromm 1966/1962:198) Stupidity is at the root of "his inability to wake up to the realistic alternatives and their consequences." (Fromm 1964:138, 142)

- In the same chapter, we recall Peck's observation that the majority of people are incapable of outgrowing their juvenile narcissism. In terms of emotional maturity, most adults remain immature, and in the sense of moral intelligence developed here, they remain morally stupid.

- In Chapter 9, we noted the role played by human stupidity in Sorokin's analysis of the causation of war. He found that the majority of people and the majority of their leaders have consistently exhibited a pattern of stupidity and self-destructiveness.

- In Chapter 10, in connection with Lorenz's study of human aggression, we noted how human aggression subverts intelligence, closely connecting aggressiveness with human stupidity. Lorenz concluded: "I consider the collective stupidity of mankind—which is somehow incapable of learning from truly negative experiences and turning them into good—very great indeed." (Lorenz 1990:163, 131) We recall that, like Lorenz, ethologist Tinbergen believed that as a species we may ultimately succumb due "to our own stupidity." (Tinbergen 1968:1418)

- In Chapter 17, in connection with ecological awareness and responsibility, we noted man's constitutional inability to make the future real in his consciousness, and so he blithely destroys other species, the environment, and breeds irresponsibly. This imagination deficit is yet another form of human stupidity.

In summary, we have commented briefly in this section on the work of researchers who have undertaken book-length studies of human stupidity, as well as the authors who have touched upon the subject of human stupidity in the context of their studies of human aggression and destructiveness. As one reads their work, we may come to suspect that some of them may have flirted with the notion that human stupidity itself should establish a new diagnostic classification, in which human stupidity and man's associated lack of awareness of it make up twin forces that contribute in a central way to the phenomenon of human evil. But none of these authors, with the exception of Heinroth, has urged such a diagnostic standard. Before psychology can answer this question, we must have before us a clearer and more integrated understanding of human stupidity, to which I now turn.

## THE PATHOLOGY OF HUMAN STUPIDITY

If you really are stupid, I would call that a disease. – James Watson, interviewed in the documentary *DNA*, which aired in Britain in March, 2003

Although it is clear that human stupidity causes great harm, it has only occasionally been characterized as a pathology. We have noted Heinroth's suggestion that stupidity is a valid psychiatric diagnostic category, and we saw that Stanovich more recently proposed a diagnostic category related to stupidity, dysrationalia, characterized by an inability to think and act rationally despite sufficient intelligence. Among others who have linked stupidity to pathology, Kardiner and Ovesey (1969/1951:332), for example, mention "hysterical stupidity" as a "diminution of intellectual capacity by emotional preoccupation." Becker (1964) identified mental illness generally as "a form of cultural and individual stupidity...." The stupidity he had in view involves what he called "meaning poverty": In the schizophrenic, according to Becker, it takes the form of a "shallowness of meaning" that "reflects insufficient participation in interpersonal experience" (131); in the depressed person, meaning poverty involves an "overly narrow repertory" of interpersonal choice. (132) From Becker's point of view, such poverty of mind, which results from a narrowed, restricted experience of the world, is characteristic of mental illness and is a kind of stupidity. Becker considered such stupidity to be an abnormality, so that for him to be "normal" means "not stupid." (6, 209) In this, we will not follow him.

Here, I wish to propose a pluralistic understanding of human stupidity in which stupidity results from the interaction of numerous affective and cognitive functions. So understood, human stupidity is both a pathology and a characteristic of the psychologically normal population. *Human stupidity* can involve any of the following elements, whose correlations with one another and relative independence we can for present purposes ignore:

1. Stupidity may include forms of behavior and thinking that are often known perfectly well to be harmful and wrong.

2. This knowledge is usually unstable and is quickly forgotten.

3. Stupidity frequently involves a deliberate evasion of facts, which, if consciously accepted and confronted, cause anxiety or fear, but which if faced intelligently could prevent much human suffering.

4. Stupidity commonly involves gullibility, suggestibility, naïveté, intellectual laziness, and a marked deficiency that often accompanies these, an absence of critical thinking ability—that is, an incapacity to engage in independent thought and to have independent emotional responses to events.

5. Hence, stupidity typically involves conformity and imitation in both thought and feeling.

6. Stupidity is often associated with a striking disinterest and disinclination to engage in any efforts that would lessen it. ("No one is listening, or wants to.")

7. Stupidity is further characterized by an often willful opposition to clear thinking. There is often a related manifest preference for irrationality and reality-denying fantasy: The stupid *prefer* their stupidity.

8. Stupidity is characterized in ordinary people by a pronounced lack of sensitivity, a thick emotional skin, a tendency to respond to events only when they reach crisis proportions that have the perceived potential to affect the stupid directly.

9. Stupid people find it difficult to make the future or the past real in their consciousness; only events that are described in the present tense are regarded as truly relevant and important.

10. Such people are motivated to engage in the various forms of projection we have distinguished (see, e.g., Chapter 6), which offer them distortions of reality that satisfy their interests and needs.

11. The stupid are stirred from the emotional monotony and intellectual lassitude of their everyday lives by the excitement of brutality, cruelty, sexual stimulation, focused hatred and prejudice, or any of the other pathologies of emotion or thought this study has examined which are used by people to achieve an emotional high that absorbs their attention. In this particular sense stupidity is a psychologically primitive readiness and need for the distraction gained from the arousal which these human intoxicants provide.

12. Stupidity is frequently exhibited in a variety of forms of emotional and cognitive immaturity: Stupid people are often confined both to a low level of juvenile narcissism, which centers their attention on themselves and their immediate groups, and to a low level of conceptual development, which is reflexively turned back upon itself so that the beliefs and ideas of the stupid come to comprise an exclusionary universe of meaning, beyond which there is perceived to be no reality, validity, or value. Narcissism confines the stupid individual and group to an emotionally self-centered universe, while their level of conceptual development does the same thing in terms of conceptual understanding, fostering rigid adherence to closed systems of belief, which produces ideological blindness.

13. Stupidity is further characterized by a reflexive inability to recognize itself. The stupid are most stupid when it comes to recognizing their own stupidity.

14. Stupid people transform their preferences into judgments of superior worth.

15. Stupidity often involves a willful avoidance of the obvious when personal and group gratifications are at stake. It fosters self-deception through a tendency to misconstrue reality, so as to satisfy personal and group interests and needs. Foremost in this pattern of stupid, willful avoidance is our species' heedless, single-minded reproduction and environmental exploitation.

16. The last characteristic I will mention here comprises a complementary variety of human stupidity to which I will refer in Part III as *epistemological stupidity*, and defer further discussion of this form of stupidity until then.

This list lends itself to lengthening, for human stupidity can assume as much variety as do the individual skills that we associate with intelligence. However, before we leave the task of summarizing principal characteristics of human stupidity, it is important that we include those particular attributes of stupidity that involve deficiencies of ability that have a moral dimension, for human stupidity often not only involves the above-mentioned general stupidities, but moral stupidity, as well. Earlier in this chapter, we considered the nature of human moral intelligence. By its absence, *human moral stupidity* includes these collaborating elements:

1. Moral stupidity can variously involve any of the pathologies we have identified earlier in this study, which make human beings receptive to the gratifications that human evil provides.

2. Moral stupidity involves the inability to feel empathy and respect for another's life, interests, and feelings.

3. The morally stupid are insensitive and uncritical in ways that encourage them to accept without distaste and without condemnation human cruelty, violence, and others forms of human evil.

4. The morally stupid lack the emotional cement, the conviction, that fuses an awareness of what is morally right with a need to act consistently with that awareness. And so in moral stupidity there is an especially evident disconnection between actual behavior and moral consciousness/rationality.

5. The previous four components of moral stupidity lead to stupidities of thought and behavior that are morally wrong, often because morally stupid perpetrators fail to make use of their existing knowledge and general abilities, or because they are stupid in other general senses defined by the previous open-ended list of characteristics.

From the practical and theoretical perspective I have proposed, human stupidity—general and moral—defines a complex pathology in the meaning of this word studied in Part I. It is a pathology not yet to be found in our nosologies of mental and emotional illness, yet it identifies a specific, unmistakable, and undeniably important diagnostic category. Stupidity qualifies as a pathology in that it is malignant: it is frequently harmful to the stupid themselves as well as to others with whom they interact, and it is contagious by virtue of the imitative mindset it promotes. From this point of view, human stupidity is one of the most common, pervasive, and genuine mental illnesses. Human stupidity is, moreover, a normal condition. It is found to varying degrees in the majority of people. The evidence for this assertion is abundantly provided by human history, and very likely at any time by current events, as well; if the reader requires a detailed inventory of examples to be convinced, the studies of human stupidity reviewed earlier in this chapter may be consulted with profit. If there is a common basis upon which the many pathologies of man rest, it is pathology of human stupidity. Gautama Buddha has correctly appraised stupidity: Among the three cardinal sources of human error which he identified—*raga*, or sensuality; *dosa*, or ill-will, and *moha*, or stupidity—he judged stupidity to be by far the worst in every respect.

✧

We have come to the end of Part II, devoted to the study of the psychology of human evil. We are in a position to look back and to take stock of the complex, convoluted interplay of very human psychological propensities that characterize the normal human population. We see a self-centered species made up of self-centered individuals and groups, all proud of their abilities, their beliefs, and their attainments, the majority of whom are assiduously committed to the perpetuation of behavior that is frequently self-destructive to the human species, and destructive to other species and to our shared environment. The psychology of human evil identifies many of the reasons why we are no better, why things stay the same, and why we should expect more of the same in the future. It is essential that we understand these things, and to realize how exceedingly hard it is for them to be changed given the many forces we have discovered that block this.

The psychology of human evil deals principally with the affective constitution of our species—its willingness to cause suffering, its aggressiveness and destructiveness, but, as we have seen in this chapter, it also deals with our species' prominent deficiencies in general and in moral intelligence. Human beings are, however, more than this psychological constitution. They are thinking beings, whose conceptual vocabulary promotes certain ways of understanding the world, other people, and other life. In Part III of this study, I turn to investigate some of these conceptual realities, which influence much of human thought and its consequences in behavior.

# PART III

# THE CONCEPTUAL PATHOLOGY OF MAN

# PART III

# THE CONCEPTUAL PATHOLOGY OF MAN

Virtually no research has been done that links patterns of human thought with the pathologies of human emotion and behavior which were the focus of Part II. The first chapter of Part III, "The Pathology of Everyday Thought," focuses attention on disorders of human thinking, and introduces this issue by discussing the psychology of delusions of misidentification. I then look at certain early, impressionistic proposals for therapeutic approaches that have been made by philosophers Wittgenstein, Wisdom, and Farrell, and by biologist-psychiatrist Bateson. With these discussions as background, I turn to summarize my own work over four decades that has led to the development of a pathology for concepts. I describe the cognitive and affective power of conceptual pathology over individual men and women and their social groups, and advance the thesis that mankind's everyday conceptual frame of reference, in terms of which people perceive and understand the world, is inherently self-destructive. I propose a rigorous approach to conceptual therapy, which makes it possible to identify and to eliminate conceptual pathologies, and examine one of these in detail, the widespread delusional belief in transcendence.

The second chapter, "Relativism, Framework-relativity, and Human Evil," takes a closer look at moral relativism, which historically has been one of the main obstacles to welding clear thinking and conviction together into a unity of reason and moral persuasion. Relativism has been and remains a theoretical and practical thorn-in-the-flesh. Today it is an especially pervasive attitude that stands in the way of human moral progress. I propose that relativism is a serious thought disorder that contributes significantly to human evil, and present a theoretically compelling refutation of relativism. I then consider how morality can be understood once moral relativism is rejected, and underscore the central role of moral intelligence in defensible morality.

The last chapter, "Reflections," looks back over the course of this study and places its conclusions in perspective. I discuss the human blinders and recalcitrance that produce resistance to an honest self-awareness of human evil. I argue that hope and forgiveness constitute second-order pathologies of man, and describe a constructive attitude that we may take that is consistent with what we know about the phenomenon of human evil. I then reflect on the purpose of writing a study such as this, evaluate its capacity to make a difference, and make some concluding remarks.

# CHAPTER 19

# THE PATHOLOGY OF EVERYDAY THOUGHT

The problems that we have created...cannot be solved at the same level of thinking at which we created them. – Einstein quoted in Perlman (2002:36)

## IDEOPATHY, OR DISORDERS OF THOUGHT

I begin this last part of our study with the recognition, based on the results of previous chapters, that psychologically average, statistically normal human beings are characterized by a large and varied set of pathological dispositions and traits. As we have seen, many of these dispositions and traits exist in people for very good reasons, because they satisfy important needs and provide deep-seated gratifications. The psychology of human evil places these needs, gratifications, and resulting attitudes and behaviors in relief so they can be identified, studied, and evaluated. This psychological focus, however, omits much that must be taken into account if we are to understand the human propensities this book is about. In this chapter, I enlarge our scope of analysis to include dimensions of human reality that have so far been given little attention by previous researchers. I look at the role of the conceptual structures that people use to define reality, to give their lives meaning, and to establish the identity of their social, political, and religious groups. Our interest in this chapter, then, will be to consider how human beings *think* in ways that are self-defeating, motivating them to engage in highly destructive forms of behavior. The discussion that follows is theoretically more abstract than is found in earlier chapters. But there is no reason to assume that pathologies that affect human beings must all exist on the same level.

The notion that mere ideas can be pathological, that they can comprise what I call *ideopathies*, can seem both startling and commonplace. As we noted in Chapter 11, "ideas can kill." They can also incite prejudice, hatred, cruelty, ideological and religious fervor, and the many other emotions and attitudes this book has been about. Max Lerner sought to underscore the destructive capacity of ideas in his book, *Ideas Are Weapons: The History and Uses of Ideas* (1991/1939). He commented: "Under the spell of...ideas a madness seems to sweep over a people, like an engulfing sea that sweeps away the dikes that rationality has painfully and prayerfully built against it over the centuries." (3) Ideas, of course, do not achieve their power over us unaided, for it requires a certain psychological constitution for people to respond aggressively and destructively to ideas that can arouse such responses. We have studied that psychological constitution in some detail now, and here need to balance our account by recognizing the existence of *pathologies of human thought*, which, as suggested earlier (Chapter 3) are inextricably involved in the phenomenon of human evil. In the present chapter, I argue that much of what we call acceptable, normal thinking is pathological—because it is wrong, harmful, and insidious, communicable in the sense of being contagious, and virulent. I will refer to "conceptual pathologies" or "ideopathies" which in psychologically normal, average individual men and women lead to a variety of dysfunctions of thought which are unrecognized and indeed universally denied. From this point of view, human history has been dominated by a kind of *twisted logic* that has so often promoted the suffering and death of others in the name of goodness, opposition to evil, moral or religious righteousness, etc. This is a subject-matter unto itself, and cannot be dealt with comprehensively in the space remaining in this volume. However, we will undertake a limited discussion here.

Among researchers whose work we have described we already find hints of this thesis. In Freud (Chapter 6), we found the beginnings in twentieth century psychiatry of a concern for ways in which ideology leads to pathology, and discussed Freud's observations concerning what he considered to be delusional, closed belief-systems in religion and philosophy, which are exclusionary and purport to account for all relevant evidence. We noted (Chapter 10) what ethologists Lorenz and Eibl-Eibesfeldt respectively called "dangerous thought habits" and "compulsions or delusions of thought..., deceptions inherent in the inaccuracy of our thinking apparatus." Social psychologists Fiske and Taylor (1991:133) (see Chapter 11 in the present work) spoke of the way in which "normal thought processes" bolster stereotypical, ethnocentric, prejudiced beliefs. Canadian psychiatrist G. B. Chisholm (1946), whose reflections on war we commented on (Chapter 14), laid the blame for human destructiveness on "a basic psychological distortion," and urged the need for an "earnest searching for the reasons we are the way we are, with *a willingness to change anything that we believe and any way that we think* if we find any of the things we *believe* or *ways that we think* are in fact liabilities rather than assets." (7, 34)

Beyond the authors we have discussed, Fish's (1967:35-9) well-known descriptive manual of psychopathologies includes "disorders of thinking," which he divided into disorders of belief and disorders of reasoning. Among the first type of disorder he included "delusions," or "false unshakeable beliefs," which are inconsistent with the believer's social and cultural background. We shall return to the subject of delusions shortly. Psychologist of terrorism Warneka (2002:110, 117) specifically referred to "thinking errors" that support aggression. What he had in mind are "cognitive distortions," i.e., thinking errors that we commonly use to evade responsibility for our actions, such as lying, blaming, denying, and rationalizing. Here, we find a contemporary again speaking of the "errors of thought" to which Canguilhem referred (Chapter 3 in the present study).

In fact, many psychologists and psychiatrists have directed attention to dysfunctional ways in which people think and believe. Philosophers and more recently cognitive scientists have also been drawn to this subject. I would like to discuss two complementary directions in which research has developed, both of which stop short of the radical thesis I will argue, that the majority of human beings often think dysfunctionally and hold self-sabotaging beliefs. But first, let us look at an important and relevant hypothesis.

## COLLINGWOOD'S HYPOTHESIS

R. G. Collingwood (1946) proposed that human conduct, to a greater extent than the conduct of nonhuman animals, is determined by thought. In his memory, I shall call this Collingwood's Hypothesis. Two important approaches to psychotherapeutic understanding have relied most heavily upon it: George Kelly's psychology of personal constructs (Kelly

1991/1955) and Albert Ellis's rational-emotive therapy (Ellis 1961, 1977). Both approaches stress the degree to which human behavior is the result of the ways in which people think and interpret events, and both seek to help people overcome harmful patterns of thinking. Kelly proposed a "grid technique" to identify an individual's personal ways of valuing experience. The "grid" makes explicit an individual's personal constructs, which form his system of meaning and establish his "reality reference space."

In a different but complementary way, Ellis sought to identify destructive ways in which people think about themselves, their interactions with others, and the world generally, and he developed a practical approach that people can use to change how they think, and hence how they will feel and behave. During the 1950s he developed an approach to psychotherapy based, one could say, on the view urged by Epictetus nearly two thousand years ago in his *Enchiridion*: "Man is not disturbed by events, but by the view he takes of them." Ellis claimed that people are largely responsible for their emotional responses. The mental habits they build up become with the passage of time ever stronger and resistant to change. But they can be broken: Rational-emotive therapy seeks to do this by systematically challenging and replacing the client's beliefs and values (concentrating attention of the "shoulds" and "oughts" the client lives by) that have attained the role of unquestioned, habitual cognitive "filters" through which people interpret, in a semi-automatic way, the world around them.

More recently and more theoretically, Watts (1992) has given a description of the dynamic in human beings that links thinking with emotion. Watts believed that two vicious circles are involved: In one, emotional states often lead to associated thoughts, and the thoughts can, in turn, augment the state of emotion. In another vicious circle, emotional states may influence how people interpret events, while their interpretations, in turn, can influence their emotional reactions. Watts concluded: "...clinicians need to consider the relative role of both thoughts/images and interpretations, and...tailor their treatment strategies accordingly." (Watts 1992:160)

There can be no doubt that habits of thought and interpretation heavily influence the emotional responses that people have to events, and also little doubt that the way people feel influences how they behave. These are distinguishable links in Collingwood's Hypothesis, and have been separately studied, with some controversy. In connection with the first link, between thought and emotion, Lazarus (1984), for example, has maintained that thoughts can control feeling and that interpretation can trigger emotion. Zazonc (1980) has argued that thinking is always tinged with emotion, and that feelings precede and arouse cognitions. Watts (1990) has claimed that feelings are independent of thought, yet produce cognitions with associated feelings. —Evidently, the exact relations between thought, emotions, and conduct have yet to be determined; it is sufficient for our present purposes to recognize that they are often connected. (See "The Influence of Thinking on Feeling" in Fewtrell 1995:33-7, and our related earlier discussion of the "moral bridge problem" in Chapter 18.) The connections exist and, as we have seen (Chapter 13), are expressed in a particularly unmistakable way in the relationship between the emotionally-laden belief-system of the fanatic and his conduct.

## DELUSIONAL MISIDENTIFICATIONS

One area in which psychiatrists and psychologists have directed attention to dysfunctional ways in which people think and believe has been that of so-called *delusions of misidentification*. They include a fascinating group of disorders in which there is an erroneous and firmly planted belief in the identity of other people, oneself, places, or objects. Among them are the Capgras delusion (in which members of the patient's family have been replaced by imposters), the Cotard delusion (the patient believes he has died), the Fregoli delusion (he is followed by people he knows, but they are in disguise), the mirrored-self misidentification (the patient's image in a mirror is not himself), reduplicative paramnesia (someone who died is still present), unilateral neglect (part of his body belongs to someone else), alien control (his behavior is controlled by someone else), thought insertion (someone is inserting thoughts into his mind), delusions of reference in which there is a belief that the actions of others have a special reference to oneself, and there are others. (See Joseph 1986.) Delusions of misidentification involve two distinguishable parts: a delusional belief and an erroneous identification. Let us look at these.

The standard *DSM* definition of 'delusion' involves four components: (i) a false belief, (ii) firmly adhered to, (iii) despite what others in the patient's social group or subculture believe, and (iv) despite incontrovertible evidence to the contrary. Going beyond the *DSM* definition, delusional people in addition (v) tend to jump to conclusions, and (vi) are vulnerable to believing ideas that are absurd or nonsensical. (Coltheart & Davies 2000:13) Furthermore, their delusional beliefs (vii) are encapsulated, that is, they are walled off from other realistic beliefs, and are, as one author put it, "cognitive impenetrable" in the sense that the delusional beliefs are immune to influence by other true and incompatible beliefs held by the person. Bisiach (1988:468) has called this immunity to influence by neighboring beliefs "pathological ideation."

There are several further characteristics of delusional beliefs I will add: They (viii) have an *inertia* of their own and in this sense are highly resistant to revision; they (ix) are *exempt from criteria of consistency* with other beliefs and (x) are similarly *exempt from criteria of rationality*. Further, they often (xi) provide a source of psychological or existential *gratification and stability* for the believer; and they (xii) are held in a *recalcitrant* manner: Although the believer may recognize their absurdity, he or she will nonetheless persist in holding them. Delusional beliefs are (xiii) often also accompanied by anosognosias, or *lack of awareness of the existence of delusion, with an accompanying denial of impairment*. We note parenthetically that usually, but not always, people with misidentification delusions have undergone some kind of right hemisphere brain damage.

Various researchers have claimed that delusions of misidentification can appropriately be classified as pathological. "It is," as one researcher put it, "quite natural to characterize delusion as a pathology of belief and to assume that this pathology is responsible for the irrationality." (Gold & Hohwy 2000:158) Researchers Coltheart and Davies (2000) have, in this context, titled their collection of papers on this subject *Pathologies of Belief.* (See also Christodoulou 1991, Roberts 1991, and Sims 2003.)

Pathologies of delusional belief involve a second element, that of erroneous identification. This is the mistake that lies at the core of the delusion. Delusional subjects, like normal people, experience the world in terms of a set of background beliefs, what I call a *conceptual structure*, which is variously the product of social and environmental factors as well as individual psychology. This conceptual structure serves as a background frame of reference, which is given specific referential content by a vocabulary of ideas in terms of which people think and interpret events. Even in normal people, this conceptual structure is usually quite biased: it leads them to prefer certain interpretations and beliefs over others, and to interpret experience in a biased light. The identifications that people make, whether true and realistic or false and delusional, take place and are made possible by this background conceptual structure. Their identifications of others, events, and themselves are contextually meaningful in this framework-relative manner. Because that conceptual structure is relied upon implicitly and habitually, the relativity of misidentifications to that overall context is usually overlooked. People, whether normal or clinically delusional, do not tend to recognize the role of their habitual conceptual vocabulary. We shall return to this important point later. Here, we observe that in psychologically normal people, as well as in those who are clinically delusional, their personal, social, political, religious, and other needs, interests, and gratifications form the fertile ground in which acceptable and sometimes mistaken or absurd beliefs take root. And, as we shall see, even when their erroneous beliefs lack evidence or are inconsistent with other beliefs, their unsupported beliefs are often accepted with amazing hardihood, and their lack of support is ignored.

Psychiatric studies of delusional misidentifications have stopped short of extending their observations and conclusions to normal subjects. We shall take this step a little later.

## PHILOSOPHY AS THERAPY

Philosophers and cognitive scientists have also been drawn to the subject of dysfunctional ways in which people think and behave. In the history of philosophy, there has always existed an interest in fallacies of thinking, formal and informal logic, prudential, plausible, and probabilistic reasoning. These approaches, however, will not concern us since here we wish to focus on the explicit association of philosophy with psychotherapy, for some philosophers and cognitive scientists have proposed ways in which philosophy can serve therapeutic needs.

There are two main approaches to therapy that have a philosophical origin: The first has emphasized the disentanglement of confusions that are due to the *misuse of language*, and was proposed by Ludwig Wittgenstein, Brian Farrell, Gilbert Ryle, John Wisdom, and others. The second has proposed a therapeutic analysis and treatment of specifically conceptual confusions that are due to a *misuse of ideas*. This approach was first proposed and developed by the present author; it was also commented upon but not developed by Gregory Bateson. Let us look briefly at the first approach here; in the next section we will discuss the second.

Wittgenstein is known for his terse, aphoristic, and fragmentary presentation, which sought to reveal through the use of examples how misuses of language can lead to the confusions that have become the grist of philosophy. He wished to provide a freely defined set of methods that would enable language-conscious philosophers to find their way out of the "fly-bottle" into which their unselfconscious abuse of language has led them. The clearest statement that emphasizes Wittgenstein's therapeutic motivation was, in my opinion, given by Brian Farrell (1946) in a two-part paper, which he called "An Appraisal of Therapeutic Positivism." Its importance in our discussion here lies in the fact that Farrell construed Wittgenstein's approach in a sufficiently broad sense so that its application was not limited to merely philosophical problems. He went about this in two ways, by arguing that "...philosophizing is an attempt to resolve a fairly general and persistent *psychological* conflict..." (147; emphasis added), and by claiming that psychopathology has limited its scope unnecessarily to "neuroses and anxiety states...caused by non-verbal factors alone." (146) Farrell believed that Wittgenstein's approach offers a therapy to deal with "anxiety states" that are produced "by the ordinary verbal habits of the person himself" (146); such anxiety states, he believed, are found in other areas of life, not just in philosophy.

He referred to Wittgenstein's general therapeutic approach as "semiotical therapy" (139), "semiotical psychiatry" (135, 144), or "therapeutic positivism." (143, 146-7) It is "a psychiatrical procedure for settling worries and conflicts of a certain type." (35) These worries and conflicts, according to Farrell, constitute a "disease" of a particular sort, one which results from "linguistic confusion." (141) What is in view, he claimed, is "a description of a certain cluster of conceptual conflicts, somewhat analogous to a description in psychiatry of the nature and pathology of (say) obsessional difficulties." (Farrell 1990:8) He went on to urge that semiotical psychiatry "be dovetailed into ordinary psychiatrical treatment," but to date this has never happened. Instead, the "therapy" proposed by Wittgenstein and others who have contributed to language analysis continues to be applied to philosophical problems, but with virtually no application beyond philosophy.

There is not space here to discuss the suggestions, all of them impressionistic, that philosophy of ordinary language might be likened to a therapy. Among them we might note the special word that Stephen Toulmin coined for the phenomena in view:

> [P]hilosophical theories were [according to Wittgenstein] to be diagnosed as symptoms of misconceptions about our *everyday* language—"cerebroses" (so to say) comparable to the neuroses which spring from misconceptions about our affective relationships. They were accordingly to be "treated" by a philosophical therapy adapted to the specific intellectual cramps of the individual patient. (Toulmin 1969:60)

And we might also mention in passing John Wisdom's use of words "with a clinical flavor" to refer to states of "philosophical stress." (Wisdom 1953; Dilman 1984, 1996) But, again, the "mental cramps" that Wittgenstein and Wisdom strove to remove are those specialized confusions found in philosophy, not those found in the conceptual structure of the common man.

## CONCEPTUAL PATHOLOGY AND HUMAN EVIL

> How is man to tell truth from error? The ignorant man solves this problem in a very simple manner: he holds that whatever he believes, he knows; and that whatever he knows is true.
> – H. L. Mencken (1993/1913: 147)

One of the earliest suggestions that philosophy should concern itself with mental illness was made by Kant. In 1797, he published a short work, *Anthropology from a Pragmatic Point of View*, which is generally regarded as Kant's main contribution to psychology. In it he attempted to catalog and describe human mental capacities. A division in Book I is devoted to "Deficiencies and Diseases of the Soul with Respect to its Cognitive Power." There, Kant offered a catalog of mental illnesses. Among them, he identified insania, in which the mind mistakes analogies "for concepts of things similar to each other," and vesania, where there is a breach with reason and the afflicted individual "fancies that he conceives the inconceivable." (Kant 1974/1797:84-5) Kant emphasized the intellectual as opposed to the emotional aspects of mental illness, and believed that the treatment of mental disorders is the province of philosophy—but then of course this was before psychiatry and psychology had become disciplines separate from philosophy. The cognitive mistakes that he distinguished, especially the second variety that involves delusional thinking, may serve as historical background relevant to the discussion that follows.

Chapter 3 briefly introduced the reader to the idea of conceptual therapy. One must adopt a new view of our species to take seriously the notion that many ordinary human ideas or concepts stand in need of real, non-metaphorical therapy. Beginning in the early 1960s, I began the development of what I have called *conceptual therapy*. It is a theory which holds that many concepts that are central to everyday as well as scientific thinking are inherently dysfunctional because they involve self-undermining forms of reference. We find, upon analysis, that such concepts do not and cannot have their intended meaning, and indeed are absurd in much the way Kant seemed to have in mind when he spoke about people who fancy they conceive of the inconceivable. In a series of studies, I have sought to avoid the impressionistic, metaphorical suggestions of philosophers, and to establish a solid, rigorously sound methodology that can reach conclusions in a clear, scientific, and intellectually compelling way. (Bartlett 1970, 1975a, 1975b, 1976, 1980, 1982, 1983a, 1983b, 1988, 1992; Bartlett & Suber 1987) This work has its roots in epistemology, which today is exerting an influence upon, and to some extent is being absorbed by, cognitive science. In its historical role as mother of the sciences, philosophy may once again be budding off part of itself to produce a separate discipline with more precise standards of justification than prevail in philosophy. Epistemology, so considered, includes not only the traditional study of the limits and conditions of knowledge, but it offers us the means to analyze the workings of both normal and abnormal claims to knowledge.

Here, the pathology of human cognition will concern us, and more specifically the pathology of human beliefs. We will focus upon certain widespread beliefs that people apply to themselves, one another, their societies, nations, ideologies, religions, and the world, generally. We will consider those beliefs in terms of the ideas they involve, ideas that are, from the epistemological standpoint I propose, recognizably and non-metaphorically pathological.

Human behavior is influenced not only by our species' underlying psychology, but, according to Collingwood's Hypothesis, by the vocabulary of ideas we use to make sense of the world and to give our lives meaning. This set of ideas, many of which are extremely basic, serves as a framework of understanding and interpretation in terms of which we, among many other things, express what we believe to be meaningful statements about ourselves, our relationships with others and with the physical world. In the mid-1960s, I proposed that this conceptual framework, which we presuppose as a common currency of communication and intelligibility of the world, is subject to malfunction. I advanced the claim that there exist pathologies of a conceptual kind, which exercise considerable influence over our thinking as well as our behavior. Epistemological pathologies of this kind frequently undermine our intentions and lead to destructive behavior.

During the following decade, Gregory Bateson took a parallel step in some of his sociological-ethnological-psychiatric publications: In 1972, he published the first of several papers in which he suggested the idea of "pathologies of epistemology," by which he, perhaps somewhat misleadingly, meant errors in human thinking that lead to errors in human action. (Bateson 1972:478-87) (He did not, that is to say, mean literally that the discipline that studies the limits and conditions of human knowledge, epistemology, itself involves pathology.) His thoughts in this area were sketchy, asserting a vague connection between errors in ordinary ways of thinking and potential human and environmental disaster. What he seems to have had in mind is the human propensity to misapprehend and misrepresent reality in ways that are self-defeating. Unfortunately, he did not develop this thesis. The view he proposed remained very general: "Epistemological error is often reinforced and therefore self-validating [sic].... [Y]ou entertain at rather deep levels of the mind premises which are simply false." (480) He concluded: "[W]e are most of us governed by epistemologies that we know to be wrong." (485)

When I first read the conclusion that Bateson drew, I believed it was wrong, and I still do. The most widespread pathologies are, I have found, simply *not* known by most people to be wrong, or even to exist. On the contrary, they are presumed without question to be right, they are made the basis of belief, and then of action, which is often tragic and destructive in its consequences. But I agreed with his observation: "epistemological lunacy...leads inevitably to various sorts of disaster." (487)

I have argued that human conceptual pathologies lead to self-undermining beliefs that, when acted upon, often lead to tragic results. I am not able in the space available here to give a full account of this approach, but will limit what I can say here to two different epistemological pathologies: the human belief in transcendence and the belief in relativism. I will deal with the first in this chapter, and the second in the chapter that follows. Before we proceed, we will need a few tools to work with.

## Epistemological Projection

All beliefs have their underpinnings in the conceptual frameworks that human beings employ when they think. A conceptual framework serves as a *reference system*, first of all, so that people can identify what they are thinking and talking about, and, secondly, so that they may successfully re-identify those objects of reference in their own thought and in communication with others. Understood in this general sense, a conceptual framework serves as a sometimes simple, often complex, system of identification. Unfortunately, although we use the ideas of identity and of identification daily and with a frequency that probably exceeds that of any other basic ideas, these ideas are often left unclear; seldom do we find an author who attempts to define them. Social scientists Moscovici and Paicheler (1978:253) admit with candor: "The concept of identity is as indispensable as it is unclear. This is why no attempt will be made to define it and we shall keep it in a zone of shaded obscurity...." When one scratches the surface in an attempt to define identity and identification, one is soon led to mathematics. Without recourse to formalization, it is enough here to remind the reader of his or her acquaintance with the familiar Cartesian coordinate system. Such a system provides us with a system for referring to individual points by their coordinates. In a Cartesian coordinate system with three axes, any point can be located by means of a set of three coordinates. The location of a point (3, -5, 5) is specified, in other words, is identified, by means of those coordinates. Anyone who is familiar with this frame of reference knows how it is used, and can locate the same point that I am referring to.

Coordinate systems are a clear-cut example of systems of reference that permit us to identify objects to which we wish to refer in totally unambiguous ways. More complex frames of reference permit us to refer to one another by name, address, Social Security number, profession, personality type, intelligence, interests, political or religious affiliation, etc. Our general, shared conceptual structure can be understood as a cluster of overlapping frames of reference that permit us to do these things. Often, we use our referential abilities in unproblematic ways, but all too often the references that we make are, so to speak, "out of bounds": We make references in an incoherent manner, and end up in referential incoherence. Unfortunately, our referential incoherence is seldom recognized, and so we proceed very much in the same way as do victims of delusions of misidentification, with one difference: Just as people who are clinically afflicted by delusional misidentification, psychologically average, normal people adhere strongly to their beliefs, despite evidence to the contrary; their delusional beliefs are walled off from their true and realistic beliefs; the delusional beliefs are highly resistant to revision; they are exempted from standards of rationality and consistency; they often provide sources of gratification and stability; they are held in a recalcitrant manner (stubbornly in the face of being shown their absurdity); and the delusion is not recognized and its existence is denied. The one difference between clinical delusions of misidentification and the kinds of referential dysfunction that characterize the nonclinical population is this: In the clinical case, the neuropsychiatrist knows the delusion is *false* (the Capgras patient's wife is not an imposter). But in the case of a psychological normal, average person, the referential misidentification is not false, it *meaningless*.

I have called the particular class of dysfunctional references that are in view here "*projective misconstructions*." (cf. Bartlett 1970, 1975b, 1976, 1982, 1983a, 1992:12ff) I chose this name because of its implicit association with the forms of projection we discussed in Chapter 6, and because of its ties to projective geometry, in which the properties of objects that are invariant under projective transformation can be studied. (Bartlett 1970:I:187n; II:124n) The conceptual error that is involved makes use of a frame of reference either (i) to predicate something of an object of reference, while intending to do this in a manner that loses sight of the reference frame that makes such a reference possible, or (ii) to deny that the object of reference has the predicated attribute(s), also in the same referentially dysfunctional manner, losing sight of the frame of reference that must necessarily be presupposed. It is as though one sought to pull the carpet out from under one's own feet, and the harder the pulling, the more firmly implanted upon the carpet one's feet become. When human beings engage in this kind of illegitimate and fundamentally incoherent mental gymnastics, they are, as the old phrase goes, hoisted by their own petards. (Bartlett 1988) The delusion of transcendence involves a projective misconstruction. Let us look at this epistemological pathology, which is widespread, has high incidence in the normal population, and is highly communicable. What we will see is a pathology which, like the autoimmune diseases mentioned in Chapter 1, involves a reflexive or self-referential malfunction.

### The Delusion of Transcendence and Human Evil

> The tendency has always been strong to believe that whatever receives a name must be an entity of being, having an independent existence of its own. And if no real entity answering to the name could be found, men did not for that reason suppose that none existed, but imagined that it was something peculiarly abstruse and mysterious. – John Stuart Mill quoted in Spearman (1927:14)

The human belief in transcendence is a disorder of thought: It involves a projective misconstruction beyond whatever reference frame is in use, plus the predication of independent existence to what is projected. This belief is common among people in all societies. It takes many forms: the child's belief that a tree must make a crashing sound when there is no one there to hear it; belief in deities who live in a heavenly dimension to which living human beings have no access; belief that a nation possesses a supervening identity and reality for which it makes sense to sacrifice life; the belief that is typical of so many ideologies—that they define an autonomous reality in which the sole, exclusionary, and unique Truth is to be found; and of course the metaphysician's belief in the reality of objects "in themselves." When these beliefs are carefully analyzed, none is found to have meaning, for the meaning they are thought to have—and the meaning they *can be thought to have*—is dependent upon the reference frames that are used to think and articulate those beliefs.

Epistemological contentions like this, however, can be intellectually slippery, for neither do the opposite claims make sense: It is equally meaningless to claim that the unobserved falling tree does *not* make a sound. —To assert this is not to espouse positivism or operationalism, but rather to endorse a framework-relative criterion of meaning, which is no more than to recognize that the identity of objects to which we refer is a framework-relative matter. It is to claim no more than that the point defined by the coordinates (3, -5, 5) has no identity if we are prevented from using a three-dimensional Cartesian coordinate system.

From this point of view, transcendence is a concept, to paraphrase Clifton Fadiman, that looks in vain for a meaning on the scrap heap of popular misuse. We have become so inured to claims that involve its use, and so comforted by the psychological and existential reassurance that it appears to offer, that we cannot see that we hold beliefs with the same tenacity as the Capgras delusionary—but here we believe in something that is not false, but *absurd*. When we make claims that involve the idea of transcendence, we trespass beyond the boundaries of meaningful reference; we step out of bounds, forget where we are, and believe with all the hardihood of the misidentification delusionary that we have thought a thought that makes good sense, or said something meaningful. In fact, we have not. (Bartlett 1982)

It should immediately be clear to the reader who has reached this point in our study how delusional misidentifications of transcendence contribute to human evil. For as long as people attribute an independent existence to the objects of their devotion and veneration, we can be assured of their willingness to sacrifice themselves and others to their causes, and in the process bring down upon themselves and others whatever suffering may be necessary to achieve the ends they prefer. We have already encountered the belief in transcendence in connection with the psychology of genocide, war, terrorism, and hatred. It is a tenacious and persistent belief, an ideopathy that is easily transmitted and accepted without question.

For a reflective, epistemologically intelligent person to believe in transcendence is intellectual hypocrisy. Paralleling the concept of moral intelligence developed in the last chapter is the concept here of *epistemological intelligence* (along with its counterpart, *epistemological stupidity*), which I do not have space to elaborate, but which I leave to the reader to imagine: Such intelligence would combine conviction and rationality in insisting upon a meaningful definition of reality, one which is, that is to say, *"de-projectively"* coherent. Intelligence of this kind is able to free itself from projective misconstructions, of which transcendence is unfortunately but one among many of the epistemologically delusional beliefs that distort the human perception of reality. Other conceptually pathological beliefs relate to commonly held notions about the identity of others and of oneself, material objects, time and space, truth, causality, etc. (Cf. Bartlett 1970, 1975b, 1983) From the point of view proposed here, to apply Marie Jahoda's criterion, "...mental health is manifested in the adequacy of an individual's *perception of reality*." (Jahoda 1974/1966:198) An adequate perception of reality is possible only when it is free of conceptual pathology.

# CHAPTER 20

## RELATIVISM, FRAMEWORK-RELATIVITY, AND HUMAN EVIL

This study's fundamental assertion, that the existence of human evil needs to be understood in terms that relate to psychologically normal people, rests on an assumption that we now need to make explicit and to justify. That assumption is that moral relativism is untenable, for if moral relativism constituted a potentially true account of human reality, the claim that there is human evil would be vulnerable to reduction to a more or less arbitrary point of view held by like-minded people who have certain moral values in common. Their moral judgments would be valid only for them: In another society, in another political system, if the prevailing ideology were different and incompatible beliefs are endorsed, morality could be quite different. If moral relativism were tenable, the study of human pathology would rest on shifting sand. "Human evil" would become the speck of dirt in one group's eye. And it is the same with any judgment that a perceived dysfunction comprises a pathology. Clinical judgments also stand or fall depending on the tenability of relativism.

In this chapter, I confront the hard questions that relativism poses for pathology and the theory of disease, and particularly for the study of human evil. We shall find that not only is moral relativism not tenable, but that as an abstract theoretical view and a set of concrete associated attitudes, it contributes to human evil as a pervasive thought disorder. We shall find that moral relativism is itself a pathology, specifically, an ideopathy. Furthermore, we shall find that the attitudes to which moral relativism gives rise have themselves contributed greatly to the phenomenon of human evil. Moral relativism forms part of the proper subject-matter of this study, for it is, as we shall see, a constituent of human evil.

During the last hundred years, relativism has come to dominate the outlook of many disciplines as well as the mindset of the public. To a great extent, discoveries in the social and behavioral sciences, and in particular in anthropology, have been responsible for the growth of relativism. Fieldwork in these disciplines has brought to light a wide range of human conceptions of moral goodness and evil. Social and cultural diversity has shown us that systems of belief are varied and often conflicting. The notion that there is a single morality and a single concept of evil has fallen into multiple pieces. Trends in contemporary philosophy, particularly in ethics and moral theory, have added to the inclination to affirm relativism.

Relativism comes in many forms. In addition to moral relativism, there are conceptual, perceptual, linguistic, and ontological relativisms, along with relativism of truth and of reason. (Edwards 1990; Harré and Krausz 1996) Each asserts a different form of dependency upon individuals and social groups; each seeks to underscore diversity and to oppose belief in uniquely established, privileged, absolutist views. Common to all varieties of relativism are these claims or suppositions: (i) The Humility Thesis, which claims that unless we can prove that our standards are objectively better than others, we have no right to impose them on others who do not accept them; (ii) the related Principle of Tolerance, which urges toleration of conflicting points of view; (iii) the Enculturation Thesis, which claims that our beliefs, perception, language, or reasoning patterns are the product of enculturation; (iv) the Generosity Maxim, which claims that it is in everyone's interests if everybody's needs are satisfied; and (v) the Denial of Unique Justification Thesis, which claims that there are no standards that are uniquely and absolutely justified. The point of view and set of attitudes that result from these five suppositions is touted as benign and broadminded, tolerant and non-judgmental. These values have an unmistakable democratic appeal. But despite these attractions, it is not difficult to show that moral relativism is untenable, and it is, as I will show, itself morally unacceptable.

Two general approaches have been used to oppose relativism: One attacks it by attempting to show that people have a universally shared nature, so that relativism is factually wrong. (See, e.g., Moody-Adams 1997). The other attacks relativism by showing that it is, on a very basic level, self-contradictory or internally inconsistent, and adds that, despite its seeming political attractiveness, relativism is morally repugnant. This is the approach I will use later in this chapter. Before we proceed, let us bring together some threads from previous chapters.

In Chapter 2, in connection with pathology, politics, and clinical judgment, we encountered the question, How are we to proceed when clinical judgments conflict and there is a state of diagnostic impasse? This is an important question, for some clinicians will no doubt disagree with the way this study identifies many normal human characteristics as pathological. Are we left with no more to say than "one man's meat is another's poison?"

In Chapter 3, I characterized pathology as a function of our acceptance of a frame of reference in terms of which (a) clinical judgments concerning pathology derive their meaning and persuasive force, and (b) a range of potential therapies is in principle suggested. This point of view led to a recognition that a condition is judged to be pathological in relation to the positive values that it negates or undermines. Are these values arbitrary? Is the identification of a pathology no more than an arbitrary classification that depends solely upon the preferences of an individual or social group? Also in the same chapter, I proposed a framework-relative theory of disease in which a disease is understood in terms of the violation of rules, the occurrence of error, or the posing of a problem to be solved. Are these so-called rules, errors, and problems nothing more than expressions of subjective preference, so that classifications of pathology disappear in a fog of uncertainty?

In Chapter 6, we saw that Freud asked the question, How are we to judge that an entire society has become psychologically pathological? What convincing standard can we apply, since "normality in that society" cannot be used?

Relativism forces us to ask these basic questions. The challenges that it seems to pose are, however, only mirages, for relativism itself is a disorder of thought.

## RELATIVISM AS A THOUGHT DISORDER

In the last chapter, I introduced an approach that seeks to identify and to treat conceptual pathology, dysfunctions in our thinking that often lead normal, average people to feel aggressive and to engage in destructive behavior. From this perspective, I discussed the human belief in transcendence, and argued that the idea of transcendence is referentially incoherent. Like the idea of transcendence, the idea of moral relativism is referentially incoherent. It involves what I have called projective misconstruction. Let us see why this is the case.

Moral relativism purports to be a coherent theory about human values. It asserts three things: that moral values are diverse among systems of belief; that from the standpoint of each belief-system, the values endorsed by its proponents are "right" or "true"; and, therefore, all moral values are dependent upon one's system of belief and can have no application beyond it. We note that, by itself, the first claim, which asserts diversity, does not on its own produce relativism; only when it is conjoined with the second claim does relativism begin to arise. In making these claims, moral relativism presupposes that the following specifically referential preconditions can be met: (1) we understand the idea of a frame of reference; (2) it is possible to refer to a plurality of morally incompatible reference frames; (3) it is possible to do this in a framework-independent manner; (4) the three previous conditions can be fulfilled in non-arbitrary ways, so that it is possible to refer meaningfully through a true and universal statement that embodies the relativist thesis. (1) and (2) are necessary in order for relativism to assert diversity; (3) is necessary in order for relativism to elevate the perception of moral diversity to the level of a framework-independent fact; and (4) caps these assumptions through the added implicit supposition that moral relativism is a true, non-arbitrary, non-relative account. From our brief discussion of epistemological pathology in the previous chapter, the reader will immediately see that conditions (3) and (4) set requirements that, in principle, cannot be fulfilled, for if relativism were true, conditions (3) and (4) could not be satisfied. As Edwards (1990:5) put this somewhat differently:

> The relativist...seems to require at least one statement of *universal* truth, this being the statement that truth is relative.... Making such general claims clearly involves the relativist in an inconsistency. The relativist thesis...is inconsistent with itself. It cannot both be the case that truth is relativised, and so restricted, to individuals or belief systems *and* that the relativist's own claim is one which is not so restricted and is true (a) for all individuals, or (b) for all belief systems. (See also Williams 1972:22-6)

Hence, moral relativism is untenable. It self-destructs. It is untenable because it pulls the carpet out from under its own feet. That is to say it is self-referentially inconsistent, and for this reason cannot make sense. It is a typical projective misconstruction, a self-sabotaging delusional belief of misidentification. It is another instance of reflexive pathology—on a cognitive level not unlike autoimmune disease on an organic level. Conditions (3) and (4) undergird the Denial of Unique Justification Thesis, which in its attempt to claim that there are no standards that are uniquely and absolutely justified, makes precisely a claim that purports to be uniquely and absolutely justified. Relativism is a disorder of thinking. As we shall see, it has consequences that are seldom noticed.

## THE HUMAN EVIL OF RELATIVISM

> [T]he revulsion against relativism is to be traced to the impact of Nazism which made ethical relativism emotionally untenable. The question had to be faced whether it could really be the case that when Nazis say it is good and fitting to torture Jews and we say it is abominable the difference is one of personal taste only. – Morris Ginsberg quoted in Farrell (1994:121-2)

The epistemological inconsistency that lies at the core of moral relativism is hardly ever noticed, and when inconsistency of this general kind is made conscious, as in clinical cases of delusional misidentification, the delusional beliefs are safely walled off from reflective evaluation even when people have some abilities of critical reflection. Moral relativism leads directly, on both an emotional and a theoretical level, to a set of concrete attitudes that need to be identified. It is important to see how a disorder of thought like moral relativism can support and strengthen a cluster of emotionally intense and often destructive attitudes.

Moral relativism is hardly an innocuous point of view. Eric Hobsbawm has argued that moral relativism opens the way for any crime, even genocide. (See Nussbaum 1999:35-6.) And yet, at the same time, we recognize that moral relativism has become a common currency of human diplomacy through its advocacy of a policy of mutual, respectful acceptance. Moral relativism contributes to the following attitudes, most of which are widely believed to be benign and praiseworthy: tolerance, respect, forgiveness, abstention from judgment, complicity, conformity, obedience, humility, and even hope. Moral relativism leads directly to *tolerance* and *respect*, since these attitudes toward conflicting points of view are among its basic suppositions. It leads to *forgiveness*, since the relativist grants to others the freedom to act in accordance with their beliefs, and does not hold others to his own moral standards. Moral relativism furthermore encourages in people *restraint from passing moral judgment*, since for the relativist to pass moral judgment is to apply one's own values "inappropriately" to the belief-system of another. Moral relativism encourages *complicity*, since the relativist is convinced that he should respect and tolerate the moral values of others, so he may feel an attraction to adopt them. This respect and tolerance make him an easy target of persuasion, and an easy pawn to demands of *conformity* and *obedience*. Moral relativism furthermore promotes the *humility* that comes from tolerance, forgiveness, restraint of judgment, complicity, and conformity. And, finally, moral relativism encourages delusional *hope* that, despite moral incompatibilities, people can live peacefully with one another—hope, that is to say, that flies in the face of the facts about human psychology and our cognitive constitution that this book has been about. We shall have further observations to make about hope in the next chapter.

More than anything else, this set of attitudes is conducive to passivity, patience, and credulity, which prevent people from taking an active stand against human malignity. This is not to say that tolerance, forgiveness, judgment abstention, complicity, conformity, and related attitudes would not exist were it not for moral relativism, but the latter clearly contributes to human pathology, especially in an egalitarian social climate that approves of relativism. A test of the pathological nature of relativism is to ask whether one would want one's physician to have these attitudes toward one's own organic disease. Would you want your doctor to tolerate pathology, accept your disease without opposing it, abstain from judgment whether it should be fought? Surely not, for the medical equivalents of tolerating a pathology, respecting and forgiving the pathogen, etc., are incompatible with the mission of any physician, which is to identify, prevent, and treat that which causes harm. Some of the attitudes I have called attention to can be benign and even desirable, but not in the context of pathology.

## MORALITY BEYOND MORAL RELATIVISM

In matters of definition there is no right or wrong.... – Hardin (1982:138)

Moral theory and theory of value have suffered from confusion regarding the types of proof and evidence that can justify value judgments. In a book about human evil, we need to give this issue some attention. In other contexts in this study, I have referred to the diverse life-worlds of human beings and other living creatures. Phenomenology has sought to describe life-worlds as constituting multiple and diverse realities. William James (1890) described a variety of such "worlds": the world of the senses, the world of scientific objects, that of myths and supernatural beliefs, etc. Similarly, Alfred Schutz (1945) wrote of "multiple realities." Today, in epistemology we still refer to "worlds," but also now to "categorial frameworks" (Körner 1970), "conceptual schemes" (Strawson 1959), and "belief systems" (Edwards 1990). In this work, I also use the language of "frames of reference." When we have moral experience in view, we can sometimes identify what I would call morally and logically primitive propositions, beliefs, or sensibilities, which serve as the fundamental presuppositions of an individual's or a group's morality. From the standpoint of the "world" or "frame of reference" of that person or group, these logically primitive propositions, beliefs, or sensibilities that concern morality are self-justifying or self-validating. They are, from the standpoint of that person or group, not tentative or provisional, but they rather possess an experienced character that is beyond relativism. In Chapter 2, we saw this position expressed by disease theorist Reznek (1987), who, we will recall, wrote:

> When I judge that Hitler is an evil man, I am making a value-judgment. However, I do not commit myself to the view that Hitler is an evil-man-for-me, but not an evil-man-for-the-Nazis. This would be to judge that I am both against Hitler and for him in the same breath, and this is incoherent. Once I have judged that Hitler is an evil man, I judge that those who disagree are wrong, and set myself against them. So if I accept that disease judgments are normative, this does not mean that I have to accept that any condition is only a disease-for-me. (211)

How does Reznek defend such assertions without incurring relativism? He does not provide an explicit justification. But it is nonetheless there, implicit in his frame of reference: The value judgment he made about Hitler is a product of the logically primitive beliefs that must be granted in order for his normative outlook to be such as it is. These fundamental beliefs cannot be denied without denying the moral point of view which *defines* Reznek's perspective. The word 'defines' is important here. As Garrett Hardin observed, there is no "right" or "wrong" in matters of definition. Here, the definition that is at issue concerns how an individual experiences reality in terms of a set of values. Those values define his reference frame; they are not themselves "right" or "wrong," but they instead determine what is "right" and "wrong" from that standpoint. In a similar way, standards of rationality are not themselves "rational" or "irrational"; they only determine what is meant by rationality. Perhaps the following analogy will make this clearer: Definitions that permit us to identify the various colors are not themselves colored; they simply act as standards.

The justification of an individual's value judgments, the proof and evidence that will justify them, requires appeal to that person's basic moral commitments. When we have identified the commitments that are truly basic—those, that is, that are logically primitive in the sense in view here—we have the proof and evidence required for moral justification. The matter is—in great measure but, as we shall see, not all— internal to the moral framework under consideration.

Does this account involve moral relativism? Reznek claims it does not but he did not elaborate. However, it is not difficult to supply the answer. Here is the justification that any disease or moral theorist can offer, if pressed, and if he or she is intellectually honest: We must, first of all, accept that moral relativism is incoherent. Second, we recognize that people differ in their moral values; hence, we recognize moral diversity. Third, we recognize that some moral values are logically primitive in a certain sense: They comprise values that cannot, from the standpoint of a given individual's moral reference frame, be denied without referential inconsistency that would destroy his sense of moral identity. And, fourth, it must be possible to situate those fundamental values in a comparative reference frame, and then to apply a standard of comparison. Let me try to make this difficult point clear, for more is involved than the simple recognition of moral diversity and the self-validating nature of moral frameworks.

Later in his life, Einstein regretted that he called his theory "relativity theory" instead of naming it *"Invariantentheorie."* (Nozick 2001:78) Although special and general relativity are theories that express physical laws in a framework-relative manner, those laws are not "relative" in the sense of being provisional or tentative; they are rather "invariants" that take framework-relativity specifically into account. This is not conceptual double-talk, for a real and important distinction is involved: Relativism, if it were tenable, would undermine the truth of any universal assertion. A *relativistic theory*, on the contrary, permits universal assertions about framework-relativity. Elsewhere (Bartlett 1975b, 1976), I have proposed a *metalogic of reference*, which is a general relativistic theory concerning the framework-relativity of reference. The results of such a metalogic are not tentative or provisional in the sense of relativism; they are *invariants* that concern the conditions of possibility of reference.

Although this is a complex idea, my proposal here involves the acceptance of the relativity of divergent moral values to their respective reference frames, but without relativism. Instead, we see before us a gamut of often incompatible moral values, which are experienced by different individuals and their groups as logically primitive. If this is the case, how, can we claim, e.g., that the values held by the Nazi doctors were "morally wrong?"

This "ultimate moral question" often raised in discussions of relativism is, in the final analysis, a question of what set of values is "better" than others, where the word 'better' implies a value judgment. This way of thinking can be misleading, since the concept of "better" derives its meaning from a set of endorsed values. To apply the term 'better' to a set of values is, so to speak, to make a grammatical mistake on the level of thought, not of language; it is as though one asked what is the color of the physical definition that specifies the color red as radiation within a certain frequency range. In other words, the "ultimate moral question" is not a meaningful question to ask.

The only meaningful response that can be given to the *issue* of moral as opposed to immoral behavior is to refer to the *level of moral development* of the person who judges the behavior. This is a developmental and evolutionary matter, a matter of moral sensibility, and has been virtually ignored in discussion of morality.

I have in this work proposed an understanding of human evil and human morality in terms of a set of abilities and capacities that define *moral intelligence*. Like cognitive intelligence, moral intelligence comes in degrees. Diversity in cognitive skills is widely recognized as a fact about the world, which many would like to equalize, usually through education. Diversity in *moral abilities* is not similarly recognized, although most people do recognize distinctions among human beings, some of whose behavior is morally to be preferred—that is, by people of high moral development.

If we accept the view that moral differences among people are an expression of diversity in moral intelligence, we begin to perceive moral goodness, and its absence in human evil, in a framework-relative manner that is free of relativism. Just as mental maturity varies among human beings, so does *moral maturity*. Both forms of maturity, of individual or group development, can be measured objectively, psychometrically: that is to say, by means of standards of measurement that define a frame of reference which is not one of relativism. Such a frame of reference defines what we mean in a public, non-arbitrary way. It provides a basis for consensus of judgment among those who apply the relevant standards.

To a man with aesthetic sensibility, a thing is beautiful or it is not. To a man with mathematical intelligence, Gödel's limitative theorems are important. To a man with moral sensibility, a behavior is good or evil. —In other words, we cannot separate judgments of value (beautiful, important, good, etc.) from the framework that is necessary in order for such judgments to have the meaning they do.

A consequence of this *metatheoretical fact* is that judgments concerned with human evil cannot be made—*or be made intelligible*—independently of the normative frameworks that allow for them. If we are interested in comparative relations between these normative frameworks, we must look at what it means to possess *moral intelligence*. Among people whose level of moral development is consistently high, it is possible for them to reach objective consensus in the sense that their shared moral judgments are invariant relative to the frame of reference common to them. Here we reach a conclusion similar to a view discussed in Chapter 1, proposed by Clouser, Culver, and Gert (1997). In formulating their theory of disease, they referred to the existence of "universal agreement among people about the nature of...basic harms and about the undesirability, absent an adequate reason, of experiencing them." (184) In another work, Gert, Culver, Clouser, and Danner (1997:111) similarly affirmed: "We believe the relativity of maladies is analogous to the relativity of morality. We regard both maladies and morality as basically universal, because both involve those harms that all rational persons everywhere avoid unless they have an adequate reason not to." The "universal agreement" of which they spoke, regarding harms that "all rational persons everywhere avoid," is never justified. Its justification lies, I believe, in the account I have given here. The refutation of moral relativism and the account of morality beyond relativism that I have proposed are abstract, but the moral issues to which they lead are far from abstract. They are issues that relate, across the linkages between thought, emotion, and behavior, to the concrete impulses people have and the choices they make—whether to behave aggressively and destructively, or whether to behave compassionately.

## PREACHING TO THE ALREADY CONVERTED

A man can do what he wishes but he is not free to wish what he wants. – Schopenhauer quoted in Planck (1933:210)

In Schopenhauer's work (1965/1841) *On the Basis of Morality*, he offers in a few succinct lines his answer how the basis of morality is justified: "...isolated individuals of superior insight have felt and become aware of the truth." (187) He went on to write: "*Legality* can be enforced through motives, but not *morality*; we can remodel *what we do*, but not really *what we will to do*, to which alone moral worth attaches." (194) People of "moral worth," whose moral attitudes and behavior are exemplary, are, according to Schopenhauer, people whose conduct toward others, human or animal, is directed by compassion:

[H]ow is it possible for a suffering which is not *mine* and does not touch *me* to become just as directly a motive as only my own normally does, and to move me to action? As I have said, only by the fact that although it is given to me merely as something external, merely by means of external intuitive perception or knowledge, I nevertheless *feel it with him, feel it as my own*, and yet not *within me*, but *in another person*. (165)

People of this kind are rare: They are isolated and distinguished from the mass of humanity by what Schopenhauer called their "superior insight." In a similar way, we saw in earlier chapters that people who have the abilities of clinical diagnostic insight (Chapters 2 and 5) are also rare, as are those who can see the larger picture in the sense proposed by Lorenz when he spoke of "persons gifted in Gestalt perception" (Chapter 10).

Elitism of diagnostic ability or moral judgment is not politically popular today—none of the elitisms are. And yet there is an unavoidable elitism that must be accepted whenever we speak of special abilities and sensibilities of any kind, which are unequally distributed in the general population. Why should moral development or moral intelligence be any different? If the reader will think back over the many researchers whose work we have discussed, he or she will find that a recognition of the elitism of perception, sensitivity, insight, problem-solving skills, and moral sensibility runs through their observations and reflections. Persons who are highly developed in Schopenhauer's sense are, unfortunately, not run-of-the-mill, everyday people. And so in this sense much that this book has to offer falls into the category of preaching to the pulpit, to the already converted, espousing moral principles and sensibility to the already morally developed. This is an unfortunate but unavoidable obstacle to the recognition of human evil, and to our determination to identify, treat, and end the many pathologies to which it gives rise. We have no other intelligent choice but to leave the matter as it was expressed by genocide scholars Israel Charny and Chanan Rapaport (1982):

> Even when we understand that nearly all of us are available to be genociders, it is also true that some of us, to some extent, are not available to be genociders. In our still so-primitive history as a species, some fortunate people have reached a more advanced point in the evolution toward a respect for life. (211)

# CHAPTER 21

# REFLECTIONS

One of the most serious problems confronting psychology is that of connecting itself with life. – Lewis M. Terman (1975/1909), opening sentence

## LOOKING BACK

In this final chapter, I gather up the threads of our discussions, reiterate certain conclusions we have reached, and reflect on the rational grounds for believing that the human species can be changed in fundamental ways that will lessen and heal human evil. We shall bring our analysis of individual pathologies to an end, and will describe the larger picture that emerges from earlier chapters.

One of the tenets of my approach to the pathology of man has been to emphasize that recognition of pathology and value-neutrality cannot co-exist. Pathology as the study of disease—here in its specialized application to the pathology of the human species—is a framework-relative science in which values play a central role. A second tenet has been the belief that the most genuinely basic solutions to human evil are to be found in psychology, psychiatry, and the expansion of their subject-matter so as to include what I have called conceptual therapy. It is only through the eyes of these disciplines that we can study the human motivations and thought processes that lead to the pathologies of behavior and of thought that we have identified, and perhaps find ways to treat them.

It has been said that a conclusion is simply the place where you got tired of thinking. This has been a long study, to which I have devoted many years. I wished it to be as comprehensive as possible, but have, as one might expect, discovered that the subject-matter is greater than can be contained within a single volume. A two-volume work was proposed to the publisher, but it was believed that a one-volume work would stand the best change of reaching the greatest number of readers. As a result of this decision, as well as constraints upon the length of a single volume, there are pathologies of man which I have not had space to discuss. Among them I wish to mention, in no specific order, the general psychology of crime, relating specifically to the motivations and to the gratifications that can be derived from criminal activity; the psychology of bullying, particularly the child psychology of aggression and hatred turned against the child's peers; the psychology of punishment, torture, and execution; the psychology of rage as manifested by drivers, shoppers, students, travelers, employees, and others; the psychology of hate crimes; the psychology of religious hatred, cruelty, and violence; the psychology of aggression when it is reflexively directed against the self, as in self-mutilation, penance, and suicide; the psychology of sports, hunting, and trapping, in which violence contributes to human entertainment; and, of course, the psychology of violent entertainment itself. There are, to be sure, other pathologies, specific pathologies that have to do with domestic conflict; cruelty in the workplace; forms of persecution that we have not directly discussed, including prejudice against gender and sexual preference; and the list could go on. Despite these limitations, I have done my best to include in this study many of the major forms of human pathology, and must leave it to others who may be similarly motivated to continue this work.

Throughout this book, I have avoided reference to a fixed "human nature"; I have also refrained from favoring a premature solution in the absence of convincing empirical data to the inherited-acculturated conflict. Instead, since this study seeks to reach reliable observational generalities about human pathology, I have adopted the neutral language of "constitutional predispositions" (as proposed by Fish 1967:6) and "predisposing factors" (as suggested by Glad 1990:12), or simply "predisposing conditions." Despite differences among the many accounts of human evil discussed in this book, there is, nonetheless, fundamental agreement as to its makeup. This is not, I believe, a remarkable coincidence, but an expression of a solid understanding and concordance of clinical judgment concerning the phenomena of human evil. In the resulting view, I have emphasized widespread patterns of human *conduct* and *thinking*, and have not wished to link these patterns with an underlying hypothesized fixed nature. The many varieties of human pathology nonetheless point to psychological, existential, and conceptual satisfactions and gratifications that are derived from human evil, and we find that comparatively very few human beings are averse to such satisfactions and gratifications. We have found that there is a great deal about our past and present emotional and cognitive constitution that reinforces human pathology, and little that obstructs it. In this context, mankind's history is the gold standard of evidence of the species' cruelty and murderous constitutional predisposition. We have found that people would have to be very significantly different not to hate and kill one another, to terrorize and condemn one another in the name of their rigid belief-systems, to refrain from devastating the world's biodiversity, etc. A great deal about human psychology and our common cognitive structure would have to be different. So much so, that the changes, if ever realized, would produce a species hardly recognizable as what we now know to be human.

Hannah Arendt proposed the phrase "the banality of evil." She sought to show how the Nazi criminals were in many ways normal people. This is one side of the equation—that perpetrators of human evil are often psychologically normal people. The other side of the equation is what much of the present study has been about—that to be normal is to possess a psychological and cognitive constitution that is pathological. When the two sides of this equation are combined, we realize that normality and pathology go hand-in-hand. The universal pathology that is involved has been almost entirely neglected, and yet it is the most serious variety of pathology the world has known.

In reaching conclusions of this sort, I have often referred to "the psychologically normal individual," the statistician's everyman, who has almost invariably been used as a standard against which to measure pathology. The evidence brought together in this study, from a multitude of researchers who have worked in different disciplines—psychopathology, normal psychology, quantitative history, ethology, phenomenological psychiatry, ecology, and cognitive science—shows us that it is necessary to question the unquestioned opposition of normality to pathology, and indeed to recognize the existence of universal pathologies that afflict the psychologically normal individual and group, usually in ways not recognized. From this point of view, normality *is* an instance of pathology; "normal behavior" and "normal thinking" are often pathogenic; and "normal people" are afflicted by dysfunctional attitudes, thought processes, patterns of emotion, and conduct. The *pathology of normality* has been neglected and even shunned. When it is recognized, we see that to be normal is to have many of the predisposing conditions that bring about human evil.

In the literature, we find many attempts to define the uniquely determining characteristics of psychological normality. As in any attempt to pin down a core meaning for a term that embraces a broad spectrum of human psychology, there has been little success in discovering factors that define "psychological normality." Out of the resulting extensive literature, only a few researchers have thought to head in the direction I have taken in this study: rather than seeking to define psychological normality, instead to identify certain psychological characteristics possessed by the majority of people, attributes which are, in various ways, pathological. Among those who have been inclined in this direction are Eissler (1960), Erickson (1968), and Offer (1974/1966). To see normality as an instance of pathology is to make a very considerable, and for some, a controversial step beyond Hannah Arendt's assertion of the banality of evil. Such a step takes us in the direction of affirming the reverse: *the human evil of normality*. A moment's reflection shows that the two affirmations are significantly different in denotation. "The human evil of normality" has a much greater range of application.

## THIS STUDY'S CONCLUSIONS

I do not propose to reiterate the results of previous chapters, but rather to place them in relief and comment on them. This study has sought to define and to understand human evil in terms of what Husserl would have called the summation of the many perspective variations of human pathology portrayed by a multitude of voices. The perspectives offered by many voices best reveal, I believe, the nature and variety of predisposing conditions that bring about human evil. In the resulting view, human evil is a multifactorial pathology.

"Why is there human evil?" is a question that is not difficult to answer now. The answer is compound, but not especially complex. There are multiple factors that contribute to the pathology of man. Each is not hard to understand. Nor are the reasons complex why human beings evade knowledge of their own pathology, for there are important needs and gratifications at stake. The pathology of man is easily observed and easily understood—provided, that is, that one is not shackled by homocentric aversion to and denial of our species' worst faults.

In the theory of disease, the identification of a malfunction is a matter of what function one has in view. Once a certain function is recognized, malfunctions become identifiable. Hence, it can only make sense to speak of malfunctions, disorders, or pathologies relative to a set of purposes. The approach I have taken in this book is essentially functional: In attempting to understand human evil, I have sought to identify the many ways in which it satisfies human needs and interests. Human evil performs definite functions for man. Unfortunately, in the process, as we well know, human pathology is highly destructive. It is in particular destructive of the values that are shared by people who have reached an equally high level of moral development. The frame of reference that such individuals share is essentially normative; it enables them to identify dysfunctions relative to their common reference frame; and allows them to make judgments that are immune to relativism.

Human evil, from this standpoint, possesses many of the characteristics associated with pathology: it has a *high prevalence* (the proportion of a population that has contracted a pathology: see Chapter 4) and *high incidence* (the rate at which new occurrences of the pathology develop); it is, as we have seen, *infectious* and *chronic*; it often leads to crises of *epidemic* proportions; it is usually *lanthanic* or latent (escaping detection for long periods). And, finally, human evil most often is made up of pathologies for which *no known effective treatment is available.* When this is the case, as we noted earlier (Chapter 4), the best that can be done is to know the nature and prognosis of the pathology, as we have sought to do in this volume.

The pathology of man affects ordinary people, who are obedient, responsive to herd emotional infection, who reproduce prolifically, and whose emotional constitution and conceptual structure are highly resistant to change and in many ways promote aggression and destruction. The behavior and attitudes of the majority toward other species are those of a pathogen, a pathogen which is in various ways also auto-pathological. Most people are characterized by many of the forms of pathology studied in this volume; such pathology affects normal humanity, and is the source of human evil. In relation to this majority, there is a very small minority of individuals who are morally intelligent, capable of independent judgment, and compassionate. But in relation to ordinary humanity, *the most inhumane act is essentially a human act.* It is, as we have seen, very often the act of normal, well-adjusted, well-intentioned, good neighbors, fellow citizens, ordinary people who invest themselves in projective beliefs, people who are emotionally gratified by belonging to their group and propounding its ideology, and who will obey their group's commandments and perpetrate the world's worst horrors in the name of common decency and human commitment to the highest goals.

In reaching these conclusions, this study has been based on certain biases or prejudices, which now need to be made explicit. One is the prejudice that is involved in all clinical judgments: the hostile bias against disease. It is what Carl Binger had in mind when he said we are prejudiced against disease

> ...in the same way that Pasteur was prejudiced against rabies; Koch against tuberculosis; Walter Reed against yellow fever; or Harvey Cushing against brain tumors. Each one of these scientists spent his genius, or his courage, or both, to attack an evil. The evil was a disease. Their method of attack was the cool and careful method of science. But they had formed a prejudgment which might be stated this way: "It is better for man to inherit the earth than it is for rabid dogs or tubercle bacilli or mosquitoes." (Ackerman & Johoda 1950:xi)

Similarly, Carl Sagan (1980:330) wrote: "Microbiologists and physicians study diseases mainly to cure people. Rarely are they rooting for the pathogen." The difference, of course, is that in the present volume we have seen how the human species has become a powerful pathogen, and yet our clinical prejudice against pathology remains in force.

The second bias of this study is the authority it recognizes in expert clinical judgment. As we have seen in previous chapters, clinical judgment involves a set of skills that are possessed only by the few. We are compelled to acknowledge the elitism of unequally distributed abilities. In particular, the conclusions of this study rest on the competence of that form of diagnostic judgment that is relied upon when new diseases are identified. This reliance on the authority of competent diagnosis is unavoidable and needs to be acknowledged. The fact that this study affirms the value of such authority will doubtless be a problem for some readers.

## BLINDERS AND RECALCITRANCE

We do not see what we prefer not to, and do not see that we do not see. – Goleman (1985:234)

Among the main elements that contribute to human evil are blindness to it and the stubborn unwillingness to see it when it is pointed out. Several characteristics play a role in obstructing consciousness of human evil. They include simple *ignorance*, or the lack of relevant information; *stupidity*, which as we saw in an earlier chapter comprises a human pathology in its own right, and which often involves the disregard or misuse of information by individuals and groups who lack intellectual or moral intelligence; *naïveté* when confronted by evidence, the response to which is marked by a lack of critical judgment; *dissimulation*, whereby relevant data are rejected and more comforting or satisfying illusions are substituted; and *commitment to an exclusionary belief system*. The ability of these five human propensities to block awareness is greatly increased by *psychological* and *epistemological projection*, which persuade people that their negative feelings, their dissatisfactions and resentments, and the objects of their beliefs have the status of externalized and autonomous realities. When all seven of these factors collaborate, blindness to human evil is assured. In such an emotionally laden and cognitively distorted context, human beings are convinced only by views they are already prepared to accept. There is then a dominating tendency "to look at things without fully perceiving them, to divert one's attention from the unpleasant to the pleasant, to suspend the process of rational inference in mid-air, and to distort one's insights to avert anxiety." (Gilbert 1950:275) This is the cry Williams James' observed (cf. Chapter 9 in the present study): "Let me not think of that! Don't speak to me of that!" H. L. Mencken (1918:123) saw this phenomenon in a somewhat different way: "The average man does not get pleasure out of an idea because he thinks it is true; he thinks it is true because he gets pleasure out of it." Psychologist Kent Bach (1994) examined ways in which human attention is constrained by the emotional investments of people, so that they become incapable of acknowledging certain realities. He found that "exclusionary categories" straightjacket what people are able to become aware of.

As a result of these mental or attentional limitations, the existence and nature of human evil go unnoticed: They pose issues contrary to the established mindset, conflicting with old neural networks and therefore blocked from consciousness. As Hardin (1982:239) expressed this, "each truth that is contrary to a well-established system [of belief] seems to have a very short half-life; such truth has to be discovered over and over again, each new statement of it being speedily transmuted into innocuous intellectual isotopes by the internal forces of Freudian denial."

The study of pathology, in particular, has been affected by this kind of denial, for it is merely a symptom of homocentric blindness to regard only non-human life forms as disease entities, and to exempt the human species from inclusion in the category of pathogens. What is at issue is a universal aversion to consciousness of human evil, along with an aversion to negativism and pessimism, to whatever is contrary to hope and optimism. But hope, too, is part of human evil, as we shall see.

## THE PATHOLOGY OF HOPE

[T]he terms 'optimism' and 'pessimism' refer to the state of one's digestion, and have nothing whatever to do with truth. – May (1982:20)

There is a deeply-embedded prejudice against studies that do not end in optimism and a glimmer of hope. As H. L. Mencken (1919:89) accurately observed: "The way to please is to proclaim in a confident manner, not what is true, but what is merely comforting." Or as Garrett Hardin (1982:196) put it most succinctly: "only optimism sells." Miller (1986:251) remarked in his study of the obedience experiments: "books that speak more glowingly regarding human nature tend to receive less scathing reviews...." This is not only true of books, but of political elections, the barometers of popularity. For example, between 1900 and 1984, out of 22 U.S. presidential elections, candidates who voiced pessimistic views lost 18 times. "It seems that voters find depressive presidential candidates repulsive. They favor aspirants with more optimistic messages, leaders who believe they can take charge and solve all problems. As Napoleon advised, a politician must be 'a dealer in hope'." (Simonton 1994:253) Another researcher remarked:

> It is safe to assume that the ultimate reaction of the public to any persistently destructive criticism will be one of rather cold distaste. Only if the disagreeable content has been well sugared...may a reasonable degree of assimilation be anticipated.... [U]nless the destructive critic is extremely tactful, he is liable to be treated as a malefactor and to have his platform turned into a pillory.... Even in modern medicine there is a faint suggestion of stigma about the Research Fellow who concentrates on diagnosis...to the exclusion of therapeutic concern. As a rule the diagnostician is forced willy-nilly to turn apothecary. (Glover 1933:73-4)

The implications of such reflections for the present study are clear. Optimism is likable and popular, but it has nothing whatever to do with the study of pathology, the investigation of disease, of the malfunction of organisms and environments. In fact, as we have noted, optimism not only can serve as a blinder, but when we have the human species in view, it can cause us to "fall victim to faith in humanity." This is one of the unsuspected sources of human evil and of our resulting lack of preparation to oppose it. Alexander Donat (1965:103) admitted: "We fell victim to our faith in mankind, our belief that humanity had set limits to the degradation and persecution of one's fellow man." The Holocaust then came to pass.

Unfortunately, people are not shocked out of moral apathy by an infusion of hope. Optimism does not effect change. The obstacles that would need to be overcome in order to lessen human evil are immense. And one of the main obstacles is hope itself.

As we have seen, a principal barrier in overcoming human evil is that the majority of people tolerate it, accepting our many human pathologies, and even approving of them. Until human pathology is recognized for what it is, this state of affairs will remain as it is. For the Greeks, hope was the worst of the evils. As Camus (1961:113) wrote: "From Pandora's box, where all the ills of humanity swarmed, the Greeks drew out hope after all the others as the most dreadful of all.... For contrary to the general belief, hope equals resignation. And to live is not to resign oneself." Foremost among the emotions that hope supports is the feeling of consolation. Pandora discovered evil, and in the process, the evil of hope's false promise. For the Greeks, since fate could not be changed, hope was an illusion, "man's curse," according to Euripides. Menninger, Mayman, and Pruser (1967/1963:381) quoted from Anouilh's adaptation of Sophocles' *Antigone*, where the heroine cries out: "We are of the tribe that asks questions, and we ask them to the bitter end—until no tiniest chance of hope remains to be strangled by our hands. We are of the tribe that hates your filthy hope, your docile, female hope; hope, your whore...." Menninger *et al.* go on to quote Cowley, Shelley, and Nietzsche, all of whom were critical of hope:

"Hope—fortune's cheating lottery, where for one prize a hundred blanks there be." – Cowley

"Worse than despair, worse than the bitterness of death, is hope." – Shelley

"Hope is the worst of all evils, for it prolongs the torment of man." – Nietzsche

Seen from this perspective, hope is synonymous with delusional thinking, and it is this association that brings hope within the scope of pathology. A seemingly unobjectionable positive outlook frequently conceals what we do not wish to see. Pathology can remain latent, lanthanic, precisely because of hope. Hope, and hope's sisters, faith and optimism, have the ability to blind us to our shortcomings so that we become unable to identify and treat our own pathology. It therefore makes sense to regard this trio as a kind of second-order pathology in its own right. They reflexively perpetuate acceptance or ignorance of the fundamental human evils to which they are ironically opposed. *Malignant hope* camouflages human evil under a curtain of denial and delusional utopian dreams. The denial of human evil through hope, faith, and optimism is genuinely delusional. The researchers whose work we have discussed in this volume have sought to see reality clearly, undistorted by delusional thinking. In their respective ways, they have advocated a study of human pathology unimpeded by wishful thinking, for only then do we apprehend reality as it is.

*The only thing that must happen for evil to triumph is for human beings to be convinced they are good.* The only optimism relevant to the study of pathology is the belief that pathology is a condition that can sometimes be reversed through treatment. But hope in the face of contrary rational expectations is unscientific and counter-productive. When effective treatment of a pathology does not as yet exist, as is the case with most of the varieties of human evil studied in this volume, it is important to have *the courage not to rely upon hope*, but to confront reality with open eyes. In the face of the deplorable, the despicable, one does not hope, but rather *condemns* and *rejects*. If we are sufficiently free to choose an intelligent attitude toward human evil, we must choose between two alternatives, which I'll call Bartlett's Wager: (1) to regard the human species in an essentially hopeful light, denying reality and dismissing obstacles that stand in the way of human betterment, or (2) to judge that the human species is unlikely to develop moral intelligence through socially acceptable means, and that, as a result, the human pattern of destructiveness, aggression, cruelty, and lack of compassion can be expected to continue.

Of the two alternatives, ironically the one that is the more positive is the second, for there the obstacles are self-consciously apprehended and the consequences that follow from the human constitution as it now is are clear and frightening—clear and frightening enough, perhaps, to motivate a relatively small number of men and women to overcome their ostrich attitudes, to endorse the attitudes of condemnation and rejection needed to oppose human evil, and to begin to take the difficult steps necessary for human improvement. In this sense, pessimism can be constructive. It sets for us the challenge posed by a clear perception of reality. William James advanced the pragmatic argument "that when confronted with two hypotheses about the nature of reality, neither of which can be proven, we must act upon that hypothesis which is most likely to enhance life." (Rubenstein 1966:85) In the framework of the present study, in the context of our recognition of the deeply rooted human needs and interests served by human evil, Bartlett's Wager suggests that it is ultimately more beneficial to see human evil for what it is than to engage in delusional distortion. Where pessimism sets a challenge to be overcome, hope encourages passivity. Holocaust scholar Richard L. Rubenstein came to feel: "I have been unable...to accept...optimism. I believe that the tragic vision is both more realistic as an account of the human predicament and more consistent with human dignity and maturity." (82) As William of Orange courageously uttered in the face of overwhelming odds: "It is not at all necessary to hope in order to endeavor, nor to succeed in order to persevere." (Rüstov 1980:xxix)

## THE PATHOLOGY OF FORGIVENESS

There can be no forgiveness; there can be no dampening of our outrage and protest against the killing of men. My desire is to understand how these terrible events come to be and what we might do to stop them, not to forgive. – Charny & Rapaport (1982:34)

Like hope in the face of human evil, forgiveness is similarly pathological. If the thesis of this book is true, we are fully justified in judging human evil to be a true pathology. Now, no one "forgives" another for an illness. It would be a strange thing to say "I forgive the illness with which you are afflicted." Within the covers of this book, the sickness I have tried to identify and shed light upon is one that afflicts the average person. There are exceptional individuals who rise above human evil by virtue of their moral intelligence, but for the great majority of children and adults, human evil is an irrefutable and constant fact. Should we "forgive" our species for its destructive, cruel, and vicious pathology? Should we instead "blame" it? Or neither?

Pathologists are most keenly motivated to treat a disease when they see firsthand the suffering and death it causes, when they are touched to the quick, feel anger toward the enemy, and dedicate themselves to fighting the pathology until it is subdued or eradicated.

There has never before been an approach to pathology that has focused on the human species as a global pathogen. Such an approach would take seriously the need to curtail very significantly the proliferation of the pathogen, and to undertake, by whatever measures are effective and socially and politically expedient, to change the basic psychological and cognitive constitution of the race.

Forgiveness does not motivate one to undertake this task. Anger perhaps does, when it is expressed in the judgment, "In the name of humanity, enough is enough!" Men and women do not need to intend evil in order to achieve it. Yet they are responsible for their actions as long as they are able to perceive a connection between their acts and their consequences. As Staub (1989:xiv) expressed this: "to understand is not necessarily to forgive. In fact, understanding can increase our awareness of the culpability of perpetrators of great evil because we can see them as human beings, not as beasts without moral capacity."

When violinist Isaac Stern visited Germany in 1999, having boycotting that country for many years after the Holocaust, he stated flatly, "I forgive nothing." Forgiveness of human evil is like hope in the face of evil: Forgiveness serves to erase and to deny that which we must remember if we are to learn from our past. Like hope, forgiveness is a second-order pathology, which contributes to the perpetuation of human evil rather than to its abatement.

## THE PURPOSE OF THIS BOOK

As the saying goes, may God preserve us from all that we can get accustomed to. – Isaac Bashevis Singer (1982:134)

Quincy Wright (1935:72) justified his study of war and its intractability by saying:

A man might wear out many pickaxes, shovels, horses and tractors in an effort to remove a rock which obstructed his view of a landscape and the more stable the rock's equilibrium the more he will waste himself in the effort. Once he realizes that the rock is but the peak of a buried mountain, that its equilibrium is so stable as to defy all his puny efforts, he will abandon the hopeless task and build an observatory on top of the rock from which he finds the view better than ever.

In this book I have sought to describe the dark and often willfully ignored side of human reality. I have said little about how human reality *should* be. It is enough for one book if what *is* has been made a little clearer. There are countless other books that claim to tell us what should—instead—be, but is not. Othello's purpose, he said, was "for the satisfaction of my thought." For many, this is enough, and if not, it is enough to build an observatory through whose lens others can see more clearly.

The diagnostic use of the phrase 'human evil', as recommended in this work, will very likely not catch on in accepted nosologies of disease. There are three main reasons for this: First, as this book has shown, human evil is a many-sided phenomenon: There are numerous human behaviors and patterns of thinking that express or embody human evil, so many that the pathologist of man is overloaded with pathologies and sub-pathologies, and sees the human species as both a pathogen and a victim of its own pathogenicity. But the logic of this reality is complex and does not fit the intellectually convenient and theoretically simple understanding of standard pathogens. Second, pathologists have sought to skirt moral issues, however hypocritically. The pride in science as a value-free enterprise dies hard. Third, the temperament, courage, and intellectual freedom required if the pathology of human evil is to be seen for what it is are qualities of person that are comparatively rare.

A label is only useful if it changes our perception of a phenomenon. The phenomenon of man includes the pathology of man. Classifying many human attitudes and types of behavior as pathologies explains much of human history retrodictively, and it allows us to anticipate, to predict, mankind's likely future. Identifying human evil as genuinely pathological serves as an explanation, that is, "as a statement which makes something unexpected appear expected." (Rapoport 1960:32) Indeed, given our understanding of human evil, it would be surprising if mankind's bloody history were other than it is. And we should be surprised if his future is not bloodier.

One of the principal values of science is prediction. In the case of human pathology, it is no different. As long as human psychological and cognitive conditions remain the same, a continuation of human evil is predictable with as much assurance as any scientific statement that brings together multiple variables in a world that is characterized by fuzzy boundaries and nonlinear processes. The effort by man to understand his own evil is one of the few ways that raises him from the chaos of uncontrolled and unreflective behavior to a level of consciousness of his own tragedy.

The famous mathematician David Hilbert once commented:

> ...whenever in our mathematical investigations we encounter a problem or conjecture a theorem, our drive for knowledge is satisfied only when we either attain a complete solution of the problem and a rigorous proof of the theorem, or, see clearly the reason for the impossibility of success and, consequently, the necessity of failure. (Wang 1987:172)

Our study of human pathology leads us to a group of *limitative results* that support a set of rational expectations. The facts we have identified about the pathogenic emotional and conceptual constitution of human beings, at this stage in the history of the species, make it relatively easy to anticipate the immediate human future, in which the psychology and epistemology of human evil will unavoidably play major roles. The roles they will play are *limitative*, that is, they make evident to us the psychological and cognitive *impossibility* of fundamental and meaningful change as long as human beings retain their present emotional and cognitive constitution. This is not a statement of pessimism, but an empirically based prediction, subject to the same kinds of disconfirmation as are other empirical claims.

We recall the main objectives of clinical diagnosis (Chapter 5): (1) to detect the occurrence of harm, (2) to group previously unrelated symptoms into constellations, connecting these with existing conditions, and (3) to situate the identified pathologies within a classification of diseases that enables us to understand them better and to suggest possible treatment. I have argued that our existing classification system in terms of which we understand pathology is inadequate because it does not take into account the existence of universal pathologies that affect statistically average individuals. We have come to recognize that many patterns of human behavior and thought are self-destructive and destructive to others, and that it is appropriate to group them together as pathological. Having done this, if we come to believe that the outlook for man is grim, "if there is no solace in the fruits of our research, there is at least some consolation in the research itself.... The effort to understand the universe is one of the very few things that lifts human life a little above the level of farce and gives it some of the grace of tragedy." (Weinberg 1977:154-5) Furthermore, it is, as Sorokin (1963:296) asserted, "the main duty of a scholar to tell the truth as he sees it, regardless of its pleasant or painful character."

If this study is successful, it by virtue of seeing things in a new way. We have come to recognize the pathological in the normal, not just Arendt's normal in the pathological.

## RESISTANCE TO THIS STUDY'S CONCLUSIONS

Man simply cannot accept human limitations as inevitable in the scheme of things. – Becker (1975:165)

This book gives a warning which, if the observations it is based upon are true, is guaranteed to be ignored or rejected. If the clinical judgments of the psychologists and psychiatrists we have discussed are correct, if the author's thesis concerning human conceptual pathology is right, then human evil in its many affective and conceptual forms will predictably stand in the way of our species' recognition of the facts this book has focused upon. Human aversion to unpleasant self-knowledge; denial; individual and group narcissism and species-wide homocentrism; the enjoyment of violence; the adrenalin rush of killing; the sense of personal empowerment of focused hatred; a steadfast and self-chosen blindness to humanity's reproductive proliferation; its self-centered avarice for land and natural resources; humanity's selfishness in its careless destruction of the world's biodiversity; the insistence of men, women, and children upon the superiority of their preferred groups and their nations and their political and religious ideologies; man's dedication to the creation, exaggeration, and strengthening of group differences; mankind's single-minded appetite only for the hopeful and the consoling; the universality of patterns of thought and a vocabulary of ideas that are self-defeating, self-undermining, and meaningless; a pronounced rigid commitment to all of these affective and cognitive habits; antagonism toward attempts to question them and to break free from the old constraints; a primitive mass level of moral development coupled with a pathological form and degree of stupidity—all of these things, which in a multitude of intertwined ways constitute the pathology of man, persuade him to turn from the realities this book has sought to portray, to raise the platitudinous objections of the injured innocent, or to nitpick a path that is more comforting and less offensive to his pride. The pathology of man—from its earliest cries of infantile narcissism to its dying satisfied sigh in the accomplishment of mass killing—is imbued with tragedy. It is the tragedy of a species that has become a pathogen to itself and to other forms of life that share this planet, but a species able to become conscious of its own dysfunctions, yet which, because its members are so amply rewarded by those very dysfunctions, ignores and denies them, and so sustains the tragic unfolding of its pathologically destructive existence.

As with any new idea, there will be resistance to the acceptance of this study, or—what most effectively stops us from hearing that which we do not want to hear—it will simply be ignored. In the present case, I believe the resistance and the covering of ears will be very considerable, since these responses themselves form part of the pathology this book has sought to study. The warning that this book expresses is what Gott (2001:235) has called a double warning, "for it cautions that the warning itself will likely not be heeded." The results of this study are psychologically and conceptually limitative, that is, we see that no meaningful changes are possible as long as human beings remain as they are, and that, given reality as it is, there do not exist plausible, appropriate, and promising methods to change the human psychological and cognitive constitution.

No book can change mankind. This study of human evil does not seek to comfort by offering false, hopeful consolation. "My courage fails me...at the thought of rising up as a prophet before my fellow-men, and I bow to their reproach that I have no consolation to offer them; for at bottom this is what they all demand...." (Freud 1952/1930:802) In another work, Freud continued this reflection on his life's work: "No doubt I might be asked here what is the point of writing these things if I am certain that they will be ineffective." (Freud 1961/1927:45) —Why, then, would one write and publish a book whose goals it is impossible to reach? This was Freud's answer: "[I]nfantilism is destined to be surmounted. Men cannot remain children for ever; they must in the end go out into 'hostile life'. We may call this *education to reality*. Need I confess to you that the sole purpose of my book is to point out the necessity for this forward step?" (63)

French physiologist Charles Richet, whose work we discussed earlier (Chapter 18), also realized he was beating his head against a wall in his wish to help mankind progress beyond stupidity. He confessed that he could not "bring about the ideal reform of my dreams," for "[m]en, with their passions, their self interest, their follies, would very soon have reduced my whole conception to dust. It would only be one more worthless book.... I am showing, or rather trying to show, the vacuity of things as they are, without even believing that any tangible good will come of it." (Richet c. 1925/1919:47) Similarly, Crawshay-Williams (1947:199), in concluding his study of human irrationality, wrote: "Whether or not I have made out a reasonable case for the views expressed in this book, I leave the reader to judge, confident that—if I am right—his opinions will probably remain unchanged whatever anyone says."

Such a conclusion is no doubt a letdown to many a reader, but I am sure that he or she can see that it takes intellectual honesty and moral courage to face, and to admit that one faces, a bleak ending. What we have come to know about the reality of human evil is not encouraging. Ervin Staub, after a life's work dedicated to understanding the psychology of genocide, admitted in his retrospective collection of papers: "I have had a very strong need to make a difference in the world, to improve the world. But the world is not visibly improving." (Staub 2003:44) There are, as we have seen, good reasons for this state of affairs. Having studied the phenomenon of human evil in detail, we see that it has a definite psychological and cognitive inevitability about it. To seek to change our cruel and destructive disposition involves contending with what stand before us as insurmountable and intractable odds.

There are few disciplines that seek to change the way people define their realities. Psychotherapy and psychiatry are, more than any other disciplines, dedicated to this effort. Religion has sought to do this, philosophy sometimes makes an indirect effort at it, and politics inculcates a definition of reality but does not usually seek explicitly for ways to change people from within. Psychology and psychiatry are today the main approaches that seek to bring about inner change that affects a person's definition of reality, his beliefs, expectations, the interpretive fabric of his life.

It is generally thought that there are four non-coercive ways to change the attitudes and behavior of those who are able to listen: through argument, through psychiatric treatment, through change of social, political, and economic conditions, and finally through condemnation. If the contentions of this study are correct, argument can only succeed to the extent that one's audience already is in fundamental agreement with the values one advocates. Psychiatric treatment, at least at present, is rendered ineffectual for large populations because of its need to treat the individual on an individualized basis. The third alternative has challenged social reformers throughout history. What it seeks to undertake is, unfortunately, most frequently undermined from within by the very dysfunctional ways of behaving and thinking that social reform attempts to change. We do not find rational grounds for hope here.

Hope, we have noted, is irrelevant, for meaningful change will not come from basking in the warm glow of human optimism. It is possible, if positive change comes at all, that some change might come from public condemnation of human evil: of its underlying attitudes, its self-centeredness, the human enjoyment of violence, the gratifications of hatred, the species' overweening desecration of the world's ecology, and, above all, mankind's obsession with having babies, the hubris in promoting fertility, and in the process blinding itself to the evil that unbridled reproduction produces. Here, change could conceivably come not only from condemnation, but from its partner, ridicule. If public education were to resort to motivational persuasion, to the tactics of astute advertising, ridicule of the human propensities that are synonymous with human evil could plausibly bring about certain benefits. But a campaign to condemn and ridicule the sources of human pathology is as unlikely as man's willingness to give up sex.

There are three main possible responses of the reader to this book. He or she may deny the pathology of the human species by overlooking, minimizing, or rationalizing human evil. Or, the reader may be convinced by the evidence summarized here, but, with the passage of time, revert to a naïve and hopeful outlook. Last—and there are very few people in this group, if the author's analysis is correct—the reader may be convinced in a lasting and unwavering way of the reality of human evil, its pervasiveness among ordinary people, and the pathogenicity of the human species in the context of other forms of life, including humanity's pathogenicity toward itself. Such a reader will regard optimism about the human species as a self-serving and delusional distortion of vision, and will choose to bridge the gulf between rationality and emotional conviction with a need to act, deliberately and decisively, to oppose the powerful human emotions and beliefs for which so many are ready to suffer and die. *Nothing prevents man from establishing a world in which cruelty, oppression, murder, and pathogenicity toward other species are avoided. Except his emotional and cognitive constitution.* Human emotions and patterns of thinking that are normal cannot in any simple way be eradicated.

More than 300 years ago, Englishman Thomas Traherne (1637-1674) wrote a little book about two years before his early death, to which an unknown hand later gave the title *Centuries of Meditation*. Traherne reached this conclusion, which will also be ours:

> Were all men wise and innocent, it were easy to be happy, for no man would injure and molest another. But he that would be happy now, must be happy among ingrateful and injurious persons.... On every side we are environed with enemies, surrounded with reproaches, encompassed with wrongs, besieged with offences, receiving evil for good, being disturbed by fools, and invaded with malice. This is the true estate of this world.... To think the world therefore a general Bedlam, or place of madmen, and oneself a physician, is the most necessary point of present wisdom.... (Traherne 1960/1908:177)

# REFERENCES

Abrams, Jeremiah & Zweig, Connie (eds.) (1991). *Meeting the Shadow: The Hidden Power of the Dark Side of Human Nature.* L.A.: Tarcher.

Ackermann, Nathan W. & Johoda, Marie (1950). *Anti-Semitism and Emotional Disorder: A Psychoanalytic Interpretation.* NY: Harper.

Actor, William (1871/1857). *The Functions and Disorders of the Reproductive Organs in Childhood, Youth, Adult Age, and Advanced Life, Considered in Their Physiological, Social, and Moral Relations.* London: Churchill. First pub. 1857.

Agich, George J. (1997). Toward a pragmatic theory of disease. In Humber & Almeder (1997:221-46).

Akhtar, Salman (1999). The psychodynamic dimension of terrorism. *Psychiatric Aspects of Terrorism* 29:6:350-5.

Alexander, Yonah & Gleason, John M. (eds.) (1981). *Behavioral and Quantitative Perspectives on Terrorism.* NY: Pergamon.

Allport, Gordon (1950). A psychological approach to the study of love and hate. In Sorokin, Pitirim A. (ed.), *Explorations in Altruistic Love and Behavior:* 145-64. Boston: Beacon.

_____ (1954). *The Nature of Prejudice.* Reading, MA: Addison-Wesley.

American Psychiatric Association (1987). *Diagnostic and Statistical Manual of Mental Disorders: DSM-III-R.* Wash., D.C.: Amer. Psychiatric Assoc .

_____ (2000). *Diagnostic and Statistical Manual of Mental Disorders: DSM-IV-TR.* Wash., D.C.: Amer. Psychiatric Assoc.

Arendt, Hannah (1964). *Eichmann in Jerusalem: A Report on the Banality of Evil.* NY: Viking.

_____ (1969). *On Violence.* NY: Harcourt, Brace & World.

Ashford, Oliver M. (1985). *Prophet—or Professor? The Life and Work of Lewis Fry Richardson.* Bristol: Hilger.

Associated Press (1999). Century's growth crowds world. *Statesman J.,* 6/27:2A.

Bach, Kent (1994). Emotional disorder and attention. In Graham, George & Stephens, G. Lynn (eds.), *Philos. Psychopathology:* 51-72. Cambridge, MA: MIT Press.

Bailey, N.T.J. (1957). *The Mathematical Theory of Epidemics.* NY: Hafner.

Bakken, L. (1983). *Moral Judgment in Adults: Its Relationship to Age, Sex, and Education.* Ph.D. dissertation, Boston Univ.

Bandura, Albert (1998). Mechanisms of moral disengagement. In Reich (1998:161-91).

Barker-Benfield, G.J. (1983). The spermatic economy: A nineteenth-century view of sexuality. In Altherr, T.L. (ed.), *Procreation or Pleasure? Sexual Attitudes in American History:* 47-70. Malabar, FL: Krieger.

Barlow, Connie (ed.) (1991). *From Gaia to Selfish Genes: Selected Writings in the Life Sciences.* Cambridge, MA: MIT Press.

Barnard, C.J. (1990). Parasitic relationships. In Barnard, C.J. & Behnke, J.M. (eds.). *Parasitism and Host Behavior:*1-33. London: Taylor & Francis.

Bartlett, Paul (1998). *Forward, Children!* Seoul, Korea: My Friend.

Bartlett, Steven J. & Suber, Peter (eds.) (1987). *Self-Reference: Reflections on Reflexivity.* Dordrecht: Nijhoff.

Bartlett, Steven J. (1969). Conviction and rationality. Research presentation, Center for the Study of Democratic Institutions.

Bartlett, Steven J. (1970). *A Relativistic Theory of Phenomenological Constitution: A Self-referential, Transcendental Approach to Conceptual Pathology*. Vol. I: French; Vol. II: English. Ph.D. dissertation, Université de Paris. Univ. Microfilms Intl. #7905583.

\_\_\_\_\_ (1975a). Towards a unified concept of reality. *Etc.: A Review of General Semantics* 32:1:43-9.

\_\_\_\_\_ (1975b). *Metalogic of Reference: A Study in the Foundations of Possibility*. Starnberg, Germany: Max-Planck-Gesellschaft.

\_\_\_\_\_ (1976). The idea of a metalogic of reference. *Methodology & Science* 9:3:85-92.

\_\_\_\_\_ (1978a). Protocol analysis in creative problem-solving. *J. of Creative Behavior* 12:3:181-92.

\_\_\_\_\_ (1978b). A metatheoretical basis for interpretations of problem-solving behavior. *Methodology & Science* 11:2:59-85.

\_\_\_\_\_ (1980). Self-reference, phenomenology, and philosophy of science. *Methodology & Science* 13:3:143-67.

\_\_\_\_\_ (1982). Referential consistency as a criterion of meaning. *Synthèse* 52:267-82.

\_\_\_\_\_ (1983a). *Conceptual Therapy: An Introduction to Framework-relative Epistemology*. St. Louis: Studies in Theory & Behavior.

\_\_\_\_\_ (1983b). Philosophy as conceptual therapy. Ed. Resources Info. Center, Natl. Inst. of Ed., Dept. of Health, Ed., & Welfare: May. Document #ED 224 402.

\_\_\_\_\_ (1986). Philosophy as ideology. *Metaphilosophy* 17:1:1-13.

\_\_\_\_\_ (1987). *When You Don't Know Where to Turn: A Self-Diagnosing Guide to Counseling and Therapy*. NY: Contemporary Bks.

\_\_\_\_\_ (1988). Hoisted by their own petards: Philosophical positions that self-destruct. *Argumentation* 2:221-32.

\_\_\_\_\_ (1990). The problem of psychotherapeutic effectiveness. *Methodology & Science* 23:2:75-86.

\_\_\_\_\_ (1993). Barbarians at the door: A psychological and historical profile of today's college students. *Modern Age* 35:4:296-310. Pub. same year in Europe in *Methodology & Science* 26:1:18-40.

\_\_\_\_\_ (2002). Roots of human resistance to animal rights: Psychological and conceptual blocks. *Animal Law* 8:143-76.

\_\_\_\_\_ (ed.) (1992). *Reflexivity: A Source-Book in Self-Reference*. Amsterdam: Elsevier.

Bateson, Gregory (1972). *Steps to an Ecology of Mind*. NY: Ballantine.

Baumeister, Roy F. (1997). *Evil: Inside Human Cruelty and Violence*. NY: W.H. Freeman.

Beaumont, Francis & Fletcher, John (1976/1647). *Love's Cure*. In Bowers, Fredson (ed.), *The Dramatic Works in the Beaumont and Fletcher Canon* III. Cambridge: Cambridge Univ. Press.

Beck, Aaron T. (2002). Prisoners of hate. *Beh. Res. & Therapy* 40:3:209-16.

Becker, Ernest (1964). *The Revolution in Psychiatry: A New Understanding of Man*. NY: Free Press.

\_\_\_\_\_ (1975). *Escape from Evil*. NY: Free Press.

Begin, Menachem (1977). *The Revolt: Story of the Irgun*. Trans. S. Katz. Jerusalem: Steimatzky's Agency.

Ben-Ze'ev, Aaron (1992). Pleasure-in-others'-misfortune. *Iyyun: The Jerusalem Philos. Q.* 41 (January):41-61.

\_\_\_\_\_ (1993). Another look at pleasure-in-others'-misfortune. *Iyyun: The Jerusalem Philos. Q.* 42 (July):431-40.

Berkeley, George (1999/1710). *Principles of Human Knowledge* and *Three Dialogues*. Robinson, Howard (ed.). Oxford: Oxford Univ. Press. First pub. 1710.

Berkowitz, Benjamin J. (1972). *Superviolence: The Civil Threat of Mass Destruction Weapons*. Santa Barbara: CA: ADCON.

Berkowitz, Leonard (1973/1968). Simple views of aggression. In Montagu (1973/1968:39-52).

\_\_\_\_\_ (1989). Frustration-aggression hypothesis: Examination and reformation. *Psych. Bull.* 106:59-73.

\_\_\_\_\_ (1990). Biological roots: Are humans inherently violent? In Glad (1990:24-40).

\_\_\_\_\_ (1993). *Aggression*. NY: McGraw-Hill.

Billig, Michael (1978). *Fascists: A Social Psychological View of the National Front*. NY: Academic Press.

Binet, Alfred & Henri, Victor (1895). La psychologie individuelle. *L'Année psychologique* 2:411-65.

Bisiach, E. (1988). Language without thought. In Weiskrantz, L. (ed.), *Thought without Language*, 464-84. Oxford: Oxford Univ. Press.

Bitter, Wilhelm (ed.) (1966/1959). *Gut und Böse in der Psychotherapie*. Stuttgart: Klett. First pub. 1959.

Bloom, Allan (1987). *The Closing of the American Mind*. NY: Simon & Schuster.

Boonz, Claudia (1995). Review of Ralf Georg Reuth, *Goebbels*. *The New York Times Book Review:* Jan.

16th:14.

Borba, Michele (2001). *Building Moral Intelligence*. San Francisco: Jossey-Bass.

Brennan, William (1995). *Dehumanizing the Vulnerable: When Word Games Take Lives*. Chicago: Loyola Univ. Press.

Brofsky, G.L. & Brand, D.J. (1980). Personality organization and psychological functioning of the Nuremberg war criminal: The Rorschach data. In Dimsdale (1980:359-403).

Brown, Roger (1986). *Social Psychology*. NY: Free Press.

Browne, Thomas (1981/1646). *Pseudodoxia Epidemica*. Robbins, Robin (ed.). 2 vols. Oxford: Clarendon Press. First pub. 1646.

Broyles, William, Jr. (1984). Why men love war. *Esquire:* Nov.:55-65.

Bruner, J. S. Tagiuri, R. (1954). The perception of people. In Lindzey, G. (ed.), *Handbook of Social Psychology:* 634-54. Reading, MA: Addison-Wesley.

Buchheim, Hans (1968). Command and compliance. Trans. R. Barry. In Krausnick *et al.* (1968/1965: 303-96).

Buck, Pearl (1931-35). *House of Earth: A House Divided*. NY: John Day.

Bucknill, John Charles & Tuke, Daniel Hack (1879/1858). *A Manual of Psychological Medicine*. London: Churchill. First pub. 1858.

Camus, Albert (1961). Summer in Algiers. In *The Myth of Sisyphus*. Trans. J. O'Brien. NY: Vintage.

Canguilhem, Georges (1978/1943). *On the Normal and Pathological*. Trans. C.R. Fawcett. Dordrecht, Holland: Reidel. Canguilhem's 1943 Strasbourg thesis with three added essays.

Caplin, A.L. (ed.) (1981). *Concepts of Health and Disease*. Reading, MA: Addison-Wesley.

Carter, John (1926). *Man Is War*. Indianapolis: Bobbs-Merrill.

Cartwright, Samuel A. (1851). Report on the diseases and physical peculiarities of the Negro race. *New Orleans Med. & Sur. J.:* May:691-715.

Chalk, Frank & Jonasson, Kurt (1990). *The History of Genocide: Analyses and Cases*. New Haven: Yale Univ. Press.

Chapman, R.N. (1928). The quantitative analysis of environmental factors. *Ecology* 9:111-22.

Charny, Israel W. & Rapaport, Chanan (1982). *How Can We Commit the Unthinkable? Genocide: The Human Cancer*. Boulder, CO: Westview.

Charny, Israel W. (1994) (ed.). *The Widening Circle of Genocide* 3: *Genocide: A Critical Bibliographic Review*. New Brunswick, N.J.: Transaction

Cheney, Lynne V. (ed.) (1992). *Telling the Truth: A Report on the State of the Humanities in Higher Education*. Wash., D.C.: Natl. Endowment for the Humanities.

Chisholm, G.B. (1946). The reëstablishment of peacetime society. *Psychiatry* IX: 2nd Series:3:1-35.

Chorover, S.L. (1979). *From Genesis to Genocide*. Cambridge, MA: MIT Press.

Christodoulou, G.N. (1991). The delusional misidentification syndromes. *Brit. J. of Psychiatry* 159: Suppl. 14:65-9.

Clouser, K. Danner; Culver, Charles M.; & Gert, Bernard (1997). Malady. In Humber & Almeder (1997:175-217).

Coles, Robert (1997). *The Moral Intelligence of Children*. NY: Random House.

Collingwood, R. G. (1946). *The Idea of History*. NY: Oxford Univ. Press.

Coltheart, Max & Davies, Martin (2000). *Pathologies of Belief*. Malden, MA: Blackwell.

Colvard, Karen (2002). The psychology of terrorists. *BMJ (Brit. Med. J.)* 324:733:359.

Combes, C. (1995). *Interactions durables: Écologie et évolution du parasitisme*. Paris: Masson.

Coronado, Raymond R. (1981). A critique of the mental disorder perspective of political terrorism. *Internatl. J. of Law & Psychiatry* 4:293-309.

Cox, V. (1974). A prize for the goose father. *Human Behavior* 3:17-22.

Craig, Wallace (1918). Appetites and aversions as constituents of instincts. *Biol. Bull. Woods Hole* 34:91-107.

Crawshay-Williams, Rupert (1947). *The Comforts of Unreason: A Study of the Motives behind Irrational Thought*. London: Kegan Paul, Trench, Trubner.

Crayton, John W. (1983). Terrorism and the psychology of the self. In Freedman, Lawrence Zelic & Alexander, Yonah (eds.), *Perspectives on Terrorism:* 33-41. Wilmington, DE: Scholarly Resources.

Crenshaw, Martha (1981). The causes of terrorism. *Comparative Politics* 13:July:379-99.

_____ (1998a). The logic of terrorism: Terrorist behavior as product of strategic choice. In Reich

(1998:7-24).

Crenshaw, Martha (1998b). Questions to be answered, research to be done, knowledge to be applied. In Reich (1998:247-60).

Crile, George W. (1916). *A Mechanistic View of War and Peace.* NY: Macmillan.

Crofton, H. D. (1971). A quantitative approach to parasitism. *Parasitology* 62:179-93.

Culver, Charles M. & Gert, Bernard (1982). *Philosophy in Medicine: Conceptual and Ethical Issues in Medicine and Psychiatry.* NY: Oxford Univ. Press.

Cunard, Nancy (ed.) (1969). *Negro: An Anthology.* NY: Negro Universities Press.

Curatorium of the C. G. Jung Institute (ed.) (1967). *Evil.* Evanston, IL: Northwestern Univ. Press.

Darwin, Charles (1872). *The Expression of Emotions in Man and Animals.* London: J. Murray.

Davies, Alan T. (1977). Response to Irving Greenberg. In Fleischner (1977:57-64).

Davies, T.R. (1973). Aggression, violence, revolution and war. In Knutson (1973:234-60).

Dawkins, Richard (1976). *The Selfish Gene.* Oxford: Oxford Univ. Press.

de Koning, A.J.J. & Jenner, F.A. (eds.) (1982). *Phenomenology and Psychiatry.* NY: Academic Press.

della Porta, Donatella (1992). Political socialization in left-wing underground organizations: Biographies of Italian and German militants. In della Porta, Donatella (ed.), *Social Movements and Violence: Participation in Underground Organizations* 4:259-90. Greenwich, CT: JAI Press.

DiGiuseppe, R.; Tafrate, R.C.; & Eckhardt, C.I. (1994). Critical issues in the treatment of anger. *Cognitive & Behavioral Practice* 1:111-32.

Dilman, Ilham (1996). Wisdom. *Philosophy* 71:278:577-90.

_____ (ed.) (1984). *Philosophy and Life: Essays on John Wisdom.* Dordrecht: Nijhoff.

Dimsdale, J.E. (ed.) (1980). *Survivors, Victims, and Perpetrators: Essays on the Nazi Holocaust.* Wash., D.C.: Hemisphere.

Dobbins, James E. & Skillings, Judith H. (2000). Racism as a clinical syndrome. *Amer. J. of Orthopsychiatry* 70:1:14-27.

Dollard, J.; Doob, L.W.; Miller, N.E.; Mowrer, O.H.; & Sears, R.R. (1939). *Frustration and Aggression.* New Haven: Yale Univ. Press.

Donat, Alexander (1965). *The Holocaust Kingdom: A Memoir.* NY: Rinehart.

Dorey, Roger (1986). L'Amour au travers de la haine. *Nouvelle Rev. de Psychanalyse* 33: Printemps:75-93: monograph issue: *L'Amour de la haine.*

Douglas, William O. (1961). The rule of law in world affairs. In Millis *et al.* (1961:145-82).

Dowie, Jack & Elstein, Arthur (eds.) (1988). *Professional Judgment.* Cambridge: Cambridge Univ. Press 1988.

Dubos, René (1987/1959). *Mirage of Health: Utopias, Progress, and Biological Change.* New Brunswick: Rutgers Univ. Press. First pub. 1959.

Dumas, Samuel & Vedel-Petersen, K.O. (1923). *Losses of Life Caused by War.* Oxford: Clarendon.

Dunn, Frederick S. (1950). *War and the Minds of Men.* NY: Harper.

Durbin, E.F.M. & Bowlby, John (1940). *Personal Aggressiveness and War.* London: Kegan Paul, Trench, Trubner.

Edwards, Steven D. (1990). *Relativism, Conceptual Schemes and Categorial Frameworks.* Aldershot, Eng.: Avebury.

Ehrlich, Paul R. (1990). *The Population Explosion.* NY: Simon & Schuster.

_____ (1997). *A World of Wounds: Ecologists and the Human Dilemma.* Oldendorf/Luhe, Germany: Ecology Inst.

Eibl-Eibesfeldt, Irenäus (1970). *Ethology: The Biology of Behavior.* NY: Holt, Rinehart & Winston.

_____ (1972). *Love and Hate: The Natural History of Behavior Patterns.* Trans. G. Strachan. NY: Holt, Rinehart & Winston. First pub. 1970.

_____ (1979). Human ethology: Concepts and implications for the sciences of man. *Behavioral and Brain Sciences* 2:1-26 and Commentaries: 26-57.

_____ (1979). *The Biology of Peace and War: Men, Animals, and Aggression.* NY: Viking 1979. First pub. 1975.

_____ (1982). Biological aspects of evil. *Australian J. of Forensic Sciences* 15:58-65.

_____ (1989). *Human Ethology.* NY: Aldine de Gruyter.

_____ (1993a). Universalien: Mit altsteinzeitlichem Erbe in der modernen Welt. In Schiefenhövel *et al.* (1993:128-33).

Eibl-Eibesfeldt, Irenäus (1993b). Subtile Ermutigung: Zur Körpersprache beim Flirten. In Schiefenhövel *et al.* (1993: 134-7).

_____ (1993c). Das 'Böse': Bedingungen menschlicher Aggression. [Evil: Conditions of human aggression.] In Schiefenhövel *et al.* (1993:142-5).

Einstein, Albert & Freud, Sigmund (1991/1933). *Why War? A Correspondence between Albert Einstein and Sigmund Freud.* Trans. S. Gilbert. Redding, CA: CAT Publishing. First pub. 1933.

Eisenberg, L. (1972). On the human nature of human nature. *Science* 176:123-8.

Eissler, K.R. (1960). The efficient soldier. *The Psychoanalytic Study of Society* I:39-97.

_____ (2000). On hatred. *The Psychoanalytic Study of the Child* 55:27-44.

Ellis, Albert (1961). *A Guide to Rational Living.* Hollywood: Wilshire Bk. Co.

_____ (1977). *Handbook of Rational Emotive Therapy.* NY: Springer.

Elmgren, John (1937). Quelques notions sur la psychologie de la haine. *Theoria* 3:267-82.

Engel, George (1961). Is grief a disease? *Psychosomatic Med.* 23:18-22.

Erasmus, Desiderius (1794/1510). *Antipolemus, or, the Plea of Reason, Religion, and Humanity against War.* London: Dilly. First pub. c. 1510.

Erickson, E.H. (1966). Ontogeny of ritualization in man. *Phil. Trans. Roy. Soc. London* B251:337-49.

Erickson, Milton (1968). The inhumanity of ordinary people. *Internatl. J. of Psychiatry* 6:277-9.

Evans, R.I. (1952). Personal values as factors in anti-Semitism. *J. of Abnormal and Soc. Psychology* 47:749-56.

Evans, Richard I. (1975). *Konrad Lorenz: The Man and His Ideas.* NY: Harcourt Brace Jovanovich.

Eysenck, Hans J. (1999). *Intelligence: A New Look.* New Brunswick: Transaction.

Farrar, Clarence B. (1909). Some origins in psychiatry: Part VIII. *Amer. J. of Insanity* 66:277-94.

_____ (1951). The word 'psychiatry'. *Amer. J. of Psychiatry* 107:8: Feb.:628; 107:11: May:868-9. (Pub. without author's name; attributed to Farrar, Editor.)

Farrell, Brian A. (1946). An appraisal of therapeutic positivism. *Mind* 55:25-48 (Part I), 133-50 (Part II).

_____ (1990). The meaning of life: A psycho-logical exploration. In Roux, A.P.J. (ed.), *Life, World and Meaning: Essays in Honor of Professor Michael Macnamara:* 1-8. Pretoria, S. Africa: Univ. of S. Africa.

_____ (1994). *Philosophy and Psychoanalysis.* NY: Macmillan.

Farrington, K. (1996). *History of Punishment and Torture.* NY: Hamlyn.

Farwell, B. (1982). *Mr. Kipling's Army.* NY: W.W. Norton.

Fein, Helen (1979). *Accounting for Genocide.* NY: Free Press.

Feinstein, Alvan R. (1967). *Clinical Judgment.* Baltimore: Williams & Wilkins.

Fenichel, Otto (1940). Psychoanalysis of antisemitism. *Amer. Imago* 1:24-39.

_____ (1946). Elements of a psychoanalytic theory of anti-semitism. In Simmel (1946:11-32).

Ferguson, Niall (1999). *The Pity of War.* NY: Basic Books.

Fewtrell, David & O'Connor, Kieron (1995). *Clinical Phenomenology and Cognitive Psychology.* NY: Routledge.

Fields, Rona M. (1978). Child terror victims and adult terrorists. *J. of Psychohistory* 7:1: Summer:71-6.

Fish, Frank (1967). *Clinical Psychopathology: Signs and Symptoms in Psychiatry.* Bristol: John Wright.

Fiske, Susan T. & Taylor, Shelley E. (1991). *Social Cognition.* NY: McGraw-Hill.

Flannery, Timothy Fridtjof (1994). *The Future Eaters: An Ecological History of the Australasian Lands and People.* NY: Braziller.

Fleischner, Eva (ed.) (1977). *Auschwitz: Beginning of a New Era? Reflections on the Holocaust.* New York: Cathedral of St. John the Divine.

Fracastoro, Girolamo (1930/1546). *Hieronymi Fracastorii De contagione et contagiosis morbis et eorum curatione, libri III.* English trans. W.C. Wright. NY: G.P. Putnam's. First pub. 1546.

Frank, Jerome (1982). *Sanity and Survival in the Nuclear Age: Psychological Aspects of War and Peace.* NY: Random House.

Frazier, Edward Franklin (1927). The pathology of race prejudice. *Forum:* June:856-62. Reprinted in Cunard (1969:116-8).

Frenkel-Brunswik, Else & Sanford, R. Nevitt (1946). The anti-Semitic personality: A research report. In Simmel (1946:96-124).

Freud, Sigmund (1921). *Group Psychology and the Analysis of the Ego.* London: Hogarth.

_____ (1952/1914). On narcissism: An introduction. Trans. C.M. Baines. *Great Books of the Western*

*World* 54:399-411. Chicago: Ency. Brit. First pub. 1914.

Freud, Sigmund (1952/1915a). Instincts and their vicissitudes. Trans. C.M. Baines. *Great Books of the Western World* 54:412-21. Chicago: Ency. Brit. First pub. 1915.

_____ (1952/1915b). Thoughts for the times on war and death. Trans. E.C. Mayne. *Great Books of the Western World* 54:755-66. Chicago: Ency. Brit. First pub. 1915.

_____ (1952/1930). *Civilization and Its Discontents.* Trans. J. Riviere. *Great Books of the Western World* 54:767-802. Chicago: Ency. Brit. First pub. 1930.

_____ (1953-74). *The Standard Edition of the Complete Psychological Works of Sigmund Freud.* 24 vols. Trans. J. Strachey (ed.), A. Freud, A. Strachey, & A. Tyson. London: Hogarth.

_____ (1953-74/1894). The neuro-psychoses of defense. In Freud (1953-74:3:43-69). First pub. 1894.

_____ (1953-74/1896). Further remarks on the neuro-psychoses of defense. In Freud (1953-74:3:159-88). First pub. 1896.

_____ (1953-74/1905). *Three Essays on the Theory of Sexuality.* In Freud (1953-74:7:125-245). First pub. 1905.

_____ (1953-74/1909). Analysis of phobia in a five-year-old boy. In Freud (1953-74:10:3-149). First pub. 1909.

_____ (1953-74/1920). *Beyond the Pleasure Principle.* In Freud (1953-74:18:3-64). First pub. 1920.

_____ (1961/1927). *The Future of an Illusion.* Trans. J. Strachey. NY: W.W. Norton. First pub. 1927.

_____ (1962/1912-13). *Totem and Taboo: Some Points of Agreement between the Mental Lives of Savages and Neurotics.* Trans. J. Strachey. NY: W.W. Norton. First pub. 1912-13.

_____ (1963/1914). *History of the Psychoanalytic Movement.* Trans. J. Riviere. NY: Collier. First pub. 1914.

Frey-Rohn, Liliane (1967). Evil from the psychological point of view. In Curatorium of the C. G. Jung Institute (1967:153-200).

Friedländer, Saul (1997). *Nazi Germany and the Jews* I: *The Years of Persecution, 1933-1939.* NY: HarperCollins.

Fromkin, D. (1975). The strategy of terrorism. *Foreign Affairs* 53:683-98.

Fromm, Erich (1963). *War within Man: A Psychological Enquiry into the Roots of Destructiveness.* Amer. Friends Serv. Committee.

_____ (1964). *The Heart of Man: Its Genius for Good and Evil.* NY: Harper & Row.

_____ (1966/1962). *Beyond the Chains of Illusion.* NY: Pocket Books. First pub. 1962.

_____ (1973). *The Anatomy of Human Destructiveness.* NY: Holt, Rinehart & Winston.

Fürth, R. (1952). Physics of social equilibrium. *Advancement of Science* 8:429-34.

Fussell, Paul (1975). *The Great War and Modern Memory.* Oxford: Oxford Univ. Press.

Galton, Francis (1869). *Hereditary Genius: An Inquiry into its Laws and Consequences.* NY: Macmillan.

Gantheret, François (1986). Les non-lieux de la mémoire. *Nouvelle Rev. de Psychanalyse* 33:11-24.

Gardner, Howard (1993). *Multiple Intelligences: The Theory in Practice.* NY: BasicBooks.

_____ (1993/1983). *Frames of Mind: The Theory of Multiple Intelligences.* NY: BasicBooks. First pub. 1983.

Gause, G.F. (1934a). Experimental investigation of the struggle for existence between *Paramaecium caudatum, Paramaecium aurelia* and *Stylonchia mytilus. Zool. J.* 13:1-17.

_____ (1934b). On the processes of destruction of one species by another in ciliate populations. *Zool. J.* 13:18-26.

_____ (1934c). *The Struggle for Existence.* Baltimore: Williams & Wilkins.

Gay, Peter (1993). *The Cultivation of Hatred.* Vol. III of *The Bourgeois Experience: Victoria to Freud.* NY: W.W. Norton.

Gaylin, Willard (2003). *Hatred: The Psychological Descent into Violence.* NY: PublicAffairs.

Geis, Gilbert; Huston, Ted L.; & Wright, Richard (1976). Compensating good Samaritans. *Crime Prevention Rev.:* 28-35.

Gert, Bernard; Culver, Charles M.; & Clouser, K. Danner (1997). *Bioethics: A Return to Fundamentals.* NY: Oxford Univ. Press.

Geyer, Horst (1954). *Über die Dummheit: Ursachen und Wirkungen der intellecktuellen Minderleistung des Menschen: Ein Essay.* Göttingen: Musterschmidt.

Gilbert, G.M. (1950). *The Psychology of Dictatorship: Based on an Examination of the Leaders of Nazi Germany.* NY: Ronald.

Gissing, George (1918). *The Private Papers of Henry Ryecroft.* NY: Modern Library.

Glad, Betty (ed.) (1990). *Psychological Dimensions of War.* Newbury Park, CA: Sage.

Glover, Edward (1933). *War, Sadism and Pacifism.* London: Allen & Unwin.

Gold, Ian & Hohwy, Jakab (2000). Rationality and schizophrenic delusion. In Coltheart & Davies (2000:145-65)

Goldhagen, Daniel (1985). The "cowardly" executioner: On disobedience in the SS. *Patterns of Prejudice* 19:2:19-32.

_____ (1996). *Hitler's Willing Executioners: Ordinary Germans and the Holocaust.* NY: Knopf.

Goldstein, J.H. & Arms, R.L. (1971). Effects of observing athletic contests on hostility. *Sociometry* 34:83-90.

Goleman, Daniel (1985). *Vital Lies, Simple Truths.* NY: Simon & Schuster.

_____ (1995). *Emotional Intelligence.* NY: Bantam.

Gott, J. Richard III (2001). *Time Travel in Einstein's Universe.* NY: Houghton Mifflin.

Gramling, O. (1942). *Free Men Are Fighting.* NY: Farrar & Rinehart.

Gray, J. Glenn (1967). *The Warriors.* NY: Harper & Row.

Greenberg, Irving (1977). Cloud of smoke, pillar of fire: Judaism, Christianity, and modernity after the Holocaust. In Fleischner (1977:7-55).

Greene, Bob (2000). *Duty: A Father, His Son, and the Man Who Won the War.* NY: Morrow.

Gregg, A. (1955). A medical aspect of the population problem. *Science* 121:3150: May 13:681-2.

Gregg, William (1970/1851). Plank roads. In *The Microbook Library of American Civilization,* microfiche #31374. Chicago: Library Resources. First pub. 1851.

Groebel, Jo & Goldstein, Jeffrey H. (eds.) (1989). *Terrorism: Psychological Perspectives.* Sevilla, Spain: Publicaciónes de la Univ. de Sevilla.

Groombridge, Brian (ed.) (1992). *Global Biodiversity: Status of the Earth's Living Resources.* NY: Chapman & Hall.

Grossman, Dave (1995). *On Killing: The Psychological Cost of Learning to Kill in War and Society.* NY: Little, Brown.

Guilford, J.P. (1967). *The Nature of Human Intelligence.* NY: McGraw-Hill.

Guillemeau, Jacques (1597). *French chirurgerye, or, All the manualle operations of chirurgerye.* Trans. A. M. (only the translator's initials were pub.) from the Dutch into English. Dort: Isaac Canin.

Gurr, Ted Robert (1970). *Why Men Rebel.* Princeton, NJ: Princeton Univ. Press.

Hacker, Frederick J. (1976). *Crusaders, Criminals, Crazies—Terror and Terrorism in Our Time.* NY: W.W. Norton.

_____ (1980). Terror and terrorism: Modern growth industry and mass entertainment. *Terrorism* 4:143-59.

Halvörsen, O. (1976). Negative interaction amongst parasites. In Kennedy (1976:99-114).

Hardin, Garrett (1982). *Naked Emperors: Essays of a Taboo-Stalker.* San Francisco: Wm. Kaufmann.

_____ (1999). *The Ostrich Factor: Our Population Myopia.* Oxford: Oxford Univ. Press.

Haret, S.C. (1910). *Méchanique sociale.* Paris: Gauthier-Villars.

Harré, Rom & Krausz, Michael (1996). *Varieties of Relativism.* Oxford: Blackwell.

Hedges, Chris (2002). *War Is a Force That Gives Us Meaning.* NY: PublicAffairs.

Heinroth, Johann Christian August (1818). *Lehrbuch der Störungen des Seelenlebens oder der Seelenstörungen und ihrer Behandlung vom rationalen Standpunkt aus entworfen.* Leipzig: F.C.W. Vogel.

_____ (1823). *Lehrbuch der Seelengesundheitskunde. Zum Behuf academischer Vorträge und zum Privatstudium. Erster Theil. Theorie und Lehre von der Leibespflege.* Leipzig: F.C.W. Vogel.

_____ (1898). *On Education and Self-formation Based upon Physical, Intellectual, Moral, and Religious Principles.* London: A. Schloss.

_____ (1975/1818). *Textbook of Disturbances of Mental Life.* 2 vols. Trans. J. Schmorak. Baltimore: Johns Hopkins Univ. Press 1975. Eng. trans. of Heinroth (1818).

Heinroth, Oskar (1910). Beiträge zur Biologie, insbesondere Psychologie und Ethologie der Anatiden. *Verh. 5. Int. Ornith. Kongr.:* 589-702.

Hennekens, Charles H. & Buring, J.E. (1987). *Epidemiology in Medicine.* Boston: Little, Brown & Co.

Herrick, C. Judson (1956). *The Evolution of Human Nature.* Austin: Univ. of Texas Press.

Hersch, Seymour (1970). *My Lai 4: A Report on the Massacre and Its Aftermath.* NY: Random House.

Heskin, Ken (1984). The psychology of terrorism in Ireland. In Alexander, Yonah & O'Day, Alan (eds.), *Terrorism in Ireland:* 88-105. NY: St. Martin's Press.

Hesse, Hermann (1969). *Damian.* Trans. W.J. Strachan. London: Panther.

Hinrichsen, Kurt (1971). Befehlsnotstand. In Adalbert Rückerl (ed.), *NS-Prozess: Nach 25 Jahren Strafverfolgung:*131-61. Karlsruhe: Müller.

Hoage, R.J. (ed.) (1985). *Animal Extinction.* Wash., D.C.: Smithsonian Institution Press.

Hoffman, Bruce (1999). The mind of the terrorist: Perspectives from social psychology. *Psychiatric Annals* 29:6:337-40.

Hoffman, M.L. (2000). *Empathy and Moral Development.* NY: Cambridge Univ. Press.

Horowitz, D.L. (2001). *The Deadly Ethnic Riot.* Berkeley: Univ. of California Press.

Hovens, J.E. (Hans) & Drozdek, Boris (2002). The terror of torture: A continuum of evil. In Stout (2002:II:75-103).

Hubbard, David G. (1983). The psychodynamics of terrorism. In Adeniran, Tunde & Alexander, Yonah (eds.), *International Violence:* 43-53. NY: Praeger.

Hudson, Rex A. (1999). *The Sociology and Psychology of Terrorism: Who Becomes a Terrorist and Why.* Wash., D.C.: Fed. Research Div., Lib. of Congress. (An electronic document accessed 11/29/02 at http://www.loc.gov/rr/frd/Sociology-Psychology%20of%20Terrorism.htm.)

Hudson, Robert P. (1983). *Disease and its Control: The Shaping of Modern Thought.* NY: Praeger.

Humber, James M. & Almeder, Robert F. (eds.) (1997). *What Is Disease?* Totowa, N.J.: Humana.

Hurst, J. Willis (1992a). Learning medicine. In Hurst, J. Willis (ed.), *Medicine for the Practicing Physician:* 2-6. Boston: Butterworth-Heinemann.

_____ (1992b). Practicing medicine. In Hurst, J. Willis (ed.), *Medicine for the Practicing Physician:* 13-5. Boston: Butterworth-Heinemann.

Hutchinson, M.C. (1978). *Revolutionary Terrorism: The FLN in Algeria 1954-1962.* Stanford: Hoover Inst. Press.

Huxley, Aldous (1934). Lettre sur la guerre et la psychologie de l'individu. Trans. H. Pernot. *Open Letters 3: L'Esprit, l'éthique et la guerre:* 55-72. Paris: League of Nations.

Illich, Ivan (1976). *Medical Nemesis.* Harmondsworth, England: Penguin.

Jäger, Herbert (1982/1967). *Verbrechen unter totalitärer Herrschaft: Studien zur nationalsozialistischen Gewaltkriminalität.* Frankfurt am Main: Suhrkamp. First pub. 1967.

Jahoda, Marie (1974/1966). The psychological meaning of various criteria for positive mental health. In Offer & Sabshin (1974/1966:197-9).

James, William (1890). *The Principles of Psychology.* 2 vols. NY: Holt.

Janet, Pierre (1932). *L'Amour et la haine.* Paris: Maloine.

Jenkins, Brian M. (1981). The study of terrorism: Definitional problems. In Alexander & Gleason (1981:3-10).

Johnson, Eric A. (1999). *Nazi Terror: The Gestapo, Jews, and Ordinary Germans.* NY: Basic Books.

Johnson, Phillip W. & Feldmann, Theodore B. (1992). Personality types and terrorism: Self-psychology perspectives. *Forensic Reports* 5:4:293-303.

Jones, Ernest (1974). War and individual psychology. In Jones, Ernest, *Psycho-myth, Psycho-history: Essays in Applied Psychoanalysis:* 55-76. NY: Hillstone.

Joseph, A.B. (1986). Focal central nervous system abnormalities in patients with misidentification syndromes. *Bibliotheca Psychiatrica* 164:68-79.

Jung, C.G. (1965). *Memories, Dreams, Reflections.* Jaffé, Aniela (ed.). Trans. R. & C. Winston. NY: Vintage.

_____ (1967-1983). *The Collected Works of C. G. Jung.* 20 vols. Trans. R.F.C. Hull. Princeton, N.J.: Princeton Univ. Press.

_____ (1967-1983/1916). General aspects of dream psychology. In Jung (1967-1983:8:237-80). First pub. 1916.

_____ (1967-1983/1916-7). *Two Essays on Analytical Psychology.* In Jung (1967-1983:7). First pub. 1916-17.

_____ (1967-1983/1919). Instinct and the unconscious. In Jung (1967-1983:8:129-38). First pub. 1919.

_____ (1967-1983/1920). The psychological foundations of belief in spirits. In Jung (1967-1983:8:301-18). First pub. 1920.

_____ (1967-1983/1928). The spiritual problem of modern man. In Jung (1967-1983:10:74-94). First pub. 1928.

_____ (1967-1983/1932). Psychotherapists or the clergy. In Jung (1967-1983:11:327-47). First pub. 1932.

_____ (1967-1983/1938a). The autonomy of the unconscious. In Jung (1967-1983:11:5-33). First pub.

1938.

Jung, C.G. (1967-1983/1938b). Dogma and natural symbols. In Jung (1967-1983:11:34-63). First pub. 1938.

_____ (1967-1983/1942). A psychological approach to the dogma of the Trinity. In Jung (1967-1983:11:109-200). First pub. 1942.

_____ (1967-1983/1945). After the catastrophe. In Jung (1967-1983:10:194-217). First pub. 1945.

_____ (1967-1983/1946a). The fight with the shadow. In Jung (1967-1983:10:218-26). First pub. 1946.

_____ (1967-1983/1946b). Epilogue to "Essays on contemporary events." In Jung (1967-1983:10:227-43). First pub. 1946.

_____ (1967-1983/1946c). The psychology of the transference. In Jung (1967-1983:16:163-323). First pub. 1946.

_____ (1967-1983/1949-58). *Aion: Researches into the Phenomenology of the Self.* In Jung (1967-1983:9:II). First pub. 1949-58.

_____ (1967-1983/1954). On the psychology of the trickster-figure. In Jung (1967-1983:9:I:255-72). First pub.1954.

_____ (1967-1983/1957). The undiscovered self. In Jung (1967-1983:10:247-305). First pub. 1957.

_____ (1967-1983/1959). Good and evil in analytical psychology. In Jung (1967-1983:10:456-68). First pub. 1959.

_____ (1977). *Jung Speaking.* Princeton: Princeton Univ. Press.

_____ (1991/1963). The problem of evil today. In Abrams & Zweig (1991:170-3). From Jung (1965).

Kalikow, T.J. (1978). Konrad Lorenz's "Brown Past": A Reply to Alec Nisbett. *J. of the Hist. of the Beh. Scs.* 14:173-9.

_____ (1983). Konrad Lorenz's ethological theory: Explanation and ideology, 1938-1943. *J. of the Hist. of Biol.* 16:39-73.

Kant, Immanuel (1974/1797). *Anthropology from a Pragmatic Point of View.* Trans. M.J. Gregor. Hague: Nijhoff. First pub. 1797.

Kaplan, Chaim Aron (1973). *The Warsaw Diary of Chaim A. Kaplan.* Trans. A.I. Katsh. NY: Collier.

Kaplan, R.D. (1994). The coming anarchy. *Atlantic Monthly:* Feb.:44-76.

Kapp, Reginald O. (1962/1960). *Towards a Unified Cosmology.* London: Sc. Bk. Guild. First pub. 1960.

Kardiner, Abram & Ovesey, Lionel (1969/1951). *The Mark of Oppression: Explorations in the Personality of the American Negro.* NY: World. First pub. 1951.

Kassinove, Howard & Sukhodolsky, Denis G. (1995). Anger disorders: Basic science and practice issues. In Kassinove (1995:1-26).

Kassinove, Howard (ed.) (1995). *Anger Disorders: Definition, Diagnosis, and Treatment.* Wash., D.C.: Taylor & Francis.

Kassirer, Jerome P.; Kuipers, Benjamin J.; & Gorry, G. Anthony (1988). Toward a theory of clinical expertise. In Dowie & Elstein (1988:212-25).

Katz, Fred E. (1993). *Ordinary People and Extraordinary Evil: A Report on the Beguilings of Evil.* Albany, NY: State Univ. of NY Press.

Kaufman, Frederik (1997). Disease: Definition and objectivity. In Humber & Almeder (1997:271-86).

Kaufmann, Walter (1980). *Discovering the Mind.* 3 vols. NY: McGraw-Hill.

Kellen, K. (1979). *Terrorists—What Are They Like? How Some Terrorist Describe Their World and Actions.* Santa Monica: Rand.

Kelley, Douglas M. (1947). *22 Cells in Nuremberg.* London: W.H. Allen.

Kelman, H. & Lawrence, L. (1972). Assignment of responsibility in the case of Lt. Calley: Preliminary report on a national survey. *J. of Soc. Issues* 28:1:177-212.

Kelman, Herbert C. & Hamilton, V. Lee (1989). *Crimes of Obedience: Toward a Social Psychology of Authority and Responsibility.* New Haven: Yale Univ. Press.

Kemmerich, Max (1912). *Aus der Geschichte der menschlichen Dummheit.* München: Langen.

Kendell, R.E. (1975). The concept of disease and its implications for psychiatry. *Brit. J. of Psychiatry* 127:305-15.

Kennedy, C.R. (ed.) (1976). *Ecological Aspects of Parasitology.* Amsterdam: N. Holland.

Kermack, W.O. & McKendrick, A.G. (1927). A contribution to the mathematical theory of epidemics. *Proc. of the Royal Soc. of London:* Series A:115:700-21.

Kernberg, Otto F. (1990). Hatred as pleasure. In Glick, Robert A. & Bone, Stanley (eds.). *Pleasure beyond the Pleasure Principle* I: *The Role of Affect in Motivation, Development, and Adaptation:* 177-88. New Haven: Yale Univ. Press.

Kitterman, David H. (1988). Those who said "no!": Germans who refused to execute civilians during World War II. *German Studies Rev.* XI:2:May:241-54.

Klee, Ernst; Dressen, Willi; & Riess, Volker (eds.) (1991). *"The Good Old Days": The Holocaust As Seen by Its Perpetrators and Bystanders.* Trans. D. Burnstone. NY: Free Press. First pub. as *Schöne Zeiten*, 1988.

Knutson, Andie L. (1965). *The Individual, Society, and Health Behavior.* NY: Russell Sage.

Knutson, Jeanne N. (ed.) (1973). *Handbook of Political Psychology.* San Francisco: Jossey-Bass.

_____ (1981). Social and psychodynamic pressures toward a negative identity. In Alexander & Gleason (1981:105-50).

Kockelmans, Joseph J. (ed.) (1987). *Phenomenological Psychology: The Dutch School.* Dordrecht: Nijhoff.

Koestler, Arthur (1978). *Janus: A Summing Up.* NY: Random House.

Kohlberg, Lawrence (1971/1969). Stage and sequence: The cognitive-developmental approach to socialization. In David A. Goslin (ed.), *Handbook of Socialization Theory and Research:* 347-480. Chicago: Rand McNally. First pub. 1969.

_____ (1981). *Essays on Moral Development* I: *The Philosophy of Moral Development: Moral Stages and the Idea of Justice.* NY: Harper & Row.

Körner, Stephen (1970). *Categorial Frameworks.* Oxford: Blackwell.

Krausnick, Helmut; Buchheim, Hans; Broszat, Martin; Jacobsen, Hans-Adolf (1968/1965). *Anatomy of the SS State.* Trans. R. Barry, M. Jackson, D. Long. London: Collins. First pub. 1965.

Kressel, Neil J. (1996). *Mass Hate: The Global Rise of Genocide and Terror.* NY: Plenum.

Kristiansen, C.M. & Zanna, M.P. (1992). Variables moderating the effects of self-confrontation on values, attitudes and behavior. Unpub. raw data.

Kristiansen, Connie M. & Hotte, Alan M. (1996). Morality and the self: Implications for the when and how of value-attitude-behavior relations. In Seligman, Clive; Olson, James M.; & Zanna, Mark P. (eds.), *The Psychology of Values: The Ontario Symposium* 8:77-105. Mahway, NJ: Erlbaum.

Kull, Steven (1985). Nuclear nonsense. *Foreign Policy* 20: Spring:28-52.

_____ (1990). War and the attraction to destruction. In Glad (1990:40-55).

Kuo, J.Y. (1932). Ontogeny of embryonic behavior in aves. *Internatl. J. of Experimental Zool.* 61:395-430, 453-89.

Kutchins, Herb & Kirk, Stuart A. (1997). *Making Us Crazy: DSM: The Psychiatric Bible and the Creation of Mental Disorders.* NY: The Free Press.

Lande, R. Gregory & Armitage, David, T. (eds.) (1997). *Principles and Practice of Military Forensic Psychiatry.* Springfield, IL: Charles C. Thomas.

Lapsley, Daniel K. (1996). *Moral Psychology.* Boulder, CO: Westview.

Laqueur, Walter (1987). *The Age of Terrorism.* Boston: Little, Brown.

Latané, Bibb & Darley, John M. (1970). *The Unresponsive Bystander: Why Doesn't He Help?.* NY: Appleton-Century-Crofts.

Lazarus, R. S. (1984). Thoughts on the relation between emotion and cognition. In Scherer, K.S. & Ekman, P. (eds.), *Approaches to Cognition:* 247-57. Hillsdale, N.J.: Erlbaum.

Lee, Vernon (1920). *Satan, The Waster: A Philosophic War Trilogy.* NY: Lane.

Lemkin, Raphael (1944). *Axis Rule in Occupied Europe.* Wash., D.C.: Carnegie Endow. for Internatl. Peace.

Lentz, Theo. F. (1955). *Towards a Science of Peace.* NY: Bookman.

Leopold, Aldo (1966). *A Sand County Almanac, with Essays from Round River.* NY: Ballantine.

Lerner, Max (1991/1939). *Ideas Are Weapons: The History and Uses of Ideas.* New Brunswick, N.J.: Transaction. First pub. 1939.

_____ (ed.) (1943). *The Mind and Faith of Justice Holmes.* NY: Modern Library.

Lerner, Melvin J. (1970). The Desire for Justice and Reactions to Victims. In Macaulay, J. & Berkowitz, L. (eds.), *Altruism and Helping Behavior:* 205-29. NY: Academic Press.

Lerner, Richard M. (1992). *Final Solutions: Biology, Prejudice, and Genocide.* Univ. Park, PA: Penn. State Univ. Press.

LeShan, Lawrence (1958). Some aspects of the positive value of hostility. *Amer. Psychologist* 13:118-9.

_____ (1992). *The Psychology of War: Comprehending Its Mystique and Its Madness.* Chicago: Noble Press.

Leslie, John (1996). *The End of the World: The Science and Ethics of Human Extinction.* London: Routledge.

Levi, Primo (1985). *Survival in Auschwitz* and *The Reawakening*. Trans. S. Woolf; "Afterword" trans. R. Feldman. NY: Summit Books. First pub. 1958 and 1963, respectively.

Lewontin, R.C.; Rose, S.; & Kamin, L.J. (1984). *Not in Our Genes: Biology, Ideology, and Human Nature.* NY: Pantheon.

Lickona, Thomas T. (ed.) (1976). *Moral Development and Behavior: Theory, Research, and Social Issues.* NY: Holt, Rinehart & Winston.

Lifton, Robert Jay (1986). *The Nazi Doctors: Medical Killing and the Psychology of Genocide.* NY: Basic Books.

Link, George K.K. (1932). The role of genetics in etiological pathology. *The Q. Rev. of Biol.* VII:2: June:127-71.

Livingstone, Neil C. (1982). *The War against Terrorism.* Lexington, Mass.: Lexington.

Llewellyn, Richard (1940). *How Green Was My Valley.* NY: Macmillan.

Loewenfeld, L. (1909). *Über die Dummheit: Eine Umschau im Gebiete menschlicher Unzulänglichkeit.* [On Stupidity: A Survey in the Area of Human Inadequacy.] Wiesbaden: Bergmann.

Lorenz, Konrad (1940). Durch Domestikation verursachte Störungen arteigenen Verhaltens. [Disorders caused by the domestication of species-specific behavior.] *Zeitschrift für angewandte Psychologie und Charackterkunde* 59:2-81.

_____ (1966). *On Aggression.* Trans. by M.K. Wilson. NY: Harcourt, Brace & World. First pub. 1963.

_____ (1970). *Studies in Animal and Human Behavior.* 2 vols. Trans. R. Martin. Cambridge: Harvard Univ. Press.

_____ (1975). The fashionable fallacy of dispensing with description. Eng. trans. in Evans (1975: 152-80). First pub. 1973.

_____ (1977). *Behind the Mirror: A Search for a Natural History of Human Knowledge.* Trans. R. Taylor. NY: Harcourt Brace Jovanovich. First pub. 1973.

_____ (1981). *The Foundations of Ethology.* Trans. K. Lorenz & R.W. Kickert. NY: Springer-Verlag. First pub. 1978.

_____ (1987). *The Waning of Humaneness.* Trans. R.W. Kickert. Boston: Little, Brown. First pub. 1983.

_____ (1990). *On Life and Living.* Trans. R.D. Bosley. NY: St. Martin's Press.

_____ (1996). *The Natural Science of the Human Species: An Introduction to Comparative Behavioral Research— The "Russian Manuscript" (1944-1948).* Ed. A. von Cranach, trans. R.D. Martin. Cambridge: MIT Press.

Lovelock, James (1979). *Gaia: A New Look at Life on Earth.* Oxford: Oxford Univ. Press.

_____ (1988). *The Ages of Gaia: A Biography of Our Living Earth.* NY: Norton.

_____ (1991). *Healing Gaia: Practical Medicine for the Planet.* NY: Harmony Books.

_____ (2000). *Gaia: The Practical Science of Planetary Medicine.* NY: Oxford Univ. Press.

Loyd, Anthony (1999). *My War Gone By, I Miss It So.* NY: Atlantic Monthly Press. First pub. 1942.

Lucretius, Carus Titus (1924/1473). *De Rerum Naturae.* Trans. W.H.D. Rouse. London: Wm. Heinemann.

MacCurdy, John Thompson (1981). *The Psychology of War.* NY: E.P. Dutton.

Macfarlane, Alan (1985). The root of all evil. In Parkin (1985:57-76).

MacFarquhar, Larissa (1997). Diagnosis: Totally sane: The *DSM* isn't crazy in the slightest. An online publication posted 11/13/1997, accessed 07/15/2004 at http://slate.msn.com/id/3138.

MacPhee, Ross D.E. & Marx, Preston A. (1997). The 40,000-year plague: Humans, hyperdisease, and first-contact extinctions. In Goodman, S.M. & Patterson, B.D., *Natural Change and Human Impact in Madagascar:* 169-217. Wash., D.C.: Smithsonian Inst.

Malitz, Bruno (1934). Die Leibesübungen in der nationalsozialistischen Idee. Munich: Verlag Brz. Eher Nacht.

Mandelbrot, Benoit B. (1983). *The Fractal Geometry of Nature.* San Francisco: W.H. Freeman.

Mantell, D.M. (1971). The potential for violence in Germany. *J. of Social Issues* 27:4:101-12.

Marcuse, Herbert (1968). *Negations: Essays in Critical Theory.* Trans. J.J. Shapiro. Boston: Beacon.

Margolin, Joseph (1977). Psychological perspectives in terrorism. In Alexander, Yonah & Finger, Seymour Maxwell (eds.), *Terrorism: Interdisciplinary Perspectives:* 270-82. NY: John Jay.

Margolis, Joseph (1976). The concept of disease. *The J. of Med. and Philosophy* 1:3:238-55.

Marquardt, William C.; Demaree, Richard S.; & Grieve, Robert B. (2000). *Parasitology and Vector Biology.* NY: Academic Press.

Martin, P.S. & Klein, R.G. (eds.) (1984). *Quaternary Extinctions, A Prehistoric Revolution.* Tucson: Univ. of

Ariz. Press.

Martin, P.S. (1984). Prehistoric overkill: The global model. In Martin & Klein (1984:354-403).

Matthews, Bernard E. (1998). *An Introduction to Parasitology*. Cambridge: Cambridge Univ. Press.

May, Rollo (1982). The problem of evil: An open letter to Carl Rogers. *J. of Humanistic Psychology* 22:3:10-21.

_____ (1985). *My Quest for Beauty*. NY: Saybrook.

May, Rollo; Angel, Ernest; & Ellenberger, Henri F. (eds.) (1958). *Existence: A New Dimension in Psychiatry and Psychology*. NY: Basic Books.

McCauley, C.R. & Segal, M.E. (1987). Social psychology of terrorist groups. In C. Hendrick (ed.), *Group Processes and Intergroup Relations* 9: *Annual Review of Social and Personality Psychology*. Beverley Hills: Sage.

McCauley, Clark (2002). Psychological issues in understanding terrorism and the response to terrorism. In Stout (2002:III:4-29).

McClintock, Jack (2000). Twenty species we may lose in the next twenty years. *Discover:* Oct.:62-7.

McDougall, William (1908). *Introduction to Social Psychology*. London: Methuen.

_____ (1927). *Janus: The Conquest of War, A Psychological Inquiry*. London: Kegan Paul, Trench, Trubner.

_____ (1927/1921). *The Group Mind*. Cambridge: Cambridge Univ. Press. First pub. 1921.

Meadows, Donella H.; Meadows, Dennis L.; & Randers, Jørgen (1992). *Beyond the Limits: Confronting Global Collapse, Envisioning a Sustainable Future*. Post Mills, Vermont: Chelsea Green Publishing.

Meadows, Donella H.; Meadows, Dennis L.; Randers, Jørgen; & Behrens, William W., III (1972). *The Limits to Growth: A Report for the Club of Rome's Project on the Predicament of Mankind*. NY: Universe.

Mechanic, David (1968). *Medical Sociology*. NY: Free Press.

Mechler, A. (1963). Das Wort 'Psychiatrie'. *Nervenartz* 34:405-6

Meeus, W.H.J. & Raaijmakers, Q.A.W. (1985). Administrative obedience: Carrying out orders to exert psychological-administrative violence. Unpub. ms., Univ. of Utrecht, Netherlands.

Megargee, E.A. (1984). Aggression and violence. In H.E. Adams & P.B. Sutker (eds.), *Comprehensive Handbook of Psychopathology:* 523-48. NY: Plenum.

Mencken, H.L. (1918). *Damn*. NY: Knopf.

_____ (1919). *Prejudices*. J.T. Farrell (ed.). NY: Random House.

_____ (1993/1913). *Friedrich Nietzsche*. NY: Transaction. First pub. 1913.

Menninger, Karl A. (1966/1938). *Man against Himself*. NY: Harcourt, Brace & World. First pub. 1938.

Menninger, Karl; Mayman, Martin; & Pruyser, Paul (1967/1963). *The Vital Balance: The Life Process in Mental Health and Illness*. NY: Viking. First pub. 1963.

Merari, Ariel & Friedland, Nehemia (1985). Social psychological aspects of terrorism. *Applied Social Psychology Annual* 6:185-205.

Mesarovic, Mihajlo & Pester, Eduard (1974). *Mankind at the Turning Point: The Second Report to the Club of Rome*. NY: Dutton.

Metzger, Wolfgang (1953). *Psychologie*. Darmstadt: Steinkopff.

Milgram, Stanley (1974). *Obedience to Authority: An Experimental View*. NY: Harper & Row.

_____ (1977). The social meaning of fanaticism. *ETC.: A Rev. of Gen. Semantics* 34:58-61.

Miller, Arthur G. (1986). *The Obedience Experiments: A Case Study of Controversy in Social Science*. NY: Praeger.

Millis, Walter (1961). A world without war. In Millis *et al.* (1961:51-108).

Millis, Walter; Niebuhr, Reinhold; Brown, Harrison; Real, James; & Douglas, William O. (1961). *A World Without War*. NY: Wash. Sq. Press.

Mills, C. Wright (1958). *The Causes of World War Three*. NY: Simon & Schuster.

Mixon, Don (1989). *Obedience and Civilization: Authorized Crime and the Normality of Evil*. Winchester, MA: Pluto.

Montagu, Ashley (1973/1968). *Man and Aggression*. NY: Oxford Univ. Press. First pub. 1968.

Moody-Adams, Michele M. (1997). *Fieldwork in Familiar Places: Morality, Culture, and Philosophy*. Cambridge, MA: Harvard Univ. Press.

Moran, Charles M.W. (1945). *Anatomy of Courage*. London: Constable.

Moreno, Francisco José (1977). *Between Faith and Reason: Basic Fear and the Human Condition*. NY: Harper & Row.

Morrell, Virginia (1999a). The Sixth Extinction. *Natl. Geographic* 195:2: Feb.:42-56.

_____ (1999b). In search of solutions. *Natl. Geographic* 195:2: Feb.:72-87.

Morris, I. (1975). *The Nobility of Failure: Tragic Heroes in the History of Japan.* London: Secker & Warburg.

Morse, Arthur (1968). *While Six Million Died: A Chronicle of American Apathy.* NY: Random House.

Moscovici, S. & Paicheler, G. (1978). Social comparison and social recognition: Two complementary processes of identification. In Tajfel (1978:251-66).

Musil, Robert (1937). *Über die Dummheit.* Vienna: Bermann-Fischer Verlag.

Myers, Norman (1979). *The Sinking Ark: A New Look at the Problem of Disappearing Species.* NY: Pergamon.

Nathan, Robert (1941). *They Went On Together.* NY: Knopf.

National Commission on the Causes and Prevention of Violence (1969). *To Establish Justice, To Insure Domestic Tranquility.* NY: Award Books.

Nettleship, M.A.; Dalegivens, R.; and Nettleship, A. (eds.) (1975). *War, Its Causes and Correlates.* The Hague: Mouton.

Neumann, Peter (1960). *The Black March.* NY: Bantam.

Nietzsche, Friedrich (1924/1880). The wanderer and his shadow. In Nietzsche, Friedrich, *Human, All-too-Human:* Part II:179-366. Trans. P.V. Cohn. *The Complete Works of Friedrich Nietzsche* 7. Levy, Oscar (ed.). NY: Macmillan. First pub. 1880.

_____ (1956). *The Birth of Tragedy* and *The Genealogy of Morals.* Trans. F. Golffing. NY: Anchor.

Nisbett, Alec (1976). *Konrad Lorenz.* NY: Harcourt Brace Jovanovich.

Novacek, Michael J. (2001). *The Biodiversity Crisis: Losing What Counts.* NY: New Press.

Nozick, Robert (2001). *Invariances: The Structure of the Objective World.* Cambridge, MA: Harvard Univ. Press.

Nussbaum, Martha (1999). *Sex and Social Justice.* NY: Oxford Univ. Press.

Nutton, Vivian (1990). The reception of Fracastoro's theory of contagion: The seed that fell among thorns? In McVaugh, Michael R. & Siraisi, Nancy G. (eds.), *Renaissance Medical Learning: Evolution of a Tradition,* comprising *Osiris* 6: 2nd Series:196-234.

O'Neill, R.V. (1996). Perspectives on economics and ecology. *Ecological Applications* 6:4:1031-3.

Odajnyk, Volodymyr Walter (1976). *Jung and Politics: The Political and Social Ideas of C. G. Jung.* NY: Harper & Row.

Offer, Daniel & Sabshin, Melvin (1974/1966). *Normality: Theoretical and Clinical Concepts of Mental Health.* NY: Basic Books. First pub. 1966.

Panati, C. (1996). *Sacred Origins of Profound Things: The Stories behind the Rites and Rituals of the World's Religions.* NY: Penguin Books.

Parkin, David (ed.) (1985). *The Anthropology of Evil.* Cambridge, MA: Basil Blackwell.

Parry, Albert (1976). *Terrorism: From Robespierre to Arafat.* NY: Vanguard Press.

Pear, T.H. (ed.) (1950). *Psychological Factors of Peace and War.* NY: Philos. Library.

Pearce, K.I. (1977). Police negotiations: A new role for the community psychiatrist. *Canadian Psychiatric Assoc. J.* 22:4:171-5.

Pearlstein, Richard M. (1991). *The Mind of the Political Terrorist.* Wilmington, DE: Scholarly Resources.

Peck, M. Scott (1983). *People of the Lie: The Hope for Healing Human Evil.* NY: Simon & Schuster.

Perlman, Diane (2002). Intersubjective dimensions of terrorism and its transcendence. In Stout (2002: I:17-47).

Philp, H. L. (1958). *Jung and the Problem of Evil.* London: Rockliff.

Piaget, Jean (1932). *The Moral Judgment of the Child.* NY: Harcourt, Brace.

Piel, G. (1994). AIDS and population "control." *Scientific Amer.* 270:2: Feb.:124.

Pilch, Judah (ed.) (1968). *The Jewish Catastrophe in Europe.* NY: Amer. Assoc. for Jewish Ed.

Piliavin, Irving A.; Rodin, Judith; & Piliavin, Jane Allyn (1969). Good Samaritanism: An underground phenomenon? *J. of Personality and Soc. Psychology* 13:289-99.

Pilisuk, Marc & Wong, Angela (2002). State terrorism: When the perpetrator is a government. In Stout (2002:II:105-32).

Pinel, Phillipe (1798). *Nosographie philosophique, ou, La Méthode de l'analyse appliquée à la médicine.* Paris: Maradan.

_____ (1801). *Traité médico-philosophique sur l'aliénation mentale ou la manie.* Paris: Richard, Caille et Ravier.

Pinsker, Lev (Leo) Semenovich (1944/1882). *Road to Freedom: Writings and Addresses.* Netanyahu, B. (ed.). Contains *Auto-Emancipation,* the Eng. trans. of Pinsker's *Auto-Emanzipation. Ein Mahnruf an seine Stammesgenossen. Von einem russischen Juden* [Self-Emancipation: A Warning Addressed to His Brethren.

by a Russian Jew]: 74-106. Trans. D.S. Blondheim. NY: Scopus. First pub. 1882.

Pitkin, Walter B. (1932). *A Short Introduction to the History of Human Stupidity*. NY: Simon & Schuster.

Planck, Max (1933). *Where Is Science Going?* London: Allen & Unwin.

Playne, Caroline E. (1925). *The Neuroses of Nations*. NY: Thomas Seltzer.

Pocock, David (1985). Unruly evil. In Parkin (1985:42-56).

Porpora, Douglas V. (1990). *How Holocausts Happen: The United States in Central America*. Philadelphia: Temple Univ. Press.

Portele, Gerhard (1985). How scientists think about science and morality. In Lind, Georg; Hartmann, Hans A.; & Wakenhut, Roland (eds.), *Moral Development and the Social Environment: Studies in the Philosophy and Psychology of Moral Judgment and Education*: 193-203. Trans. & gen. ed. T.E. Wren. Chicago: Precedent.

Post, Jerrold M. (1998). Terrorist psycho-logic: Terrorist behavior as a product of psychological forces. In Reich (1998:25-40).

———— (1990). Current understanding of terrorist motivation and psychology: Implications for a differentiated antiterrorist policy. *Terrorism* 13:1:65-71.

Poulin, Robert (1998). *Evolutionary Ecology of Parasites: From Individuals to Communities*. London: Chapman & Hall.

Poussaint, Alvin F. (1999) They hate. They kill. Are they insane? *New York Times* 148:51626:Aug. 26:A17.

Powell, Corey S. (2000). Twenty ways the world could end suddenly. *Discover:* Oct.:50-7.

Power, Samantha (2002). *"A Problem from Hell": America and the Age of Genocide*. NY: Basic Books.

Preston, E. Noel (1983 ): Is stuttering an illness? *Pediatrics* 71:1: Jan.:135-6.

Prins, Herschel (1994). Psychiatry and the concept of evil: Sick in heart or sick in mind? *Brit. J. of Psychiatry* 165:3:297-302.

Proctor, R.N. (1988). *Racial Hygiene: Medicine under the Nazis*. Cambridge, MA: Harvard Univ. Press.

Pylyshyn, Z. (1984). *Computation and Cognition: Towards a Foundation for Cognitive Science*. Cambridge, MA: MIT Press.

Pyszczynski, Tom; Solomon, Sheldon; & Greenberg, Jeff (2003). *In the Wake of 9/11: The Psychology of Terror*. Wash., D.C.: Amer. Psychological Assoc.

Rank, Otto (1961). *Psychology and the Soul*. NY: Perpetua Books.

Rapoport, Anatol (1957). Lewis F. Richardson's mathematical theory of war. *J. of Conflict Resolution* 1:3:249-99.

———— (1960). *Fights, Games, and Debates*. Ann Arbor, MI: Univ. of Michigan Press.

Rasch, W. (1979). Psychological dimensions of political terrorism in the Federal Republic of Germany. *Internatl. J. of Law and Psychiatry* 2:79-85.

Rashevsky, Nicolas (1938). *Mathematical Biophysics*. Chicago: Univ. of Chicago Press.

———— (1947). *Mathematical Theory of Human Relations*. Chicago: Univ. of Chicago Press.

———— (1951). *Mathematical Biology of Social Behavior*. Bloomington: Principia Press.

Rauschning, Hermann (1940). *The Voice of Destruction*. NY: Putnam's.

Reggia, J.A. & Tuhrim, S. (eds.) (1985). *Computers and Medicine: Computer Assisted Medical Decision Making*. 2 vols. NY: Springer.

Reich, Walter (ed.) (1998). *Origins of Terrorism: Psychologies, Theologies, and States of Mind*. Wash., D.C.: Woodrow Wilson Center Press. First pub. 1990.

Reil, Johann Christian & Hoffbauer, Johann Christophe (1808-12). *Beyträge der Medicin und ihre Verzweigungen, besonders in Beziehung auf die Berichtigung der Topik der Psychiaterie*. 2 vols. Halle: Curt.

Rest, James R. (1986). *Moral Development: Advances in Research and Theory*. NY: Praeger.

Reznek, Lawrie (1987). *The Nature of Disease*. London: Routledge & Kegan Paul.

Richards, R.J. (1987). *Darwin and the Emergence of Evolutionary Theories of Mind and Behavior*. Chicago: Univ. of Chicago Press.

Richardson, Lewis Fry (1939). *Generalized Foreign Politics: A Study in Group Psychology*. Brit. J. of Psychology *Monograph Supplement.* 23:vii-91. Cambridge: Cambridge Univ. Press.

———— (1948). War-Moods: I. *Psychometrika* 13:3: Sept.:147-74.

———— (1948a). War-Moods: II. *Psychometrika* 13:4: Dec.:197-232.

———— (1949). The persistence of national hatred and the changeability of its objects. *Brit. J. of Med. Psychology* 22:166-8.

Richardson, Lewis Fry (1950). Statistics of deadly quarrels. In Pear (1950:239-56).

_____ (1960). *Statistics of Deadly Quarrels*. Wright, Quincy & Lienau, C.C. (eds.). Pittsburgh & Chicago: Boxwood Press/Quadrangle Books.

_____ (1960a). *Arms and Insecurity: A Mathematical Study of the Causes and Origins of War*. Rashevsky, Nicolas & Trucco, Ernesto (eds.). Pittsburgh/Chicago: Boxwood Press/Quadrangle Books.

_____ (1993). *Collected Papers of Lewis Fry Richardson*. I: *Meteorology and Numerical Analysis*; II: *Quantitative Psychology and Studies of Conflict*. Ashford, Oliver M.; Charnock, H.; Drazin, P.D.; Hunt, J.C.R.; Smoker, P.; & Sutherland, Ian (eds.) Cambridge: Cambridge Univ. Press.

Richet, Charles (c. 1925/1919). *Idiot Man or The Follies of Mankind ("L'Homme Stupide")*. Trans. N. Forsythe & L. Harvey. NY: Brentano's. Eng. pub. without a date; estimated c. 1925. First pub. 1919.

Robert J. Sternberg (ed.) (2002). *Why Smart People Can Be So Stupid*. New Haven: Yale Univ. Press.

Roberts, G. (1991). Delusional belief systems and meaning in life: A preferred reality. *Brit. J. of Psychiatry* 161:298-308.

Roberts, Morley (1926). *Malignancy and Evolution: A Biological Inquiry into the Nature and Causes of Cancer*. London: Eveleigh Nash & Grayson.

_____ (1938). *Bio-Politics: An Essay in the Physiology, Pathology, and Politics of the Social and Somatic Organism*. London: Dent.

Romanes, George John (1883). *Animal Intelligence*. NY: Appleton.

_____ (1888). *Mental Evolution in Man: Origin of Human Faculty*. NY: Appleton.

_____ (1895). *Mental Evolution in Animals*. NY: Appleton.

Rosenbaum, Max (1983). *Compliant Behavior: Beyond Obedience to Authority*. NY: Human Scs.

Rosenfeld, Alvin H. & Greenberg, Irving (eds.) (1978). *Confronting the Holocaust: The Impact of Elie Wiesel*. Bloomington: Indiana Univ. Press.

Rosten, Leo C. (1935). Men like war. *Harper's Magazine:* July:189-97.

Rothchild, J. & Wolf, S.B. (1976). *The Children of the Counterculture*. NY: Doubleday.

Rubenstein, Richard L. (1966). *After Auschwitz: Radical Theology and Contemporary Judaism*. NY: Bobbs-Merrill.

Rudhyar, Dane (1971). *Directives for a New Life*. Rail Road Flat, CA: Seed Publications.

Rummel, R.J. (1994). Democide in Totalitarian States: Mortacracies and Megamurderers. In Charny (1994: 3-39).

Russell, Bertrand (1971/1915). *Why Men Fight: A Method of Abolishing the International Duel*. NY: Garland. First. pub. 1916 based on a series of lectures in 1915.

Rüstow, Alexander (1980). *Freedom and Domination: A Historical Critique of Civilization*. Trans. S. Attanasio. Princeton, N.J.: Princeton Univ. Press.

Sagan, Carl (1980). *Cosmos*. NY: Random House.

Saint-Exupéry, Antoine de (1940). *Wind, Sand and Stars*. Trans. L. Galantière. NY: Reynal & Hitchcock.

_____ (1965). *A Sense of Life*. Trans. A. Foulke. NY: Funk & Wagnalls.

Salovey, Peter & Mayer, John D. (1990). Emotional intelligence. *Imagination, Cognition, and Personality* 9:3:185-211.

Sartre, Jean-Paul (1948). *Anti-Semite and Jew*. Trans. G.J. Becker. NY: Schocken Books.

_____ (1956). *Being and Nothingness: An Essay on Phenomenological Ontology*. Trans. H.E. Barnes. NY: Philos. Library.

Schiefenhövel, Wulf; Uher, Johanna; & Krell, Renate (eds.) (1993). *Im Spiegel der Anderen: Aus dem Lebenswerk des Verhaltensforschers Irenäus Eibl-Eibesfeldt*. Munich: Realis.

Schmid, Alex P. (1983). *Political Terrorism: A Research Guide to Concepts, Theories, Data Bases, and Literature*. Amsterdam: North-Holland.

Schopenhauer, Arthur (1965/1841). *On the Basis of Morality*. Trans. E.F.J. Payne. NY: Bobbs-Merrill. First pub. 1841.

Schuman, Frederick L. (1933). *International Politics*. NY: McGraw-Hill.

Schutz, Alfred (1945). On multiple realities. *Philosophy and Phenomenological Research* V:533-76.

Sedgwick, Peter (1973). Illness—mental and otherwise. *Hastings Center Studies* I:3:19-40.

_____ (1982). *Psycho Politics*. NY: Harper & Row.

Selg, H. (1971). *The Making of Aggression: A Psychological Approach*. London: Quartet.

Shanab, M.E. & Yahya, K.A. (1978). A cross-cultural study of obedience. *Bull. of the Psychonomic Society*.

11:267-9.

Shanab, M.E. (1977). A behavioral study of obedience in children. *J. of Personality and Soc. Psychology* 35:530-6.

Shand, Alexander F. (1914). *The Foundations of Character: Being a Study of the Tendencies of the Emotions and Sentiments.* London: Macmillan.

Shaw, George Bernard (1919). *Heartbreak House, Great Catherine, and Playlets of the War.* NY: Brentano's.

Shaw, R. Paul & Wong, Yuwa (1989). *Genetic Seeds of Warfare: Evolution, Nationalism, and Patriotism.* Boston: Unwin Hyman.

Sheleff, Leon Shaskolsky (1978). *The Bystander: Behavior, Law, Ethics.* Lexington, MA: Lexington.

Sherif, M. (1966). *Group Conflict and Cooperation: Their Social Psychology.* London: Routledge & Kegan Paul.

Sherif, M.; White, B.J.; & Harvey, O.J. (1955). Status in experimentally produced groups. *Amer. J. of Sociology* 60:370-9.

Skillings, Judith H. & Dobbins, James E. (1991). Racism as disease: Etiology and treatment implications. *J. of Counseling & Development* 70:206-12.

Simmel, Ernst (ed.) (1946). *Anti-Semitism: A Social Disease.* NY: Internatl. Universities Press.

Simonton, Dean Keith (1994). *Greatness: Who Makes History and Why.* NY: Guilford.

Sims, Andrew C.P. (2003). *Symptoms in the Mind: An Introduction to Descriptive Psychopathology.* Edinburgh: Saunders.

Singer, Isaac Bashevis (1982). *The Collected Stories of Isaac Bashevis Singer.* NY: Farrar, Straus, Giroux.

Singer, J. David & Small, Melvin (1972). *The Wages of War 1816-1965: A Statistical Handbook.* NY: Wiley.

Smith, Howard K. (1942). *Last Train from Berlin.* NY: Knopf.

Sorokin, Pitirim A. (1937-41). *Social and Cultural Dynamics.* 4 vols. NY: Amer. Bk. Co.

_____ (1957). *Social and Cultural Dynamics.* Boston: Porter Sargent. A one-volume abridgment of Sorokin (1937-41).

_____ (1963). *A Long Journey: The Autobiography of Pitirim A. Sorokin.* New Haven: College & Univ. Press.

Spearman, Charles E. (1927). *The Abilities of Man.* NY: Macmillan.

Sperber, Murray A. (ed.) (1977). *Arthur Koestler: A Collection of Critical Essays.* Englewood Cliffs, N.J.: Prentice-Hall.

Spiegelberg, Herbert (1972). *Phenomenology in Psychology and Psychiatry: A Historical Introduction.* Evanston: Northwestern Univ. Press.

Spinelli, Ernesto (1989). *The Interpreted World: An Introduction to Phenomenological Psychology.* Newbury Park, CA: Sage Publications.

Spurr, Russell (1981). *A Glorious Way to Die: The Kamikaze Mission of the Battleship Yamato, April 1945.* NY: Newmarket.

Stanley-Jones, D. (1970).The biological origin of love and hate. In Arnold, Magda B. (ed.). *Feelings and Emotions: The Loyola Symposium:* 25-37. NY: Academic Press.

Stanovich, Keith E. (1993). Dysrationalia: A new specific learning disability. *J. of Learning Disabilities* 26:501-15.

_____ (1994). Reconceptualizing intelligence: Dysrationalia as an intuition pump. *Educational Researcher* 23:4:11-22.

_____ (2002). Rationality, intelligence, and levels of analysis in cognitive science: Is dysrationalia possible? In Sternberg (2002:124-58).

Staub, Ervin (1989). *The Roots of Evil: The Origins of Genocide and Other Group Violence.* Cambridge: Cambridge Univ. Press.

_____ (2003). *The Psychology of Good and Evil: Why Children, Adults, and Groups Help and Harm Others.* Cambridge: Cambridge Univ. Press.

Stein, Murray (1995). *Jung on Evil.* Princeton, N.J.: Princeton Univ. Press.

Steiner, John M. (1980). The SS yesterday and today: A sociopathological view. In Dimsdale (1980:405-56).

Stekel, Wilhelm (1953/1929). *Sadism and Masochism: The Psychology of Hatred and Cruelty.* 2 vols. Trans. L. Brink. NY: Liveright. First pub. 1929.

Sternberg, Robert J. (ed.) (2002). *Why Smart People Can Be So Stupid.* New Haven: Yale University Press.

Stevenson, Robert C. (1934). Is war inevitable? *World Unity Magazine:* 68-77.

Stewart, J.Q. (1948). Demographic gravitation: Evidence and application. *Sociometry* 11:31-57.

Stokes, Trevor (2002). Terror and violence perpetrated by children. In Stout (2002:IV:77-89).

Stone, Christopher D. (1988/1972). *Should Trees Have Standing? Toward Legal Rights for Natural Objects.* Palo Alto: Tioga Publishing. First pub. 1972.

Stout, Chris E. (ed.) (2002). *The Psychology of Terrorism.* 4 vols. Westport, CT: Praeger.

Straus, Erwin W. (1966). *Phenomenological Psychology: The Selected Papers of Erwin W. Straus.* Trans. in part E. Eng. NY: Basic Books.

Strawson, Peter (1959). *Individuals.* London: Methuen.

Sutherland, Ian. (1962). Statistics of human conflict. *J. of the Royal Statistical Society.* Series A:125:473-84.

Sutton, Henry Gawen (1886). *Lectures on Medical Pathology.* London: Baillière, Tindall.

_____ (1891). *Lectures on Pathology Delivered at the London Hospital.* Paul, Maurice Eden (ed.). London: J.A. Churchill.

Szasz, Thomas (1973). *The Second Sin.* London: Routledge & Kegan Paul.

Taft, R. (1956). Some characteristics of good judges of others. *Brit. J. Psychol.* 47:19-29.

Tagore, Rabindranath (1935). [Letter]. *Open Letters* 4: Part I: *Civilisations.* Paris: League of Nations: Internatl. Inst. of Intellectual Cooperation.

Taheri, A. (1987). *Holy Terror: The Inside Story of Islamic Terrorism.* London: Century Hutchinson.

Tajfel, Henri (ed.) (1978). *Differentiation between Social Groups: Studies in the Social Psychology of Intergroup Relations.* London: Academic Press.

_____ (1981). *Human Groups and Social Categories: Studies in Social Psychology.* Cambridge: Cambridge Univ. Press.

_____ (ed.) (1982). *Social Identity and Intergroup Relations.* Cambridge: Cambridge Univ. Press.

Tajfel, H.; Flament, C.; Billig, M.; & Bundy, R.P. (1971). Social categorization and intergroup behaviour. *European J. of Social Psychology* 1:149-78.

Taylor, David (1985). Theological thoughts about evil. In Parkin (1985:26-41).

Taylor, Maxwell (1988). *The Terrorist.* London: Brassey's.

Tec, N. (1986). *When Light Pierced the Darkness: Christian Rescue of Jews in Nazi-occupied Poland.* NY: Oxford Univ. Press.

Thomas, Alexander & Sillen, Samuel (1972). *Racism and Psychiatry.* Secaucus, N.J.: Citadel Press.

Thomas, R. Murray (1997). *Moral Development Theories—Secular and Religious.* Westport, CT: Greenwood.

Thorndike, E.L. (1920). Intelligence and its uses. *Harper's Magazine* 140:227-35.

Tilman, D. (1982). *Resource Competition and Community Structure. Monographs in Population Biol.* 17. Princeton: Princeton Univ. Press.

Tinbergen, Nikolaas (1968). On war and peace in animals and man: An ethologist's approach to the biology of aggression. *Science:* New Series:160:3835: June:1411-18.

_____ (1972). Functional ethology and the human sciences. *Proc. of the Royal Soc. of London:* B:182:385-410.

Tolkien, J.R.R. (1965). *Tree and Leaf.* Boston: Houghton Mifflin.

Toulmin, Stephen (1969). Ludwig Wittgenstein. *Encounter:* 32: January:58-71.

Trotter, W. (1920). *Instincts of the Herd in Peace and War.* London: Unwin.

Tuchman, Barbara (1978). *A Distant Mirror.* NY: Knopf.

Tuke, Daniel Hack (ed.) (1892). *A Dictionary of Psychological Medicine.* London: Churchill.

Upham, Thomas C. (1973/1840). *Outlines of Imperfect and Disordered Mental Action.* NY: Arno Press. Reprint of 1868 edition, first registered 1840.

U.S. Congress, Senate Subcommittee on Emerging Threats and Capabilities (2001). *Terrorist Organizations and Motivations.* Washington, D.C.: U.S. Government Printing Office, Nov. 15.

Valéry, Paul (1933). [Letter]. *Open Letters* 1: *A League of Minds.* Paris: League of Nations: Internatl. Inst. of Intellectual Cooperation.

Valzelli, L. (1981). *Psychobiology of Aggression and Violence.* NY: Raven.

van Creveld, Martin (1991). *The Transformation of War.* NY: Maxwell Macmillan Internatl.

van den Berg, Jan Henrik (1955). *The Phenomenological Approach to Psychiatry: An Introduction to Recent Phenomenological Psychopathology.* Springfield, IL: Charles C. Thomas.

_____ (1972). *A Different Existence: Principles of Phenomenological Psychopathology.* Pittsburgh: Duquesne Univ. Press.

_____ (1980). Phenomenology and psychotherapy. *J. of Phen. Psychology* 10:2:21-49.

Victor, George (1998). *Hitler: The Pathology of Evil.* Wash., D.C.: Brassey's.

Volkan, Vamik D. (1988). *The Need to Have Enemies & Allies.* Northvale, NJ: Aronson.

_____ (1997) *Blood Lines: From Ethnic Pride to Ethnic Terrorism.* NY: Farrar, Straus, & Giroux.

von Bernhardi, F. (1914). *Germany & the Next War.* Trans. A.H. Powdes. NY: Eron.

von Bertalanffy, Ludwig & Rapoport, Anatol (eds.) (1963). *General Systems Yearbook* VIII. NY: Society for Gen. Systems Research.

von der Gruen, Max (1980). *Howl Like the Wolves.* NY: Morrow.

von Gebsattel, V.E. (1958). The world of the compulsive. In May *et al.* (1958:170-87).

von Uexküll, Jakob Johann (1909). *Umwelt und Innenwelt der Tiere.* Berlin: Springer.

_____ (1920). *Theoretische Biologie.* Berlin: Paetel. In English: *Theoretical Biology* (1926). Trans. D.L. Mackinnon. NY: Harcourt Brace.

_____ (1957). *A Stroll through the Worlds of Animals and Men: A Picture Book of Invisible Worlds,* trans. C.H. Schiller, in Schiller, Claire H. (ed.), *Instinctive Behavior: The Development of a Modern Concept:* 5-80. NY: Internatl. Universities Press. German ed. first pub. 1934.

Waelder, Robert (1934). Lettre sur l'étiologie et l'évolution des psychoses collectives. *Correspondance: Esprit, l'éthique et la guerre* 3:85-150. Paris: Institut Internatl. de Coopération Intellectuelle, Société des Nations.

_____ (1939). *Psychological Aspects of War and Peace* (monograph vol.). *Geneva Studies* 10:2: May.

Wakefield, Jerome C. (1992). The concept of mental disorder: On the boundary between biological facts and social values. *Amer. Psychologist* 47:3: March:373-88.

Wang, Hao (1987). *Reflections on Kurt Gödel.* Cambridge, MA.: MIT Press.

Warneka, Timothy H. (2002). Everyday terrorism—The long shadow of our hidden dragon: Shared factors of terrorism and juvenile violence. In Stout (2002:IV:91-117).

Watts, Fraser N. (1990). New concepts of emotion. *The Psychologist* 14:2:75-7.

_____ (1992). Applications of current cognitive theories of the emotions to the conceptualization of emotional disorders. *Brit. J. of Clinical Psychology* 31:153-67.

Weinberg, Steven (1977). *The First Three Minutes: A Modern View of the Origin of the Universe.* NY: Basic Books.

Wells, Donald A. (1967). *The War Myth.* NY: Pegasus.

Wheeler, William Morton (1928). *Emergent Evolution.* NY: Norton.

Whitman, Charles Otis (1899). Animal behavior. *Biol. Lect. Marine Biol. Lab., Woods Hole:* 285-338.

_____ (1919). The behavior of pigeons. *Publ. Carnegie Inst.* 257:1-161.

Wiesel, Elie (1964). *The Town beyond the Wall.* NY: Atheneum.

Williams, B. (1972). *Morality: An Introduction to Ethics.* Harmondsworth, Eng.: Penguin.

Wilson, E.O. (1975). *Sociobiology: The New Synthesis.* Cambridge, MA: Harvard Univ. Press.

_____ (1998). *Consilience: The Unity of Knowledge.* NY: Knopf.

Wisdom, John (1953). *Philosophy and Psycho-analysis.* Oxford: Blackwell.

Wittgenstein, Ludwig (1953). *Philosophical Investigations,* trans. G.E.M. Anscombe. NY: Macmillan.

Woodhouse, Mark B. (1997). The concept of disease in alternative medicine. In Humber & Almeder (1997:327-55).

Wright, Quincy (1935). *The Causes of War and the Conditions of Peace.* NY: Longmans, Green.

_____ (1942). *A Study of War.* Chicago: Univ. of Chicago Press.

Wright, Quincy; Evan, William M.; & Deutsch, Morton (eds.) (1962). *Preventing World War III: Some Proposals.* NY: Simon & Schuster.

Wrightsman, L.S. (1974). The most important social psychological research in this generation? *Contemp. Psychology* 19:803-5.

Zazonc, R.B. (1980). Feeling and thinking: Preferences need no inferences. *Amer. Psychologist* 35:151-75.

Zilboorg, Gregory & Henry, George W. (1941). *A History of Medical Psychology.* NY: Norton.

Zillmer, E.A.; Archer, R.P.; & Castins, R. (1989). Rorschach records of Nazi war criminals: A reanalysis using current scoring and interpretation of practices. *J. of Personality Assessment* 53:1:85-99.

Zillmer, Eric A.; Harrower, Molly; Ritzler, Barry A.; & Archer, Robert P. (1995). *The Quest for the Nazi Personality: A Psychological Investigation of Nazi War Criminals.* Hillsdale, N.J.: Erlbaum.

Zimbardo, P.G. (1974). On "Obedience to Authority." *Amer. Psychologist* 29:566-7.

Zimmer, Carl (2000). *Parasite Rex: Inside the Bizarre World of Nature's Most Dangerous Creatures.* NY: Free Press.

Zinn, Howard (2002). *Terrorism and War.* NY: Seven Stories Press.

# INDEX

# ABOUT THE AUTHOR

S teven James Bartlett was born in Mexico City and educated in Mexico, the United States, and France. He did his undergraduate work at the University of Santa Clara and at Raymond College, an Oxford-style honors college of the University of the Pacific. He received his master's degree from the University of California, Santa Barbara; his doctorate from the Université de Paris, where his research was directed by Paul Ricoeur; and has done postdoctoral study in psychology and psychotherapy. He has been the recipient of many honors, awards, grants, scholarships, and fellowships. His research has been supported under contract or grant by the Alliance Française, the American Association for the Advancement of Science, the Center for the Study of Democratic Institutions, the Lilly Endowment, the Max-Planck-Gesellschaft, the National Science Foundation, the Rand Corporation, and others.

Bartlett brings to the present work an unusual background consisting of training in pathology, psychology, and epistemology. He is the author of eight books and monographs, and many papers and research studies in the fields of psychology, epistemology, and philosophy of science. He has taught at Saint Louis University and the University of Florida, and has held research positions at the Max-Planck-Institute in Starnberg, Germany and at the Center for the Study of Democratic Institutions in Santa Barbara. He is currently Visiting Scholar in Psychology and Philosophy at Willamette University and Senior Research Professor of Philosophy at Oregon State University.